# THE LAW OF DESIGN: DESIGN PATENT, TRADEMARK, & COPYRIGHT

## PROBLEMS, CASES, AND MATERIALS

■ ■ ■

**Edward Lee**
*Professor of Law*
*Chicago-Kent College of Law*
*Illinois Institute of Technology*

**Mark McKenna**
*Professor of Law and Notre Dame Presidential Fellow*
*University of Notre Dame Law School*

**David L. Schwartz**
*Professor of Law*
*Northwestern University Pritzker School of Law*

AMERICAN CASEBOOK SERIES®

WEST ACADEMIC PUBLISHING

444 Cedar Street, Suite 700
St. Paul, MN 55101
1-877-888-1330



Printed in the United States of America

**ISBN:** 978-0-314-29103-5

# PREFACE AND ACKNOWLEDGMENTS

"Design is a plan for arranging elements in such a way as best to accomplish a particular purpose," Charles Eames advised. In keeping with that credo, we have designed this casebook to fill a need. While many law schools offer courses on Intellectual Property (IP) law, few courses focus specifically on the protection of designs. Even law school courses that focus on some type of intellectual property—such as patents, copyrights, and trademarks—rarely spend significant time discussing the law of designs. Similarly, design schools routinely teach a range of courses related to design and design thinking, but commonly ignore instruction related to how designers might design in a way that qualifies for legal protection, thereby creating a competitive advantage. This oversight is to everyone's peril. Over time and especially more recently, the protection of designs has become more important—indeed, vital—to many busineses. We have written this casebook in response to the growing need for teaching materials in this emerging area. We have assembled an integrated discussion of the law of design as contained in the patent (design) laws, copyright laws, trademark (trade dress) laws, and international design laws.

Our casebook is designed for use by students with different backgrounds, including students without prior knowledge in IP law. Although our primary audience (we expect) are law students, we have written our casebook with much explanatory information to make our casebook accessible to students of other disciplines, including business and design. We believe that professors can use this casebook in a course on Design Law without requiring any prior courses in IP law as prerequisites. Even students who have taken prior courses in IP law will find our explanatory materials useful to refresh or solidify their previous studies. Our casebook is filled with real-world problems that capture the kinds of issues that businesses commonly face today. This problem-based approach will better prepare students not only for the final exam, but also and more importantly for legal practice as well as the demands that design protection—or lack therof—place on businesses today.

For ease of reading, we have made some deletions and changes in punctuation in the excerpted selections in our casebook without using ellipses or other notations. We have omitted most footnotes from the cases and articles we have included in our casebook. For some problems in our casebook, we copied parts of cases without quotation or citation (in part to avoid providing students with the answers to these problems).

We are grateful for the support of Harold Krent, Dean and Professor of Law at Chicago-Kent College of Law at the Illinois Institute of Technology, Daniel Rodriguez, Dean and Harold Washington Professor of Law at Northwestern Pritzker School of Law, and Nell Jessup Newton, Joseph A. Matson Dean and Professor of Law at the University of Notre Dame Law School.

We received many helpful and insightful comments from Christopher Carani. We also want to thank Alison Tan for providing us with excellent student research assistance, as well as Chicago-Kent's research librarian Scott Vanderlin and faculty assistant Nicole Lechuga for their invaluable help during the writing of this casebook. We are grateful to all the authors who granted us permission to include their materials in our casebook. We have learned a lot from their important contributions. Finally, we owe special thanks to Bonnie Karlen of West Academic for believing in our book when it was just an idea. The entire team at West, including Greg Olson and Heather Sieve, was a pleasure to work with.

No casebook is perfect, especially not in the first edition. We welcome your comments and feedback on any and every aspect of our casebook. Our goal is to keep improving its design with each edition.

EDWARD LEE
elee@kentlaw.iit.edu

MARK MCKENNA
markmckenna@nd.edu

DAVID L. SCHWARTZ
david.schwartz@law.northwestern.edu

April 2017

# SUMMARY OF CONTENTS

# TABLE OF CONTENTS

# TABLE OF CASES

**The principal cases are in bold type.**

# THE LAW OF DESIGN: DESIGN PATENT, TRADEMARK, & COPYRIGHT

## PROBLEMS, CASES, AND MATERIALS

# CHAPTER 1

# INTRODUCTION

■ ■ ■

*Design is not just what it looks like and feels like. Design is how it works.*

—Steve Jobs

*[D]esign does not stop at the form of a chair or the shape of a column. Everything man makes is design, whether with material as hard as granite or as elusive as thought.*

*Design controls our whole life.*

—Paul Jacques Grillo

Design is everywhere. Virtually every product or service—from the clothes you wear to the smartphone you use, along with the ride-sharing service you enlist via your smartphone app—has a design. According to conventional wisdom, "[d]esign is more integral to good business than ever before."[1] Indeed, the ubiquity and importance of design has even spurred graduate schools to teach and study design as a way of thinking—for application not only on products or services, but also to problem solving in general.[2]

But what is design? And why is it so important to such a wide array of businesses, ranging from Apple and Marimekko to Uber and Zara? According to one survey, companies that are driven by design have outperformed the S&P Index by a margin of 219% over the past decade.[3] Also, 20% of the top VC-backed ventures based on cumulative funding in the United States have designer co-founders, and five start-up companies co-founded by designers have raised over $2.75 billion recently.[4] Design is no longer an afterthought in business. For many businesses, it is the starting point.

Given design's importance today, businesses are seeking, not only to create great designs, but also to protect them as intellectual property (IP) in increasing numbers. The rationale for seeking such IP protection is

---

[1] Margaret Rhodes, *Take It from an Expert: Design Is More Important Than Ever*, WIRED, March 17, 2015, https://www.wired.com/2015/03/take-expert-design-important-ever/.

[2] Irving Wladawsky-Berger, *Is Design Thinking the New Liberal Arts*, WALL ST. J., Nov. 4, 2016.

[3] Tony Harmer, *4 Key Stats on the Importance of Design for Business*, CREATIVE CONNECTION BLOG (Adobe), Oct. 14, 2015, https://blogs.adobe.com/creative/design-advantage/.

[4] John Maeda, *Design in Tech Report 2015*, Kleiner Perkins Caufield & Byers, http://www.kpcb.com/blog/design-in-tech-report-2015 (slides 2, 8, and 10).

straightforward: businesses commonly attempt to protect their creations in order to recoup their investments in developing those creations. If a company spends $300 billion in developing an automated, electric car, the company would want to stop competitors from copying its car—both its design and technology—so the company can recoup a return on its investment. Intellectual property fills the vital role of providing rights to exclude others from copying certain subject matter, such as the design of products. At the same time, design law typically excludes functional elements, which are supposed to be the province of utility patents, subject to more stringent requirements and examination before being granted.

This casebook studies the various forms of intellectual property in the United States that have been used to protect designs—design patents, copyrights, and trademarks (via trade dress protection). Our main focus is to study the IP protection available for designs in the United States, with an eye to providing a solid foundation in U.S. law for students who may practice in this area. Given how global business is today, we also consider, for comparison, the system of design protection in the European Union. The casebook discusses the Community Design Regulation, which has established a popular form of design protection in the EU. The EU design right provides a good contrast with the U.S. design patent. Given space constraints, however, the casebook omits discussion of the many other design laws in other countries, such as Australia, Brazil, Japan, and South Korea. But studying design protection in this casebook should provide students with a foundation of knowledge from which they can explore other countries' design protection laws with some familiarity of recurring concepts, such as functionality. The casebook also covers the process by which entities may seek design protection in many countries via the Hague System for the International Registration of Industrial Designs. In this chapter, we introduce the topic of design and the various forms of intellectual property protection.

## A. BACKGROUND

### 1. WHAT IS DESIGN?

#### *PROBLEM 1–1*

Imagine three different creators who independently and on the exact same day create different subject matter whose shape is the same: a conical spire whose surface twists around similar to a screwdriver. Alicia, an architect, designs a sleek modern building in this shape. Green Juice Co. designs a unique bottle for its juices in this shape. Sandhya, a sculptor, designs an arresting sculpture in this shape. Imagine you are legislators in a newly formed country that is debating whether to provide any design protection. (1) In your view, do all three subject matter—the building, the bottle, and the sculpture—involve design? (2) Should all three subject matter be eligible for some form of legal protection from copying? If not, which subject matter should be excluded and why? (3) Relatedly, how should the law protect designs that involve some functional features? In thinking about these questions, consider the following discussion on the meaning of design.

---

Steve Jobs stated: "Design is not just what it looks like and feels like. Design is how it works." He also explained in an interview: "Design is a really loaded word. I don't know what it means, and so we really don't talk a lot about design around here. We just talk about how things work. Most people think, it's how they look. But it's not really how they look, it's how they work."[5]

If you apply his remarks to an Apple product, such as the iPad or iPhone, would that mean that the design of the product *includes* its functional elements that make it work—which can be encapsulated by the slogan "form follows function." Typically, U.S. law *excludes* functional elements from design protection, whether in the form of a design patent, copyright, or trade dress. The rationale is that functional elements must be protected by utility patents, which require an application and examination of whether the invention is new. Is it easy to draw the line between functional and aesthetic elements of a product if they are both part of the overall design? If form follows function, should design ever be protected?

Is design an easy concept to grasp? The more one talks to people who design things, the harder it seems to define that concept. Perhaps "everything man makes is design," as architect Paul Jacques Grillo instructs. But does Grillo's definition threaten to sweep in virtually everything into design? These problems with defining what constitutes design are not new. In thinking about what constitutes a design, also consider the following excerpt from Dr. Denman Ross, an artist, art historian, and theorist writing at the turn of the twentieth century:

## DESIGN: ITS IMPORTANCE IN LIFE

Dr. Denman W. Ross
Harvard University
13 BRUSH AND PENCIL 261–63, 265 (1904)

Design is a subject of vital importance. It is of that I am going to speak—of its place in education and in life, its importance everywhere; of this, however, very briefly. Look at anything that any one has done, any piece of work, no matter what it is; there are two elements in it which

---

[5] Dirk Beveridge, *Apple Steve Jobs on Design*, YOUTUBE (Oct. 16, 2010), https://www.youtube.com/watch?v=sPfJQmpg5zk (video at 2–20 seconds).

should be distinguished and separately considered. There is the motive of it, its intention or purpose, and there is the execution of it, the performance.

It is in the performance we see the design of it, the art of it. We see in the performance what materials have been used, what terms, how the materials or terms have been combined and arranged. We see in the performance the plan or system of the work, the ways, means, and methods which have been followed in bringing it to completion. We see in the performance the correlation of the parts, the fitness of the parts to the whole, the organic and perfect unity of the whole, and lastly, the appropriateness of the whole to its motive or purpose.

Give this motive or purpose to a hundred men. Let them work it out, each one in his own way, and no two of them will achieve the same result. When you consider the results you observe that in some cases the materials are well chosen and properly used, suitably combined, well handled; the work is done in a simple, systematic, orderly, direct way; in other cases not. In some cases the motive is well followed, the purpose well served; in other cases not. The difference is a difference of design, a difference of art. The design of any work, the art of it, is seen, not in its motive or purpose, not in its usefulness, not in its truth, not in its righteousness, but in its execution, in what I have called the performance.

The problem of life seems to resolve itself into two questions: What to do and how to do it. How to do it? That is a question of design. To do what is necessary or useful, to do what is true, beautiful, or what is right. There are no new motives. People have been following them for ages. In the art of the past we see what success they have had. Begin by reproducing the best things that have been done. Then improve upon them if you can. Bring in new elements, make new combinations and arrangements, not for the sake of change or novelty, but for the sake of the motive of the work. The end is your motive. "Art for art's sake." That is nonsense! Do we talk for the sake of talking? No; we talk because we have something to say.

How few people are able to bring this power of design into their work! They think that art is making things pretty. They don't at all understand how art is possible to all men at all times and everywhere. The habit of finding your life in your work—that is the first requisite for the artist. There is another; that is, a ceaseless and insatiable love of order. Whether it takes the forms of logic and reason, which appeal to the mind, or the forms of balance rhythm, and harmony, which appeal to the senses. As an artist, it is your ceaseless endeavor to create harmony where there is discord. What to do? There lies the wisdom of life. How to do it? There lies the power and the joy of life.

Learning how to do it means in all cases technical exercises, technical practice, leading to technical skill and ability. I know that it has been argued that technical exercises have no place in and preparatory schools, nor in the college and the university. But in the last few years we see a change of opinion. The importance of technical exercises and practices not only as a means of attaining skill or ability, but as a means of appreciating work when it is well done by others, is now at last being recognized, so that along with the history of music, of literature, of architecture, sculpture, and painting we are getting courses of technical exercises, and they are already doing great service. That means that we shall be able not merely to talk and write about works of art, but be able to take the point of view of the designer, the artist, which is always a technical point of view.

Technique is only another word for design, and design and art are one and the same thing. The artist says, I will do this or that. Having decided what to do, he no longer thinks in the abstract terms of language. Unless he proposes to speak or to write, he thinks in the materials and terms, in the forms of effort or exertions, belonging to the art in which his work is to be achieved. He thinks what he is going to do, how he is going to do it, and then he does it. He does not talk about it or write about it—he does it, using all the technical skill and ability he has. To appreciate what he has done, what he has achieved, you must also be able to think in the terms of his art. You must also be able to consider materials used and methods followed; you must also have tried to do that sort of thing to know whether it is well done or not.

But, it will be argued, it is impossible to bring all the many and various arts of life into the schools, all the variety of technical exercises. It is not proposed to bring all the arts into the schools, but only those which are most important, those which are principal or typical—gymnastics, music, speech, architecture, sculpture, and painting, which includes drawing. Surely it is not too much to propose that these principal and typical arts shall have a place in our schools and colleges, if our object is to teach people not merely what to do, but how to do it.

### *NOTES AND QUESTIONS*

1. According to Dr. Ross, how does design relate to the performance of a product? What are the goals or purposes of design? To add beauty to product? To make a product work?

2. How would you define what constitutes design? Do you agree with Steve Jobs' or Dr. Ross's description? What about this definition from the Oxford English Dictionary: "The art or action of conceiving of and producing a plan or drawing of something before it is made." In answering this question, evaluate whether you think the following items have design elements: a chair, a culinary dish, a dress, a hairstyle, a novel, a surgical technique, and a business method.

3. Do you think design is more of an artistic or technical element of a product? Or is it equally both? How do you think Ross and Jobs would have answered the question?

4. Do you think design and "design thinking" should be taught more in college and professional schools, including law schools? Can law students benefit from studying design and design thinking just as much as business and design students?

---

## 2. BRIEF HISTORY OF INDUSTRIAL DESIGN

The 19th century Industrial Revolution ushered in an era during which products were mass produced. These articles of manufacture were designed and produced for public consumption. "Industrial design" is the term that was used to describe the design features of manufactured products. Although design protection is not as old as copyright or patents, design protection dates back to at least the 18th century. France started protecting design in 1737, and England in 1787. The United States' first design patent statute was enacted in 1842. In 1883, the Paris Convention for the Protection of Intellectual Property recognized a system of priority to facilitate the seeking of industrial design protection among its member countries—a topic that will be discussed in Chapter 5.

In 1842, Henry Leavitt Ellsworth, the U.S. Commissioner of Patents, called upon Congress to enact design protection comparable to the protection in England:

> Other nations have granted this privilege, and it has afforded virtual satisfaction alike to the public and to individual applicants. Many who visit the Patent Office learn with astonishment that, no protection is given in this country to this class of persons. Competition among manufacturers for the latest patterns prompts to the highest effort to secure improvements, and calls out the inventive genius of our citizens. Such patterns are immediately pirated, at home and abroad. A pattern introduced at Lowell, for instance, with however great labor or cost, may be taken to England in 12 or 14 days, and copied and returned in 20 days more. If protection is given to designers, better patterns will, it is believed, be obtained, since the impossibility of concealment at present forbids all expense that can be avoided. It may well be asked if authors can so readily find protection in their labors, and inventors of the mechanical arts so easily secure a patent to reward their efforts, why should not discoverers of designs, the labor and expenditure of which may be far greater, have equal privileges afforded them?[6]

Congress enacted a design patent law soon after. The 1842 design statute recognized protection for "any new or original shape or

---

[6] Report from the Commissioner of Patents, Showing the operation of the Patent Office during the year 1841, S. Doc. No. 169, at 2 (2d Sess. 1842).

configuration of any article of manufacture."[7] The rationale was that such useful articles may contain a shape or configuration that was aesthetic or ornamental. One of the first design patents granted in 1843 was for the design of a candlestick holder:

**Figure 1. Drawing for Design of Blake's Girandola (1843)**

In the 19th century, the United States industries were known more for copying foreign designs rather than creating their own designs.[8] Eventually, the U.S. industries became highly innovative developers of designs. Today's design patent act was enacted as a part of the Patent Code in 1952. The ornamental feature is expressly recognized as part of the required subject matter: "Whoever invents any new, original *and ornamental* design for an article of manufacture may obtain a patent therefor, subject to the conditions and requirements of this title." 35 U.S.C. § 171 (emphasis added). We will study design patents in depth in Chapter 2.

---

[7] Patent Act of 1842, ch. 263, § 3, 5 Stat. 543, 543–44.

[8] Janice M. Mueller & Daniel Harris Brean, *Overcoming the "Impossible Issue" of Nonobviousness in Design Patents*, 99 Ky. L.J. 419, 447 (2010–11).

# B. DESIGN PROTECTION

In this section we consider both the theory and practice of design protection. Before studying the various forms of design protection, we consider the threshold question of whether designs should be protected at all. The answer is, by no means, settled today. Then we turn to a broad overview of design protection today, including a discussion of the growth of design protection and the various forms of protection offered.

## 1. DO DESIGNS NEED LEGAL PROTECTION?

It is easy to assume that designs should be protected from copying, at least for a certain period of time. But does this conventional wisdom apply in all industries? Consider the following debate over whether fashion design should be protected. Although the fashion industry may be different from other sectors in which design is important, the basic question—do designs need legal protection—is worth asking generally.

### THE PIRACY PARADOX: INNOVATION AND INTELLECTUAL PROPERTY IN FASHION DESIGN

Kal Raustiala and Christopher Sprigman
92 VA. L. REV. 1687 (2006)

II. The Piracy Paradox

*As fashion spreads, it gradually goes to its doom.*

—Georg Simmel, 1904

The orthodox view of IP law holds that piracy is a serious, even fatal threat to the incentive to engage in creative labor. Certainly, the film, music, software, and publishing industries have used the orthodox theory of IP rights to demand increased legal protections. In Congress, these industries have sought broader and more durable IP protections through new laws such as the Digital Millennium Copyright Act and the Sonny Bono Copyright Term Extension Act. In the courts, they have aggressively fought alleged pirates and their enablers. At the international level, they have pushed the executive branch to negotiate strict new bilateral IP treaties, as well as the landmark 1994 Agreement on the Trade-Related Aspects of Intellectual Property Rights ("TRIPS"), which ties signatories' enforcement of minimum IP standards to the World Trade Organization's powerful dispute resolution mechanisms.

The fashion industry, in comparison, has done none of these things. Fashion firms and designers in the United States have neither obtained expanded copyright protection applicable to apparel designs nor sui generis statutory protection. Why has the industry failed to secure U.S. copyright or quasi-copyright protection for its designs, despite what all observers agree is rampant appropriation?

The answer is not doctrinal. Later, we argue that no substantial doctrinal barrier prevents copyright's extension to fashion designs. If the law could expand to cover fashion design, why hasn't it? This Article seeks to explain why fashion's low-IP rule persists. We offer a theory of why the regime of free appropriation is a stable equilibrium, one that relevant actors have failed to overturn via the political process in the sixty-five years since the fall of the Fashion Originators' Guild. We advance two interrelated theories that we believe are foundational to the continuing viability of fashion's low-IP equilibrium, both of which relate to the economics of fashion. In doing so, we argue that the lack of design protection in fashion is not especially harmful to fashion innovators, and hence they are not incentivized to change it. Indeed, we claim that this low-IP system may paradoxically serve the industry's interests better than a high-IP system.

A. Induced Obsolescence

Clothing is a status-conferring good. Most forms of apparel above the commodity category, and even some apparel within that lowest-level category, function as what economists call "positional goods." These are goods whose value is closely tied to the perception that they are valued by others. The Economist helpfully defines positional goods as: Things that the Joneses buy. Some things are bought for their intrinsic usefulness, for instance, a hammer or a washing machine. Positional goods are bought because of what they say about the person who buys them. They are a way for a person to establish or signal their status relative to people who do not own them: fast cars, holidays in the most fashionable resorts, clothes from trendy designers. Positional goods purchases, consequently, are interdependent: what we buy is partially a function of what others buy. Put another way, the value of a positional good arises in part from social context.

The positionality of a particular good is often two-sided: its desirability may rise as some possess it, but then subsequently fall as more possess it. Take the examples used in the quote directly above. A particular fast car is most desirable when enough people possess it to signal that it is a desired object, but the value diminishes once every person in the neighborhood possesses one. Nothing about the car itself has changed, except for its ability to place its owner among the elite and to separate her from the crowd. Similarly, part of the appeal of a "fashionable" resort is that only a few people know about it, or are able to afford it. For these goods, the value of relative exclusivity may be a large part of the goods' total appeal.

Not all apparel goods are positional, but many are, and that positionality is often two-sided. Particular clothing styles and brands confer prestige. A particular dress or handbag from Gucci or Prada has value, in part, because fashionable people have it and unfashionable ones do not. As those styles diffuse to a broader clientele, frequently the prestige diminishes for the early adopters. This observation is not new. Jean Cocteau tapped into this dynamic of obsolescing attractiveness when he opined that "[a]rt produces ugly things which frequently become more beautiful with time. Fashion, on the other hand, produces beautiful things which always become ugly with time." Even earlier, sociologist Georg Simmel noted the same process: "As fashion spreads, it gradually goes to its doom. The distinctiveness which in the early stages of a set fashion assures for it a certain distribution is destroyed as the fashion spreads, and as this element wanes, the fashion also is bound to die." Perhaps Shakespeare put it most succinctly: "the fashion wears out more apparel than the man."

This process of diffusion leading to dissipation of social value occurs for at least two reasons. First, the diffusion of cheap, obviously inferior copies may tarnish by association the original article, although whether originals are in fact "tarnished" by copies is an empirical question on which there is little research. Indeed, one recent commentator has argued that such low-grade copies actually signal the desirability of the original, thus enhancing its value. Second (and, in our view, much more importantly), for the class of fashion early-adopters, the mere fact that a design is widely diffused is typically enough to diminish its value. It can no longer signify status if it widely adopted. To even a casual follower of fashion, the key point is obvious: what is initially chic rapidly becomes tacky as it diffuses into the broader public, and for true fashion junkies, nothing is less attractive than last year's hot item.

The fashion cycle has long been familiar. What is less commonly appreciated is the role of IP law in fostering the cycle. We argue that fashion's low-IP regime is paradoxically advantageous for the industry. IP rules providing for free appropriation of fashion designs accelerate the diffusion of designs and styles. We call this process "induced obsolescence." If copying were illegal, the fashion cycle would occur very slowly. Instead, the absence of protection for creative designs and the regime of free design appropriation speeds diffusion and induces more rapid obsolescence of fashion designs. As Miucci Prada put it recently, "We let others copy us. And when they do, we drop it." The fashion cycle is driven faster, in other words, by widespread design copying, because copying erodes the positional qualities of fashion goods. Designers in turn respond to this obsolescence with new designs. In short, piracy paradoxically benefits designers by inducing more rapid turnover and additional sales.

Free appropriation of clothing designs contributes to more rapid obsolescence of designs in at least two broad ways. First, copying often results in the marketing of less expensive versions, thus pricing-in consumers who otherwise would not be able to consume the design. What was elite quickly becomes mass.

As in other industries, the significance of design copying turns somewhat on the closeness of the copying. If design copies were readily discernable from originals by the casual observer, the status premium conferred by the original design would, in large part, remain. It is often quite difficult, however, to distinguish copies from originals, or to determine which version actually is the original. As the examples shown in Part I demonstrate, many copies are not visibly inferior compared with the originals, at least not without very close inspection.

Trademarks can help distinguish the original from the various copies, and thus distinguish elites from the masses. As noted above, trademarks only occasionally appear prominently on the outside of clothing. More often, they are not visible unless one looks inside an item of clothing. Where there is a visible mark, it blunts some of the effects of copying on the diffusion of innovative designs. (This may help explain what some believe is an increase in visible trademarks on apparel.) For the majority of items, however, the trademark is not visible to others, rendering the original and the copy strikingly similar.

In arguing that trademark law alone does not inhibit copying of designs, we do not wish to suggest that trademarks are unimportant. Even in a competitive environment that includes substantial freedom to copy, particular firms are known as design innovators. The Chanel firm and its head designer, Karl Lagerfeld, for example, have originated many influential styles of women's clothing. Because of the firm's reputation, and the resultant strength of its mark, Chanel is able to charge very high prices for apparel, even for apparel, such as its signature women's jacket, that is widely copied by other firms. What Chanel is not able to do, however, is establish itself as an exclusive purveyor of its own designs—an option it would have if U.S. copyright law protected Chanel's designs as well as its trademarks.

Additionally, many "copies" are not point-by-point reproductions at all, but instead new garments that appropriate design elements from the original and recast them in a derivative work. This observation brings us to the second way in which copying drives induced obsolescence. A regime of free appropriation contributes to the rapid production of substantially new designs that were creatively inspired by the original design. Importantly, this regime is precisely the opposite of the default rule under the copyright laws, which allocate to the originator the exclusive right to make or authorize derivative works. The many variations made possible by unrestricted exploitation of derivatives contributes to product differentiation that induces consumption by those who prefer a particular variation to the original. To the extent that derivatives remain visibly linked to the original design, they help diffuse the original design. This, in turn, further accelerates the process by which the design (and its derivatives) become less attractive to early adopters.

This account suggests an obvious response: if copying and derivative reworking have this effect, originating design houses would have an incentive to reproduce their original designs and variations of those designs in garments at different price levels—thus pursuing a single-firm price discrimination strategy. In other words, if this argument is correct, we should expect the originator to reproduce its own designs at lower price points, and to elaborate derivatives, rather than let competitors do it. In a recent article, Jonathan Barnett notes this puzzle and suggests further that one might even expect innovating firms to give away cheaper, visibly inferior versions of the product. Barnett argues that brand protection, the desire to maintain the exclusivity of a brand such as Gucci, stops this from occurring in the real world. Yet, the question remains why the same design could not be introduced by the same firm, but under a different brand.

The answer is that firms sometimes do pursue a single-firm strategy via bridge lines. While some fashion insiders stress the danger of bridge lines blurring a brand's identity and tarnishing a mark, many well-known design houses have a second line that is lower-priced, such as Armani's "Emporio Armani" or Dolce & Gabbana's "D & G." One way to understand the phenomenon of bridge lines is precisely as a strategy to achieve some measure of vertical integration—in essence, knocking off one's own signature designs to price discriminate among consumers. Themes developed in the premier lines are echoed in the bridge lines, but with cheaper materials, lower prices, and design variations pitched to the particular tastes of that bridge line's constituency. The most prominent user of this strategy is Armani, which has up to five distinct lines, depending on how one counts. Most fashion firms, however, do not follow the Armani model. Why the Armani model—or a model in which a single firm self-copies designs at multiple price points under different brand names—is not more prevalent is an interesting question for future research. Given the absence of IP protection and the reality faced by originating firms that other firms often will appropriate their designs at lower price levels, the economic incentives to self-appropriate via bridge lines would seem strong. Moreover, the objections to damaging the value of the brand can be overcome by using different labels and segmenting sales at different outlets. It is clear that at least some degree of self-appropriation occurs through the common practice of an (often single) bridge line. It is also clear, however, that fashion firms often do not price-discriminate via bridge lines even when they know others will do so.

While we observe some self-copying, we do not see any sustained attempt by fashion firms to prevent appropriation of their original designs by other firms. If self-appropriation through bridge lines were an optimal strategy for a large number of fashion firms, we suspect that the current low-IP equilibrium might not long endure, for a logical corollary to a more fully elaborated single-firm strategy based on bridge lines is a strategy of blocking others from appropriating one's designs. In any event, for the moment, the industry's longstanding tolerance of appropriation contributes to the rapid diffusion of original designs. Rapid diffusion leads early-adopter consumers to seek out new designs on a regular basis, which in turn leads to more copying, which fuels yet another design shift. The fashion cycle, in sum, is propelled by piracy.

## THE LAW, CULTURE, AND ECONOMICS OF FASHION

C. Scott Hemphill & Jeannie Suk
61 STAN. L. REV. 1147 (2009)

B. The Threat to Innovation

Mass copyists undermine the market for the copied good. Copies reduce the profitability of originals, thus reducing the prospective incentive to develop new designs in the first place. The predicted result, a reduced amount of innovation, is familiar from copying in other creative industries, such as file sharing of copyrighted music and films.

Fashion copying is different from file sharing, however, in an important respect. File sharing provides access to essentially every musical work. Fashion copyists, by contrast, are selective. They have a business to run and costs to recoup, and so only the most profitable designs are copied. Moreover, not all copies reduce producer profits. Some are relatively harmless.

The selectivity of copyists, combined with the uneven effects on producer profitability, reduce the incentives of some producers—and the incentive to produce some products—more than others. Thus, mass copying can be expected to affect the direction of innovation as well, as we explain below.

1. Harmful copying

Copyists target designs that are technically and legally easy to copy. Consider, for example, a floral-patterned dress introduced by designers Dana Foley and Anna Corinna (F&C). As a technical matter, the dress was easy to copy. It contained no exotic fabrics, complicated tailoring, or delicate embellishments that would make accurate outsourcing difficult. It lacked any exterior brand logo that would subject a copyist to trademark liability. Its shape and exterior details did not so powerfully call to mind F&C's identity that trade dress protection would be available. These facts made the dress a good target for copyists. [Photographs comparing the dresses are available at http://fashionista.com/2007/04/adventures-in-copyright-infringement-part-six. *Ed.*]

Moreover, for a midrange designer such as F&C, the sales of the copy substitute for and hence reduce sales of the original. The original dress sold for hundreds, not thousands of dollars, which is within the reach of copyists' customers. Sometimes the substitution is made by an aggressive retailer, rather than the final consumer. Either way, the profits of the original designer can be much reduced.

The extent of targeting, combined with the degree of substitution, explain why midrange designers account for most anecdotal complaints of design copying. They also bring most of the lawsuits that attempt to circumvent the lack of design protection by alleging copyright or trade dress violations under existing law, against Forever 21 and other fast-fashion copyists.

In addition to replacing sales, the prevalence of cheaper copies also may reduce demand for the original design. This "snob" effect may reflect a consumer's desire for distinction from lower-status consumers or from other consumers more generally. It is a negative externality of overuse with analogies in trademark and copyright. The effect is amplified, moreover, when the same shopper visits different stores—or different floors of the same department store—selling a particular design in its original and copied forms.

2. Distorting innovation

The reduced profits can be expected to have a negative effect on the amount of innovation; this is a standard result of economic theory. But in addition, there is a second effect. The lack of protection against design copying, combined with the existence of trademark, trade dress, and other protections, also distorts the direction of innovation. Designers unprotected against design copying see a disproportionate effect on their profitability, and hence are discouraged from innovating—indeed, from entering in the first place. Designers who are protected by trademark and trade dress innovate in ways that play to these legal advantages. The resulting effect on the direction of innovation is to favor innovation by designers who already enjoy existing protection by other aspects of intellectual property law, over innovation by designers—particularly small, new designers—who are not thus protected. The existence of some kinds of intellectual property protection combined with the absence of design protection also gives designers the incentive to create some kinds of products over others.

Consider, for example, trade dress, which protects features of product design that serve as a source identifier, such as the distinctive hardware of a Coach handbag. In two cases, the Supreme Court considered whether trade dress protection requires a showing that consumers have come to identify the feature with its maker, so-called "secondary meaning," or instead can rely upon the inherent distinctiveness of the feature. In the first case, outside the context of fashion designs, the Court ruled that secondary meaning was not necessary, in part because it recognized that such a requirement would place "particular burdens on the startup of small companies," because established firms are better positioned to imbue their products with secondary meaning. However, it later ruled that secondary meaning is required for trade dress in apparel and other product designs.

The result is to favor those incumbents with the resources to invest in the creation of secondary meaning.

Trademark reinforces the incumbency bias in a powerful way. Brand logos provide strong protection against copying by legitimate producers. Designers understand the value of logos as an anticopying device. Trademark protection accompanied by a lack of design protection thereby favors those firms that have strong trademarks and disproportionately encourages production of trademark-protected goods, such as articles with logos. After all, if Gucci can prohibit copies of designs that employ its trademark interlocked "G's," but not a similar work that lacks the logos, it has an incentive to employ the logo. It also encourages the production of types of items, such as handbags, for which logos (and trade dress) are highly complementary. Such "logoification" affects the communicative vocabulary that fashion provides, pulling fashion toward a status-conferring function and away from the communication of diverse messages.

Incumbents that produce luxury goods have several further advantages. Many high-end articles are hard to copy with low-cost outsourcing because they use expensive and distinctive materials and finishes. Investments in brand image provide an additional source of protection, and hence a further source of innovation distortion. A luxury image and retail buying experience insulate some high-end products from harmful copying. Brand image cements customer loyalty, a pampering in-store experience is pleasurable, and some customers value the authenticity of purchasing an original. These effects reduce substitution when copying occurs. They may also discourage copying, as they leave a copyist uncertain whether an item's appeal comes from its design, or instead from the inimitable purchase experience. Large incumbents are better able to apply that investment across high volumes and a wide variety of items. The F&Cs of the design world—less-established designers who are not large incumbents—are again at a disadvantage.

A common normative response against the idea of intellectual property protection for fashion design grows out of the assumption that fashion is a visible marker of status. On this theory, making it more difficult to copy fashion may seem undesirable because it would promote the ability of wealthy people to enjoy and signal their status through apparel that only they can have, and thwart those who want to purchase cheaper knockoffs of those goods. After all, if rampant copying makes available cheaper knockoffs, that may disrupt the ability of the wealthy to distinguish themselves as a group through the signal of fashion. On this view, perhaps permission to copy effectively softens the socially stratifying effects of fashion, while legal restrictions on copying would reinforce them.

But there is much more to fashion than signals about status. In light of the broader and more varied communicative and expressive aspects of fashion, status is only one of a wide variety of signals that fashion makes possible. Fashion has the potential to afford a broad vocabulary for the expression of a vast range of possible messages. Conscious or not, people's fashion choices signify and communicate, with meaningful individual and collective valences. We have identified this dynamic between differentiation and flocking as the key to the experience of fashion in social life. People use fashion to signal individual differences while also partaking in common movement with the collectivity. This model has informed our analysis of the formation and function of fashion trends among producers and consumers.

The current intellectual property regime, in which legal protection from design copying is lacking, tends, if anything, to push fashion consumption and production in the direction of status and luxury rather than more polyvalent innovation. In sum, we have noted two distortions. The first is toward the creation of designs that are legally more difficult to copy. Trademark and trade dress already protect the most salient status-signaling items in fashion, those adorned with logos of high-end brands. Therefore, those who want to enable effective status signal-jamming should be critical of trademark protection, and not necessarily resist copyright protection for fashion design. The second distortion is toward the creation of goods that are naturally (as opposed to legally) more difficult to copy, or goods that are more difficult for design copying to harm—for example, goods involving unusual or expensive materials or difficult workmanship.

The result of these distortions is to push creators toward the high-end realm of status and luxury, and away from devoting creative resources to design innovation. In a regime that protected original designs from copying, we would expect to see a shift in resources from developing brand-name or luxury goods or attempting close copies of designs toward developing a richer, more polycentric language of fashion that draws on and reinvents available inspirations and influences. We would expect to see greater range and variety in fashion innovation that would enlarge the vocabulary and the set of symbols with which we may produce meaning.

At bottom, though, the main reason not to accommodate the lovers of cheap fashion knockoffs is more basic. It is the same reason that we do not have a legal regime that permits people freely to make and sell photocopies of another author's book and retain the profits. It is the theory of incentives. Obviously, people always want to purchase inexpensive copies of creative works or have them for free. The reason to disallow it is not to deprive them of that benefit but rather to provide creators with an incentive to create. That is no less true in fashion.

### C. Is Piracy Really Beneficial?

The analysis so far shows that copyists reduce the amount of innovation and distort its direction. In an influential article, Kal Raustiala and Chris Sprigman (RS) have advanced the counterintuitive argument that in the fashion industry, "piracy paradoxically benefits designers."

Some observers have found their argument persuasive. Here we explain why we disagree with their argument.

RS start from the premise that derivation, inspiration, and borrowing are valuable and central to fashion and innovation. This general point is one that we too emphasize. But this does not make fashion relevantly different from music and film, where the same processes are important engines of innovation. In order to conclude, as they do, that "[w]hat works to protect the creative process in film and music will have the opposite effect on the runway," more is needed.

RS argue that the proliferation of copies of a style reduces the value of the style and renders it obsolete, which, in turn, causes consumers and hence producers to move on to new designs and trends. At first, producer profits are high. Then the copyists come in, and snob effects reduce the value of the good in the hands of existing users and would-be new users. New sales grind to a halt, and existing users become dissatisfied with the goods that they have. That, in turn, provides a new opportunity to sell new goods. RS call this "induced obsolescence." Because the opportunity to sell new goods is profitable, and entails additional innovation, RS argue that copying benefits designers and innovation. Hence the "piracy paradox." In light of this benefit, RS conclude it is a bad idea to protect designers from piracy. This type of argument has long played a role in debates over design protection. RS's analysis does not distinguish close copies from other relationships between fashion designs, such as interpretation, adaptation, homage, or remixing. In arguing that "growth and creativity in the fashion industry depend upon copying," the "piracy" part of the "piracy paradox" is seemingly meant to include both close copies and the full range of remixing and trend-joining activities.

RS treat close copying and shared trends as indistinguishable for their purposes, referring to both phenomena as "copies." We have explained above that it is important to disaggregate the phenomenon of close copying from the phenomenon of trends. Doing so helps make visible the effects on innovation of close copying as distinct from the effects of interpretation, inspiration, or homage. As we have also explained, there are also important differences among fast-fashion firms—differences between fellow designers such as Zara and H&M and copyists such as Forever 21—and their contrasting effects upon innovation. To be complete, an analysis must attend to the distinctive effect of close copyists. To consider an analogy, the argument that a broad remixing right for music benefits subsequent innovators tells us little about whether to prohibit exact copies.

RS's "induced obsolescence" account emphasizes the increased profitability of faster cycles of new fashion trends spurred by unchecked copying. The assumption of profitability calls to mind Dr. Seuss's famous fable of the Sneetches. There, the seller offered a new fashion article—stars to adorn the chest of each Sneetch. When too many Sneetches bought the stars, devaluing them, the seller provided a new service: star removal. These cycles continued, with the seller profiting from each cycle, until the Sneetches ran out of money.

This account, focused upon copies as the spur to the new, neglects the ex ante effect of the fashion cycle. What made star conferral and removal so profitable was that each Sneetch failed to recognize just how short-lived his fashion success would be, and to plan accordingly. Sneetches are not lifecycle pricers, in other words. But many fashion buyers are. If copying increases, and hence the fashion lifespan of the item falls, a consumer will recognize that fact and lower her willingness to pay. In the limiting case, producers' revenue is unchanged, as consumers make unchanged periodic payments for fashion, and profits fall due to higher (because more frequently incurred) design, materials, and other costs of production. Close copies make matters worse, reducing designer profits in the meantime by reducing sales.

The adverse effects of copying explain why many designers oppose copying, just as they oppose counterfeiting of handbags. (RS's piracy paradox argument, if correct, ought to apply to fashion trademarks and copyrights as well.) RS pitch their paradox as an explanation for the otherwise puzzling equanimity with which designers greet copyists. But that premise is faulty. In fact, many designers are vocal advocates against copying, and, as Table 1 suggests, make use of the currently limited legal tools available to curb copyists.

**Table 1. Selected U.S. Litigation Against Forever 21, 2007–2008**

| Plaintiff | Articles at Issue |
|---|---|
| Anna Sui | Seventeen articles |
| Anthropologie | Ten articles |
| Bebe Stores | Twenty-eight articles |
| Carole Hochman | Nightgown with "Marilyn Monrose" fabric design |
| Diane von Furstenberg | Four wrap dresses and one blouse |
| Harajuku Lovers | Clothing with "Heart and Heart/Box design" print |
| Harkham Industries | Dress with "Shadow Fern" design |
| Trovata | Six articles |

Vigorous designer opposition to copyists is not new. Designers cared so much in the 1930s that they set up an enormous, costly, and successful private system of self-help, the Fashion Originators' Guild of America, which boycotted retailers that did business with copyists, until it was enjoined as a violation of antitrust law. Their decades-long lobbying effort for stronger protection has been unsuccessful, not because designers are not harmed, but because they are not sufficiently powerful.

The induced obsolescence account has a further evidentiary limitation. If designers did profit from "induced obsolescence" of their products, they could induce the obsolescence themselves by taking a lax approach to counterfeits, or by engineering products designed to fall apart quickly. That they do not do so where it is currently feasible suggests that inducing obsolescence is not what fashion designers are engaged in. Even with protection, designers interested in an induced-obsolescence strategy could implement it by disclaiming protection against copying, or by burning out the trend more profitably on their own, without any help from copyists. Moreover, since, as we have explained, fashion trends do not depend on copying, designers would not need to induce obsolescence through copies in order to ensure the robust trends that comprise fashion.

### *NOTES AND QUESTIONS*

1. What is the piracy paradox for fashion designs? According to Kal Raustiala and Christopher Sprigman, how might the piracy paradox explain—and justify—copying of fashion design?

2. What is the response of C. Scott Hemphill and Jeannie Suk to the piracy paradox? What distortions result from the lack of fashion design protection, according to Hemphill and Suk?

3. Which of the two positions do you find more persuasive? Should Congress enact a law to protect new fashion designs from copying in "knock offs"?

4. *Utilitarian versus natural rights theories.* One way of thinking about the debate over protecting designs is through the debate between utilitarian and natural rights theories of intellectual property. A utilitarian approach emphasizes maximizing utility and sees intellectual property as a means to an end—enhancing social welfare. Under this approach, intellectual property is often justified as a way to provide sufficient incentives for people to create, on the fear or assumption that fewer people would create if their creations could be copied with impunity. In the debate over fashion design protection above, the scholars disputed how copying fashion designs would hurt (or not) the incentives for fashion designers to create, for example. By contrast, a natural rights approach views the act of creation as imbuing the creator with certain rewards for her labor, including a right to exclude others from copying. Which theory provides a better framework to understand how we should approach design protection?

## 2. GROWTH IN POPULARITY AND IMPORTANCE OF DESIGN PROTECTION

Although design protection has been available for a long time, we have witnessed a surge in its popularity internationally in the past decade. Since 2000, the number of applications for design patents has doubled from 18,282 in 2000 to 39,097 in 2015. Likewise, the Patent Office's granting of design patents also doubled from 17,413 in 2000 to 25,986 in 2015 (source: USPTO, patent technology monitoring team: https://www.uspto.gov/web/offices/ac/ido/oeip/taf/us_stat.htm). Table 1 below summarizes the number of design patents granted from 1991 to 2015, with subtotals by countries where the applicant was based, while Table 2 summarizes the same information by percentages of the design patents granted. Notice the growth of design patents obtained by entities of both U.S. and foreign origin starting in 2006. What do you think spurred the international growth in applications? Could it be related to development of the high-tech industries, such as the launch of the iPhone in 2007 and other smartphones thereafter? Table 3 below identifies the companies that received the most grants of design patents.

## Table 1. U.S. Design Patent Grants from 1999 to 2015 (by numbers)

Technology Assessment and Forecast Report

DESIGN PATENTS REPORT

Page A1- 1

---- Patents Granted By Date Of Patent Grant (Granted: Jan 01, 1991 - Dec 31, 2015) ----

------------ NUMBER OF PATENTS ------------

| | | Pre 2002 | 2002 | 2003 | 2004 | 2005 | 2006 | 2007 | 2008 | 2009 | 2010 | 2011 | 2012 | 2013 | 2014 | 2015 | Total |
|---|---|---|---|---|---|---|---|---|---|---|---|---|---|---|---|---|---|
| Total | | 138881 | 15451 | 16574 | 15695 | 12951 | 20965 | 24062 | 25565 | 23116 | 22799 | 21356 | 21951 | 23468 | 23657 | 25986 | 432477 |
| | U.S. Origin | 92257 | 9325 | 10045 | 9252 | 7554 | 11691 | 13494 | 13713 | 12026 | 12612 | 11756 | 12445 | 13312 | 13385 | 14335 | 257202 |
| | Foreign Origin | 46624 | 6126 | 6529 | 6443 | 5397 | 9274 | 10568 | 11852 | 11090 | 10187 | 9600 | 9506 | 10156 | 10272 | 11651 | 175275 |
| | JAPAN | 13019 | 1364 | 1567 | 1568 | 1384 | 2405 | 2416 | 2767 | 2415 | 1910 | 1869 | 1899 | 2092 | 1975 | 1878 | 40528 |
| | TAIWAN | 6498 | 1294 | 1370 | 1268 | 870 | 1553 | 1355 | 1423 | 1114 | 1348 | 1086 | 953 | 1024 | 908 | 877 | 22941 |
| | GERMANY | 3650 | 509 | 509 | 476 | 474 | 773 | 810 | 976 | 1196 | 1070 | 909 | 1051 | 960 | 930 | 1040 | 15333 |
| | KOREA, SOUTH | 1008 | 211 | 186 | 238 | 233 | 589 | 957 | 1159 | 785 | 769 | 902 | 864 | 1102 | 1630 | 2238 | 12871 |
| | CANADA | 4192 | 410 | 446 | 398 | 277 | 501 | 632 | 705 | 712 | 635 | 704 | 661 | 701 | 617 | 673 | 12264 |
| | UNITED KINGDOM | 2653 | 305 | 356 | 401 | 369 | 663 | 674 | 685 | 777 | 659 | 574 | 600 | 702 | 603 | 702 | 10723 |
| | FRANCE | 2675 | 350 | 227 | 286 | 222 | 395 | 556 | 600 | 628 | 586 | 458 | 435 | 420 | 395 | 420 | 8653 |
| | ITALY | 2070 | 205 | 292 | 358 | 294 | 416 | 524 | 544 | 485 | 439 | 437 | 412 | 418 | 393 | 425 | 7712 |
| | CHINA, PEOPLE'S REPUB | 141 | 102 | 127 | 192 | 163 | 309 | 455 | 626 | 606 | 645 | 603 | 694 | 661 | 676 | 881 | 6881 |
| | CHINA, HONG KONG S.A. | 2268 | 355 | 404 | 329 | 311 | 445 | 425 | 426 | 288 | 285 | 236 | 212 | 216 | 211 | 189 | 6600 |
| | AUSTRALIA | 1081 | 103 | 120 | 114 | 90 | 160 | 241 | 253 | 299 | 282 | 265 | 226 | 269 | 273 | 247 | 4023 |
| | SWITZERLAND | 1104 | 165 | 123 | 125 | 111 | 182 | 240 | 285 | 241 | 276 | 199 | 200 | 190 | 199 | 283 | 3923 |
| | SWEDEN | 1326 | 142 | 106 | 97 | 65 | 112 | 207 | 190 | 207 | 150 | 142 | 177 | 155 | 177 | 225 | 3478 |
| | NETHERLANDS | 769 | 69 | 79 | 50 | 63 | 107 | 124 | 127 | 102 | 113 | 148 | 117 | 165 | 98 | 186 | 2317 |
| | DENMARK | 809 | 54 | 55 | 40 | 40 | 33 | 63 | 126 | 125 | 134 | 90 | 105 | 158 | 151 | 137 | 2120 |
| | AUSTRIA | 288 | 27 | 43 | 34 | 28 | 48 | 93 | 107 | 264 | 177 | 171 | 129 | 117 | 96 | 104 | 1726 |
| | ISRAEL | 355 | 56 | 47 | 47 | 44 | 64 | 80 | 119 | 92 | 79 | 93 | 86 | 119 | 122 | 149 | 1552 |
| | BELGIUM | 449 | 66 | 64 | 50 | 55 | 69 | 90 | 85 | 92 | 62 | 128 | 112 | 71 | 72 | 78 | 1543 |
| | SPAIN | 378 | 55 | 48 | 39 | 41 | 81 | 93 | 109 | 81 | 59 | 91 | 83 | 54 | 62 | 88 | 1362 |
| | FINLAND | 274 | 46 | 77 | 35 | 31 | 53 | 92 | 82 | 132 | 82 | 65 | 60 | 65 | 116 | 100 | 1310 |
| | SINGAPORE | 105 | 11 | 33 | 36 | 29 | 55 | 56 | 49 | 56 | 27 | 49 | 30 | 59 | 60 | 82 | 737 |
| | NEW ZEALAND | 171 | 26 | 18 | 30 | 11 | 32 | 37 | 46 | 44 | 34 | 46 | 55 | 34 | 43 | 58 | 685 |
| | NORWAY | 157 | 19 | 17 | 11 | 21 | 27 | 39 | 24 | 27 | 46 | 45 | 26 | 43 | 54 | 60 | 616 |
| | BRAZIL | 76 | 15 | 50 | 55 | 21 | 26 | 23 | 29 | 44 | 43 | 39 | 59 | 32 | 28 | 58 | 598 |
| | MEXICO | 121 | 10 | 8 | 15 | 15 | 22 | 33 | 23 | 20 | 13 | 27 | 30 | 48 | 49 | 31 | 465 |
| | INDIA | 14 | 6 | 7 | 9 | 16 | 19 | 24 | 37 | 38 | 37 | 24 | 37 | 45 | 57 | 59 | 429 |
| | SOUTH AFRICA | 98 | 8 | 14 | 14 | 16 | 13 | 30 | 32 | 39 | 23 | 19 | 14 | 20 | 26 | 29 | 395 |
| | IRELAND | 90 | 15 | 19 | 10 | 13 | 22 | 15 | 24 | 8 | 18 | 14 | 16 | 28 | 23 | 37 | 352 |
| | LUXEMBOURG | 167 | 14 | 18 | 11 | 8 | 15 | 28 | 11 | 20 | 12 | 7 | 7 | 8 | 14 | 11 | 351 |
| | THAILAND | 78 | 16 | 20 | 10 | 9 | 10 | 13 | 17 | 13 | 12 | 19 | 10 | 24 | 24 | 20 | 295 |
| | MALAYSIA | 82 | 7 | 13 | 12 | 10 | 18 | 15 | 16 | 22 | 22 | 20 | 8 | 16 | 12 | 11 | 284 |
| | POLAND | 7 | 2 | 2 | 3 | 2 | 2 | 6 | 14 | 8 | 17 | 22 | 18 | 15 | 21 | 23 | 162 |
| | TURKEY | 5 | 3 | 5 | 6 | 3 | 9 | 5 | 19 | 17 | 16 | 11 | 7 | 8 | 13 | 18 | 145 |
| | RUSSIAN FEDERATION | 17 | 3 | | 3 | 2 | 2 | 4 | 4 | 7 | 12 | 9 | 7 | 14 | 3 | 41 | 128 |
| | ARGENTINA | 35 | 4 | 7 | 4 | 5 | 7 | 14 | 9 | 4 | 8 | 2 | 4 | 5 | 8 | 5 | 121 |
| | INDONESIA | 31 | 8 | 3 | 17 | 12 | 12 | 8 | 8 | 1 | | 4 | 4 | | 6 | 1 | 115 |
| | Others (92 ) | 363 | 71 | 49 | 52 | 39 | 25 | 91 | 96 | 81 | 87 | 73 | 98 | 98 | 127 | 187 | 1537 |
| Ownership: | | | | | | | | | | | | | | | | | |
| | U.S. Corporations | 55205 | 6264 | 6933 | 6421 | 5370 | 8590 | 10015 | 10325 | 8869 | 9005 | 8643 | 8947 | 9705 | 9881 | 10483 | 174656 |
| | U.S. Government | 16 | 5 | 2 | 1 | 2 | 1 | 3 | 5 | 5 | 14 | 5 | 4 | 6 | 1 | 6 | 76 |
| | U.S. Individuals | 39047 | 3202 | 3229 | 2914 | 2342 | 3270 | 3763 | 3881 | 3647 | 3874 | 3475 | 3838 | 3919 | 3865 | 4112 | 88378 |
| | Foreign Corporations | 34003 | 4605 | 4967 | 5222 | 4368 | 7712 | 8841 | 9826 | 9396 | 8653 | 8072 | 8054 | 8545 | 8682 | 10149 | 141095 |
| | Foreign Government | 2 | 1 | 2 | 2 | | 2 | 1 | 1 | 1 | 1 | | 3 | | | | 16 |
| | Foreign Individuals | 10608 | 1374 | 1441 | 1135 | 869 | 1390 | 1439 | 1527 | 1198 | 1252 | 1161 | 1105 | 1293 | 1228 | 1236 | 28256 |

(Source: https://www.uspto.gov/web/offices/ac/ido/oeip/taf/design.pdf)

## Table 2. U.S. Design Patent Grants from 1999 to 2015 (by percentages)

DESIGN PATENTS REPORT

Technology Assessment and Forecast Report

Page A1- 2

---- Patents Granted By Date Of Patent Grant (Granted: Jan 01, 1991 - Dec 31, 2015) ----

NUMBER OF PATENTS

| | Pre 2002 | 2002 | 2003 | 2004 | 2005 | 2006 | 2007 | 2008 | 2009 | 2010 | 2011 | 2012 | 2013 | 2014 | 2015 | Total |
|---|---|---|---|---|---|---|---|---|---|---|---|---|---|---|---|---|
| Total | 100 | 100 | 100 | 100 | 100 | 100 | 100 | 100 | 100 | 100 | 100 | 100 | 100 | 100 | 100 | 100 |
| U.S. Origin | 66 | 60 | 61 | 59 | 58 | 56 | 56 | 54 | 52 | 55 | 55 | 57 | 57 | 57 | 55 | 59 |
| Foreign Origin | 34 | 40 | 39 | 41 | 42 | 44 | 44 | 46 | 48 | 45 | 45 | 43 | 43 | 43 | 45 | 41 |
| JAPAN | 9 | 9 | 9 | 10 | 11 | 11 | 10 | 11 | 10 | 8 | 9 | 9 | 9 | 8 | 7 | 9 |
| TAIWAN | 5 | 8 | 8 | 8 | 7 | 7 | 6 | 6 | 5 | 6 | 5 | 4 | 4 | 4 | 3 | 5 |
| GERMANY | 3 | 3 | 3 | 3 | 4 | 4 | 3 | 4 | 5 | 5 | 4 | 5 | 4 | 4 | 4 | 4 |
| KOREA, SOUTH | 1 | 1 | 1 | 2 | 2 | 3 | 4 | 5 | 3 | 3 | 4 | 4 | 5 | 7 | 9 | 3 |
| CANADA | 3 | 3 | 3 | 3 | 2 | 2 | 3 | 3 | 3 | 3 | 3 | 3 | 3 | 3 | 3 | 3 |
| UNITED KINGDOM | 2 | 2 | 2 | 3 | 3 | 3 | 3 | 3 | 3 | 3 | 3 | 3 | 3 | 3 | 3 | 2 |
| FRANCE | 2 | 2 | 1 | 2 | 2 | 2 | 2 | 2 | 3 | 3 | 2 | 2 | 2 | 2 | 2 | 2 |
| ITALY | 1 | 1 | 2 | 2 | 2 | 2 | 2 | 2 | 2 | 2 | 2 | 2 | 2 | 2 | 2 | 2 |
| CHINA, PEOPLE'S REPUB | | 1 | 1 | 1 | 1 | 1 | 2 | 2 | 3 | 3 | 3 | 3 | 3 | 3 | 3 | 2 |
| CHINA, HONG KONG S.A. | 2 | 2 | 2 | 2 | 2 | 2 | 2 | 2 | 1 | 1 | 1 | 1 | 1 | 1 | 1 | 2 |
| AUSTRALIA | 1 | 1 | 1 | 1 | 1 | 1 | 1 | 1 | 1 | 1 | 1 | 1 | 1 | 1 | 1 | 1 |
| SWITZERLAND | 1 | 1 | 1 | 1 | 1 | 1 | 1 | 1 | 1 | 1 | 1 | 1 | 1 | 1 | 1 | 1 |
| SWEDEN | 1 | 1 | 1 | 1 | 1 | 1 | 1 | 1 | 1 | 1 | 1 | 1 | 1 | 1 | 1 | 1 |
| NETHERLANDS | 1 | | | | | 1 | 1 | | | | 1 | 1 | 1 | | 1 | 1 |
| DENMARK | 1 | | | | | | | | 1 | 1 | | | 1 | 1 | 1 | 0 |
| AUSTRIA | | | | | | | | | 1 | 1 | 1 | 1 | | | | 0 |
| ISRAEL | | | | | | | | | | | | | 1 | 1 | 1 | 0 |
| BELGIUM | | | | | | | | | | | 1 | 1 | | | | 0 |
| SPAIN | | | | | | | | | | | | | | | | 0 |
| FINLAND | | | | | | | | | 1 | | | | | | | 0 |
| SINGAPORE | | | | | | | | | | | | | | | | 0 |
| NEW ZEALAND | | | | | | | | | | | | | | | | 0 |
| NORWAY | | | | | | | | | | | | | | | | 0 |
| BRAZIL | | | | | | | | | | | | | | | | 0 |
| MEXICO | | | | | | | | | | | | | | | | 0 |
| INDIA | | | | | | | | | | | | | | | | 0 |
| SOUTH AFRICA | | | | | | | | | | | | | | | | 0 |
| IRELAND | | | | | | | | | | | | | | | | 0 |
| LUXEMBOURG | | | | | | | | | | | | | | | | 0 |
| THAILAND | | | | | | | | | | | | | | | | 0 |
| MALAYSIA | | | | | | | | | | | | | | | | 0 |
| POLAND | | | | | | | | | | | | | | | | 0 |
| TURKEY | | | | | | | | | | | | | | | | 0 |
| RUSSIAN FEDERATION | | | | | | | | | | | | | | | | 0 |
| ARGENTINA | | | | | | | | | | | | | | | | 0 |
| INDONESIA | | | | | | | | | | | | | | | | 0 |
| Others (92 ) | | | | | | | | | | | | | | 1 | 1 | 0 |
| Ownership: | | | | | | | | | | | | | | | | |
| U.S. Corporations | 40 | 41 | 42 | 41 | 41 | 41 | 42 | 40 | 38 | 39 | 40 | 41 | 41 | 42 | 40 | 40 |
| U.S. Government | | | | | | | | | | | | | | | | 0 |
| U.S. Individuals | 28 | 21 | 19 | 19 | 18 | 16 | 16 | 15 | 16 | 17 | 16 | 17 | 17 | 16 | 16 | 20 |
| Foreign Corporations | 24 | 30 | 30 | 33 | 34 | 37 | 37 | 38 | 41 | 38 | 38 | 37 | 36 | 37 | 39 | 33 |
| Foreign Government | | | | | | | | | | | | | | | | 0 |
| Foreign Individuals | 8 | 9 | 9 | 7 | 7 | 7 | 6 | 6 | 5 | 5 | 5 | 5 | 6 | 5 | 5 | 7 |

(Source: https://www.uspto.gov/web/offices/ac/ido/oeip/taf/design.pdf)

## Table 3. Top Companies for U.S. Design Patent Grants from 1999 to 2015

DESIGN PATENTS REPORT

Technology Assessment and Forecast Report

Page B - 1

Organizational Patenting (Granted: Jan 01, 1991 - Dec 31, 2015) Ranked List of Organizations with 70 or More Patents

| | Pre 2002 | 2002 | 2003 | 2004 | 2005 | 2006 | 2007 | 2008 | 2009 | 2010 | 2011 | 2012 | 2013 | 2014 | 2015 | TOTAL |
|---|---|---|---|---|---|---|---|---|---|---|---|---|---|---|---|---|
| SAMSUNG ELECTRONICS CO., LTD. | | | | | | | | | | | | | | | | |
| Patents By Year of Grant: | 81 | 3 | 3 | 8 | 80 | 261 | 622 | 768 | 465 | 383 | 328 | 378 | 515 | 836 | 1428 | 6159 |
| Patents By Year of Application: | 88 | 2 | 10 | 155 | 459 | 678 | 467 | 440 | 338 | 367 | 491 | 887 | 1326 | 438 | 13 | 6159 |
| NIKE, INC. | | | | | | | | | | | | | | | | |
| Patents By Year of Grant: | 1092 | 68 | 63 | 109 | 97 | 295 | 220 | 184 | 74 | 85 | 120 | 122 | 281 | 229 | 171 | 3210 |
| Patents By Year of Application: | 1117 | 94 | 86 | 169 | 173 | 191 | 223 | 110 | 86 | 62 | 139 | 230 | 251 | 217 | 62 | 3210 |
| SONY CORPORATION | | | | | | | | | | | | | | | | |
| Patents By Year of Grant: | 1268 | 167 | 154 | 158 | 161 | 172 | 222 | 230 | 182 | 84 | 82 | 100 | 100 | 53 | 49 | 3182 |
| Patents By Year of Application: | 1445 | 166 | 168 | 214 | 209 | 226 | 185 | 129 | 70 | 128 | 93 | 93 | 34 | 18 | 4 | 3182 |
| MICROSOFT CORPORATION | | | | | | | | | | | | | | | | |
| Patents By Year of Grant: | 114 | 12 | 17 | 32 | 40 | 153 | 327 | 286 | 257 | 214 | 182 | 302 | 409 | 329 | 318 | 2992 |
| Patents By Year of Application: | 119 | 30 | 35 | 116 | 269 | 289 | 170 | 253 | 173 | 191 | 476 | 431 | 379 | 44 | 17 | 2992 |
| LG ELECTRONICS INC. | | | | | | | | | | | | | | | | |
| Patents By Year of Grant: | 84 | 41 | 32 | 71 | 66 | 146 | 189 | 207 | 112 | 149 | 236 | 183 | 162 | 307 | 455 | 2440 |
| Patents By Year of Application: | 127 | 41 | 64 | 109 | 166 | 199 | 115 | 126 | 128 | 224 | 237 | 231 | 448 | 220 | 5 | 2440 |
| PROCTER + GAMBLE COMPANY | | | | | | | | | | | | | | | | |
| Patents By Year of Grant: | 381 | 65 | 51 | 53 | 56 | 107 | 213 | 187 | 180 | 228 | 270 | 212 | 159 | 81 | 85 | 2328 |
| Patents By Year of Application: | 461 | 54 | 73 | 111 | 135 | 205 | 169 | 185 | 224 | 226 | 274 | 75 | 96 | 39 | 1 | 2328 |
| GOODYEAR TIRE + RUBBER COMPANY | | | | | | | | | | | | | | | | |
| Patents By Year of Grant: | 759 | 88 | 89 | 83 | 54 | 91 | 124 | 126 | 140 | 80 | 80 | 55 | 42 | 47 | 63 | 1921 |
| Patents By Year of Application: | 853 | 72 | 94 | 94 | 78 | 114 | 97 | 136 | 82 | 63 | 75 | 64 | 74 | 21 | 4 | 1921 |
| HON HAI PRECISION IND. CO., LTD. | | | | | | | | | | | | | | | | |
| Patents By Year of Grant: | 270 | 117 | 93 | 145 | 72 | 174 | 150 | 142 | 123 | 158 | 114 | 74 | 57 | 51 | 27 | 1767 |
| Patents By Year of Application: | 404 | 111 | 83 | 178 | 173 | 126 | 105 | 119 | 143 | 123 | 83 | 54 | 47 | 17 | 1 | 1767 |
| HONDA GIKEN KOGYO KABUSHIKI KAISHA (HONDA MOTOR CO., LTD.) | | | | | | | | | | | | | | | | |
| Patents By Year of Grant: | 223 | 66 | 56 | 74 | 79 | 169 | 138 | 142 | 129 | 81 | 107 | 93 | 108 | 95 | 100 | 1660 |
| Patents By Year of Application: | 301 | 58 | 108 | 82 | 162 | 132 | 128 | 105 | 77 | 98 | 120 | 117 | 114 | 55 | 3 | 1660 |
| BLACK & DECKER INC. | | | | | | | | | | | | | | | | |
| Patents By Year of Grant: | 512 | 70 | 68 | 55 | 56 | 108 | 109 | 140 | 104 | 59 | 40 | 29 | 49 | 44 | 24 | 1467 |
| Patents By Year of Application: | 602 | 60 | 71 | 95 | 84 | 119 | 118 | 84 | 43 | 41 | 52 | 30 | 52 | 14 | 2 | 1467 |
| Apple, Inc. | | | | | | | | | | | | | | | | |
| Patents By Year of Grant: | 177 | 20 | 19 | 23 | 16 | 24 | 34 | 64 | 103 | 154 | 122 | 147 | 171 | 190 | 189 | 1453 |
| Patents By Year of Application: | 213 | 22 | 13 | 32 | 38 | 31 | 125 | 76 | 93 | 182 | 143 | 241 | 158 | 81 | 5 | 1453 |

(Source: https://www.uspto.gov/web/offices/ac/ido/oeip/taf/design.pdf)

Examine the companies that received the most design patents in Table 3 above. Which companies increased their applications in 2006 and following? Are you surprised Samsung, a foreign company, is at the top of the list? As shown in Table 3, the Top 11 organizations that have received design patents since 1991 are: Samsung, Nike, Sony, Microsoft, LG Electronics, Procter & Gamble, Goodyear Tire, Bon Hai Precision, Honda Motor, Black & Decker, and Apple. What do you make of the type of businesses that have received the most design patents? Are you surprised by any of the businesses on the list? What about the countries where the applicants are located? Can you guess which industries might be represented by the countries on the list?

Likewise, the number of applications to register Community designs in the European Union has doubled from 2003 (approximately 40,000) to 2015 (82,448 applications), as shown in Figure 2 below. The relative popularity of the registered Community design versus the U.S. design patent (the number of applications for the registered community design was more than triple the number of applications for U.S. design patents in 2015) may perhaps be explained by the fact that the Community design involves a "registration system" in which the EU Intellectual Property Office does not review the applications for compliance with substantive requirements. Registration occurs as long as the formalities of the application are fulfilled. By contrast, the U.S. Patent Office follows an "examination system" in which the office examines each application to determine if it meets the substantive requirements for design protection—although the amount of scrutiny of design patents by the USPTO is far less than the amount devoted by the USPTO to utility patents.

**Figure 2. Number of EU Community Designs Filed for Registration**

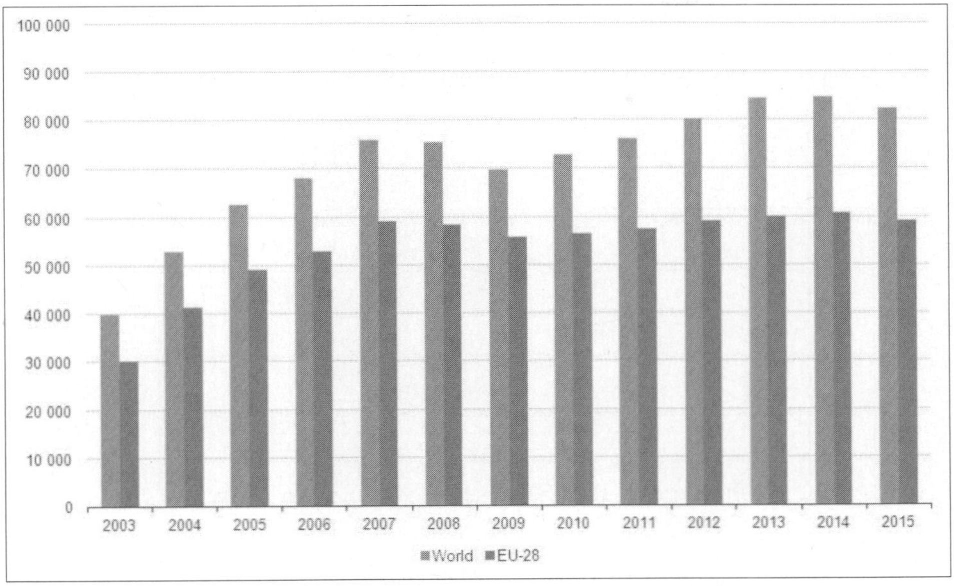


(Source: http://ec.europa.eu/eurostat/statistics-explained/index.php/File: Figure5_Total_number_of_Community_designs_CD_filed0916.PNG)

The numbers reflect the importance that businesses place on protecting the designs of their products. It also may reflect the increasing attractiveness of obtaining design protection compared to other IP forms (e.g., utility patents, copyrights, and trademarks) that might also apply to the underlying product. Typically, a rights holder does not have to limit protection of its product to just one IP form (the "election approach"). Instead, the rights holder may accumulate protection under every form of IP that is applicable (the "overlapping protection approach"). Thus, to the extent that the examination of a utility patent application may be more extensive and the requirements for a utility patent more exacting, a rights holder could benefit from seeking design protection as an alternative or a supplement to a utility patent.

## 3. FORMS OF INTELLECTUAL PROPERTY AND OVERLAPPING PROTECTION FOR DESIGN

### *PROBLEM 1–2*

**Figure 3. Hot Shots Shoe Design right side elevational view**

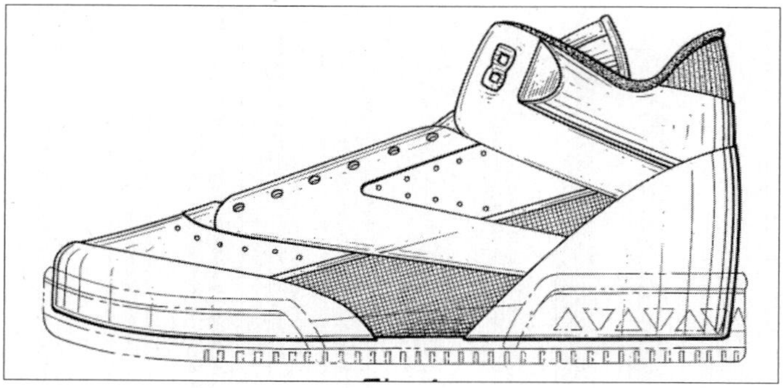

**Figure 4. Hot Shots Shoe top plan view**

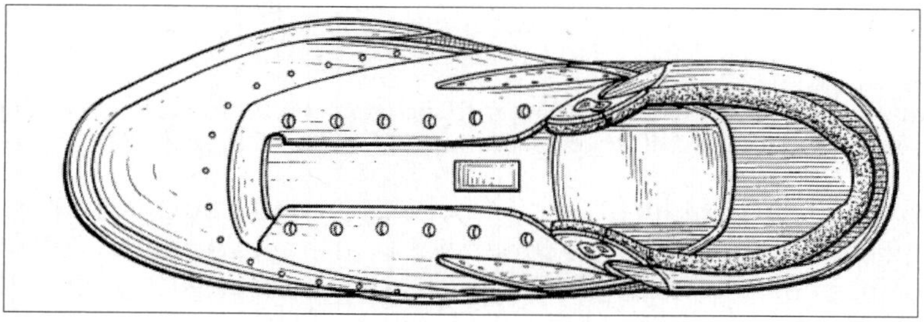

You are the General Counsel of LA Gear, a manufacturer of sports shoes and gear. Your designers have designed an athletic shoe called "Hot Shots" shoes (shown in Figures 3 and 4). LA Gear's marketing team is planning a major promotion and advertising campaign when the shoes first launch. Please advise the company whether it should seek a (i) design patent, (ii) trade dress protection, (iii) copyright, and (iv) EU Community Design right. Advise LA Gear on the following: (1) which forms of IP protection should be sought in the United States and the EU, (2) whether the protection requires an application to be filed and with whom, and (3) what potential substantive hurdles LA Gear might face in its efforts to protect the shoe design under each form of IP. Consult the following chart and discussion of the respective IP protection to answer this problem. You might not be able to answer these questions definitively at this point, but develop at least a provisional answer. As you read the following chapters, return and analyze this problem.

**Table 4. Comparison of Different Intellectual Property Systems Related to Design**

| Type of Intellectual Property | Application Required? | Is Novelty Required? | Other Key Requirements | Non-Functionality | Term |
|---|---|---|---|---|---|
| **U.S. Design Patent** | Yes.<br><br>USPTO examines application for novelty and other substantive requirements. | Yes | Ornamentality, Nonobviousness, and Originality | A corollary of ornamentality requirement.<br><br>Test is whether design is "dictated by" its function.<br><br>Existence of alternative designs for same function suggests design serves a primarily ornamental purpose. | 15 years from date of grant for applications filed on or after May 13, 2015.<br><br>14 years from date of grant for applications filed before that date. |
| **U.S. Trade Dress** | No, optional: only if one elects to register trade dress.<br><br>USPTO reviews applications for registration. | No | Distinctiveness (trade dress identifies source of the product or service) | Court made doctrine.<br><br>Test: Feature is functional if...<br>(1) Essential to use or purpose of article;<br>(2) Affects cost or quality; or<br>(3) Making it exclusive would put others at significant non-reputation related disadvantage (aesthetic functionality). | 10 years of registration from registration date, renewable indefinitely.<br><br>Unregistered trade dress can be protected indefinitely if it meets trademark requirements. |

| Type of Intellectual Property | Application Required? | Is Novelty Required? | Other Key Requirements | Non-Functionality | Term |
|---|---|---|---|---|---|
| **U.S. Copyright** | Not required for acquiring a copyright, but is required in Copyright Office for U.S. works before filing a lawsuit. | No | Originality and fixation of work | Section 101 requires separability of utilitarian features from the pictorial, graphic, or sculptural features. | Life of the author plus 70 years for individuals.<br><br>95 years from first publication or 120 years from creation, whichever expires first for corporations. |
| **EU Registered Community design (RCD)** | Yes.<br><br>EU IP Office does not examine novelty or substantive requirements. | Yes | Individual character<br><br>Must consider the degree of freedom of the designer in developing the design | CDR Article 8 functionality: feature is "solely dictated by its technical function." | 5 years from date of filing, renewable up to 5 terms for 25 years total. |
| **EU Unregistered Community design (UCD)** | No | Yes | Individual character<br>Must consider the degree of freedom of the designer in developing the design | CDR Article 8 functionality: feature is "solely dictated by its technical function." | 3 years from date design is made available to the public. |

Table 4 provides a broad overview of how the different IP regimes compare in terms of several criteria—you should periodically return to this chart as you read the following chapters. We will study each of the requirements listed above in depth in those chapters. The discussion below provides a brief overview.

### a. U.S. Design Patent

The U.S. Patent Code recognizes protection for several kinds of patents. The most well-known are utility patents for inventions that are useful or functional. Utility patents occupy the bulk of provisions in the Patent Code (35 U.S.C. §§ 100–157) and the bulk of the U.S. Patent Office's time in reviewing applications to determine if patents should be granted for the claimed inventions. In 2015, the USPTO received 589,410 utility patent applications compared to only 39,097 design patent applications.[9] By contrast, in three unusually short provisions (*id.* §§ 171–173), the Patent Code also recognizes patents for designs—commonly called "design patents" and incorporates, by reference, the provisions for utility patents to apply as well to design patents. In order to obtain a design patent (just as with a utility patent), one must file an application in the U.S. Patent and Trademark Office (USPTO). The USPTO examines the application to see if the claimed design satisfies the requirements of novelty, originality, nonobviousness, and ornamentality, although the level of scrutiny by the USPTO is less extensive for design patent applications than for utility patent applications. The design features must also not be functional. If the USPTO grants the design patent, the patent now lasts for 15 years from the date of the grant.

### b. U.S. Trade Dress

Trademark protection comes from two sources of law in the United States: state law (typically, common law) and federal law. The U.S. follows a "use-based" approach under which parties establish rights to a trademark based on the use of the mark in commerce. Under the common law, the first to use a mark in commerce is entitled to priority over the mark; no registration is required. Grademarks can be protected indefinitely as long as they satisfy distinctiveness and meet the other requirements of trademarks (such as being non-functional). Thus, there is no requirement that a trademark be registered in order to constitute a trademark. The common law still provides trademark protection. However, the federal Lanham Act provides a national registration system that is predicated on the "use-based" approach, but with additional benefits (such as constructive use of the mark and nationwide priority, *see* 15 U.S.C. § 1057) to those trademark owners who file for federal registration. In addition, applicants may file an "intent-to-use" application by filing an application first and then submitting a verified use of the mark afterwards. Federal registration lasts for 10 years, but may be renewed indefinitely with the payment of maintenance fees and satisfaction of the requirements of trademarks.

Product designs may be considered trade dress if the designs are distinctive as to the source of the product, also known as having secondary meaning. One court has defined trade dress "as the total image or overall appearance of a product, and includes, but is not limited to, such features as size, shape, color or color combinations, texture, graphics, or even a particular sales technique." *Rose Art Industries, Inc. v. Swanson*, 235 F.3d 165, 171 (3d Cir. 2000). A key requirement for trade dress is that it must be distinctive, meaning that consumers identify the source of the product or service based on the trade dress. The U.S. Supreme Court ruled that

---

[9] U.S. Patent Statistics Chart, Calendar Years 1963–2015, https://www.uspto.gov/web/offices/ac/ido/oeip/taf/us_stat.htm.

product designs can never be inherently distinctive, so the owner of the design must prove it has acquired distinctiveness as a source-identifying design in order to gain trade dress protection. *Wal-Mart Stores, Inc. v. Samara Bros., Inc.*, 529 U.S. 205, 212 (2000). By contrast, the Court recognized that the look of a restaurant can be inherently distinctive. *Two Pesos, Inc. v. Taco Cabana, Inc.*, 505 U.S. 763, 770 (1992). Even if distinctive, trade dress cannot be protected if it is functional.

### c. U.S. Copyright

The U.S. Copyright Act also may afford some protection for designs of products. In order to qualify for copyright protection, the design must contain a "pictorial, graphic, or sculptural" element that can be separated from any utilitarian aspect of the product. This is known as the test of separability, although courts have had a difficult time articulating a coherent test of separability. Section 101 defines separability in the following way: "the design of a useful article . . . shall be considered a pictorial, graphic, or sculptural work only if, and only to the extent that, such design incorporates pictorial, graphic, or sculptural features that can be identified separately from, and are capable of existing independently of, the utilitarian aspects of the article." 17 U.S.C. § 101. Likewise, "[a] "useful article" is an article having an intrinsic utilitarian function that is not merely to portray the appearance of the article or to convey information." *Id.* If a feature of a product qualifies as a pictorial, graphic, or sculptural element that is separable from the utilitarian aspects of the product, then it can be copyrighted. The term of copyright for individuals is the life of the author plus 70 years. For works made by employees in the scope of employment, the employer is treated as the author under the work-made-for-hire doctrine. For corporations and works-made-for-hire, the term of copyright lasts 95 years from first publication or 120 years from creation, whichever expires first.

### d. European Union Community Design

In 2002, the European Union enacted a *sui generis* form of design protection called the Community design right, which establishes a uniform, transnational right that applies in all EU members. There are two kinds of rights, depending on registration: (1) registered Community designs (RCDs) receive 5 years of protection, renewable for up to 25 years based on five 5-year terms; and (2) unregistered Community designs (UCDs) receive only 3 years of protection and are especially suitable for the fashion and textile industries that frequently produce designs that are commercially exploited for short periods of time. In addition to a new design, the Community Design Regulation (CDR) requires that the visual aspects of a design have individual character to qualify for protection. Under Article 6 of the CDR, "A design shall be considered to have individual character if the overall impression it produces on the informed user differs from the overall impression produced on such a user by any design which has been made available to the public: (a) in the case of an unregistered Community design, before the date on which the design for which protection is claimed has first been made available to the public; (b) in the case of a registered Community design, before the date of filing the application for registration or, if a priority is claimed, the date of priority." CDR art. 6.

## 4. THE EXCLUSION OF FUNCTIONAL ELEMENTS

### *PROBLEM 1–3*

Microsoft has developed a new kind of modular desktop computer named the Surface Studio with a touch screen that folds to a 20 degree angle so a person may comfortably use one's hands to touch and draw on the screen as if writing on a large tablet, as depicted in the Figure 5 below. You may watch a video demonstration of the Surface Studio at https://www.youtube.com/watch?v=BzMLA8YIgG0. Microsoft has already filed a utility patent in the U.S. for the Surface Studio, particularly its function in converting from a desktop to a tablet-like display. Microsoft's utility patent application is still pending before the USPTO and has not been published yet. Although there are several laptops with touchscreens that convert into tablets (including Microsoft's own Surface book), no desktop computer on the market currently has the same feature of converting from a traditional desktop computer to an adjustable surface for the user to touch and utilize at different angles down to 20 degrees.

Microsoft is eager to protect this convertibility feature as much as possible. It asks your legal advice in whether it should also pursue (i) a U.S. design patent, (ii) U.S. trade dress protection, (iii) U.S. copyright protection, and (iv) a registered Community design right for the design of the Surface Studio. Microsoft brings to your attention that Apple has a European patent from 2010 on an adjustable iMac that also folds down so a user can use a touch screen more comfortably (shown in Figure 6 below). Thus far, Apple has not manufactured such a computer, but the patent has been published. Microsoft would especially like your advice whether the Surface Studio has a design element that would not be considered functional. To answer this question, consider the discussion above in the previous section and the following discussion on functionality. Develop a provisional answer now and return back to this problem after you have studied the remaining chapters.

**Figure 5. Microsoft Surface Studio**

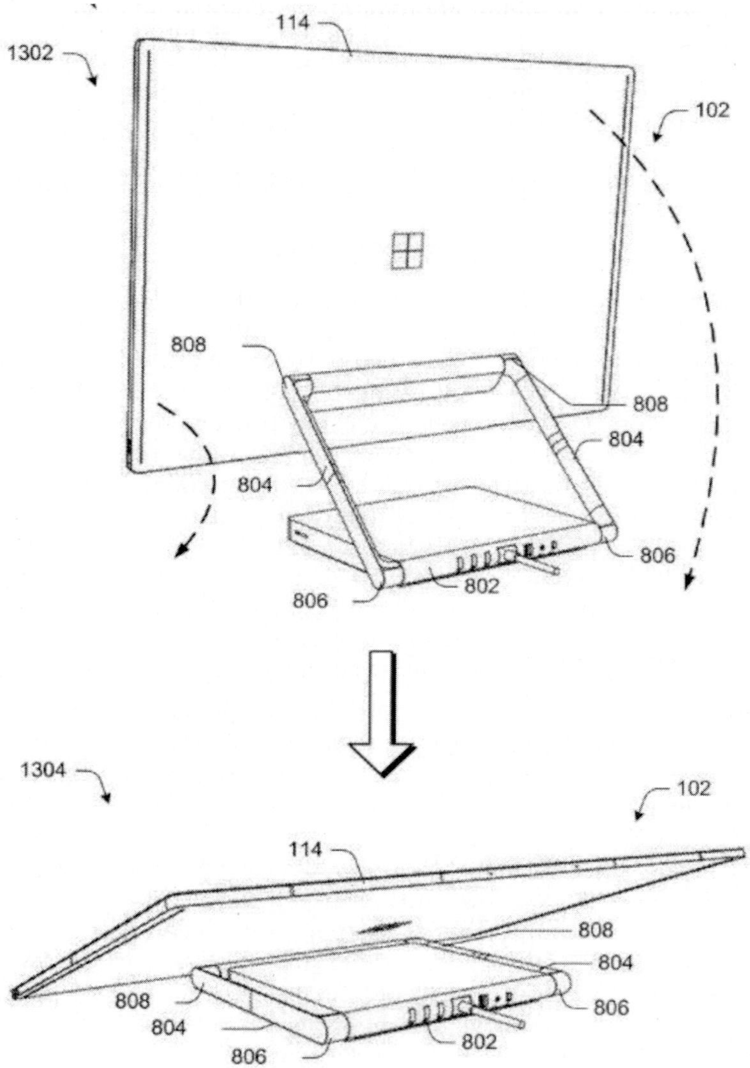

**Figure 6. Apple iMac European Patent from 2010**

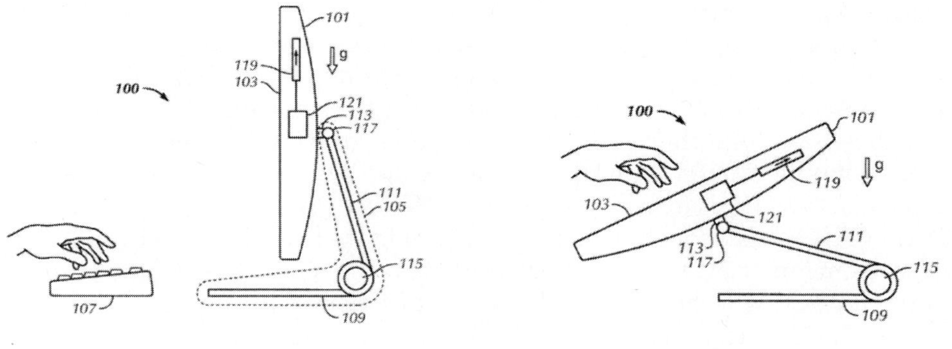


---

As indicated in Table 4 above, each form of intellectual property discussed in this casebook bars protection for *functional* elements. However, the tests for functionality are different, as outlined above. We will study each functionality test in depth in the following chapters. At the outset, though, it is worth asking, Why do all of these IP forms exclude functional elements from design protection? Would it be harmful to society and innovation if design laws also protected elements that are functional? Could part of the answer be that functional elements should be protected by utility patents that specifically govern useful inventions? Also, do you think it makes sense to have different tests of functionality depending on the IP form, each of which may be grounded in different goals? Or might it make more sense to have a single test of functionality that uniformly applied to all IP forms related to designs? Consider the following excerpt in which the author discusses some problems with the functionality doctrine in the EU and U.S.

## THE ROLE OF THE NON-FUNCTIONALITY REQUIREMENT IN DESIGN LAW

Orit Fischman Afori

20 FORDHAM INTELL. PROP. MEDIA & ENT. L.J. 847 (2010)

A. What Is a Functional Design?

Because "functionality" is a vague term that lends itself to a number of definitions, the basic principle of rejecting protection for functional features is itself unclear. The question is, therefore, how non-functional design should be defined. As explained above, the English law follows the [EU Design] Directive's language, which states the test as whether the design is "solely dictated by its technical function." This definition indicates that functionality should be examined from a technical point of view. However, this test for assessing non-functionality of designs opens a whole range of legal and theoretical questions relating to the "solely dictated" aspect of the test. When should it be concluded that a design is "solely dictated" by technical requirements? If a wholly functional article can be formed in a variety of shapes, is its design solely dictated by its function? After all, since there are several effective options for shaping the article, then the choice that is ultimately made could be based on non-technical considerations, whether aesthetic (which design would be more appealing to the eye) or economic (which design would be cheaper). The House of Lords discussed this issue in *Amp, Inc. v. Utilux Pty Ltd*, [[1971] F.S.R. 572 (H.L.) (U.K.)], and concluded that "solely dictated" by technical-functional features means that the designer decided on the shape of the article solely on the basis of whether the article would function in that manner, without considering its aesthetic appeal. This did not mean, however, that there were no other pure technical-functional possible designs for the same article. In other words, according to the House of Lords, the question of "solely dictated" by technical-function features is a subjective test which examines whether the designer had in mind only technical considerations in contrast to aesthetical considerations.

This test echoes the subjective test in *King Features Syndicate, Inc. v. O & M Kleeman, Ltd.*, [[1941] A.C. 417 (H.L.) (U.K.)], which held that, in establishing whether a design of a doll should be regarded as a copyrighted work or an industrial design, the intent of the designer was determinative. But the subjective intent of the creator or designer is a weak test, since it can be easily manipulated. Nor does it serve any of the goals underlying intellectual property law. Whether a design is "solely dictated" by functional features should depend on an objective test that can be judged solely on the basis of the design itself. The fact that many designs are commissioned, whether in the context of employment relations or not, further complicates matters if the test for functionality is the subjective intent of the designer; it raises the additional question of whether it is the commissioner's or the designer's intent that is relevant. Lord Reid himself admitted in *Amp, Inc.* that the ambiguity and controversy surrounding the eligibility of designs "has centered around the word 'dictated' which is a metaphorical word out of a place in a statutory definition." It should be mentioned that in an earlier decision the House of Lords called for an objective test, according to which the relevant question should not be the designer's intention but the effect on subsequent designers and the effective possibilities to use other alternatives in achieving the same functional outcome. Two decades later, in 2002, the ECJ similarly held that where the essential functional characteristics of the shape of a product are attributable solely to the technical result, the registration of that shape is precluded, "even if that technical result can be achieved by other shapes."[93]

[93] Case C-299/99, Koninklijke Philips Elecs. NV v. Remington Consumer Prods. Ltd., 2002 E.C.R. I-05475, P 83.

However, the ECJ refrained from construing any instructive test, whether subjective or objective, for such judicial conclusion.

It seems, then, that the question of whether a design can be regarded as "solely dictated" by functional criteria when it is merely one chosen from among a number of possibilities, each one of which is capable of delivering the same functional goal, is ultimately a question of proportionality. This question should be determined by the courts (or other relevant tribunal) by asking whether the overall impression from the shape of the object suggests a technical or an aesthetic basis for the choice. This "eye of the judge" test is a common one in design law, and it is often the ultimate test for eligibility. This test has no definable measurements and reflects the underlying preference for common law by deciding on a case-by-case basis, according to the judge's reading of the specific facts of the case.

B. Separating Function from Aesthetics

Separating the functional features of a design from its non-functional ones is an even more complicated task. The question discussed above was how to treat cases in which a functional design was motivated by obtaining a technical result but where there were other possibilities for achieving the same technical result. The answer presented is that there can be several purely functional designs for the same technical goal, and the fact that non-functional considerations led a person to choose one of the technical possibilities does not negate the design's purely functional nature. A related, overriding question is, then, how the law should treat cases in which choosing one of the purely functional designs was made due to non-functional features which are integrated with the functional shape: are the non-functional features swallowed into the functional nature? Or do the functional features become protectable because they are merged into the non-functional features?

This overriding difficulty in applying the non-functionality requirement stems from the fact that many contemporary designs combine functional and aesthetical elements, and it is impossible to separate the two. These designs follow the "Form-Follows-Function" artistic school and the philosophy of functionalism which originated in the 1920s, and which still dominates contemporary design. According to functionalism, the best designs are those in which the appearance springs truly from the structure and is a logical expression of it. However, achieving a visual effect by eliminating ornamentation must not be confused with failing to consider visual effect entirely. Functionalism is concerned specifically with aesthetics; these aesthetics, though, are merged with the function. Thus, the requirement for not protecting functional elements becomes highly problematic because it is not possible to separate physically the functional features from the non-functional features.

There are several models for dealing with this problem of merged functional and non-functional features of a design. One model is to preserve the rule rejecting protection of non-functional features, and when the features are merged, to provide no protection to the design as a whole. This is the American model, which is governed by the separability test and which is justly criticized as impossible to carry out, arbitrary, and subject to manipulation. Another model is the English one, which allows registration of merged designs. However, this model also has its shortcomings; courts have limited the possibility of registering these kinds of designs when doing so would impede the design freedom of future designers by leaving no viable options for alternative designs. The problem created by such a court-made rule is clear: on what basis, other than subjective impression, is a judge to decide that a design which merges aesthetic appeal and functionality has met the threshold requirement of limiting future options for designers? Such a decision can always be criticized as arbitrary.

C. Are Aesthetics Also a Function?

Another complication stemming from the non-functionality requirement becomes apparent when we delve into the meaning of the term "aesthetics" in the context of useful articles. One may ask what considerable efforts and investments made in the external appearance (as opposed to the underlying technology) of articles are intended to achieve. The answer is that aesthetics reflect an added value, covering everything from personal enjoyment to social status indicators. All these values contribute something real to the product and justify the consumers' choices to buy it. Therefore, it is arguable that aesthetics have a function in themselves. Another way of thinking about this is to redefine the concept of "function." If we accept the definition of function as "a way for achieving an aim," though, then aesthetics is indeed a function. Rejecting the idea of aesthetics as a "function" implies a narrow definition of "function" as technical function or even physical function. This is in fact the way the E.U. Design Directive understands the term in the context of industrial design law, as it uses the words "technical-function." Because aesthetics do not have a technical or a physical function, they are not a function as the term is used in industrial design law. As discussed above, however, aesthetics cannot be easily separated from the technical or physical features of the article.

The development of the trade dress claim in U.S. law exemplifies an attempt to determine whether aesthetics should be considered a function. Trade dress refers to the design or appearance of goods (or services). Courts were concerned that the product's dress is functional, either in the strict technical or broad aesthetic sense, and accordingly developed the concept of aesthetic functionality. Whereas strict functionality examines whether the dress adds something to the use of the article (i.e., utilitarian functionality), aesthetic functionality examines whether the dress, in addition to its sability to function as a trademark, makes the article more appealing. Aesthetic functionality applies when the appearance of a product has a significance that is not easily duplicated by substitute designs. A good example of aesthetic functionality is given in the Restatement (Third) of Unfair Competition:

> A is the first seller to market candy intended for Valentine's Day in heart-shaped boxes. Evidence establishes that the shape of the box is an important factor in the appeal of the product to a significant number of consumers. Because there are no alternative designs capable of satisfying the aesthetic desires of these prospective purchasers, the design of the box is functional. . . .

Until 2001, the approach adopted by the courts was that when articles were bought largely for their aesthetic value, their features could be functional because they contributed to their value and affected their cost, thus furthering the purpose for which the articles were intended.

In *TrafFix*, however, the Supreme Court somewhat narrowed this approach by explaining that aesthetic and utilitarian functionalities must be distinguished from each other.[115] *TrafFix* involved an expired utility patent for a road sign, which had special features that enabled the sign to withstand strong winds. Since the utility patent had expired, the plaintiff tried to pursue a trade dress claim against a competitor that had copied its design. The Supreme Court held that with respect to the design of the product no trade dress could be invoked; those specific features were the same ones that had been included in the utility patent claim, which were therefore inherently functional. The term for which protection over a utility patent was granted could not be stretched through a trade dress claim because it would undermine the legislature's intent to limit the term of protection over functional features. At the same time, the Court also held that "in a case where a manufacturer seeks to protect arbitrary, incidental, or ornamental aspects of features of a product found in the patent claims, such as arbitrary curves in the legs or an ornamental pattern painted on the springs, a different result might obtain." In other words, the Supreme Court adopted a narrow understanding of the term "functional," as including features of the type included in a utility patent, while excluding ornamental features from the functionality umbrella. In effect, the Supreme Court decided that, for purposes of industrial design, aesthetics are not a function. The decision thus narrows the functionality test because it invalidates both the competitive necessity test and the effect on the cost of the article test.

This could have resulted in a flood of trade dress cases seeking to protect ornamental features added to utilitarian products, which would have undermined the Supreme Court's declared policy not to allow over-extension of trade dress. Nevertheless, *TrafFix* did not refer to the inability

[115] TrafFix Devices, Inc. v. Mktg. Displays, Inc., 532 U.S. 23, 33 (2001).

to separate the ornamental or aesthetics of a design from its utilitarian functional features. It thus may be understood as allowing trade dress protection only when the ornamental part can be separated from the functional elements, therefore closing the floodgates of the trade dress route. In reality, however, in a number of cases after *TrafFix*, courts did recognize a trade dress claim in cases of merged ornamental and utilitarian features, and consequently the precise boundaries of the trade dress route are unclear.

Thus, even if there is a clear rule that aesthetics are not a function, and functionality in industrial design law is narrowly interpreted to mean technical, physical, or utilitarian function, there is still a fundamental problem in the actual application of the non-functional requirement. This is because the aesthetics of an article often merge with its technical, physical, and utilitarian features. Given the limitless range of possible designs, a bright-line rule cannot be formulated. This is the fundamental obstacle in industrial design law, which has resulted in considerable ambiguity and in an illogical development of this branch of intellectual property law. Yet, it is clear that it is not possible to drop the non-functionality requirement because it is critical for separating patent law from industrial design law.

### *NOTES AND QUESTIONS*

1. In determining whether a design feature is (solely) dictated by function, do you think a court should examine the subjective intent of the designer(s) in adding the feature? Or should the court examine instead the product and whether the feature, from an objective or reasonable designer's point of view, is necessary to perform a function?

2. When aesthetic and functional elements are intertwined (e.g., "form follows function"), how does U.S. copyright law and English design law attempt to determine if an element is functional?

3. Do you think the aesthetics of a product should sometimes be considered functional? For example, what about a particular pattern on athletic wear that makes a person look slimmer? Should that design be considered functional? Or is it ornamental? Both?

---

## C. SAMPLE DRAWINGS FOR DESIGN PROTECTION

Because design involves the appearance of an item, an applicant for a U.S. design patent or registered Community design must typically submit a drawing or photograph of the claimed design. The figure determines the scope of the protected design. For registered trade dress, a drawing is often submitted as well. Below we discuss examples of protected designs under a U.S. design patent, U.S. trade dress, and under a registered Community design.

## 1. U.S. DESIGN PATENT

One can search design patents at https://www.uspto.gov/patents-application-process/search-patents. Below is an example of the design of a chair that received a U.S. design patent in 2016 (D770,210). The patent claimed "[t]he ornamental design for a chair, as shown and described." In addition, "[t]he dashed broken lines in the drawings illustrate unclaimed portions of the chair and form no part of the claimed design. The dot-dashed lines in FIGS. 1–6 show the boundary between claimed and unclaimed subject matter and form no part of the unclaimed design." The Description indicates:

> Figure 1 is a perspective view of the top, front and right side of a chair showing our new design;
>
> Figure 2 is a perspective view of the top, rear and left side thereof;
>
> Figure 3 is a front view thereof;
>
> Figure 4 is a rear view thereof;
>
> Figure 5 is a left side view thereof;
>
> Figure 6 is a right side view thereof;
>
> Figure 7 is a top view thereof; and
>
> Figure 8 is a bottom view thereof.

## Drawings of Design of a Desk Chair

Fig. 1

Fig. 2

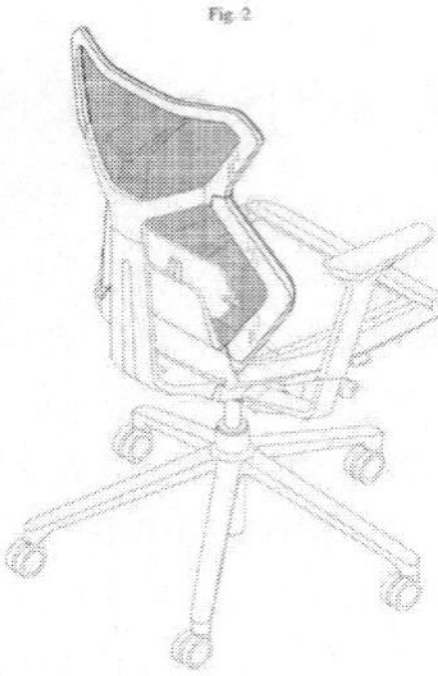

Fig. 3

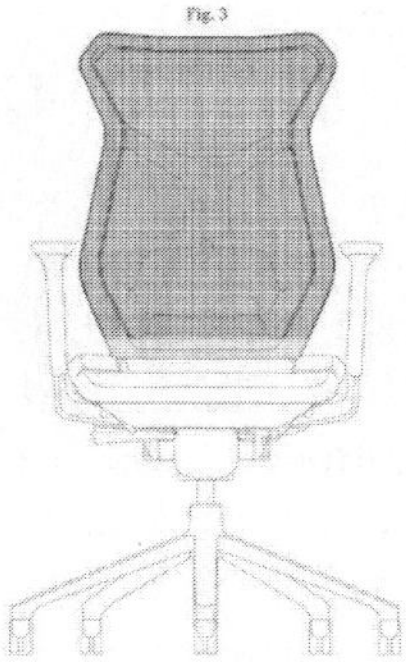

Fig. 4

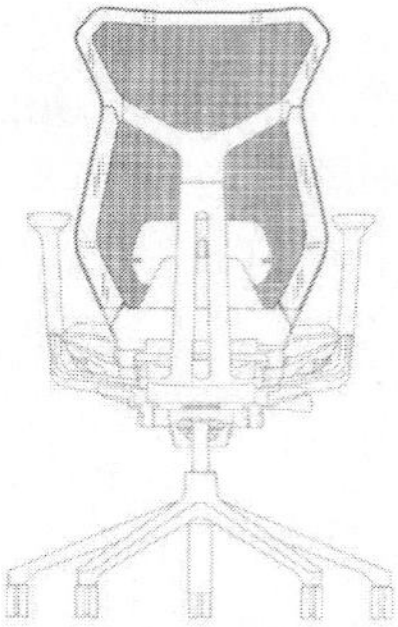

Fig. 5

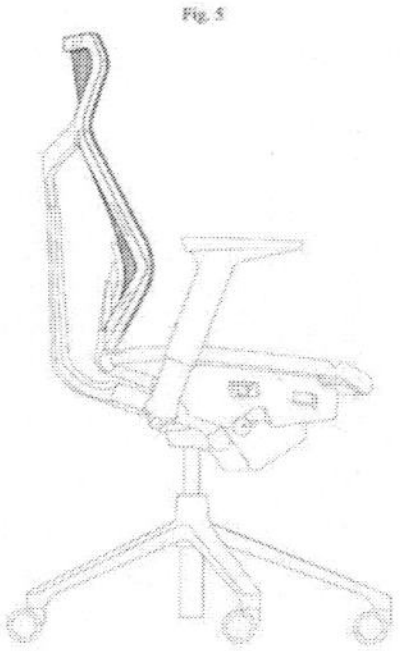

Fig. 6

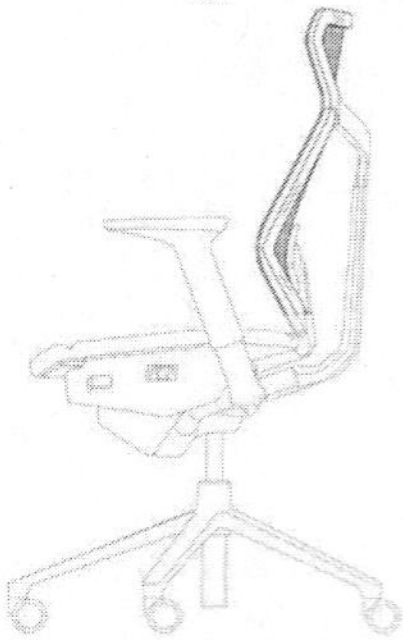

Fig. 7

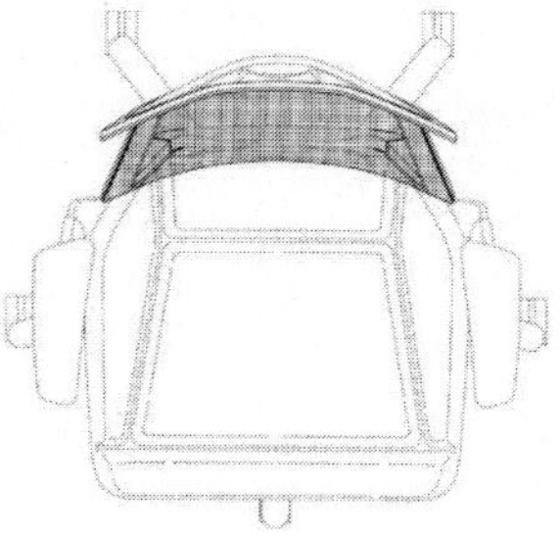

Fig. 8

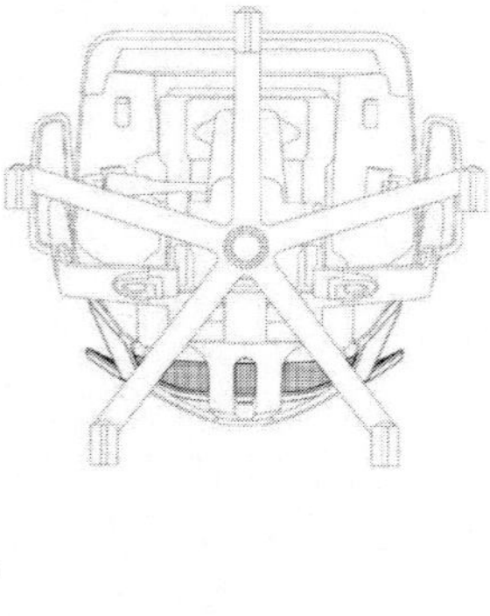

## 2. U.S. REGISTERED TRADE DRESS

One can search registered trademarks at https://www.uspto.gov/trademarks-application-process/search-trademark-database. Below is the drawing for the registered trade dress of the Coke bottle (U.S. Trademark Reg. No. 696,147.). Coca-Cola claimed "the trademark consists of the distinctively shaped contour, or confirmation, and design of the bottle as shown." A prior version of the bottle received a U.S. design patent in 1915 (D48,160), (By contrast, the British House of Lord rejected a trademark for the Coke bottle shape on the ground that it was not a mark. Application of Coca-Cola Co., [1986] 1 W.L.R. 695, 699, [1986] 2 All E.R. 274, 277 (H.L.)).

**Figure 7. Drawing of Coke Bottle Shape**

## 3. REGISTERED COMMUNITY DESIGN

One can search registered Community designs at https://euipo.europa.eu/eSearch/. In addition, one can search DesignView for a comprehensive database of WIPO, EUIPO, and over 40 national offices. Below is an example of the design of a chair that had been protected as a registered Community design until its expiration in 2015. The design's overall appearance—what is claimed for protection—should be indicated in solid lines. Typically, elements that are not claimed for protection are indicated by dotted lines. Alternatively, a photograph of the design may be submitted to satisfy the graphical representation requirement. The EU allows up to 7 different views of the design.

**Figure 8. Drawing of Design of Alpine Juliet Chair**

## *NOTES AND QUESTIONS*

1. If a drawing uses relatively few solid lines (as in the figures for the chair protected by U.S. design patent D770,210 above), would you expect the scope of the design to be broader or narrower in application? Hint: consider how many other chair designs might potentially have the same appearance?

2. Conversely, if a drawing uses all solid lines (as in Figure 8), would you expect the scope of the design to be broader or narrower in application? Hint: consider how many other chair designs might potentially have the same appearance?

3. U.S. design patents differ from utility patents in how the drawings help to define the scope of the protected design for the former, while the text of the claims define the scope of the protected invention for the latter. In design patents, the claim specifically refers to the drawings (and not much else). In utility patents, the claim does not and cannot refer to the drawings. Do you think it would be easier for an ordinary observer to determine the scope of a design patent from a well-constructed drawing than it would be for a person of ordinary skill in the art for which an invention pertains to determine the scope of a utility patent in interpreting the words of a well-constructed patent claim?

## D. ORGANIZATION AND APPROACH OF THIS CASEBOOK

This casebook focuses on the key forms of intellectual property protection for designs in the United States. The goal of this casebook is to develop your understanding of how design is protected in the United States, so that you may potentially practice in this area. By the end of the course, it is our hope that you have, not only a firm foundation in the various IP protections for design, but also the ability to discern the respective tradeoffs among the various IP forms that are used to protect design. With such knowledge, you should be equipped to analyze both legal and strategic questions about how best to protect a design in a particular situation. To that end, our casebook uses the problem method in studying the key elements of each IP form. The problems included in this casebook present "real world" situations that raise questions of design protection. Often, the problems are placed at the start of the relevant section of reading, so that you read the forthcoming passage with a greater focus as you would in representing a client. You are not asked to do any further research beyond the material in this casebook. But you should spend some time on each problem trying to apply the lessons you learned from the readings and the facts presented in the problem.

Chapter 2 begins with a study of U.S. design patent law, 35 U.S.C. §§ 171–73, which has grown dramatically in importance in the past decade. Chapters 3 and 4 then consider two general forms of intellectual property that are not specifically tailored for protecting only designs—trademark law and copyright law. Instead, these forms of IP protect source-identifying symbols and works of expression, respectively. Yet both trademark law and copyright law are used to protect design features of industrial products. Of these three forms of IP, only design patents require the filing of an application (that is examined by the Patent Office) before rights can be acquired.

After the discussion of U.S. law, Chapter 5 moves to a study of the European Union Community design right, a *sui generis* form of design protection similar, in some respects, to U.S. design patents. Chapter 5 also examines the process of obtaining registration of design internationally through the Hague Agreement Concerning the International Registration of Industrial Designs, and the minimum standards of design protection required for all World Trade Organization members under The Agreement on Trade-Related Aspects of Intellectual Property Rights (TRIPS).

Finally, continuing with our problem method, Chapter 6 provides exam-style problems to test your knowledge of the materials covered in this casebook. They are meant to help you review your learning from this casebook and prepare for a final exam. The problems will help you to hone your problem-solving abilities in situations that you could face in practice. We hope the problems are realistic, challenging, and fun.

# CHAPTER 2

# DESIGN PATENTS

■ ■ ■



---

Design patents offer a significant form of protection for ornamental design features. As set forth in this chapter, design patents have become increasingly important in recent years. Design patents are not available to primarily functional inventions, which are the province of utility patents. Design patents also lack the long duration of copyright and potentially permanent duration of trade dress protection. However, these limitations are balanced against the relative ease in obtaining design patent rights and the broad type of damages available against infringers of design patents. This chapter discusses the requirements of obtaining and enforcing a patent, relying upon cases involving design patents and with particular attention to doctrines that are central to design patents.

## A. UNDERSTANDING THE BASICS OF DESIGN PATENTS

### 1. SAMPLE DESIGN PATENT

The first design patent was issued in 1842. Since that time, over 700,000 design patents have been allowed and issued. According to data released by the U.S. Patent & Trademark Office, there were over 25,000 design patents granted in fiscal year 2015. Of those, almost 45% were granted to inventors from foreign countries. Design patents cover visual ornamental characteristics embodied in, or applied to, an article of manufacture. Since a design is manifested in appearance, the subject matter of a design patent application may relate to the configuration or shape of an article, to the surface ornamentation applied to an article, or to the combination of configuration and surface ornamentation. Design patents are common in certain industries, including athletic shoes, jewelry, tires, dishware, and electronic devices such as smartphones. The companies with the most design patents issued in 2015 were, in order, Samsung Electronics Co., Inc.; Nike, Inc.; Sony Corporation; Microsoft Corporation; LG Electronics Inc.; Procter & Gamble Company; Hon Hai Precision Ind. Co., Ltd.; Honda Motor Co.; Black & Decker, Inc.; and Apple Inc.

Design patents cover specific designs of articles of manufacture. Much like copyright, design patents cannot not cover general ideas. There are several requirements that an invention must meet in order to be eligible for patenting. These include that the invention is new, non-obvious, and with a definite scope. These requirements apply to all patents, including design patents. Design patents, however, have one special requirement, namely, that the invention be ornamental. The requirement of being ornamental, as required under 35 U.S.C. § 171, is in distinction to the requirement that utility patents be "useful" under 35 U.S.C. § 101. This section explains the contours of the legal requirements to obtain a design patent.

The requirements for obtaining a patent in the first instance and defending a patent's validity later are essentially the same. There is, though, a different burden of proof once a patent issues. Once any patent, including a design patent, has been issued by the U.S. Patent & Trademark Office, it is presumed valid. The presumption of validity is specified by 35 U.S.C. § 282 ("A patent shall be presumed valid."). The presumption of validity has been interpreted to require a patent challenger to prove by clear and convincing evidence that a patent is invalid. *Microsoft Corp. v. i4i Ltd. Partnership*, 131 S. Ct. 2238 (2011). Before a patent is granted, the applicant bears the burden of persuasion under a preponderance of the evidence standard.

Below we explain the primary requirements for design patents. You should keep in mind that there is no requirement that consumers associate the design with the inventor, nor is there any requirement of commercialization of the design.

Design patents are identified by a 6 unique digit number, preceded by the letter D. In the past, the letters "Des." instead of "D" preceded the 6 digit number. An exemplary design patent follows.

(12) **United States Design Patent**
**Shin et al.**

(10) **Patent No.:** **US D659,182 S**
(45) **Date of Patent:** ** **May 8, 2012**

(54) **EYEGLASS AND EYEGLASS COMPONENT**

(75) Inventors: **Jae Shin**, Irvine, CA (US); **Colin Baden**, Irvine, CA (US); **Peter Yee**, Irvine, CA (US)

(73) Assignee: **Oakley, Inc.**, Foothill Ranch, CA (US)

(**) Term: **14 Years**

(21) Appl. No.: **29/400,739**

(22) Filed: **Aug. 31, 2011**

(51) **LOC (9) Cl.** .......... **16-06**
(52) **U.S. Cl.** .......... **D16/326**; D16/335
(58) **Field of Classification Search** .......... D16/101, D16/300–342, 900; D29/109–110; D24/110.2; 351/41, 44, 51–52, 62, 158, 92, 103–123, 351/140, 153, 45–46; 2/426–432, 447–449, 2/441, 434–437, 13, 15; D21/483, 659–661; D14/372
See application file for complete search history.

(56) **References Cited**

U.S. PATENT DOCUMENTS

| | | | | |
|---|---|---|---|---|
| D150,924 S | | 9/1948 | Bright | |
| D158,963 S | | 6/1950 | Jonassen | |
| D192,885 S | | 5/1962 | Petitto | |
| D218,569 S | | 9/1970 | McCracken | |
| D300,226 S | | 3/1989 | Ramp | |
| D309,149 S | | 7/1990 | Pouilloux | |
| D309,618 S | | 7/1990 | Evans | |
| D330,395 S | | 10/1992 | Simioni | |
| D342,080 S | | 12/1993 | Cargle | |
| 5,537,161 A | | 7/1996 | Monroe | |
| D380,766 S | | 7/1997 | Simioni | |
| 5,712,697 A | | 1/1998 | Walton | |
| D390,864 S | | 2/1998 | Mage | |
| D399,238 S | | 10/1998 | Simioni | |
| D409,222 S | | 5/1999 | Raub | |
| D427,622 S | | 7/2000 | Conway | |
| D457,182 S | | 5/2002 | Rask | |
| D468,337 S | | 1/2003 | Chen | |
| D514,615 S | | 2/2006 | Mangum | |
| D536,027 S | | 1/2007 | Paulson | |
| D539,831 S | | 4/2007 | Hsu | |
| D539,833 S | | 4/2007 | Chuang | |
| D545,348 S | | 6/2007 | Chen | |
| D547,359 S | | 7/2007 | Krakoff et al. | |
| D549,764 S | * | 8/2007 | Teng | D16/326 |
| D561,811 S | | 2/2008 | Fox et al. | |
| D561,813 S | | 2/2008 | Baden et al. | |
| D565,088 S | | 3/2008 | Baden et al. | |
| D572,747 S | | 7/2008 | Baden et al. | |
| D581,450 S | | 11/2008 | Moritz | |
| D586,379 S | | 2/2009 | Thixton et al. | |
| D595,333 S | | 6/2009 | Markovitz et al. | |
| D599,838 S | * | 9/2009 | Rohrbach | D16/326 |
| D616,015 S | | 5/2010 | Markovitz et al. | |
| D622,302 S | | 8/2010 | Yee | |
| D623,217 S | | 9/2010 | Markovitz et al. | |
| D629,830 S | | 12/2010 | Markovitz et al. | |
| D630,674 S | * | 1/2011 | Markovitz | D16/326 |
| D645,076 S | | 9/2011 | Markovitz et al. | |
| D652,442 S | * | 1/2012 | Yee et al. | D16/326 |

* cited by examiner

*Primary Examiner* — Raphael Barkai
(74) *Attorney, Agent, or Firm* — Knobbe Martens Olson & Bear, LLP

(57) **CLAIM**

The ornamental design for an eyeglass and eyeglass component, as shown and described.

**DESCRIPTION**

FIG. **1** is a front perspective view of an eyeglass and eyeglass component of the present invention;
FIG. **2** is a front elevational view thereof;
FIG. **3** is a rear elevational view thereof;
FIG. **4** is a left side elevational view thereof, the right side elevational view being a mirror image thereof;
FIG. **5** is a top plan view thereof; and,
FIG. **6** is a bottom plan view thereof.
The broken line portions of the drawings are for illustrative purposes only and form no part of the claimed design.

**1 Claim, 4 Drawing Sheets**

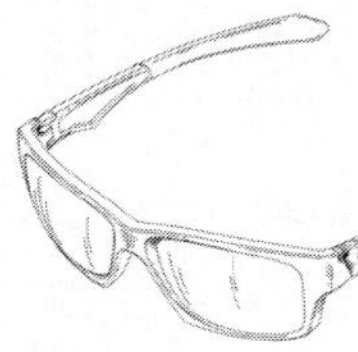

**U.S. Patent** May 8, 2012 Sheet 1 of 4 US D659,182 S

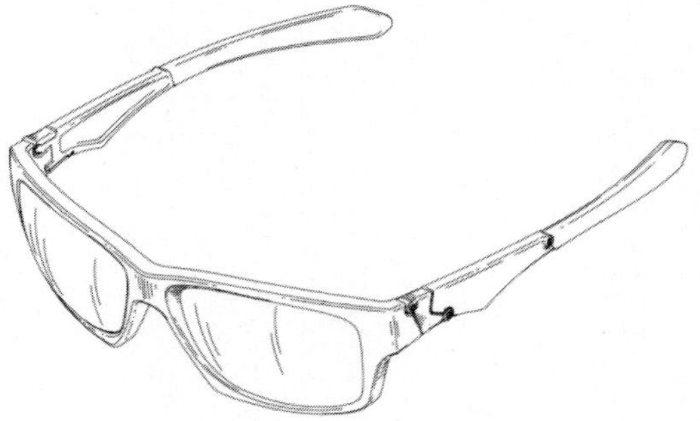

*FIG. 1*

U.S. Patent May 8, 2012 Sheet 2 of 4 US D659,182 S

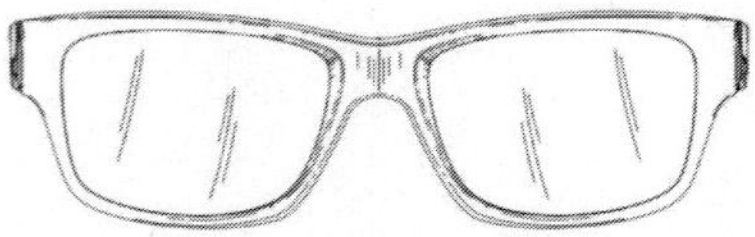

FIG. 2

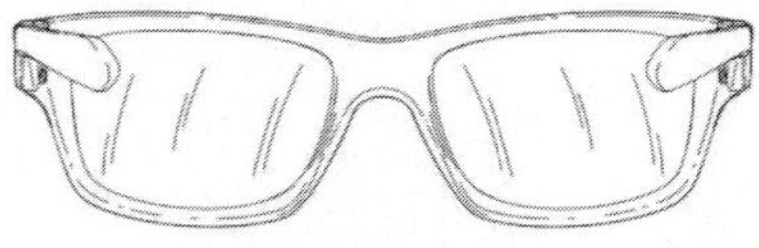

FIG. 3

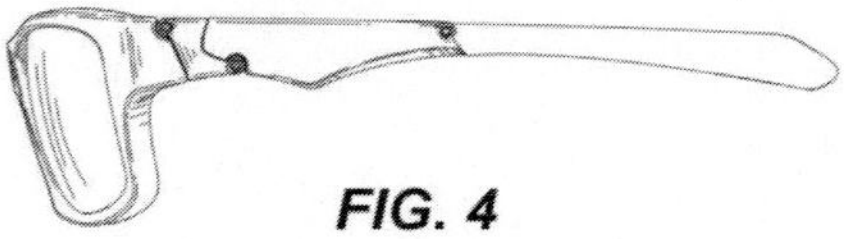

FIG. 4

U.S. Patent May 8, 2012 Sheet 3 of 4 US D659,182 S

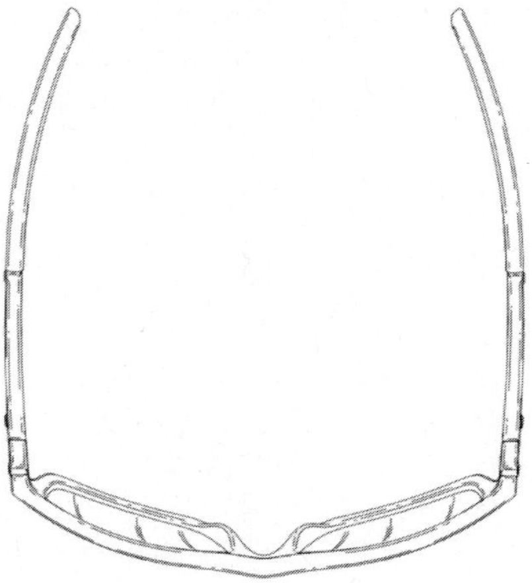

FIG. 5

U.S. Patent May 8, 2012 Sheet 4 of 4 US D659,182 S

FIG. 6

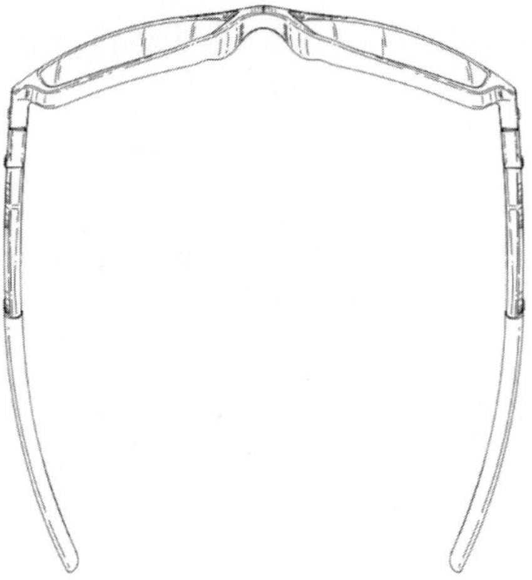

The contents of a design patent are relatively straightforward. It includes some basic demographic information about the invention, including the title, inventor's name, filing date, etc. It then includes a single claim, along with a description of each of the figures. The exact number of figures vary, but the most common number is seven views in an application. The claim, which incorporates the figures, are the important portion of the design patent. The claim of the eyeglass patent above is representative. It reads: "1. The ornamental design for an eyeglass and eyeglass component, as shown and described."

## 2. DESIGN PATENT CLAIMING STRATEGIES

The scope of design patents is determined by the claim, which in turn, references the figures. Thus, the figures or drawings are central to all design patents, even more than drawings are to utility patents. While photographs are permissible, most design patents use patent draftsmen to prepare formal engineering-style drawings such as those shown in the example in the previous section. Design patents basically protect the shape of a design. Surface ornamentation and treatment can also be claimed, as can color.

The basic rule is that "solid lines" are part of the claimed design. In the example in the previous section, all of the lines were solid; and consequently, all aspects of the figures were part of the claimed invention. It is possible for a design patent to use "dotted lines" instead of solid lines.

Dashed lines are also referred to as dotted lines, broken lines, or dashed lines. The basic rule is that dotted lines are *not* part of the claimed design. Dotted lines are for illustrative purposes only, and is provided to show part of the context or environment for the design. If an aspect of the figures is not part of the claimed design, then it is not relevant for either validity or infringement.

As an example of solid and dotted lines, see the figure below from U.S. Patent No. D647,937. The patent is assigned to Microsoft Corporation and is entitled "Electronic Camera."

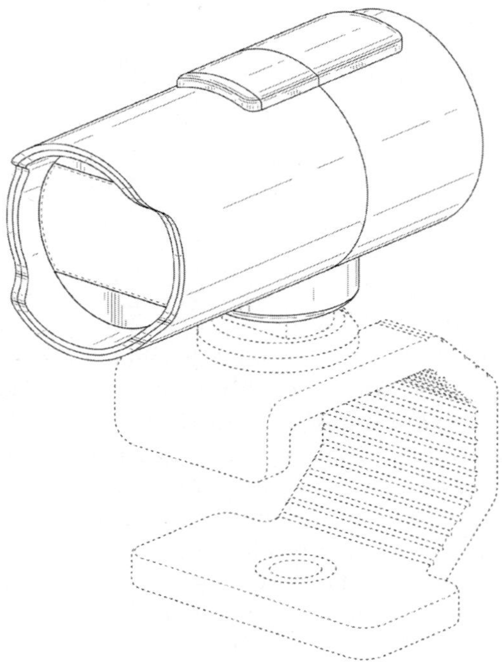

Notice the base is depicted in dotted lines, and is therefore disclaimed from the claimed design. The housing of the camera itself is depicted in solid lines, and forms part of the claimed design.

There are several other nuances in the drawings of design patents. For one, the drawings sometimes use "break lines." Break lines indicate that the length of a component is not relevant. Without a break line, the relative dimensions of items shown in the figure are part of the claimed design. An example of break lines is below in Figure 4 of U.S. Patent No. D540,595 assigned to Liberty Hardware Manufacturing, Co. and entitled "Towel Bar."

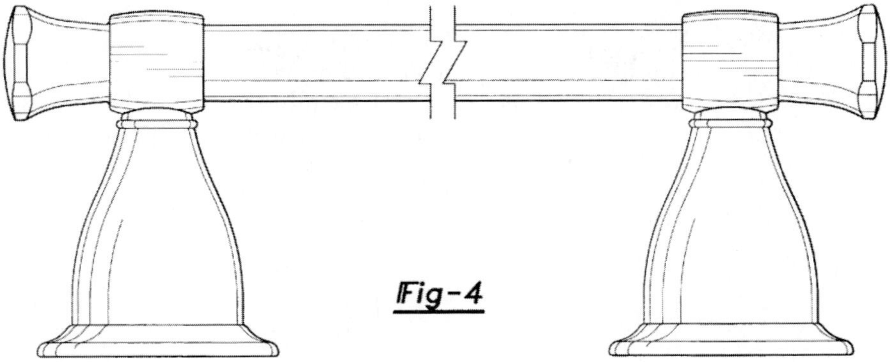

Fig-4

The break lines in the middle of the figure indicate that the length of the bar is not part of the claimed design. Thus, a bar that was five times as long as the wall mounts would be within the claim scope as much as a bar that was ten times as long as the wall mounts.

Another nuance of design patent law involves alternative embodiments. While design patents are limited to a single claim, that claim can refer to figures illustrating multiple embodiments. Several of the cases that are in this chapter address design patents with multiple embodiments. Pay attention to how courts consider alternative embodiments with respect to claim scope, as well as validity and infringement.

The *In re Owens* case below discusses the use of solid and dotted lines. *In re Owens* involves a more complicated strategy for obtaining a design patent. That strategy includes the filing of "continuation" applications. A continuation application is a second patent application filed by an applicant that is entitled to the filing date of the first application. Having the benefit of the earlier filing date is important because the earlier the filing date, the less prior art that is potentially available to render the patent invalid. Thus, an applicant can obtain multiple design patents based upon a single original patent application. The multiple design patents can vary in scope, which is advantageous to the patent holder. For a second application to be properly entitled to the priority date of the first application, it must be filed while a previously filed patent application by the same applicant is pending and it must contain an express reference to the originally filed application. *In re Owens* addresses whether applicants are permitted to change between solid lines and dotted lines in a continuation application.

As you read *In re Owens,* please think about Problem 2–1 below.

### *PROBLEM 2–1*

Maya Rose designs a new key for children. The key contains a regular blade, with teeth configured to engage with the interior of a lock. The base or bow of the key, however, is configured to look like a monkey.[10] Consider the following three different ways that a drawing for a patent application can be made. What are the differences between these three figures in terms of scope?

Example 1

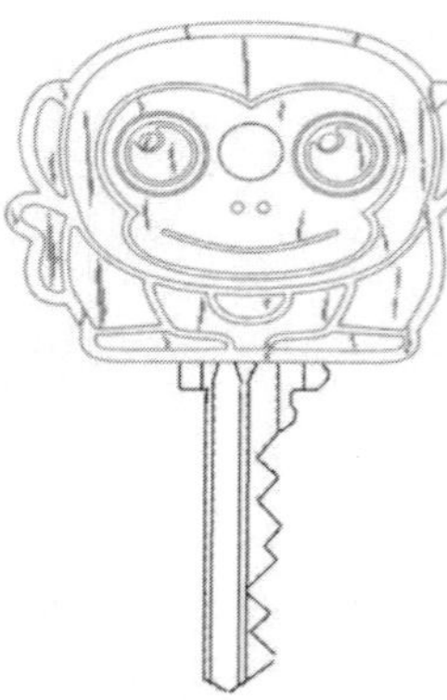

Example 2

Example 3

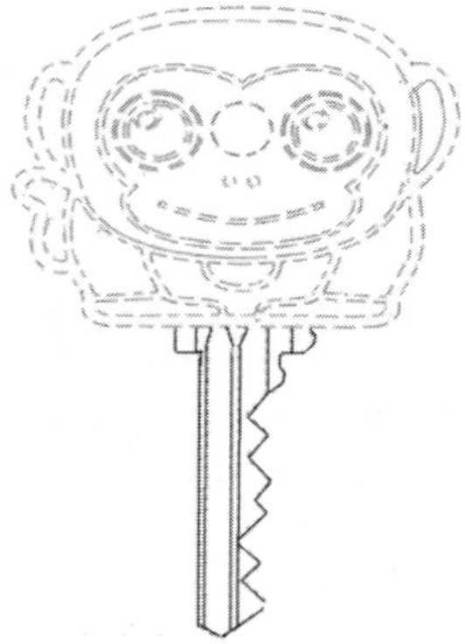

---

## IN RE OWENS

710 F.3d 1362 (Fed. Cir. 2013)

PROST, CIRCUIT JUDGE. Timothy S. Owens, et al. ("Owens") appeal a decision of the United States Patent and Trademark Office ("PTO") Board of Patent Appeals and Interferences ("Board"), *Ex parte Owens*, No. 2010–5622 (B.P.A.I. Dec. 1, 2011) ("Board Op."), affirming a rejection of his design patent application, U.S. Design Patent Application No. 29/253,172 (filed Feb. 2, 2006) ("'172 application"). For the reasons set forth below, we affirm.

The '172 application, which is the subject of this appeal, is a continuation of U.S. Design Patent Application No. 29/219,709 (filed Dec. 21, 2004) ("'709 application"). The '709 application claimed a design for a bottle with boundaries set forth in the figures below:

[10] The monkey key example is adapted from presentations given by a leading design rights attorney, Christopher Carani. We thank Christopher Carani and his firm, McAndrews Held & Malloy Ltd. in Chicago, for permission to use the example and images.

*Fig. 1*

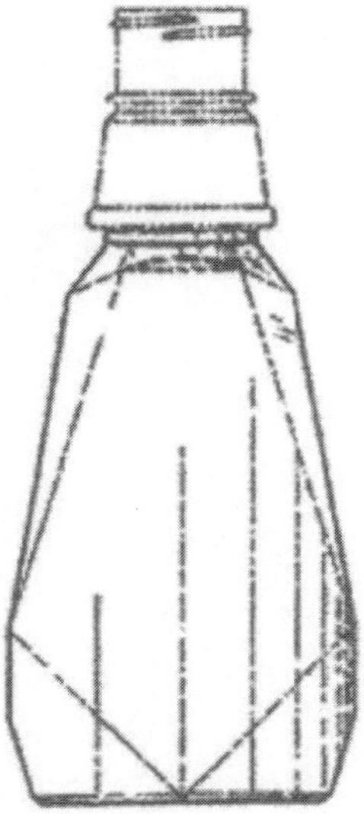

*Fig. 2*

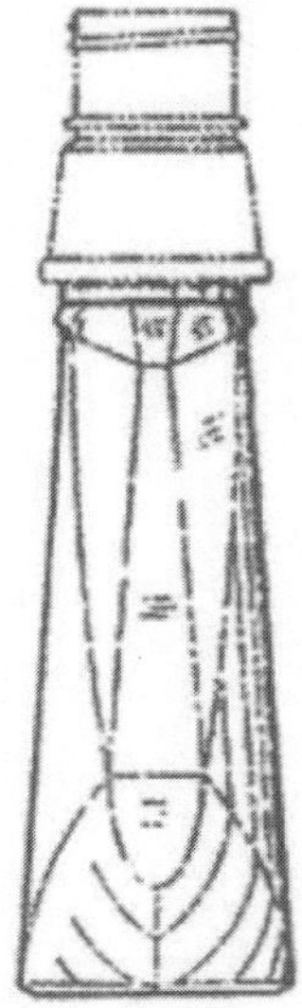

*Fig. 3*

**'709 Application Figures**

The '709 application ultimately issued as U.S. Design Patent No. D531,515 (issued Nov. 7, 2006) ("'515 patent"), and that issuance is not contested here.

Owens then filed the '172 application in 2006, seeking the benefit of the '709 application's 2004 priority date under 35 U.S.C. § 120. Owens conceded during prosecution that, if denied the earlier effective filing date, the '172 application would be unpatentable because he had sold bottles embodying his design more than one year before filing his continuation.

The '172 application claimed certain design elements found on the top and side portions of the original bottle, as depicted in Figures 1 through 3:

Fig. 1

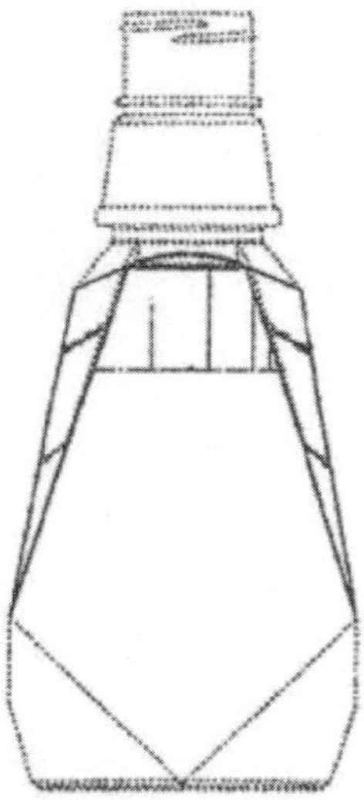

Fig. 2

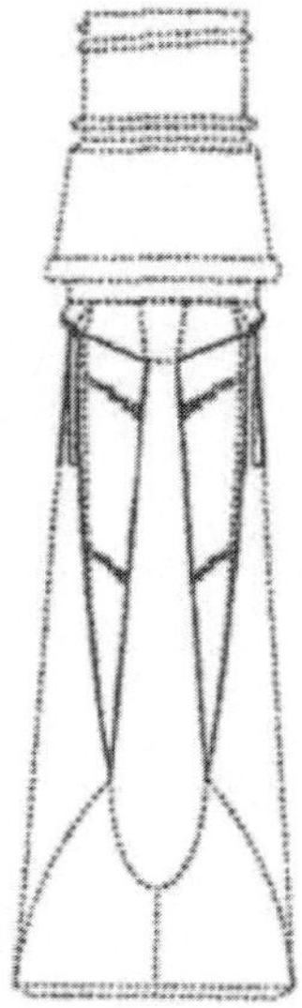

Fig. 3

**'172 Application Figures**

The '172 application claimed three design elements: (1) the small crescent-shaped area on the front and back of the bottle near the cap; (2) the narrow triangular areas along the bottle's "shoulders;" and (3) an upper portion of the bottle's pentagonal center panel. To indicate what portion of the center was claimed, Owens bisected the top of his panel with a broken line.

The examiner rejected the '172 application. The basis for the rejection was the addition of the broken line, which the examiner understood as defining an entirely new "trapezoidal"-shaped surface that was considered new matter:

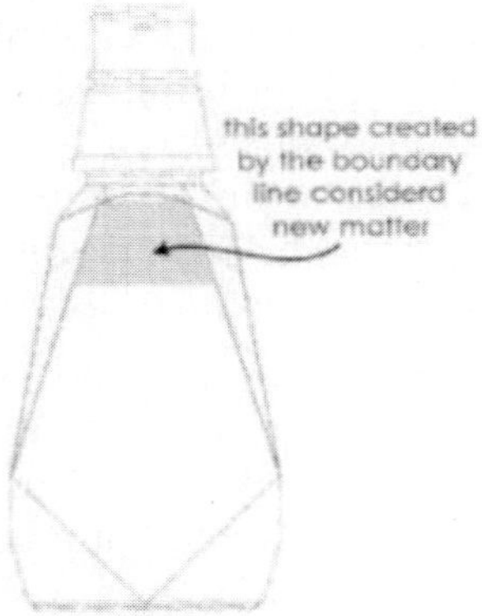


*Fig. 2*

The examiner found no evidence that Owens originally possessed such a trapezoidal region in the '709 application. As such, the examiner rejected the '172 application for lack of written description under 35 U.S.C. § 112 and furthermore rejected the application as unpatentably obvious in view of the earlier-sold bottles under 35 U.S.C. § 103(a).

Owens appealed to the Board, which noted . . . that the correctness of the examiner's § 103(a) rejection depended on whether the '172 application was entitled to the benefit of the '709 application's filing date. That hinged on whether the '709 application contained a written description sufficient to convey to an ordinary designer that Owens possessed the subject matter of the '172 application as of the earlier filing date.

The Board focused upon the difference between the parent and the continuation's front panels—namely, the continuation's introduction of a broken line bisecting the parent's pentagonal front panel. Like the examiner, the Board understood this to indicate that Owens had claimed previously undisclosed "trapezoidal sections occupying part, but not all, of the surface area of the front and back panels." The Board affirmed the examiner's rejections.

To be entitled to a parent's effective filing date, a continuation must comply with the written description requirement of 35 U.S.C. § 112. Whether a claimed invention is supported by an adequate written description is a question of fact that we review for substantial evidence.

The test for sufficiency of the written description [is] "whether the disclosure of the application relied upon reasonably conveys to those skilled in the art that the inventor had possession of the claimed subject matter as of the filing date." In the context of design patents, the drawings provide the written description of the invention. When an issue of priority arises one looks to the drawings of the earlier application for disclosure of the subject matter claimed later.

The subject of this appeal is the broken line that Owens introduced in his continuation application. The parent application discloses no boundary that corresponds (either explicitly or implicitly) to this newly-added broken line. However, the parties also agree that a design patentee may, under certain circumstances, introduce via amendment a straight broken line without adding new matter, even "[w]here no [corresponding] boundary line is shown in a design application as originally filed."

The parties refer to these broken-line boundaries as "unclaimed boundary" lines because the lines are "not intended to form part of the claimed design" and do "not exist in reality in the article embodying the design." Rather, when an unclaimed boundary line is introduced via amendment or continuation, it is "understood that the claimed design extends to the [unclaimed] boundary but does not include the [unclaimed] boundary."

When an unclaimed boundary line divides a previously claimed area, it indicates that the applicant has disclaimed the portion beyond the boundary while claiming the area within it. Unclaimed boundary lines allow the patentee to adjust his patent coverage and encompass embodiments that differ slightly but insignificantly from the originally-filed design. These lines must comply the written description requirement to receive the benefit of priority under § 120.

We turn to the merits of Owens's case. The Board rejected the '172 application because it believed that, as a prerequisite to patentability, Owens needed to demonstrate prior possession of a bottle with a trapezoidal section occupying part, but not all, of the surface area of the center-front panel. Owens made no such showing before the Board, nor does he do so on appeal.

Instead, Owens attacks the very notion that his continuation claims a trapezoidal-shaped area at all. Owens insists that in order to claim a new design element, one must first claim a new boundary. Yet his newly-introduced broken line is, as all parties agree, "unclaimed." He believes the Board applied the wrong written description test to his case, one which erroneously treated his unclaimed boundary as though it was claimed.

Owens misconstrues our holding in *In re Daniels,* 144 F.3d 1452 (Fed. Cir. 1998). The patentee in *Daniels* did not introduce any new unclaimed lines, he removed an entire design element. It does not follow from *Daniels* that an applicant, having been granted a claim to a particular design element, may proceed to subdivide that element in subsequent continuations however he pleases.

Owens's parent application discloses a design for a bottle with an undivided pentagonal center-front panel, whereas the continuation claims only the trapezoidal top portion of that center-front panel . . . [T]he question for written description purposes is whether a skilled artisan would recognize upon reading the parent's disclosure that the trapezoidal top portion of the front panel might be claimed separately from the remainder of that area.

The Board answered this factual question in the negative, finding that nothing in the parent application's disclosure suggested anything uniquely patentable about the top portion of the bottle's front panel. This . . . is supported by substantial evidence because the parent disclosure does not distinguish the now-claimed top trapezoidal portion of the panel from the rest of the pentagon in any way . . . We must affirm the Board's decision.

Lastly, we turn to a question raised implicitly in Owen's appeal and explicitly in amicus briefing—whether, and under what circumstances, Owens could introduce an unclaimed boundary line on his center-front panel and still receive the benefit of § 120.

The Manual of Patent Examining Procedure ("MPEP") provides some direction in this regard, saying that unclaimed boundary lines "may" be acceptable when "connecting the ends of existing full lines." MPEP § 1503.02. Were this the rule, it might be acceptable for Owens to bisect his front panel with a broken line along the pentagon's widest point. However, it seems that such a boundary would simply outline a larger trapezoidal area, and so the resulting claim would suffer from the same description problems as the '172 application.

In our view, the best advice for future applicants [is] that unclaimed boundary lines typically should satisfy the written description requirement only if they make explicit a boundary that already exists, but was unclaimed, in the original disclosure. This rule comports with our understanding of how unclaimed boundary lines generally should affect entitlement to an earlier filing date under § 112, ¶1, and § 120. Its implications for Owens's case should be obvious.

### *NOTES AND QUESTIONS*

1. Why would an applicant want to include in its patent figures an unclaimed boundary line? If the line is not included within the claim scope, then it is not necessary for an accused infringer to appropriate for there to be infringement. On the other hand, the same unclaimed boundary line may not be the basis for overcoming a rejection based upon anticipation or obviousness.

2. For trade dress to be protectable in a product configuration, there must be secondary meaning in the design. As we explain in detail in Chapter 3, this means that consumers must associate the design with a single source. In contrast, design patents lack such a requirement. Can you think of policy or practical reasons why secondary meaning or an analogous showing is not required for design patents?

3. Why don't all applicants obtain coverage via design patents with unclaimed boundary lines? Applicants can file one design patent application

with all solid lines, and another with some solid lines and some unclaimed boundary lines. Such approach provides a range of claim scope. Converting a drawing with solid (claimed) boundary lines to one with unclaimed boundary lines is extremely inexpensive. The cost to an applicant to filing multiple applications using a variety of types of boundary is relatively small.

---

## B. REQUIREMENTS FOR A VALID DESIGN PATENT

### 1. ORNAMENTALITY AND NON-FUNCTIONALITY

A key attribute of design patent law is that it protects ornamental aspects of creations and inventions. The patent laws, which cover utility patents, design patents, and plant patents, are all addressed in 35 U.S.C. § 101 *et. seq.* Design patents are distinct from utility patents, which protect functional inventions, and also from plant patents, which protect "asexually reproduced a distinct and new variety of plant, other than a tuber propagated plant or a plant found in an uncultivated state." 35 U.S.C. § 161.

The ornamentality requirement of design patent law is codified in § 171(a) of the Patent Act. It reads: "Whoever invents any new, original and ornamental design for an article of manufacture may obtain a patent therefor, subject to the conditions and requirements of this title." The ornamentality restriction is enforced, in part, by the prohibition against using design patents to protect functional aspects of an article. Ornamentality is an affirmative and positive requirement. As we will see later, some courts treat functionality differently in trade dress law, imposing the burden of persuasion of functionality on the challenger rather than the rights holder.

Design patents claim the appearance of an "article of manufacture." Unlike utility patents which cover the mechanical structures and functions of articles, design patents protect the visual look of an article. The line between the aesthetic appearance and function, however, is not always clear. The Supreme Court has held that "To qualify for protection, a design must present an . . . appearance that is not dictated by function alone, and must satisfy the other criteria of patentability." *Bonito Boats v. Thunder Craft Boats,* 489 U.S. 141, 148 (1989). Relying up this Supreme Court statement, the Federal Circuit has held that the design of a useful article is deemed functional where "the appearance of the claimed design is 'dictated by' the use or purpose of the article." *Ethicon Endo-Surgery, Inc. v. Covidien, Inc.,* 796 F.3d 1312 (Fed. Cir. 2015). Several decisions follow, which set forth more fully and discuss the functionality requirement.

As you read the following cases, notice the diverse set of industries which have obtained and enforced design patents. Please pay attention to how the courts grapple with whether a design is primarily functional. As you are doing so, think about whether the court is using the same test for ornamentality in *Oddzon Products, Inc. v. Just Toys, Inc.* as it is in the most recent *Ethicon Endo-Surgery, Inc. v. Covidien, Inc.*

## ODDZON PRODUCTS, INC. V. JUST TOYS, INC.

122 F.3d 1396 (Fed. Cir. 1997)

LOURIE, CIRCUIT JUDGE. OddzOn is a toy and sporting goods company that sells the popular "Vortex" tossing ball, a foam football-shaped ball with a tail and fin structure. The Vortex ball is OddzOn's commercial embodiment of its design patent, U.S. Patent D 346,001, which issued on April 12, 1994. Figure 1 of the patent is shown below:

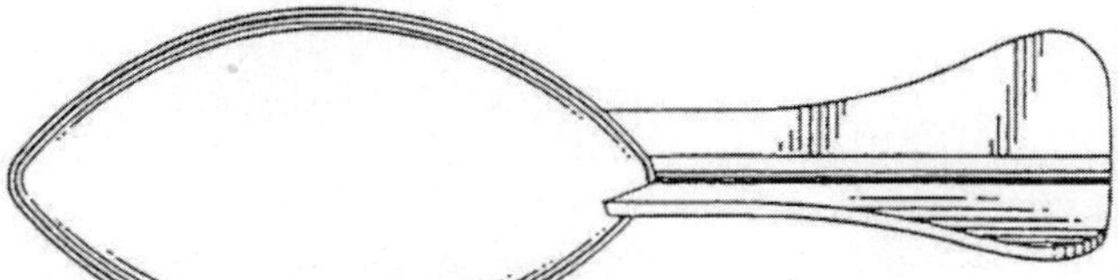

Fig. 1

Just Toys, Inc., another toy and sporting goods company, sells a competing line of "Ultra Pass" balls. Two versions of the allegedly infringing Ultra Pass balls are shown below:

OddzOn sued Just Toys for design patent infringement, trade dress infringement, and state-law unfair competition, asserting that the Ultra Pass line of tossing balls was likely to be confused with OddzOn's Vortex ball . . . Just Toys denied infringement and asserted that the patent was invalid. On cross-motions for summary judgment, the district court held that the patent was not shown to be invalid and was not infringed. The court also held that Just Toys did not infringe OddzOn's trade dress.

The district court determined that two confidential designs that had been disclosed to the inventor qualified as subject matter . . . these designs could be combined with other prior art designs for purposes of a challenge to the validity of the patent. The district court held that the patented design would not have been obvious in light of the prior art . . . The court construed the single claim of the patent as being directed to the design for:

> a ball shaped like a football, with a slender, straight tailshaft projecting from the rear of the football. In addition, the '001 Patent design has three fins symmetrically arranged around the tailshaft, each of which has a gentle curve up and outward which creates a fin with a larger surface area at the end furthest from the ball. The fins flare outwardly along the entire length of the tailshaft, with the front end of the fin extending slightly up along the side of the football so that the fins seemingly protrude from the inside of the football.

After construing the claim, the court held that the patented design was not dictated solely by function and thus that it was not invalid on that ground . . . The district court considered OddzOn's proffered consumer survey evidence of similarity, but held that it was not probative on the question whether the accused balls were substantially similar to the patented design in terms of its protectable features. The district court concluded that the survey evidence demonstrated nothing more than that any ball with a tail and fins, regardless of its ornamental features, would appear to be similar to the patented design.

Whether a design patent is infringed is determined by first construing the claim to the design, when appropriate, and then comparing it to the design of the accused device. *Elmer v. ICC Fabricating, Inc.* A design patent only protects the novel, ornamental features of the patented design. *See Lee v. Dayton-Hudson Corp.,* ("[I]t is the non-functional, design aspects that are pertinent to determinations of infringement.") Where a design contains both functional and non-functional elements, the scope of the claim must be construed in order to identify the non-functional aspects of the design as shown in the patent.

In *Gorham,* the claimed elements were purely ornamental, being limited to the scroll work on the handle portion of flatware. If . . . a design contains both functional and ornamental features, the patentee must show that the perceived similarity is based on the ornamental features of the design. The patentee "must establish that an ordinary person would be deceived by reason of the common features in the claimed and accused designs which are ornamental." *Read Corp. v. Portec, Inc.*

In construing the claim of OddzOn's patent, the district court carefully noted the ornamental features that produced the overall "rocket-like" appearance of the design. We agree with the district court's claim construction, which properly limits the scope of the patent to its overall ornamental visual impression, rather than to the broader general design concept of a rocket-like tossing ball. We therefore reject OddzOn's contention that overall similarity of the "rocket-like" appearance is sufficient to show infringement.

OddzOn next argues that the survey establishes not only overall similarity, but that the similarity is due to common ornamental features. OddzOn argues that the various features identified by survey respondents, including the ends of the fins, the football shape, the rocket-like tail, and a ball in front with triangular fins in back, are ornamental "because they are not required for a tossing ball." Thus, OddzOn argues, the survey is sufficient to show infringement because it establishes that the common features are ornamental. We disagree. The survey fails to establish a link between the similarity reported by respondents and the patented ornamental aspects of the design. Many of the respondents indicated that the balls were similar. When asked why, they responded by pointing to specific features, some general, some more specific, some functional, some not. However, the survey did not ask the respondents whether they believed that there was overall similarity apart from the fact that both the design and the accused products were essentially footballs with tails and fins.

OddzOn argues that the shape of a football with an arrow-like tail is an ornamental feature because "it is not required for a tossing ball." . . . It is the football shape combined with fins on a tail that give the design these functional qualities. The tail and fins on OddzOn's design add stability in the same manner as do the tail and fins found on darts or rockets. They are no less functional simply because "tossing balls" can be designed without them. [C]ontrary to Just Toys' arguments in its cross-appeal, these functional characteristics do not invalidate the design patent, but merely limit the scope of the protected subject matter. The district court's claim construction . . . captures the overall ornamental quality of the design.

Because the accused products are clearly similar to OddzOn's design in terms of their football shape and their tail and fins, it was incumbent on OddzOn to submit evidence establishing that the ornamental aspects of their football-with-tail-and-fin combination accounted for the similarity perceived by the survey participants. None of the evidence, when viewed in the light most favorable to OddzOn, would support a jury verdict that the accused devices are similar to the patented design with its football-shaped ball, slender tailshaft, and three fins which seemingly protrude out of the football and gently flare outwardly.

## ETHICON ENDO-SURGERY, INC. V. COVIDIEN, INC.

796 F.3d 1312 (Fed. Cir. 2015)

CHEN, CIRCUIT JUDGE. Plaintiffs-appellants Ethicon Endo-Surgery, Inc. and Ethicon Endo-Surgery, LLC (collectively, Ethicon) sued defendants-appellees Covidien, Inc. and Covidien LP (collectively, Covidien) in the U.S. District Court for the Southern District of Ohio for alleged infringement of several utility and design patents related to ultrasonic surgical devices. After the close of the discovery, the district court granted Covidien's motions for summary judgment, concluding that 1) U.S. Patent No. 8,182,501 (the '501 patent) is valid as indefinite, 2) U.S. Patent No. 5,989,275 (the '275 patent) is not infringed by Covidien's accused products, and 3) U.S. Patent Nos. D661,801 (the D'801 patent), D661,802 (the D'802 patent), D661,803 (the D'803 patent), and D661,804 (the D'804 patent) (collectively, the Design Patents) are invalid as functional and in the alternative, not infringed. The district court entered final judgment in favor of Covidien, and Ethicon now appeals.

As for the Design Patents, we reverse the district court's grant of invalidity based on functionality. The district court evaluated the claimed designs using too high a level of abstraction, focusing on the unclaimed utilitarian aspects instead of the claimed ornamental designs. We affirm the district court's grant of summary judgment of noninfringement of the Design Patents. After the functional aspects are properly excluded from the infringement analysis, the claimed ornamental designs are plainly dissimilar from the ornamental design of Covidien's accused products. . . .

The Design Patents claim particular ornamental designs of an ultrasonic surgical device. The D'801 patent claims a particular ornamental design of an inverted "U"-shaped trigger. The D'802 patent claims the overall appearance of the ornamental design of the "U"-shaped trigger and the particular ornamental design of a rounded and fluted torque knob positioned above and forward from the trigger. The D'803 patent claims the overall appearance of the ornamental design of the "U"-shaped trigger and the particular ornamental design of a rounded activation button positioned directly above the trigger. The D'804 patent claims the overall appearance of the ornamental designs of the "U"-shaped trigger, the fluted torque knob, and the rounded activation button, with the torque knob and the button positioned relative to the trigger as in the D'802 and D'803 patents, respectively. A figure from the D'804 patent, depicting the ornamental designs of the trigger, torque knob, and button claimed in various combinations and relative positions by the Design Patents, is reproduced below:

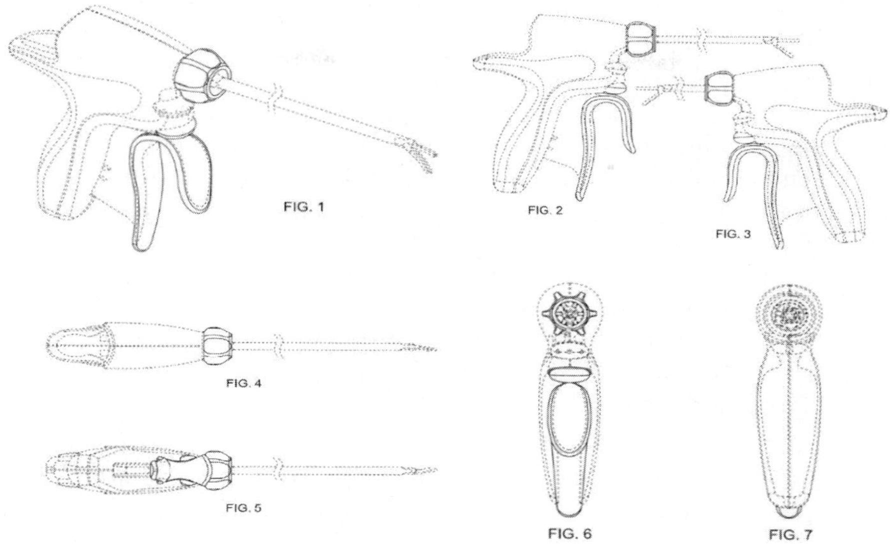


**Fig. 1 is a left perspective view of a user interface for a surgical instrument showing our design. Fig. 2 and Fig. 3 is a left side view and right side view thereof, respectively. Fig. 4 and Fig. 5 is a top view and a bottom view thereof, respectively. Fig. 6 and Fig. 7 is a front view and a rear view thereof, respectively.**

The district court concluded that the claimed designs in the Design Patents were all dictated by function and were therefore invalid. Under each consideration for assessing functionality, Ethicon's claimed designs were dictated by function. The district court found that because each of the designs of the trigger, torque knob, and button must be "factored out", the Design Patents had no scope, and therefore Covidien's accused design could not infringe the Design Patents. Even if the functional elements were not factored out, there was no infringement under the ordinary observer test laid out in *Egyptian Goddess, Inc. v. Swisa, Inc.* The district court found that the "highly sophisticated" ordinary observer in the "highly complex medical device purchasing process" would find that the claimed designs and the design of Covidien's accused ultrasonic shears were plainly dissimilar.

Design patents enjoy the same presumption of validity as utility patents under 35 U.S.C. § 282. Thus, Covidien has the burden to prove invalidity of the Design Patents by clear and convincing evidence. We have described as "stringent" this standard as it applies to invalidating design patents on grounds of functionality.

Articles of manufacture necessarily serve a utilitarian purpose, but design patents are directed to ornamental designs. If a particular design is essential to the use of an article, it cannot be the subject of a design patent. We have found designs to be essential to the use of an article when the claimed design is "dictated by" the use or purpose of the article. Design patents on such primarily functional rather than ornamental designs are invalid.

In determining whether a claimed design is primarily functional, "[t]he function of the article itself must not be confused with 'functionality' of the design of the article." In *Hupp*, we separated the function inherent in a concrete mold is an aesthetic design choice. Even though the claimed design pattern was embedded within the functional concrete mold, the proper analysis required a determination of whether the design pattern within the mold—and not the concrete mold itself—was "dictated by" its function. We determined that the claimed design was "primarily ornamental," and not invalid as functional. A claimed design was not invalid as functional simply because the "primary features" of the design could perform functions.

The overall appearance of the article is the basis of the relevant inquiry, not the functionality of elements of the claimed design viewed in isolation. We explained that "the utility of each of the various elements that comprise the design is not the relevant inquiry with respect to a design patent" because whether a design is primarily functional or primarily ornamental requires viewing the claimed design "in its entirety."

The availability of alternative designs [is] an important factor in evaluating the legal functionality of a claimed design. The district court in *L.A. Gear* referenced the evidence of many alternative designs that accomplished the same functionality associated with the underlying athletic sneaker. We noted that "[w]hen there are several ways to achieve the function of an article of manufacture, the design of the article is more likely to serve a primarily ornamental purpose.

The district court appeared to discount the existence and availability of alternative designs in determining that the claimed Design Patents were "primarily functional" based on its evaluation of the five considerations. We explained that where the existence of alternative designs is not dispositive of the invalidity inquiry, the district court may look to several other factors for its analysis:

> whether the protected design represents the best design; whether alternative designs would adversely affect the utility of the specified article; whether there are any concomitant utility patents; whether the advertising touts particular features of the design as having specific utility; and whether there are any elements in the design or an overall appearance clearly not dictated by function.

Evaluating these other considerations "might" be relevant to assessing whether the overall appearance of a claimed design is dictated by functional considerations. An inquiry into whether a claimed design is primarily functional should begin with an inquiry into the existence of alternative designs.

Ethicon presented evidence of alternative ornamental designs that could provide the same or similar functionality of the underlying ultrasonic shears. Ethicon's expert testified that "there [we]re many different designs that would function just as well" as the designs claimed. Covidien's expert admitted that other trigger designs . . . would "work well" but "look different." Indeed, Covidien does not contend that there are no alternatives, but merely argues that such designs cannot be considered true alternatives because they did not work "equally well" as the claimed designs.

The foregoing evidence does not support the district court's grant of summary judgment that the claimed designs are primarily functional for two reasons. The district court's determination that the designs did not work "equally well" apparently describes the preferences of surgeons for certain basic design concepts, not differences in functionality. In supporting . . . that alternative designs "would not have worked as well" as the claimed design, the district court pointed to testimony that surgeons preferred ultrasonic shears with certain basic design features like activation buttons on the front . . . "open" triggers and forward positions for placement of the torque knob.

The alternative design must simply provide "the same or similar functional capabilities." *Rosco*, 304 F.3d at 1378. Here, there is no dispute that the underlying ultrasonic shears could still function in the same manner with a differently-shaped open trigger, activation button, and torque knob, and different relative locations of the trigger, button, and torque knob. Covidien identifies no evidence or testimony that the particular appearance and shape of the open trigger, torque knob, or activation button provided utilitarian advantages over other ornamental designs of those elements.

The district court supported its conclusion that the claimed designs were "primarily functional" using testimony from Ethicon witnesses that the chosen design was "the best design ergonomically". This same evaluation of an open trigger guided the district court's determination that alternative designs would not have worked as well as an open trigger because surgeons preferred the chosen design to alternatives. The surgeon-preferred design was not the specific patented design, but rather the general concept of an "open trigger" versus a "closed trigger" design.

The district court found significant Ethicon applied for utility patents that included figures similar to those of the claimed designs. The district court noted that the utility patents described an "ergonomically formed" trigger with a proximal and distal portion having different lengths, a rounded button, and a fluted rotation knob. This focuses on the concepts of an open trigger, button, and torque knob, rather than the specifically claimed design conceptions.

Ethicon's Design Patents cover only the specific ornamental conceptions of the features shown in their figures, and not the general concepts of an open trigger, a rounded button, and a fluted torque knob oriented in some configuration as part of an ultrasonic surgical device. The analysis ... must also be performed at a level of particularity commensurate with the scope of the claims. The district court performed its functionality analysis at too high a level of abstraction, focusing on the general concepts of an open trigger, torque knob, and activation button rather than the ornamental designs adorning those elements.

Moreover, Covidien has not shown by clear and convincing evidence that no designs other than those claimed in the Design Patents allow the underlying ultrasonic shears to perform their intended function. The district court clearly erred in finding that Ethicon's patented designs are dictated by functional considerations and are therefore invalid as primarily functional. We reverse the district court's grant of summary judgment of invalidity of the Design Patents for functionality.

## *PROBLEM 2–2*

Turning back to Maya Rose's monkey key design, reproduced below, which of the examples satisfy the ornamentality requirement of design patent law.

Example 1

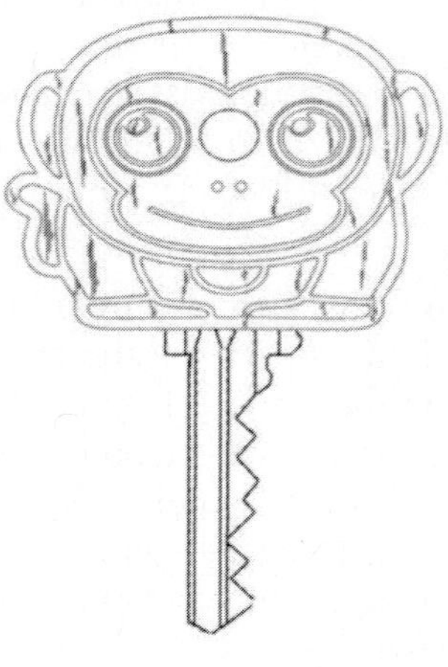

Example 2

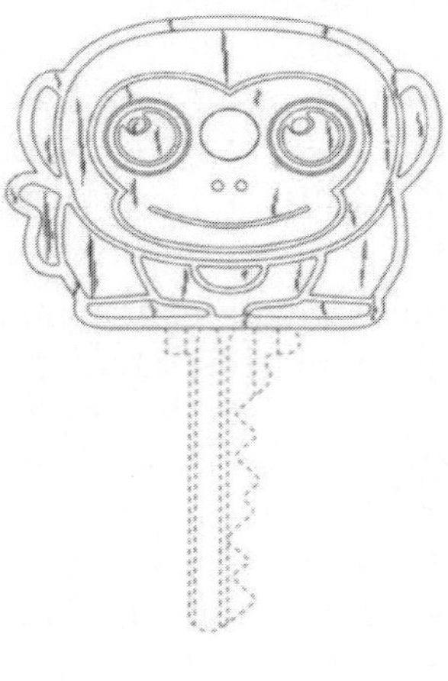

Example 3

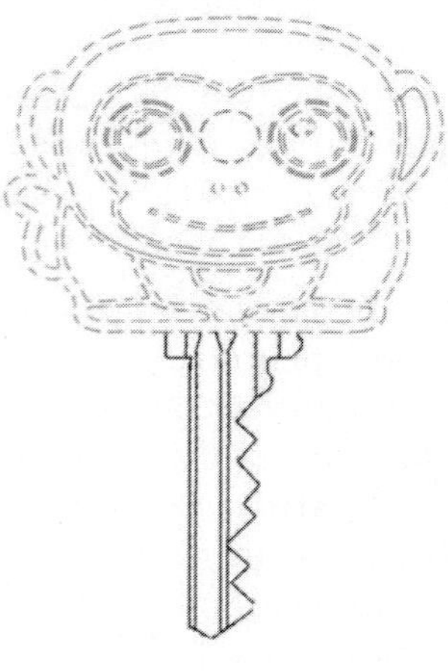

## *NOTES AND QUESTIONS*

1. How should the functionality doctrine apply to items that are not visible to consumers? In *Static Control Components, Inc. v. Lexmark Intern., Inc.*, 697 F.3d 387 (6th Cir. 2012), Lexmark obtained several design patents covering its toner cartridges for laser printers. The cartridges were visible to consumers at

some points, but at no point was their appearance important to the end-user. Furthermore, the design of the cartridges was primarily dictated by the design of the printer. The Sixth Circuit affirmed a finding that Lexmark's design patents were invalid as functional. Should it matter that the cartridges were sold online with photographs of the products? Should consumer surveys be required to prove whether consumers thought the product was functional? In *Lexmark*, the Sixth Circuit affirmed a finding of invalidity without survey evidence.

2. What happens when there are numerous functional aspects of a design? In *Rip-It Holdings, LLC v. Wilson Hunt Intern., Ltd.*, 2002 U.S. Dist. LEXIS 4490 (M.D. Fla. 2012), Rip-It Holdings obtained a design patent for a fielders' face mask to be used by softball and baseball players to protect their faces from being hit by a ball. The drawings in the design patent were:

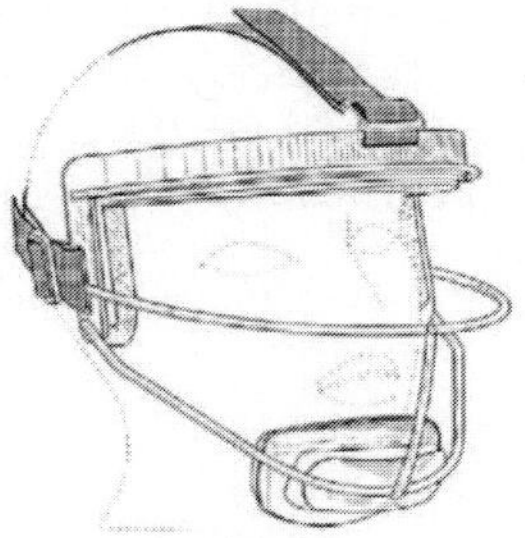
FIG. 1

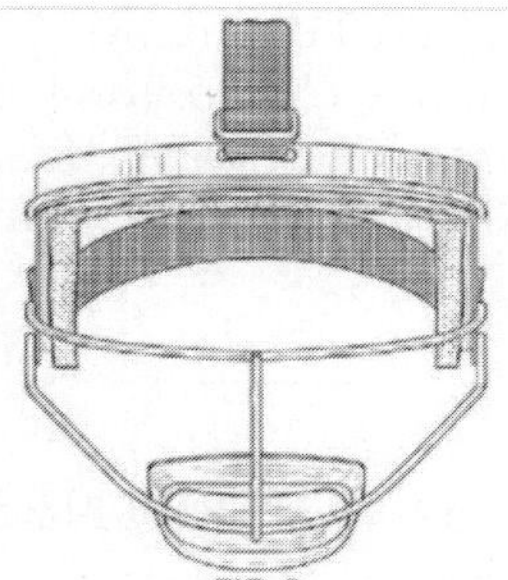
FIG. 2

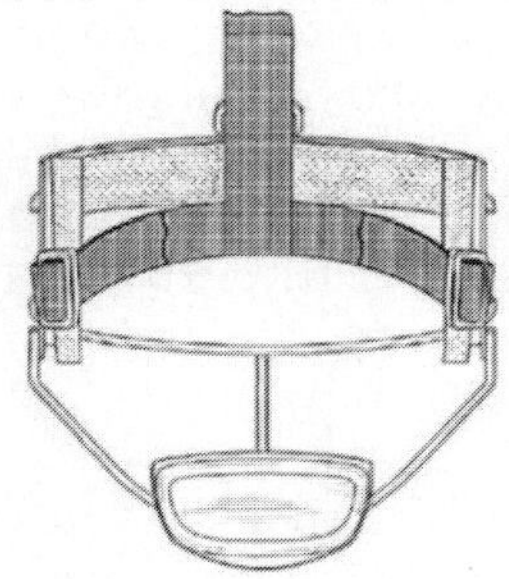
FIG. 3

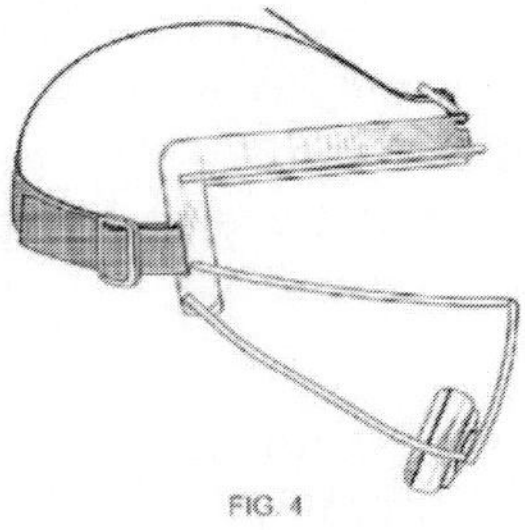
FIG. 4

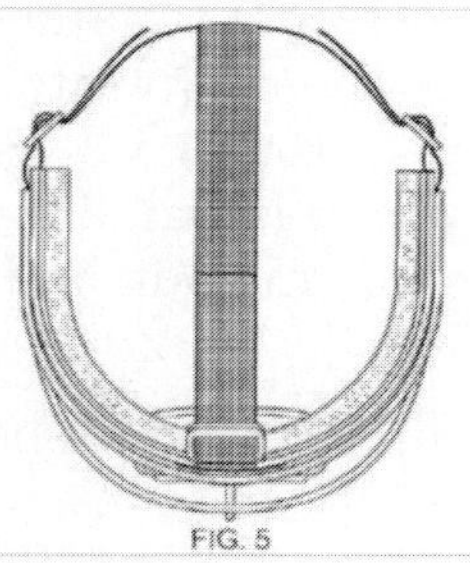
FIG. 5

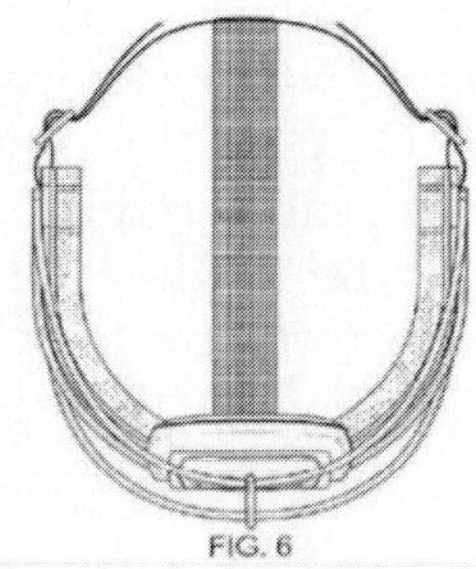
FIG. 6

The accused infringer argued that there were numerous uses or purposes of the mask. While the patent holder conceded that the basic purpose was to protect player's faces, there were also evidence (including promotional statement on the patent owner's website) that the mask was intended to be lightweight and provide a wide field of vision. While the focus must be on the overall appearance of the design, the court stated that in the functionality analysis, the purposes of the particular elements of the design necessarily must be considered. In denying a preliminary injunction, the court held that "[t]he mere fact that each element of a design serves some functional purpose does not necessarily mean that the overall design is dictated by function, but when the function of each element cannot be separated from the overall design, it indicates that the entire design is dictated by function."

3. Keep the ornamentality and lack of functionality requirements in mind when you read about the functionality requirement in trade dress. While the requirements are ostensibly directed toward the same concern, the tests differ. Does the test for ornamentality in design patent make sense as a mechanism to police the boundary between utility and design patents? For a proposal on design patent functionality, see Christopher Carani, *Design Patent Functionality: A Sensible Proposal*, LANDSLIDE 19 (Nov./Dec. 2014).

4. One area of design patenting is graphical user interfaces (GUIs). Apple, Samsung, and many other companies have obtained design patents covering GUIs for creative computer software displays. Software displays have traditionally been protected via the copyright system. Design patents do not permit the same equitable defenses, such as fair use, as copyrights do. Does it make sense to permit design patents on GUIs? For a discussion of design patents on GUIs, see Michael Risch, *Functionality and Graphical User Interface Design Patents,* 17 STAN. TECH. L. REV. 53 (2013); see also William J. Seymour & Andrew W. Torrance, *(R)evolution in Design Patentable Subject Matter: The Shifting Meaning of "Article of Manufacture,"* 17 STAN. TECH. L. REV. 183 (2013); Jason J. DuMont & Mark D. Janus, *Virtual Designs,* 17 STAN. TECH. L. REV. 107 (2013).

---

## 2. DEFINITENESS

The patent laws require that "The specification shall conclude with one or more claims particularly pointing out and distinctly claiming the subject matter which the inventor or a joint inventor regards as the invention." 35 U.S.C. § 112(b) [renumbered from 35 U.S.C. § 112 ¶ 2 in 2011]. The definiteness requirement, which is found within that sentences, requires that the claim "particularly point out and distinctly claim the subject matter" sought to be patented."

As previously discussed, the patent specification of a design patent largely is made up of figures. Sometimes, the figures themselves will be inconsistent with each other, even other illustrating the same design. In this instance, one can be unable to understand the meets and bounds of the claimed invention. The *Seed Lighting v. Home Depot* case that follows explains the doctrine for design patents. Another potential problem with design patent figures is when an aspect of the design is unclear, even after reviewing all of the figures. If portions of the design are left to conjecture, then the claim can be found as indefinite.

### SEED LIGHTING V. HOME DEPOT

2005 WL 1868152 (N.D. Cal. 2005)

ARMSTRONG, DISTRICT JUDGE. Plaintiff Seed Lighting Design Co., Ltd. ("Seed Lighting"), a company based in Taiwan, is the owner of a design patent protecting the ornamental features of a dual-head halogen desk lamp, U.S. Design Patent No. 407,519 (the " '519 Patent"). Home Depot, Inc. ("Home Depot") is a Delaware corporation doing business in numerous districts throughout the United States. Seed Lighting manufactures a lamp called the "Oligio" lamp (hereinafter referred to as the "Subject Lamp").

On May 6, 1998, Seed Lighting filed its design patent application for the '519 Patent in the United States. The Subject Lamp is the embodiment of the '519 Patent.

Defendants have . . . moved for summary judgment on Seed Lighting's patent infringement claim on the grounds that Seed Lighting's design patent is invalid for non-enablement.

The second paragraph of § 112 provides that "[t]he specification shall conclude with one or more claims particularly pointing out and distinctively claiming the subject matter which the applicant regards as his invention." "Determining whether a claim is definite requires an analysis of whether one skilled in the art would understand the bounds of the claim when read in light of the specification." *Personalized Media Communications v. Int'l Trade Comm'n.* Because, in a design patent, "the drawings or photograph constitute[ ] the entire visual disclosure of the claims[,] it is of utmost importance that the drawing or photo be clear and complete, and that *nothing* regarding the design sought to be patented is left to conjecture." *[S]ince* the '591 Patent survived the full patent examination process, it is presumed valid pursuant to 35 U.S.C. § 282. Defendants must therefore prove their invalidity defense by clear and convincing evidence.

To meet their burden of proof, Defendants have cited to a report prepared by their expert, Cooper Woodring, as well as certain admissions made by the inventor of the lamp, Meiric Chen. Defendants contend, and Seed Lighting does not dispute, that:

1) Mr. Woodring and Mr. Chen are experts skilled in the art of industrial design.

2) Mr. Woodring has identified certain mistakes and ambiguities in the drawings of the '591 Patent.

3) Mr. Chen has conceded that, due to certain ambiguities in the '519 Patent's drawings, even he cannot clearly articulate the precise scope of the patent.

As Mr. Woodring explains . . . the '519 Patent consists of one claim, which itself consists of ten separate figures on six drawing sheets. The mistakes and ambiguities in the Patent's drawings fall within three of the six major components of the Subject Lamp: (1) the base, (2) the shades, and (3) the disk at the top of the vertical rods. These components contain the following inconsistencies and flaws:

- The base of the Subject Lamp is depicted as a thin, flat, disk-like plate in Figure 1 and as a raised, domed shape in Figures 2 and 3.

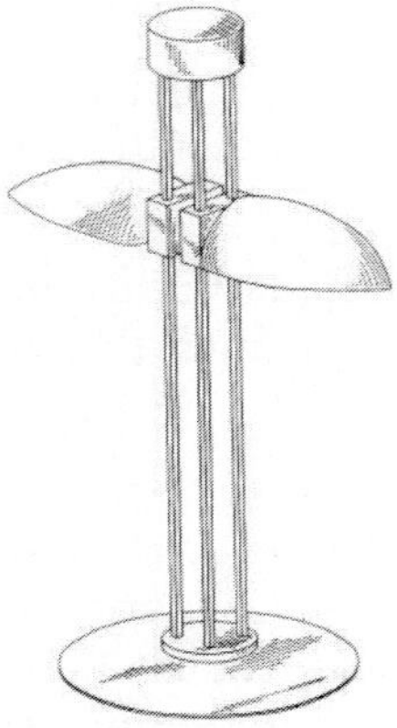

FIG.1

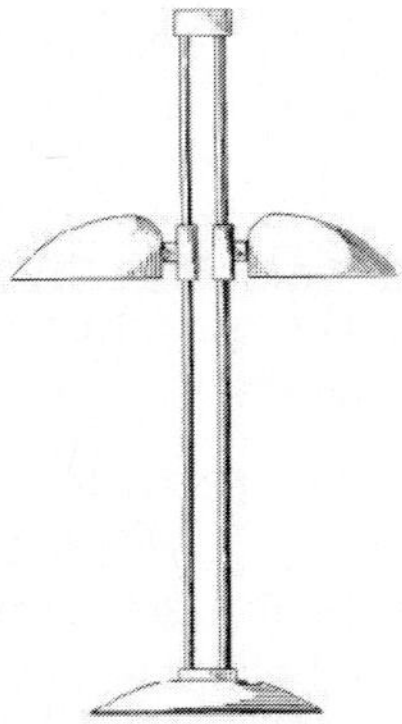

FIG. 2

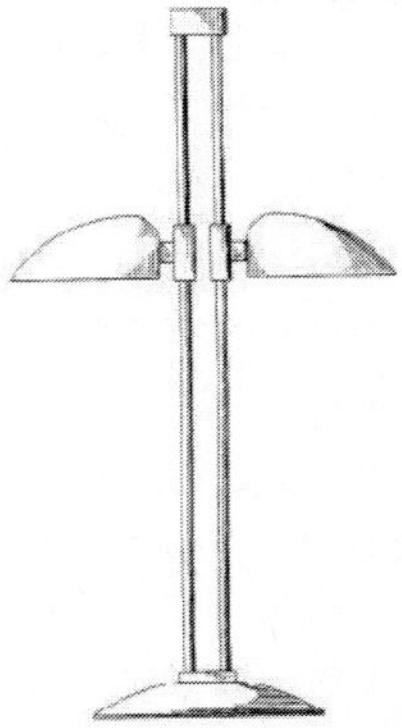

FIG.3

- The underside of the Subject Lamp is depicted in Figure 8 as having a specific edge and wall thickness around the perimeter of the shade and in Figure 5 as consisting of a solid surface with no edge or wall thickness.

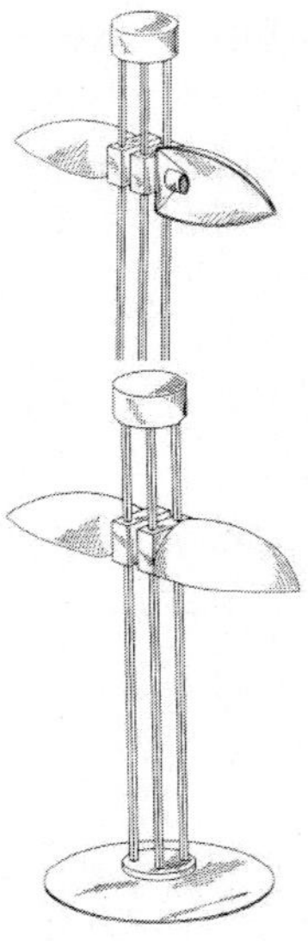

FIG.1

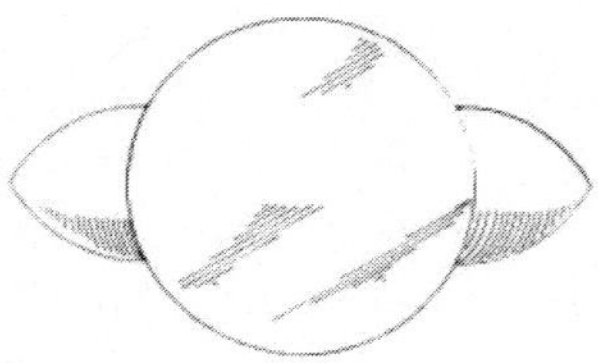

FIG.5

- The disk at the top of the vertical rods of the Subject Lamp is shown in Figure 1 as having the same outer dimension as the square formed by the "sliders" that move the shades up and down and in Figure 4 as being small enough to fit within the square formed by those sliders.

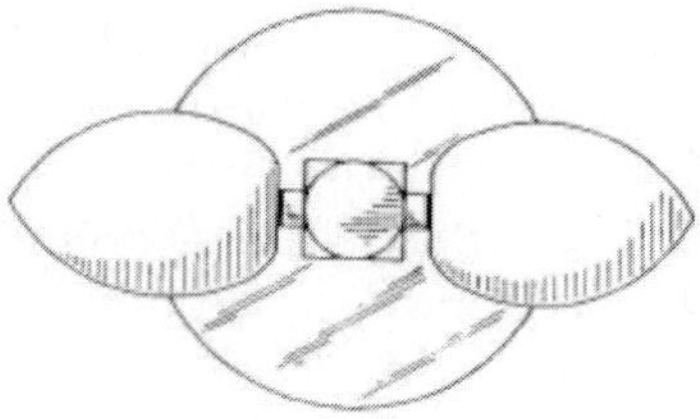

FIG.4

Due to these inconsistencies, after reviewing the '591 Patent during his deposition, Mr. Chen-the *inventor* of the patent-agreed that he could not determine whether the base of the claimed lamp was a flat disk or a rounded dome. Mr. Chen also stated in his deposition that Figure 5 of the '591 Patent-which appears to show a solid surface with no edge-is not supposed to depict a solid surface, but, rather, the underside of the shade.

In its opposition, Seed Lighting does not identify a single piece of evidence or testimony that would demonstrate to the Court that a person skilled in the art would understand the bounds of the '519 Patent's claim. To the contrary, even Seed Lighting's *own* witness appears to agree that the patent drawings are flawed and unclear. Further, Seed Lighting's sole response to Defendants' evidence is that "the slight differences or vagaries contained within the nine figures which make up the '519 Patent are so insubstantial and inconsequential as to render Home Depo's indefiniteness argument meaningless." The bare, unsupported belief of Seed Lighting's *counsel* that the vagaries are "insubstantial," however, is not sufficient to overcome summary judgment. Without any evidence, facts, or expert testimony, the Court finds that Seed Lighting has utterly failed to demonstrate the existence of genuine factual issues sufficient to preclude summary judgment on its patent claim.

---

The recent *Apple v. Samsung* lawsuit raised most of the core design patent issues, including definiteness. The case is a closer case than the *Seed Lighting* case above.

## APPLE, INC. V. SAMSUNG ELECTRONICS CO., LTD.

932 F. Supp.2d 1076 (2013)

KOH, DISTRICT JUDGE. In this patent case, a jury found that Samsung had infringed several of Apple's patents, including Claim 50 of U.S. Patent No. 7,864,163 ("the '163 Patent") and four design patents: No. D618,677 ("the D'677 Patent"); No. D593,087 ("the D'087 Patent"); No. D604,305 ("the D'305 Patent"); and No. D504,889 ("the D'889 Patent"). Samsung now argues that . . . all four design patents are invalid for failure to meet the definiteness requirement of 35 U.S.C. § 112. . . .

### II. DESIGN PATENT INDEFINITENESS

### A. LEGAL STANDARD

The definiteness requirement applies to design patents as well as utility patents. Even in design patents, "[c]laims are considered indefinite when they are not amenable to construction or are insolubly ambiguous. Indefiniteness requires a determination whether those skilled in the art would understand what is claimed." *Young v. Lumenis, Inc.* There is little clear precedent. Courts considering the question have analyzed whether "a person of skill in the art" would get "an overall understanding of the total substance of the designs." *Antonious v. Spalding & Evenflo Companies, Inc.*

As indefiniteness is intimately linked to claim construction, the cases discussing claim construction in design patents bear on the indefiniteness analysis. Further, the test for infringement certainly bears on the test for indefiniteness, since the ultimate inquiry for indefiniteness is whether a person having ordinary skill in the art could tell what is claimed—and therefore, what infringes. Design patents protect "overall designs" rather than individual specific features. Design patents are infringed when "an ordinary observer, familiar with the prior art designs, would be deceived into believing that the accused product is the same as the patented design." *Crocs, Inc. v. Int'l Trade Comm'n.* In construing design patent claims, a district court "[i]s not obligated to issue a detailed verbal description of the design," *Egyptian Goddess*, but "can usefully guide the finder of fact by describing the role of particular conventions in design patent drafting, such as the role of broken lines; assessing and describing the effect of any representations that may have been made in the course of the prosecution history; and distinguishing between those features of the claimed design that are ornamental and those that are purely functional." Samsung must show by clear and convincing evidence that a designer of ordinary skill in the art would not understand what is claimed.

### B. DISCUSSION

Specifically, Samsung argues that the D'889 Patent is indefinite for four reasons: (1) drawings showing the design oriented in different directions make it impossible to know which way the design is supposed to be oriented or where features actually appear; (2) the use of broken lines is inconsistent, making it difficult to tell which elements are claimed; (3) the use of surface shading is different in different pictures, making it unclear what type of surface is being represented; and (4) the 035 Mockup and iPad 2 embody the design, while the original iPad [does] not. Samsung then presents a single argument for indefiniteness of the D'305 Patent: that the use of color in one drawing but not another makes it impossible to tell whether color is necessary. Finally indefiniteness of the related D'677 and D'087 Patents: (1) that the drawing does not make clear whether the "lozenge" shape and rectangular shape are beneath the surface, a break in the surface, or resting on top of the surface; and (2) that the lack of shading on the D'087 drawing makes it impossible to see that there is a display area below a transparent surface.

Several of Samsung's arguments concern use of drafting techniques (broken lines and shading) where inconsistent use of broken lines is per se indefinite. *In re Blum,* 374 F.2d 904 (C.C.P.A. 1967). The *Blum* court noted that "[d]otted and broken lines may mean different things in different circumstances" and that "in each case it must be made entirely clear what they do mean" to avoid indefiniteness. It makes clear that it "is the examiner's responsibility to obtain such definiteness." When the patent has already issued, the patent comes with a strong presumption of validity. Claim construction shows that these features *are* amenable to construction. Given that [they] have construed the claims in these patents, they are not "insolubly ambiguous" or "not amenable to construction." *Young.*

Moreover, the Federal Circuit has explicitly recognized that it is appropriate for district courts to issue interpretations of drafting conventions. If the use of drafting conventions had to be facially obvious for the patent to be valid, no such interpretations would ever be necessary. Regarding the differently oriented drawings in the D'889 Patent, the Court sees nothing inconsistent about these drawings. They show a device facing different directions, but there is no place in which an identifiable feature of the design appears in two different places in two different figures. The fact that a feature may be invisible in one of the figures due to the resolution and orientation of the drawing does not make it impossible to determine whether or not the feature is part of the design. The Court cannot be certain as to what features Samsung intends to refer, the Court sees no inconsistency. There is simply no requirement that a claimed design must have a particular preferred orientation. The fact that the D'889 Patent shows a design in different orientations merely shows that the particular orientation is not part of what is claimed.

Samsung also argues that the fact that the iPad 2 and the 035 Mockup both embody the D'889 Patent necessarily renders the patent indefinite but the same design patent can have multiple embodiments. If two objects as different as the iPad 2 and the 035 Mockup can both embody the patented design . . . the patent simply must be indefinite. But Samsung presents no evidence to support its assertion that the 035 Mockup and iPad2 are less similar in relevant ways than the original iPad, and a mere assertion in a brief that objects are similar or dissimilar cannot serve as a basis for invalidating a patent. Given the strong presumption of validity accompanying issued patents, this Court cannot find that the similarities and differences between these three articles and the patent itself warrant a finding of indefiniteness.

Samsung claims that because only one of the figures in the D'305 Patent is in color, there is no possible way to know whether color is part of the claimed design. As Samsung acknowledges, the Model of Patent Examining Procedure explains that color drawings are allowed where "color is an integral part of the claimed design." By including a color drawing, Apple has made clear that color *is* necessary to the design. The regulations governing color drawings make clear that they are to be used only rarely and only where necessary to convey what is claimed. Nowhere do the regulations say that if one drawing is in color, all drawings must be in color. Given the presumption of validity afforded to issued patents, the Court declines to adopt a rule requiring [this] for color to be part of the claimed design.

Samsung argues that the D'677 and D'087 Patents are indefinite because it is unclear whether the lozenge and rectangle shapes are below, in, or on top of the surface. But it does not matter . . . as long as any of those could produce interchangeable visual effects that would appear "substantially the same to the ordinary observer." *Egyptian Goddess.* A design patent protects an overall visual impression, and "it will be for the jury to decide whether the accused device's 'lozenge-shaped element would appear as it does in the figures.' " The design patent need not specify how the lozenge shape is created. It need only provide the visual standard. It may be possible to produce the same overall visual impression in any one of those three positions. There may be more than one way to manufacture an article that embodies the claimed design.

Finally, Samsung argues that Apple's "named inventors and other witnesses" testified "that they could not understand the designs reflected in Apple's patents." The witnesses express a lack of familiarity, or a lack of understanding about design patents. The witnesses' reluctance to verbally interpret the drawings does not establish indefiniteness. Rather, the testimony consistently indicates a lack of familiarity with design patent conventions. Witnesses' ignorance of drafting conventions does not establish that the patents cannot be construed so as to clearly delineate what design is claimed. Definiteness does not require that persons of skill in the art be able to clearly describe the designs in words; they must simply be able to replicate the patented design.

Apple presents some trial testimony of witnesses who *were* able to interpret the drawings. Samsung's design expert testified that the designs were obvious and functional. Apple [says] it would be difficult to have an opinion that a given design was obvious without understanding what the design actually was. Samsung's arguments, which all concern the quality and specificity of the drawings, are in contrast to the types of defects that courts have found constituted design patent indefiniteness. The distinction between drafting inconsistencies and actual ambiguity is especially relevant, where the Court has been able to construe the drafting techniques. All of Samsung's alleged sources of indefiniteness concern how the design is represented, rather than the nature of the design itself. Samsung has not established indefiniteness by clear and convincing evidence, and Apple's design patents remain valid.

### *NOTES AND QUESTIONS*

1. The definiteness requirement ensures that the claim which references the drawings provided by the inventor are sufficient. The definiteness requirement can make fatal Inconsistencies among various views of the patented design or ambiguities in the figures.

2. The U.S. Supreme Court in 2015 changed the standard for determining definiteness for utility patents. *Nautilus, Inc. v. Biosig Instruments, Inc.*, 134 S. Ct. 2120 (2014). The Supreme Court rejected the Federal Circuit's previous test which required that a claim be "insolubly ambiguous" or "not amenable to construction" to be indefinite. Instead, the Supreme Court held that a claim is indefinite if a person having ordinary skill in the art cannot discern the scope with reasonable clarity from the claim, specification, and the remaining documents relating to the patent. While the holding in *Nautilus* likely applies in the design patent context as well, it remains to be seen whether the change in legal test affects the outcomes in cases like *Seed Lighting* and *Apple v. Samsung*.

3. The (utility) patent law treats the disclosure requirements as necessary for the Constitutional requirement that patents "promote progress of . . . the useful arts." U.S. Const. Art. I, cl. 8, § 8. Copyright, which does not have a disclosure or publication requirement, is geared toward promoting the creative arts. A work does not have to be published to be copyrightable. The Courts have held that design patents are meant to "give encouragement to the decorative arts." *Gorham v. White,* 81 U.S. 551. Does a strong disclosure requirement make sense for design patents, given their difference in purpose from utility patents?

---

## 3. NOVELTY

A bedrock principle of patent law is that one cannot obtain a patent for an invention that is old. The rationale is straightforward: if someone else has already invented the items, then the market reward of a patent is unnecessary. In fact, a patent in such circumstances would remove items from the public domain; in their place would be exclusive private property rights. This bedrock principle applies for design patent the same as it does for utility patents. It is codified in the U.S. patent laws at 35 U.S.C. § 102.

The newness requirement is referred to by courts and lawyers as the "novelty requirement." Alternatively, the requirement can be referred to in the negative—the invention cannot be anticipated or else it is unpatentable or otherwise invalid. Below are portions of two cases that illuminate the requirement of novelty or lack of anticipation as it pertains to design patents.

The first case sets forth the current law on anticipation, and explains why a previous test employed by the courts is no longer used. Basically, to anticipate, a single prior art reference must show the same subject matter as that of the patent, and must be identical in all material respects. Please pay particular attention to whether the designs need to be visible to the consumer. The second case provides a recent exemplary analysis of the novelty and anticipation requirement.

## INTERNATIONAL SEAWAY TRADING CORP. V. WALGREENS CORP.

589 F.3d 1233 (Fed. Cir. 2009)

DYK, CIRCUIT JUDGE. Plaintiff-Appellant International Seaway Trading Corporation ("Seaway") filed suit against Walgreens Corporation ("Walgreens") and Touchsport Footwear USA, Inc. ("Touchsport") claiming infringement of Seaway's patents, U.S. Design Patents Nos. D529,263 ("the '263 patent"), D545,032 ("the '032 patent"), and D545,033 ("the '033 patent"). The district court granted summary judgment for defendants, finding that the claims of the asserted patents were invalid under 35 U.S.C. § 102 as anticipated by a patent assigned to Crocs, Inc. ("Crocs"), U.S. Design Patent No. D517,789 ("the Crocs '789 patent").

On appeal, Seaway contends that the district court erred by basing its invalidity determination solely on the ordinary observer test and by failing to apply the point of novelty test. We agree with the district court that the point of novelty test should not be utilized for anticipation, and that only the ordinary observer test applies. However, while we conclude that the exterior appearance of the patented designs would be substantially similar to the prior art in the eyes of an ordinary observer, we conclude that the district court erred in failing to compare the insoles of the patents-in-suit with the prior art from the perspective of the ordinary observer.

Plaintiff-Appellant Seaway is an Ohio corporation that acts as a buyer's agent and/or importer of footwear to mass merchandise retailers [and] creates its own shoe and boot designs and pursues design patents for them. Defendant-Appellee Walgreens is an Illinois corporation with retail drug stores across the country that sell footwear, among other products.

Seaway's '263, '032, and '033 patents (collectively "the patents-in-suit") claim designs for casual, lightweight footwear, which are typically referred to as "clogs." It is undisputed that the '032 and '033 patents are "substantially the same as the '263 patent design" except that the heel strap is in a forward position overlying a portion of the clog upper in the '032 patent and that the heel strap is not part of the claimed design for the '033 patent.

During prosecution of the '263 patent application, the examiner considered and found the '263 patent design patentable over: (a) four pages from the website of Crocs that depicted various models of Crocs clogs, including the Beach model clog; (b) five pages of photographs of the Crocs Beach model clog; and (c) a December 2002 archival version of the Crocs website, depicting various views of a Crocs clog. In the examination of the '263 patent application, the examiner did not have the benefit of the Crocs '789 patent, which depicted the Crocs Beach model clog, even though the '789 patent issued before the examination was concluded. For the '032 and '033 patent applications, the examiner considered and found these patentable over the references considered during the '263 prosecution as well as the '789 patent.

On February 15, 2008, Seaway filed a complaint against Walgreens and Touchsport . . . alleging that they were infringing its '263, '032 and '033 patents. [The district court found the three patents invalid as anticipated by the Crocs '789 patent.] Figures depicting the design in the '789 patent, and the design in the '263 patent, which is representative of the designs in the '032 and '033 patents, are set forth below.

**Figure 1 in the Crocs '789 Patent (Prior Art)**

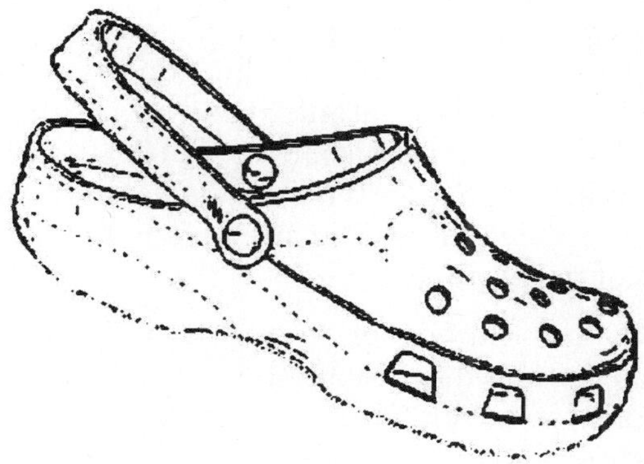

**Figure 2 in the '263 Patent**

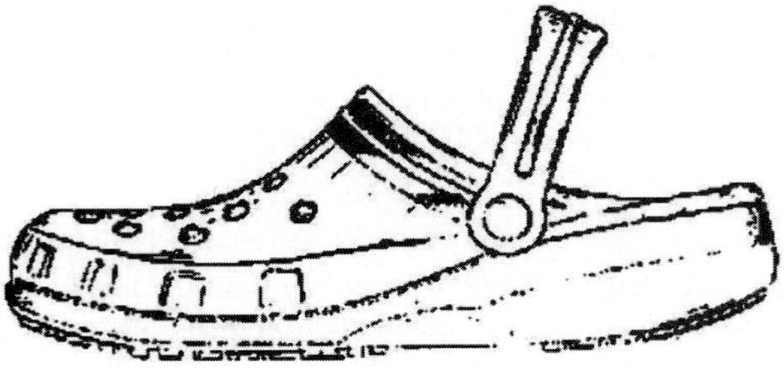

Seaway first contends that the district court should have applied the point of novelty test in addition to the ordinary observer test during its anticipation analysis. Our decision in *Egyptian Goddess, Inc. v. Swisa, Inc.*, changed the test for infringement: "the 'point of novelty' test should no longer be used in the analysis of a claim of design patent infringement" and that "the 'ordinary observer' test should be the sole test for determining whether a design patent has been infringed." The issue remains whether *Egyptian Goddess* also requires a similar change in the test for invalidity . . . [W]e have concluded that the district court was correct in concluding that *Egyptian Goddess* necessarily requires a change in the standard for anticipation.

"Whoever invents any new, original and ornamental design for an article of manufacture may obtain a patent therefor, subject to the conditions and requirements of this title." 35 U.S.C. § 171. Section 171 excludes the word "useful" (to distinguish design patents from utility patents) and adds the word "original." The courts have not construed the word "original" as requiring that design patents be treated differently than utility patents. Section 171 requires that the "conditions and requirements of this title" be applied to design patents, thus requiring application of the provisions of sections 102 (anticipation) and 103 (invalidity). Our cases have recognized that in the past we have applied a dual test for anticipation identical to the then-applicable test for infringement, namely the ordinary observer and point of novelty tests.

[I]n applying the ordinary observer test . . . in the case of anticipation, we compared the patented design with the alleged anticipatory reference. In applying the point of novelty test . . . in the case of anticipation, we compared the patented design with the alleged anticipatory reference to see if it appropriated the points of novelty of the prior art reference. The points of novelty of the prior art reference were determined by looking to earlier prior art to determine the points of novelty in the anticipatory reference. The ordinary observer and point of novelty tests were applied in the same manner for obviousness as for anticipation, except that in the case of obviousness the features of the prior art could be combined to create a single anticipatory reference or an earlier single reference could be modified based on the knowledge of a skilled artisan.

While our cases have utilized the point of novelty test for infringement and anticipation, this test was not mandated by *Smith v. Whitman Saddle Co.,* or precedent from other courts. In *Whitman,* the Supreme Court utilized only the ordinary observer test for determining infringement and invalidity . . .

Moreover, it has been well established for over a century that the same test must be used for both infringement and anticipation. The same rule applies for design patents. In *Egyptian Goddess,* we abandoned the point of novelty test for design patent infringement and held that the ordinary observer test should serve as the sole test for design patent infringement. The ordinary observer test originated in 1871 when the Supreme Court held that if, in the eye of an ordinary observer, giving such attention as a purchaser usually gives, two designs are substantially the same, if the resemblance is such as to deceive such an observer, inducing him to purchase one supposing it to be the other, the first one patented is infringed by the other . . . [W]e also refined the ordinary observer test by characterizing the ordinary observer as being "deemed to view the differences between the patented design and the accused product in the context of the prior art," where:

> When the differences between the claimed and accused design are viewed in light of the prior art, the attention of the hypothetical ordinary observer will be drawn to those aspects of the claimed design that differ from the prior art. And when the claimed design is close to the prior art designs, small differences between the accused design and the claimed design are likely to be important to the eye of the hypothetical ordinary observer.

We further determined that the point of novelty test, as a second and free-standing requirement for proof of design patent infringement, was inconsistent with the ordinary observer test laid down in *Gorham.* In light of Supreme Court precedent and our precedent holding that the same tests must be applied to infringement and anticipation, and our holding in *Egyptian Goddess* that the ordinary observer test is the sole test for infringement, we now conclude that the ordinary observer test must logically be the sole test for anticipation as well.

The problems inherent in the point of novelty test in the infringement context also exist in the anticipation context. The test is just as difficult to apply in the context of anticipation as in . . . infringement, encouraging the focus on minor differences between the allegedly anticipatory reference and the patented design. [A]pplying the point of novelty test in the context of anticipation, as in . . . infringement, creates the need to canvass the entire prior art . . .

In summary, the district court did not err in concluding that the ordinary observer test is the sole test for design patent invalidity under § 102.

Seaway's second contention is that the district court misapplied the ordinary observer test by failing to compare the entirety of the patented designs, including the clogs' insoles, with the Crocs '789 patent. The district court, relying on *Contessa,* held "that the law requires a court to consider only those portions of the product that are visible during normal use, regardless of whether those portions are visible during the point of sale." The court did "not consider any aspects of the insoles of the shoes" because the insoles are "hidden by the user's foot." We conclude that the district court erred. We vacate and remand for a determination of whether the differences between the insole patterns in the patents-in-suit and in the prior Crocs art bar a finding of anticipation or obviousness.

The district court here misconstrued *Contessa* as requiring that the normal use of a clog be limited to the time when it is worn. *Contessa* did not exclude the point of sale from the normal use of a product. The sale of a clog occurs after it has been manufactured and before it is ultimately destroyed. The point of sale for a clog clearly occurs during its normal use lifetime. At the point of sale, the insole is visible to potential purchasers when the clog is displayed on a shelf or rack and when the clog is picked up for examination. Removing a clog from a wearer's foot also occurs after manufacture and before destruction of the clog . . . it falls squarely within the clog's normal use lifetime.

Walgreens and Touchsport acknowledge that the district court misinterpreted *Contessa* but argue that it was harmless error. They assert that it was a harmless error because insoles have an insignificant effect on the overall visual appearance of the clogs: there is a "universal truth that consumers buy shoes primarily for their exterior appearance. The insole therefore contributes little to the overall appearance of the shoe to an ordinary observer with knowledge of the prior art." We reject this argument. Walgreens and Touchsport had the burden to establish by clear and convincing evidence that consumers do not consider the insoles of shoes to be significant. The appellees failed to present any evidence in support of this argument.

Walgreens and Touchsport also argue that the district court's error was harmless because the asserted differences between the insoles of the patents-in-suit and the prior art "were at most slight variations of design elements already present in the Crocs prior art." We disagree. The insole pattern for the patents-in-suit is distinctly different than the Crocs insole pattern.

**Figure 6 in the Crocs '789 Patent**

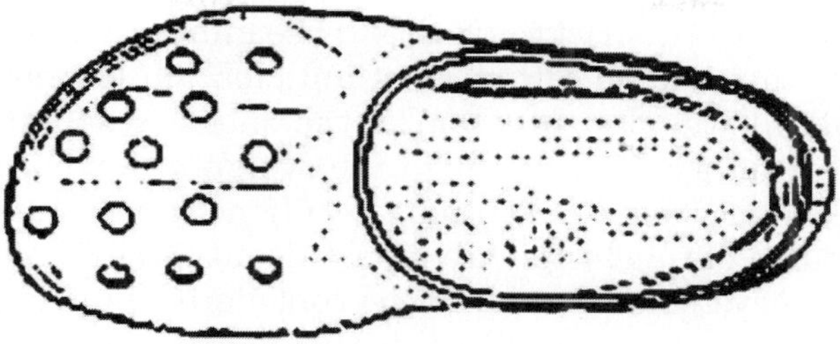

**Figure 6 in the '263 Patent**

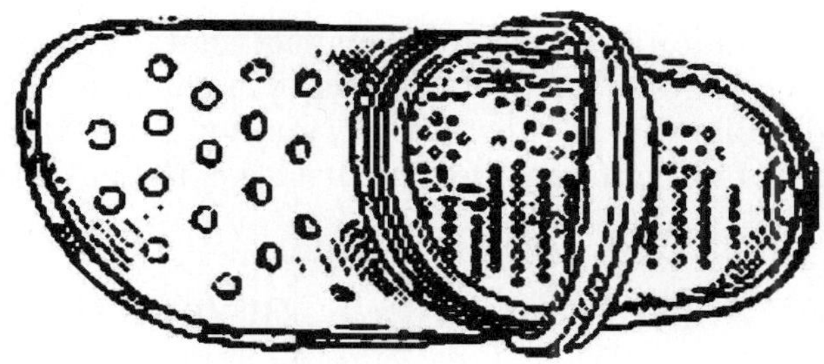

The Crocs '789 patent, as shown above, contains a long, U-shaped dimpling pattern on the insole. In contrast, the patents-in-suit . . . have a dimpling pattern that includes multiple short rows of dimples.

Beyond the insole features of its patented designs, Seaway argues that a genuine issue of material fact exists as to whether the exterior features of its designs preclude a finding of anticipation. It claims that four exterior features differ from the prior art to the degree necessary to preclude summary judgment: (1) the number and arrangement of the circular openings on the upper of the clog; (2) the number and position of the rectangular cut-outs in the lower portion of the upper of the clog; (3) the shape of the toe portion of the clog; and (4) the raised pattern of the outsole of the clog. These features are identical in all three of Seaway's patents-in-suit.

With regard to these alleged dissimilarities, the district court stated:

> Slight variations on the number and position of the circular holes on the top of the shoe, the rectangular holes on the toe of the shoe as well as the design of different shaped rectangles on the sole of the shoe would not convince a reasonable jury, or an ordinary observer with knowledge of the prior art, that the limitations were not inherently disclosed in the '789 patent. This conclusion does not change merely because plaintiff slightly changed the

arrangement of the textured portions on the top and around the bottom portion of the sides of the shoe.

We agree with the district court that these minor variations in the shoe are insufficient to preclude a finding of anticipation because they do not change the overall visual impression of the shoe. Although the ordinary observer test requires consideration of the design as a whole . . . this does not prevent the district court on summary judgment from determining that individual features of the design are insignificant from the point of view of the ordinary observer and should not be considered as part of the overall comparison . . . Just as "minor differences between a patented design and an accused article's design cannot, and shall not, prevent a finding of infringement," so too minor differences cannot prevent a finding of anticipation.

We thus conclude that, while the district court correctly determined that there was no genuine issue of material fact that the exterior features of the patented designs were substantially similar to the Crocs 789 patent, the court erred by failing to consider the insoles of the patents-in-suit in its invalidity analysis.

## HIGH POINT DESIGN LLC v. BUYER'S DIRECT

621 Fed. Appx. 632 (Fed. Cir. 2015) (unpublished decision)

CHEN, CIRCUIT JUDGE. On remand [after a previous appeal], the district court again granted summary judgment, finding that: (1) the asserted patent was anticipated; (2) the accused products did not infringe; [and two other rulings.]]

BDI owns a design patent for the ornamental appearance of a fuzzy slipper, U.S. Patent No. D598,183 (the D'183 patent). The D'183 patent is entitled "Slipper," and recites one claim for "the ornamental design for a slipper, as shown and described" in eight figures. Exemplary Figures 1 and 4 are reproduced below:

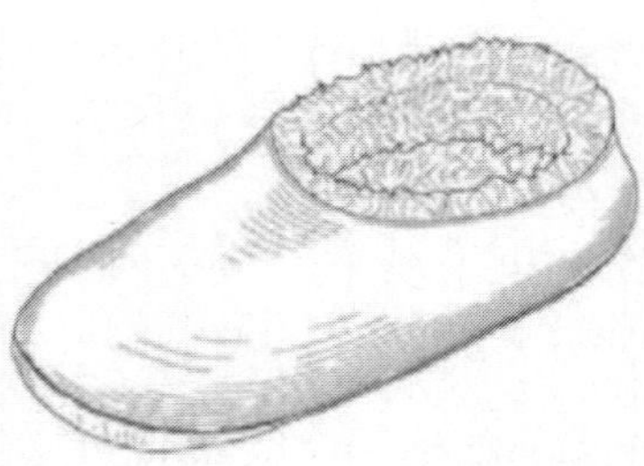

Fig. 1

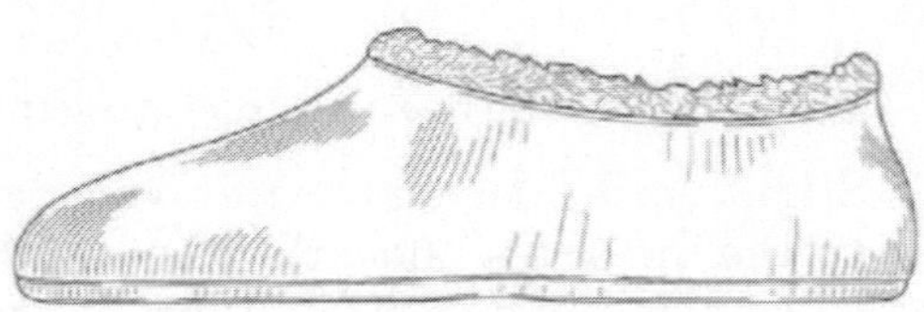

Fig. 4

The claimed design discloses two embodiments for the slipper soles. One embodiment has a sole with two groups of raised dots (Figure 7 on the left), and the other has a sole with a smooth bottom (Figure 8 on the right).

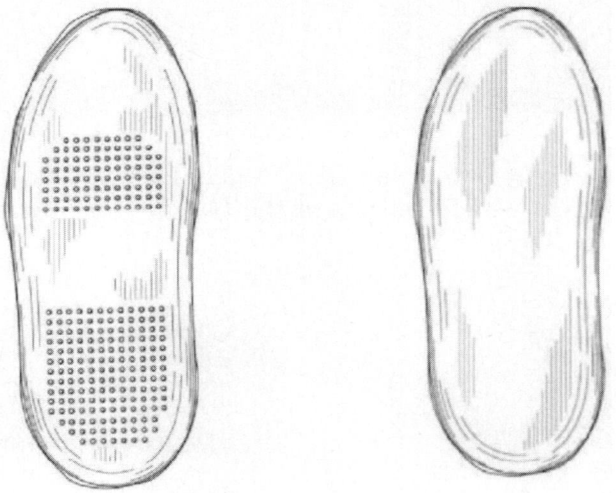

BDI manufactures a slipper called the SNOOZIE® (Snoozie), which it contends is an embodiment of the design disclosed in the D'183 patent. An exemplary Snoozie slipper is shown below:

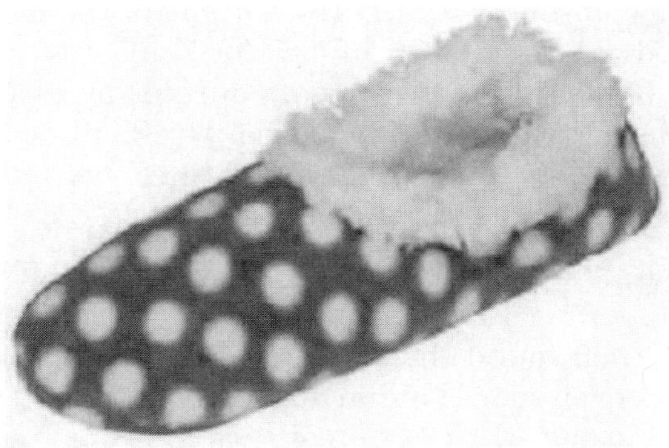

High Point Design LLC (High Point) manufactures and distributes the accused FUZZY BABBA® slipper (Fuzzy Babba). Fuzzy Babba slippers are sold through various retailers, including Meijer, Sears, and Wal-mart (collectively Retailers) and are alleged to compete with Snoozie. An exemplary Fuzzy Babba slipper is shown below:

The district court found that the D'183 patent was anticipated by the Woolrich Prior Art, which consists of the Laurel Hill and Penta slippers (below).

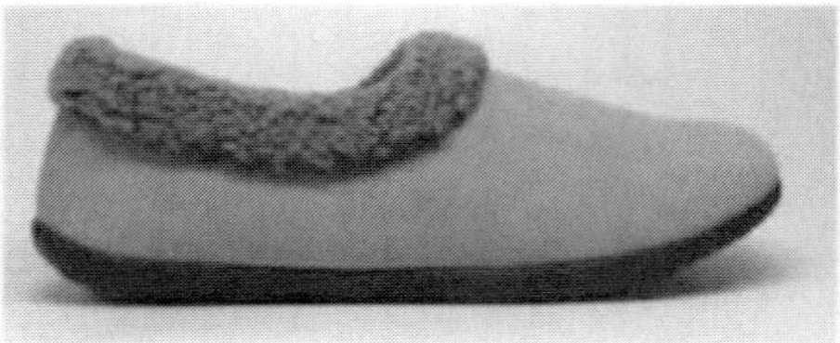

Laurel Hill

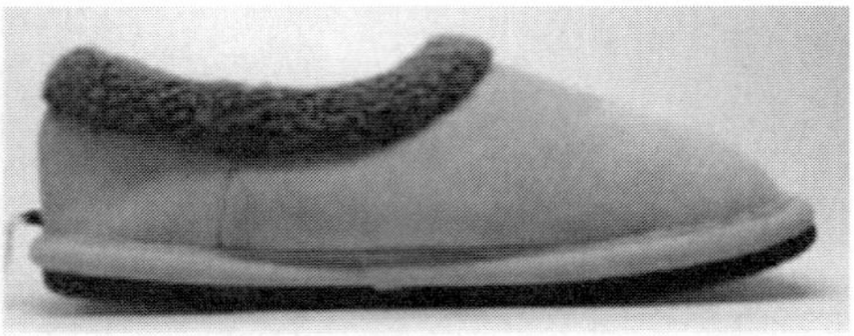

Penta

The district court offered the following description of the claimed design in support of its decision:

To an ordinary observer, the D'183 Patent is the design of a slipper with a formed body, a protrusion of fuzz or fluff, and a sole with some solidity. The outside of the slipper appears durable and looks to be made of a relatively tough material; the inside looks soft, plush, and made of a warm material. The sole appears to be fairly thick and looks sturdy.

The district court first determined that the Laurel Hill anticipated because it also had "a structured body, a softlooking fluff surrounding the opening of the slipper, and a sole that appears durable and fairly thick." The district court then found that the Penta also anticipated, concluding that the Penta was even more similar to the D'183 patent than the Laurel Hill. The court found that the Penta "conveys the visual effect of a slipper, the body and sole of which have some defined shape and solidity but which has a protrusion of fluff or fuzz emanating from the foot opening." Although . . . a close study of the patented and prior art designs revealed differences, those differences were "minor" and insufficient to defeat anticipation.

We turn first to the district court's grant of summary judgment on anticipation.

Design patents are presumed to be valid. 35 U.S.C. § 282(a). A party seeking to invalidate a patent on the basis of anticipation must do so by clear and convincing evidence. Design patent anticipation requires a showing that a single prior art reference is "identical in all material respects" to the claimed invention (quoting *Hupp v. Siroflex of Am., Inc.*). The two designs must be substantially the same (applying design patent infringement test from *Gorham Mfg. Co. v. White,* 14 Wall. 511, 81 U.S. 511, 528 (1871), as the test for anticipation). Two designs are substantially the same "if the resemblance is such as to deceive [an ordinary observer], inducing him to purchase one supposing it to be the other." Anticipation is a question of fact. *Int'l Seaway Trading Corp. v. Walgreens Corp.* Summary judgment is proper only when the evidence underlying anticipation is clear and convincing such that no reasonable fact-finder could find otherwise. Viewing all evidence in the light most favorable to the non-moving party—a reasonable jury could have found there was not clear and convincing evidence of anticipation.

In *High Point I,* we instructed that on remand, the district court should "add sufficient detail to its verbal description of the claimed design to evoke a visual image consonant with [the] claimed design." The district court should perform a side-by-side comparison of the claimed and prior art designs as part of the proper obviousness determination. Notably, we cautioned that there appeared to be "genuine issues of material fact as to whether the Woolrich Prior Art are, in fact, proper primary references" for obviousness purposes under 35 U.S.C. § 103.

On remand, the district court did not perform a side-by-side comparison, but concluded that the claimed and prior art designs share the "same characteristics" because they share "a structured body, a soft-looking fluff surrounding the opening of the slipper, and a sole that appears durable and fairly thick." We find again that the district court fundamentally erred in its analysis by analyzing the designs from "too high a level of abstraction" and failing to focus "on the distinctive visual appearances of the reference and the claimed design." The court's description does little more than point out the main concepts of the claimed design: a structured slipper having fuzzy material at the foot opening. The court failed to properly consider the ornamental aspects of the designs at issue. There are numerous such features in the body, the fuzzy material, and the sole of the designs, all of which were overlooked in the district court's analysis.

There are meaningful differences between the curvatures of the slipper body designs. The body of the patented design has a distinct 'S' curve between the foot opening and the front of the slipper as viewed from the side, which ends in a downward slope toward the front of the body. The Laurel Hill has a prominent upward curve near the front. The Penta is also different because it has a noticeably flatter, more even slope from the foot opening towards the front.

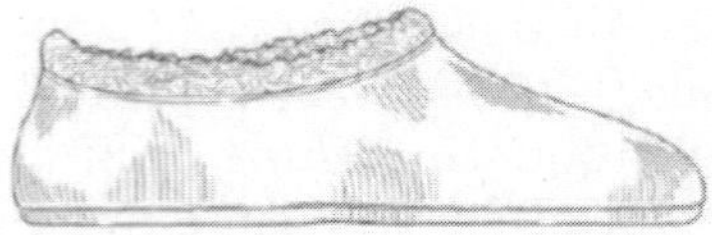

D'183 patent, Figure 5

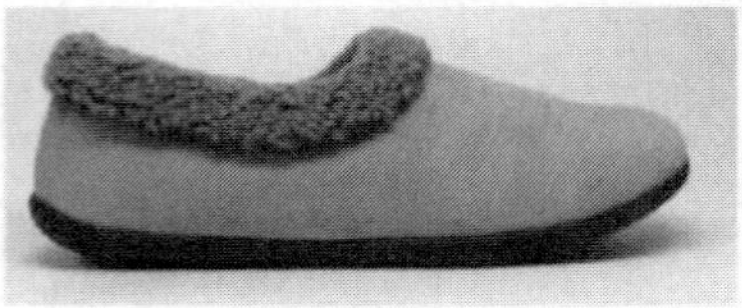

Laurel Hill Prior Art

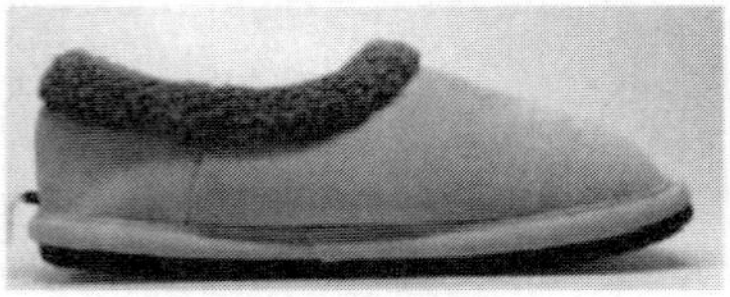

Penta Prior Art

There are also clear differences between the protruding fuzz of the claimed and prior art designs. In particular, the Woolrich Prior Art appears to differ . . . in that both prior art slippers have a pronounced fleece overlap oriented outward and which obscures the top edge of the foot opening. By contrast, no such overlap is visible in the patented design. The district court failed to take into consideration the substantial differences between the ornamental aspects of the soles of the claimed design and the prior art designs. The district court did not address the ornamental aspects of the soles, but stated in the *2012 Order* that "[t]he only difference between the slippers relates to the sole of the slippers, which is quite minor in the context of the overall slipper." We disagree. There are unmistakable differences between the sole design of the D'183 patent and the Woolrich Prior Art. The patent claims one embodiment, shown in Figure 7, where the sole has dots . . . arranged in a uniformly spaced pattern of rows and columns in two separate groups. One group is positioned closer to the front of the slipper, and narrows slightly toward the toe area. The other group is placed closer to the rear, and has a corresponding taper toward the rear area. The other embodiment, shown in Figure 8, has a smooth sole. Neither of the Woolrich Prior Art designs has either of these design components.

The prior art designs instead each have their own distinct ornamental designs. The Laurel Hill sole has embedded within it images of four trees and two moose. The Laurel Hill also has a grooved border not present in the claimed design. The Penta sole has a large "WOOLRICH" image imprinted thereon and is also decorated with a distinct pattern. Like the Laurel Hill—but unlike the claimed design—the Penta also has a grooved border.

As we cautioned in *High Point I,* there appeared to be genuine issues of material fact regarding whether the Woolrich Prior Art properly served as base references under this court's obviousness law. We now similarly hold that the evidence is not so clear and convincing such that a reasonable fact-finder could not find for BDI on anticipation. For these reasons, we reverse summary judgment of invalidity.

## *NOTES AND QUESTIONS*

1. Do you agree with the Federal Circuit's conclusion on whether the prior art shippers anticipated BDI's slippers? Do you think an ordinary observer would have found the differences between the prior art and BDI's slippers material?

2. The threshold for anticipation of a design patent is tied to the ordinary observer. In contrast, the threshold for anticipation of a utility patent is limited to how a scientific person in the field would view the prior art. For utility patents, if a prior art reference falls within the scope of the claimed invention, then the claim lacks novelty. Do you think this difference makes it easier or harder to anticipate a design patent? Why do we include the ordinary observer in the test for anticipation of design patents?

3. One researcher found evidence that courts tend to favor more attractive designs over less attractive ones. Andrew W. Torrance, *Beauty Fades: An Experimental Study of Federal Circuit Design Patent Aesthetics*, 19 J. INTEL. PROP. L. 389 (2012). Why would the attractiveness of a design matter to a trier of fact? Should it matter?

4. Novelty is distinct from the copyright requirement of originality, discussed in Chapter 4. Some have argued that the copyright originality requirement is embodied in the design patent laws in 35 U.S.C. § 171 ("Whoever invents any new, *original*, and ornamental design. . . .") (emphasis added). The Federal Circuit found that the purpose of the term "original" in the design patent laws is unclear. *Int'l Seaway Trading Corp. v. Walgreens Corp.*, 589 F.3d 1233 (Fed. Cir. 2009). Although the originality requirement was present in the first design patent laws enacted in 1842, "[t]he purpose of incorporating an originality requirement is unclear; it likely was designed to incorporate the copyright concept of originality—requiring that the work be original with the author, although this concept did not find its way into the language of the Copyright Act until 1909." *Id.* at 1238. Other cases assert that the originality requirement for design patents simply requires the applicant's design to be "the product of the inventive process." *See Durdin v. Kuryakyn Holdings, Inc.*, 440 F. Supp. 2d 921, 923 (W.D. Wis. 2006); *Smith v. Whitman Saddle Co.*, 148 U.S. 674, 679 (1893).

5. Anticipation or novelty requires that a single reference disclose all elements of a claimed invention. In the next section, we study the non-obviousness requirement that permits the combination of multiple references together.

## 4. NON-OBVIOUSNESS

The requirement that an invention be non-obvious is intended to preclude patents for trivial inventions. The requirement is a cornerstone of utility patent law, with the inquiry focusing on whether an ordinary person in the art would have found the claimed invention, as a whole, obvious in light of the prior art. The obviousness requirement, codified at 35 U.S.C. § 103(a), is on its face directed towards functional inventions rather than designs. It reads: "A patent for a claimed invention may not be obtained, notwithstanding that the claimed invention is not identically disclosed as set forth in section 102, if the differences between the claimed invention and the prior art are such that the claimed invention as a whole would have been obvious before the effective filing date of the claimed invention to a person having ordinary skill in the art."

The seminal Supreme Court decision of *Graham v. John Deere*, 383 U.S. 1 (1966) sets forth a logical framework for analyzing obviousness of utility patents. First, the scope and content of the prior art are catalogued. Then, the focus turns to the differences between the prior art and the claimed invention. Finally, one must consider the skill of the ordinary person in the field. After using the *Graham* framework, the obviousness inquiry is whether there is an apparent reason to combine the prior art references to reach the claimed invention. *See KSR v. Teleflex,* 550 U.S. 398 (2006). In assessing whether an invention is obvious, the U.S. Supreme Court held that one must consider secondary considerations of nonobviousness. *Graham*, 383 U.S. at 17–18. A patent owner faced with an obviousness challenge in litigation generally bears the burden of establishing these existence and scope of secondary considerations. These include, for example, (1) the invention's commercial success; (2) long felt but unresolved needs; (3) the failure of others; (4) skepticism by experts; (5) praise by others; (6) unexpected results; (7) licensing of the invention by other; and (8) copying of the invention by competitors. The patent owner generally must establish a nexus between each secondary consideration and the benefits of the patented invention. Secondary considerations, also known as objective indicia of non-obviousness, are meant to aid the decision-maker in correctly determining whether a claimed invention is obvious. Secondary considerations can provide evidence relating to how the market perceived the particular invention, and can aid the decision-maker in avoiding "hindsight bias."

The requirement does not seem to translate well into design patents. For one, there is no person of ordinary skill in the art for design patents. Despite its imperfect fit, the design patent laws have wholeheartedly adopted a non-obviousness requirement. For design patents, the general inquiry is whether it is obvious to combine the prior art in view of the "ordinary designer" where the primary reference is basically the same as the claimed design. In other words, are the design references so related that the appearance of certain ornamental features in one reference would suggest the application of those features to the other reference? Design patent law requires that there be a "primary reference" which contains "basically the same" design as the claimed invention, plus other references or knowledge by the ordinary designer to arrive at the claimed design. In other words, there must be a reference, a something in existence, the design characteristics of which are basically the same as the claimed design in order to support a holding of obviousness. The primary reference requirement is meant to prevent a finding of obviousness when only bits and pieces of the claimed design are found in any given reference. The concern is that all designs build upon things done before, and that all design may appear obvious in hindsight. Below, we provide examples of how the court considers non-obviousness for design patents.

## MRC INNOVATIONS, INC. V. HUNTER MFG, LLP

747 F.3d 1326 (Fed. Cir. 2014)

PROST, CIRCUIT JUDGE. MRC Innovations, Inc. appeals from a final judgment of the U.S. District Court for the Northern District of Ohio granting summary judgment of invalidity with respect to U.S. Design Patent Nos. D634,488 S ("'488 patent") and D634, 487 S ("'487 patent"). For the reasons stated below, we affirm.

MRC is the owner by assignment of both patents-in-suit. The '488 patent claims an ornamental design for a football jersey for a dog, while the '487 patent does the same for a baseball jersey, as shown below:

| '488 Patent | '487 Patent |
|---|---|
|  | 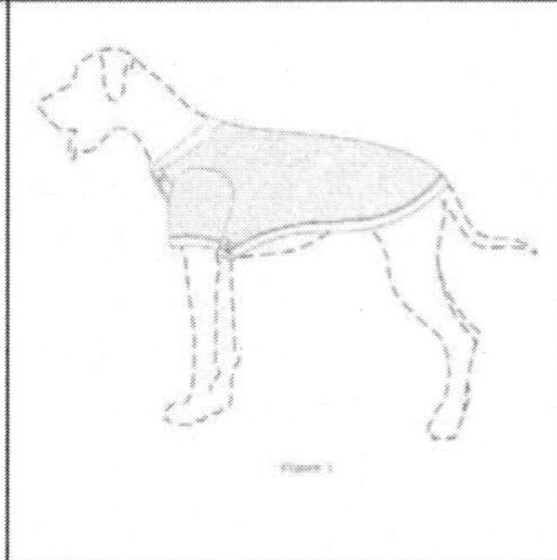 |
| 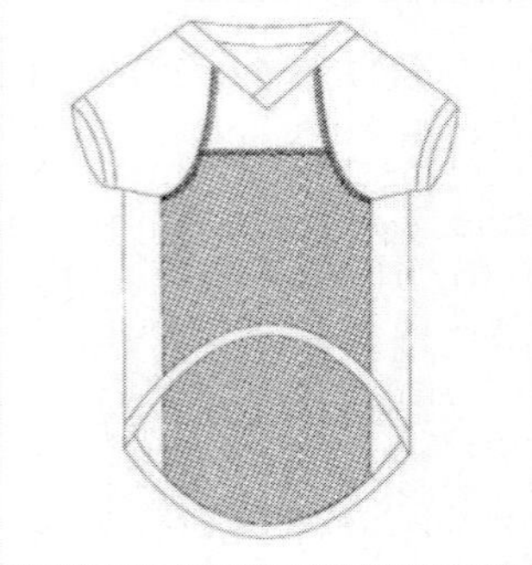 | 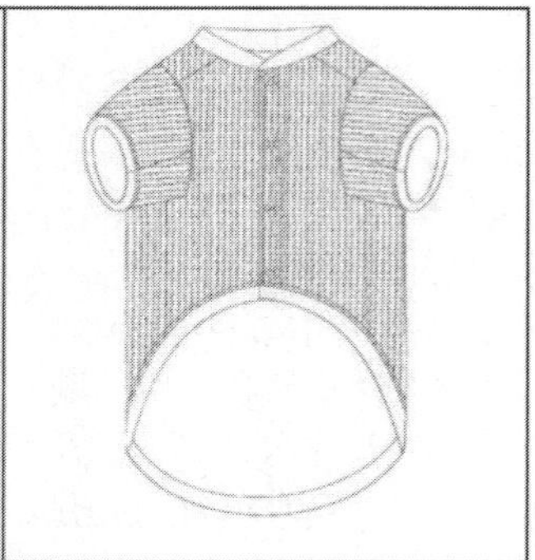 |
|  |  |

Mark Cohen is the named inventor of both patents; he is the principal shareholder of MRC and assigned his rights in both patents to that company. Appellee Hunter Manufacturing, LLP, is a retailer of licensed sports consumer products, including pet jerseys. Prior to September 9, 2009, Hunter purchased pet jerseys for dogs from Mark Cohen through companies with which he was affiliated. Cohen supplied Hunter with a "V2" football jersey through the Stephen Gould Corporation and through Fun-in-Games, Inc. ("FiG"). Similarly, Cohen supplied Hunter, through FiG, with a green pet jersey bearing a Philadelphia Eagles logo, which Hunter then sold through third-party retailers such as Wal-Mart and

PetSmart prior to July 30, 2009. The V2 and Eagles jerseys are depicted below:

| V2 Jersey | Eagles Jersey |
|---|---|
| 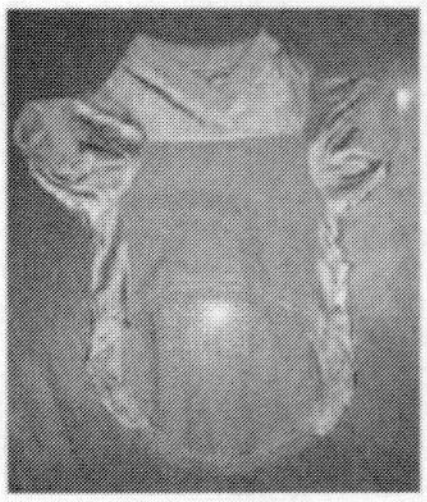 | 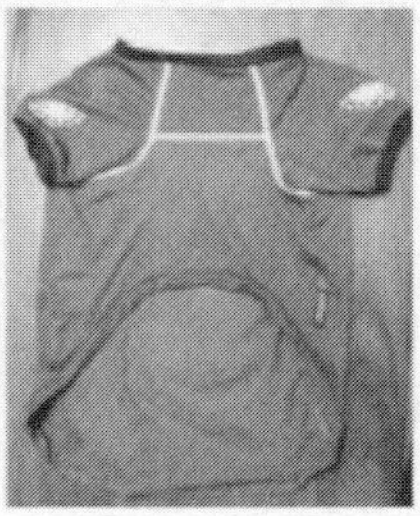 |
| 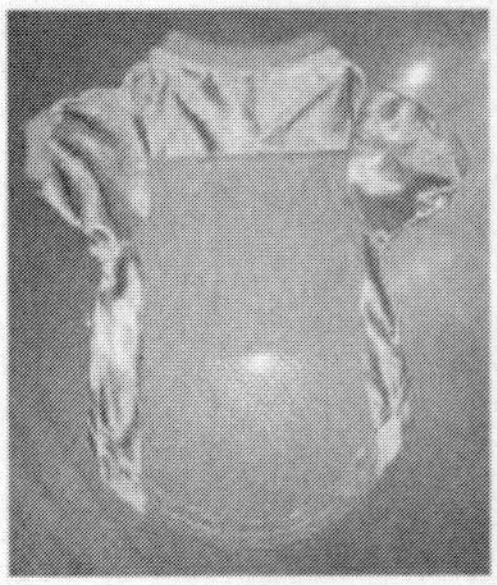 |  |

Cohen asserts that in 2009 he designed another pet jersey, known as the "V3" jersey, which later became the subject of the '488 patent. Hunter began purchasing the V3 jersey from FiG after September 8, 2009. On September 8, 2010, Cohen filed a patent application for both the V3 jersey and the baseball equivalent that would later become the subject of the '487 patent.

In December 2010, Cohen informed Hunter that he no longer intended to do business with Hunter because Hunter was having difficulty making payments. Hunter then sought proposals from other companies to manufacture and supply it with pet jerseys like the V3. Ultimately, Hunter contracted with another supplier, appellee CDI International, Inc., to supply Hunter with pet jerseys. MRC filed suit against both Hunter and CDI for willful infringement of both patents. The district court granted summary judgment in favor of Hunter and CDI on the grounds that both patents are invalid as obvious under 35 U.S.C. § 103(a). The district court denied summary judgment of invalidity based on 35 U.S.C. § 112.

MRC appealed the grant of summary judgment.

This court reviews a district court's grant of summary judgment under the law of the regional circuit. The Sixth Circuit reviews a district court's grant of summary judgment de novo. Summary judgment is appropriate if . . . the movant shows that there is no genuine dispute as to any material fact and the movant is entitled to judgment as a matter of law.

I. The '488 Patent

The district court concluded that the '488 patent would have been obvious in view of several prior art pet jerseys. MRC now appeals. Obviousness is a question of law that is reviewed de novo, based on underlying factual questions that are reviewed for clear error following a bench trial. The underlying factual inquiries include: (1) the scope and content of the prior art; (2) the level of ordinary skill in the art; (3) the differences between the claimed invention and the prior art; and (4) objective evidence of non-obviousness. *Graham v. John Deere Co. of Kan. City,* 383 U.S. 1, 17 (1966). Summary judgment of obviousness is appropriate if "the content of the prior art, the scope of the patent claim, and the level of ordinary skill in the art are not in material dispute, and the obviousness of the claim is apparent in light of these factors." *TriMed, Inc. v. Stryker Corp.* (citing *KSR Int'l Co. v. Teleflex Inc.*).

In the context of design patents, " 'the ultimate inquiry under section 103 is whether the claimed design would have been obvious to a designer of ordinary skill who designs articles of the type involved.' " *Titan Tire Corp. v. Case New Holland, Inc.* [A] court must first determine "whether one of ordinary skill would have combined teachings of the prior art to create the same overall visual appearance as the claimed design." The court must identify "a single reference, 'a something in existence, the design characteristics of which are basically the same as the claimed design.' " The "basically the same" test requires consideration of the "visual impression created by the patented design as a whole." We have noted . . . " the trial court judge may determine almost instinctively whether the two designs create basically the same visual impression," but "must communicate the reasoning behind that decision."

Once the primary reference is found, other "secondary" references "may be used to modify it to create a design that has the same overall visual appearance as the claimed design." These secondary references must be " 'so related [to the primary reference] that the appearance of certain ornamental features in one would suggest the application of those features to the other.' "

The district court used the "Eagles" pet jersey as the "primary reference" under step one of the *Durling* analysis. MRC argues that this was legally erroneous because there are significant differences between the Eagles jersey and the patented design of the '488 patent. [T]here are three differences: (1) the patented design has a V-neck collar where the Eagles jersey has a round neck; (2) the patented design contains an interlock fabric panel on the side portion of the design rather than mesh; and (3) the patented design contains additional ornamental surge stitching on the rear portion of the jersey. MRC argues that the district court overlooked these differences by focusing on the claimed design at "too high a level of abstraction." If the district court had translated the claimed design into a verbal description as required by *High Point,* it would have concluded that neither the Eagles jersey nor any other prior art reference contained design characteristics that were "basically the same" as the claimed design.

The district court pointed out three key similarities between the claimed design and the Eagles jersey: an opening at the collar portion for the head, two openings and sleeves stitched to the body of the jersey for limbs, and a body portion on which a football logo is applied. However, the district court went on to point out two additional similarities between the two designs: first, the Eagles jersey is made "primarily of a mesh and interlock fabric"; and second, it contains at least some ornamental surge stitching—both features found in the '488 claimed design. The district court also went on to acknowledge the three major differences between the two designs that are enumerated above. Taking all of those things together . . . the district court painted a clear picture of the claimed design. [I]t thoroughly considered the "distinctive 'visual appearances' of the reference and the claimed design." *Apple, Inc. v. Samsung Elecs., Inc.,* 678 F.3d 1314, 1332 (Fed. Cir. 2012) (quoting *Durling,* 101 F.3d at 104). Thus, the district court did not err by failing to provide an express verbal description of the claimed design; it described the claimed design in the context of comparing it to the prior art.

Nor did the district court err in finding that the design characteristics of the '488 design created "basically the same" overall visual impression as the Eagles jersey prior art reference. As the district court noted, both designs contain the same overall shape, similar fabric, and ornamental surge stitching. That there are slight differences in the precise placement of the interlock fabric and the ornamental stitching does not defeat a claim of obviousness; if the designs were identical, no obviousness analysis would be required. Indeed, we have permitted prior art designs to serve as "primary references" when their differences are as great or greater than the differences in this case.

*Apple,* on which MRC relies, is not to the contrary. There, we faulted the district court for finding that the prior art Fidler tablet could serve as a primary reference to the patented tablet design. However, in that case we noted "substantial differences in the overall visual appearance between the patented design and the Fidler reference," and described no fewer than six differences between the two products. The Fidler tablet was asymmetrical where the patented tablet was symmetrical; it contained a sunken screen that created a "picture frame" effect rather than the visual impression of "an unbroken slab of glass extending from edge to edge on the front side of the [patented] tablet"; and it contained two card-like projections and an indentation on its sides rather than the smooth sides of the claimed design. These differences rendered the Fidler tablet significantly different in overall visual appearance from the patented design; the same cannot be said of the '488 patented design and the Eagles jersey, which we agree are "basically the same."

In support of the non-obviousness of its patents, MRC submitted evidence relating to commercial success, copying, and acceptance by others. First, with respect to commercial success, MRC argued that the sales of the V3 jersey were more successful than sales of the V2 design it replaced. Second, MRC alleged that Hunter and CDI chose to copy the patented V3 design rather than other available non-patented designs. And third, MRC points out that it has granted a license on the '488 patent.

The district court noted that the only evidence in support of these secondary considerations was the testimony of the inventor himself, which was "unpersuasive to demonstrate a genuine dispute" of fact sufficient to defeat summary judgment of obviousness. MRC argues that the district court effectively dismissed the uncontroverted secondary considerations evidence as if it did not exist, rather than construing the evidence in the favor of the non-moving party. MRC also points out that Hunter and CDI failed to provide any evidence of another explanation for those secondary considerations besides a nexus with the claimed design.

MRC has the standard backwards. As the patentee, it was MRC's burden of production to demonstrate a nexus between the claimed design and the secondary considerations. MRC presented no evidence whatsoever that the commercial success and copying were related to the merits of the claimed invention. [A]lthough the district court's analysis of secondary considerations was admittedly somewhat cursory, we do not believe that the evidence of record before the district court created a genuine dispute of *material* fact . . . MRC had not established a nexus between the secondary considerations and the claimed design that was sufficient to overcome the other evidence of obviousness.

---

The *MRC Innovations, Inc. v. Hunter Mfg, L.L.P.* is a useful case to help in understanding the role of a primary reference in obviousness determinations. The *Apple v. Samsung* excerpt below provides a full discussion of obviousness in the context of electronic devices.

## APPLE, INC. V. SAMSUNG ELECTRONICS CO.

786 F.3d 983 (Fed. Cir. 2015) (rev'd in part on other grounds)

BRYSON, CIRCUIT JUDGE. Apple, Inc., is the owner of several design and utility patents pertaining to smartphones and tablet computers. U.S. Design Patent Nos. D593,087 ("the D'087 patent") and D618,677 ("the D'677 patent") are directed to designs that Apple contends are generally embodied in the iPhone, Apple's popular smartphone. Those patents issued on May 26, 2009, and June 29, 2010, respectively. Both patents claim a minimalist design for a rectangular smartphone consisting of a large rectangular display occupying most of the phone's front face. The corners of the phone are rounded. Aside from a rectangular speaker slot above the display and a circular button below the display claimed in several figures of the patent, the design contains no ornamentation. The D'087 patent claims a bezel surrounding the perimeter of the phone's front face and extending from the front of the phone partway down the phone's side. The parts of the side beyond the bezel, as well as the phone's back, are disclaimed, as indicated by the use of broken lines in the patent figures. The D'677 patent does not claim a bezel but instead shows a black, highly polished, reflective surface over the entire front face of the phone. The D'677 patent disclaims the sides and back of the device. Below are representative depictions of the designs:

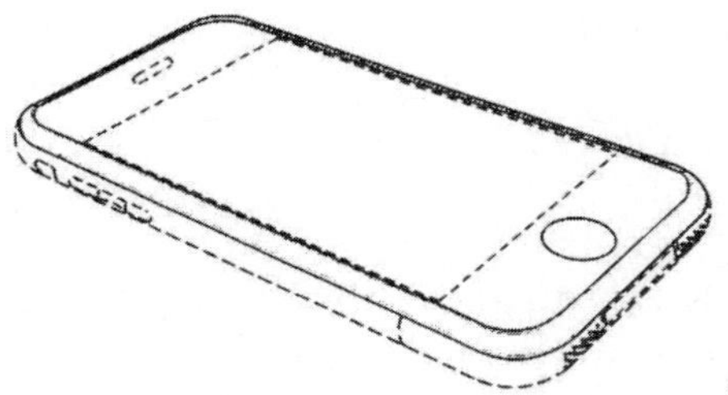

(D'087 Patent, Fig. 1)

44

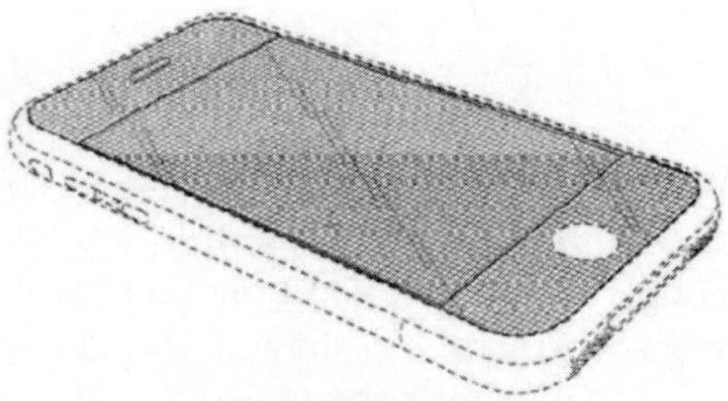

(D'677 Patent, Fig. 1)

Apple also owns U.S. Design Patent No. D504,889 ("the D'889 patent"), which is directed to the design of a tablet computer. The patent depicts a rectangular tablet with a polished reflective surface extending to the edge of the front side of the device. Within that surface, broken lines delineate a slightly smaller rectangular display area. The front face of the patented design has rounded corners, and a thin bezel surrounds the front surface along its perimeter. The front surface has no ornamentation, buttons, speaker slots, holes, or raised surfaces. The back and sides of the design are also claimed; the figures depict a flat, unadorned back transitioning into the sides through a rounded-over edge. Apple claims that its iPad tablet computer embodies the design of the D'889 patent. A figure representing the claimed design shows the following:

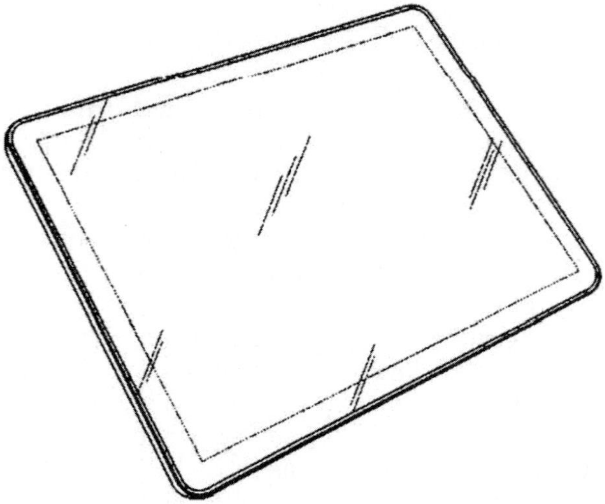

**(D'889 Patent, Fig. 1)**

The court then addressed the D'677 patent. The court again looked to the '638 patent as a primary reference but concluded that the '638 design was sufficiently different from the D'677 patent that it would not have been obvious to a designer to adopt a "flat, black, translucent front screen." The court concluded that Samsung had not raised a substantial question regarding the validity of the D'677 patent. As to infringement, the court found that both the Galaxy S 4G and the Infuse 4G phones had an overall design that an ordinary observer would likely find substantially the same as the claimed D'677 design and that those phones were likely to infringe.

Although the court found that the design claimed by the D'889 patents was not dictated by functionality, it concluded that Samsung had raised a substantial question about whether the patented design would have been obvious in light of a combination of prior art references.

At the outset of its obviousness analysis, the court characterized the visual impression of the patented design as a "broad, simple design that gives the overall visual impression of a rectangular shape with four evenly rounded corners, a flat glass-like surface without any ornamentation[,] a rim surrounding the front surface, . . . [a] flat [back] panel that rounds up near the edges[, and an] overall design [that] creates a thin form factor." The design created basically the same visual impression as a prototype tablet developed in 1994 by Roger Fidler. Although the Fidler tablet lacked a "flat glass-like surface," the court found that difference not to "detract from the fact that the 'overall visual impression' created by the D'889 patent is the same as the 1994 Fidler tablet." The court used Fidler as a primary reference in its obviousness analysis. For the flat glass screen, the court turned to the 2002 Hewlett-Packard Compaq Tablet TC1000, which "contains a flat glass screen that covers the top surface of the tablet and a thin rim that surrounds the front face of the device."

The court found that the combination of Fidler and the TC1000 would likely render the D'889 patent obvious. The court rejected Apple's secondary consideration evidence . . . because the court found the evidence of skepticism to be inconclusive and the evidence of commercial success not to show "the requisite nexus between the patented design and the success of the iPad." The court concluded that Apple's secondary consideration evidence failed to overcome the substantial questions of invalidity and that Apple had not established that it is "likely to succeed at trial against Samsung's challenge to the validity of the D'889 patent."

**(1994 Fidler Tablet)**

**(Hewlett–Packard Compaq Tablet TC1000)**

In addressing a claim of obviousness in a design patent, "the ultimate inquiry . . . is whether the claimed design would have been obvious to a designer of ordinary skill who designs articles of the type involved." *Titan Tire,* 566 F.3d at 1375, quoting *Durling v. Spectrum Furniture Co.,* 101 F.3d 100, 103 (Fed. Cir. 1996). To determine whether "one of ordinary skill would have combined teachings of the prior art to create the same overall visual appearance as the claimed design," the finder of fact must employ a two-step process. First, "one must find a single reference, 'a something in existence, the design characteristics of which are basically the same as the claimed design.'" *Durling,* quoting *In re Rosen.* Second, "other references may be used to modify [the primary reference] to create a design that has the same overall visual appearance as the claimed design." However, the "secondary references may only be used to modify the primary reference if they are 'so related to the primary reference that the appearance of certain ornamental features in one would suggest the application of those features to the other.'"

The district court began its obviousness analysis by finding that the Fidler reference "creates basically the same visual impression as the D'889 patent" because both are rectangular tablets with four evenly rounded corners and a flat reflective surface for the front screen surrounded by a rim on all four sides . . . [T]he back of the Fidler reference as being "essentially flat." It then concluded that although the Fidler reference did not have a flat glass surface, that did not prevent it from creating the same overall visual impression as the D'889 design. The court looked to the TC1000 tablet to supply the missing flat glass screen and the thin rim that surrounds the front face of the device. The court relied on the testimony of Samsung's expert, who concluded that "a designer of ordinary skill . . . would have found it obvious to create the D'889 tablet consisting of a rectangular design with four evenly rounded corners, a relatively thin depth, a smooth back that curves up . . . and a flat, clear front surface that extended beyond the edges of the display."

The district court erred in finding that the Fidler tablet created the same visual impression as the D'889 patent. A side-by-side comparison of the two designs shows substantial differences in the overall visual appearance between the patented design and the Fidler reference.

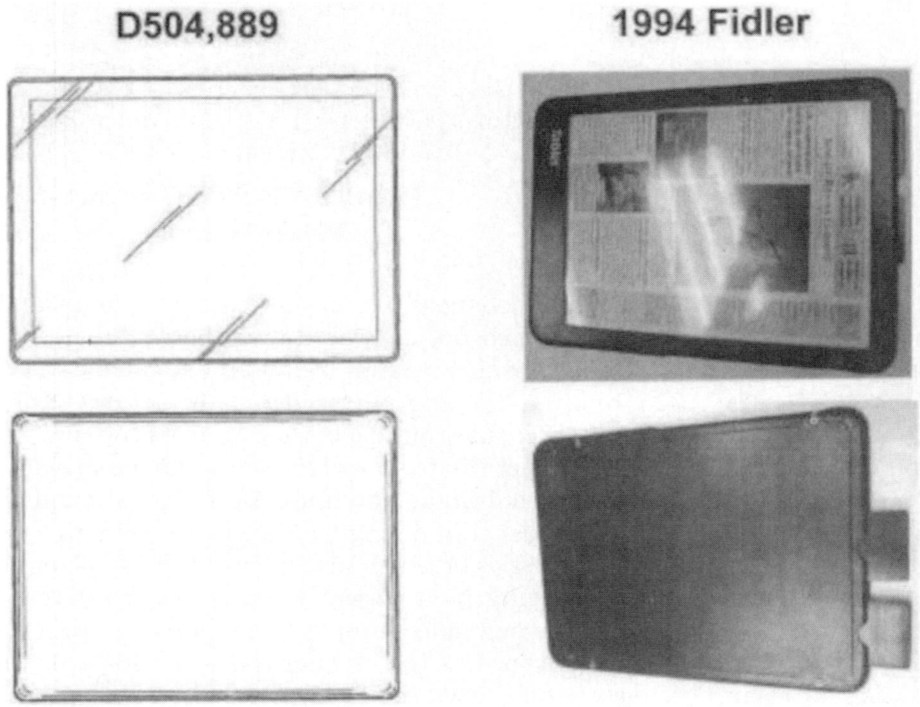


First, the Fidler tablet is not symmetrical: The bottom edge is noticeably wider than the others. The frame of the Fidler tablet creates a very different impression from the "unframed" D'889 design . . . [T]he frame surrounding the screen contrasts sharply with the screen itself. The

Fidler screen appears to sink into the frame, creating a "picture frame" effect and breaking the continuity between the frame and the screen embedded within it. The transparent glass-like front surface of the D'889 patent, however, covers essentially the entire front face of the patented design without any breaks or interruptions. As a result, the D'889 design creates the visual impression of an unbroken slab of glass extending from edge to edge on the front side of the tablet. The Fidler reference does not. . . .

There are other noticeable differences between the Fidler tablet and the D'889 patent that contribute to the distinct visual appearance of the two designs. Unlike the D'889 patent, the Fidler reference contains no thin bezel surrounding the edge of the front side. One corner of the frame in the Fidler reference contains multiple perforations. In contrast to the D'889 patent, the sides of the Fidler reference are neither smooth nor symmetrical; it has two card-like projections extending out from its top edge and an indentation in one of its sides. And the back of the Fidler reference also conveys a visual impression different from that of the D'889 design.

In design patent obviousness analysis, a primary reference must be "something in existence, the design characteristics of which are basically the same as the claimed design in order to support a holding of obviousness." *In re Rosen*. Based on the differences . . . we hold that the Fidler tablet does not give the same visual impression as the D'889 patent, and therefore the district court erred in looking to Fidler as the primary reference against the D'889 patent.

Even assuming that Fidler qualified as a primary reference, the TC1000 secondary reference could not bridge the gap between Fidler and the D'889 design. First, while the TC1000 has a flat glass front, the screen area of that device is surrounded by a gray area that frames the screen. In addition, the perimeter of the TC1000 is encircled by a wide rounded-over metallic rim. And the screen area contains indicator lights in several places, unlike the minimalist design claimed in the D'889 patent. "[T]he teachings of prior art designs may be combined only when the designs are 'so related that the appearance of certain ornamental features in one [design] would suggest the application of those features to the other.' " The TC1000 is so different in visual appearance from the Fidler reference that it does not qualify as a comparison reference under that standard.

Samsung contends that the district court properly focused on overall visual appearance rather than on the "design concepts" highlighted by Apple. In our assessment . . . the district court's error was to view the various designs from too high a level of abstraction. Fidler does not qualify as a primary reference simply by disclosing a rectangular tablet with four evenly rounded corners and a flat back. Rather than looking to the "general concept" of a tablet, the district court should have focused on the distinctive "visual appearances" of the reference and the claimed design. When those visual impressions are compared, it becomes apparent that the Fidler reference, with or without the TC1000, cannot serve to render the D'889 patent invalid for obviousness.

## *PROBLEM 2–3*

Consider a design covering a coffee table. The top is transparent and circular. It is supported by means of slots cut into three V- or L-shaped legs. A design patent application for the design of the coffee table is rejected by the U.S. Patent & Trademark Office as obvious in light of patents on a desk, display stand, and tables. Below are the claimed design and the prior art references. Is the patent examiner's obviousness rejection correct?

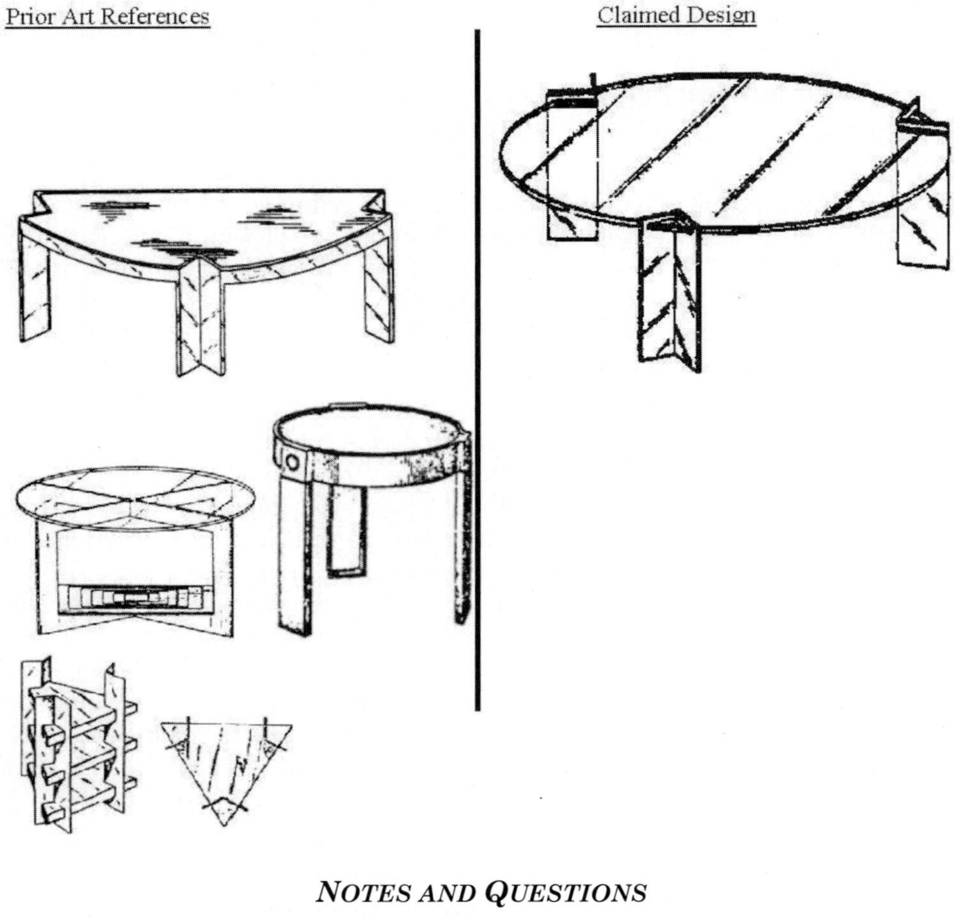


## *NOTES AND QUESTIONS*

1. For an explanation and thorough discussion of the history of the non-obviousness requirement in design patent law, see Jason J. DuMont, *A Non-Obvious Design: Reexamining the Origins of the Design Patent Standard,* 45 GONZAGA L. REV. 531 (2010).

2. The non-obviousness requirement fits squarely with the purpose of utility patent law, where most innovation is incremental and cumulative. Does design work the same way? For an interesting discussion of non-obviousness with respect to design patent law, see Mark P. McKenna & Katherine J. Strandburg, *Progress and Competition in Design,* 17 STAN. TECH. L. REV. 1 (2013). See also Sarah Burstein, *Moving Beyond the Standard Criticisms of Design Patents,* 17 STAN. TECH. L. REV. 305 (2013).

3. How much, if at all, should the complexity of the design matter? Are more complex and ornate designs more likely to be obvious or more likely to be non-obvious?

---

## C. THE BASICS OF DESIGN PATENT PROSECUTION

We pause here to discuss the process for procuring and enforcing design patents. This process is referred to as "patent prosecution." To file a design patent, it costs about $1,800 in filing and examination costs, although those amounts are substantially lower for very small applicants known as "microentities." Only registered patent attorneys or patent agents may represent a client, such as the inventor of a new design, during patent prosecution. To qualify as a registered patent attorney or agent, an individual must pass an examination administered by the U.S. Patent & Trademark Office. In addition, the individual is generally required to have a technical degree, such as in engineering, chemistry, computer science, or physics. United States design patents are substantively examined by the U.S. Patent & Trademark Office. Until such examination has been successfully navigated by an inventor, no legal rights are available. The process commences with an applicant submitting a design patent application to the U.S. Patent & Trademark Office. The application consists of drawings from various perspectives of the design. It also includes a single "claim." For design patents, the claim must be in a formal format. More precisely, the claim must read: "The ornamental design for (the article which embodies the design or to which it is applied) as shown." The U.S. Patent & Trademark Office publishes a helpful "Guide to filing a Design Patent Application." (A copy of the guide is available at http://www.uspto.gov/web/offices/com/iip/pdf/brochure_05.pdf).

Design patent applications are examined relatively expeditiously by the U.S. Patent & Trademark Office. During prosecution, the application is maintained as confidential by the U.S. Patent & Trademark Office. Unlike utility patent applications, the application is not published by the patent office. After a design application has been filed, it is assigned to one of the roughly 100 design patent examiners. These examiners specialize in reviewing and evaluating design patent applications.

Historically, the majority of design patents were issued within one year of filing. See http://patentlyo.com/patent/2013/01/design-patents-are-still-relatively-quick.html. One commentator has noted that over three quarters of design patents issue without any rejection from the U.S. Patent & Trademark Office. http://www.patentlyo.com/patent/2010/01/design-patent-rejections.html. If the U.S. If Patent & Trademark Office rejects the claim of a design patent, the applicant has the ability to contest the rejection. It can do this both with the original patent examiner, and on an administrative appeal within the U.S. Patent & Trademark Office to the Patent Trial & Appeal Board or "PTAB." If the applicant is dissatisfied with the decision of the PTAB, it can appeal in federal court, as discussed below.

In general, patent applicants are permitted to file multiple patent applications based upon a single disclosure. Filing an additional patent application based upon an earlier application is known as a "continuation" application. The continuation application is entitled to the filing date of the original patent application (known as the "parent" application). The earlier filing date is important, as the filing date determines what counts as prior art for the purposes of showing the invention is not novel.

All appeals from the U.S. Patent & Trademark Office are heard by a single federal court of appeals in Washington D.C. That court, the United States Court of Appeals for the Federal Circuit or the "Federal Circuit," is a quasi-specialized court. The Federal Circuit hears all disputes involving patent infringement, and it also hears all appeals of decision from the U.S. Patent & Trademark Office, including appeals of denials of design patents. While patents make up about fifty percent of the Federal Circuit's docket, the Federal Circuit also hears many other types of cases. The Federal Circuit hears appeals from the U.S. Court of Federal Claims involving claims against the government (including takings claims), veteran appeals, appeals from the United States Merit Systems Protection Board, and several other areas. Appeals from decisions of the Federal Circuit are brought to the U.S. Supreme Court, which has discretion whether to hear the case. The Supreme Court takes very few cases overall (typically around 80 per year in recent years), and until this year, had not decided a design patent case since the 1890s.

When issued by the U.S. Patent & Trademark Office, a design patent lasts for fifteen years from the issuance date. The fifteen-year term is a recent change. Before December 2013, the term of a design patent was fourteen years from issuance.

Absent a contrary agreement or understanding, design patents typically are owned by the inventor. Most businesses today require employees involved in designing products to execute an employment agreement. A typical employment agreement includes an invention assignment provision, which contractually assigns inventions (including design patents) to the employer. Many states also have common law rules for employees who were "hired to invent." The inventions of employees who fall within this category, including most engineers, are automatically assigned to the employer. Note that there is no 'work for hire' doctrine applicable to design patents. As discussed in the Chapter about Copyright, the work for hire doctrine automatically vests the copyright in the employer when an employee creates a copyrightable work within the scope of her employment.

## D. LITIGATION

Design patents provide the right to exclude others from making, selling, using, offering for sale, and importation of the design during the term of the patent. It is important to note that an owner of a design patent does not need to manufacture any products. The design patent is valid and enforceable (or invalid and unforceable) regardless of whether the owner manufactures a physical product embodying the design. There is no working requirement as it is called. As for enforcement, patent litigation cannot be filed in the state courts. Congress has expressly placed original jurisdiction for all patent infringement claims, including design patent infringement claims, with the federal courts. 35 U.S.C. § 1338. If infringement of a design patent involves importation of goods into the United States, the suit may be brought in the United States International Trade Commission. These proceedings, known as Section 337 Investigations, may be brought in parallel with an action in U.S. district court. After the trial tribunal adjudicates the design patent dispute, all patents are heard by a single federal court of appeals in Washington D.C., the United States Court of Appeals for the Federal Circuit.

### 1. CLAIM CONSTRUCTION

In order to determine whether a patent claim is valid or infringed, it is necessary to determine the legal scope of the patent holder's right. In litigation, the parties almost always dispute the proper scope of the claim. Determining the scope of the claim is critical, and often dispositive, in many cases. It explains the reach of the patent, which makes it easier to determine whether the patent overlaps with the prior art (and consequently is invalid as anticipated or obvious), or whether an accused product is covered by the patent (and consequently an infringer may owe damages). In utility patents, the claims typically consist of words. These meaning of these words are debated. The U.S. Supreme Court in 1996 required that the judge—as opposed to the jury—determine the meaning of words in a utility patent, a process called interchangeably claim construction or claim interpretation. There was some debate whether a formal claim construction was necessary for design patents, which primarily consist of drawings. In 2009, the Federal Circuit sat *en banc* with all of its judges to address claim construction in design patents.

## EGYPTIAN GODDESS, INC. V. SWISA, INC.

543 F.3d 665 (Fed. Cir. 2008) (en banc)

BRYSON, CIRCUIT JUDGE. One of the issues raised by this court was whether trial courts should conduct claim construction in design patent cases. While this court has held that trial courts have a duty to conduct claim construction in design patent cases, as in utility patent cases, the court has not prescribed any particular form that the claim construction must take. To the contrary, the court has recognized that design patents "typically are claimed as shown in drawings," and that claim construction "is adapted accordingly." This court has not required that the trial court attempt to provide a detailed verbal description of the claimed design, as is typically done in the case of utility patents.

As the Supreme Court has recognized, a design is better represented by an illustration "than it could be by any description and a description would probably not be intelligible without the illustration." The preferable course will be for a district court not to attempt to "construe" a design patent claim by providing a detailed verbal description of the claimed design.

It is important to emphasize that the court's decision to issue a relatively detailed claim construction will not be reversible error. The court is not obligated to issue a detailed verbal description of the design if it does not regard verbal elaboration as necessary. In deciding whether to attempt a verbal description of the claimed design, the court should recognize the risks entailed in such a description.

While it may be unwise to attempt a full description of the claimed design, a court may find it helpful to point out various features of the claimed design as they relate to the accused design and the prior art. There would be nothing wrong with the court pointing out to a jury that in the patented design only three sides have buffers attached, while in the accused product (and in the three-sided Nailco patent), all of the sides have buffers attached. It would similarly be permissible for the court to point out that although the FaIley Buffer Block has four sides, it is not hollow, unlike the '389 patent, the Nailco patent, and the accused Swisa product.

Apart from attempting to provide a verbal description of the design, a trial court can usefully guide by addressing a number of other issues that bear on the scope of the claim. Those include such matters as describing the role of particular conventions in design patent drafting, such as the role of broken lines assessing and describing the effect of any representations that may have been made in the course of the prosecution history and distinguishing between those features of the claimed design that are ornamental and those that are purely functional.

We therefore leave the question of verbal characterization of the claimed designs to the discretion of trial judges, with the proviso that those courts should not treat the process of claim construction as requiring a detailed verbal description of the claimed design, as would typically be true in the case of utility patents.

### *NOTES AND QUESTIONS*

1. Claim construction is a central issue in utility patent infringement law. The parties almost always dispute the proper definition of at least one claim term. Much of this may be attributable to inherent vagaries of language used in utility patent claims. Is the same concern present in design patent construction? Should we expect more or fewer disputes?

2. Do you think a verbal description of the scope of a design patent results in broader or narrower scope than merely pointing to the figures? Which approach do you think requires more judicial resources?

The *Egyptian Goddess* case lays out a general framework. The Court in *Egyptian Goddess* notes that courts can use language to define the claimed invention, or it can refer to the figures themselves. This difference is important since the court's claim construction is provided to the jury. After *Egpytian Goddess,* the vast majority of district courts have opted to construe claims by reference to the figures, as opposed to a detailed verbal construction.

---

The next case, *Ethicon Endo-Surgery, Inc. v. Covidien*, provides a current example of how the courts apply this framework. We read an excerpt from this case earlier in the chapter with respect to ornamentality. The case helps explain how non-ornamental aspects of a design should be treated during claim construction. There are similar discussions in the case law about how to treat novel v. ordinary design features and significant v. insignificant design aspects. The courts generally do not atomize designs into each component part. The drawings themselves are primary in the analysis, and the design needs to be considered as a whole. The actual task of determining the scope of a design patent and the subsequent infringement analysis is complex and difficult, and is frequently contested in design patent litigation.

## ETHICON ENDO-SURGERY, INC. V. COVIDIEN, INC.

796 F.3d 1312 (Fed. Cir. 2015)

CHEN, CIRCUIT JUDGE. We move to the district court's grant of Covidien's motion for summary judgment of noninfringement. The district court found the claimed trigger, torque knob, and activation button elements to be "based on functional considerations." The district court construed each claim of the Design Patents to encompass "nothing," factoring out and removing every element from the scope of the claimed designs.

Any underlying factual findings supporting the construction for clear error. Because a claimed design is better represented by an illustration rather than a description, unlike utility patents, "the preferable course ordinarily will be for a district court not to attempt to 'construe' a design patent claim by providing a detailed verbal description of the claimed design." *Egyptian Goddess*, 543 F.3d at 679.

A design patent is invalid if its overall appearance is dictated by function . . . and primarily functional. If the overall appearance of a claimed design is not primarily functional, the design claim is not invalid, even if certain elements have functional purposes.

The district court found that the "U"-shaped trigger, the torque knob, and the rounded button claimed in various combinations by the Design Patents are dictated by function. Its "open" design allows the user to exert higher input forces by employing multiple fingers, thus lessening hand fatigue and strain. The torque knob and rounded button provide functional controls for the ultrasonic shears. Their placement relative to the trigger offers ergonomic access, and the fluted shape of the torque knob permits a user to operate the knob with one finger. The district court's construction to have no scope whatsoever fails to account for the particular ornamentation of the claimed design and departs from our established legal framework.

There is no evidence that any of the ornamental designs adorning those underlying articles are essential to the use of the article. Although the Design Patents do not protect the general design concept . . . in a particular configuration, they nevertheless have some scope. We therefore vacate the district court's construction that the Design Patents cover "nothing." The scope encompasses the depicted ornamental aspects of certain combinations of the trigger, torque knob, and activation button elements of ultrasonic surgical shears, in specific relative positions and orientations.

### *NOTES AND QUESTIONS*

1. In litigation, it is possible that patent owners and accused infringers display strategic behavior on claim construction. In the same dispute, the patent owner may seek a broad claim construction for infringement (to cover as many different designs as possible), while a narrow claim construction for validity (to overcome the prior art). Accused infringers have the opposite tendency. For an interesting discussion of this dilemma, see Mark A. Lemley & Mark P. McKenna, *Scope,* 57 WM. & MARY L. REV. 2197 (2016).

2. Another recent Federal Circuit case cautions against deconstructing features of a claimed design. See *Sport Dimension, Inc. v. The Coleman Co.,* 820 F.3d 1316 (Fed. Cir. 2016) (considering how functional elements relate to claim scope). There, the Federal Circuit rejected a district court's claim construction of an ornamental design for a personal floatation device, finding

that the lower court's construction resulted in the design patent at issue to have "no scope whatsoever." *Id.* at 1322. The Federal Circuit stated that "design patents protect the overall ornamentation of a design, not an aggregation of separable elements." *Id.*

## 2. INFRINGEMENT TESTS

After the patent claim has been construed, the court still needs to assess infringement. Infringement refers to whether the accused product falls within the scope of the patent claim. If the accused product falls within the scope of the claim, it is called infringement. If the product infringes and the design patent is valid, then the court assesses remedies.

The courts have set forth several tests for infringement of design patents, which has caused much uncertainty over the years. The original and seminal case, *Gorham Co. v. White*, follows. The basic inquiry seeks to understand what the views of an ordinary observer of the design patent and accused product. It focuses on the *overall* ornamental appearance of the claimed design, not selected ornamental features. More specifically, the test is whether, in the eye of an ordinary observer, giving such attention as a purchaser usually gives, two designs are substantially the same, if the resemblance is such as to deceive such an observer, inducing him to purchase one supposing it to be the other, the first one patented is infringed by the other. Compare this test with the infringement tests for trade dress, copyrights, and the EU Community design in the following respective chapters.

As you read the cases and consider how to determine infringement, think about Problem 2–4 below.

### *PROBLEM 2–4*

Noah Miller develops a multi-functional carpentry tool called a "stepclaw." He obtains a design patent that claims the design for the stepclaw that combines a conventional hammer with a stud climbing tool and a crowbar. He later finds a competitor on the market and asks whether the product infringes. How would you advise him?

Patented Design

Accused Product

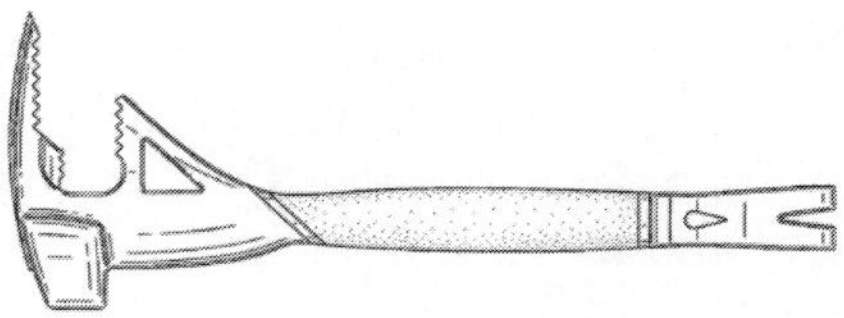

## GORHAM CO. V. WHITE

81 U.S. 551 (1871)

JUSTICE STRONG. Gorham & Co., in July 1861 obtained a patent for a new design for the handles of tablespoons and forks, which under the name of the "cottage pattern" became extremely popular; the most successful plain pattern, indeed, that had been in the market for many years. Gorham & Co. subsequently transferred their patent to the Gorham Manufacturing Company.

In the year 1867 one White obtained a patent for a design which he alleged to be original with him for the same things; the handles, namely, of forks and spoons; and in 1868 a patent for still another design . . .

Manufacturing and selling quantities of spoons and forks of these last two patterns, White interfered largely with the interests of the Gorham Manufacturing Company, and that company accordingly filed a bill in the court below to enjoin his making and selling spoons and forks under either of his patents.

Patented Desgn — White, 1867 accused design — White, 1868 accused design

The sole question is one of fact. The acts of Congress, which authorize the grant of patents for designs, were plainly intended to give encouragement to the decorative arts. They contemplate not so much utility as appearance. The law manifestly contemplates that giving certain new and original appearances to a manufactured article may enhance its salable value, may enlarge the demand for it, and may be a meritorious service to the public. It therefore proposes to secure for a limited time to the ingenious producer of those appearances the advantages. It is the appearance itself, which attracts attention and calls out favor or dislike. The appearance may be the result of peculiarity of configuration, or of ornament alone, or of both conjointly, but, in whatever way produced, it is the new thing, or product, which the patent law regards. To speak of the invention as a combination or process, or to treat it as such, is to overlook its peculiarities. As the acts of Congress embrace only designs applied, or to be applied, they must refer to finished products of invention. A patent for a product is a distinct thing from a patent for the elements entering into it, or for the ingredients of which it is composed, or for the combination that causes it.

We do not say that in determining whether two designs are substantially the same, differences in the lines, the configuration, or the modes by which the aspects they exhibit are not to be considered; but we think the controlling consideration is the resultant effect.

The true test of identity of design must be sameness of appearance. [M]ere difference of lines in the drawing or sketch, a greater or smaller number of lines, or slight variances in configuration will not destroy the substantial identity. An engraving that has many lines may present to the eye the same picture, and to the mind the same idea or conception as another with much fewer lines. The design, however, would be the same. The same conception was in the mind of the designer, and to that conception he gave expression.

If identity of appearance, or sameness of effect upon the eye, is the main test of substantial identity of design, the only remaining question is whether it is essential that the appearance should be the same to the eye of an expert. The court below was of opinion that the test of a patent for a design is not the eye of an ordinary observer. The learned judge thought there could be no infringement unless there was "substantial identity" "in view of the observation of a person versed in designs in the particular trade in question who sees and examines the articles containing them side by side." There must be a comparison of the features, which make up the two designs. Such a test would destroy all the protection, which the act of Congress intended to give. There never could be piracy of a patented design, for human ingenuity has never yet produced a design, in all its details, exactly like another, so like that an expert could not distinguish them. Experts, therefore, are not the persons to be deceived. Much less than that which would be substantial identity in their eyes would be undistinguishable in the eyes of men generally. For example, they are led to purchase forks or spoons, deceived by an apparent resemblance into the belief that they bear the "cottage" design, and, therefore, are the production of the holders of the Gorham, Thurber, and Dexter patent, when in fact they are not. The purpose of the law must be effected if possible; but it cannot be if minor differences of detail in the manner in which the appearance is produced, observable by experts, but not noticed by ordinary observers, by those who buy and use, are sufficient to relieve an imitating design from condemnation as an infringement.

We hold, therefore, that if, in the eye of an ordinary observer, giving such attention as a purchaser usually gives, two designs are substantially the same, if the resemblance is such as to deceive such an observer, inducing him to purchase one supposing it to be the other, the first one patented is infringed by the other.

The Gorham design, and the two designs sold by the defendant, which were patented to White, one in 1867, and the other in 1868, are alike the result of peculiarities of outline, or configuration, and of ornamentation. These make up whatever is distinctive in appearance, and of these, the outline or configuration is most impressive to the eye. Comparing the figure or outline of the plaintiffs' design with that of the White design of 1867, it is apparent there is no substantial difference. Even the minor differences are so minute as to escape observation unless observation is stimulated by a suspicion that there may be diversity. In all the designs, the ornament is, in part, a rounded moulding or bead along the edge with scrolls at the shoulders and near the top. There are, however, some diversities in this ornament, which are discoverable when attention is called to them . . . but there are the same number of scrolls in all the designs, and they are similarly located. No doubt to the eye of an expert they are all real . . .

Both the White designs we think are proved to be infringements of the Gorham patent. A large number of witnesses, familiar with designs, and most of them engaged in the trade, testify that, in their opinion, there is no substantial difference in the three designs, and that ordinary purchasers would be likely to mistake the White designs for the "cottage". This opinion is repeated in many forms of expression, as, that they are the same pattern; that the essential features are the same; that seven out of ten customers who buy silverware would consider them the same; that manufacturers as well as customers would consider them the same; that the trade generally would so consider them; that, though there are differences, they would not be noticed without a critical examination; that they are one and the same pattern. Some think the White designs were intended to imitate the other, and they all agree that they are so nearly identical that ordinary purchasers of silverware would mistake one for the other. On the other hand a large number of witnesses have testified on behalf of the defendant that the designs are substantially unlike, but when they attempt to define the dissimilarity they specify only the minor differences in the ornamentation, of which we have heretofore spoken. Not one of them denies that the appearance of the designs is substantially the same, or asserts that the effect upon the eye of an observer is different, or that ordinary purchasers, or even persons in the trade, would not be led by their similarity to mistake one for another. They give little importance to configuration, and none to general aspect. Such evidence leaves undisputed the facts that whatever differences there may be between the plaintiffs' design and those of the defendant in details of ornament, they are still the same in general appearance and effect, so much alike that in the market and with purchasers they would pass for the same thing—so much alike that even persons in the trade would be in danger of being deceived.

Unless, therefore, the patent is to receive such a construction that the act of Congress will afford no protection to a designer against imitations of his invention, we must hold that the sale by the defendant of spoons and forks bearing the designs patented to White in 1867 and 1868 is an infringement of the complainants' rights.

---

In an attempt to clarify the law of infringement, the entire Federal Circuit addressed the issue in 2009. Below is an excerpt from that case, *Egyptian Goddess, Inc. v. Swisa, Inc.* (We previously read a different portion of the case pertaining to claim construction). The en banc *Egyptian Goddess* decision is important in that it streamlined the test for infringement of a design patent. Before the Federal Circuit decision, design patent holders had to satisfy several different tests for infringement, including the difficult to prove "point of novelty" test. As will be seen below, the Federal Circuit found that the "point of novelty" test was inappropriate.

## EGYPTIAN GODDESS, INC. V. SWISA, INC.

543 F.3d 665 (Fed. Cir. 2008) (en banc)

BRYSON, CIRCUIT JUDGE. We granted rehearing en banc in this design patent case to address the appropriate legal standard to be used in assessing claims of design patent infringement.

Appellant Egyptian Goddess, Inc., ("EGI") brought this action in the United States District Court for the Northern District of Texas, alleging that Swisa, Inc., and Dror Swisa (collectively, "Swisa") had infringed EGI's U.S. Design Patent No. 467,389 ("the '389 patent"). The patent claimed a design for a nail buffer, consisting of a rectangular, hollow tube having a generally square cross-section and featuring buffer surfaces on three of its four sides. Swisa's accused product consists of a rectangular, hollow tube having a square cross-section, but featuring buffer surfaces on all four of its sides.

The district court first issued an order construing the claim of the '389 patent. In so doing, the district court sought to describe in words the design set forth in Figure 1 of the patent, which is depicted below:

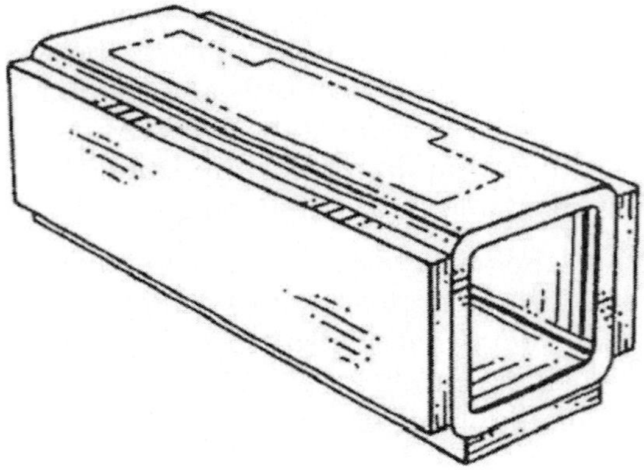

Upon study of the claimed design, the court described it as follows:

> A hollow tubular frame of generally square cross section, where the square has sides of length S, the frame has a length of approximately 3S, and the frame has a thickness of approximately T = 0.1S . . . with rectangular abrasive pads of thickness T affixed to three of the sides of the frame, covering the flat portion of the sides while leaving the curved radius uncovered, with the fourth side of the frame bare.

The district court ruled that "Swisa has not shown that the appearance of the Buffer Patent is dictated by its utilitarian purpose." The court therefore held that the patent is not invalid on the ground that the design was governed solely by function.

Swisa then moved for summary judgment of noninfringement. The district court granted the motion . . . [stating] that the plaintiff in a design patent case must prove both (1) that the accused device is "substantially similar" to the claimed design under what is referred to as the "ordinary observer" test, and (2) that the accused device contains "substantially the same points of novelty that distinguished the patented design from the prior art." *Egyptian Goddess, Inc. v. Swisa, Inc.* After comparing the claimed design and the accused product, the court held that Swisa's allegedly infringing product did not incorporate the "point of novelty" of the '389 patent, which the court identified as "a fourth, bare side to the buffer."

The district court noted that the parties disagreed as to the points of novelty in the '389 patent. EGI identified four elements . . . and for each element it identified prior art that did not embody that element. EGI therefore contended that the point of novelty is the combination of those four elements. The district court declined to address whether the point of novelty could be found in the combination of elements not present in various prior art references, because the court found that a single prior art reference, United States Design Patent No. 416,648 ("the Nailco patent"), contained all but one of the elements of the '389 design. The only element of the '389 patent design that was not present in the Nailco patent was "the addition of the fourth side without a pad, thereby transforming the equilateral triangular cross-section into a square." Because the Swisa product does not incorporate the point of novelty of the '389 patent—a fourth side without a pad—the court concluded that there was no infringement.

EGI appealed, and a panel of this court agreed with the district court that there was no issue of material fact as to whether the accused Swisa buffer "appropriates the point of novelty of the claimed design." *Egyptian Goddess, Inc. v. Swisa, Inc.,* 498 F.3d 1354, 1355 (Fed. Cir. 2007). The panel stated that the point of novelty in a patented design "can be either a single novel design element or a combination of elements that are individually known in the prior art." *Id.* at 1357. In order for a combination of individually known design elements to constitute a point of novelty, "the combination must be a non-trivial advance over the prior art."

This court granted rehearing en banc and asked the parties to address . . . whether the "point of novelty" test should continue to be used as a test for infringement of a design patent; whether the court should adopt the "non-trivial advance test", how the point of novelty test should be administered, particularly when numerous features of the design differ from certain prior art designs; and whether district courts should perform formal claim construction in design patent cases.

The starting point for any discussion of the law of design patents is the Supreme Court's decision in *Gorham Co. v. White,* 81 U.S. 511, 20 L. Ed. 731 (1871). In its analysis of claim infringement, the Court stated that the test of identity of design "must be sameness of appearance, and mere difference of lines in the drawing or sketch . . . or slight variances in configuration . . . will not destroy the substantial identity." Identity of appearance . . . or "sameness of effect upon the eye, is the main test of substantial identity of design"; the two need not be the same "to the eye of an expert" . . .

Since the decision in *Gorham,* the test articulated by the Court has been referred to as the "ordinary observer" test and has been recognized . . . as the proper standard for determining design patent infringement. The court in *Litton Systems* wrote:

> For a design patent to be infringed . . . no matter how similar two items look, "the accused device must appropriate the novelty in the patented device which distinguishes it from the prior art." That is, even though the court compares two items through the eyes of the ordinary observer, it must nevertheless . . . attribute their similarity to the novelty which distinguishes the patented device from the prior art.

The court held that the accused design had none of those features and therefore did not infringe. The extent to which the point of novelty test has been a separate test has not always been clear. More recently this court has described the ordinary observer and point of novelty tests as "two distinct tests" and has stated that "[t]he merger of the point of novelty test and the ordinary observer test is legal error."

The point of novelty test has proved reasonably easy to apply . . . in which the claimed design is based on a single prior art reference and departs from that reference in a single respect. In particular, applying the point of novelty test where multiple features and multiple prior art references are in play has led to disagreement over whether combinations of features, or the overall appearance of a design, can constitute the point of novelty of the claimed design.

EGI argues this court should no longer recognize the point of novelty test as a second part of the test for design patent infringement, distinct from the ordinary observer test established in *Gorham*. EGI contends that the ordinary observer test can fulfill the purposes for which the point of novelty test was designed, but with less risk of confusion. As long as the ordinary observer test focuses on the "appearance that distinguishes the patented design from the prior art" it will enable the fact-finder to address the proper inquiry, i.e., whether an ordinary observer, familiar with the prior art, would be deceived into thinking that the accused design was the same as the patented design. Relatedly, EGI argues that if the ordinary observer test is performed from the perspective of an ordinary observer who is familiar with the prior art, there is no need for a separate "non-trivial advance" test, because the attention of an ordinary observer familiar with prior art designs will naturally be drawn to the features of the claimed and accused designs that render them distinct from the prior art.

Swisa counters that this court may not abandon the point of novelty test. According to Swisa, the point of novelty test was adopted by the Supreme Court in *Smith v. Whitman Saddle Co.,* Swisa interprets that case as dictating the use of the point of novelty test as a second and distinct test for design patent infringement, separate from the ordinary observer test. Subsequent decisions of this court and others applying the point of novelty test are soundly based on *Whitman Saddle.*

We disagree with Swisa's submission . . . The Supreme Court did not adopt a separate point of novelty test for design patent infringement case. We conclude that the point of novelty test is inconsistent with the ordinary observer test laid down in *Gorham,* is not mandated by *Whitman Saddle* or precedent from other courts, and is not needed to protect against unduly broad assertions of design patent rights. The Court emphasized the importance of "invention" to the patentability of a design. If, however, the selection and adaptation of an existing form is more than the exercise of the imitative faculty, and the result is in effect a new creation, the design may be patentable.

Although the trial court, sitting in equity, concluded that the design was patentable, the Supreme Court disagreed. The Court wrote, "Nothing more was done in this instance than to put the two halves of these saddles together in the exercise of the ordinary skill of workmen of the trade, and in the way and manner ordinarily done."

If this drop were material to the design, and rendered it patentable as a complete and integral whole, there was no infringement. As before said, the design of the patent had two features of difference as compared with the Granger saddle and, unless there was infringement as to the latter there was none at all, since the saddle design of the patent does not otherwise differ from the old saddle with the old cantle added. Moreover, that difference was so marked that in our judgment the defendant's saddle could not be mistaken for the saddle of the complainant.

The Court did not distinguish sharply between its analysis of patentability and its discussion of infringement. Within the same passage, the Court moved from stating that it could not agree with the trial court that the design in issue was patentable to the conclusion that if the design were patentable because of the drop at the rear of the pommel, there was no infringement. The accused design did not contain the single feature that would have made it appear distinctively similar to the patented design rather than like the numerous prior art designs. The accused design did not infringe.

The *Sears, Roebuck & Co. v. Talge,* 140 F.2d 395 (8th Cir. 1944) and *Applied Arts Corp. v. Grand Rapids Metalcraft Corp.*, 67 F.2d 428 (6th Cir. 1933) cases became the principal precedents relied upon by this court to which this court's precedents dealing with the point of novelty test trace their origin. When the differences between the claimed and accused design are viewed in light of the prior art, the hypothetical ordinary observer will be drawn to those aspects of the claimed design that differ from the prior art. When the claimed design is close to the prior art designs, small differences are likely to be important to the eye of the hypothetical ordinary observer.

Not only is this approach consistent with the precedents discussed above, but it makes sense as a matter of logic as well. It can be difficult to answer the question whether one thing is like another without being given a frame of reference. The context in which the claimed and accused designs are compared, i.e., the background prior art, provides such a frame of reference and is therefore often useful in the process of comparison.

In addition, the more novel the design, the more opportunities there are for a defendant to argue that its design does not infringe because it does not copy all of the points of novelty even though it may give the overall appearance of being identical to the claimed design.

An ordinary observer will attach importance to differences between the claimed design and the prior art depending on the overall effect of those differences on the design. If the claimed design consists of a combination of old features that creates an appearance deceptively similar to the accused design, even to an observer familiar with similar prior art designs, a finding of infringement would be justified. Otherwise, infringement would not be found.

One function that has been served by the point of novelty test is to cabin unduly broad assertions of design patent scope by ensuring that a design that merely embodies or is substantially similar to prior art designs is not found to infringe. We believe that the preferable way to achieve that is to do so by relying on the ordinary observer test, conducted in light of the prior art. Examining the novel features of the claimed design can be an important component of the comparison.

On the basis of the foregoing analysis the "point of novelty" test should no longer be used in the analysis of a claim of design patent infringement. We also do not adopt the "non-trivial advance" test, which is a refinement of the "point of novelty" test. Instead, in accordance with *Gorham* and subsequent decisions, we hold that the "ordinary observer" test should be the sole test for determining whether a design patent has been infringed.

In some instances, the claimed design and the accused design will be sufficiently distinct that it will be clear without more that the patentee has not met its burden of proving the two designs would appear "substantially the same" to the ordinary observer, as required by *Gorham*. Where there are many examples of similar prior art designs differences between the claimed and accused designs that might not be noticeable in the abstract can become significant to the hypothetical ordinary observer who is conversant with the prior art.

We emphasize that although the approach we adopt will frequently involve comparisons between the claimed design and the prior art, it is designed solely as a test of infringement. The burden of proof as to infringement remains on the patentee. However, if the accused infringer elects to rely on the comparison prior art as part of its defense against the claim of infringement, the burden of production of that prior art is on the accused infringer. Under the ordinary observer test, it makes sense to impose the burden of production as to any comparison prior art on the accused infringer.

It is agreed that the general shape of the accused nail buffer at issue is the same as that of the patented buffer design. The difference between the two is that the accused buffer has raised buffing pads on all four sides, while the patented buffer has buffing pads on only three sides. The two closest prior art nail buffers before the court were the Falley nail buffer, which has a solid, rectangular cross section with slightly raised buffers on all sides, and the Nailco patent, which shows a nail buffer design having a triangular shape and a hollow cross section, and in which raised buffing pads are located on all three sides. The four nail buffers are pictured below:

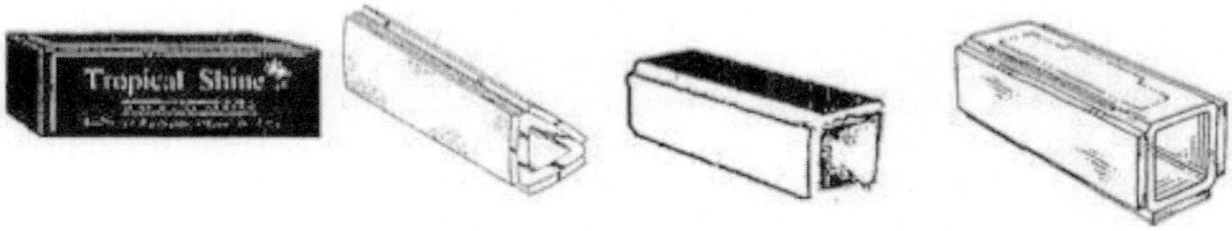


The question before this court under the standard we have set forth above is whether an ordinary observer, familiar with the prior art Falley and Nailco designs, would be deceived into believing the Swisa buffer is the same as the patented buffer. EGI argues that such an observer would notice a difference between the prior art and the '389 patent, consisting of "the hollow tube that is square in cross section and that has raised pads with exposed gaps at the corners." EGI invokes the declaration of its expert witness, Kathleen Eaton [who] concluded that the patented and accused designs would "confuse an ordinary observer into purchasing the accused buffer thinking it to be the patented buffer design. The substantially similar appearance results from both designs having a hollow tube, square in cross section and rectangular in length, with multiple raised rectangular pads mounted on the sides . . . that do not cover the corners of the tube."

Swisa counters that the '389 patent closely tracks the design of the Nailco nail buffer, except that it "add[s] a fourth side without an abrasive pad, resulting in square ends." In light of the close prior art buffers. Swisa argues that an ordinary observer would notice the difference between the claimed and accused designs. Swisa cites the declaration of its expert, Steve Falley [who] addressed the differences among the prior art designs, the accused design, and patented design, and he concluded that you could simply add to the Nailco Buffer a fourth side without an abrasive on it. This merely takes the Nailco Buffer to the block shape of the original Falley Buffer Block, while keeping [its] hollow aspect. As there had already been on the market for a long time 3-way buffer blocks that had no abrasive on one side, it was also obvious that you could have a three way hollow buffer that had four sides but with no abrasive on one side.

Mr. Falley added that "four-way" nail buffers having four different abrasive surfaces have been made since 1985, and that four-sided "buffer blocks" have been on the market since 1987. The difference between a buffer with abrasive on three sides and a buffer with abrasive on four sides is immediately apparent to any consumer used to buying nail buffers.

The problem with Ms. Eaton's declaration is that she characterized the accused and patented designs as similar because they both have square cross sections and "multiple" raised buffer pads, without directly acknowledging that the patented design has three pads while the accused design has four. She also failed to address the fact that the design of the Nailco patent is identical to the accused device except that the Nailco design has three sides rather than four. Nothing about Ms. Eaton's declaration explains why an ordinary observer would regard the accused design as being closer to the claimed design than to the Nailco prior art patent. Eaton's reference to the prior art buffers is limited to that an ordinary observer and purchaser of nail buffers would consider the patented design and the accused buffer to be substantially similar . . .

No reasonable fact-finder could find that EGI met its burden of showing that an ordinary observer would believe the accused design to be the same as the patented design. We reach the same conclusion—although by using the ordinary observer test as informed by the prior art. After analyzing the Nailco patent and the claimed design the district court concluded, "a fourth side without a pad is not substantially the same as a fourth side with a pad." Although we do not adopt the "non-trivial advance" test employed by the panel in this case our analysis under the ordinary observer test is parallel to the panel's approach. The panel focused on viewing the difference between the claimed and accused designs in light of the prior art. "The Swisa buffers have raised, abrasive pads on *all four* sides . . . this difference cannot be considered minor." That point captures the essence of the rationale of our decision today, even though the panel decision employed a different analytical approach. We sustain the district court's entry of summary judgment of no infringement, but we do so under the ordinary observer test without using the point of novelty test that we have disapproved. Under *Gorham*, we hold that the accused design could not reasonably be viewed as so similar to the claimed design that a purchaser familiar with the prior art would be deceived by the similarity between the claimed and accused designs, "inducing him to purchase one supposing it to be the other."

---

A more recent example of the court's approach to determining infringement of a design patent is found below.

## REVISION MILITARY, INC. V. BALBOA MFG. CO.

700 F.3d 524 (Fed. Cir. 2012)

NEWMAN, CIRCUIT JUDGE. Revision Military, Inc., and Balboa Manufacturing Co. design, manufacture, and sell protective eyewear. Revision markets its ballistic protective eyewear primarily to military establishments and law enforcement agencies, and also to others who require eye protection, such as hunters and range shooters. Revision alleges that Balboa's new "Bravo" design protective goggles (also called "Bobster Bravo") copied and infringes Revision's "Bullet Ant" goggles covered by U.S. Design Patents No. 537,098 (the '098 patent) and No. 620,039 (the '039 patent). After this infringement suit was filed Revision moved for a preliminary injunction, seeking to enjoin Balboa from making and selling the Bobster Bravo goggles while the litigation is pending. Revision stated that it is likely to succeed on the merits, that if the infringement is not enjoined it is likely to suffer irreparable harm, that the equities are balanced in its favor, and that public policy favors grant of a preliminary injunction on the merits and equities of this case.

The law of design patent infringement is stated in *Gorham Co. v. White*, as whether "in the eye of an ordinary observer, giving such attention as a purchaser usually gives, [the] two designs are substantially the same." In *Egyptian Goddess, Inc. v. Swisa, Inc.* the court confirmed that "in accordance with *Gorham* . . . we hold that the 'ordinary observer' test should be the sole test for determining whether a design patent has been infringed." The court's purpose was to lay to rest the "point of novelty" test for design patent infringement, and to reinforce the principles established in Gorham. We conclude that the point of novelty test, as a second and freestanding requirement for proof of design patent infringement, is inconsistent with the ordinary observer test laid down in Gorham.

Revision states that to the eye of the ordinary observer, and viewing the designs as a whole, the designs here at issue are substantially the same. Revision offers a comparison of the patented designs in the '098 and '039 patents, and photographs of the Bobster Bravo:

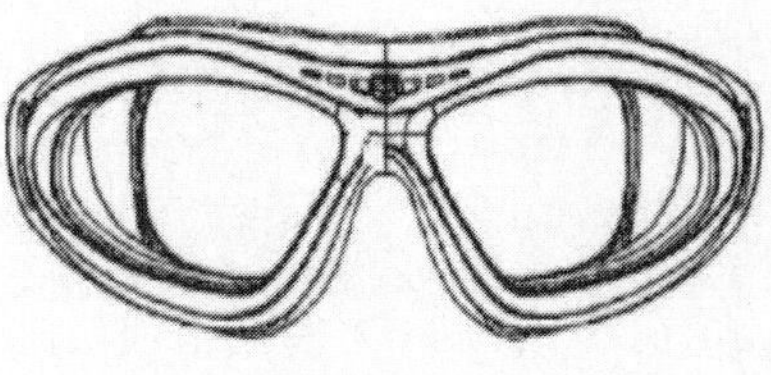

**'039 Patent Figure 2**

**Bobster Bravo**

**'098 Patent Figure 2**

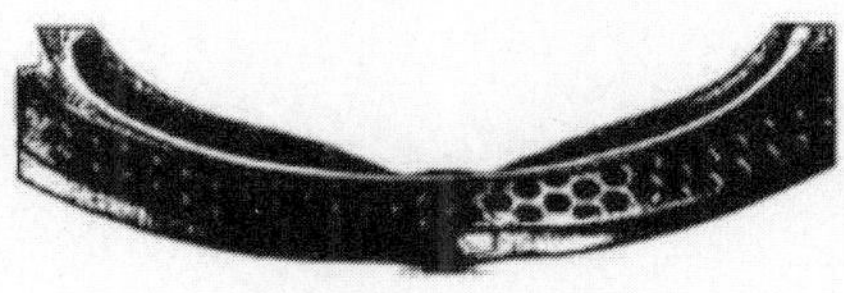

**Bobster Bravo**

*Revision* states that the criteria of *Gorham* and *Egyptian Goddess* are met. Infringement is more likely that not to be found at trial.

Although the district court stated the correct "overall design" standard, citing *Crocs, Inc. v. International Trade Commission,* the court focused on features that "stand out as dissimilar," reciting the shape and sizes of the lenses, the concavity of the nose bridge, and the venting along the top and bottoms. The design of the Bravo goggles and the patented goggles is substantially the same and the ordinary observer would not notice any differences.

Although individual features may indeed serve in assessing the "impact on the overall appearance", in determining whether apparently minor differences between specific features would be recognized as distinguishing the designs, it is often helpful to refer to any prior art with which the ordinary observer would reasonably be familiar. As stated in *Egyptian Goddess,* "the background prior art, provides . . . a frame of reference and is therefore often useful in the process of comparison." The district court did not consider the prior art context in which the ordinary observer test is applied. Although the district court stated that "[b]ecause this is not a particularly close case, the court does not need prior art as a 'frame of reference' to apply the 'ordinary observer test' ", the record suggests otherwise. On remand, the district court may redetermine, applying the design-as-a-whole criterion and the more-likely-than-not standard.

It is the role of the district court to determine, in the first instance, whether a preliminary injunction is warranted on the law, facts, and equities of the case. We vacate the denial of the preliminary injunction, and remand for redetermination in accordance with Federal Circuit criteria.

---

Finally, we consider deference to the jury in findings of infringement in a hotly contested case in the Smartphone patent wars. We have previously viewed a lower court ruling in this dispute as it related to indefiniteness. There were many design patents at issue in the *Apple v. Samsung* dispute, including some on graphic user interfaces. The case combines the issues in claim construction—including how to assess functional aspects of a design—with infringement.

## APPLE INC. V. SAMSUNG ELECTRONICS CO., LTD.

786 F.3d 983 (Fed. Cir. 2015) (rev'd in part on other grounds)

PROST, CHIEF JUDGE.

### I. Design Patents

The design patents on appeal claim certain design elements embodied in the iPhone. The D'677 patent focuses on design elements on the front face of the iPhone:

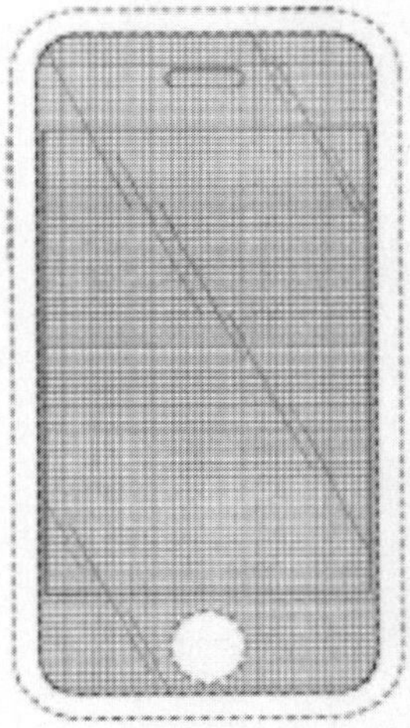

FIG. 3

FIG. 7

FIG. 8

The D'087 patent claims another set of design features that extend to the bezel of the iPhone:

FIG. 19

FIG. 23

FIG. 24

The D'305 patent claims "the ornamental design for a graphical user interface for a display screen or portion thereof" as shown in the following drawing:

Samsung contends that it should not have been found liable for infringement of the asserted design patents because any similarity was limited to the basic or functional elements in the design patents. There was no evidence of actual deception of consumers and the differences between the accused smartphones and the asserted design patents should have been clear if prior art designs were properly considered.

Samsung raises three issues—functionality, actual deception, and comparison to prior art—in the context of the jury instructions and the sufficiency of evidence to support the infringement verdict. Samsung argues that the district court legally erred in allowing the jury to award as damages Samsung's entire profits on its infringing smartphones. We do not find any of these challenges persuasive as discussed below.

### A. Infringement

#### 1. Jury Instructions

##### a. Functional Aspects in the Asserted Design Patents

"Where a design contains both functional and nonfunctional elements, the scope of the claim must be construed in order to identify the non-functional aspects of the design as shown in the patent."... Samsung contends that the district court erred in failing to exclude the functional aspects of the design patents ... The district court should have excluded elements that are " 'dictated by their functional purpose,' or cover the 'structural ... aspects of the article.' " Such elements ... should be "ignored" in their entirety from the design patent claim scope. For example, Samsung contends that rectangular form and rounded corners are among such elements that should be ignored in the infringement analysis.

Our case law does not support Samsung's position. In *Richardson,* the design patent at issue depicted a multifunction tool with numerous components that were "dictated by their functional purpose." 597 F.3d at 1294. But the claim construction in *Richardson* [*v. Stanley Works, Inc.*, 597 F.3d 1288 (Fed. Cir. 2010)] did not exclude those components in their entirety. The claim construction included the ornamental aspects of those components: "the standard shape of the hammer-head, the diamond-shaped flare of the crow-bar and the top of the jaw, the rounded neck, the orientation of the crow-bar relative to the head of the tool, and the plain, undecorated handle." The language "dictated by their functional purpose" was only a description of the facts there; it did not establish a rule to eliminate entire elements from the claim scope as Samsung argues.

Our case law likewise does not support Samsung's proposed rule of eliminating any "structural" aspect from the claim scope. Samsung arrives at its proposed rule by selecting a few words from the following statement in *Lee [v. Dayton-Hudson Corp.*, 838 F.2d 1186 (Fed. Cir. 1988)]: "[d]esign patents do not and cannot include claims to the structural or functional aspects of the article. . . ." But that statement addressed design patent validity. It did not specify a rule, as Samsung represents, to eliminate elements from the claim scope of a valid patent in analyzing infringement.

More directly applicable to the claim scope issue at hand, *Lee* stated elsewhere that "it is the non-functional, design aspects that are pertinent to determinations of infringement." That principle was properly reflected ... in the district court's construction of the design patents as claiming only "the ornamental design" as shown in the patent figures. Samsung has not persuasively shown how the district court's claim constructions were legally erroneous under *Lee* or *Richardson.*

Samsung asserted during oral argument that the jury should have been instructed to compare the accused Samsung smartphones to the "overall *ornamental* appearance" of a patented design, instead of simply "the overall appearance" as the district court provided. According to Samsung, "crucially, what's missing there is the word 'ornamental.'" *Id.* at 4:25–4:28. The jury instructions . . . already limited the scope of the asserted design patents to the "ornamental" elements through the claim constructions as discussed earlier: the design patents were each construed as claiming "the ornamental design" as shown in the patent figures. Samsung has failed to show prejudicial error in the jury instructions as a whole that would warrant a new trial.

b. Actual Deception and Role of Prior Art

Samsung further contends that the infringement instruction was erroneous for stating that actual deception was not required. A design patent is infringed if an ordinary observer would have been deceived: "if, in the eye of an ordinary observer, giving such attention as a purchaser usually gives, two designs are substantially the same, if the resemblance is such as to deceive such an observer, inducing him to purchase one supposing it to be the other, the first one patented is infringed by the other." *Gorham Co. v. White.* Moreover, an infringement analysis must include a comparison of the asserted design against the prior art: "[i]f the accused design has copied a particular feature of the claimed design that departs conspicuously from the prior art, the accused design is naturally more likely to be regarded as deceptively similar to the claimed design, and thus infringing." *Egyptian Goddess, Inc. v. Swisa, Inc.*

These holdings were reflected in the infringement instruction . . . Samsung does not contend otherwise. Samsung argues that the portions in the infringement instruction highlighted below made the lack of actual deception irrelevant and led the jury to disregard the prior art:

> Two designs are substantially the same if, in the eye of an ordinary observer, giving such attention as a purchaser usually gives, the resemblance between the two designs is such as to deceive such an observer, inducing him to purchase one supposing it to be the other. *You do not need, however, to find that any purchasers actually were deceived or confused by the appearance of the accused Samsung products. . . .*
>
> This determination of whether two designs are substantially the same will benefit from comparing the two designs with prior art. You must familiarize yourself with the prior art admitted at trial in making your determination of . . . direct infringement.

We conclude instead that the jury instruction clarified that actual deception was not required, which is an accurate reflection of the Gorham analysis. The jury instruction expressly required that each juror "must" consider the prior art admitted at trial. The jury instruction's guidelines did not reduce the entire prior art analysis to a mere option as Samsung contends. Samsung again has failed to show that "when, looking to the instructions as a whole, the substance of the applicable law was [not] fairly and correctly covered."

### 2. Supporting Evidence

Samsung contends that the infringement verdict was not supported by substantial evidence. Samsung's contentions . . . are premised on the same issues—functionality, actual deception, and comparison to prior art—it raises in the context of the jury instructions.

Having rejected the jury instruction challenges, we likewise find Samsung's parallel substantial evidence complaints unpersuasive. Apple's witnesses provided sufficient testimonies to allow the jury to account for any functional aspects in the asserted design patents. The witnesses testified on the similar overall visual impressions of the accused products to the asserted design patents such that an ordinary observer would likely be deceived. Apple's experts also testified about the differences between the asserted patents and both the prior art and other competing designs. The jury could have reasonably relied on the evidence in the record to reach its infringement verdict.

### 3. Preclusion of Evidence

Samsung appeals the district court's preclusion of testimony on Samsung's independent development of its F700 phone that pre-dated the iPhone to rebut an allegation of copying. The evidence on the F700 was previously excluded as a prior art reference under a Rule 37 sanction due to Samsung's failure to timely disclose the evidence during discovery.

The district court found that Samsung's witness did not design any of the accused devices and was unaware that any of the accused devices was based on the F700. The district court determined that the proffered testimony of Samsung's witness would have limited probative value on the question of whether Samsung copied any of Apple's design patents because she lacked first-hand knowledge relevant to the underlying issue. The district court concluded that the limited probative value of the testimony was outweighed by the likelihood that it would be considered by the jury for the prohibited purpose under the earlier Rule 37 sanction.

We find that the district court acted within its discretion in precluding Samsung's proffered testimony to rebut an allegation of copying.

There was no prejudicial legal error in the infringement jury instructions on the three issues that Samsung raises: functionality, actual deception, and comparison to prior art. Thee district court did not abuse its discretion in excluding Samsung's evidence of independent development and that there was substantial evidence to support the jury's infringement findings. We therefore affirm the district court's denial of Samsung's motion for judgment as a matter of law on design patent infringement and Samsung's alternative motion for a new trial.

### *NOTES AND QUESTIONS*

1. Do you think the test for infringement of a design patent is easy for courts to apply with consistency?

2. Who is the "ordinary observer"? Should the ordinary observer be an expert in the field? The courts have held it cannot be an expert, but instead of a "purchase of things of similar design." How should the court treat products that are sold to a "middleman" before reaching the ultimate consumer. Is the ordinary observer the middleman or the end user? See *Arminak v. Saint-Gobain Calmar, Inc.*, 501 F.3d 1314 (Fed. Cir. 2007) (finding an industrial purchaser to be the ordinary observer for design patent infringement).

3. As discussed in Chapter 3, the test for trade dress infringement differs from the test for design patent infringement? Trade dress infringement is focused on customers rather than ordinary observers. More importantly, the trade dress infringement analysis focuses on how consumers confront the designs *in the marketplace*. This can include other contextual clues to similarity. In contrast, the ordinary observer in design patent infringement considers the designs in the abstract. Which test do you think makes more sense from a policy perspective? Does it make sense to have divergent tests for two forms of intellectual property that protect similar attributes? For a brief discuss of these issues, see Sarah Burstein, *Commentary: Faux Amis in Design Law,* 105 TRADEMARK REP. 1455 (2015).

4. One commentator argues that frequently "designs involve non-novel or functional features, and are only protectable because of other novel features, or because of a novel combination of otherwise familiar features." If this is so, how are judges and juries about to avoid finding infringement (and consequently providing too broad a scope of design patent protection) when the similarities between the accused product and the patented design are due to unpatentable features. For an interesting analysis of this issue, see Rebecca Tushnet, *The Eye Alone is the Judge: Images and Design Patents*, 19 J. INTELL. PROP. L. 409 (2012).

5. How are graphical user interfaces are visual ways of interacting with computers. They are not physically manufactured; instead they are typically displayed on a screen. Are graphical user interfaces clearly "articles of manufacture" for purposes of design patent law?

---

## 3. LIMITS ON INFRINGEMENT

Design patent infringement has incorporated an important limitation that is present in utility patent infringement. To understand this limitation, one must understand a difference between the infringement tests. Patent holders asserting infringement of a utility patent can prove infringement in either of two ways. They can show that the accused product literally infringes. Literal infringement means that each limitation in the claim is identically found in the accused device. Patent owners can also show infringement under the "doctrine of equivalents." The doctrine of equivalents permits patent holders to show that the accused product has only "insubstantial differences" or it performs the same function, in the same way, to achieve substantially the same result. Design patent law combines these two inquiries—literal infringement and infringement under the doctrine of equivalents—into a single inquiry.

Utility patent law has long recognized limits on the patent owners' ability to assert the doctrine of equivalents. One long-standing limit, known as "prosecution history estoppel," addresses when a patent owner narrows its patent claims when interacting with the U.S. Patent & Trademark Office, and then attempts to argue that the disclaimed claim scope is "equivalent." The basic rationale behind prosecution history estoppel is that a patent owner cannot narrow the patent claims in order to win allowance before the U.S. Patent & Trademark Office, and then argue that the claims are entitled to a broad range of 'equivalents' in litigation. The patent owner was in a position to draft appropriately scoped patent claims during the pendency of the patent application, and also controlled whether to appeal or acquiesce in any rejections of the claims.

The *Pacific Coast Marine Windshields* case below shows how the doctrine of prosecution history estoppel affects the design patent infringement analysis.

## PACIFIC COAST MARINE WINDSHIELDS LTD. V. MALIBU BOATS, LLC

739 F.3d 694 (Fed. Cir. 2014)

DYK, CIRCUIT JUDGE. Pacific Coast Marine Windshields Limited ("Pacific Coast") is the assignee of all rights in U.S. Patent No. D555,070 ("the '070 patent") for an ornamental boat windshield design. Pacific Coast brought suit against Malibu Boats, LLC, Marine Hardware, Inc., Tressmark, Inc., MH Windows, LLC, and John F. Pugh (collectively "Malibu Boats") in the Middle District of Florida, alleging infringement. The district court granted Malibu Boats' motion for summary judgment of non-infringement, finding that prosecution history estoppel barred the infringement claim. Pacific Coast appeals. We hold that the principles of prosecution history estoppel apply to design patents, but reverse the district court's summary judgment of non-infringement because the accused infringing design was not within the scope of the subject matter surrendered during prosecution, and remand for further proceedings.

Darren A. Bach, the owner and chief executive officer of Pacific Coast, filed a design patent application on April 27, 2006, claiming an "ornamental design of a marine windshield with a frame, a tapered corner post with vent holes and without said vent holes, and with a hatch and without said hatch, as shown and described."

The accompanying figures depicted various embodiments of the claimed design with different vent hole configurations. The drawings also showed designs that included and excluded a hatch on the front of the windshield. Shown below are submitted figures representative of the various embodiments:

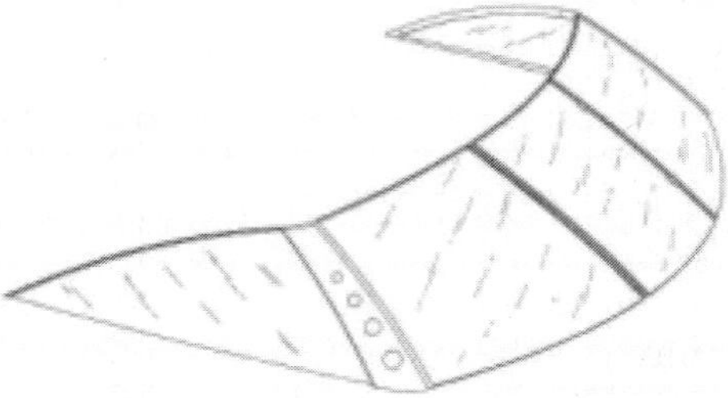

**Representative drawing figure of US D555,070**

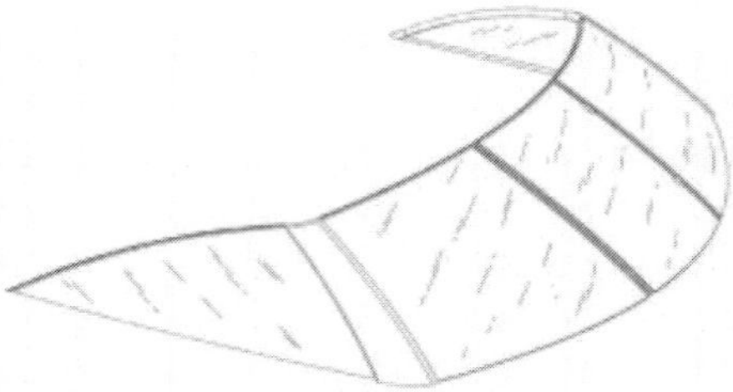

**Representative drawing figure of US D569,782**

The examiner determined that the multiple embodiments represented five "patentably distinct groups of designs" and issued a restriction requirement, identifying the five distinct groups of designs as windshields with: (1) four circular holes and a hatch (Fig. 1); (2) four circular or square holes and no hatch (Figs. 7 & 12); (3) no holes and a hatch (Fig. 8); (4) no holes and no hatch (Fig. 9); and (5) two oval or rectangular holes and a hatch (Figs. 10 & 11).

Fig. 1

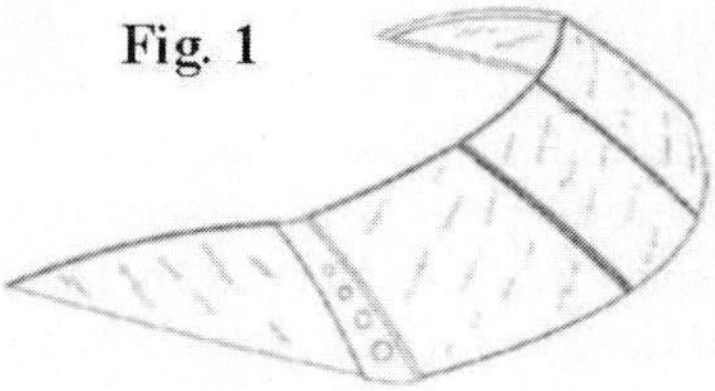

Fig. 7

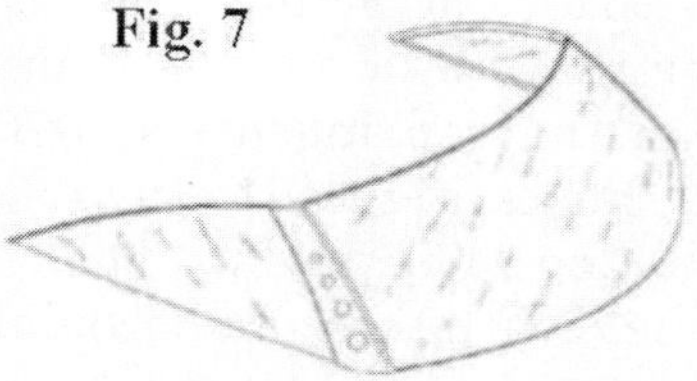

Fig. 8

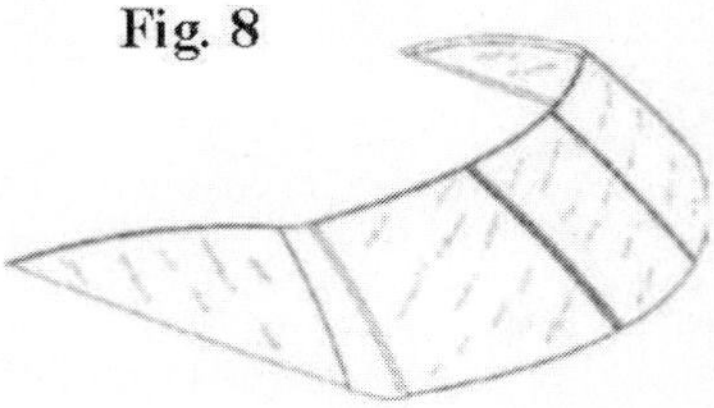

Fig. 9

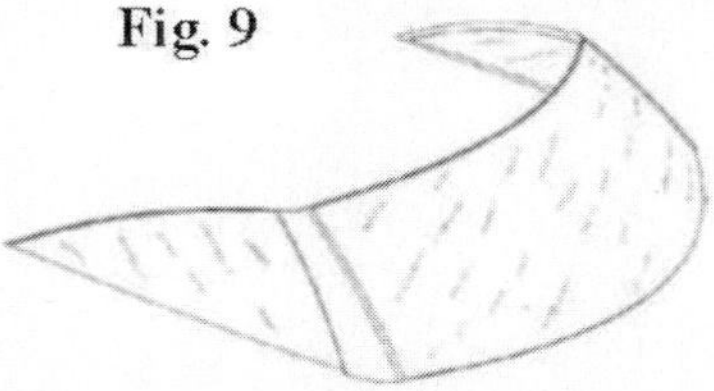

Fig. 10

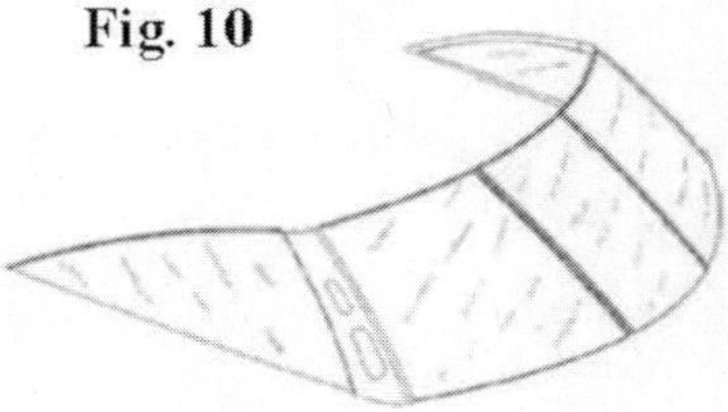

Fig. 11

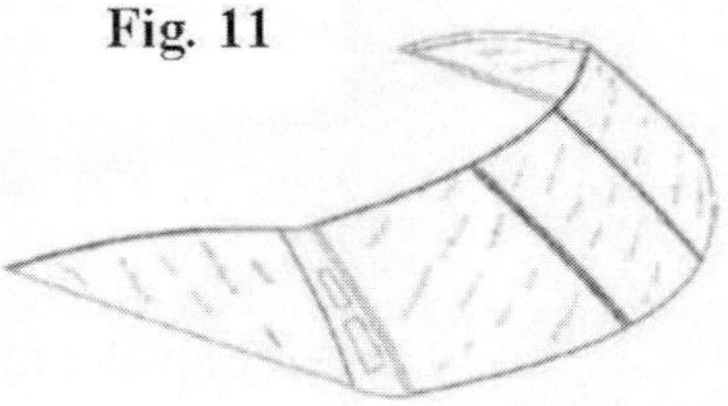

Fig. 12

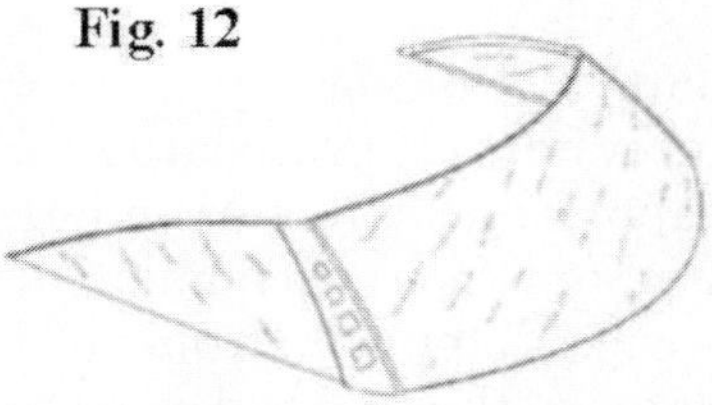

**Five "Patentably Distinct Groups of Designs"**

The applicant was required to elect a single group for the pending application although the applicant was entitled to file additional applications for each of the remaining groups.

The applicant elected "Group I, Embodiment 1," corresponding to Fig.1 above, depicting four vent holes and a hatch. He amended the claim to recite "the ornamental design of a marine windshield with a frame, and a pair of tapered corner posts" removing the original claim language stating "with vent holes and without said vent holes, and with a hatch and without said hatch." The amended application issued as the '070 patent on November 13, 2007. As issued, the '070 patent claims "[t]he ornamental design for a marine windshield, as shown and described." The inventor assigned all rights in the '070 patent to his wholly owned company, Pacific Coast, in June, 2011. The inventor later obtained a patent for the design with no holes in the corner post as a divisional of the originally-filed application, but did not file another divisional application with respect to any of the other embodiments.

In 2011, Pacific Coast brought suit in the Middle District of Florida, alleging that Malibu Boats manufactured and sold boat windshields with a design that infringed the '070 patent. Pacific Coast also alleged that Malibu Boats induced others, including customers and distributors, to infringe the '070 patent. The accused infringing design was in a boat windshield with three trapezoidal holes on the corner post, as shown below.

**Accused Infringing Design of Malibu Boats' Marine Windshield**

The district court granted Malibu Boats' motion for partial summary judgment of non-infringement on the grounds of prosecution history estoppel. The district court found the applicant had surrendered the designs reflected in the canceled figures and amended the claim "in order to obtain the patent." The patentee was estopped from asserting infringement against the accused design, where "the accused design is still clearly within 'the territory [surrendered] between the original claim and amended claim.' " The court also found that the patentee failed to overcome the presumption of prosecution history estoppel and entered a judgment of non-infringement based on the finding of prosecution history estoppel.

Pacific Coast appealed. Whether the presumption of prosecution history estoppel precludes a patentee from asserting infringement against an alleged equivalent of an amended claim element is a question of law that we review without deference.

The Federal Circuit held as an issue of first impression that the concept of prosecution history estoppel applies to design patents as well as utility patents. For doctrine of equivalents purposes, the accused and claimed elements are equivalent if there are only "insubstantial differences" between them. For design patents, the concepts of literal infringement and equivalents infringement are intertwined. The statutory provision on design patent infringement does not require literal identity, imposing liability on anyone who "without license of the owner, (1) applies the patented design, *or any colorable imitation thereof,* to any article of manufacture for the purpose of sale, or (2) sells or exposes for sale any article of manufacture to which such design or *colorable imitation* has been applied" 35 U.S.C. § 289.

Under the leading Supreme Court case, the test for design patent infringement is whether in the eye of an ordinary observer two designs are substantially the same. If the resemblance is such as to deceive such an observer, inducing him to purchase one supposing it to be the other, the first one patented is infringed by the other. *Gorham Mfg. Co. v. White.* The test for design patent infringement is not identity, but rather sufficient similarity—whether "the accused design could not reasonably be viewed as so similar to the claimed design that a purchaser familiar with the prior art would be deceived by the similarity between the designs". *Egyptian Goddess, Inc. v. Swisa, Inc.*

Pacific Coast argued that prosecution history estoppel should not apply to design patents at all. At oral argument, Pacific Coast conceded that a patentee should not be able to assert infringement against a particular design that was abandoned during prosecution for reasons of patentability. Prosecution history estoppel in design patents promotes the "clarity [that] is essential to promote progress." *Festo.* In design patents, the claimed scope is defined by drawings rather than language, but does not argue against application of prosecution history estoppel principles. We conclude that the principles of prosecution history estoppel apply to design patents as well.

Having determined that the principles of prosecution history estoppel apply to design patents, we consider: (1) whether there was a surrender; (2) whether it was for reasons of patentability; and (3) whether the accused design is within the scope of the surrender.

There was a surrender of claim scope during prosecution. While we look primarily to the wording of the claims in utility patents for the purpose of prosecution history estoppel, we must look at the requisite drawings in design patents to determine whether a surrender has occurred. The applicant amended the claim by cancelling figures associated with all but one of the patentably distinct groups of designs identified by the examiner—the four-hole embodiment. The applicant surrendered such designs and conceded that the claim was limited to what the remaining figure showed—and colorable imitations thereof. By removing broad claim language referring to alternate configurations and cancelling the individual figures, the applicant narrowed the scope of his original application and surrendered subject matter.

The surrender was not made to avoid prior art but because of a restriction requirement under 35 U.S.C. § 121. The examiner imposed a restriction requirement on the ground that the different drawings showed "patentably distinct groups of designs," contravening the requirement that design patents must claim only one design. The examiner identified the specific design groups, giving the applicant the option to elect one. Pacific

Coast argues that only surrenders to avoid prior art are within the doctrine. We think broader. The surrender resulting from a restriction requirement invokes prosecution history estoppel if the surrender was necessary "to secure the patent." *Festo.*

The final question is whether the accused design is within the scope of the surrender. Prosecution history estoppel only bars an infringement claim if the accused design fell within the scope of the surrendered subject matter. The surrendered designs included windshields with two holes on the corner post. Although the accused design had a three-hole configuration, the court found that "the accused design is still clearly within the 'territory between the original claim and the amended claim' ". Malibu Boats argues that by abandoning a design with two holes and obtaining patents on designs with four holes and no holes, the applicant abandoned the range. This range concept does not work in the context of design patents where ranges are not claimed, but rather individual designs. The record only reflects the surrender of the two-hole.

The defendant here did not argue that the scope of the surrendered two-hole embodiment extended to the three-hole embodiment because the three-hole embodiment was not colorably different from the two-hole embodiment. The patentee here does not argue that the accused design was within the scope of the surrendered two-hole embodiment, and no presumption of prosecution history estoppel could arise. Prosecution history estoppel principles do not bar Pacific Coast's infringement claim, and remand for further proceedings.

### *NOTES AND QUESTIONS*

1. Historically design patents have been rarely amended during prosecution, perhaps due to the relatively high grant rate of nearly 90%. *See* Jason J. DuMont & Mark D. Janus, *Virtual Designs*, 17 STAN. TECH. L. REV. 107, 148 (2013). In fact, the leading patent law blog found that the U.S. Patent & Trademark Office issued over 80% of design applications filed from 2005 to 2009 without any rejections whatsoever. Design Patent Rejections, Patently-O Blog, Jan. 19, 2010 (available at http://patentlyo.com/patent/2010/01/design-patent-rejections.html). If most design patents have no substantive prosecution history, the limitations on design patent infringement will likely be minimal.

2. In utility patent law, there is a clear distinction between two forms of infringement: literal infringement and infringement under the doctrine of equivalents. The U.S. Supreme Court has held that one purpose of the doctrine of equivalents is prevent a "pirate" from making minor changes to a patented invention to avoid liability. Design patent law combines the overall infringement inquiry, and has no distinct doctrine of equivalents. Do you think that the design patent infringement test provides enough flexibility to capture "pirate" behavior? Does it provide too much flexibility to the patent owner?

## 4. DAMAGES, THE MARKING REQUIREMENT & OTHER REMEDIES

If a design patent is found to be infringed and not invalid, then the patent owner is entitled to a remedy. The remedy includes both monetary damages and a potential injunction. The monetary damages for design patent infringement can governed by two sections of the Patent Act, 35 U.S.C. §§ 284 and 289. Section 284 is the general damages statute for patent infringement. It reads, in operative part, that the court shall award "damages adequate to compensate for the infringement, but in no event less than a reasonable royalty for the use made of the invention by the infringer." Thus, the statute sets the floor on damages as the reasonable royalty. Under well-established damages doctrine relating to utility patents, the patentee can sometimes obtain its (the patent owner's) lost profits.

Design patent infringement has an additional statutory remedy not available to owners of utility patents. Section 289 reads (emphasis added):

> Whoever during the term of a patent for a design, without license of the owner, (1) applies the patented design, or any colorable imitation thereof, to any article of manufacture for the purpose of sale, or (2) sells or exposes for sale any article of manufacture to which such design or colorable imitation has been applied **shall be liable to the owner to the extent of his total profit**, but not less than $250, recoverable in any United States district court having jurisdiction of the parties.
>
> Nothing in this section shall prevent, lessen, or impeach any other remedy which an owner of an infringed patent has under the provisions of this title, but he shall not twice recover the profit made from the infringement.

In December 2016, the U.S. Supreme Court ruled on the scope of § 289 in multiple component products in the *Apple v. Samsung* case below. While the Supreme Court opinion below only dealt with issues relating to damages, readers may recall that we previously read two rulings from this dispute relating to indefiniteness and infringement. The Supreme Court opinion was issued by a unanimous court. Did the Court articulate a test for determining the "article of manufacture" for purposes of calculating damages?

## SAMSUNG ELECTRONICS CO., LTD. V. APPLE INC.

137 S.Ct. 429, 580 U.S. ___ (2016)

JUSTICE SOTOMAYOR. Section 289 of the Patent Act provides a damages remedy specific to design patent infringement. A person who manufactures or sells "any article of manufacture to which [a patented] design or colorable imitation has been applied shall be liable to the owner to the extent of his total profit." 35 U.S.C. § 289. In the case of a design for a single-component product, such as a dinner plate, the product is the "article of manufacture" to which the design has been applied. In the case of a design for a multicomponent product, such as a kitchen oven, identifying the "article of manufacture" to which the design has been applied is a more difficult task.

This case involves the infringement of designs for smartphones. The United States Court of Appeals for the Federal Circuit identified the entire smartphone as the only permissible "article of manufacture" for the purpose of calculating § 289 damages because consumers could not separately purchase components of the smartphones. The question before us is whether that reading is consistent with § 289. We hold that it is not.

### I

### A

The federal patent laws have long permitted those who invent designs for manufactured articles to patent their designs. See Patent Act of 1842, § 3, 5 Stat. 543–544. Patent protection is available for a "new, original and ornamental design for an article of manufacture." 35 U.S.C. § 171(a). A patentable design "gives a peculiar or distinctive appearance to the manufacture, or article to which it may be applied, or to which it gives form." *Gorham Co. v. White*, 14 Wall. 511, 525 (1872). This Court has explained that a design patent is infringed "if, in the eye of an ordinary observer, giving such attention as a purchaser usually gives, two designs are substantially the same." Id., at 528.

In 1885, this Court limited the damages available for design patent infringement. The statute in effect at the time allowed a holder of a design patent to recover "the actual damages sustained" from infringement. Rev. Stat. § 4919. In *Dobson v. Hartford Carpet Co.,* 114 U.S. 439 (1885), the lower courts had awarded the holders of design patents on carpets damages in the amount of "the entire profit to the [patent holders], per yard, in the manufacture and sale of carpets of the patented designs, and not merely the value which the designs contributed to the carpets." Id., at 443. This Court reversed the damages award and construed the statute to require proof that the profits were "due to" the design rather than other aspects of the carpets. Id., at 444; *see also Dobson v. Dornan*, 118 U.S. 10, 17 (1886) ("The plaintiff must show what profits or damages are attributable to the use of the infringing design").

In 1887, in response to the *Dobson* cases, Congress enacted a specific damages remedy for design patent infringement. See S. Rep. No. 206, 49th Cong., 1st Sess., 1–2 (1886); H.R. Rep. No.1966, 49th Cong., 1st Sess., 1–2 (1886). The new provision made it unlawful to manufacture or sell an article of manufacture to which a patented design or a colorable imitation thereof had been applied. An act to amend the law relating to patents, trademarks, and copyright, § 1, 24 Stat. 387. It went on to make a design patent infringer "liable in the amount of" $250 or "the total profit made by him from the manufacture or sale . . . of the article or articles to which the design, or colorable imitation thereof, has been applied."

The Patent Act of 1952 codified this provision in § 289. 66 Stat. 813. That codified language now reads, in relevant part:

> "Whoever during the term of a patent for a design, without license of the owner, (1) applies the patented design, or any colorable imitation thereof, to any article of manufacture for the purpose of sale, or (2) sells or exposes for sale any article of manufacture to which such design or colorable imitation has been applied shall be liable to the owner to the extent of his total profit, but not less than $250. . . ."

B

Apple Inc. released its first-generation iPhone in 2007. The iPhone is a smartphone, a "cell phone with a broad range of other functions based on advanced computing capability, large storage capacity, and Internet connectivity." *Riley v. California*, 573 U.S. ___, ___ (2014). Apple secured many design patents in connection with the release. Among those patents were the D618,677 patent, covering a black rectangular front face with rounded corners, the D593,087 patent, covering a rectangular front face with rounded corners and a raised rim, and the D604,305 patent, covering a grid of 16 colorful icons on a black screen.

Samsung Electronics Co., Samsung Electronics America, Inc., and Samsung Telecommunications America, LLC (Samsung), also manufacture smartphones. After Apple released its iPhone, Samsung released a series of smartphones that resembled the iPhone.

Apple sued Samsung in 2011, alleging, as relevant here, that various Samsung smartphones infringed Apple's D593,087, D618,677, and D604,305 design patents. A jury found that several Samsung smartphones did infringe those patents. All told, Apple was awarded $399 million in damages for Samsung's design patent infringement, the entire profit Samsung made from its sales of the infringing smartphones.

The Federal Circuit affirmed the design patent infringement damages award.[11] In doing so, it rejected Samsung's argument "that the profits

[11] Samsung raised a host of challenges on appeal related to other claims in the litigation between Apple and Samsung. The Federal Circuit affirmed in part—with respect to the design

awarded should have been limited to the infringing 'article of manufacture' "—for example, the screen or case of the smartphone—"not the entire infringing product"—the smartphone. 786 F.3d 983, 1002 (2015). It reasoned that "limit[ing] the damages" award was not required because the "innards of Samsung's smartphones were not sold separately from their shells as distinct articles of manufacture to ordinary purchasers." Ibid.

We granted certiorari, and now reverse and remand.

II

Section 289 allows a patent holder to recover the total profit an infringer makes from the infringement. It does so by first prohibiting the unlicensed "appli[cation]" of a "patented design, or any colorable imitation thereof, to any article of manufacture for the purpose of sale" or the unlicensed sale or exposure to sale of "any article of manufacture to which [a patented] design or colorable imitation has been applied." 35 U.S.C. § 289. It then makes a person who violates that prohibition "liable to the owner to the extent of his total profit, but not less than $250." Ibid. "Total," of course, means all. See American Heritage Dictionary 1836 (5th ed.2011) ("[t]he whole amount of something; the entirety"). The "total profit" for which § 289 makes an infringer liable is thus all of the profit made from the prohibited conduct, that is, from the manufacture or sale of the "article of manufacture to which [the patented] design or colorable imitation has been applied."

Arriving at a damages award under § 289 thus involves two steps. First, identify the "article of manufacture" to which the infringed design has been applied. Second, calculate the infringer's total profit made on that article of manufacture.

This case requires us to address a threshold matter: the scope of the term "article of manufacture." The only question we resolve today is whether, in the case of a multicomponent product, the relevant "article of manufacture" must always be the end product sold to the consumer or whether it can also be a component of that product. Under the former interpretation, a patent holder will always be entitled to the infringer's total profit from the end product. Under the latter interpretation, a patent holder will sometimes be entitled to the infringer's total profit from a component of the end product.[12]

patent infringement finding, the validity of two utility patent claims, and the design and utility patent infringement damages awards—and reversed and remanded in part—with respect to trade dress dilution. Only the design patent infringement award is at issue here.

[12] In its petition for certiorari and in its briefing, Samsung challenged the decision below on a second ground. It argued that 35 U.S.C. § 289 contains a causation requirement, which limits a § 289 damages award to the total profit the infringer made because of the infringement. Samsung abandoned this theory at argument, and so we do not address it.

A

The text resolves this case. The term "article of manufacture," as used in § 289, encompasses both a product sold to a consumer and a component of that product.

"Article of manufacture" has a broad meaning. An "article" is just "a particular thing." J. Stormonth, A Dictionary of the English Language 53 (1885) (Stormonth); see also American Heritage Dictionary, at 101 ("[a]n individual thing or element of a class; a particular object or item"). And "manufacture" means "the conversion of raw materials by the hand, or by machinery, into articles suitable for the use of man" and "the articles so made." Stormonth 589; see also American Heritage Dictionary, at 1070 ("[t]he act, craft, or process of manufacturing products, especially on a large scale" or "[a] product that is manufactured"). An article of manufacture, then, is simply a thing made by hand or machine.

So understood, the term "article of manufacture" is broad enough to encompass both a product sold to a consumer as well as a component of that product. A component of a product, no less than the product itself, is a thing made by hand or machine. That a component may be integrated into a larger product, in other words, does not put it outside the category of articles of manufacture.

This reading of article of manufacture in § 289 is consistent with 35 U.S.C. § 171(a), which makes "new, original and ornamental design[s] for an article of manufacture" eligible for design patent protection.[13] The Patent Office and the courts have understood § 171 to permit a design patent for a design extending to only a component of a multicomponent product. See, e.g., *Ex parte Adams*, 84 Off. Gaz. Pat. Office 311 (1898) ("The several articles of manufacture of peculiar shape which when combined produce a machine or structure having movable parts may each separately be patented as a design . . . "); *Application of Zahn*, 617 F.2d 261, 268 (CCPA 1980) ("Section 171 authorizes patents on ornamental designs for articles of manufacture. While the design must be embodied in some articles, the statute is not limited to designs for complete articles, or 'discrete' articles, and certainly not to articles separately sold . . . ").

This reading is also consistent with 35 U.S.C. § 101, which makes "any new and useful . . . manufacture . . . or any new and useful improvement thereof" eligible for utility patent protection. Cf. 8 D. Chisum, Patents § 23.03[2], pp. 23–12 to 23–13 (2014) (noting that "article of manufacture" in § 171 includes "what would be considered a 'manufacture' within the

[13] As originally enacted, the provision protected "any new and original design for a manufacture." § 3, 5 Stat. 544. The provision listed examples, including a design "worked into or worked on, or printed or painted or cast or otherwise fixed on, any article of manufacture" and a "shape or configuration of any article of manufacture." Ibid. A streamlined version enacted in 1902 protected "any new, original, and ornamental design for an article of manufacture." Ch. 783, 32 Stat. 193. The Patent Act of 1952 retained that language. See § 171, 66 Stat. 813.

meaning of Section 101"). "[T]his Court has read the term 'manufacture' in § 101 . . . to mean 'the production of articles for use from raw or prepared materials by giving to these materials new forms, qualities, properties, or combinations, whether by hand-labor or by machinery.'" *Diamond v. Chakrabarty*, 447 U.S. 303, 308, 100 S.Ct. 2204, 65 L.Ed.2d 144 (1980) (quoting *American Fruit Growers, Inc. v. Brogdex* Co., 283 U.S. 1, 11, 51 S.Ct. 328, 75 L.Ed. 801 (1931)). The broad term includes "the parts of a machine considered separately from the machine itself." 1 W. Robinson, The Law of Patents for Useful Inventions § 183, p. 270 (1890).

B

The Federal Circuit's narrower reading of "article of manufacture" cannot be squared with the text of § 289. The Federal Circuit found that components of the infringing smartphones could not be the relevant article of manufacture because consumers could not purchase those components separately from the smartphones. See 786 F.3d, at 1002 (declining to limit a § 289 award to a component of the smartphone because "[t]he innards of Samsung's smartphones were not sold separately from their shells as distinct articles of manufacture to ordinary purchasers"); *see also Nordock, Inc. v. Systems Inc.,* 803 F.3d 1344, 1355 (C.A.Fed.2015) (declining to limit a § 289 award to a design for a "'lip and hinge plate'" because it was "welded together" with a leveler and "there was no evidence" it was sold "separate[ly] from the leveler as a complete unit"). But, for the reasons given above, the term "article of manufacture" is broad enough to embrace both a product sold to a consumer and a component of that product, whether sold separately or not. Thus, reading "article of manufacture" in § 289 to cover only an end product sold to a consumer gives too narrow a meaning to the phrase.

The parties ask us to go further and resolve whether, for each of the design patents at issue here, the relevant article of manufacture is the smartphone, or a particular smartphone component. Doing so would require us to set out a test for identifying the relevant article of manufacture at the first step of the § 289 damages inquiry and to parse the record to apply that test in this case. The United States as amicus curiae suggested a test, see Brief for United States as Amicus Curiae 27–29, but Samsung and Apple did not brief the issue. We decline to lay out a test for the first step of the § 289 damages inquiry in the absence of adequate briefing by the parties. Doing so is not necessary to resolve the question presented in this case, and the Federal Circuit may address any remaining issues on remand.

III

The judgment of the United States Court of Appeals for the Federal Circuit is therefore reversed, and the case is remanded for further proceedings consistent with this opinion.

---

The Patent Act places special requirements on patent owners that produce products. More specifically, patent owners are required to mark their products with an identification of relevant patents. As previously mentioned, a patent owner need not manufacture products to have a valid design patent. However, if a patent owner elects to manufacture or sell products covered by the design patent, then it must satisfy the marking requirements in order to obtain damages.

The marking requirement is codified at 35 U.S.C. § 287. The penalty for a failure to appropriately mark products is a loss of damages. The *Nike Inc.* case below explains the marking requirement as it pertains to design patent damages, with an explanation of the history and policy rationales for the doctrine.

## NIKE INC. V. WAL-MART STORES, INC.

138 F.3d 1437 (Fed. Cir. 1998)

NEWMAN, CIRCUIT JUDGE. Wal-Mart Stores, Inc., and Hawe Yue, Inc. appeal the judgment of the United States District Court for the Eastern District of Virginia, concerning United States Design Patent No. 348,765 (the D'765 patent), owned by Nike, Inc. The court held the patent valid and infringed, and awarded the infringers' profits to the patentee in accordance with 35 U.S.C. § 289. The appellants do not appeal the rulings of validity and infringement, but raise issues of patent marking, notice, the measure of compensation, and accounting.

We reverse the district court's holding that the marking statute does not apply when remedy for infringement is obtained under 35 U.S.C. § 289, and remand for findings concerning Nike's compliance with the marking statute. The court's accounting methodology is affirmed.

The D'765 patent is for Nike's "Air Mada Mid" model athletic shoe design, illustrated as:

FIG. 1

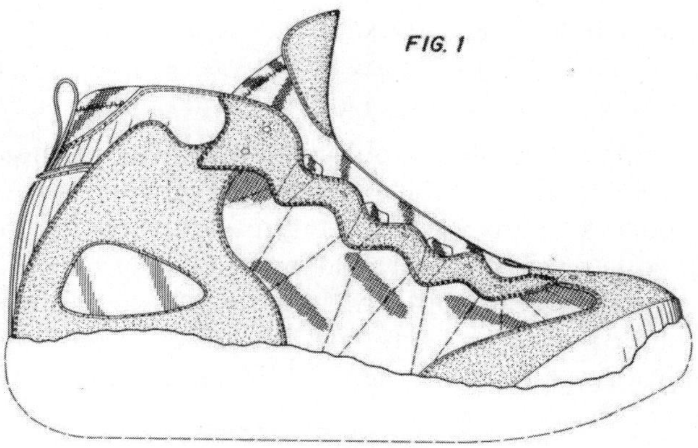

The D'765 patent was applied for on October 13, 1993, and issued on July 19, 1994 upon Nike's expedited prosecution. Nike introduced these shoes into the marketplace in April 1994. Significant numbers of shoes had already been manufactured and sold, or were already in the distribution chain, at the time of patent issuance; these shoes were unmarked with the patent number. Nike implemented marking procedures after patent issuance.

Hawe Yue imported copies of the Air Mada Mid design shoes starting in April 1995, and Wal-Mart's first retail sales were in May 1995. On January 18, 1996 Nike filed suit in the Eastern District of Virginia. The appellants' position is that the presence in the marketplace and the sale of unmarked shoes before and after Nike's asserted marking precludes Nike's recovery for any infringement that occurred before suit was filed, citing the marking statute, 35 U.S.C. § 287(a):

> Patentees . . . may give notice to the public that the same is patented, either by fixing thereon the word 'patent' or the abbreviation 'pat.', together with the number of the patent, or when, from the character of the article, this can not be done, by affixing to it, or to the package wherein one or more of them is contained, a label containing a like notice. In the event of a failure to so mark, no damages shall be recovered by the patentee in any action for infringement, except on proof that the infringer was notified of the infringement and continued to infringe thereafter, in which event damages may be recovered only for infringement occurring after such notice. Filing of an action for infringement shall constitute such notice.

The district court held that the marking statute applies when the requested remedy is "damages," *e.g.*, the remedy provided for in the general damages provision, 35 U.S.C. § 284:

> Upon finding for the claimant the court shall award the claimant damages adequate to compensate for the infringement, but in no event less than a reasonable royalty . . .

However, the court held that the marking statute does not apply to limit recovery of the infringer's profit, an alternate remedy for design patent infringement, codified at 35 U.S.C. § 289:

> Whoever during the term of a patent for a design, without license of the owner, (1) applies the patented design, or any colorable imitation thereof, to any article of manufacture for the purpose of sale, or (2) sells or exposes for sale any article of manufacture to which such design or colorable imitation has been applied shall be liable to the owner to the extent of his total profit, but not less than $250, recoverable in any United States district court having jurisdiction of the parties . . .

Holding that marking is not required by statute when recovery of the infringer's profit is sought under § 289, the district court awarded Nike the appellants' profits for all of the infringing sales. Wal-Mart and Hawe Yue appeal this ruling, contending that Nike's sale of unmarked shoes precludes any recovery for infringement . . . before suit was filed. Nike responds that the district court correctly held that § 287(a) does not apply. Nike states that its marking procedures complied with § 287(a).

## I. MARKING

The district court considered the provision in § 287(a) that "in the event of a failure to mark, no damages shall be recovered by the patentee in any action for infringement." The court held that the provision is unambiguous, and . . . the distinction between damages and profits requires that the marking statute with its limitation on "damages" does not apply to a recovery of the infringer's "profit" under § 289.

The appellants contend that "damages" is used in § 287(a) in its general and ordinary meaning of money recovered from a wrongdoer, however the recovery is measured. Nike responds that the historical distinction between profits and damages supports and indeed requires the district court's ruling. Nike proposes that since these statutory provisions are unambiguous no further inquiry is warranted.

We conclude that the term "damages" as it appears in the marking statute is not limited to the recovery at law but includes recovery measured by the infringer's profits, and continues to be so used although such recovery is now limited to design patent infringement. The statutory history establishes that the marking requirement has always applied, and continues to apply, to both recovery of the infringer's profit under § 289, and recovery of damages, however measured, under § 284.

### A. Damages and Profits

The equitable remedy of injunction in patent cases was authorized in 1819. By the Patent Act of 1836 a patentee could elect to proceed in equity and recover the infringer's profits, or to proceed in law and recover "as damages, compensation for the pecuniary injury he suffered by the infringement." However, the patentee was required to choose between these paths of recovery. As remedy, the Act of 1870 authorized the court in equity to award both the infringer's profits and compensatory damages . . . [T]he Court held that damages should be awarded only to the extent that "the injury sustained by the infringement is plainly greater than the aggregate of what was made by the [infringer]." *Birdsall*, 93 U.S. at 69.

As explained in W. Robinson, *The Law of Patents* § 1091 at 406 (1890), a plaintiff in equity could recover the infringer's profit and "damages also where [the plaintiff's] loss exceeded the defendant's profit." Thus the Act of 1870 provided for the recovery of damages in equity, but it did not allow for recovery of the infringer's profit as such in an action at law.

Because both the patentee's losses and the infringer's profits could be obtained in equity, whereas only the patentee's losses were recoverable at law, after 1870 a patentee had incentive to invoke equity jurisdiction even when injunctive relief was not important.

Referring to *Dobson*, Congress reported that: It now appears that the design patent laws provide no effectual money recovery for infringement. The Act of 1887 removed the apportionment requirement when recovery of the infringer's profit was sought:

> § 1. Hereafter, during the term of letters patent for a design, it shall be unlawful for any person other than the owner of said letters patent, without the license of such owner, to apply the design secured by such letters patent, or any colorable imitation thereof, to any article of manufacture for the purpose of sale, or to sell or expose for sale any article of manufacture to which such design or colorable imitation shall, without the license of the owner, have been applied, knowing that the same has been so applied. Any person violating the provisions, or either of them, of this section, shall be liable in the amount of two hundred and fifty dollars, he shall be further liable for the excess of such profit over and above [that sum, the full amount recoverable] either by action at law or upon a bill in equity for an injunction to restrain such infringement.
>
> § 2. That nothing in this Act contained shall prevent, lessen, impeach, or avoid any remedy at law or in equity which any owner of letters patent for a design, aggrieved by the infringement of the same might have had if this act had not been passed; but such owner shall not twice recover the profit made from the infringement.

Act of 1887, 24 Stat. 387. The Act of 1887 thus authorized recovery by the patentee of the infringer's profit when the infringer appropriated the patented design "knowing that the same has been so applied."

The difference for design patents in 1887 was the removal of the need to apportion the infringer's profits between the patented design and the article bearing the design. Although Nike argues that the 1946 Act should be read to have eliminated the marking requirement for design patents, the 1946 Act does not mention design patents and does not mention marking . . .

The statutory record shows the origins in law and equity of remedy for patent infringement, initially and until 1887 without distinction between utility and design patents. The additional remedy created in 1887 for design patents was enacted to overcome the allocation problem for designs, and did not deplete the remedies available for either utility or design patent infringement. Further, the general damages statutes, which authorized recovery of the infringer's profits as well as the patentee's losses, continued in effect for both utility and design patents.

B. The Marking Statutes

The marking statute serves three related purposes: 1) helping to avoid innocent infringement; 2) encouraging patentees to give notice to the public that the article is patented; and 3) aiding the public to identify whether an article is patented.

The early patent statutes contained no marking requirement. A duty to mark was imposed by the Patent Act of 1842, which required "all patentees and assignees of patents to stamp on each article vended, or offered for sale, the date of the patent." Act of 1842, 5 Stat. 543, 544. If the patentee failed to mark each article, the penalty was a fine of "not less than one hundred dollars." In 1861 the statute was amended to place a limitation on the patentee's right to recover for infringement. The Patent Act of 1861, 12 Stat. 246, 249, provided that "no damage shall be recovered by the plaintiff" unless that person marked the article as patented or the infringer received actual notice of the patent.

The marking provision has not been substantially changed since 1861. The 1952 Act, 35 U.S.C. § 287(a), provides that "in the event of failure so to mark, no damages shall be recovered by the patentee in any action for infringement." These provisions remained constant through the various changes in remedy for patent infringement . . .

In cases decided around the time of enactment of the 1861 marking statute, the Supreme Court and other courts used the word "damage" or "damages" to encompass the patentee's monetary recovery whether it was derived from the infringer's profits or the patentee's losses.

In 1922 the Eighth Circuit conducted an exhaustive review of Supreme Court and lower court case law, and concluded: The great weight of authority is that the term 'damages' in section 4900 is used in its general sense and includes profits as a measure of damages.

We concur in the analysis that the courts have not distinguished between remedies in requiring either actual or constructive notice, whether the proposed remedy is the infringer's profits or the patentee's losses. Precedent and the marking statutes have used the term "damages" to encompass both sources of recovery.

The conclusion that the marking statute with its use of the word "damages" applies broadly to include recovery of the infringer's profits is strongly reinforced by concern about notice for design patent infringement. The Act of 1887 was accompanied by assurances that the infringer would not be liable if he did not know that the design was patented. The statute imposed liability only upon a person who acts "knowing that the [design] has been so applied" without authority.

With such steady emphasis on knowledge of or notice of the patent, as a matter of fairness, we doubt that both actual and constructive notice were silently abandoned as applied to § 289 and design patents. Although in the 1952 codification the phrase "knowing that the same has been so applied" was omitted in writing § 289, that omission is explicable only on the ground of redundancy with the marking statute codified at § 287.

Nike stresses this court's decision in *Braun*, wherein the court held that the provision for enhancement of "damages" of § 284 does not authorize enhancement of profits recovered under § 289. However, the decision was based not on drawing a rigorous distinction between "damages" and "profits," but on the provision of § 289 that bars the design patentee, upon recovering the infringer's profits, from "twice recovering the profit made from the infringement." Nike argues that a ruling that § 287(a) controls a recovery under § 289 would give the term "damages" different meanings. Nike points to the anomaly if the "damages" provision of § 287(a) is held to embrace profits and thus to require marking for recovery under § 289, while the treble "damages" provision of § 284 under *Braun* does not apply to recovery of profits under § 289. We agree that the result is anomalous. However, *Braun* relates to multiplied recovery, not to notice, and is distinguishable.

Although there is a natural presumption that identical words used in different parts of the same act are intended to have the same meaning, "it is not unusual for the same word to be used with different meanings in the same act, and there is no rule of statutory construction which precludes the courts from giving to the word the meaning which the Legislature intended it should have in each instance."

Should this court now limit the word "damages" in the marking statute to a compensatory recovery at law, we negate the purpose of the marking statute, *i.e.*, to give notice and thus to prevent innocent infringement. Indeed, a general principle of the common law is that although there may be liability without actual or constructive notice of adverse rights, damages therefor are rarely greater than nominal. Statute and precedent have shown concern for the principles of fairness that underlie this principle.

Upon review of statute, legislative history, policy, and precedent, we conclude that the marking requirement, § 287(a), applies to design patents whether remedy for infringement is sought under § 284 or § 289.

* * *

### *NOTES AND QUESTIONS*

1. Neither copyright law nor trademark law requires marking to recover damages for infringement, as the following chapters discuss. Should marking be required in these other areas of intellectual property?

2. Are the athletic shoes at issue in *Nike* single-component products or multiple component products? How should damages for the athletic shoes be determined under *Apple v. Samsung?*

---

In general, patent owners in certain circumstances are permitted to recover enhanced damages. Enhanced damages permit the court to increase the actual damages by up to three times. 35 U.S.C. § 284. The U.S. Supreme Court recently chimed in on when enhanced damages are available, overruling a line of Federal Circuit precedent. In *Halo Electronics, Inc. v. Pulse Electronics, Inc.*, 579 U.S. ___ (2016), the Supreme Court held that enhanced damages were available if the infringement represented an egregious case typified by willful infringement. While the Patent Act does not distinguish design patents from utility patents for enhanced damages, the courts have.

## BRAUN INC. V. DYNAMICS CORPORATION OF AMERICA

975 F.2d 815 (Fed. Cir. 1992)

COHN, DISTRICT JUDGE (sitting by designation). Plaintiffs/cross-appellants, Braun, Inc., and Braun Aktiengesellschaft (Braun), are the owners of U.S. design patent No. 271,176, which relates to a hand held electric blender. Defendant-appellant, Dynamics Corporation of America's Waring Products Division (Waring), manufactures a competing hand held electric blender. On February 1, 1988, Braun sued Waring in the United States District Court for the District of Connecticut, alleging: (1) design patent infringement, 35 U.S.C. § 271, (2) false designation of origin, including trade dress infringement, pursuant to section 43(a) of the Lanham Act, 15 U.S.C. § 1125(a), and (3) unfair competition and passing off under Connecticut common law and statutory law.

There are two separate reasons why the district court erred in awarding Braun three times Waring's total profit. First, the district court's award of treble damages was based on the jury's erroneous determination that Waring willfully infringed Braun's design patent. Whether infringement is willful is a question of fact, and the jury's determination as to willfulness is therefore reviewable under the substantial evidence standard.

We must determine whether there is substantial evidence, when viewed as a whole, upon which a jury could determine under the clear and convincing evidence standard that Waring willfully infringed Braun's patent. We find insufficient evidence upon which the jury could rely.

Assuming *arguendo* that there is substantial evidence that Waring willfully infringed Braun's design, the district court nevertheless erroneously awarded Braun three times Waring's total profit. Braun elected to recover Waring's total profits under 35 USC § 289, not 35 USC § 284, which provides that a patentee may recover "damages adequate to compensate for the infringement" which "the court may increase . . . up to three times." Nothing in 35 USC § 289 authorizes an increase in a patentee's total profit. In fact, 35 USC § 289 explicitly precludes a patentee from "twice recover[ing] the profits made from the infringement." *See Bergstrom v. Sears, Roebuck and Co.* ("the purpose of this latter phrase is to insure that a patentee not recover both the profit of an infringer and some additional damage remedy from the same infringer, such as reasonable royalty"). As a result, by trebling Waring's total profit, the district court clearly exceeded its statutory authority.

In trebling Waring's total profits, the district court reasoned: (1) there is little substantive difference between damages under 35 USC § 284 and profits under § 289, and (2) as a result, it may increase profits as well as damages. This analysis ignores the longstanding distinction in patent law between damages and profits. Recovery of compensatory damages for infringement evolved in courts of law and could be increased, but recovery of an infringer's profits evolved in courts of equity and could not be increased. *See generally* D. Chisum, *Patents* (drew a "sharp cleavage" between profits and damages). Although a utility patentee could recover an infringer's profit prior to 1946, just as a design patentee may do so today, courts uniformly held that the infringer's profit could not be increased. The Supreme Court further distinguished damages from profits by holding that only damages were recoverable under 35 USC § 284.

### *NOTES AND QUESTIONS*

1. Does it make sense for a design patent owner to be able to obtain all profits made from an infringing device, even if the device contains numerous other design and functional features not covered by the design patent. Many scholars argue that it makes no sense from a policy perspective. See Mark A. Lemley, *A Rational System of Design Patent Remedies,* 17 STAN. TECH. L. REV. 219 (2013). The Supreme Court did not directly answer this question in *Apple v. Samsung*, instead focusing on the definition of "article of manufacture."

2. The original language from Section 289 was adopted in 1887. That statute, which was rewritten unchanged in the 1952 Patent Act, overturned two Supreme Court cases from 1885 and 1886. The Supreme Court had ruled that design patent owners were entitled to damages of merely six cents for infringement. The infringers had argued that the infringing articles of manufacture, carpets, were purchased due to the "intrinsic merits of quality and structure" of the carpet, not the design. Accordingly, the Supreme Court ruled that the adjudicated damages should be apportioned and that (essentially) none of the damages were due to design patent infringement. Congress overturned these cases and chose to disgorge profits in cases of design patent infringement. For a detailed read of the history of these events, see Jason J. DuMont & Mark D. Janus, *Brief of Amicus Curiae by James J.*

*DuMont and Mark D. Janus in Support of Appellee Apple Inc.* (available at http://papers.ssrn.com/sol3/papers.cfm?abstract_id=2511893).

Injunctions are also available in design patent cases. Like injunctions in utility patent infringement cases, injunctions are awarded based upon four equitable factors: (1) whether the patent owner has suffered an irreparable injury; (2) that remedies available at law are inadequate to compensate for the infringement; (3) that considering the balancing of the hardships between the plaintiff and the defendant, a remedy in equity is warranted; and (4) that the public interest would not be disserved by a permanent injunction. *eBay Inc. v. MercExchange, L.L.C.,* 547 U.S. 388 (2006).

# CHAPTER 3

# TRADEMARK LAW

■ ■ ■



---

A trademark is "any word, name, symbol, or device, or any combination thereof" that is used by a party "to identify and distinguish his or her goods, including a unique product, from those manufactured or sold by others and to indicate the source of the goods, even if that source is unknown." 15 U.S.C. § 1127. Though words and logos are prototypical trademarks, the statutory language describes the universe of protectable trademarks in the broadest of terms. Indeed, as the Supreme Court has said, "[s]ince human beings might use as a 'symbol' or 'device' almost anything at all that is capable of carrying meaning, this language, read literally, is not restrictive." *Qualitex Co. v. Jacobson Prods. Co., Inc.*, 514 U.S. 159, 162 (1995). Thus, courts and the Trademark Office have recognized as valid trademarks a wide range of subject matter including colors, sounds, and even scents. Significantly for our purposes here, they have also recognized "trade dress"—"a category that originally included only the packaging, or 'dressing,' of a product, but in recent years has been expanded . . . to encompass the design of a product." *Wal-Mart Store, Inc. v. Samara Bros., Inc.*, 529 U.S. 205, 209 (2000). Like any trademark, trade dress must be distinctive of the *source* of the product or service in order to receive protection. It also must not be functional.

This chapter focuses on the particular challenges that arise when parties attempt to use trademark law to protect design. In reading this chapter, consider how trade dress protection is different from design patent protection—does one form of protection offer any advantages over the other?

## A. HISTORICAL DEVELOPMENT OF UNFAIR COMPETITION

In order to understand the evolution of trademark law to encompass protection for product design, we must first study the historical development of common law unfair competition. Many decades before Congress passed the Lanham Act in 1946, courts wrestled with the basic question of whether they should prohibit copying of unpatented designs, or if instead they should limit relief to accompanying labels or other disclosures.

### 1. TRADITIONAL UNFAIR COMPETITION

As we noted above, the Lanham Act defines a trademark as "any word, name, symbol, or device, or any combination thereof" that is used by a party to indicate the source of its goods and to identify and distinguish those goods from goods manufactured or sold by others. 15 U.S.C. § 1127. Modern interpretation of that definition includes within trademark law much more than it once did. Trademark law traditionally focused on words or symbols that unequivocally indicated the commercial origin of a party's goods. These "technical trademarks" could be federally registered, and federal law provided a cause of action for their protection. Other kinds of terms that were susceptible of multiple meanings—terms that described the goods or identified their geographic origin, for example—could not be registered (because they were not technically trademarks), and they were therefore not enforceable under federal law. But parties could sometimes get relief against others that used similar terms or devices under the common law of unfair competition.

Trademark law was typically conceived of as part of this broader law of unfair competition in the sense that all of unfair competition law aimed to prevent sellers from passing off their goods as those of another. Use of a competitor's technical trademark was a particularly clear form of unfair competition; hence, the owners of technical trademarks needed only to prove that another party used the same or a similar mark for directly competing goods. But parties could sometimes pass their goods off without using a competitor's trademark, and unfair competition law provided a remedy in those cases. Since cases not involving technical trademarks by definition involved more ambiguous designators, however, unfair competition claimants had to prove intent to pass off and the remedies available typically were more limited.

One way a party might have attempted to pass off its goods as those of a competitor without using that competitor's technical trademark was by designing the product or its packaging in the same way. As the initial cases in this chapter suggest, courts were often conflicted about those claims insofar as they sought control over the design of products themselves, as opposed to their labeling. In reading these cases, try to identify the conflicting policy interests the courts attempted to balance.

## FLAGG MFG. CO. V. HOLWAY

178 Mass. 83 (1901)

HOLMES, C. J. This is a bill brought to restrain the defendant from selling zithers which imitate the plaintiff's, or with strings arranged and spaced as the plaintiff's strings are arranged and spaced, and specifically to restrain it from selling a particular form of zither heretofore sold by it and exhibited by the bill. The case was sent to a master, who reported what is manifest on inspection, when the time of the respective manufactures is known, that the defendant deliberately copied the plaintiff's instrument in all essential and many nonessential details, adding that this was done for a wrongful purpose. The Superior Court made a decree for the plaintiff, in terms almost as broad as the prayers of the bill, and the defendant appealed.

We are of opinion that the decree was wrong in principle. Both zithers are adapted for the use of patented sheets of music, but the zithers are not patented. Under such circumstances the defendant has the same right that the plaintiff has to manufacture instruments in the present form, to imitate the arrangement of the plaintiff's strings or the shape of the body. In the absence of a patent the freedom of manufacture cannot be cut down under the name of preventing unfair competition. *Stamping Co. v. Fellows*, 163 Mass. 191, 40 N. E. 105. *See Singer Mfg. Co. v. June Mfg. Co.*, 163 U.S. 169. All that can be asked is that precautions shall be taken, so far as are consistent with the defendant's fundamental right to make and sell what it chooses, to prevent the deception which no doubt it desires to practice.

It is true that a defendant's freedom of action with regard to some subsidiary matter of ornament or label may be restrained, although a right of the same nature with its freedom to determine the shape of the articles which it sells. But the label or ornament is a relatively small and incidental affair, which would not exist at all, or at least would not exist in that shape but for the intent to deceive; whereas the instrument sold is made as it is, partly at least, because of a supposed or established desire of the public for instruments in that form. The defendant has the right to get the benefit of that desire even if created by the plaintiff. The only thing it has not the right to steal is the good will attaching to the plaintiff's personality, the benefit of the public's desire to have goods made by the plaintiff. Probably if there were an absolute conflict between the defendant's right as we have stated it and that of the plaintiff's, the defendant's would prevail. *American Waltham Watch Co. v. United States Watch Co.*, 173 Mass. 85, 86, 87. But the plaintiff's right can be protected sufficiently by requiring the defendant's zithers to be clearly marked so as to indicate unmistakably that they are the defendant's and not the plaintiff's goods. This is the relief which the master found to be proper, and we are of opinion that he was right. To go further is to save the plaintiff from a competition from which it has no right to be exempt. Decree reversed.

## CRESCENT TOOL CO. V. KILBORN & BISHOP CO.

247 F. 299 (2d Cir. 1917)

LEARNED HAND, DISTRICT JUDGE. The cases of so-called 'nonfunctional' unfair competition, starting with the 'coffee mill case,' *Enterprise Mfg. Co. v. Landers, Frary & Clark*, 131 Fed. 240, are only instances of the doctrine of 'secondary' meaning. All of them presuppose that the appearance of the article, like its descriptive title in true cases of 'secondary' meaning, has become associated in the public mind with the first comer as manufacturer or source, and, if a second comer imitates the article exactly, that the public will believe his goods have come from the first, and will buy, in part, at least, because of that deception. Therefore it is apparent that it is an absolute condition to any relief whatever that the plaintiff in such cases show that the appearance of his wares has in fact come to mean that some particular person—the plaintiff may not be individually known—makes them, and that the public cares who does make them, and not merely for their appearance and structure. It will not be enough only to show how pleasing they are, because all the features of beauty or utility which commend them to the public are by hypothesis already in the public domain. The defendant has as much right to copy the 'nonfunctional' features of the article as any others, so long as they have not become associated with the plaintiff as manufacturer or source. The critical question of fact at the outset always is whether the public is moved in any degree to buy the article because of its source and what are the features by which it distinguishes that source. Unless the plaintiff can answer this question he can take no step forward; no degree of imitation of details is actionable in its absence.

In the case at bar it nowhere appears that before 1910, when the defendant began to make its wrenches, the general appearance of the plaintiff's wrench had come to indicate to the public any one maker as its source, or that the wrench had been sold in any part because of its source, as distinct from its utility or neat appearance. It is not enough to show that the wrench became popular under the name 'Crescent'; the plaintiff must prove that before 1910 the public had already established the habit of buying it, not solely because they wanted that kind of wrench, but because they also wanted a Crescent, and thought all such wrenches were Crescents.

Upon the trial the plaintiff may, however, be able to establish this, and it is only fair to indicate broadly the considerations which will then determine the scope of his relief. In such cases neither side has an absolute right, because their mutual rights conflict. Thus the plaintiff has the right not to lose his customers through false representations that those are his wares which in fact are not, but he may not monopolize any design or pattern, however trifling. The defendant, on the other hand, may copy the plaintiff's goods slavishly down to the minutest detail; but he may not represent himself as the plaintiff in their sale. When the appearance of the goods has in fact come to represent a given person as their source, and that person is in fact the plaintiff, it is impossible to make these rights absolute; compromise is essential, exactly as it is with the right to use the common language in cases of 'secondary' meaning. We can only say that the court must require such changes in appearance as will effectively distinguish the defendant's wares with the least expense to him; in no event may the plaintiff suppress the defendant's sale altogether. The proper meaning of the phrase 'nonfunctional,' is only this: That in such cases the injunction is usually confined to nonessential elements, since these are usually enough to distinguish the goods, and are the least burdensome for the defendant to change. Whether changes in them are in all conceivable cases the limit of the plaintiff's right is a matter not before us. If a case should arise in which no effective distinction was possible without change in functional elements, it would demand consideration; but the District Court may well find an escape here from that predicament. Certainly the precise extent and kind of relief must in the first instance be a matter for the discretion of that court. Order reversed, and motion denied.

### *NOTES AND QUESTIONS*

1. These cases reflect courts' attempts to balance concerns about passing off with the general presumption that others have a right to copy unpatented designs. What concerns animate courts in striking that balance? Do these cases balance the parties' interests in the same way?

2. Why would courts emphasize that the designs at issue in these cases were unpatented? Is it because parties should only be able to get protection for designs using patent law (a sort of conflict preemption)? Is it that the defendants in these cases copied particular sorts of features that we associate with patent law because those features relate to the product's function? Is it that the features they copied were particularly important to effective competition? To what extent are this distinct questions?

3. What is Chief Justice Holmes's solution to any possible confusion that might be caused by the similarity of the zithers? Do you think the solution is adequate?

## KELLOGG CO. V. NATIONAL BISCUIT CO.

305 U.S. 674 (1938)

JUSTICE BRANDEIS. This suit was brought in the federal court for Delaware by National Biscuit Company against Kellogg Company to enjoin alleged unfair competition by the manufacture and sale of the breakfast food commonly known as shredded wheat. The competition was alleged to be unfair mainly because Kellogg Company uses, like the plaintiff, the name shredded wheat and, like the plaintiff, produces its biscuit in pillow-shaped form.

Shredded wheat is a product composed of whole wheat which has been boiled, partially dried, then drawn or pressed out into thin shreds and baked. The shredded wheat biscuit generally known is pillow-shaped in form. It was introduced in 1893 by Henry D. Perky, of Colorado; and he was connected until his death in 1908 with companies formed to make and market the article. Commercial success was not attained until the Natural Food Company built, in 1901, a large factory at Niagara Falls, New York. In 1908, its corporate name was changed to 'The Shredded Wheat Company'; and in 1930 its business and goodwill were acquired by National Biscuit Company.

Kellogg Company has been in the business of manufacturing breakfast food cereals since its organization in 1905. For a period commencing in 1912 and ending in 1919 it made a product whose form was somewhat like the product in question, but whose manufacture was different, the wheat being reduced to a dough before being pressed into shreds. For a short period in 1922 it manufactured the article in question. In 1927, it resumed manufacturing the product. In 1928, the plaintiff sued for alleged unfair competition two dealers in Kellogg shredded wheat biscuits. That suit was discontinued by stipulation in 1930. On June 11, 1932, the present suit was brought. Much evidence was introduced; but the determinative facts are relatively few; and as to most of these there is no conflict.

In 1935, the District Court dismissed the bill. It found that the name 'Shredded Wheat' is a term describing alike the product of the plaintiff and of the defendant; and that no passing off or deception had been shown. It held that upon the expiration of the Perky patent No. 548,086 issued October 15, 1895, the name of the patented article passed into the public domain. In 1936, the Circuit Court of Appeals affirmed that decree. Upon rehearing, it vacated, in 1937, its own decree and reversed that of the District Court, with direction 'to enter a decree enjoining the defendant from the use of the name 'Shredded Wheat' as its trade-name and from advertising or offering for sale its product in the form and shape of plaintiff's biscuit in violation of its trade-mark; and with further directions to order an accounting for damages and profits.' In its opinion the court described the trade-mark as 'consisting of a dish, containing two biscuits submerged in milk'. We denied Kellogg Company's petition for a writ of certiorari, and denied rehearing.

On January 5, 1938, the District Court entered its mandate in the exact language of the order of the Circuit Court of Appeals, and issued a permanent injunction. Shortly thereafter National Biscuit Company petitioned the Circuit Court of Appeals to recall its mandate 'for purposes of clarification.' It alleged that Kellogg Company was insisting, contrary to the court's intention, that the effect to the mandate and writ of injunction was to forbid it from selling its product only when the trade name 'Shredded Wheat' is applied to a biscuit in the form and shape of the plaintiff's biscuit and is accompanied by a representation of a dish with biscuits in in; and that it was not enjoined from making its biscuit in the form and shape of the plaintiff's biscuit, nor from calling it 'Shredded Wheat,' unless at the same time it uses upon its cartons plaintiff's trade-mark consisting of a dish with two biscuits in it. On May 5, 1938, the Circuit Court of Appeals granted the petition for clarification and directed the District Court to enter a decree enjoining Kellogg:

> '(1) from the use of the name 'Shredded Wheat' as its trade name, (2) from advertising or offering for sale its product in the form and shape of plaintiff's biscuit, and (3) from doing either.'

Kellogg Company then filed a petition for a writ of certiorari to review the decree as so clarified, and also sought reconsideration of our denial of its petition for certiorari to review the decree as entered in its original form.

The plaintiff concedes that it does not possess the exclusive right to make shredded wheat. But it claims the exclusive right to the trade name 'Shredded Wheat' and the exclusive right to make shredded wheat biscuits pillow-shaped. It charges that the defendant, by using the name and shape, and otherwise, is passing off, or enabling others to pass off, Kellogg goods for those of the plaintiff. Kellogg Company denies that the plaintiff is entitled to the exclusive use of the name or of the pillow-shape; denies any passing off; asserts that it has used every reasonable effort to distinguish its produce from that of the plaintiff; and contends that in honestly competing for a part of the market for shredded wheat it is exercising the common right freely to manufacturer and sell an article of commerce unprotected by patent.

First. The plaintiff has no exclusive right to the use of the term 'Shredded Wheat' as a trade name. For that is the generic term of the article, which describes it with a fair degree of accuracy; and is the term by which the biscuit in pillow-shaped form is generally known by the public. Since the term is generic, the original maker of the product acquired no exclusive right to use it. As Kellogg Company had the right to make the article, it had, also, the right to use the term by which the public knows it. Ever since 1894 the article has been known to the public as shredded wheat. For many years, there was no attempt to use the term 'Shredded

Wheat' as a trade-mark. When in 1905 plaintiff's predecessor, Natural Food Company, applied for registration of the words 'Shredded Whole Wheat' as a trade-mark under the so-called 'ten year clause' of the Act of February 20, 1905, William E. Williams gave notice of opposition. Upon the hearing it appeared that Williams had, as early as 1894, built a machine for making shredded wheat, and that he made and sold its product as 'Shredded Whole Wheat'. The Commissioner of Patents refused registration. The Court of Appeals of the District of Columbia affirmed his decision, holding that 'these words accurately and aptly describe an article of food which * * * has been produced for more than ten years * * * .'

Moreover, the name 'Shredded Wheat', as well as the product, the process and the machinery employed in making it, has been dedicated to the public. The basic patent for the product and for the process of making it, and many other patents for special machinery to be used in making the article, issued to Perky. In those patents the term 'shredded' is repeatedly used as descriptive of the product. The basic patent expired October 15, 1912; the others soon after. Since during the life of the patents 'Shredded Wheat' was the general designation of the patented product, there passed to the public upon the expiration of the patent, not only the right to make the article as it was made during the patent period, but also the right to apply thereto the name by which it had become known. As was said in *Singer Mfg. Co. v. June Mfg. Co.*, 163 U.S. 169:

> 'It equally follows from the cessation of the monopoly and the falling of the patented device into the domain of things public that along with the public ownership of the device there must also necessarily pass to the public the generic designation of the thing which has arisen during the monopoly.
>
> 'To say otherwise would be to hold that, although the public had acquired the device covered by the patent, yet the owner of the patent or the manufacturer of the patented thing had retained the designated name which was essentially necessary to vest the public with the full enjoyment of that which had become theirs by the disappearance of the monopoly.'

It is contended that the plaintiff has the exclusive right to the name 'Shredded Wheat', because those words acquired the 'secondary meaning' of shredded wheat made at Niagara Falls by the plaintiff's predecessor. There is no basis here for applying the doctrine of secondary meaning. The evidence shows only that due to the long period in which the plaintiff or its predecessor was the only manufacturer of the product, many people have come to associate the product, and as a consequence the name by which the product is generally known, with the plaintiff's factory at Niagara Falls. But to establish a trade name in the term 'shredded wheat' the plaintiff must show more than a subordinate meaning which applies to it. It must show that the primary significance of the term in the minds of the consuming public is not the product but the producer. This it has not done. The showing which it has made does not entitle it to the exclusive use of the term shredded wheat but merely entitles it to require that the defendant use reasonable care to inform the public of the source of its product.

The plaintiff seems to contend that even if Kellogg Company acquired upon the expiration of the patents the right to use the name shredded wheat, the right was lost by delay. The argument is that Kellogg Company, although the largest producer of breakfast cereals in the country, did not seriously attempt to make shredded wheat, or to challenge plaintiff's right to that name until 1927, and that meanwhile plaintiff's predecessor had expended more than $17,000,000 in making the name a household word and identifying the product with its manufacture. Those facts are without legal significance. Kellogg Company's right was not one dependent upon diligent exercise. Like every other member of the public, it was, and remained, free to make shredded wheat when it chose to do so; and to call the product by its generic name. The only obligation resting upon Kellogg Company was to identify its own product lest it be mistaken for that of the plaintiff.

Second. The plaintiff has not the exclusive right to sell shredded wheat in the form of a pillow-shaped biscuit—the form in which the article became known to the public. That is the form in which shredded wheat was made under the basic patent. The patented machines used were designed to produce only the pillow-shaped biscuits. And a design patent was taken out to cover the pillow-shaped form.[4] Hence, upon expiration of the patents the form, as well as the name, was dedicated to the public. As was said in *Singer Mfg. Co. v. June Mfg. Co.*: 'It is self-evident that on the expiration of a patent the monopoly granted by it ceases to exist, and the right to make the thing formerly covered by the patent becomes public property. It is upon this condition that the patent is granted. It follows, as a matter of course, that on the termination of the patent there passes to the public the right to make the machine in the form in which it was constructed during the patent. We may therefore dismiss without further comment the complaint as to the form in which the defendant made his machines.'

Where an article may be manufactured by all, a particular manufacturer can no more assert exclusive rights in a form in which the public has become accustomed to see the article and which, in the minds of the public, is primarily associated with the article rather than a particular producer, than it can in the case of a name with similar connections in the public mind. Kellogg Company was free to use the pillow-shaped form,

[4] The design patent would have expired by limitations in 1909. In 1908 it was declared invalid by a district judge on the ground that the design had been in public use for more than two years prior to the application for the patent and theretofore had already been dedicated to the public.

subject only to the obligation to identify its product lest it be mistaken for that of the plaintiff.

Third. The question remains whether Kellogg Company in exercising its right to use the name 'Shredded Wheat' and the pillow-shaped biscuit, is doing so fairly. Fairness requires that it be done in a manner which reasonably distinguishes its product from that of plaintiff.

Each company sells its biscuits only in cartons. The standard Kellogg carton contains fifteen biscuits; the plaintiff's twelve. The Kellogg cartons are distinctive. They do not resemble those used by the plaintiff either in size, form, or color. And the difference in the labels is striking. The Kellogg cartons bear in bold script the names 'Kellogg's Whole Wheat Biscuit' or 'Kellogg's Shredded Whole Wheat Biscuit' so sized and spaced as to strike the eye as being a Kellogg product. It is true that on some of its cartons it had a picture of two shredded wheat biscuits in a bowl of milk which was quite similar to one of the plaintiff's registered trade-marks. But the name Kellogg was so prominent on all of the defendant's cartons as to minimize the possibility of confusion.

Some hotels, restaurants, and lunchrooms serve biscuits not in cartons, and guests so served may conceivably suppose that a Kellogg biscuit served is one of the plaintiff's make. But no person familiar with plaintiff's product would be misled. The Kellogg biscuit is about two-thirds the size of plaintiff's; and differs from it in appearance. Moreover, the field in which deception could be practiced is negligibly small. Only 2 ½ per cent of the Kellogg biscuits are sold to hotels, restaurants and lunchrooms. Of those so sold 98 per cent are sold in individual cartons containing two biscuits. These cartons are distinctive and bear prominently the Kellogg name. To put upon the individual biscuit some mark which would identify it as the Kellogg product is not commercially possible. Relatively few biscuits will be removed from the individual cartons before they reach the consumer. The obligation resting upon Kellogg Company is not to insure that every purchaser will know it to be the maker but to use every reasonable means to prevent confusion.

It is urged that all possibility of deception or confusion would be removed if Kellogg Company should refrain from using the name 'Shredded Wheat' and adopt some form other than the pillow-shape. But the name and form are integral parts of the goodwill of the article. To share fully in the goodwill, it must use the name and the pillow-shape. And in the goodwill Kellogg Company is as free to share as the plaintiff. Moreover, the pillow-shape must be used for another reason. The evidence is persuasive that this form is functional—that the cost of the biscuit would be increased and its high quality lessened if some other form were substituted for the pillow-shape.

Kellogg Company is undoubtedly sharing in the goodwill of the article known as 'Shredded Wheat'; and thus is sharing in a market which was created by the skill and judgment of plaintiff's predecessor and has been widely extended by vast expenditures in advertising persistently made. But that is not unfair. Sharing in the goodwill of an article unprotected by patent or trade-mark is the exercise of a right possessed by all—and in the free exercise of which the consuming public is deeply interested. There is no evidence of passing off or deception on the part of the Kellogg Company;[5] and it has taken every reasonable precaution to prevent confusion or the practice of deception in the sale of its product.

Fourth. By its 'clarifying' decree, the Circuit Court of Appeals enjoined Kellogg Company from using the picture of the two shredded wheat biscuits in the bowl only in connection with an injunction against manufacturing the pillow-shaped biscuits and the use of the term shredded wheat, on the grounds of unfair competition.[6] The use of this picture was not enjoined on the independent ground of trade-mark infringement. Since the National Biscuit Company did not petition for certiorari, the question whether use of the picture is a violation of that trade-mark although Kellogg Company is free to use the name and the pillow-shaped biscuit is not here for review.

Mr. Justice McREYNOLDS and Mr. Justice BUTLER are of opinion that the decree of the Circuit Court of Appeals is correct and should be affirmed. To them it seems sufficiently clear that the Kellogg Company is fraudulently seeking to appropriate to itself the benefits of a goodwill built up at great cost by the respondent and its predecessors.

## *NOTES AND QUESTIONS*

1. Was the concern in *Kellogg* regarding the shape of the shredded wheat biscuits that National Biscuit Company was trying to enforce rights in the shape of a product that had already received patent protection? That only patent law can provide protection for designs (such that unpatented designs simply should not receive any form of legal protection)? That this particular design could not be protected because it was the result of a comparatively cheap or effective method of manufacture?

---

5 Attention is called to the fact that the label on these Kellogg cartons bears, in small letters, the words: 'The original has this (W. K. Kellogg's) signature.' Objection to their use was not charged in the bill; no such issue was raised at the trial; and the use was not enjoined. Counsel for the Company admitted in the argument before us that its use, common as applied to other Kellogg products, should not have been made on cartons of shredded wheat; and stated that the use had been discontinued long before entry of the 'clarifying' decree.

6 In its opinion clarifying the mandate, the Circuit Court of Appeals, after considering the provisions concerning the name and the form of the biscuit, said: 'The only remaining question is whether, in view of the fact that the order of April 12, 1937, did not specifically provide for an injunction against the violation of the two-biscuit-in-a-dish trade-mark (although it was intended to do so) we have any jurisdiction to amend the mandate so as to include specifically such a provision. As there may be some doubt on this question, we will not amend the mandate so as to provide a specific injunction against the use of the two-biscuit-in-a-dish trade-mark. Its use on a carton or in advertising matter, when the defendant is not permitted to use the word 'Shredded Wheat' as a trade-name or to advertise or sell biscuits in the pillow-shaped form, would manifestly be so improper and so likely to mislead that we will assume that the appellee will not use it.'

2. The Court in *Kellogg* fairly emphatically rejected the idea that National Biscuit Company could prevent Kellogg from making biscuits in the same basic shape. At the same time, the Court contemplated that there could be liability if, in selling biscuits of the same shape, Kellogg tried to pass of its cereal as though it were National Biscuit Company's. Though it rejected the idea that the use of the words "shredded wheat" could constitute passing off, the Court suggested that a court could enjoin misleading labeling or packaging such as the "two biscuits in a bowl" picture on the cartons. That distinction between relief relating to copying of the product itself and relief relating to labeling or packaging resonates with the court's statement in *Flagg Mfg.* that relief should be focused on "a defendant's freedom of action with regard to some subsidiary matter of ornament or label." Does that form of relief strike an appropriate balance?

3. When a the relevant consuming public understands a claimed term to signify the type of product or service rather than its source, that term is deemed generic and therefore unprotectable. Genericism is concept typically associated with word marks, such as "shredded wheat." Would it be helpful to apply this analysis also to trade dress, such as the shape of the cereal or a pretzel? Are the concerns about protecting generic words the same as those regarding unpatented designs?

---

## 2. PREEMPTION OF STATE UNFAIR COMPETITION CLAIMS

*Kellogg* was decided in an era in which trademark and unfair competition law were related but distinct bodies of law. Federal law provided a mechanism for registration of trademarks and a federal cause of action for infringement of registered marks. Common law unfair competition claims dealt with unregistered (and often unregistrable) subject matter, which could not be enforced under federal law. After *Erie Railroad v. Tompkins*, 304 U.S. 64 (1938), those law unfair competition claims were understood to be state law claims. For that reason, the longstanding concerns about use of unfair competition law to protect unpatented designs took on a different valence, raising preemption concerns. The following case analyzes federal preemption of state law claims.

### SEARS, ROEBUCK & CO. V. STIFFEL CO.

376 U.S. 973 (1964)

JUSTICE BLACK. The question in this case is whether a State's unfair competition law can, consistently with the federal patent laws, impose liability for or prohibit the copying of an article which is protected by neither a federal patent nor a copyright. The respondent, Stiffel Company, secured design and mechanical patents on a 'pole lamp'—a vertical tube having lamp fixtures along the outside, the tube being made so that it will stand upright between the floor and ceiling of a room. Pole lamps proved a decided commercial success, and soon after Stiffel brought them on the market Sears, Roebuck & Company put on the market a substantially identical lamp, which it sold more cheaply, Sears' retail price being about the same as Stiffel's wholesale price. Stiffel then brought this action against Sears in the United States District Court for the Northern District of Illinois, claiming in its first count that by copying its design Sears had infringed Stiffel's patents and in its second count that by selling copies of Stiffel's lamp Sears had caused confusion in the trade as to the source of the lamps and had thereby engaged in unfair competition under Illinois law. There was evidence that identifying tags were not attached to the Sears lamps although labels appeared on the cartons in which they were delivered to customers, that customers had asked Stiffel whether its lamps differed from Sears', and that in two cases customers who had bought Stiffel lamps had complained to Stiffel on learning that Sears was selling substantially identical lamps at a much lower price.

The District Court, after holding the patents, invalid for want of invention, went on to find as a fact that Sears' lamp was 'a substantially exact copy' of Stiffel's and that the two lamps were so much alike, both in appearance and in functional details, 'that confusion between them is likely, and some confusion has already occurred.' On these findings the court held Sears guilty of unfair competition, enjoined Sears 'from unfairly competing with (Stiffel) by selling or attempting to sell pole lamps identical to or confusingly similar to' Stiffel's lamp, and ordered an accounting to fix profits and damages resulting from Sears' 'unfair competition.'

The Court of Appeals affirmed. That court held that, to make out a case of unfair competition under Illinois law, there was no need to show that Sears had been 'palming off' its lamps as Stiffel lamps; Stiffel had only to prove that there was a 'likelihood of confusion as to the source of the products'—that the two articles were sufficiently identical that customers could not tell who had made a particular one. Impressed by the 'remarkable sameness of appearance' of the lamps, the Court of Appeals upheld the trial court's findings of likelihood of confusion and some actual confusion, findings which the appellate court construed to mean confusion 'as to the source of the lamps.' The Court of Appeals thought this enough under Illinois law to sustain the trial court's holding of unfair competition, and thus held Sears liable under Illinois law for doing no more than copying and marketing an unpatented article. We granted certiorari to consider whether this use of a State's law of unfair competition is compatible with the federal patent law.

Before the Constitution was adopted, some States had granted patents either by special act or by general statute, but when the Constitution was adopted provision for a federal patent law was made one of the enumerated powers of Congress because, as Madison put it in The Federalist No. 43, the States 'cannot separately make effectual provision' for either patents or copyrights. That constitutional provision is Art. 1, s 8, cl. 8, which empowers Congress 'To promote the Progress of Science and useful Arts, by securing for limited Times to Authors and Inventors the exclusive Right to their respective Writings and Discoveries.' Pursuant to this constitutional authority, Congress in 1790 enacted the first federal patent and copyright law, 1 Stat. 109, and ever since that time has fixed the condition upon which patents and copyrights shall be granted, see. These laws, like other laws of the United States enacted pursuant to constitutional authority, are the supreme law of the land. When state law touches upon the area of these federal statutes, it is 'familiar doctrine' that the federal policy 'may not be set at naught, or its benefits denied' by the state law. This is true, of course, even if the state law is enacted in the exercise of otherwise undoubted state power.

The grant of a patent is the grant of a statutory monopoly; indeed, the grant of patents in England was an explicit exception to the statute of James I prohibiting monopolies. Patents are not given as favors, as was the case of monopolies given by the Tudor monarchs, but are meant to encourage invention by rewarding the inventor with the right, limited to a term of years fixed by the patent, to exclude others from the use of his invention. During that period of time no one may make use, or sell the patented product without the patentee's authority. But in rewarding useful invention, the 'rights and welfare of the community must be fairly dealt with and effectually guarded.' To that end the prerequisites to obtaining a patent are strictly observed, and when the patent has issued the limitations on its exercise are equally strictly enforced. To begin with, a genuine 'invention' or 'discovery' must be demonstrated 'lest in the constant demand for new appliances the heavy hand of tribute be laid on each slight technological advance in an art.' Once the patent issues, it is strictly construed, it cannot be used to secure any monopoly beyond that contained in the patent, the patentee's control over the product when it leaves his hands is sharply limited, and the patent monopoly may not be used in disregard of the antitrust laws. Finally, and especially relevant here, when the patent expires the monopoly created by it expires, too, and the right to make the article—including the right to make it in precisely the shape it carried when patented—passes to the public. *Kellogg Co. v. National Biscuit Co.*, 305 U.S. 111, 120–122 (1938); *Singer Mfg. Co. v. June Mfg. Co.*, 163 U.S. 169, 185 (1896).

Thus the patent system is one in which uniform federal standards are carefully used to promote invention while at the same time preserving free competition. Obviously a State could not, consistently with the Supremacy Clause of the Constitution, extend the life of a patent beyond its expiration date or give a patent on an article which lacked the level of invention required for federal patents. To do either would run counter to the policy of

Congress of granting patents only to true inventions, and then only for a limited time. Just as a State cannot encroach upon the federal patent laws directly, it cannot, under some other law, such as that forbidding unfair competition, give protection of a kind that clashes with the objectives of the federal patent laws.

In the present case the 'pole lamp' sold by Stiffel has been held not to be entitled to the protection of either a mechanical or a design patent. An unpatentable article, like an article on which the patent has expired, is in the public domain and may be made and sold by whoever chooses to do so. What Sears did was to copy Stiffel's design and to sell lamps almost identical to those sold by Stiffel. This it had every right to do under the federal patent laws. That Stiffel originated the pole lamp and made it popular is immaterial. 'Sharing in the goodwill of an article unprotected by patent or trade-mark is the exercise of a right possessed by all—and in the free exercise of which the consuming public is deeply interested.' *Kellogg Co. v. National Biscuit Co.*, *supra*, 305 U.S. at 122. To allow a State by use of its law of unfair competition to prevent the copying of an article which represents too slight an advance to be patented would be to permit the State to block off from the public something which federal law has said belongs to the public. The result would be that while federal law grants only 14 or 17 years' protection to genuine inventions, States could allow perpetual protection to articles too lacking in novelty to merit any patent at all under federal constitutional standards. This would be too great an encroachment on the federal patent system to be tolerated.

Sears has been held liable here for unfair competition because of a finding of likelihood of confusion based only on the fact that Sears' lamp was copied from Stiffel's unpatented lamp and that consequently the two looked exactly alike. Of course there could be 'confusion' as to who had manufactured these nearly identical articles. But mere inability of the public to tell two identical articles apart is not enough to support an injunction against copying or an award of damages for copying that which the federal patent laws permit to be copied. Doubtless a State may, in appropriate circumstances, require that goods, whether patented or unpatented, be labeled or that other precautionary steps be taken to prevent customers from being misled as to the source, just as it may protect businesses in the use of their trademarks, labels, or distinctive dress in the packaging of goods so as to prevent others, by imitating such markings, from misleading purchasers as to the source of the goods. But because of the federal patent laws a State may not, when the article is unpatented and uncopyrighted, prohibit the copying of the article itself or award damages for such copying. The judgment below did both and in so doing gave Stiffel the equivalent of a patent monopoly on its unpatented lamp. That was error, and Sears is entitled to a judgment in its favor.

## *NOTE*

Stiffel's original complaint in *Sears* alleged infringement of design and utility patents as well as unfair competition. The District Court found both patents invalid "for want of invention," leaving only the unfair competition claim. Thus, the Supreme Court's statements about unpatented designs clearly were meant to refer to designs not covered by utility or design patents—that is, *Sears* was not exclusively about a conflict with utility patent law. Likewise, Day-Brite had received a design patent on the lighting fixture at issue in *Compco Corp. v. Day-Brite Lighting, Inc.*, 376 U.S. 234, 237–38 (1964), *Sears*'s companion case, and it alleged design patent infringement along with unfair competition. The design patent claim was no longer at issue when the case reached the Supreme Court because the the plaintiff did not appeal the Seventh Circuit's affirmance of the district court's finding that the design patent was invalid on the ground that the design was functional. *Day-Brite Lighting, Inc. v. Compco Corp.*, 311 F.2d 26, 27 (7th Cir. 1963).

*Compco* sounded the same preemption note, perhaps even more strongly than *Sears*:

> Here Day-Brite's fixture has been held not to be entitled to a design or mechanical patent. Under the federal patent laws it is, therefore, in the public domain and can be copied in every detail by whoever pleases. It is true that the trial court found that the configuration of Day-Brite's fixture identified Day-Brite to the trade because the arrangement of the ribbing had, like a trademark, acquired a "secondary meaning" by which that particular design was associated with Day-Brite. But if the design is not entitled to a design patent or other federal statutory protection, then it can be copied at will.

And *Compco* reiterated that labeling was the only legitimate remedy in these cases, even if the claimed features are nonfunctional and have secondary meaning:

> A State of course has power to impose liability upon those who, knowing that the public is relying upon an original manufacturer's reputation for quality and integrity, deceive the public by palming off their copies as the original. That an article copied from an unpatented article could be made in some other way, that the design is "nonfunctional" and not essential to the use of either article, that the configuration of the article copied may have a "secondary meaning" which identifies the maker to the trade, or that there may be "confusion" among purchasers as to which article is which or as to who is the maker, *may be relevant evidence in applying a State's law requiring such precautions as labeling*; however, and regardless of the copier's motives, neither these facts nor any others can furnish a basis for imposing liability for or prohibiting the actual acts of copying and selling.

Preemption is question of the relationship between federal and state law, of course, so it is relevant only in cases involving claims under state law.

Congress has the power to enact a federal law of unfair competition or otherwise assimilate protection for designs into trademark law, and preemption would not apply to claims made under such laws. And in the next section, we examine how the Lanham Act, enacted by Congress in 1946, was interpreted to extend to uses that once would have been actionable under the common law of unfair competition. As you read these cases, consider whether the concerns that animated the Supreme Court's *Sears* and *Compco* decisions were merely about preemption, and if not, how courts have addressed broader concerns about protecting unpatented designs with trademark law.

---

## B. TRADE DRESS IN THE MODERN ERA

After the Supreme Court's decision in *Erie*, many advocates sought a federal statutory basis for unfair competition, and some claimed that the Lanham Act had in fact provided such a basis. Starting in the 1950's, courts began to interpret § 43(a) to ground federal unfair competition claims in cases not involving trademarks but other false statements, and then eventually to allow federal claims for infringement of unregistered trademarks and trade dress. *See, e.g.*, *Scarves by Vera, Inc. v. United Merchants and Mfrs., Inc.*, 173 F. Supp. 625 (S.D.N.Y. 1959); *Catalina, Inc. v. Gem Swimwear, Inc.*, 162 F. Supp. 911 (S.D.N.Y. 1958).

Over the decades that followed, courts began recognizing a much broader range of identifiers as trademark subject matter (and therefore potentially registrable)— including product packaging and design, colors, sounds, and even scents. Those designators previously would not have been considered trademarks, and consequently, use of those designators by third parties would have been remediable only through (common law) unfair competition claims. Having assimilated them into the law of trademarks, however, courts needed a way to assess the protectability of particular claimed trade dress features. That has required some modification of trademark law's basic eligibility rules, since those were developed primarily to assess word marks.

By definition, a trademark is *distinctive of source*—meaning that it uniquely identify's the commercial source of the goods or services with which it is used. Distinctiveness of word marks is classically determined by placing the claimed mark in one of four categories typically associated with *Abercrombie & Fitch v. Hunting World*, 537 F.2d 4 (2d Cir. 1976).

"Arrayed in an ascending order which roughly reflects their eligibility to trademark status and the degree of protection accorded, these classes are (1) generic, (2) descriptive, (3) suggestive, and (4) arbitrary or fanciful." *Id.* A generic term is one that refers, or has come to be understood as referring, to the "genus of which the particular product is a species," and generic terms are never protectable. A term is descriptive if it conveys an immediate idea of the ingredients, qualities or characteristics of the goods, and descriptive terms are protectable only when they have acquired "secondary meaning." Secondary meaning, perhaps more appropriately labeled "acquired meaning," exists when the "primary significance of the term refers to the producer rather than the product." A term is suggestive if it requires imagination, thought and perception to reach a conclusion as to the nature of goods (PENGUIN for freezers). Suggestive terms are protectable without evidence of secondary meaning. Arbitrary terms are existing words that are used in a way what is disconnected from their ordinary semantic meaning (APPLE for computers). Fanciful terms are coined—they have no non-trademark meaning (EXXON for oil and gas). Arbitrary and fanciful terms are also protectable without evidence of secondary meaning.

Collectively suggestive, arbitrary, and fanciful terms are classified as *inherently distinctive* because they have no direct connection to the goods or services with which they are used. When used in connection with computers, for example, the word APPLE offers consumers no information about the nature of the products. Computers obviously are not apples, and "apple" does not even offer indirect information about any of the features or characteristics of computers. Trademark law assumes that, because there is no other way to understand the significance of the word APPLE on computers, consumers will interpret use of that word as an indication of the source of the computer. It does not matter whether consumers know that an APPLE computer is manufactured by the Apple Computer Company, only that they believe all computers that bear the word APPLE come from the same source.

Descriptive terms have ambiguous meaning in the context in which they are being used. The words "Best Buy," for example, offer consumers significantly more information when used by a retail store than APPLE does when used in connection with computers. When consumers see or hear "Best Buy," they might reasonably conclude that the store using those words offers good deals. As a result, unlike APPLE for computers, we cannot be confident consumers will interpret "Best Buy" as an indicator of source rather than simply as a descriptor of the store's services. Descriptive terms like "Best Buy" are therefore not considered to be inherently distinctive, but they may become distinctive if consumers begin to associate them with a particular seller over time because of experience with the seller and/or its advertising efforts (as very likely has happened with BEST BUY the electronics store). Descriptive terms that become distinctive in this way have *acquired distinctiveness* or *secondary meaning*, and they can be protected as trademarks on that basis. But marks that are protected on the basis of secondary meaning, while protectable, are not entirely equal to inherently distinctive marks: Inherently distinctive marks, such as APPLE for computers or EXXON for gasoline, are considered stronger marks than descriptive marks that have acquired secondary meaning and, all else equal, receive greater legal protection.

Two points deserve emphasis here. First is that these basic categories are used to assess the distinctiveness of both registered and unregistered marks. Implicit here is the fact that trademark rights do not depend on registration—those rights arise through use, not registration, and registration is not required for any type of mark. Federal registration does confer certain advantages, however. First, contigent on registration, the mark owner may claim nationwide constructive use of the mark as of the date of application, "conferring a right of priority, nationwide in effect." Thus, the trademark registrant does not have to rely on actual use of the mark in all 50 states in order to establish a mark that is national in scope. Registration also creates "constructive notice of the registrant's claim of ownership." 15 U.S.C. § 1072.

Federal registration also serves as "prima facie evidence of the validity of the registered mark and of the registration of the mark, of the owner's ownership of the mark, and of the owner's exclusive right to use the registered mark in commerce on or in connection with the goods or services specified in the certificate." *Id.* § 1057(b). After five years of registration, the registrant may request that the registration acheive "incontestable" status, which limits the grounds on which others may challenge the validity of the mark. *Id.* §§ 1065, 1115(b).

Today, there are two primary bases on which a party can seek registration: (1) on the basis of prior use of the mark in interstate commerce ("Section 1(a) application"); and (2) on the basis of the applicant's bona fide intent to use the mark ("Section 1(b) or ITU application"). 15 U.S.C. § 1051(a), (b). In both cases, registration ultimately depends on use of the mark, but an intent to use application allows the applicant to seek registration before making the use. The applicant has 6 months from the date of filing to demonstrate that it has made use (a period that may be extended in 6 month increments up to 3 years). *Id.* § 1051(d).*

Second, the *Abercrombie* spectrum was developed as a means for assessing the distinctiveness of word marks—the approach focuses on the extent to which the word mark provides information about the type of goods or services with which it is used. Before getting to the particular rules for trade dress, the next case considers the ways distinctiveness rules might need to be modified for other non-word marks—in this case, a logo. Consider whether logos raise the same concerns as trade dress, or whether the rules developed here could fruitfully be applied to trade dress as well.

---

* Most applications are filed online using the Trademark Electronic Application System (TEAS). The fees range from $225 to $325 per application. https://www.uspto.gov/trademarks-application-process/filing-online. In FY 2015, over 500,000 applications were filed. USPTO, PERFORMANCE AND ACCOUNTABILITY REPORT FY 2015, at 199.

## 1. DISTINCTIVENESS OF NON-WORD MARKS

### AMAZING SPACES, INC. V. METRO MINI STORAGE

608 F.3d 225 (5th Cir. 2010)

KING, CIRCUIT JUDGE. Amazing Spaces, Inc., and Metro Mini Storage are rival self-storage businesses in Houston, Texas. Amazing Spaces brought this action against Metro and Landmark Interest Corporation, a construction company, alleging infringement of a star design that it claims as a service mark. The district court concluded that the design was not a legally protectable mark and dismissed Amazing Spaces's claims on summary judgment. We agree that the design was not legally protectable, and we affirm the judgment dismissing Amazing Spaces's service mark infringement claims. However, we also conclude that the district court erred in dismissing Amazing Spaces's claims relating to infringement of its trade dress, and we reverse and remand for further proceedings.

I. Background

Amazing Spaces and Metro compete directly with each other in providing self-storage services in Houston, Texas. Landmark has built facilities for both Amazing Spaces and Metro. Amazing Spaces claims, in connection with providing storage services, exclusive use rights in a design consisting of a raised, five-pointed star set within a circle (the "Star Symbol").[1] Metro uses a similar star design on its buildings. In response to this use, Amazing Spaces brought suit against Metro and Landmark in federal district court, alleging federal and state causes of action. With respect to the Star Symbol alone, Amazing Spaces brought a federal claim for service mark infringement under the Lanham Act and state law claims for common law infringement and statutory dilution. With respect to its trade dress, of which the Star Symbol comprises one element, Amazing Spaces brought federal claims for trade dress infringement under the Lanham Act and copyright infringement and state law claims for common law unfair competition and statutory dilution.

Amazing Spaces was founded in 1998 by Scott and Kathy Tautenhahn, and it currently operates three storage facilities in the greater Houston area. The facilities opened in 1998, 2001, and 2006, respectively. Landmark was hired to build each of these facilities and, at Amazing Spaces's request, installed the Star Symbol under the peaks of the facilities' gabled roofs. Amazing Spaces has used the Star Symbol in its facilities' architecture and in its advertising, and it claims to have done so since at least April 1998. One trade magazine has recognized Amazing Spaces for its storage

---

[1] The parties and the district court used varying terminology in describing the design at issue. Amazing Spaces refers to it as the "Star Logo," Metro refers to it as the "Texas Star," and the district court's opinion refers to it as the "star mark." Except where alluding to a different design or quoting from either the parties or the district court, we will employ the term "Star Symbol."

services, and the magazine displayed the Star Symbol in connection with the accompanying article. Amazing Spaces has also used the Star Symbol to designate the locations of its facilities on maps, and it claims to have directed customers—through telephone advertisements—to "look for the star."

The Star Symbol is registered as a service mark with the United States Patent and Trademark Office (PTO). Prior to applying for registration, Amazing Spaces engaged a company to perform a database search to determine whether other storage companies had registered a similar star mark; the search revealed no such registrations. Amazing Spaces's application stated that it believed no other person or business was entitled to use the Star Symbol or a deceptively similar design as a mark for storage services. On July 6, 2004, the PTO issued U.S. Service Mark Registration No. 2,859,845 (the " '845 Registration") for the Star Symbol. . . . Amazing Spaces also holds a registration for another design (the "Peaks and Sky Symbol") that features a series of roof peaks, including stars on the gables, placed below a sky expanse, with the words "AMAZING SPACES" underneath.

Landmark has also constructed self-storage facilities for Metro; these facilities feature a similar five-pointed-star-in-a-circle design (but not raised) on their gables. Despite Amazing Spaces's demand that Metro cease its use of a star, Metro continued to use its design and remodeled existing facilities to include the design. According to Amazing Spaces, this has caused confusion among its customers, who mistook Metro's facilities for new Amazing Spaces facilities. According to Kathy Tautenhahn, existing or prospective customers have inquired about whether new Amazing Spaces facilities had opened where Metro facilities were located. The record also includes a declaration from a customer to similar effect. In the present case, Amazing Spaces has submitted a declaration by its alarm technician that the technician was confused by the appearance of Community's facility and believed it to be an Amazing Spaces facility.

Metro refused to cease using its star design, and Amazing Spaces proceeded to file the lawsuit at issue. Metro and Landmark each filed an answer, asserting various affirmative defenses and counterclaims. One of these counterclaims was a request that the trademark be canceled for invalidity. The district court recognized early on that "[t]here does seem to be a question about the trademarkability of the Texas star logo." Accordingly, the court ordered discovery to proceed in stages, with the first stage limited to "the threshold issues raised by the 'trademarkability' of the Texas star and similar issues affecting copyright and trade dress."

Following discovery, Metro[3] moved for summary judgment on the ground that the Star Symbol was not a valid service mark. It argued primarily that the Star Symbol was not inherently distinctive and that Amazing Spaces could not establish that it had acquired secondary meaning. It supported this contention by presenting evidence that the same or a similar five-pointed star was used in commerce "in at least 63 different industries and businesses on buildings, property, and as part of logos" and on the buildings of "at least 28 other self-storage locations."[4] The court concluded that "[t]he ubiquitous nature of the five-pointed star set within a circle precludes a finding that it is inherently distinctive or that it can serve as an indicator of origin for a particular business," and that "the record d[id] not raise a fact issue material to determining whether the star mark has acquired distinctiveness through a secondary meaning."

III. Discussion

A. The Star Symbol

In reviewing whether the Star Symbol qualifies for protection as a mark, we begin with the definitions provided by the Lanham Act. Section 45 of the Lanham Act separately defines "trademark" and "service mark," but the terms essentially include:

> any word, name, symbol, or device, or any combination thereof . . . used by a person . . . to identify and distinguish his or her goods [or services] . . . from those manufactured or sold [or provided] by others and to indicate the source of the goods [or services], even if that source is unknown.

Lanham Act § 45, 15 U.S.C. § 1127; accord *Two Pesos*, 505 U.S. at 768 ("In order to be registered [and thus legally protectable], a mark must be capable of distinguishing the applicant's goods from those of others." (citing Lanham Act § 2, 15 U.S.C. § 1052)). "To be protectable, a mark must be distinctive. . . ."; 1 MCCARTHY ON TRADEMARKS § 3:1, at 3–3 ("In determining what can qualify as a trademark, it is crucial that the symbol in question be so distinctive that it is capable of performing the function of identifying and distinguishing the goods that bear the symbol.").

---

3 Although Metro and Landmark play distinct roles in Amazing Spaces's allegations of infringement, they asserted the same arguments at the summary judgment stage and now assert the same arguments on appeal. Thus, for ease of reference, unless we note otherwise or it is made apparent from context, further references in this opinion to Metro extend to Landmark as well.

4 Metro submitted an affidavit from the former owner of one such storage facility attesting to the use of a raised, five-pointed star within a circle on the storage facility—on walls and on gables beneath roof peaks—prior to April 1998.

> [A] mark can be distinctive in one of two ways. First, a mark is inherently distinctive if its intrinsic nature serves to identify a particular source.... Second, a mark has acquired distinctiveness, even if it is not inherently distinctive, if it has developed secondary meaning, which occurs when, in the minds of the public, the primary significance of a mark is to identify the source of the product rather than the product itself.

*Wal-Mart Stores, Inc. v. Samara Bros., Inc.*, 529 U.S. 205, 210–11 (2000).

Amazing Spaces claims that the Star Symbol is sufficiently distinctive to warrant protection as a service mark. The requisite distinctiveness, it claims, is shown in three distinct manners: (1) the statutory presumption of validity flowing from the '845 Registration; (2) the Star Symbol's inherent distinctiveness; and (3) evidence that the Star Symbol has acquired secondary meaning. In response, Metro rejects each claimed source of distinctiveness and further requests that we order cancellation of the '845 Registration. We address each argument in turn.

2. Inherent Distinctiveness

As mentioned above, "a mark is inherently distinctive if 'its intrinsic nature serves to identify a particular source.'" *Wal-Mart Stores*. Inherent distinctiveness is attributable to a mark when the mark "almost automatically tells a customer that it refers to a brand and . . . immediately signal[s] a brand or a product source." *Id.* at 212. The parties disagree over not only the answer to whether the Star Symbol is inherently distinctive but also over the proper method for conducting the inquiry. Metro urges that the familiar *Abercrombie* test cannot be used to categorize the Star Symbol and instead asks that we apply the *Seabrook Foods* test to determine that the Star Symbol is not inherently distinctive. Amazing Spaces, by contrast, presses the application of the Abercrombie test, under which it claims the Star Symbol is inherently distinctive, and it argues alternatively that the Star Symbol is inherently distinctive under the *Seabrook Foods* test.

a. *Abercrombie*

In *Abercrombie*, Judge Friendly sought to arrange the universe of marks into a spectrum of distinctiveness. As the Supreme Court has noted, "[m]arks are often classified in categories of generally increasing distinctiveness; following the classic formulation set out by Judge Friendly, they may be (1) generic; (2) descriptive; (3) suggestive; (4) arbitrary; or (5) fanciful." *Two Pesos*. Under this scheme, "'[t]he latter three categories of marks, because their intrinsic nature serves to identify a particular source of a product, are deemed inherently distinctive and are entitled to protection,'" while "[g]eneric terms receive no trademark protection, [and] descriptive terms merit protection only if they have secondary meaning."

We agree with Metro that the Star Symbol resists categorization under the *Abercrombie* test, and we consequently do not rely on a rote application of its categories in determining whether the Star Symbol is inherently distinctive. The Supreme Court's most recent recitation of the *Abercrombie* categories noted its use only in the context of marks consisting of words. See *Wal-Mart Stores*, 529 U.S. at 210 ("*In the context of word marks*, courts have applied the now-classic test originally formulated by Judge Friendly. . . ." (emphasis added) (citing *Abercrombie*, 537 F.2d at 10–11)). The Court's precedent also supports the proposition that some marks, although deserving of legal protection, do not fit within the *Abercrombie* spectrum. In *Qualitex*, the Court declined to apply the *Abercrombie* test to a mark consisting purely of a shade of color used in a product's trade dress, holding that the mark could constitute a legally protectable mark only through a showing of secondary meaning. The Court further extended that logic when, in *Wal-Mart Stores*, it stated that "[i]t seems to us that [product] design, like color, is not inherently distinctive" and held that marks consisting of a product's design were protectable only upon proof of secondary meaning—a conclusion it could not have reached had it applied the *Abercrombie* test. Professor McCarthy, a luminary in the field of trademark law, has likewise suggested that the *Abercrombie* test may not apply to all marks, stating that "[u]se of the spectrum of descriptive, suggestive, arbitrary and fanciful is largely confined to word marks. It is usually not suitable for nonword designations such as shapes and images . . . [, which] must be judged by other guidelines." The *Restatement*, in a section addressed to symbols, graphic designs, and colors, agrees. RESTATEMENT § 13 cmt. D, at 107.

As the district court discovered, the challenge of placing the Star Symbol into *Abercrombie*'s constellation of categories is a futile endeavor. The district court briefly probed the utility of applying the *Abercrombie* test and concluded that the Star Symbol did not fit as a generic, descriptive, or suggestive mark. The district court first rejected the notion that the Star Symbol was generic because "[a] five-pointed star within a circle does not refer to a product or service provided by a self-storage company" and "[t]he evidence of widespread use of a five-point star or a five-point star set within a circle by many diverse businesses and government offices supports the conclusion that the star mark is not related to or a generic symbol for self-storage goods or services." It next determined that the Star Symbol was not descriptive because "[i]t does not identify a characteristic or quality of self-storage service, such as its function or quality." Nor was the Star Symbol suggestive, according to the district court, because "[t]here is no basis to conclude that a five-pointed star set within a circle suggests an attribute of self-storage services." We discern no flaws in the district court's analysis with respect to these three categories. However, the logical extension of the district court's analysis is the conclusion that the Star Symbol is arbitrary or fanciful, which under the *Abercrombie* test would render it inherently distinctive and thus entitled to protection. Yet the district court refused to so conclude, stating that "the star mark cannot be classified as arbitrary or fanciful unless it is inherently distinctive so as to serve as a source identifier for Amazing Spaces." It then turned to the *Seabrook Foods* test in conducting its inquiry into the Star Symbol's inherent distinctiveness.

We agree that the Star Symbol—indeed, any mark—lacks inherent distinctiveness if its intrinsic nature does not serve to identify its source. Furthermore, as we have already indicated, we approve the district court's decision to apply a test other than *Abercrombie* in this case. Both the Supreme Court and scholars have questioned the applicability of the *Abercrombie* test to marks other than words. . . . We do not go so far as to hold that the *Abercrombie* test is eclipsed every time a mark other than a word is at issue. Instead, we hold that the *Abercrombie* test fails to illuminate the fundamental inquiry in this case: whether the Star Symbol's " 'intrinsic nature serves to identify' " Amazing Spaces and its storage services. For the answer to that question, we now turn to the *Seabrook Foods* test employed by the district court.

b. *Seabrook Foods*

In contrast to the *Abercrombie* test, the *Seabrook Foods* test, articulated by the U.S. Court of Customs and Patent Appeals in 1977, applies expressly to marks consisting of symbols and designs:

> In determining whether a design is arbitrary or distinctive this court has looked to [1] whether it was a "common" basic shape or design, [2] whether it was unique or unusual in a particular field, [3] whether it was a mere refinement of a commonly-adopted and well-known form of ornamentation for a particular class of goods viewed by the public as a dress or ornamentation for the goods, or [4] whether it was capable of creating a commercial impression distinct from the accompanying words.

The first three of the *Seabrook Foods* " 'questions are merely different ways to ask whether the design, shape or combination of elements is so unique, unusual or unexpected in this market that one can assume without proof that it will automatically be perceived by customers as an indicator of origin—a trademark.' " As is true of the *Abercrombie* test, the *Seabrook Foods* test seeks an answer to the question whether a mark's " 'intrinsic nature serves to identify a particular source.' "[16]

We agree . . . that the *Seabrook Foods* factors are variations on a theme rather than discrete inquiries. In *Star Industries v. Bacardi & Co.*, the Second Circuit noted that " '[c]ommon basic shapes' or letters are, as a matter of law, not inherently distinctive . . . , [but] stylized shapes or letters

[16] Metro submitted an affidavit from the former owner of one such storage facility attesting to the use of a raised, five-pointed star within a circle on the storage facility—on walls and on gables beneath roof peaks—prior to April 1998.

may qualify, provided the design is not commonplace but rather unique or unusual in the relevant market." 412 F.3d 373, 382 (2d Cir. 2005). This statement, turning on whether the symbol or design is "common," comprises, essentially, the first two *Seabrook Foods* factors. However, the third *Seabrook Foods* factor similarly asks whether a symbol or design is "common" in the sense that it is likely to be perceived by the public as ornamentation rather than a mark.[17] A "common" symbol or design—lacking inherent distinctiveness—is the antithesis of a symbol or design that " 'is so unique, unusual or unexpected in this market that one can assume without proof that it will automatically be perceived by customers as an indicator of origin—a trademark.' " *I.P. Lund Trading*, 163 F.3d at 40 (quoting 1 MCCARTHY ON TRADEMARKS § 8:13, at 8–58.5); accord RESTATEMENT § 13 cmt. d, at 107 ("Commonplace symbols and designs are not inherently distinctive since their appearance on numerous products makes it unlikely that consumers will view them as distinctive of the goods or services of a particular seller.").

The district court determined that the Star Symbol was "not a plain five-pointed star" but was instead "shaded and set within a circle," rendering it "sufficient[ly] styliz[ed]" to be "more than a common geometric shape." It then proceeded to conclude that the Star Symbol "[wa]s not inherently distinctive and d[id] not act as an indicator of origin for any self-storage business, including Amazing Spaces." It supported this assertion with a discussion of "[t]he ubiquitous nature of the five-pointed star set within a circle" in Texas, specifically its "use[ ] as a decoration or ornamentation on innumerable buildings, signs, roads, and products." The court concluded that this ubiquity—including use of the same or a similar star design in 63 industries businesses and 28 other self-storage locations—"preclude[d] a finding that [the Star Symbol wa]s inherently distinctive or that it c[ould] serve as an indicator of origin for a particular business."

Undoubtedly, the Star Symbol is stylized relative to an unshaded five-pointed star design not set within a circle. However, we disagree that the issue of stylization revolves around comparing a design's actual appearance to its corresponding platonic form. Instead, as discussed above, asking whether a shape is stylized is merely another way of asking whether

---

[17] The interrelationship between these inquiries is also reflected in Professor McCarthy's discussion of common geometric shapes:

> Most common geometric shapes are regarded as not being inherently distinctive, in view of the common use of such shapes in all areas of advertising. Thus, such ordinary shapes as circles, ovals, squares, etc., either when used alone or as a background for a word mark, cannot function as a separate mark unless (1) the shape is likely to create a commercial impression on the buyer separate from the word mark or any other indicia and (2) the shape is proven to have secondary meaning. . . . The rationale is that such designs have been so widely and commonly used as mere decorative graphic elements that the origin-indicating ability of such designs has been diminished.

1 MCCARTHY ON TRADEMARKS AND UNFAIR COMPETITION § 7:29, at 7–73–74 (footnotes omitted).

the design is "commonplace" or "unique or unusual in the relevant market," *Star Indus.*, 412 F.3d at 382, or whether it is "a mere refinement of a commonly-adopted and well-known form of ornamentation for a particular class of goods viewed by the public as a dress or ornamentation," *Seabrook Foods*, 568 F.2d at 1344.[18] The stylization inquiry is properly conceived of asking whether a particular symbol or design is stylized such that prospective purchasers of goods or services are likely to differentiate it from other, similar symbols or designs.[19] See *Wiley*, 762 F.2d at 142 (holding that a red heart on a teddy bear "carrie[d] no distinctive message of origin to the consumer . . . given the heart shape's widespread use as decoration for any number of products put out by many different companies; 1 MCCARTHY ON TRADEMARKS § 3.3, at 3–11 ("Usually, if when viewed in context, it is not immediately obvious that a certain designation is being used as an indication of origin, then it probably is not. In that case, it is not a trademark."). The record evidence is replete with similar or

---

[18] The parties dispute the scope of the "relevant market"—specifically, whether the district court correctly considered use of a similar or identical star design beyond the self-storage service industry. Amazing Spaces contends that we should limit our analysis to the self-storage services industry, while Metro argues that we may take into account uses of star designs in a larger context. The second *Seabrook Foods* factor refers to uniqueness or unusualness "in a particular field," 568 F.2d at 1344, and the Second Circuit has stated that a stylized design may be protectable when it "is not commonplace but rather unique or unusual in the relevant market," *Star Indus.*, 412 F.3d at 382. Similarly, the third factor refers to whether a mark is commonly used as ornamentation for a "particular class of goods." *Seabrook Foods*, 568 F.2d at 1344. In contrast, the First Circuit, in considering whether a red heart on the chest of a teddy bear was inherently distinctive, appeared to consider the broader use of red hearts in determining whether the use at issue was unique or unusual. See *Wiley*, 762 F.2d at 142 ("[T]he record contains so many examples of use of a red heart motif on teddy bears and other stuffed animals, not to mention all manner of other toys and paraphernalia, that no reasonable argument on this point can be made." (emphasis added)). The rule in the Restatement asks whether, "because of the nature of the designation and the context in which it is used, prospective purchasers are likely to perceive it as a designation that . . . identifies goods or services produced or sponsored by a particular person." RESTATEMENT § 13(a), at 104 (emphasis added). It further explains that

> [c]ommonplace symbols and designs are not inherently distinctive since their appearance on numerous products makes it unlikely that consumers will view them as distinctive of the goods or services of a particular seller. Thus, unless the symbol or design is striking, unusual, or otherwise likely to differentiate the products of a particular producer, the designation is not inherently distinctive.

*Id.* § 13 cmt. d, at 107. Finally, and most importantly, the Lanham Act defines "service mark" as a mark used "to identify and distinguish the services of one person . . . from the services of others and to indicate the source of the services." Lanham Act § 45, 15 U.S.C. § 1127. Because a mark must distinguish one person's services from another, we agree that our inquiry is whether the Star Symbol identifies and distinguishes Amazing Spaces's self-storage services from others' self-storage services. This does not mean, however, that we must blind ourselves to uses beyond the self-storage services industry: the fact that the same or a similar star is used in countless other ways certainly bears on whether it is "likely that prospective purchasers will perceive [a given star design] as an indication of source" within a particular industry because a "[c]ommonplace symbol[']s . . . appearance on numerous products makes it unlikely that consumers will view [it] as distinctive of the goods or services of a particular seller." RESTATEMENT § 13 cmt. d, at 107.

[19] Under this analysis, use by third parties of a design bears on whether the design is inherently distinctive, not merely whether the design "is a 'strong' or a 'weak' [ ]mark." *Exxon Corp. v. Tex. Motor Exchange of Houston, Inc.*, 628 F.2d 500, 504 (5th Cir. 1980); *cf. Union Nat'l Bank of Tex., Laredo, Tex.*, 909 F.2d at 848 n.25 (noting that widespread industry use can render a mark not inherently distinctive, but third-party use otherwise typically affects the issue of whether there is a likelihood of confusion between marks).

identical five-pointed stars, both raised and set in circles, and used in similar manners, such that—notwithstanding the residual evidence of the presumption of validity—no reasonable jury could find that the Star Symbol is even a mere refinement of this commonly adopted and well-known form of ornamentation. The Star Symbol is thus not " 'so unique, unusual or unexpected in this market that one can assume without proof that it will automatically be perceived by customers as an indicator of origin—a trademark,' " *I.P. Lund Trading*, 163 F.3d at 40 (quoting 1 MCCARTHY ON TRADEMARKS § 8:13, at 8–58.5), and it "does not almost automatically tell a customer that it refers to a brand . . . [or] immediately signal a brand or a product source," *Wal-Mart Stores*, 529 U.S. at 212 (alterations and internal quotation marks omitted). Because the Star Symbol does not, by " 'its intrinsic nature[,] serve[ ] to identify a particular source," *id.* at 210, it is not inherently distinctive, and it can be protected only upon a showing of secondary meaning.

3. Secondary Meaning

The parties disagree over whether the Star Symbol has acquired distinctiveness through secondary meaning. "Secondary meaning occurs when, in the minds of the public, the primary significance of a mark is to identify the source of the product rather than the product itself." *Wal-Mart Stores*, 529 U.S. at 211).[21]

> Secondary meaning is used generally to indicate that a mark or dress has come through use to be uniquely associated with a specific source. To establish secondary meaning, a manufacturer must show that, in the minds of the public, the primary significance of a product feature or term is to identify the source of the product rather than the product itself.

*Two Pesos*, 505 U.S. at 766 n.4 "The inquiry is one of the public's mental association between the mark and the alleged mark holder." *Smack Apparel*, 550 F.3d at 476. "Because the primary element of secondary meaning is a mental association in buyer[s'] minds between the alleged mark and a single source of the product, the determination whether a mark or dress has acquired secondary meaning is primarily an empirical inquiry." *Sunbeam Prods.*, 123 F.3d at 253.

In the context of trade dress, we have articulated seven factors to consider in determining whether secondary meaning has been shown:

> (1) length and manner of use of the mark or trade dress, (2) volume of sales, (3) amount and manner of advertising, (4) nature of use of the mark or trade dress in newspapers and magazines, (5)

---

[21] The *Wal-Mart Stores* Court noted that the term "secondary meaning" "is often a misnomer in th[e] context [of nonword marks], since nonword marks ordinarily have no 'primary' meaning." 529 U.S. at 211 n.*. The Court suggested that a clearer description of the concept would use the term "acquired meaning," but the Court followed "the conventional terminology" of "secondary meaning." We follow it as well.

consumer-survey evidence, (6) direct consumer testimony, and (7) the defendant's intent in copying the trade dress.

*Smack Apparel*, 550 F.3d at 476.[22] "In considering this evidence, the focus is on how it demonstrates that the meaning of the mark or trade dress has been altered in the minds of consumers." *Pebble Beach*, 155 F.3d at 541 (citing *Zatarain's*, 698 F.2d at 795); accord *Zatarain's*, 698 F.2d at 795 ("'[T]he question is not the extent of promotional efforts, but their effectiveness in altering the meaning of the term to the consuming public.'" We have consistently expressed a preference for "an objective survey of the public's perception of" the mark at issue.

The district court considered the following evidence that Amazing Spaces claimed raise a fact issue regarding secondary meaning: (1) the Star Symbol was used for ten years; (2) Amazing Spaces had spent nearly $725,000 in advertising and promoting the Star Symbol; (3) Amazing Spaces had realized over $11.5 million in revenue since it first began using the Star Symbol; (4) Kathy Tautenhahn's statement in her declaration that the Star Symbol identifies Amazing Spaces's self-storage services; and (5) declarations of a customer and an alarm technician about confusion when seeing rival self-storage facilities (Metro and Community) that displayed symbols similar to the Star Symbol. The district court concluded that no fact issue was raised. It based this conclusion partly on the absence of survey evidence, but primarily on its determination that the remaining evidence was not probative regarding secondary meaning: the advertisements did not prominently display the Star Symbol but instead prominently featured the Peaks and Sky Symbol, and the declarations described confusion only in reference to the overall architecture of the facilities.

We agree with the district court that no fact issue has been raised regarding the existence of secondary meaning. As we discussed above, Amazing Spaces's use of the Star Symbol has been primarily decorative and ornamental. Moreover, the record discloses that the Star Symbol was almost invariably used not as a stand-alone mark but was rather, as Amazing Spaces states in its brief, "an integral part of several marks that Amazing Spaces uses—indeed it is the one common element across its non-word marks." While this argument might support secondary meaning as to those other marks, it does not support secondary meaning as to the Star Symbol. This logic extends to the advertising present in the record. While the Star Symbol (or a variation thereof) constitutes a minor piece of the Peaks and Sky Symbol, marks Amazing Spaces's locations on a map, or replaces the bullet in a bulleted list, it is virtually absent as a stand-alone mark from Amazing Spaces's advertising in the record. This predominant advertising use belies the force Amazing Spaces would attribute to its

[22] We recognize that these factors may apply with varying force depending on whether the mark is a service mark or whether it consists of a symbol or design.

telephonic advertising directing customers to "look for the star." Nor does Amazing Spaces's volume of sales—to the extent that it applies to a service mark rather than a trademark, trade dress, or product design—reveal secondary meaning: the advertising attempted to attract customers using marks other than the Star Symbol.

We also agree with the district court's assessment that the two declarations evidencing consumer confusion do not bear on the secondary meaning of the Star Symbol. Shane Flores averred that he was confused by the appearance of a Metro facility's "use of a star logo in conjunction with the similarity in the architectural features and designs" and believed it to be an Amazing Spaces facility. Glen Gilmore averred similarly with respect to a Community facility. While these instances of confusion may bear on Amazing Spaces's trade dress claims, they do not have relevance as to the secondary meaning of the Star Symbol itself.[24] Amazing Spaces also claims that intentional copying has been shown because Metro constructed a facility that incorporated a star design after this lawsuit had been filed. But this chronology does not bear on whether Metro's use of a common design was intentional copying of Amazing Spaces's design. Amazing Spaces also contends that the district court placed undue emphasis on the lack of a survey. We have already noted this court's preference for survey evidence as proof of secondary meaning, and we also note that the other factors do not weigh in Amazing Spaces's favor. As Professor McCarthy has stated, "in a borderline case where it is not at all obvious that [a] designation has been used as a mark, survey evidence may be necessary to prove trademark perception." 1 MCCARTHY ON TRADEMARKS § 3.3, at 3–8.

In conclusion, we agree with the district court's assessment that Amazing Spaces has failed to raise a fact issue regarding the existence of secondary meaning with respect to the Star Symbol. In light of the overwhelming evidence that the Star Symbol is not distinctive, we hold that it does not serve "to identify and distinguish the services of" Amazing Spaces. Lanham Act § 45, 15 U.S.C. § 1127.

### *NOTES AND QUESTIONS*

Several circuits have used variations of the *Seabrook Foods* test to evaluate the inherent distinctiveness of non-word marks. *See, e.g., In re Pacer Technology*, 338 F.3d 1348 (Fed. Cir. 2003) (applying the *Seabrook* test and finding configuration of a cap for a container for adhesives not inherently distinctive); *AmBrit, Inc. v. Kraft, Inc.*, 805 F.2d 974 (11th Cir. 1986), *opinion superseded*, 812 F.2d 1531 (11th Cir. 1986), *cert. denied*, 481 U.S. 1041 (1987) (finding square size, bright colored, pebbled textured ice cream bar packaging with images of polar bear and sunburst to be inherently distinctive trade dress under the *Seabrook* test). Is the *Seabrook* test a good one to determine whether

[24] This is also true with respect to Kathy Tautenhahn's declaration, in which she averred that managers had reported inquiries about whether Amazing Spaces had facilities where Metro facilities were located.

a non-word mark is inherently distinctive? Is it consistent with the principles on which the *Abercrombie* spectrum was based?

Other circuits have insisted that the *Abercrombie* test can be used to evaluate the distinctiveness of any claimed subject matter. The Second Circuit, after having embraced something like the *Seabrook Foods* approach in some earlier trade dress cases, confined that analysis to product design cases (where, as discussed below, inherent distinctiveness is no longer relevant in light of *Wal-Mart*). In *Fun-Damental Too, Ltd. v. Gemmy Indus. Corp.*, 111 F.3d 993 (2d Cir. 1997), the court said it "[saw] no reason to abandon the *Abercrombie* distinctiveness spectrum" in a product packaging case because, while there may be a "finite set of ways to configure a product, the variety of packaging available for a given product is limited only by the bounds of imagination." *See also Nora Beverages, Inc. v. Perrier Group of Am., Inc.*, 164 F.3d 736 (2d Cir. 1998) (applying *Abercrombie* spectrum to packaging), later proceedings 269 F.3d 114 (2d Cir. 2001) (finding 1.5 liter clear, ribbed polyethylene bottle for spring water "generic"). The Second Circuit has not, however, always been entirely consistent on this point. *See Landscape Forms, Inc. v. Columbia Cascade Co.*, 113 F.3d 373 (2d Cir. 1997) ("We are not so confident [as the *Fun-Damental* court] that the *Abercrombie* analysis is more naturally fit for direct application to product packaging cases than configuration cases.").

Courts in other circuits have also attempted to apply the *Abercrombie* spectrum to trade dress, though most of those cases predate *Wal-Mart* and involve product configuration. *See, e.g., Stuart Hall Co. v. Ampad Corp.*, 51 F.3d 780 (8th Cir. 1995) (holding that the *Abercrombie* spectrum should be applied to trade dress); *Insty*Bit v. Poly-Tech Industries, Inc.*, 95 F.3d 663 (8th Cir. 1996) (applying spectrum to product shape trade dress); *Shakespeare Co. v. Silstar Corp. of Am.*, 110 F.3d 234 (4th Cir. 1997) (finding gray-based graphite and clear-tipped fiberglass fishing rod "descriptive" because those colors "describe[d] to the consumer the properties of those materials that make them suitable for their function"); *Sunbeam Prods. Inc. v. West Bend Co.*, 123 F.3d 246 (5th Cir. 1997) (applying the *Abercrombie* spectrum of distinctiveness to product shape trade dress); *Pebble Beach Co. v. Tour 18 I, Ltd.*, 155 F.3d 526 (5th Cir. 1998) (applying *Abercrombie* to determine distinctiveness of design of golf course hole designs); *Ashley Furniture Industries, Inc. v. San Giacomo N.A. Ltd.*, 187 F.3d 363 (4th Cir. 1999) (combining the *Abercrombie* test with the *Seabrook* test to determine distinctiveness of a line of furniture); *Sally Beauty Co., Inc. v. Beautyco, Inc.*, 304 F.3d 964 (10th Cir. 2002) (asking whether plaintiff's white bullet-shaped bottle with a flat, black cap was "descriptive").

What are the advantages and disadvantages of these different approaches? Which approach do you think courts should adopt?

---

## 2. TRADE DRESS DISTINCTIVENESS

### *PROBLEM 3–1*

Ferrari is a world famous designer and manufacturer of sports cars. Between 1969 and 1973, Ferrari produced the 365 GTB/4 Daytona (see http://auto.ferrari.com/en_EN/sports-cars-models/past-models/365-gtb4/). In order to create an aura of exclusivity, Ferrari limited production to 1,400 Daytonas, only 100 of which were originally built as Spyders (soft-top convertibles). Daytona Spyders now sell for $1.0 to $2.0 million. Although Ferrari no longer makes Daytona Spyders, it has continuously produced mechanical parts and body panels and provided repair service for the cars. In 1984, Ferrari began producing another sportscar it called the Testarossa (see http://auto.ferrari.com/en_US/sports-cars-models/past-models/testarossa/). Ferrari limits production of the Testarossa as well; it has produced approximately 7,000 Testarossas since it began production. A new Testarossa sells for approximately $230,000.

Hart Car Productions is in the business of selling "kit cars." Kit cars are replicas of luxury cars that mimic their exterior, with fiberglass shells that are assembled onto the bodies of cars that are typically much cheaper. For example, Hart Car sells kit cars that imitate the designs of the Daytona and Testarossa, and those kit cars are assembled by attaching fiberglass shells onto the undercarriage of a Corvette. The kits sell for $10,000 each.

Ferrari has hired your law firm to analyze its potential trade dress claim against Hart Car Productions. Ferrari has not registered the car designs in the Trademark Office. How, if at all, Ferrari can establish that it owns rights in the shapes of its Daytona and Testarossa cars. What evidence, if any, would Ferrari need in order to prove the designs of its cars are valid trade dress? (ii) Would the functionality doctrine bar Ferrari's claim?

### *PROBLEM 3–2*

Bear Company has designed an ornament to cover a trailer hitch on the back of a vehicle, such as a pick-up truck. The ornament covers the hitch, but it also has a decorative device that resembles a marine propeller of a motor boat. The device spins from the force of the air when a car using the hitch cover is driven. A drawing of the device is shown below:

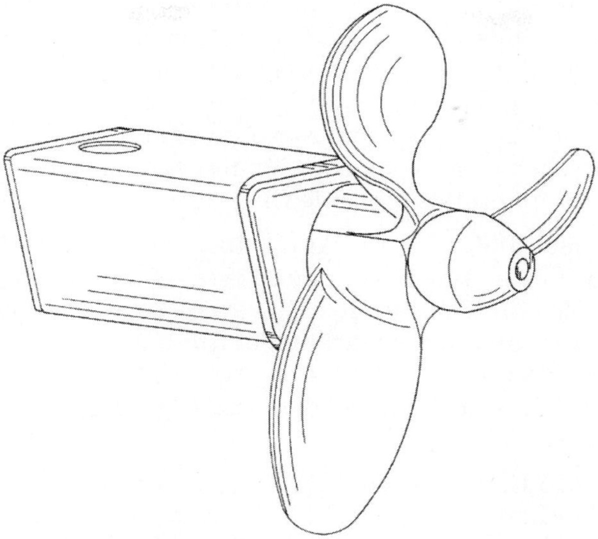

Bear Company has not yet marketed its hitch cover. It would like your legal advice on whether it can claim trade dress protection for its hitch cover, and whether there are further steps it can take to bolster its potential claims.

---

In the time period between 1992 and 2000, the U.S. Supreme Court decided three major trademark cases dealing with the protectability of non-word marks and trade dress. The Court issued a broad ruling with respect to trade dress in *Two Pesos*, and then appeared to back away from the broad ruling in *Qualitex* and *Wal-Mart*. While reading *Two Pesos, Qualitex*, and *Wal-Mart,* think about how these cases can be reconciled. Considering all three cases together, how difficult is it to claim trade dress rights? Does it depend on the type of trade dress claimed?

## TWO PESOS, INC. V. TACO CABANA, INC.

505 U.S. 763 (1992)

JUSTICE WHITE. The issue in this case is whether the trade dress of a restaurant may be protected under § 43(a) of the Trademark Act of 1946 (Lanham Act), based on a finding of inherent distinctiveness, without proof that the trade dress has secondary meaning.

Respondent Taco Cabana, Inc., operates a chain of fast-food restaurants in Texas. The restaurants serve Mexican food. The first Taco Cabana restaurant was opened in San Antonio in September 1978, and five more restaurants had been opened in San Antonio by 1985. Taco Cabana describes its Mexican trade dress as a festive eating atmosphere having interior dining and patio areas decorated with artifacts, bright colors, paintings and murals. The patio includes interior and exterior areas with the interior patio capable of being sealed off from the outside patio by overhead garage doors. The stepped exterior of the building is a festive and vivid color scheme using top border paint and neon stripes. Bright awnings and umbrellas continue the theme.

In December 1985, a Two Pesos, Inc., restaurant was opened in Houston. Two Pesos adopted a motif very similar to the foregoing description of Taco Cabana's trade dress. Two Pesos restaurants expanded rapidly in Houston and other markets, but did not enter San Antonio. In 1986, Taco Cabana entered the Houston and Austin markets and expanded into other Texas cities, including Dallas and El Paso where Two Pesos was also doing business.

In 1987, Taco Cabana sued Two Pesos in the United States District Court for the Southern District of Texas for trade dress infringement under § 43(a) of the Lanham Act, 15 U.S.C. § 1125(a), and for theft of trade secrets under Texas common law. The case was tried to a jury, which was instructed to return its verdict in the form of answers to five questions propounded by the trial judge. The jury's answers were: Taco Cabana has a trade dress; taken as a whole, the trade dress is nonfunctional; the trade dress is inherently distinctive; the trade dress has not acquired a secondary meaning in the Texas market; and the alleged infringement creates a likelihood of confusion on the part of ordinary customers as to the source or association of the restaurant's goods or services. Because, as the jury was told, Taco Cabana's trade dress was protected if it either was inherently distinctive or had acquired a secondary meaning, judgment was entered awarding damages to Taco Cabana. In the course of calculating damages, the trial court held that Two Pesos had intentionally and deliberately infringed Taco Cabana's trade dress.

The Lanham Act was intended to make "actionable the deceptive and misleading use of marks" and "to protect persons engaged in . . . commerce against unfair competition." § 45, 15 U.S.C. § 1127. Section 43(a) "prohibits a broader range of practices than does § 32," which applies to registered marks, *Inwood Laboratories, Inc. v. Ives Laboratories, Inc.*, 456 U.S. 844, 858 (1982), but it is common ground that § 43(a) protects qualifying unregistered trademarks and that the general principles qualifying a mark for registration under § 2 of the Lanham Act are for the most part applicable in determining whether an unregistered mark is entitled to protection under § 43(a).

A trademark is defined in 15 U.S.C. § 1127 as including "any word, name, symbol, or device or any combination thereof" used by any person "to identify and distinguish his or her goods, including a unique product, from those manufactured or sold by others and to indicate the source of the goods, even if that source is unknown." In order to be registered, a mark must be capable of distinguishing the applicant's goods from those of others. § 1052. Marks are often classified in categories of generally increasing distinctiveness; following the classic formulation set out by Judge Friendly, they may be (1) generic; (2) descriptive; (3) suggestive; (4) arbitrary; or (5) fanciful. See *Abercrombie & Fitch Co. v. Hunting World, Inc.*, 537 F.2d 4, 9 (2d Cir. 1976). The Court of Appeals followed this classification and petitioner accepts it. The latter three categories of marks, because their intrinsic nature serves to identify a particular source of a product, are deemed inherently distinctive and are entitled to protection. In contrast, generic marks—those that "refe[r] to the genus of which the particular product is a species," *Park 'N Fly, Inc. v. Dollar Park & Fly, Inc.*, 469 U.S. 189, 194 (1985), citing *Abercrombie & Fitch, supra*, at 9—are not registrable as trademarks.

The general rule regarding distinctiveness is clear: An identifying mark is distinctive and capable of being protected if it *either* (1) is inherently distinctive *or* (2) has acquired distinctiveness through secondary meaning. It is also clear that eligibility for protection under § 43(a) depends on nonfunctionality. It is, of course, also undisputed that liability under § 43(a) requires proof of the likelihood of confusion. . . .

Petitioner argues that the jury's finding that the trade dress has not acquired a secondary meaning shows conclusively that the trade dress is not inherently distinctive. The Court of Appeals' disposition of this issue was sound:

> Two Pesos' argument—that the jury finding of inherent distinctiveness contradicts its finding of no secondary meaning in the Texas market—ignores the law in this circuit. While the necessarily imperfect (and often prohibitively difficult) methods for assessing secondary meaning address the empirical question of current consumer association, the legal recognition of an inherently distinctive trademark or trade dress acknowledges the owner's legitimate proprietary interest in its unique and valuable informational device, regardless of whether substantial consumer association yet bestows the additional empirical protection of secondary meaning.

Although petitioner makes the above argument, it appears to concede elsewhere in its brief that it is possible for a trade dress, even a restaurant trade dress, to be inherently distinctive and thus eligible for protection under § 43(a). Recognizing that a general requirement of secondary meaning imposes "an unfair prospect of theft [or] financial loss" on the developer of fanciful or arbitrary trade dress at the outset of its use, petitioner suggests that such trade dress should receive limited protection without proof of secondary meaning. Petitioner argues that such protection should be only temporary and subject to defeasance when over time the dress has failed to acquire a secondary meaning. This approach is also vulnerable for the reasons given by the Court of Appeals. If temporary protection is available from the earliest use of the trade dress, it must be because it is neither functional nor descriptive, but an inherently distinctive dress that is capable of identifying a particular source of the product. Such a trade dress, or mark, is not subject to copying by concerns that have an equal opportunity to choose their own inherently distinctive trade dress. To terminate protection for failure to gain secondary meaning over some unspecified time could not be based on the failure of the dress to retain its fanciful, arbitrary, or suggestive nature, but on the failure of the user of the dress to be successful enough in the marketplace. This is not a valid basis to find a dress or mark ineligible for protection. The user of such a trade dress should be able to maintain what competitive position it has and continue to seek wider identification among potential customers.

This brings us to the line of decisions by the Court of Appeals for the Second Circuit that would find protection for trade dress unavailable absent proof of secondary meaning, a position that petitioner concedes would have to be modified if the temporary protection that it suggests is to be recognized. In *Vibrant Sales, Inc. v. New Body Boutique, Inc.*, 652 F.2d 299 (1981), the plaintiff claimed protection under § 43(a) for a product whose features the defendant had allegedly copied. The Court of Appeals held that unregistered marks did not enjoy the "presumptive source association" enjoyed by registered marks and hence could not qualify for protection under § 43(a) without proof of secondary meaning. The court's rationale seemingly denied protection for unregistered, but inherently distinctive, marks of all kinds, whether the claimed mark used distinctive words or symbols or distinctive product design. The court thus did not accept the arguments that an unregistered mark was capable of identifying a source and that copying such a mark could be making any kind of a false statement or representation under § 43(a).

This holding is in considerable tension with the provisions of the Lanham Act. If a verbal or symbolic mark or the features of a product design may be registered under § 2, it necessarily is a mark "by which the goods of the applicant may be distinguished from the goods of others," and must be registered unless otherwise disqualified. Since § 2 requires secondary meaning only as a condition to registering descriptive marks, there are plainly marks that are registrable without showing secondary meaning. These same marks, even if not registered, remain inherently capable of distinguishing the goods of the users of these marks. Furthermore, the copier of such a mark may be seen as falsely claiming that his products may for some reason be thought of as originating from the plaintiff.

The Fifth Circuit was quite right in *Chevron*, and in this case, to follow the *Abercrombie* classifications consistently and to inquire whether trade dress for which protection is claimed under § 43(a) is inherently distinctive. If it is, it is capable of identifying products or services as coming from a specific source and secondary meaning is not required. This is the rule generally applicable to trademarks, and the protection of trademarks and trade dress under § 43(a) serves the same statutory purpose of preventing deception and unfair competition. There is no persuasive reason to apply different analysis to the two.

It would be a different matter if there were textual basis in § 43(a) for treating inherently distinctive verbal or symbolic trademarks differently from inherently distinctive trade dress. But there is none. The section does not mention trademarks or trade dress, whether they be called generic, descriptive, suggestive, arbitrary, fanciful, or functional. Nor does the concept of secondary meaning appear in the text of § 43(a). Where secondary meaning does appear in the statute, it is a requirement that applies only to merely descriptive marks and not to inherently distinctive ones. We see no basis for requiring secondary meaning for inherently distinctive trade dress protection under § 43(a) but not for other distinctive words, symbols, or devices capable of identifying a producer's product.

Engrafting onto § 43(a) a requirement of secondary meaning for inherently distinctive trade dress also would undermine the purposes of the Lanham Act. Protection of trade dress, no less than of trademarks, serves the Act's purpose to "secure to the owner of the mark the goodwill of his business and to protect the ability of consumers to distinguish among competing producers. National protection of trademarks is desirable, Congress concluded, because trademarks foster competition and the maintenance of quality by securing to the producer the benefits of good reputation." *Park 'N Fly*, 469 U.S., at 198. By making more difficult the identification of a producer with its product, a secondary meaning requirement for a nondescriptive trade dress would hinder improving or maintaining the producer's competitive position.

Suggestions that under the Fifth Circuit's law, the initial user of any shape or design would cut off competition from products of like design and shape are not persuasive. Only nonfunctional, distinctive trade dress is protected under § 43(a). The Fifth Circuit holds that a design is legally functional, and thus unprotectible, if it is one of a limited number of equally efficient options available to competitors and free competition would be unduly hindered by according the design trademark protection. This serves to assure that competition will not be stifled by the exhaustion of a limited number of trade dresses.

On the other hand, adding a secondary meaning requirement could have anticompetitive effects, creating particular burdens on the startup of small companies. It would present special difficulties for a business, such as respondent, that seeks to start a new product in a limited area and then expand into new markets. Denying protection for inherently distinctive nonfunctional trade dress until after secondary meaning has been established would allow a competitor, which has not adopted a distinctive trade dress of its own, to appropriate the originator's dress in other markets and to deter the originator from expanding into and competing in these areas.

As noted above, petitioner concedes that protecting an inherently distinctive trade dress from its inception may be critical to new entrants to the market and that withholding protection until secondary meaning has been established would be contrary to the goals of the Lanham Act. Petitioner specifically suggests, however, that the solution is to dispense with the requirement of secondary meaning for a reasonable, but brief, period at the outset of the use of a trade dress. If § 43(a) does not require secondary meaning at the outset of a business' adoption of trade dress, there is no basis in the statute to support the suggestion that such a requirement comes into being after some unspecified time.

We agree with the Court of Appeals that proof of secondary meaning is not required to prevail on a claim under § 43(a) of the Lanham Act where the trade dress at issue is inherently distinctive, and accordingly the judgment of that court is affirmed. It is so ordered.

## QUALITEX CO. V. JACOBSON PRODS. CO., INC.

514 U.S. 159 (1995)

JUSTICE BREYER. The question in this case is whether the Trademark Act of 1946 (Lanham Act), 15 U.S.C. §§ 1051–1127, permits the registration of a trademark that consists purely and simply, of a color. We conclude that, sometimes, a color will meet ordinary legal trademark requirements. And, when it does so, no special legal rule prevents color alone from serving as a trademark.

The case before us grows out of petitioner Qualitex Company's use (since the 1950's) of a special shade of green-gold color on the pads that it makes and sells to dry cleaning firms for use on dry cleaning presses. In 1989, respondent Jacobson Products (a Qualitex rival) began to sell its own press pads to dry cleaning firms; and it colored those pads a similar green gold. In 1991, Qualitex registered the special green-gold color on press pads with the Patent and Trademark Office as a trademark. Registration No. 1,633,711. Qualitex subsequently added a trademark infringement count, 15 U.S.C. § 1114(1), to an unfair competition claim, § 1125(a), in a lawsuit it had already filed challenging Jacobson's use of the green-gold color.

Qualitex won the lawsuit in the District Court. But, the Court of Appeals for the Ninth Circuit set aside the judgment in Qualitex's favor on the trademark infringement claim because, in that Circuit's view, the Lanham Act does not permit Qualitex, or anyone else, to register "color alone" as a trademark. This Court granted certiorari. We now hold that there is no rule absolutely barring the use of color alone, and we reverse the judgment of the Ninth Circuit.

### *II*

The Lanham Act gives a seller or producer the exclusive right to "register" a trademark, 15 U.S.C. § 1052, and to prevent his or her competitors from using that trademark, § 1114(1). Both the language of the Act and the basic underlying principles of trademark law would seem to include color within the universe of things that can qualify as a trademark. The language of the Lanham Act describes that universe in the broadest of terms. It says that trademarks "includ[e] any word, name, symbol, or device, or any combination thereof." § 1127. Since human beings might use as a "symbol" or "device" almost anything at all that is capable of carrying meaning, this language, read literally, is not restrictive. The courts and the Patent and Trademark Office have authorized for use as a mark a particular shape (of a Coca-Cola bottle), a particular sound (of NBC's three chimes), and even a particular scent (of plumeria blossoms on sewing thread). See, *e.g.*, Registration No. 696,147; Registration Nos. 523,616 and 916,522; *In re Clarke*, 17 U.S.P.Q. 2d 1238, 1240 (T.T.A.B. 1990). If a shape, a sound, and a fragrance can act as symbols why, one might ask, can a color not do the same?

A color is also capable of satisfying the more important part of the statutory definition of a trademark, which requires that a person "us[e]" or "inten[d] to use" the mark "to identify and distinguish his or her goods, including a unique product, from those manufactured or sold by others and to indicate the source of the goods, even if that source is unknown." 15 U.S.C. § 1127.

True, a product's color is unlike "fanciful," "arbitrary," or "suggestive" words or designs, which almost *automatically* tell a customer that they refer to a brand. *Abercrombie & Fitch Co. v. Hunting World, Inc.*, 537 F.2d 4, 9–10 (2d Cir. 1976) (Friendly, J.); *see Two Pesos, Inc. v. Taco Cabana, Inc.*, 505 U.S. 763, 768 (1992). The imaginary word "Suntost," or the words "Suntost Marmalade," on a jar of orange jam immediately would signal a brand or a product "source"; the jam's orange color does not do so. But, over time, customers may come to treat a particular color on a product or its packaging (say, a color that in context seems unusual, such as pink on a firm's insulating material or red on the head of a large industrial bolt) as signifying a brand. And, if so, that color would have come to identify and distinguish the goods—*i.e.*, "to indicate" their "source"—much in the way that descriptive words on a product (say, "Trim" on nail clippers or "Car-Freshner" on deodorizer) can come to indicate a product's origin. *See, e.g., J. Wiss & Sons Co. v. W.E. Bassett Co.*, 462 F.2d 567, 569 (C.C.P.A. 1972). In this circumstance, trademark law says that the word (*e.g.*, "Trim"), although not inherently distinctive, has developed "secondary meaning." See *Inwood Laboratories, Inc. v. Ives Laboratories*, 456 U.S. 844, 851, n.11

(1982) ("[S]econdary meaning" is acquired when "in the minds of the public, the primary significance of a product feature . . . is to identify the source of the product rather than the product itself"). Again, one might ask, if trademark law permits a descriptive word with secondary meaning to act as a mark, why would it not permit a color, under similar circumstances, to do the same?

We cannot find in the basic objectives of trademark law any obvious theoretical objection to the use of color alone as a trademark, where that color has attained "secondary meaning" and therefore identifies and distinguishes a particular brand (and thus indicates its "source"). In principle, trademark law, by preventing others from copying a source-identifying mark, "reduce[s] the customer's costs of shopping and making purchasing decisions," 1 J. MCCARTHY, MCCARTHY ON TRADEMARKS AND UNFAIR COMPETITION § 2.01[2], p. 2–3 (3d ed. 1994) (hereinafter McCarthy), for it quickly and easily assures a potential customer that *this* item—the item with this mark—is made by the same producer as other similarly marked items that he or she liked (or disliked) in the past. At the same time, the law helps assure a producer that it (and not an imitating competitor) will reap the financial, reputation-related rewards associated with a desirable product. The law thereby "encourage[s] the production of quality products," *ibid.*, and simultaneously discourages those who hope to sell inferior products by capitalizing on a consumer's inability quickly to evaluate the quality of an item offered for sale. It is the source-distinguishing ability of a mark—not its ontological status as color, shape, fragrance, word, or sign—that permits it to serve these basic purposes. *See* Landes & Posner, *Trademark Law: An Economic Perspective*, 30 J. LAW & ECON. 265, 290 (1987). And, for that reason, it is difficult to find, in basic trademark objectives, a reason to disqualify absolutely the use of a color as a mark.

[The court then found that the functionality doctrine does not create an absolute bar to the use of color alone as a mark, though color may in particular cases be determined functional.]

It would seem, then, that color alone, at least sometimes, can meet the basic legal requirements for use as a trademark. It can act as a symbol that distinguishes a firm's goods and identifies their source, without serving any other significant function. *See* Trademark Manual of Examining Procedure § 1202.04(e), p. 1202–13 (approving trademark registration of color alone where it "has become distinctive of the applicant's goods in commerce," provided that "there is [no] competitive need for colors to remain available in the industry" and the color is not "functional"); *see also* 1 MCCARTHY §§ 3.01[1], 7.26, pp. 3–2, 7–113 ("requirements for qualification of a word or symbol as a trademark" are that it be (1) a "symbol," (2) "use[d] . . . as a mark," (3) "to identify and distinguish the seller's goods from goods made or sold by others," but that it not be "functional"). Indeed, the District Court, in this case, entered findings (accepted by the Ninth Circuit) that show Qualitex's green-gold press pad color has met these requirements. The green-gold color acts as a symbol. Having developed secondary meaning (for customers identified the green-gold color as Qualitex's), it identifies the press pads' source. And, the green-gold color serves no other function. Although it is important to use *some* color on press pads to avoid noticeable stains, the court found "no competitive need in the press pad industry for the green-gold color, since other colors are equally usable." 21 U.S.P.Q. 2d at 1460. Accordingly, unless there is some special reason that convincingly militates against the use of color alone as a trademark, trademark law would protect Qualitex's use of the green-gold color on its press pads.

### *III*

Respondent Jacobson Products says that there are four special reasons why the law should forbid the use of color alone as a trademark. We shall explain, in turn, why we, ultimately, find them unpersuasive.

*First*, Jacobson says that, if the law permits the use of color as a trademark, it will produce uncertainty and unresolvable court disputes about what shades of a color a competitor may lawfully use. Because lighting (morning sun, twilight mist) will affect perceptions of protected color, competitors and courts will suffer from "shade confusion" as they try to decide whether use of a similar color on a similar product does, or does not, confuse customers and thereby infringe a trademark. Jacobson adds that the "shade confusion" problem is "more difficult" and "far different from" the "determination of the similarity of words or symbols."

We do not believe, however, that color, in this respect, is special. Courts traditionally decide quite difficult questions about whether two words or phrases or symbols are sufficiently similar, in context, to confuse buyers. They have had to compare, for example, such words as "Bonamine" and "Dramamine" (motion-sickness remedies); "Huggies" and "Dougies" (diapers); "Cheracol" and "Syrocol" (cough syrup); "Cyclone" and "Tornado" (wire fences); and "Mattres" and "1-800-Mattres" (mattress franchisor telephone numbers). *See, e.g., G.D. Searle & Co., v. Chas Pfizer & Co.*, 265 F.2d 385, 389 (7th Cir. 1959); *Kimberly-Clark Corp. v. H. Douglas Enterprises, Ltd.*, 774 F.2d 1144, 1146–47 (Fed. Cir. 1985); *Upjohn Co. v. Schwartz*, 246 F.2d 254, 262 (2d Cir. 1957); *Hancock v. American Steel & Wire Co. of N.J.*, 203 F.2d 737, 740–41 (C.C.P.A. 1953); *Dial-A-Mattress Franchise Crop. v. Page*, 880 F.2d 675, 678 (2d Cir. 1989). Legal standards exist to guide courts in making such comparisons. *See, e.g.*, 2 MCCARTHY § 15.08; 1 MCCARTHY §§ 11.24–11.25 ("[S]trong" marks, with greater secondary meaning, receive broader protection than "weak" marks). We do not see why courts could not apply those standards to a color, replicating, if necessary, lighting conditions under which a colored product is normally sold. *See* Ebert, *Trademark Protection in Color: Do It By the Numbers!*, 84

TRADEMARK REP. 379, 405 (1994). Indeed, courts already have done so in cases where a trademark consists of a color plus a design, *i.e.,* a colored symbol such as a gold stripe (around a sewer pipe), a yellow strand of wire rope, or a "brilliant yellow" band (on ampules). *See, e.g., Youngstown Sheet & Tube Co. v. Tallman Conduit Co.*, 149 U.S.P.Q. 656, 657 (T.T.A.B. 1966); *Amsted Industries, Inc., v. West Coast Wire Rope & Rigging Inc.*, 2 U.S.P.Q. 2d 1755, 1760 (T.T.A.B. 1987); *In re Hodes-Lange Corp.*, 167 U.S.P.Q. 255, 256 (T.T.A.B. 1970).

*Second*, Jacobson argues, as have others, that colors are in limited supply. Jacobson claims that, if one of many competitors can appropriate a particular color for use as a trademark, and each competitor then tries to do the same, the supply of colors will soon be depleted. Put in its strongest form, this argument would concede that "[h]undreds of color pigments are manufactured and thousands of colors can be obtained by mixing." L. CHESKIN, COLORS: WHAT THEY CAN DO FOR YOU 47 (1947). But, it would add that, in the context of a particular product, only some colors are usable. By the time one discards colors that, say, for reasons of customer appeal, are not usable, and adds the shades that competitors cannot use lest they risk infringing a similar, registered shade, then one is left with only a handful of possible colors. And, under these circumstances, to permit one, or a few, producers to use colors as trademarks will "deplete" the supply of usable colors to the point where a competitor's inability to find a suitable color will put that competitor at a significant disadvantage.

This argument is unpersuasive, however, largely because it relies on an occasional problem to justify a blanket prohibition. When a color serves as a mark, normally alternative colors will likely be available for similar use by others. *See, e.g., Owens-Corning*, 774 F.2d at 1121 (pink insulation). Moreover, if that is not so—if a "color depletion" or "color scarcity" problem does arise—the trademark doctrine of "functionality" normally would seem available to prevent the anticompetitive consequences that Jacobson's argument posits, thereby minimizing that argument's practical force.

*Third*, Jacobson points to many older cases—including Supreme Court cases—in support of its position. In 1878, this Court described the common-law definition of trademark rather broadly to "consist of a name, symbol, figure, letter, form, or device, if adopted and used by a manufacturer or merchant in order to designate the goods he manufactures or sells to distinguish the same from those manufactured or sold by another." *McLean v. Fleming*, 96 U.S. 245, 254 (1877). Yet, in interpreting the Trademark Acts of 1881 and 1905, 21 Stat. 502, 33 Stat. 724, which retained that common-law definition, the Court questioned "[w]hether mere color can constitute a valid trade-mark," *A. Leschen & Sons Rope Co. v. Broderick & Bascom Rope Co.*, 201 U.S. 166, 171 (1906), and suggested that the "product including the coloring matter is free to all who make it," *Coca-Cola Co. v. Koke Co. of America*, 254 U.S. 143, 147 (1920). Even though these statements amounted to dicta, lower courts interpreted them as forbidding protection for color alone. *See, e.g., Campbell Soup Co. v. Armour & Co.*, 175 F.2d 795, 798, n.9 (3d Cir. 1949); *Life Savers Corp. v. Curtiss Candy Co.*, 182 F.2d 4, 9 (7th Cir. 1950).

These Supreme Court cases, however, interpreted trademark law as it existed *before* 1946, when Congress enacted the Lanham Act. The Lanham Act significantly changed and liberalized the common law to "dispense with mere technical prohibitions," S. Rep. No. 1333, 79th Cong., 2d Sess., 3 (1946), most notably, by permitting trademark registration of descriptive words (say, "U-Build-It" model airplanes) where they had acquired "secondary meaning." *See Abercrombie & Fitch Co.*, 537 F.2d at 9. The Lanham Act extended protection to descriptive marks by making clear that (with certain explicit exceptions not relevant here) "nothing . . . shall prevent the registration of a mark used by the applicant which has become distinctive of the applicant's goods in commerce." 15 U.S.C. § 1052(f).

This language permits an ordinary word, normally used for a nontrademark purpose (*e.g.*, description), to act as a trademark where it has gained "secondary meaning." Its logic would appear to apply to color as well. Indeed, in 1985, the Federal Circuit considered the significance of the Lanham Act's changes as they related to color and held that trademark protection for color was consistent with the "jurisprudence under the Lanham Act developed in accordance with the statutory principle that if a mark is capable of being or becoming distinctive of [the] applicant's goods in commerce, then it is capable of serving as a trademark." *Owens-Corning*, 774 F.2d at 1120.

In 1988, Congress amended the Lanham Act, revising portions of the definitional language, but left unchanged the language here relevant. 15 U.S.C. § 1127. It enacted these amendments against the following background: (1) the Federal Circuit had decided *Owens-Corning*; (2) the Patent and Trademark Office had adopted a clear policy (which it still maintains) permitting registration of color as a trademark, *see* PTO Manual § 1202.04(e) (at p. 1200–12 of the January 1986 edition and p. 1202–13 of the May 1993 edition); and (3) the Trademark Commission had written a report, which recommended that "the terms 'symbol, or device' . . . not be deleted or narrowed to preclude registration of such things as a color, shape, smell, sound, or configuration which functions as a mark," The United States Trademark Association Trademark Review Commission Report and Recommendations to USTA President and Board of Directors, 77 T.M. Rep. 375, 421 (1987); *see also* 133 Cong. Rec. 32812 (1987) (statement of Sen. DeConcini) ("The bill I am introducing today is based on the Commission's report and recommendations"). This background strongly suggests that the language "any word, name, symbol, or device," 15 U.S.C. § 1127, had come to include color. And, when it amended the statute, Congress retained these terms. Indeed, the Senate

Report accompanying the Lanham Act revision explicitly referred to this background understanding, in saying that the "revised definition intentionally retains . . . the words 'symbol or device' so as not to preclude the registration of colors, shapes, sounds or configurations where they function as trademarks." S. Rep. No. 100–515, at 44 U.S. Code Cong. & Admin. News, 1988, p. 5607. (In addition, the statute retained language providing that "[n]o trademark by which the goods of the applicant may be distinguished from the goods of others shall be refused registration . . . on account of its nature" (except for certain specified reasons not relevant here). 15 U.S.C. § 1052.)

This history undercuts the authority of the precedent on which Jacobson relies. Much of the pre-1985 case law rested on statements in Supreme Court opinions that interpreted pre-Lanham Act trademark law and were not directly related to the holdings in those cases. Moreover, we believe the Federal Circuit was right in 1985 when it found that the 1946 Lanham Act embodied crucial legal changes that liberalized the law to permit the use of color alone as a trademark (under appropriate circumstances). At a minimum, the Lanham Act's changes left the courts free to reevaluate the preexisting legal precedent which had absolutely forbidden the use of color alone as a trademark. Finally, when Congress reenacted the terms "word, name, symbol, or device" in 1988, it did so against a legal background in which those terms had come to include color, and its statutory revision embraced that understanding.

*Fourth*, Jacobson argues that there is no need to permit color alone to function as a trademark because a firm already may use color as part of a trademark, say, as a colored circle or colored letter or colored word, and may rely upon "trade dress" protection, under § 43(a) of the Lanham Act, if a competitor copies its color and thereby causes consumer confusion regarding the overall appearance of the competing products or their packaging, *see* 15 U.S.C. § 1125(a). The first part of this argument begs the question. One can understand why a firm might find it difficult to place a usable symbol or word on a product (say, a large industrial bolt that customers normally see from a distance); and, in such instances, a firm might want to use color, pure and simple, instead of color as part of a design. Neither is the second portion of the argument convincing. Trademark law helps the holder of a mark in many ways that "trade dress" protection does not. *See* 15 U.S.C. § 1124 (ability to prevent importation of confusingly similar goods); § 1072 (constructive notice of ownership); § 1065 (incontestible status); § 1057(b) (prima facie evidence of validity and ownership). Thus, one can easily find reasons why the law might provide trademark protection in addition to trade dress protection.

## *IV*

Having determined that a color may sometimes meet the basic legal requirements for use as a trademark and that respondent Jacobson's arguments do not justify a special legal rule preventing color alone from serving as a trademark (and, in light of the District Court's here undisputed findings that Qualitex's use of the green-gold color on its press pads meets the basic trademark requirements), we conclude that the Ninth Circuit erred in barring Qualitex's use of color as a trademark. For these reasons, the judgment of the Ninth Circuit is reversed.

## WAL-MART STORES, INC. V. SAMARA BROS., INC.

529 U.S. 205 (2000)

JUSTICE SCALIA. In this case, we decide under what circumstances a product's design is distinctive, and therefore protectible, in an action for infringement of unregistered trade dress under § 43(a) of the Trademark Act of 1946 (Lanham Act).

Respondent Samara Brothers, Inc., designs and manufactures children's clothing. Its primary product is a line of spring/summer one-piece seersucker outfits decorated with appliqués of hearts, flowers, fruits, and the like. A number of chain stores, including JC Penney, sell this line of clothing under contract with Samara.

Petitioner Wal-Mart Stores, Inc., is one of the Nation's best known retailers, selling among other things children's clothing. In 1995, Wal-Mart contracted with one of its suppliers, Judy-Philippine, Inc., to manufacture a line of children's outfits for sale in the 1996 spring/summer season. Wal-Mart sent Judy-Philippine photographs of a number of garments from Samara's line, on which Judy-Philippine's garments were to be based; Judy-Philippine duly copied, with only minor modifications, 16 of Samara's garments, many of which contained copyrighted elements. In 1996, Wal-Mart briskly sold the so-called knockoffs, generating more than $1.15 million in gross profits.

In June 1996, a buyer for JC Penney called a representative at Samara to complain that she had seen Samara garments on sale at Wal-Mart for a lower price than JC Penney was allowed to charge under its contract with Samara. The Samara representative told the buyer that Samara did not supply its clothing to Wal-Mart. Their suspicions aroused, however, Samara officials launched an investigation, which disclosed that Wal-Mart and several other major retailers—Kmart, Caldor, Hills, and Goody's—were selling the knockoffs of Samara's outfits produced by Judy-Philippine.

After sending cease-and-desist letters, Samara brought this action in the United States District Court for the Southern District of New York against Wal-Mart, Judy-Philippine, Kmart, Caldor, Hills, and Goody's for copyright infringement under federal law, consumer fraud and unfair competition under New York law, and—most relevant for our purposes—infringement of unregistered trade dress under § 43(a) of the Lanham Act,

15 U.S.C. § 1125(a). All of the defendants except Wal-Mart settled before trial.

After a weeklong trial, the jury found in favor of Samara on all of its claims. Wal-Mart then renewed a motion for judgment as a matter of law, claiming, *inter alia*, that there was insufficient evidence to support a conclusion that Samara's clothing designs could be legally protected as distinctive trade dress for purposes of § 43(a). The District Court denied the motion, and awarded Samara damages, interest, costs, and fees totaling almost $1.6 million, together with injunctive relief. The Second Circuit affirmed the denial of the motion for judgment as a matter of law, and we granted certiorari.

The Lanham Act provides for the registration of trademarks, which it defines in § 45 to include "any word, name, symbol, or device, or any combination thereof [used or intended to be used] to identify and distinguish [a producer's] goods . . . from those manufactured or sold by others and to indicate the source of the goods. . . ." 15 U.S.C. § 1127. . . .

The text of § 43(a) provides little guidance as to the circumstances under which unregistered trade dress may be protected. It does require that a producer show that the allegedly infringing feature is not "functional," and is likely to cause confusion with the product for which protection is sought. Nothing in § 43(a) explicitly requires a producer to show that its trade dress is distinctive, but courts have universally imposed that requirement, since without distinctiveness the trade dress would not "cause confusion as to the origin, sponsorship, or approval of [the] goods," as the section requires. Distinctiveness is, moreover, an explicit prerequisite for registration of trade dress under § 2, and "the general principles qualifying a mark for registration under § 2 of the Lanham Act are for the most part applicable in determining whether an unregistered mark is entitled to protection under § 43(a)." *Two Pesos, Inc. v. Taco Cabana, Inc.*, 505 U.S. 763 (1992).

In evaluating the distinctiveness of a mark under § 2 (and therefore, by analogy, under § 43(a)), courts have held that a mark can be distinctive in one of two ways. First, a mark is inherently distinctive if "[its] intrinsic nature serves to identify a particular source." *Id.* . . . . Second, a mark has acquired distinctiveness, even if it is not inherently distinctive, if it has developed secondary meaning, which occurs when, "in the minds of the public, the primary significance of a [mark] is to identify the source of the product rather than the product itself." *Inwood Laboratories, Inc. v. Ives Laboratories, Inc.*, 456 U.S. 844, 851, n.11 (1982).

The judicial differentiation between marks that are inherently distinctive and those that have developed secondary meaning has solid foundation in the statute itself. Section 2 requires that registration be granted to any trademark "by which the goods of the applicant may be distinguished from the goods of others"—subject to various limited exceptions. It also provides, again with limited exceptions, that "nothing in this chapter shall prevent the registration of a mark used by the applicant which has become distinctive of the applicant's goods in commerce"—that is, which is not inherently distinctive but has become so only through secondary meaning. § 2(f). Nothing in § 2, however, demands the conclusion that every category of mark necessarily includes some marks "by which the goods of the applicant may be distinguished from the goods of others" *without* secondary meaning—that in every category some marks are inherently distinctive.

Indeed, with respect to at least one category of mark—colors—we have held that no mark can ever be inherently distinctive. *See Qualitex Co. v. Jacobson Products Co.*, 514 U.S. 159, 162–63 (1995). In *Qualitex*, petitioner manufactured and sold green-gold dry-cleaning press pads. After respondent began selling pads of a similar color, petitioner brought suit under § 43(a), then added a claim under § 32 after obtaining registration for the color of its pads. We held that a color could be protected as a trademark, but only upon a showing of secondary meaning. Reasoning by analogy to the *Abercrombie & Fitch* test developed for word marks, we noted that a product's color is unlike a "fanciful," "arbitrary," or "suggestive" mark, since it does not "almost *automatically* tell a customer that [it] refer[s] to a brand," 514 U.S., at 162–163, and does not "immediately . . . signal a brand or a product 'source,' " *id.*, at 163. However, we noted that, "over time, customers may come to treat a particular color on a product or its packaging . . . as signifying a brand." *Ibid.* Because a color, like a "descriptive" word mark, could eventually "come to indicate a product's origin," we concluded that it could be protected *upon a showing of secondary meaning. Ibid.*

It seems to us that design, like color, is not inherently distinctive. The attribution of inherent distinctiveness to certain categories of word marks and product packaging derives from the fact that the very purpose of attaching a particular word to a product, or encasing it in a distinctive packaging, is most often to identify the source of the product. Although the words and packaging can serve subsidiary functions—a suggestive word mark (such as "Tide" for laundry detergent), for instance, may invoke positive connotations in the consumer's mind, and a garish form of packaging (such as Tide's squat, brightly decorated plastic bottles for its liquid laundry detergent) may attract an otherwise indifferent consumer's attention on a crowded store shelf—their predominant function remains source identification. Consumers are therefore predisposed to regard those symbols as indication of the producer, which is why such symbols "almost *automatically* tell a customer that they refer to a brand," *id.*, at 162–163, and "immediately . . . signal a brand or a product 'source,' " *id.*, at 163. And where it is not reasonable to assume consumer predisposition to take an affixed word or packaging as indication of source—where, for example, the affixed word is descriptive of the product ("Tasty" bread) or of a geographic origin ("Georgia" peaches)—inherent distinctiveness will not be found. That is why the statute generally excludes, from those word marks that can be registered as inherently distinctive, words that are "merely descriptive" of the goods, or "primarily geographically descriptive of them." In the case of product design, as in the case of color, we think consumer predisposition to equate the feature with the source does not exist. Consumers are aware of the reality that, almost invariably, even the most unusual of product designs—such as a cocktail shaker shaped like a penguin—is intended not to identify the source, but to render the product itself more useful or more appealing.

The fact that product design almost invariably serves purposes other than source identification not only renders inherent distinctiveness problematic; it also renders application of an inherent-distinctiveness principle more harmful to other consumer interests. Consumers should not be deprived of the benefits of competition with regard to the utilitarian and esthetic purposes that product design ordinarily serves by a rule of law that facilitates plausible threats of suit against new entrants based upon alleged inherent distinctiveness. How easy it is to mount a plausible suit depends, of course, upon the clarity of the test for inherent distinctiveness, and where product design is concerned we have little confidence that a reasonably clear test can be devised. Respondent and the United States as *amicus curiae* urge us to adopt for product design relevant portions of the test formulated by the Court of Customs and Patent Appeals for product packaging in *Seabrook Foods, Inc. v. Bar-Well Foods, Ltd.*, 568 F.2d 1342 (1977). That opinion, in determining the inherent distinctiveness of a product's packaging, considered, among other things, "whether it was a 'common' basic shape or design, whether it was unique or unusual in a particular field, [and] whether it was a mere refinement of a commonly-adopted and well-known form of ornamentation for a particular class of goods viewed by the public as a dress or ornamentation for the goods." *Id.*, at 1344 (footnotes omitted). Such a test would rarely provide the basis for summary disposition of an anticompetitive strike suit. Indeed, at oral argument, counsel for the United States quite understandably would not give a definitive answer as to whether the test was met in this very case, saying only that "[t]his is a very difficult case for that purpose." Tr. of Oral Arg. 19. . . .

Respondent contends that our decision in *Two Pesos* forecloses a conclusion that product-design trade dress can never be inherently distinctive. In that case, we held that the trade dress of a chain of Mexican restaurants, which the plaintiff described as "a festive eating atmosphere having interior dining and patio areas decorated with artifacts, bright colors, paintings and murals," 505 U.S., at 765, could be protected under § 43(a) without a showing of secondary meaning. *Two Pesos* unquestionably establishes the legal principle that trade dress can be inherently distinctive, but it does not establish that *product-design* trade dress can be. *Two Pesos* is inapposite to our holding here because the trade dress at issue, the décor of a restaurant, seems to us not to constitute product *design*. It was either product packaging—which, as we have discussed, normally *is* taken by the consumer to indicate origin—or else some *tertium quid* that is akin to product packaging and has no bearing on the present case.

Respondent replies that this manner of distinguishing *Two Pesos* will force courts to draw difficult lines between product-design and product-packaging trade dress. There will indeed be some hard cases at the margin: a classic glass Coca-Cola bottle, for instance, may constitute packaging for those consumers who drink the Coke and then discard the bottle, but may constitute the product itself for those consumers who are bottle collectors, or part of the product itself for those consumers who buy Coke in the classic glass bottle, rather than a can, because they think it more stylish to drink from the former. We believe, however, that the frequency and the difficulty of having to distinguish between product design and product packaging will be much less than the frequency and the difficulty of having to decide when a product design is inherently distinctive. To the extent there are close cases, we believe that courts should err on the side of caution and classify ambiguous trade dress as product design, thereby requiring secondary meaning. The very closeness will suggest the existence of relatively small utility in adopting an inherent-distinctiveness principle, and relatively great consumer benefit in requiring a demonstration of secondary meaning.

We hold that, in an action for infringement of unregistered trade dress under § 43(a) of the Lanham Act, a product's design is distinctive, and therefore protectible, only upon a showing of secondary meaning. The judgment of the Second Circuit is reversed, and the case is remanded for further proceedings consistent with this opinion.

### *NOTES AND QUESTIONS*

1. After *Two Pesos*, trade dress is protectable if it is either inherently distinctive or has acquired distinctiveness, and inherently distinctive, non-functional trade dress is protectable without evidence of secondary meaning. *Qualitex* limited the *Two Pesos* holding by declaring that certain subject matter (color in particular) is categorically incapable of being inherently distinctive. *Wal-Mart* further limited *Two Pesos*, holding that product design is also incapable of being inherently distinctive. According to the Court, product design differs from product packaging because consumers generally do not treat product design features as indications of source. Was that conclusion based on an empirical assessment of consumer understanding of product packaging and product design features? Do you agree that consumers see product packaging and design differently in this regard? Is there a textual basis for the distinction in the Lanham Act?

2. In *Wal-Mart*, the Court recognized the difficulty of distinguishing between product packaging and product design. As Justice Scalia's COKE bottle

illustration demonstrates, features that clearly serve as product packaging in most settings may serve as features of a product in other other circumstances. Given the difficulty of differentiating packaging and design, and the stakes of the determination, it is perhaps surprising that the Court failed to identify any principles to guide lower courts in distinguishing between the two. Instead the Court seemed to create a presumption in favor of treating the claimed trade dress as product design. Specifically, the Court instructed that, in close cases, "courts should err on the side of caution and classify ambiguous trade dress as product design, thereby requiring secondary meaning." But the Court then muddied the waters by suggesting the interior design of the Mexican restaurant at issue in *Two Pesos*, which did not fit in either the product design or product packaging category, should not follow the default rule the Court had just created. Instead, the Court said that the restaurant design was some "*tertium quid* that is akin to product packaging." This complicated things because it suggested that some features are neither design nor packaging and may not be treated under the default rule equating them to product design.

Thus far, courts have been relatively conservative and have tended to resolve any doubts by requiring secondary meaning. In *In re Slokevage*, 441 F.3d 957 (Fed. Cir. 2006), for example, the court reviewed the Trademark Office's refusal to register without evidence of secondary meaning a design consisting of v-shaped cut-outs and flaps on the backside of clothing (jeans, for instance).

The court noted that the Supreme Court in *Wal-Mart* had emphasized the need for proof of secondary meaning "whenever the purchase implicates a utilitarian or aesthetic purpose, rather than a source-identifying function." In the case of the cut-out features on the back of clothing, consumers might purchase the garment for aesthetic reasons. The proposed mark was not clearly "packaging," and Slokevage had referred to the proposed mark as a "cut-away flap design" in the application. In light of the Supreme Court's default rule, the Federal Circuit believed it should err on the side of product design and require evidence of secondary meaning

---

## YANKEE CANDLE COMPANY, INC. V. BRIDGEWATER CANDLE CO.

259 F.3d 25 (1st Cir. 2001)

TORRUELLA, CIRCUIT JUDGE. Yankee Candle Company ("Yankee"), a leading manufacturer of scented candles, sued competitor Bridgewater Candle Company ("Bridgewater") on counts of copyright infringement and trade dress infringement under federal law, as well as on state claims of common law trade dress infringement, tortious interference, and deceptive trade practices under Mass. Gen. Laws ch. 93A. The district court granted summary judgment to Bridgewater on all claims except those of tortious interference and violation of 93A. In a later memorandum, the district court determined that Yankee's evidentiary support for its federal copyright and trade dress claims was irrelevant with respect to the state claim for tortious interference, and substantially limited Yankee's ability to introduce such evidence.

On appeal, Yankee challenges: (i) the grant of summary judgment on its copyright claims; (ii) the grant of summary judgment on its federal trade dress claims; (iii) the district court's decision to narrow the scope of trial and severely limit allowable evidence; and (iv) the grant of summary judgment on the 93A claim. For the reasons explained herein, we affirm the opinions of the district court.

### II. Trade Dress Claims

#### A. Purposes and Scope of Trade Dress Protection

Yankee's second set of claims, for trade dress infringement, is brought pursuant to § 43(a) of the Lanham Act, which provides protection against the use of "any word, term, name, symbol, or device" that "is likely to cause confusion, or to cause mistake, or to deceive" as to the source of a product. 15 U.S.C. § 1125(a). The Lanham Act extends protection not only to words and symbols, but also to "trade dress," defined as "the design and appearance of a product together with the elements making up the overall image that serves to identify the product presented to the consumer." *Chrysler Corp. v. Silva,* 118 F.3d 56, 58 (1st Cir. 1997). The primary purpose of trade dress protection is to protect that which identifies a product's source. *I.P. Lund Trading ApS v. Kohler Co.,* 163 F.3d 27, 35 (1st Cir. 1998). Courts recognize trade dress claims based both on product packaging and on "product design/configuration." *See, e.g., Wal-Mart Stores v. Samara Bros., Inc.,* 529 U.S. 205, 213–14 (2000).

In order for trade dress to be protected under § 43(a), a plaintiff must prove that the dress is: (i) used in commerce; (ii) non-functional; and (iii) distinctive. Distinctiveness may be either "inherent," that is, the "intrinsic nature [of the trade dress] serves to identify a particular source," *Wal-Mart,* 529 U.S. at 210 (citing *Two Pesos, Inc. v. Taco Cabana, Inc.,* 505 U.S. 763, 768 (1992)), or "acquired," i.e., the trade dress has acquired a "secondary meaning" whereby the public views its "primary significance . . . as identify[ing] the source of the product rather than the product itself," *id.* at 211 (quoting *Inwood Labs., Inc. v. Ives Labs., Inc.* , 456 U.S. 844, 851 n. 11 (1982)). Finally, to prove infringement of protected trade dress, the plaintiff must show that another's use of a similar trade dress is likely to cause confusion among consumers as to the product's source. *Lund,* 163 F.3d at 43–44.

#### B. The District Court Analysis

The district court identified three ways in which Yankee claimed that Bridgewater had infringed its trade dress: (i) by copying Yankee's method of shelving and displaying candles in its stores, called the "Vertical Display

System"; (ii) by copying the overall "look and feel" of Yankee's Housewarmer line of candles; and (iii) by copying the design of Yankee's merchandise catalog, specifically its one fragrance per page layout. The court first held that the Vertical Display System was "manifestly functional," both in its arrangement of candles by color and in its use of wooden shelving, and concluded that "Yankee cannot invoke the Lanham Act to appropriate such a conventional method of presenting its wares."

The court then turned to the "look and feel" of the Housewarmer line of candles and the layout of the Yankee catalog. It concluded, with little explanation, that both claims alleged trade dress infringement of a product design/configuration, rather than infringement of product packaging. In accordance with the Supreme Court's decision in *Wal-Mart,* the district court thus held that neither aspect of Yankee's trade dress could be inherently distinctive as a matter of law. *See Wal-Mart,* 529 U.S. at 213–14 (holding that product design/configuration trade dress may never be inherently distinctive). The district court therefore turned to a determination of whether a genuine issue of material fact existed with respect to secondary meaning.

As to the Housewarmer line of candles, the district court determined that the evidence introduced by Yankee had fallen far short of the "vigorous" evidentiary standard required to show secondary meaning in a product design/configuration case. Lastly, although it had not found any of Yankee's trade dress sufficiently distinctive to qualify for protection, the district court held in the alternative that "no reasonable juror could conclude that there is a likelihood of confusion, where clearly marked company names are featured on the face of the products and catalogues." *Id.* at 156.

C. Yankee's Claims

On appeal, Yankee argues that the district court erred in several ways. First, Yankee contends that the district court ignored its "combination" claim defining its trade dress as the *combination* of its Housewarmer series of labels, its choice of candle sizes and styles, its Vertical Design System, and its catalog layout. By disaggregating the features of its trade dress, says Yankee, the district court failed to analyze the "look and feel" of the entire Yankee product. Second, Yankee argues that the district court erroneously defined its trade dress as product design/configuration, and in so doing, proceeded directly to the question of secondary meaning without considering that the dress might be inherently distinctive. Third, Yankee argues that it introduced sufficient evidence of secondary meaning to survive summary judgment. Fourth, Yankee argues that it introduced sufficient evidence of likelihood of confusion to survive summary judgment had the district court needed to reach that issue. Although we agree with Yankee that the district court failed to address its combination claim as such and we entertain the possibility that the court incorrectly analyzed

Yankee's claims under a product design/configuration rubric, we ultimately reach the same conclusion as the district court and affirm the grant of summary judgment, albeit using a different analysis.

1. Yankee's Trade Dress

We begin by sketching Yankee's claimed trade dress, which we read on appeal as defined in two possible ways. First, Yankee suggests that its trade dress is a combination of: (i) the Vertical Display System;[8] (ii) the catalog, with an emphasis on its "one fragrance per page" layout; (iii) its candle shapes and sizes; (iv) the quantities of candles it sells as a unit; and (v) the Housewarmer labels, specifically their inclusion of (a) a full-bleed photograph, (b) a superimposed title plate with gold edging and lettering on a white background, (c) a rectangular shape, and (d) a reflective border.[9] Alternatively, Yankee describes its trade dress as the elements common to its Housewarmer labels, of which we have provided greater detail in the copyright section of this opinion.

2. Inherent Distinctiveness

a. The Combination Claim

Yankee argues that the distinct combination of elements comprising its candle sizes and shapes, quantities sold, labels, Vertical Design System, and catalog stem from "arbitrary" choices and are thus "inherently distinctive" and entitled to trademark protection. Certain types of trade dress, however, can never be inherently distinctive. *Wal-Mart,* 529 U.S. at 212–14 (product design/configuration cannot be inherently distinctive); *Qualitex Co. v. Jacobson Prods. Co.,* 514 U.S. 159, 162 (1995) (color cannot be inherently distinctive). We find that Yankee's combination claim falls under the category of product design/configuration, and thus Yankee must prove that the dress has attained secondary meaning in order for it to be protected under the Lanham Act. *Wal-Mart,* 529 U.S. at 215.

Yankee argues that because its products are candles, all the trappings associated with the sale of the candle—i.e., the candle-holders, the Vertical Display System, the labels, and the catalog—constitute product packaging,

---

[8] The district court found that the Vertical Display System is entirely functional, and therefore not entitled to trade dress protection. Although we agree as to the functionality of the display, we note that a combination of functional elements may itself be entitled to trade dress protection. *Lund,* 163 F.3d at 37.

[9] We note that Yankee has not been entirely consistent in its definition of its trade dress in its appellate brief. At times, it appears that Yankee is arguing that individual *features* of its product line, namely its labels, its catalogues and its Vertical Display System, deserve trade dress protection. This was the analysis undertaken by the district court. At other points, however, Yankee disclaims such an approach. We note that the burden to clearly identify the trade dress at issue is on the plaintiff. *See, e.g., Landscape Forms v. Columbia Cascade Co.,* 113 F.3d 373, 381 (2d Cir.1997). Moreover, at least one federal court has previously criticized Yankee for failing in this regard. *Yankee Candle Co. v. New England Candle Co.,* 14 F. Supp. 2d 154, 162 (D. Mass.1998), *vacated pursuant to settlement,* 29 F. Supp. 2d 44 (D. Mass.1998). After a careful review of the record, we conclude that Yankee has been sufficiently consistent as to these two descriptions of its trade dress for us to evaluate them on appeal.

or at the very least a "*tertium quid* . . . akin to product packaging," categories of trade dress that may be inherently distinctive. *See Wal-Mart,* 529 U.S. at 215 (citing *Two Pesos,* 505 U.S. at 773).

Although, as we explain below, Yankee's Housewarmer *labels* are product packaging and thus may be inherently distinctive, when combined with actual candle features, candle containers, the catalog,[10] and the in-store display system, the claim is no longer clearly a product-packaging one. Nor can the claim be categorized as product design/configuration, as that term has generally been defined to be limited to features inherent to the actual physical product: here, the candles. *See Wal-Mart,* 529 U.S. at 212 (describing cocktail shaker shaped as penguin as a product design); *Lund,* 163 F.3d at 34–36 (kitchen faucets). We also do not see this claim as akin to the restaurant decor upheld as potentially inherently distinctive in *Two Pesos,* which the Supreme Court later described as a "*tertium quid* that is akin to product packaging." *Wal-Mart,* 529 U.S. at 215; *see also Best Cellars Inc. v. Grape Finds at Dupont, Inc.,* 90 F. Supp. 2d 431, 451–53 (S.D.N.Y. 2000) (finding that the overall layout of a wine store could be, and was, inherently distinctive). Yankee has not made a claim as to the overall appearance of an entire store, but has instead isolated certain characteristics of its candle display in stores. This strikes us as far closer to the design/configuration category. The fact that Yankee points to particular aspects of the candles themselves, namely their shapes and sizes, only confirms our categorization.

In *Wal-Mart,* the Supreme Court instructed us how to deal with claims that were at the margin of product design/configuration: "To the extent that there are close cases, we believe that courts should err on the side of caution and classify ambiguous trade dress as product design, thereby requiring secondary meaning." 529 U.S. at 215. We follow that advice here. To prevail on its combination claim, Yankee must show that its trade dress has acquired secondary meaning.

b. Labels

Yankee also claims that unique features of its Housewarmer labels constitute an inherently distinctive trade dress. The district court found that the labels were also product configuration/design, and thus could not be inherently distinctive as a matter of law. We disagree. Detachable labels

---

[10] We note that we are troubled by the inclusion of Yankee's catalog in its combination trade dress claim. A combination trade dress claim is one that includes a number of different features of a product or its packaging which, *taken together,* are potentially indicative of source. In this case, although the candles, their labels, and the Vertical Display System are all seen at the same time, the catalog is a separate item mailed to consumers at their homes. Moreover, Bridgewater's catalog is a wholesale one, sent only to retailers. Even if we were willing to accept that Yankee's catalog may constitute part of its trade dress, and even if Bridgewater's catalog is eerily similar to Yankee's, we do not see how that similarity could contribute to any consumer confusion. At any rate, because we conclude that Yankee must establish that its combination has acquired secondary meaning, and has not in fact done so, whether the catalog is included or not in the combination claim is ultimately irrelevant.

are a classic case of product packaging, and therefore may be inherently distinctive. *See, e.g., Fun-Damental Too,* 111 F.3d at 1000–01. Although the district court did not determine whether the Housewarmer labels were inherently distinctive, we are convinced that the label elements highlighted by Yankee do not meet the inherent distinctiveness test of *Abercrombie & Fitch Co. v. Hunting World, Inc.,* 537 F.2d 4 (2d Cir. 1976). We therefore uphold the district court's grant of summary judgment on this basis.

Under *Abercrombie,* trademarks are divided into five categories: generic, descriptive, suggestive, arbitrary, and fanciful. If a mark falls into one of the latter three categories, it is deemed to be inherently distinctive. Because the *Abercrombie* test was first applied to word marks, *see Abercrombie,* 537 F.2d at 9, it may be difficult to apply to visual marks or trade dress, *Lund,* 163 F.3d at 39. The Supreme Court, however, has endorsed the use of the *Abercrombie* test in the evaluation of visual marks, as well as in the assessment of product packaging trade dress claims. *Id.* (citing *Two Pesos,* 505 U.S. at 768–69).

This Court, however, has noted that "[w]e do not believe that the Supreme Court's endorsement of the *Abercrombie* test in *Two Pesos* requires a strict application of the *Abercrombie* test in all contexts. . . ." *Id.* at 40. Instead, we have found it appropriate to supplement the somewhat bare-boned *Abercrombie* categories with the questions asked in *Seabrook Foods, Inc. v. Bar-Well Foods Ltd.,* 568 F.2d 1342 (C.C.P.A. 1977). In *Seabrook,* inherent distinctiveness was determined by reference to: (i) whether the design was a common or basic one; (ii) whether it was "unique or unusual" in the field; (iii) whether it was a refinement of a common form of ornamentation; and (iv) "whether it was capable of creating a commercial impression distinct from the accompanying words."[11] *Wiley v. Am. Greetings Corp.,* 762 F.2d 139, 141 (1st Cir. 1985) (quoting *Seabrook,* 568 F.2d at 1344). "In reality [the question is] whether the [dress] is so unique, unusual or unexpected in this market that it will automatically be perceived by customers as an indicator of origin." *Lund,* 163 F.3d at 40 (citing 1 J. McCarthy, *McCarthy on Trademarks and Unfair Competition* § 8.13 (4th ed. 1996)); *see also McKernan v. Burek,* 118 F. Supp. 2d 119, 124 (D.Mass. 2000) (describing this question as the "*Lund* test" for inherent distinctiveness).

Furthermore, in evaluating the inherent distinctiveness of Yankee's packaging, we must consider the fact that although Yankee's Housewarmer labels have obvious similarities, they also differ significantly from one another, in that they necessarily display different pictures

[11] We note that other circuits may be less willing to apply this "gloss" on the *Abercrombie* test when product packaging is at issue. For example, despite noting that "[w]e are not so confident that the *Abercrombie* analysis is more naturally fit for product packaging cases" than is a *Seabrook*-like test, the Second Circuit has resisted the temptation to refine the *Abercrombie* test for visual marks or trade dress. *Landscape Forms,* 113 F.3d at 379.

corresponding to their particular candle fragrance. In other words, Yankee seeks to protect features common to a set of labels, as opposed to a specific label common to a host of Yankee goods. A trade dress plaintiff seeking to protect a series or line of products faces a particularly difficult challenge, as it must show that the appearance of the several products is "sufficiently distinct and unique to merit protection." *Landscape Forms,* 113 F.3d at 380; *Jeffrey Milstein, Inc. v. Greger, Lawlor, Roth, Inc.*, 58 F.3d 27, 32–33 (2d Cir. 1995). Moreover, trade dress claims across a line of products present special concerns in their ability to artificially limit competition, as such claims are generally broader in scope than claims relating to an individual item. *Landscape Forms,* 113 F.3d at 381.

Yankee has focused on the "arbitrary" choices it made in designing its label, and has for this reason introduced into evidence numerous possibilities of alternative label designs. While we appreciate that there are many different potential ways of creating a candle label, we think Yankee's approach ignores the focus of the inherent distinctiveness inquiry. As we detailed in the copyright section of this opinion, Yankee's label is essentially a combination of functional and common features. *See Pubs. Int'l,* 164 F.3d at 341 (gold coloring is a prime example of aesthetic functionality, because it connotes opulence). Although such a combination may be entitled to protection where secondary meaning is shown, *Lund,* 163 F.3d at 37, it is less likely to qualify as inherently distinctive, *Jeffrey Milstein,* 58 F.3d at 32. While the particular combination of common features may indeed be "arbitrary," we do not think that any reasonable juror could conclude that these elements are so "unique and unusual" that they are source-indicative in the absence of secondary meaning. *Lund,* 163 F.3d at 40.

3. Secondary Meaning

Having concluded that neither trade dress claim made by Yankee qualifies for protection based on its inherent distinctiveness, we next address whether Yankee has introduced sufficient evidence to survive summary judgment on the question of secondary meaning. As evidence of secondary meaning,[12] Yankee points to: (i) its advertising campaign featuring pictures of its products with the claimed trade dress; (ii) its continuous and virtually exclusive use of its trade dress since 1995; (iii) its high sales figures for Housewarmer candles; (iv) evidence from Bridgewater's files indicating that retailers identify a resemblance between Bridgewater's styles and Yankee's; (v) testimony by a Bridgewater's sales agent as to the distinctiveness of the Yankee trade dress; (vi) testimony by Bridgewater and Yankee employees as to the

[12] With respect to the question of secondary meaning, Yankee does not clearly distinguish the evidentiary support for its label claim from that supporting its combination claim. For purposes of this analysis, we assume that the adduced evidence may be relevant to both aspects of its claimed trade dress. We note, however, that secondary meaning faces a higher threshold in a product design/configuration case. *See Lund,* 163 F.3d at 42; *Duraco,* 40 F.3d at 1435.

distinctiveness of Yankee's claimed trade dress; (vii) evidence of actual consumer confusion between Bridgewater and Yankee products; and (viii) evidence of intentional copying by Bridgewater.

This Court has said that "[p]roof of secondary meaning entails vigorous evidentiary requirements." *Boston Beer,* 9 F.3d at 181 (quoting *Perini Corp. v. Perini Constr.,* 915 F.2d 121, 125 (4th Cir. 1990)). The only direct evidence probative of secondary meaning is consumer surveys and testimony by individual consumers. *Id.* Although survey evidence is not required, "it is a valuable method of showing secondary meaning." *Lund,* 163 F.3d at 42. Yankee has introduced no survey evidence here.[13] Yankee also cites no evidence that individual consumers associate the particular features at issue with Yankee.

Secondary meaning may also be proven through circumstantial evidence, specifically the length and manner of the use of the trade dress, the nature and extent of advertising and promotion of the trade dress, and the efforts made to promote a conscious connection by the public between the trade dress and the product's source. *See Boston Beer,* 9 F.3d at 182. Other factors may include the product's "established place in the market" and proof of intentional copying. *Lund,* 163 F.3d at 42. Yankee has introduced substantial evidence that the Housewarmer line of candles and corresponding display have been in circulation since 1995, that Yankee spends significant resources advertising its Housewarmer line, and that sales of Housewarmer candles have been extremely successful. However, in concluding that Yankee had not made a sufficient evidentiary showing of secondary meaning, the district court focused on the lack of evidence as to advertising of the *specific* trade dress claimed, as well as the lack of evidence demonstrating a conscious connection by the public between the claimed trade dress and the product's source.

We believe the district court emphasized the relevant issues in conducting its analysis of secondary meaning. Proof of secondary meaning requires at least *some* evidence that consumers associate the trade dress with the source. Although evidence of the pervasiveness of the trade dress may support the conclusion that a mark has acquired secondary meaning, it cannot stand alone. To find otherwise would provide trade dress protection for any successful product, or for the packaging of any successful product. *See Seabrook,* 568 F.2d at 1344 (evidence of sales volume may be relevant to secondary meaning, but "is not necessarily indicative"). Such an open standard hardly comports with the "vigorous" evidentiary showing required by this Court, nor does it comport with the purposes of trade dress protection, namely "to protect that which identifies a product's source." *Lund,* 163 F.3d at 35. In the absence of *any* evidence that the claimed trade

[13] Yankee has cited surveys, taken by Bridgewater, indicating that Bridgewater's trade dress is substantially similar to Yankee's. Although this evidence, if admissible, would be probative of a likelihood of confusion, it does not indicate that Yankee's trade dress has acquired secondary meaning.

dress actually *does* identify a product's source, the trade dress should not be entitled to protection.

That being said, Yankee argues that, because its advertising contained pictures of its products incorporating the claimed trade dress, it was the type of "look-for" advertising that can, on its own, support a finding of secondary meaning. *See First Brands Corp. v. Fred Meyer, Inc.,* 809 F.2d 1378, 1383 (9th Cir. 1987). "Look-for" advertising is such that "encourages consumers to identify the claimed trade dress with the particular producer." *Thomas & Betts Corp. v. Panduit Corp.,* 65 F.3d 654, 662 (7th Cir. 1995). In other words, it is advertising that specifically directs a consumer's attention to a particular aspect of the product. To be probative of secondary meaning, the advertising must direct the consumer to those features claimed as trade dress. *Id.* Merely "featuring" the relevant aspect of the product in advertising is no more probative of secondary meaning than are strong sales; again, to provide protection based on extensive advertising would extend trade dress protection to the label (or to the combination claim) without any showing that the consumer associated the dress with the product's source. *See Int'l Jensen, Inc. v. Metrosound U.S.A., Inc.,* 4 F.3d 819, 824 (9th Cir. 1993) ("While evidence of a manufacturer's sales, advertising and promotional activities may be relevant in determining secondary meaning, the true test of secondary meaning is the *effectiveness* of this effort to create it.") (emphasis added). The district court found that Yankee's advertising did not emphasize any particular element of its trade dress, and thus could not be probative of secondary meaning. We agree.

We also do not find Yankee's evidence of intentional copying probative of secondary meaning. First, to the extent Yankee seeks to use such evidence as secondary meaning of its *combination* trade dress, intent plays a particularly minor role in product design/configuration cases. *See, e.g., Duraco,* 40 F.3d at 1453 ("[A]ttempts to copy a product configuration [may] not be probative [because] the copier may very well be exploiting a particularly desirable feature, rather than seeking to confuse consumers as to the source of the product."). Given the highly functional nature of certain elements of Yankee's claimed combination trade dress, the concern that protection could prevent healthy competition in the scented candle field weighs heavily in this case.

The testimony that Bridgewater designers were, at times, told to make the labels look more like Yankee's is more troubling. *See Blau Plumbing, Inc. v. S.O.S. Fix-it, Inc.,* 781 F.2d 604, 611 (7th Cir. 1986) (defendant's belief that trade dress has acquired secondary meaning provides some evidence that it actually has acquired secondary meaning). However, the relevant intent is not just the intent to copy, but to "pass off" one's goods as those of another. *Id.* Given that Bridgewater prominently displayed its trade name on its candles, we do not think that the evidence of copying was sufficiently probative of secondary meaning.

In sum, Yankee has not introduced any of the direct evidence—surveys or consumer testimony—traditionally used to establish secondary meaning. Although it has introduced some of the circumstantial evidence often used to support such a finding, the lack of any evidence that actual consumers associated the claimed trade dress with Yankee, as well as the lack of evidence as to confusion on the part of actual consumers,[15] renders this circumstantial evidence insufficient for a reasonable juror to find that the trade dress had acquired a secondary meaning. Yankee has not made the vigorous evidentiary showing required by this Court. The grant of summary judgment on Yankee's Lanham Act claim is affirmed.

### *NOTES AND QUESTIONS*

1. The court in *Yankee Candle* treated Yankee's combination trade dress as product configuration rather than product packaging or the elusive *tertium quid*. That determination required Yankee to establish secondary meaning (because product configuration cannot, under *Wal-Mart*, be considered inherently distinctive). Why was a combination that included features one wouldn't naturally consider product configuration (including labels, the layout of a store, and the design of a catalog) treated as configuration? Was this a conclusion Yankee could have avoided by characterizing its trade dress differently?

2. The *Yankee Candle* court repeatedly stated that it is more difficult to establish the secondary meaning of product configuration, compared to product packaging or other indications that are not inherently distinctive. Why would courts hold product design to a higher standard? What evidence would have satisfied the court that the combination trade dress had secondary meaning? How does that compare to the kind of evidence courts ordinarily find persuasive in, say, descriptive word mark cases?

---

## C. FUNCTIONALITY

In addition to the difficulty of assessing trade dress distinctiveness, features claimed as trade dress—particularly though not exclusively

---

[15] Yankee does point to several consumer affidavits as indicative of actual consumer confusion. A close examination of these affidavits indicates that all of the confusion was premised on alleged misrepresentations by retail employees. For example, in one case, an employee allegedly told a consumer that Yankee had been taken over by Bridgewater; the consumer believed this story because the candles had somewhat similar labels. Yankee has adduced *no* evidence, as far as we can tell, that any consumer (on their own accord) examined a Bridgewater candle and thought that it had been made by Yankee. The fact that Bridgewater candles prominently display the Bridgewater trade name makes this lack of evidence unsurprising. *Pampered Chef, Ltd. v. Magic Kitchen, Inc.*, 12 F. Supp. 2d 785, 795 (N.D.Ill. 1998); *Swisher Mower & Mach. Co. v. Haban Mfg., Inc.*, 931 F. Supp. 645, 650 (W.D. Mo.1996).

product design—often contribute to the article's performance in some way. Granting protection to features that have some utility is potentially problematic because competitors may need to use those design features to compete effectively. Moreover, trademark protection for such features may conflict with patent law, which establishes the criteria for legal protection of useful inventions. We have already studied this same issue in the context of design patents. It may be no easier to solve for trademarks.

## 1. THE SUPREME COURT'S FUNCTIONALITY JURISPRUDENCE

Recall that the Supreme Court touched on the issue of functionality in its *Qualitex* decision. There the court said that concerns about competitors' need to use certain colors could adequately be addressed with the functionality doctrine in particular cases and were not a reason to exclude colors from trademark protection categorically. The *Qualitex* Court's discussion of functionality is reproduced below. The case that follows, *TrafFix Devices, Inc. v. Marketing Displays, Inc.*, the court addresses the proper test for functionality and the relationship between trademark and patent law.

### QUALITEX CO. V. JACOBSON PRODUCTS CO.

514 U.S. 159 (1995)

JUSTICE BREYER. The functionality doctrine prevents trademark law, which seeks to promote competition by protecting a firm's reputation, from instead inhibiting legitimate competition by allowing a producer to control a useful product feature. It is the province of patent law, not trademark law, to encourage invention by granting inventors a monopoly over new product designs or functions for a limited time, 35 U.S.C. §§ 154, 173, after which competitors are free to use the innovation. If a product's functional features could be used as trademarks, however, a monopoly over such features could be obtained without regard to whether they qualify as patents and could be extended forever (because trademarks may be renewed in perpetuity). See *Kellogg Co. v. National Biscuit Co.*, 305 U.S. 111, 119–20 (1938) (Brandeis, J.); *Inwood Labs.*, 456 U.S. at 863 (White, J., concurring in result) ("A functional characteristic is 'an important ingredient in the commercial success of the product,' and, after expiration of a patent, it is no more the property of the originator than the product itself") (citation omitted).

Functionality doctrine therefore would require, to take an imaginary example, that even if customers have come to identify the special illumination-enhancing shape of a new patented light bulb with a particular manufacturer, the manufacturer may not use that shape as a trademark, for doing so, after the patent had expired, would impede competition—not by protecting the reputation of the original bulb maker, but by frustrating competitors' legitimate efforts to produce an equivalent illumination-enhancing bulb. *See, e.g.*, *Kellogg*, 305 U.S. at 119–20 (trademark law cannot be used to extend monopoly over "pillow" shape of shredded wheat biscuit after the patent for that shape had expired). This Court consequently has explained that, "[i]n general terms, a product feature is functional," and cannot serve as a trademark, "if it is essential to the use or purpose of the article or if it affects the cost or quality of the article," that is, if exclusive use of the feature would put competitors at a significant non-reputation-related disadvantage. *Inwood Labs.*, 456 U.S. at 850 n.10. Although sometimes color plays an important role (unrelated to source identification) in making a product more desirable, sometimes it does not. And, this latter fact—the fact that sometimes color is not essential to a product's use or purpose and does not affect cost or quality—indicates that the doctrine of "functionality" does not create an absolute bar to the use of color alone as a mark. *See Owens-Corning*, 774 F.2d at 1123 (pink color of insulation in wall "performs no nontrademark function").

* * *

The functionality doctrine, as we have said, forbids the use of a product's feature as a trademark where doing so will put a competitor at a significant disadvantage because the feature is "essential to the use or purpose of the article" or "affects [its] cost or quality." *Inwood Labs.*, 456 U.S. at 850 n.10. The functionality doctrine thus protects competitors against a disadvantage (unrelated to recognition or reputation) that trademark protection might otherwise impose, namely, their inability reasonably to replicate important non-reputation-related product features. For example, this Court has written that competitors might be free to copy the color of a medical pill where that color serves to identify the kind of medication (*e.g.*, a type of blood medicine) in addition to its source. See *id.* at 853, 858 n.20 ("[S]ome patients commingle medications in a container and rely on color to differentiate one from another"); see also J. GINSBURG, D. GOLDBERG, & A. GREENBAUM, TRADEMARK AND UNFAIR COMPETITION LAW 194–195 (1991) (noting that drug color cases "have more to do with public health policy" regarding generic drug substitution "than with trademark law"). And, the federal courts have demonstrated that they can apply this doctrine in a careful and reasoned manner, with sensitivity to the effect on competition. See *Deere & Co. v. Farmhand, Inc.*, 560 F. Supp. 85, 98 (S.D. Iowa 1982), *aff'd*, 721 F.2d 253 (8th Cir. 1983) [allowing "competitors to copy the green color of farm machinery (because customers wanted their farm equipment to match)"]; *Brunswick Corp. v. British Seagull Ltd.*, 35 F.3d 1527, 1532 (Fed. Cir. 1994) ["barr[ing] the use of black as a trademark on outboard boat motors (because black has the special functional attributes of decreasing the apparent size of the motor and ensuring compatibility with many different boat colors"]; *see also Nor-Am Chemical v. O.M. Scott & Sons Co.*, 4 U.S.P.Q. 2d 1316, 1320 (E.D. Pa.

1987) (blue color of fertilizer held functional because it indicated the presence of nitrogen). The Restatement (Third) of Unfair Competition adds that, if a design's "aesthetic value" lies in its ability to "confe[r] a significant benefit that cannot practically be duplicated by the use of alternative designs," then the design is "functional." Restatement § 17, Comment *c,* pp. 175–176 (1993). The "ultimate test of aesthetic functionality," it explains, "is whether the recognition of trademark rights would significantly hinder competition." *Id.*, at 176.

The upshot is that, where a color serves a significant nontrademark function—whether to distinguish a heart pill from a digestive medicine or to satisfy the "noble instinct for giving the right touch of beauty to common and necessary things," G. CHESTERTON, SIMPLICITY AND TOLSTOY 61 (1912)—courts will examine whether its use as a mark would permit one competitor (or a group) to interfere with legitimate (nontrademark-related) competition through actual or potential exclusive use of an important product ingredient. That examination should not discourage firms from creating esthetically pleasing mark designs, for it is open to their competitors to do the same. But, ordinarily, it should prevent the anticompetitive consequences of Jacobson's hypothetical "color depletion" argument, when, and if, the circumstances of a particular case threaten "color depletion."

## TRAFFIX DEVICES, INC. V. MARKETING DISPLAYS, INC.

532 U.S. 23 (2001)

JUSTICE KENNEDY. Temporary road signs with warnings like "Road Work Ahead" or "Left Shoulder Closed" must withstand strong gusts of wind. An inventor named Robert Sarkisian obtained two utility patents for a mechanism built upon two springs (the dual-spring design) to keep these and other outdoor signs upright despite adverse wind conditions. The holder of the now-expired Sarkisian patents, respondent Marketing Displays, Inc. (MDI), established a successful business in the manufacture and sale of sign stands incorporating the patented feature. MDI's stands for road signs were recognizable to buyers and users (it says) because the dual-spring design was visible near the base of the sign.

This litigation followed after the patents expired and a competitor, TrafFix Devices, Inc., sold sign stands with a visible spring mechanism that looked like MDI's. MDI and TrafFix products looked alike because they were. When TrafFix started in business, it sent an MDI product abroad to have it reverse engineered, that is to say copied. Complicating matters, TrafFix marketed its sign stands under a name similar to MDI's. MDI used the name "Wind-Master," while TrafFix, its new competitor, used "WindBuster."

MDI brought suit under the Trademark Act of 1946 (Lanham Act) against TrafFix for trademark infringement (based on the similar names), trade dress infringement (based on the copied dual-spring design), and unfair competition.

We are concerned with the trade dress question. The District Court ruled against MDI on its trade dress claim. After determining that the one element of MDI's trade dress at issue was the dual-spring design, it held that "no reasonable trier of fact could determine that MDI has established secondary meaning" in its alleged trade dress, *id.*, at 269. In other words, consumers did not associate the look of the dual-spring design with MDI. As a second, independent reason to grant summary judgment in favor of TrafFix, the District Court determined the dual-spring design was functional. On this rationale secondary meaning is irrelevant because there can be no trade dress protection in any event. In ruling on the functional aspect of the design, the District Court noted that Sixth Circuit precedent indicated that the burden was on MDI to prove that its trade dress was nonfunctional, and not on TrafFix to show that it was functional (a rule since adopted by Congress) and then went on to consider MDI's arguments that the dual-spring design was subject to trade dress protection. Finding none of MDI's contentions persuasive, the District Court concluded MDI had not "proffered sufficient evidence which would enable a reasonable trier of fact to find that MDI's vertical dual-spring design is *non*-functional." 971 F. Supp., at 276. Summary judgment was entered against MDI on its trade dress claims.

The Court of Appeals for the Sixth Circuit reversed the trade dress ruling. The Court of Appeals held the District Court had erred in ruling MDI failed to show a genuine issue of material fact regarding whether it had secondary meaning in its alleged trade dress and had erred further in determining that MDI could not prevail in any event because the alleged trade dress was in fact a functional product configuration. The Court of Appeals suggested the District Court committed legal error by looking only to the dual-spring design when evaluating MDI's trade dress. Basic to its reasoning was the Court of Appeals' observation that it took "little imagination to conceive of a hidden dual-spring mechanism or a tri or quad-spring mechanism that might avoid infringing [MDI's] trade dress." *Ibid.* The Court of Appeals explained that "[i]f TrafFix or another competitor chooses to use [MDI's] dual-spring design, then it will have to find *some other way* to set its sign apart to avoid infringing [MDI's] trade dress." *Ibid.* It was not sufficient, according to the Court of Appeals, that allowing exclusive use of a particular feature such as the dual-spring design in the guise of trade dress would "hinde[r] competition somewhat." Rather, [e]xclusive use of a feature must 'put competitors at a *significant* non-reputation-related disadvantage' before trade dress protection is denied on functionality grounds. *Ibid.* (quoting *Qualitex Co. v. Jacobson Products Co.*, 514 U.S. 159, 165 (1995)). In its criticism of the District Court's ruling on the trade dress question, the Court of Appeals took note of a split among Courts of Appeals in various other Circuits on the issue whether the existence of an expired utility patent forecloses the possibility of the patentee's claiming trade dress protection in the product's design. To resolve the conflict, we granted certiorari.

It is well established that trade dress can be protected under federal law. The design or packaging of a product may acquire a distinctiveness which serves to identify the product with its manufacturer or source; and a design or package which acquires this secondary meaning, assuming other requisites are met, is a trade dress which may not be used in a manner likely to cause confusion as to the origin, sponsorship, or approval of the goods. In these respects protection for trade dress exists to promote competition. As we explained just last Term, see *Wal-Mart Stores, Inc. v. Samara Brothers, Inc.*, 529 U.S. 205 (2000), various Courts of Appeals have allowed claims of trade dress infringement relying on the general provision of the Lanham Act which provides a cause of action to one who is injured when a person uses "any word, term name, symbol, or device, or any combination thereof . . . which is likely to cause confusion . . . as to the origin, sponsorship, or approval of his or her goods." 15 U.S.C. § 1125(a)(1)(A). Congress confirmed this statutory protection for trade dress by amending the Lanham Act to recognize the concept. Title 15 U.S.C. § 1125(a)(3) (1994 ed., Supp. V) provides: "In a civil action for trade dress infringement under this chapter for trade dress not registered on the principal register, the person who asserts trade dress protection has the burden of proving that the matter sought to be protected is not functional." This burden of proof gives force to the well-established rule that trade dress protection may not be claimed for product features that are functional. *Qualitex, supra*, at 164–165; *Two Pesos, Inc. v. Taco Cabana, Inc.*, 505 U.S. 763, 775 (1992). And in *Wal-Mart, supra*, we were careful to caution against misuse or overextension of trade dress. We noted that "product design almost invariably serves purposes other than source identification." *Id.*, at 213.

Trade dress protection must subsist with the recognition that in many instances there is no prohibition against copying goods and products. In general, unless an intellectual property right such as a patent or copyright protects an item, it will be subject to copying. As the Court has explained, copying is not always discouraged or disfavored by the laws which preserve our competitive economy. *Bonito Boats, Inc. v. Thunder Craft Boats, Inc.*, 489 U.S. 141, 160 (1989). Allowing competitors to copy will have salutary effects in many instances. "Reverse engineering of chemical and mechanical articles in the public domain often leads to significant advances in technology." *Ibid.*

The principal question in this case is the effect of an expired patent on a claim of trade dress infringement. A prior patent, we conclude, has vital significance in resolving the trade dress claim. A utility patent is strong evidence that the features therein claimed are functional. If trade dress protection is sought for those features the strong evidence of functionality based on the previous patent adds great weight to the statutory presumption that features are deemed functional until proved otherwise by the party seeking trade dress protection. Where the expired patent claimed the features in question, one who seeks to establish trade dress protection must carry the heavy burden of showing that the feature is not functional, for instance by showing that it is merely an ornamental, incidental, or arbitrary aspect of the device.

In the case before us, the central advance claimed in the expired utility patents (the Sarkisian patents) is the dual-spring design; and the dual-spring design is the essential feature of the trade dress MDI now seeks to establish and to protect. The rule we have explained bars the trade dress claim, for MDI did not, and cannot, carry the burden of overcoming the strong evidentiary inference of functionality based on the disclosure of the dual-spring design in the claims of the expired patents.

The dual springs shown in the Sarkisian patents were well apart (at either end of a frame for holding a rectangular sign when one full side is the base) while the dual springs at issue here are close together (in a frame designed to hold a sign by one of its corners). As the District Court recognized, this makes little difference. The point is that the springs are necessary to the operation of the device. . . .

The rationale for the rule that the disclosure of a feature in the claims of a utility patent constitutes strong evidence of functionality is well illustrated in this case. The dual-spring design serves the important purpose of keeping the sign upright even in heavy wind conditions; and, as confirmed by the statements in the expired patents, it does so in a unique and useful manner. . . . The dual-spring design allows sign stands to resist toppling in strong winds. Using a dual-spring design rather than a single spring achieves important operational advantages. For example, the specifications of the patents note that the "use of a pair of springs . . . as opposed to the use of a single spring to support the frame structure prevents canting or twisting of the sign around a vertical axis," and that, if not prevented, twisting "may cause damage to the spring structure and may result in tipping of the device." U.S. Patent No. 3,646,696, col. 3. In the course of patent prosecution, it was said that "[t]he use of a pair of spring connections as opposed to a single spring connection . . . forms an important part of this combination" because it "forc[es] the sign frame to tip along the longitudinal axis of the elongated ground-engaging members." App. 218. The dual-spring design affects the cost of the device as well; it was acknowledged that the device "could use three springs but this would unnecessarily increase the cost of the device." *Id.*, at 217. These statements made in the patent applications and in the course of procuring the patents demonstrate the functionality of the design. MDI does not assert that any of these representations are mistaken or inaccurate, and this is further strong evidence of the functionality of the dual-spring design. . . .

Discussing trademarks, we have said " '[i]n general terms, a product feature is functional,' and cannot serve as a trademark, 'if it is essential to the use or purpose of the article or if it affects the cost or quality of the article.' " *Qualitex*, 514 U.S., at 165 (quoting *Inwood Laboratories, Inc. v. Ives Laboratories, Inc.*, 456 U.S. 844, 850, n.10 (1982)). Expanding upon the meaning of this phrase, we have observed that a functional feature is one the "exclusive use of [which] would put competitors at a significant non-reputation-related disadvantage." 514 U.S., at 165. The Court of Appeals in the instant case seemed to interpret this language to mean that a necessary test for functionality is "whether the particular product configuration is a competitive necessity." 200 F.3d, at 940. This was incorrect as a comprehensive definition. As explained in *Qualitex*, *supra*, and *Inwood*, *supra*, a feature is also functional when it is essential to the use or purpose of the device or when it affects the cost or quality of the device. The *Qualitex* decision did not purport to displace this traditional rule. Instead, it quoted the rule as *Inwood* had set it forth. It is proper to inquire into a "significant non-reputation-related disadvantage" in cases of esthetic functionality, the question involved in *Qualitex*. Where the design is functional under the *Inwood* formulation there is no need to proceed further to consider if there is a competitive necessity for the feature. In *Qualitex*, by contrast, esthetic functionality was the central question, there having been no indication that the green-gold color of the laundry press pad had any bearing on the use or purpose of the product or its cost or quality.

The Court has allowed trade dress protection to certain product features that are inherently distinctive. *Two Pesos*, 505 U.S., at 774. In *Two Pesos*, however, the Court at the outset made the explicit analytic assumption that the trade dress features in question (decorations and other features to evoke a Mexican theme in a restaurant) were not functional. *Id.*, at 767, n.6. The trade dress in those cases did not bar competitors from copying functional product design features. In the instant case, beyond serving the purpose of informing consumers that the sign stands are made by MDI (assuming it does so), the dual-spring design provides a unique and useful mechanism to resist the force of the wind. Functionality having been established, whether MDI's dual-spring design has acquired secondary meaning need not be considered.

There is no need, furthermore, to engage, as did the Court of Appeals, in speculation about other design possibilities, such as using three or four springs which might serve the same purpose. Here, the functionality of the spring design means that competitors need not explore whether other spring juxtapositions might be used. The dual-spring design is not an arbitrary flourish in the configuration of MDI's product; it is the reason the device works. Other designs need not be attempted. . . .

The Lanham Act does not exist to reward manufacturers for their innovation in creating a particular device; that is the purpose of the patent law and its period of exclusivity. The Lanham Act, furthermore, does not protect trade dress in a functional design simply because an investment has been made to encourage the public to associate a particular functional feature with a single manufacturer or seller. The Court of Appeals erred in viewing MDI as possessing the right to exclude competitors from using a design identical to MDI's and to require those competitors to adopt a different design simply to avoid copying it. MDI cannot gain the exclusive right to produce sign stands using the dual-spring design by asserting that consumers associate it with the look of the invention itself. Whether a utility patent has expired or there has been no utility patent at all, a product design which has a particular appearance may be functional because it is "essential to the use or purpose of the article" or "affects the cost or quality of the article." *Inwood*, 456 U.S., at 850, n.10. The judgment of the Court of Appeals is reversed, and the case is remanded for further proceedings consistent with this opinion.

### *NOTES AND QUESTIONS*

1. The functionality doctrine was originally created by courts and was treated as a basis for denying relief in infringement cases and as grounds to refuse registration of a mark. Both uses of the functionality doctrine are now incorporated into the Lanham Act. Section 1052(e)(5) makes functionality a ground for refusing registration of a mark. For this reason, marks that are registered are presumed not to be functional, though that presumption may be rebutted even after a mark has achieved "incontestable status." 15 U.S.C. § 1065. Section 1125(a)(3) assigns the plaintiff in a case involving unregistered trade dress the burden to prove the claimed features are not functional.

2. The *TrafFix* decision identifies two policy reasons for denying protection to functional features: promoting competition and avoiding conflict with utility patent law by channeling protection for features that could be the subject of patent protection to that regime. These policy considerations are obviously related in the sense that utility patent law is generally understood to set the conditions on which parties can restrict access to useful product features. More specifically, utility patent protection is an exception to a general background rule of free copying. If parties could use trademark law as an alternative mechanism for protecting the sorts of useful features that are the subject of patent law, they could undermine the balance Congress sought in developing patent eligibility criteria. But, prior to *TrafFix*, some courts had been determining functionality almost exclusively by reference to competitive need, finding even previously patented features non-functional because alternative designs were available. One way to understand the *TrafFix* decision is as a

correction to those courts that had lost sight of the importance of the channeling function of the functionality doctrine.

3. In *TrafFix*, the Supreme Court held that once a design element is found to be functional, there is no need to consider "whether the particular product configuration is a competitive necessity." The Court held that the Sixth Circuit had erred in speculating about other design possibilities for the spring mechanism, such as using three or four springs rather than two. Consideration of whether competitors would be at a disadvantage without access to the product configuration in question was based on language from the Supreme Court's opinion in *Qualitex*. In *Qualitex*, the Court said that a product feature is functional if it is essential to the use or purpose of the article or if it affects the cost or quality of the article; that is, if exclusive use of the feature would put competitors at a *significant non-reputation-related disadvantage*. The italicized words suggest that courts must consider the competitive significance of granting exclusive rights in the feature. And prior to *TrafFix*, most courts evaluated functionality this way—typically relying on a framework articulated in *In re Morton-Norwich Prods., Inc.*, 671 F.2d 1332 (C.C.P.A. 1982).

In that case, the Federal Circuit's predecessor described functionality as referring to the utility of an object's design, which "is determined in light of 'utility,' which is determined in light of 'superiority of design,' and rests upon the foundation 'essential to effective competition.'" Because, in that court's view, "the effect upon competition 'is really the crux of the matter'" in functionality cases, the issue is "not the *right* to slavishly copy articles [that] are not protected by patent or copyright, but the *need* to copy those articles, which is more properly termed the right to compete *effectively*." The fact that the utilitarian advantages of the claimed features were disclosed in an expired utility patent is relevant to functionality under this approach, but it is not dispositive. Courts also were instructed to consider (1) whether the originator of the design touts the design's utilitarian advantages through advertising; (2) whether alternative designs are available; and (3) whether the design results from a comparatively simple or cheap method of manufacturing the article.

In *TrafFix*, however, the Court deemphasized competitive consequences and instructed courts to find functionality if a feature is essential to the use or purpose of an article, even if other designs are available. Subsequent to *TrafFix*, lower courts have focused primarily on how to determine whether a particular feature is "essential to the use or purpose of the article." In particular, courts have differed over the continuing relevance of alternative designs. We take that issue up below in the section on Utilitarian (Mechanical) Functionality.

4. The Court in *TrafFix* distinguished two types of functionality: utilitarian functionality, which was at issue in that case, and aesthetic functionality, which it suggested was at issue in *Qualitex*. Aesthetically functional features do not contribute to the utilitarian function of an object, but their appearance contributes to consumer demand for the product. The orange color of orange soda, for example, is entirely artificial. There is nothing about the ingredients of the orange soda that necessarily makes it orange, and the orange coloration

is not essential to the soda's taste. Producers of orange soda artificially color the soda, however, because consumers expect orange soda to be orange. Forcing other sellers of orange-flavored soda to use another color would place them at a "significant, non-reputation-related disadvantage." Because these features do not contribute to the utilitarian function of the product, they do not raise the same concerns about conflict with utility patent law. Hence, though there is a sense in which these kinds of features can be considered "essential to the use or purpose of the article," the court in *TrafFix* suggested that courts in aesthetic functionality cases properly focus on whether exclusive use of a particular feature would have such competitive consequences.

5. Recall that *Sears* and *Compco* both involved designs that had been claimed in design patents, and the Supreme Court did not distinguish design patents from utility patents when it ruled out unfair competition claims for unpatented designs. Since those cases involved state law unfair competition claims, however, courts later understood them primarily as preemption cases. When courts began interpreting the Lanham Act to provide a federal cause of action for infringement of unregistered trademarks, including trade dress, they began to see *Sears* and *Compco* as less directly relevant. The functionality doctrine essentially took the place of what had been a rather categorical rejection of protection. But as *TrafFix* indicates, courts have understood the functionality doctrine primarily as a means of policing the boundary between trademark and *utility* patent; design patent has fallen out of the picture. Indeed, some courts have gone so far as to say that the fact that a feature was once the subject of a design patent is evidence of *non*-functionality (since design patents cover the ornamental design of an article of manufacture). *See, e.g., In re Becton-Dickson*, 675 F.3d 1368, 1380 (2012) (applying *In re Morton-Norwich Prods., Inc.*, 671 F.2d 1332, 1342 n.3 (C.C.P.A. 1982)).

---

## 2. UTILITARIAN (MECHANICAL) FUNCTIONALITY

As the *TrafFix* decision suggested, courts often regard functionality as having two different forms: (i) utilitarian or mechanical functionality; and (ii) aesthetic functionality. We discuss the former in this section and then the latter in the following section.

### *PROBLEM 3–3*

In 2015, Apple finished developing a wireless pair of headphones it calls AirPods. Each AirPod fits into a person's ear canal. The AirPod is designed to transmit sound into the ear, as well as to receive audio wirelessly from an iPhone and to remain in the ear canal without falling out from normal activities, such as jogging. Jony Ive, the Chief Design Officer of Apple, said that the shape of the AirPod also embodies an "uncompromising symmetry between form and function—it's the modern headset reduced to simplicity and art. The shape is a sculpture of modern beauty." You can view the AirPods at http://www.apple.com/airpods/. A diagram of one ear piece is below:

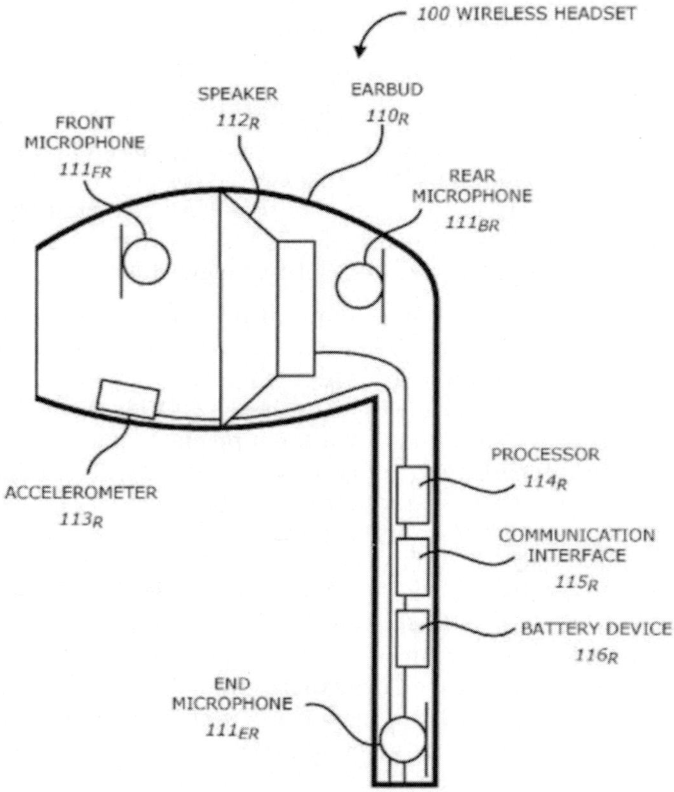


It is December 2015 and the Apple has not yet released the AirPods. It has hired your law firm to analyze whether the shape of the AirPods or the combination of the shape and the color white on the AirPods can be protected as trade dress. Many consumers associate the color white on earphones with Apple, since Apple has exclusively used white for its earphones since it began selling its first iPod in 2001. Tim Cook, the CEO of Apple, said he would spend "as much money as it takes" to establish that consumers identify white earphones with Apple.

Apple would also like your opinion also on whether seeking a design or utility patent on the AirPods might affect its claims to the trade dress.

---

We have read several decisions from the *Apple v. Samsung* dispute in Chapter 2 on design patents. Apple also asserted trade dress infringement claims in the lawsuit. Below is an excerpt of an appellate decision dealing with the trade dress issues.

## APPLE, INC. V. SAMSUNG ELECTRONICS CO., LTD.

786 F.3d 983 (Fed. Cir. 2015)

PROST, CHIEF JUDGE. Samsung appeals from a final judgment of the U.S. District Court for the Northern District of California in favor of Apple. A jury found that Samsung infringed Apple's design and utility patents and diluted Apple's trade dresses. For the reasons that follow, we affirm the jury's verdict on the design patent infringements, the validity of two utility patent claims, and the damages awarded for the design and utility patent infringements appealed by Samsung. However, we reverse the jury's findings that the asserted trade dresses are protectable. We therefore vacate the jury's damages awards against the Samsung products that were found liable for trade dress dilution and remand for further proceedings consistent with this opinion.

### BACKGROUND

Apple Sued Samsung in April 2011. On August 24, 2012, the first jury reached a verdict that numerous Samsung smartphones infringed and diluted Apple's patents and trade dresses in various combinations and awarded over $1 billion in damages. The diluted trade dresses are Trademark Registration No. 3,470,983 (" '983 trade dress") and an unregistered trade dress defined in terms of certain elements in the configuration of the iPhone. Following the first jury trial, the district court upheld the jury's infringement, dilution, and validity findings over Samsung's post-trial motion.

### DISCUSSION

#### I. Trade Dresses

The jury found Samsung liable for the likely dilution of Apple's iPhone trade dresses under the Lanham Act. When reviewing Lanham Act claims, we look to the law of the regional circuit where the district court sits. We therefore apply Ninth Circuit law.

The Ninth Circuit has explained that "[t]rade dress is the totality of elements in which a product or service is packaged or presented." *Stephen W. Boney, Inc. v. Boney Servs., Inc.*, 127 F.3d 821, 828 (9th Cir. 1997). The essential purpose of a trade dress is the same as that of a trademarked word: to identify the source of the product.

The protection for source identification, however, must be balanced against "*a fundamental right to compete through imitation of a competitor's product. . . .*" *Leatherman Tool Grp., Inc. v. Cooper Indus., Inc.*, 199 F.3d 1009, 1011–12 (9th Cir. 1999). This "right can only be *temporarily* denied by the patent or copyright laws." *Id.* In contrast, trademark law allows for a perpetual monopoly and its use in the protection of "physical details and design of a product" must be limited to those that are "nonfunctional." *Id.* at 1011–12; *see also Qualitex Co. v. Jacobson Prods. Co.*, 514 U.S. 159, 164–

65 (1995) ("If a product's functional features could be used as trademarks, however, a monopoly over such features could be obtained without regard to whether they qualify as patents and could be extended forever (because trademarks may be renewed in perpetuity)."). Thus, it is necessary for us to determine first whether Apple's asserted trade dresses, claiming elements from its iPhone product, are nonfunctional and therefore protectable.

"In general terms, a product feature is functional if it is essential to the use or purpose of the article or if it affects the cost or quality of the article." *Inwood Labs., Inc. v. Ives Labs., Inc.,* 456 U.S. 844, 850 n. 10 (1982). "A product feature need only have *some* utilitarian advantage to be considered functional." *Disc Golf Ass'n v. Champion Discs, Inc.,* 158 F.3d 1002, 1007 (9th Cir. 1998). A trade dress, taken as a whole, is functional if it is "in its particular shape *because it works better in this shape.*" *Leatherman,* 199 F.3d at 1013.

"[C]ourts have noted that it is, and should be, more difficult to claim product configuration trade dress than other forms of trade dress." *Id.* at 1012–13 (discussing cases). Accordingly, the Supreme Court and the Ninth Circuit have repeatedly found product configuration trade dresses functional and therefore non-protectable. *See, e.g., TrafFix,* 532 U.S. at 26–27, 35 (reversing the Sixth Circuit's reversal of the district court's grant of summary judgment that a trade dress on a dual-spring design for temporary road sign stands was functional); *Secalt S.A. v. Wuxi Shenxi Const. Mach. Co.,* 668 F.3d 677, 687 (9th Cir. 2012) (affirming summary judgment that a trade dress on a hoist design was functional); *Disc Golf,* 158 F.3d at 1006 (affirming summary judgment that a trade dress on a disc entrapment design was functional).

Moreover, federal trademark registrations have been found insufficient to save product configuration trade dresses from conclusions of functionality. *See, e.g., Talking Rain Beverage Co. v. S. Beach Beverage,* 349 F.3d 601, 602 (9th Cir. 2003) (affirming summary judgment that registered trade dress covering a bottle design with a grip handle was functional); *Tie Tech, Inc. v. Kinedyne Corp.,* 296 F.3d 778, 782–83 (9th Cir. 2002) (affirming summary judgment that registered trade dress covering a handheld cutter design was functional). The Ninth Circuit has even reversed a jury verdict of non-functionality of a product configuration trade dress. *See Leatherman,* 199 F.3d at 1013 (reversing jury verdict that a trade dress on the overall appearance of a pocket tool was non-functional). Apple conceded during oral argument that it had not cited a single Ninth Circuit case that found a product configuration trade dress to be non-functional.

The Ninth Circuit's high bar for non-functionality frames our review of the two iPhone trade dresses on appeal. While the parties argue without distinguishing the two trade dresses, the unregistered trade dress and the registered '983 trade dress claim different details and are afforded different evidentiary presumptions under the Lanham Act. We analyze the two trade dresses separately below.

A. Unregistered Trade Dress

Apple claims elements from its iPhone 3G and 3GS products to define the asserted unregistered trade dress:

> a rectangular product with four evenly rounded corners;
>
> a flat, clear surface covering the front of the product;
>
> a display screen under the clear surface;
>
> substantial black borders above and below the display screen and narrower black borders on either side of the screen; and
>
> when the device is on, a row of small dots on the display screen, a matrix of colorful square icons with evenly rounded corners within the display screen, and an unchanging bottom dock of colorful square icons with evenly rounded corners set off from the display's other icons.

As this trade dress is not registered on the principal federal trademark register, Apple "has the burden of proving that the claimed trade dress, taken as a whole, is not functional. . . ." *See* 15 U.S.C. § 1125(c)(4)(A).

Apple argues that the unregistered trade dress is nonfunctional under each of the *Disc Golf* factors that the Ninth Circuit uses to analyze functionality: "(1) whether the design yields a utilitarian advantage, (2) whether alternative designs are available, (3) whether advertising touts the utilitarian advantages of the design, and (4) whether the particular design results from a comparatively simple or inexpensive method of manufacture." *See Disc Golf,* 158 F.3d at 1006. However, the Supreme Court has more recently held that "a feature is also functional . . . when it affects the cost or quality of the device." *See TrafFix,* 532 U.S. at 33. The Supreme Court's holding was recognized by the Ninth Circuit as "short circuiting some of the *Disc Golf* factors." *Secalt,* 668 F.3d at 686–87. Nevertheless, we explore Apple's contentions on each of the *Disc Golf* factors and conclude that there was insufficient evidence to support a jury finding in favor of non-functionality on any factor.

1. Utilitarian Advantage

Apple argues that "the iPhone's physical design did not 'contribute unusually . . . to the usability' of the device." Apple further contends that the unregistered trade dress was "developed . . . not for 'superior performance.' " Neither "unusual usability" nor "superior performance," however, is the standard used by the Ninth Circuit to determine whether there is any utilitarian advantage. The Ninth Circuit "has never held, as [plaintiff] suggests, that the product feature must provide *superior* utilitarian advantages. To the contrary, [the Ninth Circuit] has suggested that in order to establish nonfunctionality the party with the burden must demonstrate that the product feature serves *no purpose* other than identification." *Disc Golf,* 158 F.3d at 1007 (internal quotation marks omitted).

The requirement that the unregistered trade dress "serves *no purpose* other than identification" cannot be reasonably inferred from the evidence. Apple emphasizes a single aspect of its design, beauty, to imply the lack of other advantages. But the evidence showed that the iPhone's design pursued more than just beauty. Specifically, Apple's executive testified that the theme for the design of the iPhone was:

> to create a new breakthrough design for a phone that was beautiful and simple and *easy to use* and created a beautiful, smooth surface that had a touchscreen and went right to the rim with the bezel around it and looking for a look that we found was beautiful and *easy to use* and appealing.

Moreover, Samsung cites extensive evidence in the record that showed the usability function of every single element in the unregistered trade dress. For example, rounded corners improve "pocketability" and "durability" and rectangular shape maximizes the display that can be accommodated. A flat clear surface on the front of the phone facilitates touch operation by fingers over a large display. The bezel protects the glass from impact when the phone is dropped. The borders around the display are sized to accommodate other components while minimizing the overall product dimensions. The row of dots in the user interface indicates multiple pages of application screens that are available. The icons allow users to differentiate the applications available to the users and the bottom dock of unchanging icons allows for quick access to the most commonly used applications. Apple rebuts none of this evidence.

Apple conceded during oral argument that its trade dress "improved the quality [of the iPhone] in some respects." It is thus clear that the unregistered trade dress has a utilitarian advantage. *See Disc Golf,* 158 F.3d at 1007.

### 2. Alternative Designs

The next factor requires that purported alternative designs "offer *exactly* the same features" as the asserted trade dress in order to show non-functionality. *Tie Tech,* 296 F.3d at 786 (quoting *Leatherman,* 199 F.3d at 1013–14). A manufacturer "does not have rights under trade dress law to compel its competitors to resort to alternative designs which have a different set of advantages and disadvantages." *Id.*

Apple, while asserting that there were "*numerous* alternative designs," fails to show that any of these alternatives offered exactly the same features as the asserted trade dress. Apple simply catalogs the mere existence of other design possibilities embodied in rejected iPhone prototypes and other manufacturers' smartphones. The "mere existence" of other designs, however, does not prove that the unregistered trade dress is non-functional. *See Talking Rain,* 349 F.3d at 604.

### 3. Advertising of Utilitarian Advantages

"If a seller advertises the utilitarian advantages of a particular feature, this constitutes strong evidence of functionality." *Disc Golf,* 158 F.3d at 1009. An "inference" of a product feature's utility in the plaintiff's advertisement is enough to weigh in favor of functionality of a trade dress encompassing that feature. *Id.*

Apple argues that its advertising was "[f]ar from touting any utilitarian advantage of the iPhone design. . . ." Apple relies on its executive's testimony that an iPhone advertisement, portraying "the distinctive design very clearly," was based on Apple's "product as hero" approach. The "product as hero" approach refers to Apple's stylistic choice of making "the product the biggest, clearest, most obvious thing in [its] advertisements, often at the expense of anything else around it, to remove all the other elements of communication so [the viewer] see[s] the product most predominantly in the marketing."

Apple's arguments focusing on its stylistic choice, however, fail to address the substance of its advertisements. The substance of the iPhone advertisement relied upon by Apple gave viewers "the ability to see a bit about how it might work," for example, "how flicking and scrolling and tapping and all these multitouch ideas simply [sic]." Another advertisement cited by Apple similarly displayed the message, "[t]ouching is believing," under a picture showing a user's hand interacting with the graphical user interface of an iPhone. Apple fails to show that, on the substance, these demonstrations of the user interface on iPhone's touch screen involved the elements claimed in Apple's unregistered trade dress and why they were not touting the utilitarian advantage of the unregistered trade dress.

### 4. Method of Manufacture

The fourth factor considers whether a functional benefit in the asserted trade dress arises from "economies in manufacture or use," such as being "relatively simple or inexpensive to manufacture." *Disc Golf,* 158 F.3d at 1009.

Apple contends that "[t]he iPhone design did not result from a 'comparatively simple or inexpensive method of manufacture' " because Apple experienced manufacturing challenges. Apple's manufacturing challenges, however, resulted from the durability considerations for the iPhone and not from the design of the unregistered trade dress. According to Apple's witnesses, difficulties resulted from its choices of materials in using "hardened steel"; "very high, high grade of steel"; and, "glass that was not breakable enough, scratch resistant enough." These materials were chosen, for example, for the iPhone to survive a drop:

> If you drop this, you don't have to worry about the ground hitting the glass. You have to worry about the band of steel surrounding the glass hitting the glass. . . . In order to, to make it work, we had to use very high, high grade of steel because we couldn't have it sort of deflecting into the glass.

The durability advantages that resulted from the manufacturing challenges, however, are outside the scope of what Apple defines as its unregistered trade dress. For the design elements that comprise Apple's unregistered trade dress, Apple points to no evidence in the record to show they were not relatively simple or inexpensive to manufacture. *See Disc Golf,* 158 F.3d at 1009 ("[Plaintiff], which has the burden of proof, offered no evidence that the [asserted] design was not relatively simple or inexpensive to manufacture.").

In sum, Apple has failed to show that there was substantial evidence in the record to support a jury finding in favor of non-functionality for the unregistered trade dress on any of the *Disc Golf* factors. Apple fails to rebut the evidence that the elements in the unregistered trade dress serve the functional purpose of improving usability. Rather, Apple focuses on the "beauty" of its design, even though Apple pursued both "beauty" and functionality in the design of the iPhone. We therefore reverse the district court's denial of Samsung's motion for judgment as a matter of law that the unregistered trade dress is functional and therefore not protectable.

### B. The Registered '983 Trade Dress

In contrast to the unregistered trade dress, the '983 trade dress is a federally registered trademark. The federal trademark registration provides "prima facie evidence" of non-functionality. *Tie Tech,* 296 F.3d at 782–83. This presumption "shift[s] the burden of production to the defendant . . . to provide evidence of functionality." *Id.* at 783. Once this presumption is overcome, the registration loses its legal significance on the issue of functionality. *Id.* ("In the face of sufficient and undisputed facts demonstrating functionality, . . . the registration loses its evidentiary significance.").

The '983 trade dress claims the design details in each of the sixteen icons on the iPhone's home screen framed by the iPhone's rounded-rectangular shape with silver edges and a black background:

> The first icon depicts the letters "SMS" in green inside a white speech bubble on a green background; . . .
>
> the seventh icon depicts a map with yellow and orange roads, a pin with a red head, and a red-and-blue road sign with the numeral "280" in white; . . .

> the sixteenth icon depicts the distinctive configuration of applicant's media player device in white over an orange background.

'983 trade dress (omitting thirteen other icon design details for brevity).

It is clear that individual elements claimed by the '983 trade dress are functional. For example, there is no dispute that the claimed details such as "the seventh icon depicts a map with yellow and orange roads, a pin with a red head, and a red-and-blue road sign with the numeral '280' in white" are functional. *See id.* Apple's user interface expert testified on how icon designs promote usability. This expert agreed that "the whole point of an icon on a smartphone is to communicate to the consumer using that product, that if they hit that icon, certain functionality will occur on the phone." The expert further explained that icons are "[v]isual shorthand for something" and that "rectangular containers" for icons provide "more real estate" to accommodate the icon design. Apple rebuts none of this evidence.

Apple contends instead that Samsung improperly disaggregates the '983 trade dress into individual elements to argue functionality. But Apple fails to explain how the total combination of the sixteen icon designs in the context of iPhone's screen-dominated rounded-rectangular shape—all part of the iPhone's "easy to use" design theme—somehow negates the undisputed usability function of the individual elements. Apple's own brief even relies on its expert's testimony about the "instant recognizability due to highly intuitive icon usage" on "the home screen of the iPhone." Apple's expert was discussing an analysis of the iPhone's overall combination of icon designs that allowed a user to recognize quickly particular applications to use. The iPhone's usability advantage from the combination of its icon designs shows that the '983 trade dress viewed as a whole "is nothing other than the assemblage of functional parts. . . ." *See Tie Tech,* 296 F.3d at 786 (quoting *Leatherman,* 199 F.3d at 1013). There is no "separate 'overall appearance' which is non-functional." *Id.* (quoting *Leatherman,* 199 F.3d at 1013). The undisputed facts thus demonstrate the functionality of the '983 trade dress. "In the face of sufficient and undisputed facts demonstrating functionality, as in our case, the registration loses its evidentiary significance." *See id.* at 783.

The burden thus shifts back to Apple. *See id.* But Apple offers no analysis of the icon designs claimed by the '983 trade dress. Rather, Apple argues generically for its two trade dresses without distinction under the *Disc Golf* factors. Among Apple's lengthy citations to the record, we can find only two pieces of information that involve icon designs. One is Apple's user interface expert discussing other possible icon designs. The other is a citation to a print iPhone advertisement that included the icon designs claimed in the '983 trade dress. These two citations, viewed in the most favorable light to Apple, would be relevant to only two of the *Disc Golf* factors: "alternative design" and "advertising." But the cited evidence suffers from the same defects as discussed in subsections I.A.2 and I.A.3. Specifically, the expert's discussion of other icon design possibilities does not show that the other design possibilities "offer[ed] *exactly* the same features" as the '983 trade dress. *See Tie Tech,* 296 F.3d at 786 (quoting *Leatherman,* 199 F.3d at 1013–14). The print iPhone advertisement also fails to establish that, on the substance, it was not touting the utilitarian advantage of the '983 trade dress. The evidence cited by Apple therefore does not show the non-functionality of the '983 trade dress.

In sum, the undisputed evidence shows the functionality of the registered '983 trade dress and shifts the burden of proving non-functionality back to Apple. Apple, however, has failed to show that there was substantial evidence in the record to support a jury finding in favor of non-functionality for the '983 trade dress on any of the *Disc Golf* factors. We therefore reverse the district court's denial of Samsung's motion for judgment as a matter of law that the '983 trade dress is functional and therefore not protectable.

Because we conclude that the jury's findings of non-functionality of the asserted trade dresses were not supported by substantial evidence, we do not reach Samsung's arguments on the fame and likely dilution of the asserted trade dresses, the Patent Clause of the Constitution, or the dilution damages.

### *NOTES AND QUESTIONS*

1. Compare the Federal Circuit's consideration of functionality in the context of Apple's design patent claims with its treatment of functionality in the context of Apple's trade dress claims. Why did the court find the trade dress was functional when it concluded that functionality did not invalidate the design patents? Is there a policy reason for utilizing different tests for functionality for design patents and trade dress, particularly when both claims are asserted regarding the same commercial product?

2. Courts applying *TrafFix* have differed over the role of alternative designs. In *Valu Engineering, Inc. v. Rexnord Corp.*, 278 F.3d 1268 (Fed. Cir. 2002), the court understood the question of whether a design feature is "essential to the use or purpose" to be a relative one: Design features are only essential, in the Federal Circuit's view, when viable alternatives are lacking. Hence, while *TrafFix* commanded that courts find functionality without regard to any "significant non-reputation-related disadvantage" whenever the features are essential to the use or purpose of the article, the Federal Circuit concluded that the availability of alternative designs was relevant to the determination of essentiality in the first place. In *Apple v. Samsung*, the Federal Circuit, applying Ninth Circuit law, said that alternative designs were relevant only if those alternatives offered "*exactly* the same features" as the claimed design. According to the court, the "mere existence" of other designs does not prove that the unregistered trade dress is non-functional. Other courts have declared that alternative designs are irrelevant altogether. In *Eppendorf-Netheler-Hinz*

*GMBH v. Ritter GMBH*, 289 F.3d 351 (5th Cir. 2002), the Fifth Circuit held the availability of alternative designs irrelevant once it concluded that the features the plaintiff claimed were essential to the use or purpose of its disposable pipette tips. Moreover, the Fifth Circuit evaluated whether the design features were essential in that case simply by asking whether they contributed at all to the product's function. More specifically, the Fifth Circuit contrasted "essential" features with arbitrary ones, finding the claimed features "essential to the use or purpose of the article" because they were not "arbitrary flourish[es] which serve[d] no purpose in the Combitips."

Most courts have been closer to the Fifth and Ninth Circuit approaches, which substantially limit the evidentiary value of alternative designs. *See, e.g., Specialized Seating, Inc. v. Greenwich Industries, LP*, 616 F.3d 722 (7th Cir. 2010) ("A design such as Clarin's x-frame chair is functional not because it is the only way to do things, but because it represents one of many solutions to a problem. . . What this says to us is that *all* of the designs are functional, in the sense that they represent different compromises along the axes of weight, strength, kind of material, ease of setup, ability to connect ("gang") the chairs together for maximum seating density, and so on."); *Tie Tech, Inc. v. Kinedyne Corp.*, 296 F.3d 778, 786 (9th Cir. 2002) ("[A] product's manufacturer does not have rights under trade dress law to compel its competition to resort to alternative designs which have a different set of advantages and disadvantages. Such is the realm of patent law.").

3. Courts have also differed to some extent over the role of utility patents, notwithstanding *TrafFix*. One aspect of the problem is that *TrafFix* was somewhat unclear about when the claimed features implicate a patent. The Supreme Court referred to the dual spring design as the "central advance" of the expired utility patent, even though that patent claimed dual springs that were spaced apart and the claimed trade dress consisted of dual springs positioned close together. Thus, it was clear in *TrafFix* that the utility patent could have "vital significance" even if the trade dress was not identical to the device claimed in the patent (though in TrafFix the plaintiff had previously claimed that devices with dual springs close together still infringed the patent under the doctrine of equivalents).

But must the features claimed as trade dress have been claimed in a utility patent in order for the patent to have evidentiary value? Or must the utility of the features merely be disclosed in the patent? *Compare Fuji Kogyo Co., Ltd. v. Pacific Bay Int'l, Inc.*, 461 F.3d 675, 688-89 (6th Cir. 2006) (interpreting *TrafFix* to give utility patents significant weight only when the claimed trade dress would have infringed the patent, literally or under the doctrine of equivalents); with *Jay Franco & Sons, Inc. v. Franek*, 615 F.3d 855, 858 (7th Cir. 2010) ("Proving patent infringement can be *sufficient* to show that a trademarked design is useful, as it means that the infringing design is quite similar to a useful invention. But such proof is unnecessary. Functionality is determined by a feature's usefulness, not its patentability or its infringement of a patent.").

How specifically must the features be disclosed in the patent to be considered "covered" by the patent? In *Georgia-Pacific Consumer Prods. LP v. Kimberly-Clark Corp.*, 647 F.3d 723 (7th Cir. 2011), the court treated Georgia-Pacific's utility patents as strong evidence of the functionality its claimed trade dress in the following designs.

Reg. No. 2,710,741

Reg. No. 1,778,352

Reg. No. 1,806,076

Reg. No. 1,979,345

It did so noting that the same designs were disclosed in the utility patents, even though those patents claimed the design at a higher level of generality than the trade dress. Specifically, the utility patents disclosed a diamond lattice pattern with signature bosses, and they claimed the benefits of that design as the "central advance." Id. at 728. The patents did not call specifically for hearts and flowers, the particular designs included in Georgia-Pacific's trade dress.

By contrast, in *McAirlaids, Inc. v. Kimberly-Clark Corp.*, 756 F.3d 307 (4th Cir. 2014), the court downplayed the significance of utility patents that covered a fiber-fusing process and absorbent material. According to the court, the patents did not weigh heavily because, while they required some embossing pattern and the choices were constrained, the patents did not require the particular pixel pattern claimed by McAirlaids. In fact, the court went so far as to say that, because the utility patents did not constitute the same strong evidence of functionality as the patent in *TrafFix*, *TrafFix*'s holding about alternative designs was inapplicable. Is that holding consistent with the Supreme Court's treatment of utility patents?

## 3. AESTHETIC FUNCTIONALITY

### *PROBLEM 3–4*

John Deere & Company is a leading producer of farm machinery and equipment. In 1972, John Deere introduced its front-end loader, an apparatus that attaches to a farm tractor and that is designed to scoop and move materials, especially manure and snow. These Deere loaders are designed for use with Deere tractors. Since at least 1955, John Deere has used the same shade of green as the predominant color of its entire line of farm machinery and equipment. Deere has sophisticated procedures, tests, and devices for assuring that the color it uses will not vary from factory to factory or from year to year. One such device is a "color-eye," which measures the weathering of paint finishes. Deere requires its paint suppliers to pass rigid paint performance tests, and it discontinues its relationships with suppliers that do not meet its standards. Deere's advertising prominently and continuously features the shade of green known in the industry as "John Deere green." You can view a Deere front-end loader at https://www.deere.com/en_US/products/equipment/front-end-loaders/front-end-loaders-category.page.

Nobilo Company also manufactures front-end loaders for use on tractors manufactured by other companies. Nobilo's best-selling loader is a front-end loader that is compatible with John Deere tractors. These Nobilo loaders are the exact shade of green of John Deere's equipment. Nobilo believes that using the same color has a signaling function because it helps farmers understand that Nobilo's front-end loader is compatible with Deere tractors. Also, several farmers have told Nobilo that it's more attractive to have a front-end loader that matches the color of the tractor. John Deere has sent Nobilo a cease-and-desist letter demanding that Nobilo stop using the "John Deere green" color on Nobilo's equipment. Deere has not yet registered the color as a trademark in the Trademark Office. Nobilo has hired you to analyze John Deere's potential trade dress claim, including the issue of functionality. To answer this problem, consider the following two cases, *Franek and Loboutin.*

---

## JAY FRANCO & SONS, INC. V. FRANEK

615 F.3d 855 (7th Cir. 2010)

EASTERBROOK, CHIEF JUDGE. The same year Huey Lewis and the News informed America that it's "Hip To Be Square," Clemens Franek sought to trademark the circular beach towel. His company, CLM Design, Inc., pitched the towel as a fashion statement—"the most radical beach fashion item since the bikini," declared one advertisement. "Bound to be round! Don't be square!" proclaimed another. CLM also targeted lazy sunbathers: "The round shape eliminates the need to constantly get up and move your towel as the sun moves across the sky. Instead merely reposition yourself."

The product enjoyed some initial success. Buoyed by an investment and promotional help from the actor Woody Harrelson (then a bartender on the TV show *Cheers*), CLM had sold more than 30,000 round beach towels in 32 states by the end of 1987. To secure its status as the premier circular-towel maker, the company in 1986 applied for a trademark on the towel's round design. The Patent and Trademark Office registered the "configuration of a round beach towel" as trademark No. 1,502,261 in 1988. But this was not enough to save CLM: Six years later it dissolved. The mark was assigned to Franek, who continues to sell circular towels.

In 2006 Franek discovered that Jay Franco & Sons, a distributor of bath, bedding, and beach accessories, was selling round beach towels.

Franek sued two of Jay Franco's customers, Target and Walmart, for unauthorized use of his registered trademark in violation of § 32 of the Lanham Act, 15 U.S.C. § 1114. Jay Franco had agreed to indemnify and defend its customers in such suits, so it sued Franek to invalidate his mark. The district judge granted summary judgment in Jay Franco's favor, and dismissed the remaining claims and counterclaims. Franek appeals from that judgment.

One way to void a trademark is to challenge its distinctiveness. A valid trademark identifies the source of the good it marks. Designs do not inherently communicate that information, so to be valid a product-design mark must have acquired a "secondary meaning"—a link in the minds of consumers between the marked item and its source. But this type of invalidation is unavailable to Jay Franco. Franek (and before him CLM) has continuously used the round-towel mark since its 1988 registration. That makes the mark "incontestable," 15 U.S.C. § 1065.

Unfortunately for Franek, incontestable marks are not invincible. The Lanham Act lists a number of affirmative defenses an alleged infringer can parry with; one is a showing that the mark is "functional." *See* § 1115(b)(8); *Specialized Seating, Inc. v. Greenwich Industries, L.P.*, 616 F.3d 722, 724 (7th Cir. 2010) (discussing functionality and other ways to defeat incontestable marks). [P]atent law alone protects useful designs from mimicry; the functionality doctrine polices the division of responsibilities between patent and trademark law by invalidating marks on useful designs. This was the route Jay Franco pursued. The district judge agreed, finding Franek's mark "functional" under the definition the Supreme Court gave that concept in *TrafFix Devices, Inc. v. Marketing Displays, Inc.*, 532 U.S. 23 (2001). The judge got it right.

*TrafFix* says that a design is functional when it is "essential to the use or purpose of the device or when it affects the cost or quality of the device," a definition cribbed from *Inwood Laboratories, Inc. v. Ives Laboratories, Inc.*, 456 U.S. 844, 850 n.10 (1982). So if a design enables a product to operate, or improves on a substitute design in some way (such as by making the product cheaper, faster, lighter, or stronger), then the design cannot be trademarked; it is functional because consumers would pay to have it rather than be indifferent toward or pay to avoid it. A qualification is that any pleasure a customer derives from the design's identification of the product's source—the joy of buying a marked good over an identical generic version because the consumer prefers the status conferred by the mark—doesn't count. That broad a theory of functionality would penalize companies for developing brands with cachet to distinguish themselves from competitors, which is the very purpose of trademark law. In short, a design that produces a benefit other than source identification is functional.

Figuring out which designs meet this criterion can be tricky. Utility patents serve as excellent cheat sheets because any design claimed in a patent is supposed to be useful. *See* 35 U.S.C. § 101; *Brenner v. Manson,* 383 U.S. 519, 528–36 (1966). For this reason, *TrafFix* held that expired utility patents provide "strong evidence that the features therein claimed are functional." 532 U.S. at 29. The parties in this case wrangle over the relevance of a handful of utility patents that claim circular towels. We need discuss only one (No. 4,794,029), which describes a round beach towel laced with drawstrings that can be pulled to turn the towel into a satchel. This patent's first two claims are:

1. A towel-bag construction comprising:

   a non-rectangular towel;

   a casing formed at the perimeter of said towel;

   a cord threaded through said casing; and

   a section of relatively non-stretchable fabric of a shape geometrically similar to that of said towel attached with its edges equidistant from the edges of said towel.

2. A towel-bag construction as set forth in claim 1 wherein said towel is circular in shape, whereby a user while sunbathing may reposition his or her body towards the changing angle of the sun while the towel remains stationary.

Claim 2 sounds like Franek's advertisements, which we quoted above. The patent's specification also reiterates, in both the summary and the detailed description, that a circular towel is central to the invention because of its benefit to lazy sunbathers.

Franek argues that claim 2 does not trigger the *TrafFix* presumption of functionality because his towel does not infringe the '029 patent. He notes that claim 2 incorporates claim 1 (in patent parlance, claim 1 is "independent" and claim 2 "dependent," *see* 35 U.S.C. § 112) with the added condition that the towel be circular. An item can infringe a dependent claim only if it also violates the independent claim incorporated by the dependent claim. *See Monsanto Co. v. Syngenta Seeds, Inc.*, 503 F.3d 1352, 1359 (Fed. Cir. 2007). Franek reasons that because his towel lacks a perimeter casing, drawstring, and non-stretchable section of fabric, it does not infringe claim 1, and thus cannot infringe claim 2. Even if his towel could infringe claim 2, Franek maintains that the claim is invalid because the towel-to-bag patent was sought in 1987, two years after Franek started selling a round beach towel, and thus too late to claim its invention. *See* 35 U.S.C. § 102(b); *Pfaff v. Wells Electronics, Inc.,* 525 U.S. 55 (1998).

Proving patent infringement can be *sufficient* to show that a trademarked design is useful, as it means that the infringing design is quite similar to a useful invention. *See Raytheon Co. v. Roper Corp.,* 724

F.2d 951, 959 (Fed. Cir. 1983). But such proof is unnecessary. Functionality is determined by a feature's usefulness, not its patentability or its infringement of a patent. *TrafFix*'s ruling that an expired patent (which by definition can no longer be infringed) may evince a design's functionality demonstrates that proof of infringement is unnecessary. If an invention is too useless to be patentable, or too dissimilar to a design to shed light on its functions, then the lack of proof of patent infringement is meaningful. Otherwise it is irrelevant. A design may not infringe a patented invention because the invention is obvious or taught by prior art, *see* 35 U.S.C. §§ 102(a), 103(a), but those and other disqualifiers do not mean that the design is not useful. Just so here: Franek's towel may lack some of the components in claim 1 necessary to infringe claim 2, but claim 2's coverage of a circular beach towel for sunbathing is enough to signal that a round-towel design is useful for sunbathers. Each claim in a patent is evaluated individually, *see Altoona Publix Theatres, Inc. v. American Tri-Ergon Corp.*, 294 U.S. 477, 487 (1935), each must be substantially different, *see* 37 C.F.R. § 1.75(b); Manual of Patent Examining Procedure § 2173.05(n)(b) (8th ed., July 2010 rev.), and each is presumed valid, 35 U.S.C. § 282. We must therefore presume that the unique component in claim 2—the round shape of the towel—is useful.

Nor does it matter that the '029 patent application was filed two years after Franek began selling round towels. As we've explained, a patent's invalidity for a reason other than uselessness says nothing about the claimed design's functionality. And a design patented yesterday can be as good evidence of a mark's functionality as a design patented 50 years ago. Indeed, more recent patents are often *better* evidence because technological change can render designs that were functional years ago no longer so. *See Eco Manufacturing LLC v. Honeywell International Inc.*, 357 F.3d 649, 653 (7th Cir. 2003). The Court in *TrafFix* may have dealt only with *expired* utility patents, but the logic it employed is not limited to them.

To put things another way, a trademark holder cannot block innovation by appropriating designs that under-gird further improvements. Patent holders can do this, but a patent's life is short; trademarks can last forever, so granting trademark holders this power could permanently stifle product development. If we found Franek's trademark nonfunctional, then inventors seeking to build an improved round beach towel would be out of luck. They'd have to license Franek's mark or quell their inventiveness. That result does not jibe with the purposes of patent or trademark law.

This "strong evidence" of the round towel's functionality is bolstered by Franek's own advertisements, which highlight two functional aspects of the round beach towel's design. One, also discussed in the '029 patent, is that roundness enables heliotropic sunbathers—tanners who swivel their bodies in unison with the sun's apparent motion in order to maintain an even tan—to remain on their towels as they rotate rather than exert the energy to stand up and reposition their towels every so often, as conventional rectangular towels require.

Franek responds that whatever its shape (golden-ratio rectangle, square, nonagon) any towel can satisfy a heliotropic tanner if it has enough surface area—the issue is size, not shape. That's true, and it is enough to keep the roundness of his towel from being functional under the first prong of *TrafFix*'s definition ("essential to the use or purpose of the device") but not the second. For heliotropic sunbathers, a circle surpasses other shapes because it provides the most rotational space without waste. Any non-circle polygon will either limit full rotations (spinning on a normal beach towel leads to sandy hair and feet) or not use all the surface area (a 6' tall person swiveling on a 6' by 6' square towel won't touch the corners). Compared to other shapes that permit full rotations, the round towel requires less material, which makes it easier to fold and carry. That's evidence that the towel's circularity "affects the . . . quality of the device." (The reduction in needed material also suggests that round towels are cheaper to produce than other-shaped towels, though Franek contends that cutting and hemming expenses make them costlier. We express no view on the matter.)

But let us suppose with Franek—who opposed summary judgment and who is thus entitled to all reasonable inferences—that round towels are not measurably better for spinning with the sun. After all, other shapes (squircles, regular icosagons) are similar enough to circles that any qualitative difference may be lost on tanners. Plus, the ability to rotate 180 degrees may be an undesired luxury. Few lie out from dawn 'til dusk (if only to avoid skin cancer) and the daily change in the sun's declination means it will rise due east and set due west just twice a year, during the vernal and autumnal equinoxes. A towel shaped like a curved hourglass that allows only 150 or 120 degrees of rotation (or even fewer) may be all a heliotropic tanner wants. No matter. Franek's mark still is functional.

Franek's advertisements declare that the round towel is a fashion statement. Fashion is a form of function. A design's aesthetic appeal can be as functional as its tangible characteristics. *See Qualitex Co. v. Jacobson Products Co.,* 514 U.S. 159, 169–70 (1995); *Wal-Mart,* 529 U.S. at 214; *TrafFix,* 532 U.S. at 33. And many cases say that fashionable designs can be freely copied unless protected by patent law. *See, e.g., Bonito Boats, Inc. v. Thunder Craft Boats, Inc.,* 489 U.S. 141 (1989).

The chief difficulty is distinguishing between designs that are fashionable enough to be functional and those that are merely pleasing. Only the latter group can be protected, because trademark law would be a cruel joke if it limited companies to tepid or repugnant brands that discourage customers from buying the marked wares. We discussed this problem at length in *Keene. See also Eco Manufacturing,* 357 F.3d at 654; *Schwinn Bicycle Co. v. Ross Bicycles, Inc.,* 870 F.2d 1176, 1188–91 (7th Cir.

1989). The Supreme Court broached the subject in *Qualitex* when it discussed the functionality of the green-gold color of a dry cleaning pad. Unwilling to say that the pad required a green-gold hue or was improved by it, the Court still thought that the color would be functional if its exclusive use by a single designer "would put competitors at a significant non-reputation-related disadvantage." 514 U.S. at 165. This is a problem for Franek's round-towel mark.

Franek wants a trademark on the circle. Granting a producer the exclusive use of a basic element of design (shape, material, color, and so forth) impoverishes other designers' palettes. *See, e.g., Brunswick Corp. v. British Seagull Ltd.,* 35 F.3d 1527 (Fed. Cir. 1994) (black color of boat engines is functional because it is compatible with boats of many different colors). *Qualitex*'s determination that "color alone, at least sometimes, can meet the basic legal requirements for use as a trademark" (514 U.S. at 166), means that there is no per se rule against this practice. *See also Thomas & Betts Corp. v. Panduit Corp.,* 138 F.3d 277, 299 (7th Cir. 1998). The composition of the relevant market matters. But the more rudimentary and general the element—all six-sided shapes rather than an irregular, perforated hexagon; all labels made from tin rather than a specific tin label; all shades of the color purple rather than a single shade—the more likely it is that restricting its use will significantly impair competition. *See, e.g., Keene*, 778 F.2d at 343; *Lorillard v. Pride*, 28 F. 434 (C.C.N.D. Ill. 1886); *Saint-Gobain Corp. v. 3M Co.,* 90 U.S.P.Q. 2d 1425 (T.T.A.B. 2007). Franek's towel is of this ilk. He has trademarked the "configuration of a round beach towel." Every other beach towel manufacturer is barred from using the entire shape as well as any other design similar enough that consumers are likely to confuse it with Franek's circle (most regular polygons, for example).

Contrast Franek's mark with the irregular hexagon at issue in *Keene* or the green-gold hue in *Qualitex.* Those marks restrict few design options for competitors. Indeed, they are so distinctive that competitors' only reason to copy them would be to trade on the goodwill of the original designer. *Cf. Service Ideas, Inc. v. Traex Corp.,* 846 F.2d 1118, 1123–24 (7th Cir. 1988) (purposeful copying of a beverage server's arbitrary design indicated a lack of aesthetic functionality). That's not so here. A circle is the kind of basic design that a producer like Jay Franco adopts because alternatives are scarce and some consumers want the shape regardless of who manufactures it. There are only so many geometric shapes; few are both attractive and simple enough to fabricate cheaply. *Cf. Qualitex*, 514 U.S. at 168–69 (functionality doctrine invalidates marks that would create color scarcity in a particular market). And some consumers crave round towels—beachgoers who prefer curved edges to sharp corners, those who don't want to be "square," and those who relish the circle's simplicity. A producer barred from selling such towels loses a profitable portion of the market. The record does not divulge much on these matters, but any holes in the evidence are filled by the *TrafFix* presumption that Franek's mark is functional, a presumption he has failed to rebut.

Franek chose to pursue a trademark, not a design patent, to protect the stylish circularity of his beach towel. He must live with that choice. We cannot permit him to keep the indefinite competitive advantage in producing beach towels this trademark creates.

If Franek is worried that consumers will confuse Jay Franco's round beach towels with his, he can imprint a distinctive verbal or pictorial mark on his towels. *See Publications International*, 164 F.3d at 343. That will enable him to reap the benefits of his brand while still permitting healthy competition in the beach towel market.

### *NOTES AND QUESTIONS*

1. Courts have typically distinguished between mechanical or utilitarian functionality, on the one hand, and aesthetic functionality on the other hand, applying different tests to each. Can you articulate why the court found the design of the round beach towel functional?

2. What role did the '029 patent play in the court's holding? How did the court understand the purposes of functionality doctrine, and particularly the relationship between trademark and patent law?

3. According to the court in *Jay Franco & Sons*, "the composition of the relevant market matters" in determining whether exclusive use of the claimed features would put competitors at a significant non-reputation-related disadvantage. Yet the court did not feel compelled to define the relevant market in that case because it was satisfied that Franek claimed a feature that was so "rudimentary and general" that restricting its use was likely to impair competition. Is that a reasonable rule of thumb—that basic shapes can be presumed functional? Would that kind of approach be redundant of distinctiveness if a court were to apply the *Seabrook* test described above in the context of non-word marks?

4. In *Dippin' Dots, Inc. v. Frosty Bites Distribution, Inc.*, 369 F.3d 1197 (11th Cir. 2004), the court confronted a similar market definition issue. In that case, Dippin' Dots argued that Frosty Bites did not need to copy the shape, size, and color of Dippin' Dots' flash-frozen ice cream beads because Frosty Bites could easily enter the ice cream market selling other types of ice cream (for example, soft-serve ice cream). The Eleventh Circuit rejected that argument because Frosty Bites "[did] not want to compete in the ice cream business; it want[ed] to compete in the flash-frozen ice cream business, which [was] in a different market from more traditional forms of ice cream." Why is the flash-frozen ice cream market a distinct market? Why *isn't* the relevant market the ice cream market, or perhaps even more broadly, the dessert market?

5. The Eleventh Circuit in *Dippin' Dots* also rejected the plaintiff's argument that, even if certain colors generally are functional (e.g., the color pink for strawberry ice cream), Frosty Bites unnecessarily copied the "identical Pantone®

colors" of its ice cream. The court acknowledged Frosty Bites did not need to copy the identical colors, but it still denied Dippin' Dots' claim. Noting that the Supreme Court in *TrafFix* had rejected a focus on competitive necessity, the Eleventh Circuit held that the "functionality [of the color of the ice cream beads] having been established . . . [t]here [was] no need . . . to engage . . . in speculation about other design possibilities." But *TrafFix* was a mechanical functionality case, and the Supreme Court was concerned in that case about the overlap between trademark and utility patent law, an issue that was not implicated with respect to the colors at issue in *Dippin' Dots*. Should Dippin' Dots have prevailed if it had defined its trade dress in terms of the precise Pantone® colors it employed and conceded that Frosty Bites could use other versions of pink?

---

## CHRISTIAN LOUBOUTIN S.A. V. YVES SAINT LAURENT AMERICA HOLDING, INC.

696 F.3d 206 (2d Cir. 2012)

JOSÉ A. CABRANES, CIRCUIT JUDGE. The question presented is whether a single color may serve as a legally protected trademark in the fashion industry and, in particular, as the mark for a particular style of high fashion women's footwear. Christian Louboutin, a designer of high-fashion women's footwear and accessories, has since 1992 painted the "outsoles" of his women's high-heeled shoes with a high-gloss red lacquer. In 2008, he registered the red lacquered outsole as a trademark with the United States Patent and Trade Office ("PTO").[1] We are asked to decide whether that mark is protectable under federal trademark law.

Louboutin, Christian Louboutin S.A., and Christian Louboutin, L.L.C. (jointly, "Louboutin"), bring this interlocutory appeal from an August 10, 2011 order of the United States District Court for the Southern District of New York (Victor Marrero, Judge) denying a motion for a preliminary injunction against alleged trademark infringement by Yves Saint Laurent America Holding, Inc., Yves Saint Laurent S.A.S., and Yves Saint Laurent America, Inc. (jointly, "YSL"). The District Court, in addressing a difficult and novel issue of trademark law, held that, because a single color can never be protected by trademark in the fashion industry, Louboutin's trademark was likely not enforceable. It therefore declined to enter a preliminary injunction to restrain YSL's alleged use of the mark.

We conclude that the District Court's holding that a single color can never serve as a trademark in the fashion industry is inconsistent with the Supreme Court's decision in *Qualitex Co. v. Jacobson Products Co.,* 514 U.S. 159, 162 (1995) ("*Qualitex*"), and that the District Court therefore erred by resting its denial of Louboutin's preliminary injunction motion on

---

[1] Specifically, the registration for the Louboutin mark states: "The color(s) red is/are claimed as a feature of the mark. The mark consists of a lacquered red sole on footwear."

that ground. We further conclude that Louboutin's trademark, which covers the red, lacquered outsole of a woman's high fashion shoe, has acquired limited "secondary meaning" as a distinctive symbol that identifies the Louboutin brand. As explained below, pursuant to Section 37 of the Lanham Act, 15 U.S.C. § 1119, we limit the trademark to uses in which the red outsole contrasts with the remainder of the shoe (known as the "upper"). We conclude that the trademark, as thus modified, is entitled to trademark protection. Finally, we conclude that, because the monochrome design employed by YSL is not a use of Louboutin's modified trademark, we need not, and indeed should not, address whether YSL's use of a red outsole risks consumer confusion or whether the Louboutin mark, as modified, is "functional."

We therefore (1) affirm in part the order of the District Court, insofar as it declined to enjoin the use of all red lacquered outsoles; (2) reverse in part the order of the District Court insofar as it purported to deny trademark protection to Louboutin's use of *contrasting* red lacquered outsoles; and (3) enter judgment accordingly.

Background

This appeal arises out of an action for injunctive relief and enforcement of a trademark brought by Louboutin, together with the corporate entities that constitute his eponymous French fashion house, against YSL, a venerable French fashion institution. Louboutin is best known for his emphasis upon the otherwise-largely-ignored outsole of the shoe. Since their development in 1992, Louboutin's shoes have been characterized by their most striking feature: a bright, lacquered red outsole, which nearly always contrasts sharply with the color of the rest of the shoe.

Christian Louboutin introduced his signature footwear to the fashion market in 1992. Since then, his shoes have grown in popularity, appearing regularly on various celebrities and fashion icons. The District Court concluded, and YSL does not dispute, that "Louboutin [had] invested substantial amounts of capital building a reputation and good will, as well as promoting and protecting Louboutin's claim to exclusive ownership of the mark as its signature in women's high fashion footwear." The District Court further found that Louboutin had succeeded in promoting his shoes "to the point where, in the high-stakes commercial markets and social circles in which these things matter a great deal, the red outsole became closely associated with Louboutin. Leading designers have said it, including YSL, however begrudgingly." As a result of Louboutin's marketing efforts, the District Court found, the "flash of a red sole" is today "instantly" recognizable, to "those in the know," as Louboutin's handiwork.

On the strength of the fashion world's asserted recognition of the red sole, Louboutin on March 27, 2007 filed an application with the PTO to protect his mark (the "Red Sole Mark" or the "Mark"). The trademark was granted in January 2008, and stated: "The color(s) red is/are claimed as a feature of the mark. The mark consists of a lacquered red sole on footwear." The written description was accompanied by a diagram indicating the placement of the color:

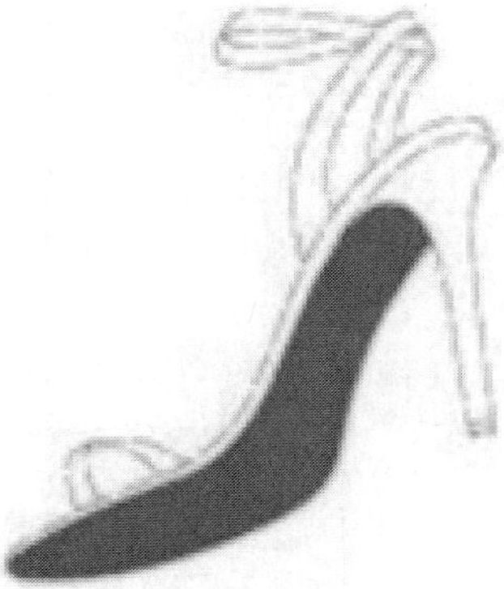

In 2011, YSL prepared to market a line of "monochrome" shoes in purple, green, yellow, and red. YSL shoes in the monochrome style feature the same color on the entire shoe, so that the red version is all red, including a red insole, heel, upper, and outsole. This was not the first time that YSL had designed a monochrome footwear line, or even a line of footwear with red soles; indeed, YSL maintains that since the 1970s it had sold such shoes in red and other colors.

In January 2011, Louboutin avers, his fashion house learned that YSL was marketing and selling a monochrome red shoe with a red sole. Louboutin filed this action on April 7, 2011, asserting claims under the Lanham Act, 15 U.S.C. § 1051 *et seq.,* for trademark infringement. Louboutin also sought a preliminary injunction preventing YSL from marketing, during the pendency of the action, any shoes, including red monochrome shoes, bearing outsoles in a shade of red identical to the Red Sole Mark, or in any shade which so resembles the Red Sole Mark as to cause confusion among consumers.

In response, YSL asserted two counterclaims: (1) seeking cancellation of the Red Sole Mark on the grounds that (a) it is not "distinctive," but instead merely "ornamental,"[4] (b) it is "functional."

On August 10, 2011, the District Court issued a Decision and Order denying the injunction and holding that the Louboutin fashion house had

[4] An ornamental feature is one that "do[es] not serve a purpose" in the design of a product. *See TrafFix Devices, Inc. v. Marketing Displays, Inc.*, 532 U.S. 23, 35 (2001); *see also Wallace Int'l Silversmiths, Inc. v. Godinger Silver Art Co., Inc.*, 916 F.2d 76, 80 (2d Cir. 1990) (holding that "the features at issue are strictly ornamental because they neither affect the use of the [product] nor contribute to its efficient manufacture").

not shown a likelihood of success on the merits of its claims. This appeal followed.

Discussion

II. Trademark Protection of Single-Color Marks

A. The Analytical Framework

We analyze trademark infringement claims in two stages. In order for a trademark to be protectable, the mark must be "distinctive" and not "generic." A mark is said to be "inherently" distinctive if "[its] intrinsic nature serves to identify a particular source." *Two Pesos, Inc. v. Taco Cabana, Inc.*, 505 U.S. 763, 768 (1992).[9] Even a mark that is not inherently distinctive may nonetheless "acquire" distinctiveness by developing "secondary meaning" in the public mind. A mark has acquired "secondary meaning" when, "in the minds of the public, the primary significance of a product feature . . . is to identify the source of the product rather than the product itself."

Second, if (and only if) the plaintiff's trademark is "distinctive" within the meaning of trademark law and is therefore valid and protectable, we must then determine "whether [the] defendant's use of a similar mark is likely to cause consumer confusion." In this second stage, if a markholder has successfully demonstrated that its mark is valid and that the competitor's mark is likely to cause confusion, "the competitor can [nevertheless] prevail . . . by showing that the [mark] is functional"—a traditional defense to the enforcement of a trademark. The "functionality" of a mark can be demonstrated by, *inter alia,* showing that the mark has either traditional "utilitarian" functionality or "aesthetic" functionality.

C. Single-Color Marks Today

The question of whether a color can be protected as a trademark or trade dress was finally resolved in 1995 by the Supreme Court's decision in *Qualitex,* which involved a claim for trade dress protection of the green-gold color of a dry cleaning press pad. The question presented was "whether the [Lanham Act] permits the registration of a trademark that consists, purely and simply, of a color." *Qualitex,* 514 U.S. at 160–61 (citation omitted). The Court observed that "it is difficult to find, in basic trademark objectives, a reason to disqualify absolutely the use of a color as a mark." *Id.* at 164. The Court held, among other things, that it could find no "principled objection to the use of color as a mark in the important 'functionality' doctrine of trademark law." *Id.* It concluded that "color alone, *at least sometimes,* can meet the basic legal requirements for use as a

[9] Although *Two Pesos,* and several of the other cases we rely upon, discuss unregistered trade dress rather than a registered trademark, the infringement analysis is the same. *See Wal-Mart Stores, Inc. v. Samara Bros., Inc.,* 529 U.S. 205, 210–11 (2000) (noting with approval instances in which courts analyzed distinctiveness with regard to trade dress by analogy to the law of registered trademarks).

trademark. It can act as a symbol that distinguishes a firm's goods and identifies their source, without serving any other significant function." *Id.* at 166 (emphasis added).

III. The "Functionality" Defense

As the Supreme Court observed in *Qualitex,* aspects of a product that are "functional" generally "cannot serve as a trademark." *Id.* at 165. We have observed that "[t]he doctrine of functionality prevents trademark law from inhibiting legitimate competition by giving monopoly control to a producer over a useful product." *Nora Beverages, Inc.,* 269 F.3d at 120 n.4. This is so because functional features can be protected only through the patent system, which grants a limited monopoly over such features until they are released into general use (typically after either 14 or 20 years, depending on the type of patent).

As noted above, two forms of the functionality doctrine are relevant to us today: "traditional" or "utilitarian" functionality, and "aesthetic" functionality. Both forms serve as an affirmative defense to a trademark infringement claim.

A. "Traditional" or "Utilitarian" Functionality

According to our traditional understanding of functionality, a product feature is considered to be "functional" in a utilitarian sense if it is (1) "essential to the use or purpose of the article," or if it (2) "affects the cost or quality of the article." *Inwood Labs.,* 456 U.S. at 850 n.10. A feature is essential " 'if [it] is dictated by the functions to be performed' " by the article. It affects the cost or quality of the article where it " 'permits the article to be manufactured at a lower cost' or 'constitutes an improvement in the operation of the goods.' " *Id.* A finding that a product feature is functional according to the *Inwood* test will ordinarily render the feature ineligible for trademark protection.

B. "Aesthetic Functionality"

Generally, "[w]here [a product's] design is functional under the *Inwood* formulation there is no need to proceed further." *TrafFix Devices, Inc. v. Marketing Displays, Inc.,* 532 U.S. 23, 33 (2001) ("*TrafFix*"). Nevertheless, as the Supreme Court had held in 1995 in *Qualitex,* when the aesthetic design of a product is *itself* the mark for which protection is sought, we may also deem the mark functional if giving the markholder the right to use it exclusively "would put competitors at a significant non-reputation-related disadvantage," *Qualitex,* 514 U.S. at 165. This remains true even if there is "no indication that [the mark has] any bearing on the use or purpose of the product or its cost or quality." *TrafFix,* 532 U.S. at 33; *see Landscape Forms, Inc. v. Colum. Cascade Co.,* 70 F.3d 251, 253 (2d Cir. 1995) (when evaluating design trademarks we consider whether "certain features of the design are essential to effective competition in [the] particular market").

As set forth below, the test for aesthetic functionality is threefold: At the start, we address the two prongs of the *Inwood* test, asking whether the design feature is either "essential to the use or purpose" or "affects the cost or quality" of the product at issue. Next, if necessary, we turn to a third prong, which is the competition inquiry set forth in *Qualitex*. In other words, if a design feature would, from a traditional utilitarian perspective, be considered "essential to the use or purpose" of the article, or to affect its cost or quality, then the design feature is functional under *Inwood* and our inquiry ends. But if the design feature is not "functional" from a traditional perspective, it must still pass the fact-intensive *Qualitex* test and be shown not to have a significant effect on competition in order to receive trademark protection.

i. The Development of the Aesthetic Functionality Doctrine

Although the theory of aesthetic functionality was proposed as early as 1938,[16] the first court to adopt the theory as the basis for denial of protection of a design was the United States Court of Appeals for the Ninth Circuit in *Pagliero v. Wallace China Co.,* 198 F.2d 339 (9th Cir. 1952). In *Pagliero,* the Court of Appeals determined that the Wallace China Company was not entitled to the exclusive use of a particular floral design on hotel china, despite its "creat[ion of] a substantial market for its products bearing these designs by virtue of extensive advertising." *Id.* at 340. The design, the Court held, was "functional" because it satisfied "a demand for the aesthetic as well as for the utilitarian." *Id.* at 343–44. Because the "particular feature is an *important ingredient* in the commercial success of the product, the interest in free competition permits its imitation in the absence of a patent or copyright." *Id.* at 343 (emphasis added).

Despite its apparent counterintuitiveness (how can the purely aesthetic be deemed functional, one might ask?), our Court has long accepted the doctrine of aesthetic functionality.[17] We have rejected,

[16] In 1938, the Restatement of Torts stated that "[a] feature of goods is functional . . . if it affects their purpose, action or performance, or the facility or economy of processing, handling or using them; it is non-functional if it does not have any of such effects." RESTATEMENT OF TORTS § 742 (1938). In the official comment to that Section, the Restatement explained several ways in which," goods or their features might be functional. With regard to "goods [that] are bought largely for their aesthetic value," the Restatement suggested that "their features may be functional because they definitely contribute to that value and thus aid the performance of an object for which the goods are intended." *Id.* § 742, cmt. a. This was the first time that a commentator had proposed that an aesthetic product feature might be functional.

[17] The doctrine of aesthetic functionality remains controversial in our sister circuits, which have applied the doctrine in varying ways (and some not at all). For example, the Seventh Circuit has applied the doctrine of aesthetic functionality liberally, holding that "[f]ashion is a form of function." *See Jay Franco & Sons, Inc. v. Franek,* 615 F.3d 855, 860 (7th Cir. 2010). The Sixth Circuit recently discussed the doctrine, but made clear that it has not yet decided whether or not to adopt it. *See Maker's Mark Distillery, Inc. v. Diageo N. Am., Inc.,* 679 F.3d 410, 417–19 (6th Cir. 2012). The Ninth Circuit has applied the doctrine inconsistently. The Fifth Circuit rejects the doctrine of aesthetic functionality entirely. *Bd. of Supervisors for La. State Univ. Agric. & Mech. Coll. v. Smack Apparel Co.,* 550 F.3d 465, 487–88 (5th Cir. 2008) (arguing that the Supreme Court

however, the circular "important ingredient" test formulated by the *Pagliero* court, which inevitably penalized markholders for their success in promoting their product.[18] Instead, we have concluded that "Lanham Act protection does not extend to configurations of ornamental features which would *significantly* limit the range of competitive designs available." *Coach Leatherware Co. v. AnnTaylor, Inc.,* 933 F.2d 162, 171 (2d Cir. 1991) (emphasis added). Accordingly, we have held that the doctrine of aesthetic functionality bars protection of a mark that is "necessary to compete in the [relevant] market." *Villeroy & Boch Keramische Werke K.G. v. THC Sys., Inc.,* 999 F.2d 619, 622 (2d Cir. 1993).

ii. A Modern Formulation of the Aesthetic Functionality Doctrine

In 1995, the Supreme Court in *Qualitex* gave its imprimatur to the aesthetic functionality doctrine, holding that "[t]he ultimate test of aesthetic functionality . . . is whether the recognition of trademark rights [in an aesthetic design feature] would significantly hinder competition." *Qualitex,* 514 U.S. at 170 (quoting Restatement (Third) of Unfair Competition § 17, cmt. c, at 176 (1993)). Six years later, reiterating its *Qualitex* analysis, the Supreme Court in *TrafFix* declared that where "[a]esthetic functionality [is] the central question courts must "inquire" as to whether recognizing the trademark "would put competitors at a significant non-reputation-related disadvantage." *TrafFix,* 532 U.S. at 32–33.

Although we have not recently had occasion to apply the doctrine of aesthetic functionality thus enunciated by the Supreme Court, it is clear that the combined effect of *Qualitex* and *TrafFix* was to validate the aesthetic functionality doctrine as it had already been developed by this Court. . . .

On the one hand, " '[w]here an ornamental feature is claimed as a trademark and trademark protection would significantly hinder competition by limiting the range of adequate alternative designs, the aesthetic functionality doctrine denies such protection.' " *Forschner Grp., Inc. v. Arrow Trading Co.,* 124 F.3d 402, 409–10 (2d Cir. 1997). But on the other hand, " 'distinctive and arbitrary arrangements of predominantly ornamental features that do *not* hinder potential competitors from entering the same market with differently dressed versions of the product are non-

has recognized the aesthetic functionality doctrine only in *dicta,* and that therefore the Fifth Circuit's long-standing rejection of the doctrine was not abrogated by *Qualitex* and *TrafFix*).

[18] *See Wallace Int'l Silversmiths,* 916 F.2d at 80 ("We rejected *Pagliero*['s 'important ingredient' formulation] in [*Le*] *Sportsac* and reiterate that rejection here."); Mark P. McKenna, *(Dys)functionality,* 48 Hous. L. Rev. 823, 851 (2011) ("Courts that apply the aesthetic functionality doctrine today overwhelmingly rely on the test the Supreme Court endorsed in *TrafFix* [rather than the *Pagliero* test], . . . asking whether exclusive use of the claimed feature put competitors at a significant non-reputation-related disadvantage.").

functional[,] and [are] hence eligible for [trademark protection].' " *Fabrication Enters., Inc.,* 64 F.3d at 59 (emphasis added).

In short, a mark is aesthetically functional, and therefore ineligible for protection under the Lanham Act, where protection of the mark *significantly* undermines competitors' ability to compete in the relevant market. In making this determination, courts must carefully weigh "the competitive benefits of protecting the source-identifying aspects" of a mark against the "competitive costs of precluding competitors from using the feature." *Fabrication Enters., Inc.,* 64 F.3d at 59.

Finally, we note that a product feature's successful source indication can sometimes be difficult to distinguish from the feature's aesthetic function, if any. Therefore, in determining whether a mark has an aesthetic function so as to preclude trademark protection, we take care to ensure that the mark's very success in denoting (and promoting) its source does not itself defeat the markholder's right to protect that mark.

Because aesthetic function and branding success can sometimes be difficult to distinguish, the aesthetic functionality analysis is highly fact-specific. In conducting this inquiry, courts must consider both the markholder's right to enjoy the benefits of its effort to distinguish its product and the public's right to the "vigorously competitive market [ ]" protected by the Lanham Act, which an overly broad trademark might hinder. *Yurman Design, Inc.,* 262 F.3d at 115. In sum, courts must avoid jumping to the conclusion that an aesthetic feature is functional merely because it denotes the product's desirable source.

iii. Aesthetic Functionality in the Fashion Industry

We now turn to the *per se* rule of functionality for color marks in the fashion industry adopted by the District Court—a rule that would effectively deny trademark protection to any deployment of a single color in an item of apparel. As noted above, the *Qualitex* Court expressly held that "sometimes [ ] a color will meet ordinary legal trademark requirements[, a]nd, when it does so, no special legal rule prevents color alone from serving as a trademark." *Qualitex,* 514 U.S. at 161. In other words, the Supreme Court specifically forbade the implementation of a *per se* rule that would deny protection for the use of a single color as a trademark in a particular industrial context. *Qualitex* requires an individualized, fact-based inquiry into the nature of the trademark, and cannot be read to sanction an industry-based *per se* rule. The District Court created just such a rule, on the theory that "there is something unique about the fashion world that militates against extending trademark protection to a single color." *Louboutin,* 778 F. Supp. 2d at 451.

Even if *Qualitex* could be read to permit an industry-specific *per se* rule of functionality (a reading we think doubtful), such a rule would be neither necessary nor appropriate here. We readily acknowledge that the fashion industry, like other industries, has special concerns in the operation of trademark law; it has been argued forcefully that United States law does not protect fashion design adequately.[19] Indeed, the case on appeal is particularly difficult precisely because, as the District Court well noted, in the fashion industry, color can serve as a tool in the palette of a designer, rather than as mere ornamentation.

Nevertheless, the functionality defense does not guarantee a competitor "the greatest range for [his] creative outlet," *id.* at 452–53, but only the ability to fairly compete within a given market.[20] The purpose of the functionality defense "is to prevent advances in functional design from being *monopolized* by the owner of [the mark] . . . in order to encourage competition and the broadest dissemination of useful design features." *Fabrication Enters., Inc.,* 64 F.3d at 58 (emphasis added).

In short, "[b]y focusing upon hindrances to legitimate competition, the [aesthetic] functionality test, carefully applied, can accommodate consumers' somewhat conflicting interests in being assured enough product differentiation to avoid confusion as to source and in being afforded the benefits of competition among producers." *Stormy Clime,* 809 F.2d at 978–79.

### IV. The Red Sole Mark

Having determined that no *per se* rule governs the protection of single-color marks in the fashion industry, any more than it can do so in any other industry, we turn our attention to the Red Sole Mark. As we have explained, Part II.A, *ante,* we analyze a trademark infringement claim in two stages, asking first whether the mark "merits protection" and, second, whether the allegedly infringing use of the mark (or a similar mark) is "likely to cause consumer confusion." The functionality defense (including

[19] The intellectual property protection of fashion design has been for years a subject of controversy among commentators. Some have proposed working within the confines of the current intellectual property system, while others have advocated that fashion design may be an appropriate area for *sui generis* statutory protection. *See generally* C. Scott Hemphill & Jeannie Suk, *The Law, Culture, and Economics of Fashion,* 61 Stan. L. Rev. 1147 (2009); *see also id.* at 1184–90. (Indeed, suggested legislation creating such protection has been considered several times by Congress, although not adopted. *See, e.g.,* Design Piracy Prohibition Act, H.R. 2033, 110th Cong. § 2(c) (2007); Design Piracy Prohibition Act, S. 1957, 110th Cong. § 2(c) (2007).) Still other commentators have suggested that intellectual property protection of fashion design would be damaging to the industry and should be avoided. *See* Kal Raustiala & Christopher Sprigman, *The Piracy Paradox: Innovation and Intellectual Property in Fashion Design,* 92 Va. L. Rev. 1687, 1775–77 (2006).

[20] The trademark system, in this way, stands in sharp contrast to the copyright system. Copyright, unlike trademark, rewards creativity and originality even if they interfere with the rights of an existing copyright holder. In the copyright system there is a defense to infringement known as "independent creation": if a writer or musician, through the creative process, independently arrives at an arrangement of words or notes that is the subject of a copyright, he may market the result of his creativity despite the existing copyright. The trademark system, unlike the copyright system, aims to prevent consumer confusion even at the expense of a manufacturer's creativity: in trademark, if a branding specialist produces a mark that is identical to one already trademarked by another individual or corporation, he must "go back to the drawing board."

the tripartite aesthetic functionality test) is an affirmative defense that we consider at the second stage of this analysis.

We have stated the basic rule that "[a] certificate of registration with the PTO is prima facie evidence that the mark is registered and valid (*i.e.*, protect[a]ble), that the registrant owns the mark, and that the registrant has the exclusive right to use the mark in commerce." *Lane Capital Mgmt., Inc.*, 192 F.3d at 345. As the District Court correctly noted, "Louboutin's certificate of registration of the Red Sole Mark gives rise to a statutory presumption that the mark is valid." *Louboutin,* 778 F. Supp. 2d at 450 (citing 15 U.S.C. § 1057(b)). But the District Court found, in effect, that YSL had rebutted that presumption by showing that the Red Sole Mark is ineligible for protection because a single color can never achieve trademark protection in the fashion industry. As explained above, that holding was error.

Although, as set forth below, we determine that the Mark as it currently stands is ineligible for protection insofar as it would preclude competitors' use of red outsoles in *all* situations, including the monochromatic use now before us, we conclude that the Mark has acquired secondary meaning—and thus the requisite "distinctness" to merit protection—when used as a red outsole *contrasting* with the remainder of the shoe. Because in this case we determine that the Red Sole Mark merits protection only as modified, and because YSL's use of a red outsole on monochromatic red shoes does not infringe on the Mark as modified, we need not, and do not, reach the issues of customer confusion and functionality at the second stage of the trademark infringement analysis described above.

In light of the evidence in the record, including extensive consumer surveys submitted by both parties during the preliminary injunction proceedings, and of the factual findings of the District Court, we think it plain that Louboutin's marketing efforts have created what the able district judge described as "a . . . brand with worldwide recognition," *Louboutin,* 778 F. Supp. 2d at 448. By placing the color red "in [a] context [that] seems unusual," *Qualitex,* 514 U.S. at 162, and deliberately tying that color to his product, Louboutin has created an identifying mark firmly associated with his brand which, "to those in the know," "instantly" denotes his shoes' source, *Louboutin,* 778 F. Supp. 2d at 448. These findings of fact by the District Court in addressing a motion for a preliminary injunction are not clearly erroneous. We hold that the lacquered red outsole, as applied to a shoe with an "upper" of a different color, has "come to identify and distinguish" the Louboutin brand, *Qualitex,* 514 U.S. at 163, and is therefore a distinctive symbol that qualifies for trademark protection.

We further hold that the record fails to demonstrate that the secondary meaning of the Red Sole Mark extends to uses in which the sole *does not* contrast with the upper—in other words, when a red sole is used on a monochromatic red shoe. As the District Court observed, "[w]hen Hollywood starlets cross red carpets and high fashion models strut down runways, and heads turn and eyes drop to the celebrities' feet, lacquered red outsoles on *high-heeled, black shoes* flaunt a glamorous statement that *pops out* at once." As clearly suggested by the District Court, it is the *contrast* between the sole and the upper that causes the sole to "pop," and to distinguish its creator.

The evidentiary record further demonstrates that the Louboutin mark is closely associated with contrast. For example, Pinault, the chief executive of YSL's parent company, wrote that the "distinctive signature" of the Mark is in its "contrast with the general presentation of the [shoe], particularly its upper." Of the hundreds of pictures of Louboutin shoes submitted to the District Court, only *four* were monochrome red. And Louboutin's own consumer surveys show that when consumers were shown the YSL monochrome red shoe, of those consumers who misidentified the pictured shoes as Louboutin-made, nearly every one cited the red *sole* of the shoe, rather than its general red color. We conclude, based upon the record before us, that Louboutin has not established secondary meaning in an application of a red sole to a red shoe, but *only* where the red sole contrasts with the "upper" of the shoe. The use of a red lacquer on the outsole of a red shoe of the same color is not a use of the Red Sole Mark.

Because we conclude that the secondary meaning of the mark held by Louboutin extends only to the use of a lacquered red outsole that contrasts with the adjoining portion of the shoe, we modify the Red Sole Mark, pursuant to Section 37 of the Lanham Act insofar as it is sought to be applied to any shoe bearing the same color "upper" as the outsole. We therefore instruct the Director of the Patent and Trade Office to limit the registration of the Red Sole Mark to only those situations in which the red lacquered outsole contrasts in color with the adjoining "upper" of the shoe. *See id.*

In sum, we hold that the Red Sole Mark is valid and enforceable as modified. This holding disposes of the Lanham Act claims brought by both Louboutin and YSL because the red sole on YSL's monochrome shoes is neither a use of, nor confusingly similar to, the Red Sole Mark. We therefore affirm the denial of the preliminary injunction insofar as Louboutin could not have shown a likelihood of success on the merits in the absence of an infringing use of the Red Sole Mark by YSL.

### *NOTES AND QUESTIONS*

1. Do you agree with the Second Circuit's refusal to declare a per se rule disqualifying single-color trademarks in the fashion context? Or are there legitimate concerns that exclusive use of basic colors will stifle competition? Is the functionality doctrine sufficient to avoid the problem?

2. Should some colors be considered generic for certain fashion—e.g., blue jeans, blue blazer, and black dress? Should those single colors be categorically barred from trademark as to those clothing items?

3. By resolving the case on secondary meaning rather than functionality, the Second Circuit left open a number of difficult questions about the scope of Louboutin's rights. If Prada began selling pink, contrasting-sole women's shoes, would Prada would be infringing Loboutin's trademark? What about women's pumps with red lacquered heels? What if Burberry began selling men's shoes with red contrasting soles? Are these questions sufficiently difficult that the court would have been better off addressing functionality?

---

## D. TRADE DRESS INFRINGEMENT

The Lanham Act has two infringement provisions: § 32 provides remedies for infringement of registered marks and § 43(a) for, among other things, infringement of unregistered marks. 15 U.S.C. §§ 1114, 1125(a). Though the language of those provisions differs slightly, courts have uniformly interpreted them to be equivalent as to infringement. To prove infringement under either provisions, a plaintiff must prove that an appreciable number of reasonably prudent purchasers are likely to be confused about the source of the defendant's goods, or as to some sponsorship or affiliation between the parties. Each Circuit has adopted its own list of factors for determining likelihood of confusion. While the number of factors and their specific articulation varies somewhat from circuit to circuit, there is a great deal of similarity among them. All circuits take into account the similarity of the marks and of the goods or services, evidence of actual confusion and intent, the strength of the mark, and the nature of the markets in which the parties use their marks including the sophistication and similarity of the parties' customers. The list of factors is flexible, and courts frequently say that no one factor is dispositive. *See, e.g., Nora Beverages, Inc. v. Perrier Group, Inc.*, 269 F.3d 114, 119 (2d Cir. 2001) (noting that although the *Polaroid* factors are important in determining infringement, no one factor is dispositive and courts should focus on "the ultimate question of whether consumers are likely to be confused").

These factors were designed primarily to assess confusion in cases involving the use of word marks or logos for non-competing goods, but courts typically have used the same frameworks to evaluate the likelihood of confusion in trade dress cases. As the *Groeneveld* decision demonstrates, courts sometimes weight the factors somewhat differently in those cases, particularly where the claimed features are arguably functional.

### *PROBLEM 3–5*

Gibson Guitar Company has designed a "Les Paul" electric guitar starting in 1952. Les Paul was a famous guitarist who licensed his name to Gibson for use on the guitar he helped to design and popularize. The Les Paul guitar has a solid body with a single cutaway or U-shaped indentation near where the guitar body meets the guitar neck. Gibson registered the shape of the Les Paul guitar as a trademark in 1993, submitting both a drawing and a photograph as shown below. The registration is still live in the U.S. Trademark Office. In 1999, the registration became incontestable.

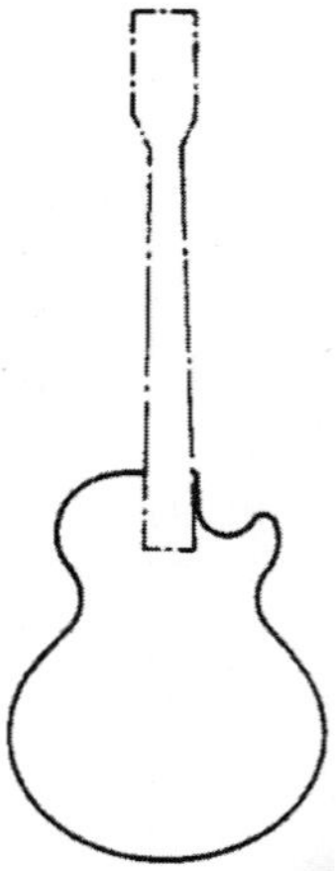

**Gibson's Les Paul guitar shape®** **Photo of Gibson Les Paul guitar**

Meanwhile, Paul Reed Smith Guitars (PRS), a competitor, began selling a single cutaway electric guitar in 2000. A photograph of PRS's guitar is below:

**Photo of Paul Reed Smith guitar**

You can also compare the Gibson and PRS guitars at http://www.gibson.com/Products/Electric-Guitars/Les-Paul.aspx and http://www.prsguitars.com/index.php/electrics/core/p245.

Gibson has sued PRS for trade dress infringement. You are a law clerk to the district court judge trying the case. In addition to the evidence above, the parties have submitted the following evidence:

1. The Gibson Les Paul guitar very well known among guitarists. Knowledgeable consumers of guitars identify that shape as signifying a "Les Paul guitar."

2. Gibson spent more than $2.2 million advertising the Les Paul, including with photographs of the guitar.

3. PRS developed its single cutaway guitar to fill a need in the market due to Gibson's dispute with retail music stores selling guitars. The stores informed PRS that they wanted an alternative single cutaway guitar to sell instead of the Gibson guitar.

4. PRS added features to its guitar to help distinguish it from a Gibson Les Paul. The PRS guitar has a longer scale length, different headstock colors, a vertical instead of a horizontal logo on the headstock, a one-piece bridge, a belly carve in the back, a contoured neck joint (as opposed to a right angle), a thinner body,

a significantly different outside shape, and a differently shaped truss rod cover. The PRS guitar also lacks binding (contrasting color striping around the body and neck), a pickguard, and the ring around the toggle switch, all of which are found in the Les Paul design. PRS also included its own characteristic three-dimensional "scoop" in the cutaway portion of the guitar body, the PRS trademarked headstock shape, the PRS logo on the headstock, distinctive PRS bird inlay on the fretboard, and accompanying materials such as tags that hang from the guitar when it is displayed for sale.

5. Both Gibson and PRS manufacture and sell guitars in the $1,800 to $3,500 price range. Both companies compete in the same market and sell their guitars in the same outlents (i.e., retail stores where customers can personally examine the products). Expensive guitars are not "impulse items."

6. There is no evidence of any actual confusion at the point of sale about the source of a PRS guitar. However, Gibson submitted evidence of several consumers who mistakenly thought the PRS guitar was a Gibson Les Paul guitar when the consumers first saw the guitar on display in stores. The confusion was erased once the consumers were close enough to inspect the guitar and its label.

7. There are a variety of ways that single cutaway guitars (particularly the angle, shape, and depth of the cutaway portion and "horn" that the cutaway portion leaves) can be designed without materially altering the sound or performance of the guitar.

Please prepare a bench memorandum advising the Judge on the following: (1) what is the legal test for determining trade dress infringement; and (2) what are your recommendations for how the Judge should apply the test to the evidence in the case as set forth above. Answer this problem first as a court in the Sixth Circuit would and then as a court in a different circuit that is not required to follow the Sixth Circuit's approach (such as to initial interest and post-sale confusion). To answer this problem, consider the following two cases and discussion.

## GROENEVELD TRANSPORT EFFICIENCY, INC. V. LUBECORE INTERNATIONAL, INC.

730 F.3d 494 (6th Cir. 2013)

GILMAN, CIRCUIT JUDGE. The key issue in this case is whether a company can use trade-dress law to protect its functional product design from competition with a "copycat" design made by another company where there is no reasonable likelihood that consumers would confuse the two companies' products as emanating from a single source. We hold that it cannot. In so holding, we reaffirm that trademark law is designed to promote brand recognition, not to insulate product manufacturers from lawful competition.

Groeneveld Transport Efficiency, Inc. sued Lubecore International, Inc., claiming that Lubecore's automotive grease pump is a "virtually identical" copy of Groeneveld's automotive grease pump. The complaint asserts that such copying constitutes trade-dress infringement in violation of § 43(a) of the Lanham (Trademark) Act, 15 U.S.C. § 1125(a), and further violates a number of related federal and Ohio laws. All the claims except trade-dress infringement were dismissed. The trade-dress claim went to the jury, which found for Groeneveld and awarded it $1,225,000 in damages.

Lubecore appeals the denial of its Rule 50 motion with respect to the trade-dress claim. Groeneveld in turn cross-appeals from the dismissal of its other claims. For the reasons set forth below, we REVERSE the judgment of the district court denying Lubecore's Rule 50 motion with respect to Groeneveld's trade-dress claim, AFFIRM the district court's dismissal of Groeneveld's other claims, and REMAND the case with instructions to enter judgment as a matter of law in favor of Lubecore on all claims.

## I. BACKGROUND

### A. Factual background

This case, like many trademark cases before it, is a contest between an oldtimer and a newcomer. Their battle is over a relatively obscure product—the grease pump used in an automated lubrication system (ALS) for commercial trucks. An ALS, as the name implies, is a system for delivering a controlled amount of lubricant to different parts of a machine (in this case a commercial truck) while the machine is in operation. Automated lubrication saves time, increases operational efficiency, and minimizes corrosion by obviating the need for frequent manual lubrication. The primary component of an ALS is a grease pump that forces grease through injectors and hoses to targeted areas at timed intervals.

Groeneveld is the American branch of a Dutch company that has been in the ALS business for over 40 years. It began marketing the grease pump at issue in the present case—designated by Groeneveld as its EP0 pump—in the 1980s. The Groeneveld family of companies employs thousands of people and has a well-established international presence.

Lubecore, by contrast, is the new kid on the block. It was founded in 2007 by Jan Eisses, who had previously sold another company of his to Groeneveld and had been a Groeneveld employee for approximately three years. Lubecore is located in Canada, is owned by Eisses and his wife, and employed 12 people at the time of pretrial discovery. It designed the grease pump at issue in this case in December 2007 and began selling it first in Canada (starting in April 2008) and then in the United States (starting in

March 2009). The two companies' competing grease pumps are shown below:

B. Procedural background

In April 2010, Groeneveld brought suit against Lubecore in the United States District Court for the Northern District of Ohio. The complaint alleged that Lubecore was marketing a grease pump that was "virtually identical" to Groeneveld's pump with the intent to confuse consumers into believing that the two pumps were made by the same company, thus freeriding on Groeneveld's established goodwill by passing off Lubecore pumps as Groeneveld pumps. Groeneveld further alleged that, of all competing manufacturers, only Lubecore made a pump that had essentially the same design as Groeneveld's.

A seven-day jury trial was held in October 2011. At the close of Groeneveld's proof, Lubecore moved for judgment as a matter of law under Rule 50 of the Federal Rules of Civil Procedure, which motion it renewed at the close of all the evidence. The district court granted Lubecore's Rule 50 motion with respect to Counts 2–6 of the complaint, but reserved ruling on Count 1, the trade-dress claim.

Count 1 was subsequently submitted to the jury in the form of the following three interrogatories, which track the three elements of a trade-dress claim:

1. Do you find that Plaintiff Groeneveld proved by a preponderance of the evidence that its Trade Dress (the external shape and appearance of the pump, including logo and color) are non-functional?

2. Do you find that Plaintiff Groeneveld proved by a preponderance of the evidence that its Trade Dress (the external shape and appearance of the pump, including logo and color) is distinctive in the marketplace, that is has it acquired secondary meaning?

3. Do you find that Plaintiff Groeneveld proved by a preponderance of the evidence that there is a likelihood of confusion in the minds of consumers of EP[0] pumps as to the source of Defendant Lubecore's EP[0] pump?

The jury answered "yes" to all three interrogatories and awarded Groeneveld damages in the amount of $1,225,000. On the following day, the jury returned to hear arguments as to whether Lubecore's trade-dress infringement had been willful (which would be a relevant consideration for the purpose of damages in the event that Groeneveld's other claims were revived on appeal). It answered "yes" to this question also. The district court accepted the jury's answers and entered judgment in favor of Groeneveld. It also entered a permanent injunction barring Lubecore from selling its grease pump in the United States. Lubecore's timely appeal and Groeneveld's cross-appeal followed.

D. The likelihood of confusion

An element that Groeneveld must prove in order to prevail on its trade-dress claim is that an ordinary consumer of grease pumps would likely be confused into thinking that the two pumps at issue were manufactured by the same company or were associated or affiliated with the same company. *See Abercrombie & Fitch Stores, Inc. v. Am. Eagle Outfitters, Inc.,* 280 F.3d 619, 645 (6th Cir. 2002). The appropriate benchmark for assessing the likelihood of confusion is the ordinary consumer who would consider buying the product at issue. *Frisch's Restaurant, Inc. v. Shoney's, Inc.,* 759 F.2d 1261, 1266 (6th Cir. 1985). And the focus is on "the typical buyer exercising ordinary caution," *Daddy's Junky Music,* 109 F.3d at 285, not "the most obtuse consumer," *Abercrombie,* 280 F.3d at 648.

This court has enumerated eight factors to consider in determining whether the trade dresses of competing products present a sufficient likelihood of confusion: "(1) strength of the plaintiff's [trade dress]; (2) relatedness of the goods; (3) similarity of the [trade dresses]; (4) evidence of actual confusion; (5) marketing channels used; (6) likely degree of purchaser care; (7) defendant's intent in selecting the [trade dress]; (8) likelihood of expansion of the product lines." *Frisch's,* 759 F.2d at 1264.

These factors are helpful guides rather than rigid requirements, *Daddy's Junky Music,* 109 F.3d at 280, with "[t]he ultimate question remain [ing] whether relevant consumers are likely to believe that the products or services offered by the parties are affiliated in some way." *Id.* The *Frisch* factors are therefore not always weighed consistently in this court's caselaw, and a particular factor might receive a greater or lesser weight depending on the circumstances. Accordingly, this court has sometimes resolved the question of confusion by reference to only one or a few of these factors, without inquiring into the rest.

In the present case, Groeneveld's and Lubecore's logos and trademarks appearing on their respective product designs are unmistakably different, as shown in the product photos at the beginning of this opinion. The former is green with a large "G" mark and says "GROENEVELD"; the latter is red with a maple-leaf mark and says "lubecore." And the evidence is undisputed that the same logos appear on the parties' sales and marketing literature. In light of such a stark visual difference in branding, no reasonable consumer would think that the two grease pumps belong to the same company.

Groeneveld does not dispute that potential purchasers of grease pumps are knowledgeable and sophisticated people. Such purchasers are therefore not likely to ignore the stark difference in labeling and mistakenly purchase a Lubecore ALS when they intend to purchase a Groeneveld ALS. As this court has stated,

> when a buyer has expertise or is otherwise more sophisticated with respect to the purchase of the services at issue, a higher standard [of consumer confusion] is proper. Similarly, when services are expensive or unusual, the buyer can be expected to exercise greater care in her purchases. When services are sold to such buyers, other things being equal, there is less likelihood of confusion.

*Daddy's Junky Music*, 109 F.3d at 285.

Groeneveld argues, however, that the two pumps' starkly different labeling would not distinguish the pumps in the eyes of their sophisticated consumers because "(1) labels are not the predominant brand identifiers in the industry; (2) corporate mergers and acquisitions are frequent, so competitor affiliations are constantly changing; (3) many pumps bear multiple company names; (4) a pump's label does not identify who made it or where it was manufactured; (5) Lubecore is a newcomer and has no independent brand recognition; and (6) witnesses who saw the Lubecores were still confused, notwithstanding the Lubecore label." We find none of these arguments persuasive.

Points (2) and (5) simply have no bearing on the issue of whether the pumps' different labels are sufficient to tell them apart. Point (1) is similarly irrelevant and, in any event, is not supported by the record evidence cited by Groeneveld. The most that the cited testimony shows is that certain witnesses were able to distinguish Groeneveld's pumps from pumps other than Lubecore's without even looking at the labels, which says nothing about whether a consumer would be able to distinguish a Groeneveld pump from a Lubecore pump with the labels. Points (3) and (4), on the other hand, plainly do not apply to the labels at issue in the present case. Finally, point (6), which is really Groeneveld's only relevant argument on this issue, will be discussed below under the "actual confusion" factor. The upshot is that Groeneveld has at most identified possible reasons why—hypothetically—differential branding might not be sufficient to distinguish the sources of competing products, but it did not present any evidence to show that any of those hypothetical reasons actually applies in the present case.

We therefore conclude that the starkly different branding of the two grease pumps and the high degree of care presumably exercised by the pumps' sophisticated consumers—factors 3 and 6 of the *Frisch* factors—compel the conclusion that, as a matter of law, Groeneveld has failed to carry its burden of raising a triable issue regarding the likelihood of confusion. Nevertheless, in order to give Groeneveld the benefit of all favorable inferences, we will proceed to analyze all of the *Frisch* factors to see whether, taken together, they would enable a reasonable jury to find for Groeneveld on this issue.

### *1. Lubecore's intent in selecting the trade dress*

Because Groeneveld makes Lubecore's intent the centerpiece of its likelihood-of-confusion analysis, we will start with this factor and then proceed to the other *Frisch* factors. Groeneveld argues that Lubecore intended to copy Groeneveld's trade dress (minus the label) and that this "bad intent," for which Lubecore has offered "no innocent explanation whatsoever," is sufficient to prove the likelihood of confusion.

The similarities in the two pumps' appearance (excluding the labels), the fact that other manufacturers' pumps do not have a similar look, and the fact that Lubecore's founder used to be a Groeneveld employee constitute circumstantial evidence of an intent to copy. But Groeneveld is mistaken about the legal significance of such copying. In particular, its assertion that the intentional copying of its trade dress constitutes "bad intent" that creates a "presumption of confusing similarity" indicates a fundamental misapprehension of the purposes of trademark law.

Groeneveld's argument fails to appreciate that trademark law does not prohibit *copying* as such; that is the province of copyrights and patents. *See TrafFix Devices, Inc. v. Mktg. Displays, Inc.*, 532 U.S. 23, 34 (2001) ("The Lanham Act does not exist to reward manufacturers for their innovation in creating a particular device; that is the purpose of the patent law and its period of exclusivity."); *Fuji Kogyo Co. v. Pac. Bay Int'l, Inc.*, 461 F.3d 675, 686 (6th Cir. 2006) ("Trademark law cannot properly make an end run around the strict requirements of utility patent law by giving equivalent rights to exclude.").

A manufacturer who desires protection against copying must satisfy the requirements of protectability under the copyright or patent regimes and must also submit itself to the limited time periods of protection afforded under those regimes. Those requirements and their attendant restrictions incentivize valuable artistic and scientific creations while ensuring that the social costs of monopoly are contained within reasonable bounds. *See* U.S. Const. art. I, § 8, cl. 8 (the Copyright and Patent Clause) ("The Congress shall have Power . . . To promote the Progress of Science and useful Arts, by securing for limited Times to Authors and Inventors the exclusive Right to their respective Writings and Discoveries."); *Bonito Boats, Inc. v. Thunder Craft Boats, Inc.,* 489 U.S. 141, 146–51 (1989) (explicating the policies and tradeoffs of the patent system); *Sony Corp. of Am. v. Universal City Studios, Inc.,* 464 U.S. 417, 428–29 (1984) (explicating the policies and tradeoffs of copyright law). The public policy behind the patent regime is perhaps most clearly set out in *Sears, Roebuck & Co. v. Stiffel Co.,* 376 U.S. 225 (1964) ["Thus the patent system is one in which uniform federal standards are carefully used to promote invention while at the same time preserving free competition."].

Trademark law's likelihood-of-confusion requirement, in contrast, is designed to promote informational integrity in the marketplace. By ensuring that consumers are not confused about what they are buying, trademark law allows them to allocate their capital efficiently to the brands that they find most deserving. This, in turn, incentivizes manufacturers to create robust brand recognition by consistently offering good products and good services, which results in more consumer satisfaction. That is the virtuous cycle envisioned by trademark law, including its trade-dress branch. As stated in *Qualitex Co. v. Jacobson Products Co., Inc.,* 514 U.S. 159 (1995):

> In principle, trademark law, by preventing others from copying a source-identifying mark, reduces the customer's costs of shopping and making purchasing decisions, for it quickly and easily assures a potential customer that *this* item—the item with this mark—is made by the same producer as other similarly marked items that he or she liked (or disliked) in the past. At the same time, the law helps assure a producer that it (and not an imitating competitor) will reap the financial, reputation-related rewards associated with a desirable product. The law thereby encourages the production of quality products, and simultaneously discourages those who hope to sell inferior products by capitalizing on a consumer's inability quickly to evaluate the quality of an item offered for sale. It is the source-distinguishing ability of a mark . . . that permits it to serve these basic purposes.

Such an incentive structure would of course be disrupted if a manufacturer's hard-won brand recognition were open to appropriation by other manufacturers who confused consumers into believing that the two brands are affiliated or are one and the same. If manufacturers' qualitative efforts were subject to such skimming off, they would have less incentive to improve their offerings and build a robust brand in the first place.

No harm is done to this incentive structure, however, by the copying of a product design that does *not* confuse consumers as to the product's source. As long as a consumer can easily identify the source based on the trademark, the consumer will still be able to allocate his or her capital freely and efficiently, and manufacturers will retain the incentive to improve their offerings and solidify their brands. So trademark law, like the law of unfair competition of which it is a part, focuses not on copying per se but on confusion:

> The law of unfair competition has its roots in the common-law tort of deceit: its general concern is with protecting consumers from confusion as to source. While that concern may result in the creation of 'quasi-property rights' in communicative symbols, the focus is on the protection of consumers, not the protection of producers as an incentive to product innovation. Judge Hand captured the distinction well in *Crescent Tool Co. v. Kilborn & Bishop Co.,* 247 F. 299, 301 (2d Cir.1917), where he wrote: "The plaintiff has the right not to lose his customers through false representations that those are his wares which in fact are not, but he may not monopolize any design or pattern, however trifling. The defendant, on the other hand, may copy plaintiff's goods slavishly down to the minutest detail: but he may not represent himself as the plaintiff in their sale."

*Bonito Boats, Inc. v. Thunder Craft Boats, Inc.,* 489 U.S. 141, 157 (1989) (brackets and emphasis omitted).

That is why, in the absence of consumer confusion, and in the absence of any copyright or patent protection, copying is perfectly legal. Indeed, such copying is more than just legal; it is often beneficial:

> Trade dress protection must subsist with the recognition that in many instances there is no prohibition against copying goods and products. In general, unless an intellectual property right such as a patent or copyright protects an item, it will be subject to copying. As the Court has explained, copying is not always discouraged or disfavored by the laws which preserve our competitive economy. Allowing competitors to copy will have salutary effects in many instances. Reverse engineering of chemical and mechanical articles in the public domain often leads to significant advances in technology.

*TrafFix Devices, Inc. v. Mktg. Displays, Inc.,* 532 U.S. 23, 29 (2001). The same principle has been affirmed repeatedly by this court. *See Antioch Co. v. W. Trimming Corp.,* 347 F.3d 150, 160 (6th Cir.2003).

The clear import of the twin principles that copying in the absence of copyright or patent protection often serves useful purposes, and that the concern of trademark law is not about copying per se but about copying that engenders consumer confusion, is that the appropriate "intent" to focus on is not the intent to *copy* but rather the intent to *deceive* or *confuse.*

*See Maker's Mark Distillery, Inc. v. Diageo N. Am., Inc.,* 679 F.3d 410, 424 (6th Cir.2012).

If the law were otherwise, an act that is not only legal but also often beneficial would be transformed into evidence—or worse, as Groeneveld suggests, a "presumption"—of unlawfulness. Such an interpretation would contravene *TrafFix Devices* and the other decisions cited above and would subvert the fundamental purposes of trademark law. We recognize that the intent to copy might be probative in proving secondary meaning, *see, e.g., Abercrombie,* 280 F.3d at 639, but such intent standing alone has no bearing on the likelihood-of-confusion issue.

The principle that copying can have salutary effects is illustrated by the circumstances of the present case. Contrary to Groeneveld's protestation that Lubecore's copying of Groeneveld's design (minus the logo) has "no innocent explanation," the similarity serves the procompetitive purpose of signaling the existence of a competitive alternative by alerting potential consumers that the pumps might work the same because they look the same.

By making the appearance of its pump essentially the same as Groeneveld's (other than the label), Lubecore has specifically targeted consumers who are familiar with the Groeneveld pump and offered them a competitive option. The Supreme Court has unanimously confirmed that using a functional product's look to promote a competitive offering is a procompetitive practice. *See TrafFix Devices,* 532 U.S. at 34 ("If buyers are assured the product serves its purpose by seeing the operative mechanism[,] that in itself serves an important market need.").

Lubecore's targeting of Groeneveld's customers would of course be unfair and anticompetitive if Lubecore masqueraded as Groeneveld and confused them about the product they were buying. But Lubecore has in fact scrupulously avoided such confusion by choosing a starkly different logo that it prominently displays on its pumps and on all its sales and marketing literature. That is why the differential labeling is critical—it transforms a practice that would otherwise be anticompetitive into one that is procompetitive. And by specifically targeting Groeneveld customers, Lubecore focuses its competitive activity on those who are most interested in such competition, thereby decreasing the consumers' search costs and intensifying competition where it matters most. None of this is to say, of course, that consumers should switch from Groeneveld to Lubecore or that Lubecore makes a better pump. The point, rather, is that the state of affairs where consumers are aggressively courted and offered competitive options is beneficial as a matter of public policy.

These points are borne out by one of Groeneveld's witnesses, Dean Osborn, who testified that he likes the way the Groeneveld pump works but does not particularly care who manufactures it. Therefore, when Lubecore offered him *its* pump as an alternative to the Groeneveld pump, he considered and ultimately bought the Lubecore pump. Osborn testified that he has been satisfied with both the Groeneveld and the Lubecore pumps that he has owned, and that he has never been confused between the two brands:

> [Osborn:] [W]hat I would think is if you just, if you took off the top half of the thing and you took all the labels off of these things, take the red thing off and the black one and you take the label off here and you put that base with this off and that off and you look at the bases, to me I would not tell the difference. And to me that means I'm comfortable with the product. If it be whose product it is, I don't care. I have a good experience with it. So I'm very comfortable with it. Whatever labels you put on it or sticker, you know, I mean it doesn't matter. I'm looking at the mechanism that functions the grease to go to the spots where the greasing, that's all I'm—that's all I care about.
>
> [Groeneveld's Counsel:] Sir, would you have considered or bought the Lubecores if the pump didn't look so much like the Groeneveld pump?
>
> [Osborn:] It made me very comfortable when it—when that looks like a Groeneveld. . . . The Lubecore, the comfort zone of knowing that it looks identical to it and it probably operates the same thing, they, you know, in the literature they have the blocks of where the main grease goes to the different blocks and then it goes out. Everything to me resembles the same, you know what I mean. The Lubecore and Groeneveld, they look like sister machines, okay. They look like twins. And for me making my decision on buying a greaser, that's easy. I like these two systems. Who owns it doesn't matter to me. I just want the grease to go to the places to where [it should go] and I want a place here to service it.
>
> [Lubecore's Counsel:] . . . When you bought the four Lubecore systems, it was clear to you that you were buying Lubecore systems, not Groeneveld systems, correct?
>
> [Osborn:] Correct.
>
> [Lubecore's Counsel:] Garvin [an independent distributor through which both parties sold their ALS systems] has told you as much himself?
>
> [Osborn:] Um-hum, yes.
>
> [Lubecore's Counsel:] And the product has got Lubecore's label on it more than one place, right?
>
> [Osborn:] Yes.
>
> [Lubecore's Counsel:] So there was no confusion on your part about whose product you were buying?

[Osborn:] Correct.

Groeneveld objects to Lubecore's targeted competition, arguing that Lubecore's pumps are of "diminish[ed] . . . quality," have been subject to recalls, and "have been seen leaking grease." It also points to Lubecore's practice of offering to extend Groeneveld's warranty and to replace Groeneveld pumps and parts with Lubecore products.

These allegations, however, do not strengthen Groeneveld's trade-dress claim or make Lubecore's competition unfair. If Lubecore's pumps are in fact inferior, all the better for Groeneveld: Consumers would soon realize the difference in quality on the clearly labeled pumps and flock to Groeneveld. But that is a business judgment to be made by consumers as they see fit, not a legal judgment to be dictated by trade-dress law. The free market, not the courts, should pick winners and losers in the business world. As stated in *TrafFix Devices,* 532 U.S. at 28, "protection for trade dress exists to promote competition," not to hinder it.

Groeneveld's protestations against slavish copying admittedly have a certain emotional appeal and presumably swayed the jury. After all, people generally dislike copycats. But, as the foregoing discussion demonstrates, the proper application of trademark law requires us to focus our analysis not on the intent to copy the product design, but on the likelihood of consumer confusion. Evidence of Lubecore's intent to copy Groeneveld's product design is therefore of no help to Groeneveld. Such evidence, if anything, shows the procompetitive benefits of Lubecore's practices and cautions against allowing the issue to go to the jury. *See Wal-Mart Stores, Inc. v. Samara Bros.,* 529 U.S. 205, 214 (2000) (discussing the desirability of "summary disposition of an anticompetitive strike suit" in the trade-dress context).

*2. Strength of Groeneveld's trade dress*

This factor "focuses on the distinctiveness of a mark and its recognition among the public." *Maker's Mark Distillery, Inc. v. Diageo N. Am., Inc.,* 679 F.3d 410, 419 (6th Cir. 2012). Groeneveld submitted evidence of its prominence and pedigree in the industry, its extensive advertising, and, most importantly, witnesses who testified that they recognized the pump's design and associated it with Groeneveld. This evidence is sufficient to support a factual finding that Groeneveld's trade dress is strong. But such a finding is of no help to Groeneveld in the absence of any evidence that consumers are likely to confuse the source of the competing grease pumps.

*3. Relatedness of the goods*

The parties do not dispute that Groeneveld's and Lubecore's grease pumps perform the same function and directly compete in the industry. So this factor would also favor Groeneveld if it had any proof of the likelihood of confusion.

*4. Similarity of the marks*

As discussed above, the starkly different labels and trademarks on the competing products serve to dispel any likelihood of confusion between the two pumps. This factor weighs heavily against Groeneveld.

*5. Evidence of actual confusion*

Nothing shows the likelihood of confusion more than the fact of actual confusion. So evidence of actual consumer confusion, though not necessary, would be immensely helpful to Groeneveld. *See Frisch's Restaurant, Inc. v. Shoney's, Inc.*, 759 F.2d 1261, 1267 (6th Cir. 1985) (noting that evidence of actual confusion "is not necessary," but "it is obviously the most probative proof of likelihood of confusion").

But Groeneveld submitted no surveys showing whether a sample of the relevant consumer population was actually confused as between the parties' products. Groeneveld instead offered the testimony a single customer, Dean Osborn, in support of its actual-confusion claim. Osborn, however, unequivocally testified on cross-examination that he was *not* confused as to the origin of the pumps, as reflected in the transcript quoted above.

Groeneveld also cites the testimony of some of its own employees and affiliates professing "shock" and "surprise" that Lubecore's pump "looks the same" as Groeneveld's, saying that it "looks like a Groeneveld with a Lubecore sticker on it." None of these witnesses, however, were consumers, and none of them were actually confused as to the origin of the two pumps. Indeed, Groeneveld admitted at oral argument that it had no evidence of actual confusion. In sum, there is simply no evidence of actual confusion in the record.

*6. Marketing channels used*

The record contains evidence that both parties often attended the same industry trade shows, that they marketed their products over the Internet, and that certain distributors sold both parties' ALS systems. Such evidence is sufficient to show that there is a commonality in how the ALS systems are marketed. But, again, this evidence would be helpful to Groeneveld only if there were any showing of the likelihood of confusion.

*7. Likely degree of purchaser care*

As previously discussed, consumers of grease pumps are knowledgeable and sophisticated about the market, and they are unlikely to buy an expensive ALS system without exercising a substantial degree of care. This factor strongly favors Lubecore, especially when coupled with the stark dissimilarity in labeling.

*8. Likelihood of market expansion*

The only evidence regarding the likelihood of market expansion with respect to either company was the testimony of Eisses, Lubecore's founder, that he "really would like to move into the United States," but could not do so because of the lawsuit. This factor, however, does not alter our analysis in the absence of any evidence of confusing similarity.

*9. Summary of the Frisch factors*

The upshot of the likelihood-of-confusion analysis is that (1) the overall trade dresses of the two pumps are dissimilar because they are distinguished by starkly different logos, (2) the sophisticated purchasers of the expensive ALS systems presumably exercise a high degree of care in making their purchases, (3) there is no evidence of actual confusion, and (4) the intent and effect of Lubecore's choice of design is procompetitive. These *Frisch* factors all weigh in Lubecore's favor. By contrast, the factors that weigh in Groeneveld's favor (giving it the benefit of all reasonable inferences) are that (1) Groeneveld's trade dress is strong, (2) the parties' products are related, and (3) the parties use similar marketing channels. But these latter factors standing alone do not raise a triable issue of fact regarding the likelihood of confusion in the absence of any evidence showing that a potential consumer exercising ordinary care would confuse the grease pumps in question. In sum, no reasonable jury could conclude on the basis of the evidence before it that Groeneveld has met its burden of proving the likelihood of confusion.

E. Groeneveld's additional trade-dress theories

Beyond the so-called "point-of-sale confusion," which has been discussed in Part II.D. above, Groeneveld claims that the Lanham Act protects against other kinds of confusion and harm as well. The additional theories put forth by Groeneveld are (1) initial-interest confusion, and (2) dilution.

*1. Initial-interest confusion*

The usual focus of trademark law is on whether consumers are misled as to the source of the goods they purchase. But in certain circumstances trademark law protects against confusion even if it is ultimately dissipated before the moment of purchase. "Initial-interest confusion takes place when a manufacturer improperly uses a trademark to create initial customer interest in a product, even if the customer realizes, prior to purchase, that the product was not actually manufactured by the trademark-holder." *Gibson Guitar Corp. v. Paul Reed Smith Guitars, LP*, 423 F.3d 539, 549 (6th Cir. 2005).

The following example demonstrates why protection against initial-interest confusion might make sense under the right circumstances: Suppose that you are taking a long roadtrip, you have become very hungry, and you are keeping an eye out for a McDonald's, which is your fast-food restaurant of choice. Soon you spot a "McDonald's" sign by an exit. You take the exit and follow the signs, looking forward to your favorite McDonald's hamburger. But—behold—it's a Burger King. The signs were misleading. You are not so fond of Burger King but, having already made the detour and loath to waste even more time, you reluctantly buy a Whopper and get on with your trip. *See Brookfield Commc'ns, Inc. v. W. Coast Entm't Corp.*, 174 F.3d 1036, 1064 (9th Cir. 1999) (using a similar example with video rental stores). One does not have to be an economist to see that such a deceitful creation of an initial interest is harmful to consumer interests, brand-development incentives, and efficient allocation of capital, even if the confusion is ultimately dissipated by the time of purchase.

But the circumstances of the present case do not remotely approach those of a paradigmatic initial-interest case. To begin with, Groeneveld presented no proof as to how, in view of the two pumps' starkly different labels and logos, there would be any initial-interest confusion at all. Nor does Groeneveld explain why, assuming that such initial confusion were to take place, it would not be instantly dissipated without any harm. Simply invoking the term "initial-interest confusion" does not state a viable claim, let alone create a triable issue of fact. This court has held that alleging a hypothetical chance that a consumer might think for an instant that two products come from the same source is simply not enough:

> We decline to adopt such a broad reading of the initial-interest-confusion doctrine. Many, if not most, consumer products will tend to appear like their competitors at a sufficient distance. Where product shapes themselves are trademarked, such a theory would prevent competitors from producing even *dissimilar* products which might appear, from the far end of an aisle in a warehouse store, somewhat similar to a trademarked shape.

*Gibson Guitar,* 423 F.3d at 552 (emphasis in original) (internal citations omitted); *see also* 4 J. Thomas McCarthy, *McCarthy on Trademarks and Unfair Competition* § 23:9 ("Confusion means more than that the junior user's mark merely calls to mind the senior user's mark." (internal quotation marks omitted)).

In the final analysis, what appears to concern Groeneveld is not so much initial-interest *confusion,* but initial interest, period. Groeneveld, in other words, simply does not want its customers to become interested in Lubecore as a potential competitor and possibly switch over. We cannot ascribe any other interpretation to Groeneveld's rather startling claim that evidence of diverted sales and declining revenues, which are the normal signs of a market opening up to competition, create "a reasonable inference of confusion and its likelihood." Groeneveld's desire to be the only game in town is perfectly natural; most companies would hope for that status. But

Groeneveld cannot get any help from trade-dress law in suppressing lawful competition.

F. Trade-dress summary

In sum, because Groeneveld failed to present sufficient evidence to enable a reasonable jury to find both that Groeneveld's product design is nonfunctional and that ordinary consumers would likely confuse its trade dress with Lubecore's, judgment as a matter of law should have been entered for Lubecore. We therefore reverse the district court's denial of Lubecore's motion for judgment as a matter of law, set aside the jury's award of damages, and dissolve the injunction.

## *NOTES AND QUESTIONS*

1. The *Groeneveld* court puts significant weight on the parties' use of clearly distinct labels and word marks, suggesting that consumers would not be confused by similarity in product design because of those labels. That approach is to some extent reminiscent of earlier unfair competition cases, in which courts would often refuse to enforce exclusive rights in the design of a product itself but would provide relief in the form of labeling or other means of distinguishing products. It is also reminiscent of more recent cases in which courts in word mark cases consider the presence of a "house mark" (a prominent company name) in evaluating the likelihood of confusion between two trademarks.

In some cases, courts have credited the defendant's use of a house mark as a factor that decreases the likelihood of confusion. *See, e.g., Freedom Card, Inc. v. JPMorgan Chase & Co.*, 432 F.3d 463, 476 (3d Cir. 2005) (finding that the use of the house mark "Chase" with the term "freedom" decreased the likelihood of confusion with the previously registered "Freedom Card"); *Autozone, Inc. v. Tandy Corp.*, 373 F.3d 786, 797 (6th Cir. 2004) (finding that the defendant's use of the "Radio Shack" house mark in proximity to the "Autozone" mark for electronics reduced the likelihood of confusion with the plaintiff's "Autozone" mark for automotive products); *Nabisco, Inc. v. Warner-Lambert Co.*, 220 F.3d 43, 45 (2d Cir. 2000) (determining that the use of the house mark "Dentyne" significantly reduced the likelihood of confusion between "Dentyne Ice" and "Ice Breakers" chewing gum); *Luigino's, Inc. v. Stouffer Corp.*, 170 F.3d 827, 831 (8th Cir. 1999) (determining that the prominent display of a house mark lessens the likelihood of consumer confusion).

In other cases, courts have seen the presence of a house mark as "an aggravation and not a justification, for it is openly trading in the name of another upon the reputation acquired by the device of the true proprietor." *Menendez v. Holt*, 128 U.S. 514, 521 (1888). *See also Sands, Taylor, and Wood, Co. v. Quaker Oats Co.*, 978 F.2d 947, 954 (7th Cir. 1992) ("[I]n the related context of determining likelihood of confusion, some courts have observed that the conjunction of defendant's trademark and the allegedly infringed term 'may actually increase the misappropriation by linking defendant's name to plaintiff's goodwill.' " (quoting *Banff, Ltd. v. Federated Department Stores, Inc.*, 841 F.2d 486, 492 (2d Cir. 1988)). In recent years, courts have found the presence of a house mark to increase the likelihood of confusion only in reverse confusion cases (cases in which the plaintiff alleges that the defendant's use will cause confusion about the source of the plaintiff's goods). *Cf. Americana Trading, Inc. v. Russ Berrie & Co.*, 966 F.2d 1284, 1288 (9th Cir. 1992) ("[T]he prominence of Russ's housemark may serve to create reverse confusion that Russ, and not Amtra, is the source of Amtra's 'Wedding Bears.' Russ's housemark therefore does not, as a matter of law, render its use of 'Wedding Bear' non-similar to Amtra's trademark.").

Should courts put special weight on labeling in trade dress cases? If so, is it because consumers in fact rely more heavily on word marks than on the design of products to determine source? Or is it simply that policy concerns about protecting design suggests that we should tolerate some amount of confusion relating to design when labels can be used to ameliorate the harm?

2. In word mark cases, courts treat intent to cause confusion as strong evidence that confusion is likely. As the *Groeneveld* court noted, courts typically "presume that the person who sets out to infringe on another's trademark has more brains than scruples, and will likely succeed." *Sara Lee Corp. v. Kayser-Roth Corp.*, 81 F.3d 455, 466 (4th Cir. 1996). Indeed, Barton Beebe's research suggests that a finding of intent is practically dispositive in infringement determinations. *See* Barton Beebe, *An Empirical Study of the Multifactor Tests for Trademark Infringement*, 95 CAL. L. REV. 1581 (2006). But the majority in *Groeneveld* emphasized that *intent to copy* is not enough, particularly in trade dress cases; the plaintiff must prove *intent to cause confusion*. Given the policy interests favoring copying of functional features, the court suggested, that distinction is particularly important in trade dress cases. Why did the majority think the plaintiff's evidence of intent was inadequate? Why did the dissent disagree?

3. The Sixth Circuit in *Groeneveld* rejected the alternative theory of initial interest confusion. The doctrine of initial interest confusion deals with circumstances in which a party uses another's mark in a way that might initially draw consumers' attention, but any confusion is dispelled before purchase. Many courts have described these uses as a sort of bait-and-switch: having been attracted to the defendant because of its use of the mark, consumers might never return to the mark owner. Though initial interest confusion was recognized by courts prior to the internet era, the doctrine is primarily associated with internet advertising cases. In early versions of these cases, trademark owners argued that the mere use of their marks as keywords would cause initial interest confusion, because the confusion would result at the point the keyword was entered into the search engine. But recent cases have been more skeptical of the doctrine, focusing not on the initial search but on the text of the advertisements consumers see after the search is completed and the behavior of consumers in interacting with those ads. Where those ads are clearly labeled, courts have tended not to find liability. *See, e.g., 1-800 Contacts, Inc. v. Lens.com,* 722 F.3d 1229 (10th Cir. 2013); *Multi Time*

*Machine, Inc. v. Amazon.com, Inc.*, 804 F.3d 930 (9th Cir. 2015). Are there particular reasons to be skeptical of initial interest confusion in trade dress cases?

4. *Dilution of famous marks.* Since 1995, the Lanham Act has provided a cause of action against dilution of famous trademarks. 15 U.S.C. § 1125(c), Dilution does not require a likelihood of confusion; instead, it requires either (i) blurring of the famous mark created by "association arising from the similarity between a mark or trade name and a famous mark that impairs the distinctiveness of the famous mark" or (ii) tarnishment of the famous mark created by "association arising from the similarity between a mark or trade name and a famous mark that harms the reputation of the famous mark." *Id.* § 1125(c)(2). However, only nationally famous marks qualify for protection against dilution. "[A] mark is famous if it is widely recognized by the general consuming public of the United States as a designation of source of the goods or services of the mark's owner." *Id.* § 1125(c)(2). Given the high standard of fame, it is difficult for trade dress consisting of product design to qualify as a nationally famous mark. In an omitted portion of the *Groeneveld* decision, the court rejected Groeneveld's dilution claim because its trade dress was not famous. 730 F.3d at 519.

---

## GENERAL MOTORS CORP. V. KEYSTONE AUTOMOTIVE INDUSTRIES

453 F.3d 351 (6th Cir. 2006)

MERRITT, CIRCUIT JUDGE. GM, currently the world's largest automaker, manufactures and sells replacement parts for its vehicles. Tong Yang produces and sells aftermarket replacement parts for automobiles, including some manufactured by GM. Tong Yang sells these parts to distributors like Keystone, which in turn sells most of the parts to collision repair shops (including some owned by GM) and also sells some parts to individuals over the internet.

GM owns registered trademarks in the Chevrolet "bow tie" design and the "GMC" design. The instant case arose out of Tong Yang's manufacturing and Keystone's distribution of replacement grilles with "placeholders" bearing these two designs.

For Chevrolets, the placeholder is a recessed space on the front of the grille in the shape of a bow tie in which a heavy plastic GM "bow tie" emblem is inserted. For GMC vehicles, the placeholder is a raised pedestal upon which a red-lettered "GMC" emblem is mounted. Each emblem is a separate part always purchased from GM and is secured to the placeholder with studs or pins extending from the back of the emblem so as to pass through holes in the placeholder. After inserted and secured in the placeholder of a Chevrolet grille, the "bow tie" emblem partially or wholly fills the "bow tie" recess. Similarly, when mounted onto a placeholder of a

GMC grille, the "GMC" emblem wholly or partially covers the underlying "GMC" logo on the placeholder.

After GM filed suit, Tong Yang changed its grilles to remove the trademarked "bow tie" and "GMC" designs from its placeholders. These modifications have apparently decreased demand for the Tong Yang grilles. GM's complaint alleges that the defendants' use of the trademarks constitutes [*inter alia*]: trademark infringement under 15 U.S.C. § 1114(1). . . . The District Court granted summary judgment in favor of the defendants, holding that there is no likelihood of confusion. This appeal ensued.

GM's trademark infringement and unfair competition claims under state and federal law are closely related, and their resolution hinges on the central issue of likelihood of confusion. This Court has joined the vast majority of courts in extending the likelihood of confusion inquiry beyond only the point of sale. *See Ferrari S.p.A. Esercizio v. Roberts,* 944 F.2d 1235, 1245 (6th Cir. 1991); 3 McCarthy, *supra,* at § 23:5. Accordingly, we will first address likelihood of confusion at the point of sale before venturing downstream.

Likelihood of confusion at the point of sale involves a purchaser's confusion as to a product's origin or sponsorship occurring at the time of purchase. The points of sale for most of Tong Yang's grilles are collision repair shops, but some are sold directly to individuals over the internet. We need not exhaustively apply the eight-factor test to reach the rather obvious conclusion that there is no likelihood of confusion at the point of sale because buyers are expressly informed that they are not purchasing GM grilles. . . .

In addition to point-of-sale confusion, the Sixth Circuit recognizes that a likelihood of downstream confusion, also called "post-sale" confusion, is actionable: "Since Congress intended to protect the reputation of the manufacturer as well as to protect purchasers, the Act's protection is not limited to confusion at the point of sale." *Ferrari S.p.A. Esercizio*, 944 F.2d at 1245. Thus, injection of knockoffs into the stream of commerce may lead to a likelihood of confusion among the general public. To assess the likelihood of downstream confusion, we first apply the eight-factor test [from *Frisch's Rest., Inc. v. Shoney's Inc.*, 759 F.2d 1261, 1264 (6th Cir. 1985)] and then discuss the potential harm from the influx of Tong Yang's grilles into the stream of commerce.

### 1. Eight-Factor Test

Applying the eight-factor test to this case favors a finding of likelihood of confusion among the general viewing public.

i. Strength of the Plaintiff's Mark

It is beyond dispute that Chevrolet's "bow tie" and the "GMC" design are strong trademarks in that the public readily accepts them as hallmarks of GM. This factor, therefore, favors a likelihood of confusion.

ii. Relatedness of the Goods

The goods are at least somewhat closely related. The goods are identical in that, as the District Court noted, "both parties produce replacement grilles for the same GM vehicles." (J.A. at 0165.) The grilles, however, are generally not directly competitive because, again in the words of the District Court, "the parties generally sell their goods to different buyers." (Id.) Accordingly, this factor also favors GM.

iii. Similarity of the Marks

In general, "[s]imilarity of marks is a factor of considerable weight." *Daddy's Junky Music Stores, Inc. v. Big Daddy's Family Music Ctr.*, 109 F.3d 275, 283 (6th Cir. 1997). The trademarks at issue are virtually identical apparently with only trivial differences. This factor further points towards a likelihood of confusion.

iv. Evidence of Actual Confusion

For obvious reasons, evidence of actual confusion is the most important factor in assessing a likelihood of confusion. Due to the rarity of this type of evidence, however, this factor is weighed heavily only when such evidence exists. GM has "theorized possible methods for Defendants' customers to defraud subsequent purchasers" and has cited an instance where a collision repair shop attempted unsuccessfully to return to GM a grille manufactured neither by GM nor Tong Yang, but GM has not proved that any member of the general public has mistaken a Tong Yang grille for a GM grille. Thus, GM has not presented evidence of actual confusion.

v. Marketing Channels Used

"This factor . . . consists of considerations of how and to whom the respective goods or services of the parties are sold." *Homeowners Group, Inc. v. Home Mktg. Specialists, Inc.*, 931 F.2d 1100, 1110 (6th Cir. 1991). This factor involves two considerations: (1) whether the parties use the same means to market the product, and (2) whether the "predominant customers" are the same. *Daddy's Junky Music Stores, Inc.*, 109 F.3d at 285. There is less likelihood of confusion "if the services of one party are sold through different marketing media in a different marketing context than those of another seller." *Homeowners Group, Inc.*, 931 F.2d at 1110. The same is true "[i]f one mark user sells exclusively at retail and the other exclusively to commercial buyers . . . since no one buyer ever buys both products." *Id.* (quoting 2 McCarthy, *supra,* at § 24:7 (2d ed. 1984)). Since this factor focuses on the point of sale, it has little bearing on the question of downstream confusion. *See Ferrari S.p.A. Esercizio*, 944 F.2d at 1245.

vi. Likely Degree of Purchaser Care

This factor involves assessing (1) the type of goods at issue, and (2) the level of sophistication of the purchaser. As to the first inquiry, "when services are expensive or unusual, the buyer can be expected to exercise greater care in her purchases," and there is accordingly less likelihood of confusion. *Homeowners Group, Inc.*, 931 F.2d at 1111. A sophisticated purchaser exercises a high degree of care and is less likely to be confused as to a product's origin. This factor also focuses on the point of sale and is, therefore, generally inapplicable to downstream confusion.

vii. Defendant's Intent in Selecting the Mark

"If a party chooses a mark with the intent of causing confusion, that fact alone may be sufficient to justify an inference of confusing similarity." *Homeowners Group, Inc.*, 931 F.2d at 1111. "Intent is relevant because purposeful copying indicates that the alleged infringer, who has at least as much knowledge as the trier of fact regarding the likelihood of confusion, believes that his copying may divert some business from the senior user." *Daddy's Junky Music Stores, Inc.*, 109 F.3d at 286. Intent can be proven by direct or circumstantial evidence. *Id.* There can be little question that Tong Yang intentionally copied GM's trademarks. Tong Yang reverse engineers the grilles to look as close as possible to the original equipment manufactured by GM. Accordingly, this factor favors GM.

viii. Likelihood of Expansion of the Product Lines

"[A] 'strong possibility' that either party will expand his business to compete with the other or be marketed to the same consumers will weigh in favor of finding that the present use is infringing." *Homeowners Group, Inc.*, 931 F.2d at 1112. Expansion could be geographic or an increase in products or services. *Daddy's Junky Music Stores, Inc.*, 109 F.3d at 287. The District Court noted that there is no evidence that either party plans to expand its grille manufacturing business. Accordingly, this factor favors the defendants.

In sum, although the eight-factor test is arguably less important in assessing downstream confusion than point-of-sale confusion since two of the factors (5 and 6) focus on the point of sale, the analysis favors a likelihood of downstream confusion here because, of the remaining six factors, four (1, 2, 3 and 7) favor GM, and only two (4 and 8) favor Tong Yang.

2. Downstream Harm

Our review of cases discussing the harm of injecting knockoffs into the stream of commerce further signals the likelihood of downstream confusion in this case. Even without point-of-sale confusion, knockoffs can harm the public and the original manufacturer in a number of ways, including: (1) the viewing public, as well as subsequent purchasers, may be deceived if expertise is required to distinguish the original from the counterfeit; (2) the purchaser of an original may be harmed if the widespread existence of knockoffs decreases the original's value by making the previously scarce commonplace; (3) consumers desiring high quality products may be harmed if the original manufacturer decreases its investment in quality in order to compete more economically with less expensive knockoffs; (4) the original manufacturer's reputation for quality may be damaged if individuals mistake an inferior counterfeit for the original; (5) the original manufacturer's reputation for rarity may be harmed by the influx of knockoffs onto the market; and (6) the original manufacturer may be harmed if sales decline due to the public's fear that what they are purchasing may not be the original. On the other hand, courts should be wary of overprotecting public domain ideas and works whose exploitation can lead to economic efficiency, greater competition, and lower costs for consumers.

Applying these principles in *Ferrari S.p.A. Esercizio v. Roberts*, 944 F.2d 1235 (6th Cir. 1991), this Court upheld the verdict of a bench trial enjoining the production of knockoff Ferrari automobiles which could damage Ferrari's reputation for quality and rarity. Other courts have reached similar conclusions in cases involving knockoff Rolex watches, designer purses, and other products.

The instant case carries similar potential for downstream confusion and corresponding harm to GM and the public—if the public can actually see the underlying placeholders after the "bow tie" or "GMC" emblems are affixed to the grilles. Unaided by the defendants' conspicuously marked packaging, the invoice disclaimer, or a collision shop's expertise, the viewing public could mistake a Tong Yang grille for a GM grille. Such confusion could damage GM's reputation for quality if the public associates any inferior attributes (e.g., improper fit or cracking) of Tong Yang's grilles with GM. Other types of possible downstream harm, such as that resulting from a product's reduced scarcity, however, are largely inapplicable to this case. Nonetheless, visibility of the placeholder after the automobile is repaired and returned to the road may harm the public and GM. . . .

We hold that the defendants' use of GM's Chevrolet "bow tie" and "GMC" trademarks does not pose a likelihood of point-of-sale confusion. We also hold that there are genuine disputes of material fact regarding whether the defendants' placeholders remain visible after the "bow tie" or "GMC" emblem is affixed to the defendants' replacement grilles, and, if so, whether that visibility is sufficient to create a likelihood of downstream confusion. Accordingly, we reverse the District Court's grant of summary judgment in favor of the defendants and denial of GM's motion for summary judgment. We remand this case for further proceedings consistent with this opinion.

## *NOTE*

Post-sale confusion cases differ from other infringement cases because they focus on confusion after the point of sale, and generally among non-purchasers. In *General Motors*, purchasers were not confused. The collision repair shops and individuals purchasing online were likely to know that the replacement grilles did not come from General Motors Corporation. But the court though that others who viewed the car after they had been fitted with the replacement grilles might believe that General Motors had supplied the part. That is the concept of post-sale confusion—confusion by non-purchasers who view a product after it has been purchased and is in use. The *General Motors* court identifies several harms from such confusion. Do you find the court's arguments persuasive? Who is harmed by any such "confusion"? Couldn't that confusion be dispelled by proper labeling?

## *PROBLEM 3–6*

Chudleigh's Bakery is a well-known producer of various baked goods, primarily baked apple pies and related desserts. Chudleigh's sells its products primarily through its apple farm and bakery in Ontario, Canada, and grocery stores throughout Canada and the United States. Since the mid-1990's, Chudleigh's has been selling "Blossoms," which it describes as "single-serve, fully-baked" desserts with fruit fillings. Chudleigh's makes a hand-folded version of its Blossom, which appears to be created by folding a single circular piece of dough upwards and in a clockwise direction around the filling, creating six pleats, and a machine-folded version, which is created by folding six rounded petals upwards around the filling so that they overlap slightly. According to Chudleigh's marketing, the Crumble Crunch Apple Blossoms, to take one example, "start with a flaky pastry made from our own Chudleigh's #3 flower blend. Snuggled up inside is a delectable mix of fresh-peeled, locally sourced Northern Spy apples, natural cane sugar and cinnamon, and topped with a simple, delicious mixture of pastry crumbs, creamy butter, light brown sugar, rolled oats and more cinnamon. And every blossom is hand finished, for an extra hug to send them on their way to your plate."

Sweet Street manufactures and sells desserts to restaurant chains, including Applebee's, and distributors. In 2010, Applebee's asked Sweet Street to develop a single-serving apple dessert for its restaurants. Sweet Street proposed a round "apple pocket" that consisted of a unitary, pie-like bottom with an open top covered by six rectangular pieces of dough folded around the filling in a counter-clockwise spiral pattern, depicted below.

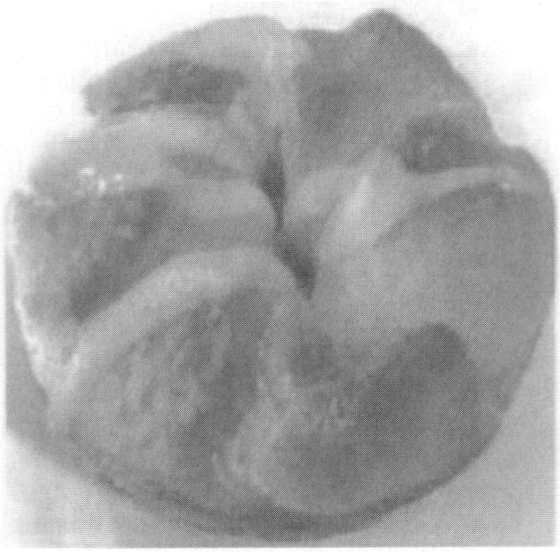

Chudleigh's promply sued Sweet Street, alleging that Sweet Street's new dessert infringed Chudleigh's rights in its Blossom shape trade dress. Chudleigh's describes its Blossom Design as follows:

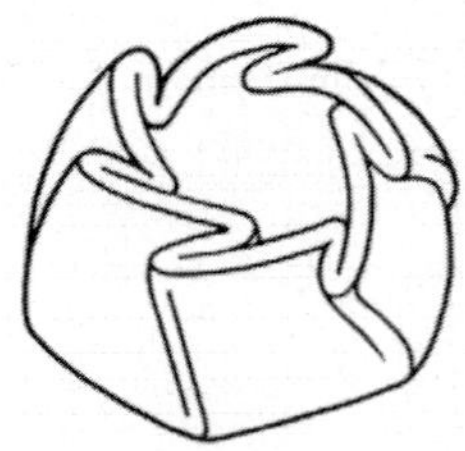

1. A single-served dessert item;
2. A round shape;
3. Six folds or petals of dough;
4. Such folds or petals being folded upward and around a filling;
5. Such upward folding resulting in the folds or petals partially overlapping each other;
6. Such upward folding yielding a regular spiral pattern resembling the shape of a blossom; and

7. Such upward folding leaving an opening at the top.

Is the Blossom Design a valid trade dress? If so, is Chudleigh's likely to prevail on its trade dress infringement claim against Sweet Street? Review the readings above to answer this problem.

---

## E. PERMISSIBLE USES OF TRADEMARKS

Aside from the fact that trademark rights are not rights in gross, some particular types of uses uses of trademarks by third parties are generally permitted. This section considers two types of such uses: (1) distribution of trademarked goods after an authorized first sale; and (2) uses of trademarks in expressive works.

### 1. FIRST SALE (EXHAUSTION)

Trademark rights, like other intellectual property rights, are often "exhausted" on the sale of a genuine product bearing the mark. Used car dealers operate every day on this basic premise—resellers and consumers would both be harmed, and competition would suffer, if used car dealers could not truthfully identify genuine vehicles as FORDS or HONDAS. But a lot here depends on the assumption that the dealer is actually selling genuine FORDS or HONDAS. What does it mean to say that the goods are "genuine"? Two lines of cases are particularly relevant to these questions.

One line of cases, associated with *Prestonettes Inc. v. Coty,* 264 U.S. 359 (1924), deals with whether a party can use another's mark to describe the contents of its product, usually after having repackaged the original mark owner's goods. In *Prestonettes,* the Supreme Court held that a repackager of Coty's famous perfume and powder was permitted to describe the contents of its goods truthfully by using the plaintiff's original mark. More recently, a court held that a tuna salad maker could legitimately use the Bumble Bee trademark to state truthfully, but without permission, that its tuna salad was "Made with Bumble Bee Tuna." *See Bumble Bee Seafoods L.L.C. v. UFS Industries, Inc.*, 71 U.S.P.Q.2d 1684 (S.D.N.Y. 2004). At first blush, these cases suggest that, so long as the goods actually originated with the mark owner, a party can use the original mark to identify the repacakaged goods, and it can do so even if it modifies the mark holder's goods and produces an inferior product. But many courts have limited the reach of *Prestonettes* where the defendant's repackaging made a material difference in the quality of the plaintiff's product. As the court described in *Enesco Corp. v. Price/Costco Inc.*, 146, F.3d 1083, 1087 (9th Cir. 1998), "[c]ourts have recognized a quality control exception from the first sale doctrine where there is "some defect (or potential defect) in the product itself that the customer would not readily be able to detect." In *Shell Oil Co. v. Commercial Petroleum, Inc.*, 928 F.2d 104 (4th Cir. 1991), the court prohibited the defendant from selling oil under the Shell trademarks because the defendant did not observe Shell's tank and pump cleaning requirements. Courts also are careful in repackaging and component cases to say that consumers must not be deceived into thinking that the defendant's ultimate product and the component parts emanate from the same source. *See William Grant & Sons Ltd. v. European Beverages Co. Inc.*, 668 F. Supp. 1421 (C.D. Cal. 1987) (ordering the defendant to use a disclaimer because "a label which merely states that defendants' product was distilled at the Glenfiddich or Balvenie Distillery and bottled by defendant would be confusing and misleading to most customers.")

The second line of cases is associated with the Supreme Court's ruling in *Champion Spark Plug Co. v. Sanders*, 331 U.S. 125 (1947), which dealt with the question of whether a party can continue to use the original trademark for products that have been reconditioned. In *Champion Spark Plug*, the repaired spark plugs did not give the product a new design and the defendants tried to restore the products as closely as possible to their original condition. The Court acknowledged that it was possible repairs might be so extensive that "it would be a misnomer to call the article by its original name," but did not feel the defendant's reconditioning crossed that threshold. It did, however, require the defendant to label its products using a term such as "renewed," "restored," or "reconditioned" to avoid confusion.

## NITRO LEISURE PRODUCTS, L.L.C. V. ACUSHNET CO.

341 F.3d 1356 (Fed. Cir. 2003)

LINN, CIRCUIT JUDGE. Acushnet Company ("Acushnet") appeals from the denial of its motion for a preliminary injunction by the United States District Court for the Southern District of Florida. Because the district court did not abuse its discretion in denying Acushnet's motion in view of Acushnet's failure to show a reasonable likelihood of success on the merits of its claims, we affirm.

### BACKGROUND

Acushnet manufactures and sells golfing equipment, and in particular, golf balls. Acushnet owns and has federally registered the trademarks TITLEIST, ACUSHNET, PINNACLE, and PRO V1. Of particular interest in this case, Acushnet manufactures and markets new golf balls under the TITLEIST name and trademark, including the TITLEIST PRO V1, asserted by Acushnet to be the best selling golf ball in the United States since February 2001.

Nitro obtains and sells two categories of used golf balls at a discounted rate. The first category of balls are "recycled" balls. The recycled balls are those found in relatively good condition, needing little more than washing, and are repackaged for resale. Recycled balls represent approximately 30% of Nitro's sales. The second category includes balls that are found with stains, scuffs or blemishes, requiring "refurbishing." Nitro's refurbishing process includes cosmetically treating the balls by removing the base coat of paint, the clear coat layer, and the trademark and model markings without damaging the covers of the balls, and then repainting the balls, adding a clear coat, and reaffixing the original manufacturer's trademark. Nitro also applies directly to each "refurbished" ball the legend "USED & REFURBISHED BY SECOND CHANCE" or "USED AND REFURBISHED BY GOLFBALLSDIRECT.COM." In these statements, the terms "Second Chance" and "Golfballsdirect.com" refer to businesses of Nitro. Some, but not all, of the refurbished balls also bear a Nitro trademark. Nitro's refurbished balls are packaged in containers displaying the following disclaimer:

> ATTENTION USED/REFURBISHED GOLF BALLS: The enclosed contents of used/refurbished golf balls are USED GOLF BALLS. Used/Refurbished golf balls are subject to performance variations from new ones. These used/refurbished balls were processed via one or more of the following steps: stripping, painting, stamping and/or clear coating in our factory. This product has NOT been endorsed or approved by the original manufacturer and the balls DO NOT fall under the original manufacturer's warranty.

According to Nitro, there is a large market for used golf balls. In 2001, Nitro saw annual sales of approximately $10 million, including $4.8 million for refurbished balls.

On April 23, 2002, Acushnet moved for a preliminary injunction on its trademark and patent claims. As to the trademark claims, Acushnet concedes that it has no trademark claim with respect to "recycled" balls and does not object to those sales. As to the "refurbished" balls, however, Acushnet asserts that "Nitro's refurbishing process produces a golf ball that bears no resemblance to a genuine Acushnet product in performance, quality or appearance" and that "Nitro's refurbishing process so alters the basic composition of Acushnet's golf balls that 'it would be a misnomer to call the article by its original name.' " Following oral argument, the district court on August 9, 2002, issued its *Order*, concluding that Acushnet had failed to show a likelihood of success on the merits and denying preliminary injunctive relief on both the trademark and the patent law claims.

Before this court, Acushnet seeks review of the denial of its motion for preliminary injunction only as to its trademark infringement and dilution claims.

## DISCUSSION

### II. Trademark Infringement

### A. The Applicable Standard

Acushnet first argues that the district court failed to apply the correct legal standard to the trademark infringement claim. Acushnet asserts that the district court misapplied *Champion Spark Plug Co. v. Sanders*, 331 U.S. 125 (1947), and Eleventh Circuit law by failing to extend the "material difference" test applied in the context of altered new goods in *Davidoff*, 263 F.3d at 1302, to the used and refurbished goods involved in the present case. Acushnet also contends that the district court's reliance on *Champion* was misplaced because the refurbished goods in this case differed from the original goods not by the ordinary wear and tear expected in used products but by the refurbishing actions taken by Nitro. Acushnet argues that the "undisputed evidence" presented, when analyzed under the correct legal standard, would have established the requisite likelihood of success on the merits to warrant a preliminary injunction, and that denial of the requested preliminary injunction was an abuse of discretion. We disagree and find no abuse of discretion.

To succeed in its request for a preliminary injunction on its trademark infringement claim, Acushnet must show, *inter alia*, a likelihood of success on the merits. This means that it must show a likelihood of success on its claim that the sale by Nitro of its refurbished golf balls bearing re-applied Acushnet trademarks is likely to cause confusion. In considering this issue, the district court looked to *Champion*—clear precedent in the used goods context—and concluded, on the record presented at this preliminary stage, that the differences between Acushnet's new golf balls and Nitro's refurbished golf balls were not so great as to be a misnomer and that it was not an act of infringement, warranting preliminary injunctive relief, for Nitro to re-apply Acushnet's trademarks to the Acushnet balls refurbished by Nitro and to re-sell those balls in packaging identifying them as used or refurbished.

The Eleventh Circuit looks to the following factors in assessing a likelihood of confusion in trademark cases:

1. Type of mark
2. Similarity of mark
3. Similarity of the products the marks represent
4. Similarity of the parties' retail outlets (trade channels) and customers
5. Similarity of advertising media
6. Defendant's intent
7. Actual confusion

*Frehling Enters., Inc. v. Int'l Select Group, Inc.*, 192 F.3d 1330, 1335 (11th Cir. 1999). In the present case, the dispute centers around the differences between new and refurbished Acushnet golf balls, thus implicating the "similarity of the products" factor. Specifically, the question presented is the propriety of the re-application by Nitro of the Acushnet trademark, without Acushnet's consent, to genuine Acushnet golf balls that have been used, subjected to Nitro's refurbishing process, and then re-sold by Nitro as refurbished balls.

The district court assessed that question by applying the standards applied to used and refurbished goods by the Supreme Court in the *Champion* case. The district court cited *Davidoff* but did not directly apply the "material differences" test articulated in that case. Acushnet urges us to conclude that the district court erred in not recognizing from *Davidoff* that the "material differences" standard used to assess likelihood of confusion in the sale by unrelated parties of new, genuine trademarked goods would also be used in the Eleventh Circuit as the standard for assessing trademark infringement in the sale of used, genuine trademarked goods. Acushnet argues from this that had the district court applied the *Davidoff* test, it would have found the refurbished golf balls sold by Nitro and bearing the Nitro re-applied Acushnet trademarks to be "materially different" from the original trademarked goods and thus an infringement of Acushnet's trademarks, warranting preliminary injunctive relief. Nitro argues that *Davidoff* is simply inapplicable, and attempts to distinguish this case from *Davidoff*, based on the fact that *Davidoff* considered new goods and because *Davidoff* did not include disclaimers. Nitro also attempts to distinguish the cases cited by Acushnet in support of adoption of the *Davidoff* "material differences" standard; namely, *Rolex Watch USA, Inc. v. Michel*, 179 F.3d 704 (9th Cir. 1999), *Rolex Watch USA, Inc. v. Meece*, 158 F.3d 816 (5th Cir. 1998), and *Intel Corp. v. Terabyte International, Inc.*, 6 F.3d 614 (9th Cir. 1993).

Under 15 U.S.C. §§ 1114(1) and 1125(a)(1), any person who uses the trademark of another, without consent, in a manner that is likely to cause confusion, mistake, or to deceive may be liable in a civil action for trademark infringement. *McDonald's Corp.*, 147 F.3d at 1307. In the *Champion* case, a seminal opinion on the use of trademarks on used goods, the accused infringer collected genuine used Champion spark plugs, repaired and reconditioned the spark plugs, painted the spark plugs for aesthetic reasons, and resold the spark plugs, each labeled "Renewed." 331 U.S. at 126. The issue before the Supreme Court was simply whether the lower courts erred in not requiring the accused infringer to remove Champion's trademark name from the repaired and reconditioned spark plugs. *Id.* at 128. The Supreme Court acknowledged that, in some cases, used and repaired goods can be sold under the trademark of the original manufacturer, without "deceiv[ing] the public," so long as the accused infringer had attempted to restore "so far as possible" the original condition of the goods and full disclosure is made about the true nature of the goods, for example, as "used" or "repaired." *Id.* at 129–30. In *Champion*, the Supreme Court stated that "[w]hen the mark is used in a way that does not deceive the public we see no such sanctity in the word as to prevent its being used to tell the truth." *Id.* at 129.

The Supreme Court recognized that this standard results in the second-hand dealer getting some advantage from the trademark; however, this windfall is "wholly permissible so long as the manufacturer is not identified with the inferior qualities of the product." *Id.* at 130 (citing *Prestonettes, Inc. v. Coty*, 264 U.S. 359 (1924)). This advantage is not inconsistent with the stated purposes of the Lanham Act. In passing the Lanham Act, Congress noted that the purpose was "to protect legitimate business and consumers of the country." 92 Cong. Rec. 7524 (1946). To fulfill this purpose, the Act "protect[s] the public so it may be confident that, in purchasing a product bearing a particular trade-mark which it favorably knows, it will get the product which it asks for and wants to get." S. Rep. No. 79–1333 at 3 (1946), reprinted in 1946 U.S.S.C.A.N. 1274. Further, the owner of the trademark must have the energy and effort he expended in building goodwill in his trademark protected from misappropriation. *Id.* However, so long as the customer is getting a product with the expected characteristics, and so long as the goodwill built up by the trademark owner is not eroded by being identified with inferior quality, the Lanham Act does not prevent the truthful use of trademarks, even if such use results in the enrichment of others.

The *Champion* court, while concluding that the facts of that case did not establish a likelihood of confusion, cautioned that there are limits on the use of a trademark by another on a used or repaired item. The Supreme Court explained that "[c]ases may be imagined where the reconditioning or repair would be so extensive or so basic that it would be a misnomer to call the article by its original name, even though the words 'used' or 'repaired' were added." 331 U.S. at 129. In *Champion*, the repair was such that it "[did] not give [the product] a new design," and the accused infringers had sought to restore the product "so far as possible, [to its] original condition," *Id.* Thus, no infringement was found.

Similar to the admonition expressed by the Supreme Court in connection with the sale of refurbished goods in *Champion*, the Eleventh Circuit in *Davidoff* cautioned that there are limits to the permissible uses of a trademark by re-sellers even on new, genuine trademarked goods. In *Davidoff*, the Eleventh Circuit found infringement in the use of a trademark by a party unrelated to the trademark owner for new, genuine trademarked goods sold in packaging that had been altered. In that case, accused infringer PLD purchased genuine bottles of Davidoff's perfumes and, prior to re-sale, etched and altered the bottles to remove batch code information from the bottoms of the bottles. Davidoff sought to end this practice, arguing that the etching of the bottles altered the product in a way that caused consumer confusion. The Eleventh Circuit agreed, holding that the removal of the batch code information was a material alteration that would affect a consumer's decision whether to purchase the product in question.

The fundamental question examined in *Davidoff* was the same question considered in *Champion*—likelihood of confusion—but presented in the context of re-sales of new goods. The context is important because consumers of new goods have different expectations than consumers of used goods. For new goods, any variation of the product from a new condition—even as relatively modest as the obliteration of a name or batch number from the bottom of a container—may signal imitation, counterfeiting, falsity or some other irregularity affecting a customer's decision whether to purchase the product. *See, e.g., Societe Des Produits Nestle S.A. v. Casa Helvetia, Inc.*, 982 F.2d 633, 644 (1st Cir. 1992) (finding such differences as configuration, i.e., the number of different shapes of chocolates, and packaging, i.e., whether the packaging is shiny or matte and the colors of the packaging, to be material). For new goods, consumers are likely to be confused by the presence of such "material differences." *Davidoff*, 263 F.3d at 1302 (11th Cir. 2001).

For used or refurbished goods, customers have a different expectation. They do not expect the product to be in the same condition as a new product. *Champion*, 331 U.S. at 129. There is an understanding on the part of consumers of used or refurbished products that such products will be degraded or will show signs of wear and tear and will not measure up to or perform at the same level as if new. *Id.* at 129–30. For used or refurbished products, consumers are not likely to be confused by—and indeed expect—differences in the goods compared to new, unused goods. *Id.* Thus, the tests applied to assess likelihood of confusion by courts will not necessarily be the same when determining trademark infringement in the resale of altered new goods and when considering trademark infringement in the resale of used and refurbished goods.

Both *Champion* and *Davidoff* sought to define the boundaries of when the use of a trademark on genuine trademarked goods is no longer permitted. The tests applied in both cases focus on the similarities and differences between the accused infringing goods and the genuine trademarked goods and assess the likelihood of confusion resulting from contemporaneous sales of those goods.

The *Davidoff* test looks to the effect on a consumer's decision to purchase of differences in an altered or modified new product from the original. It is a reasonable and workable test of the likelihood of confusion and the loss of goodwill represented by the trademark applied to the product, given consumer expectations as to the nature and quality of new products as offered for sale. The test has been adopted and applied to new, genuine trademarked goods in the First, Second, Third, Fifth, and Ninth Circuits. *See, e.g., Nestle*, 982 F.2d at 644 (1st Cir.) (finding material differences based on quality control, composition, configuration, packaging, and price); *Original Appalachian Artworks, Inc. v. Granada Elecs., Inc.*, 816 F.2d 68, 73 (2d Cir. 1987) (finding material differences where an imported doll comes with foreign language "adoption papers" and is not permitted to be "adopted" domestically); *Iberia Foods Corp. v. Romeo*, 150 F.3d 298, 302 (3d Cir. 1998) (finding material differences where quality control measures differ); *Martin's Herend Imports Inc. v. Diamond & Gem Trading USA, Co.*, 112 F.3d 1296, 1302 (5th Cir. 1997) (finding material differences when the trademark holder had chosen to sell only selected pieces in the United States and the accused infringer was selling other, genuine pieces in the United States); *Enesco Corp. v. Price/Costco Inc.*, 146 F.3d 1083, 1087 (9th Cir. 1998) (finding material differences where quality control measures differ).

The *Champion* Court recognizes that consumers do not expect used or refurbished goods to be the same as new goods and that for such goods, "material differences" do not necessarily measure consumer confusion. According to *Champion*, what is more telling on the question of likelihood of confusion in the context of used goods is whether the used or refurbished goods are so different from the original that it would be a misnomer for them to be designated by the original trademark. We see no basis to conclude that the district court's reliance on *Champion* was improper.

The district court in this case properly assessed likelihood of confusion in concluding: (1) that on the evidence before it, the differences in the goods were nothing more than what would be expected for used golf balls; (2) that it was therefore not a misnomer to apply the Acushnet mark to the used Acushnet balls; and (3) that Acushnet had not established a likelihood of success on the merits of its trademark "likelihood of confusion" case. This is all that was required, and there is no basis to conclude that the district court applied the wrong test or otherwise abused its discretion. This court need not predict whether the Eleventh Circuit would apply *Davidoff* to used goods. It would only be necessary to make such a prediction if application of the "material differences" test must be satisfied in all cases involving genuine trademarked goods. But *Davidoff* does not go that far and cannot be read to supplant the statutory "likelihood of confusion" test with a "material differences" test applicable to all cases involving the resale of genuine trademarked goods, both new and used.

Alternatively, Acushnet argues that the district court's reliance on *Champion* is misplaced. Acushnet attempts to distinguish *Champion*, arguing first that Nitro does not restore "so far as possible" the used balls to their original condition, but rather masks the balls' condition, and second, that by masking rather than restoring, Nitro makes it more likely that customers will associate inferior performance with Acushnet. Acushnet argues that, although there was repainting of the spark plugs in *Champion*, such painting was merely cosmetic. Acushnet contends that the district court failed to recognize that Nitro's process of stripping and repainting was more than cosmetic and changed the fundamental attributes of the reprocessed balls. Moreover, Acushnet argues that it is Nitro's refurbishing process, not normal wear and tear, that degraded the quality of Nitro's used golf balls. Acushnet thus asserts that *Champion* is distinguishable on its facts and should not apply. We disagree with Acushnet's distinctions.

First, while it is true that the spark plugs were repainted in *Champion*, the reconditioning also involved removing burned and pitted portions of the center electrodes, welding new metal to the side electrodes, wearing away the plug's porcelain insulators through sandblasting, and then cleaning and painting the spark plug. *Champion Spark Plug Co. v. Sanders*, 156 F.2d 488, 489 (2d Cir. 1946). The refurbishing process in *Champion,* then, was not merely cosmetic, and cannot be distinguished from the present case on that basis. Second, *Champion* also held that the source of any inferiority, whether the reconditioning or the refurbishing, is irrelevant, stating that inferiority is immaterial as long as the original manufacturer "is not identified with the inferior qualities of the product *resulting from wear and tear or the reconditioning.*" *Champion*, 331 U.S. at 130, (emphasis added). In the *Champion* case, the district court noted that there was no proof whether the inferior qualities stemmed from either "wear and tear prior to the discarding of the plug by the original user, or to the process of repair as conducted by the defendants." *Champion Spark Plug Co. v. Sanders*, 61 F. Supp. 247, 248–49 (E.D.N.Y. 1945). Acushnet's distinction on this point is similarly untenable.

In this case, the district court carefully considered the extent of the alterations made by Nitro. The district court also looked to a number of factors, outlined by the Ninth Circuit, to determine if the alterations resulted in a new product. *Order* at 9 ("These factors 'include the nature and extent of the alterations, the nature of the device and how it is designed . . . , whether a market has developed for service or spare parts . . . and, most importantly, whether end users of the product are likely to be misled as to the party responsible for the composition of the product.' *Karl Storz Endoscopy-America, Inc. v. Surgical Technologies, Inc.*, 285 F.3d 848, 856–57 (9th Cir. 2002)."). The district court also considered: (a) evidence proffered by Nitro that the performance differences were not as extensive as claimed by Acushnet; (b) evidence of the use of disclaimers; and (c) evidence from customers of both Acushnet and Nitro on the question of confusion. On this record, the district court concluded that "Acushnet has not presented sufficient evidence to support its claim that the golf balls are so extensively repaired that they cannot be truly labeled with the Titleist marks."

Because the district court properly considered the *Frehling* factors; fully and carefully assessed the differences between Acushnet's new golf balls and Nitro's refurbished golf balls in determining likelihood of confusion; and correctly looked to *Champion* for the applicable legal standard, we find no abuse of discretion in the district court's denial of Acushnet's requested preliminary injunction based on its trademark infringement claim.

### *NOTES AND QUESTIONS*

1. Does *Nitro Leisure* give any further guidance about the point at which repairs might be so extensive that "it would be a misnomer to call the article by its original name"? If you were advising a client considering selling repaired or refurbished goods, how would you advise them about that line?

2. Are repackaging and reconditioning the only circumstances in which exhaustion should arise? What if, for example, an ice cream shop began selling mixed confections that included pieces of KIT-KAT bars? Is that a "repackaging" or a "reconditioning" of the KIT-KAT bars? Would the ice cream shop be able to use the KIT-KAT mark to describe its confections? Would it matter if consumers believed that ice cream shops needed permission from candy manufacturers to include their candy products in their ice cream? Would the quality of the ice cream product matter?

---

## 2. EXPRESSIVE USES OF TRADEMARKS

Under what circumstances can a trade dress owner prevent the depiction of its trade dress in a creative work? As you read the case below about the University of Alabama football uniforms, consider both the financial interests of the parties and the role of the First Amendment in regulating and creating expressive uses of trade dress.

### THE UNIVERSITY OF ALABAMA BOARD OF TRUSTEES V. NEW LIFE ART, INC.

683 F.3d 1266 (11th Cir. 2012)

ANDERSON, CIRCUIT JUDGE. Since 1979, Daniel A. Moore has painted famous football scenes involving the University of Alabama (the "University" or "Alabama"). The paintings feature realistic portrayals of the University's uniforms, including helmets, jerseys, and crimson and white colors. Moore has reproduced his paintings as prints and calendars, as well as on mugs and other articles.

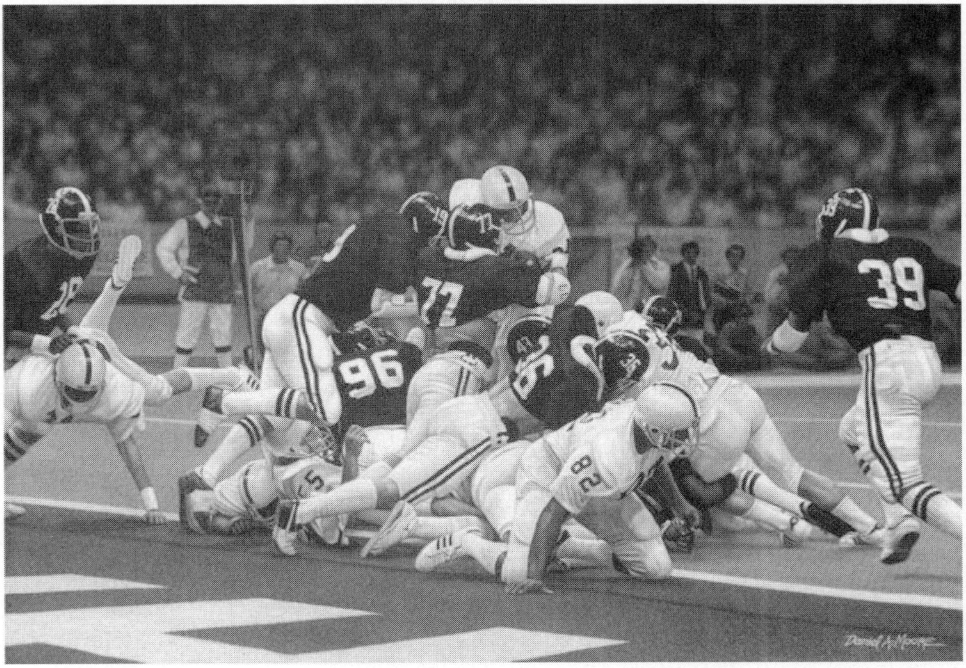

In 2002, the University told Moore that he would need permission to depict the University's uniforms because they are trademarks. Moore contended that he did not need permission because the uniforms were being used to realistically portray historical events. The parties could not reach a resolution, and in March 2005, the University sued Moore in the Northern District of Alabama for breach of contract, trademark infringement, and unfair competition. The outcome at the district court was split. The court granted summary judgment to Moore with respect to paintings and prints, and granted summary judgment to the University with respect to calendars, mugs, and other "mundane products." This appeal resulted. We affirm in part, reverse in part, and remand.

## I. FACTS

From 1979 to 1990, Moore painted historical Alabama football scenes without any kind of formal or informal relationship with the University. From 1991 to 1999, Moore signed a dozen licensing agreements with the University to produce and market specific items, which would often include additional Alabama trademarks on the border or packaging, or would come with a certificate or stamp saying they were officially licensed products.

From 1991 to 2002, Moore produced other Alabama-related paintings and prints that were not the subject of any licensing agreements. He also continued to sell paintings and prints of images that had originally been issued before 1991. He did not pay royalties for any of these items, nor did the University request that he do so. Moore said that he would enter into a licensing agreement if he felt that it would help increase the sales of that particular product, or if he wanted the University—his alma mater—to benefit from royalties.

During this time, the University issued Moore press credentials so he could obtain material for his work. The University also asked Moore to produce an unlicensed painting on live television during a football game. However, in January 2002, the University told Moore that he would need to license all of his Alabama-related products because they featured the University's trademarks. In particular, the University asserted that Moore needed permission to portray the University's uniforms, including the jersey and helmet designs and the crimson and white colors.

Moore contended that he did not need permission to paint historical events and that there was no trademark violation so long as he did not use any of the University's trademarks outside of the "image area" of the painting (i.e., outside the original painting). Despite this disagreement, the University still sold Moore's unlicensed calendars in its campus stores for several years. It also displayed unlicensed paintings at its Bryant Museum and athletic department office.

The parties were unable to reach a satisfactory resolution, and the University brought suit on March 18, 2005, in the Northern District of Alabama. The University contended that . . . Moore's paintings, prints, calendars, mugs, and other objects violated the Lanham Act by infringing the University's trademark rights in its football uniforms. *See* 15 U.S.C. § 1125(a).

The only issues on appeal in this case are those decided by Judge Propst, who concluded in November 2009 that (3) Moore's depiction of the uniforms in paintings and prints was protected by the First Amendment and also was a fair use; and (4) Moore's depiction of the uniforms on mugs, calendars, and other "mundane products" was not protected by the First Amendment, was not a fair use, and would likely result in consumer confusion.

First we address the arguments of the respective parties with respect to a category of objects composed of paintings, prints, and calendars. Then we address the arguments of the parties with respect to a second category of objects composed of mugs and other "mundane products."

## II. PAINTINGS, PRINTS, AND CALENDARS

In accordance with the district court's rulings, the University is appellant with respect to paintings and prints that "are of the same or larger sizes and of the same or better quality of such paintings and prints previously created, produced, manufactured and distributed by [Moore]." Moore is appellant for calendars. We address these items together.

The University's claim is that Moore's unlicensed paintings, prints, and calendars infringe on the University's trademarks because the inclusion in these products of the University's football uniforms (showing the University's crimson and white colors) creates a likelihood of confusion on the part of buyers that the University sponsored or endorsed the product.

The University argues that its uniforms are "strong" trademarks and that its survey provides strong evidence of confusion sufficient to establish a likelihood of confusion to sustain a Lanham Act violation by Moore. *See* 15 U.S.C. § 1125(a); *Two Pesos, Inc. v. Taco Cabana, Inc.,* 505 U.S. 763, 769 (1992). . . . [W]e need not in this case settle upon a precise evaluation of the strength of the mark or the degree of likelihood of confusion. As our discussion below indicates, we conclude that the First Amendment interests in artistic expression so clearly outweigh whatever consumer confusion that might exist on these facts that we must necessarily conclude that there has been no violation of the Lanham Act with respect to the paintings, prints, and calendars.

The First Amendment's protections extend beyond written and spoken words. "[P]ictures, films, paintings, drawings, and engravings . . . have First Amendment protection[.]" *Kaplan v. California,* 413 U.S. 115, 119–20 (1973).

The University argues that Moore's paintings, prints, and calendars "are more commercial than expressive speech and, therefore, entitled to a lower degree" of First Amendment protection. *See Cent. Hudson Gas & Elec. Corp. v. Pub. Serv. Comm'n of N.Y.,* 447 U.S. 557, 562–63 (1980) ("The Constitution . . . accords a lesser protection to commercial speech than to other constitutionally guaranteed expression."). However, these items certainly do more than "propos[e] a commercial transaction." *Id.* at 562. Naturally, Moore sells these items for money, but it "is of course no matter that the dissemination [of speech] takes place under commercial auspices." *Smith v. California,* 361 U.S. 147, 150 (1959). Like other expressive speech, Moore's paintings, prints, and calendars are entitled to full protection under the First Amendment.

Thus, we must decide whether Moore's First Amendment rights will give way to the University's trademark rights. We are not the first circuit to confront this issue. In 1989, the Second Circuit decided *Rogers v. Grimaldi,* 875 F.2d 994 (2d Cir. 1989), which is the landmark case for balancing trademark and First Amendment rights. In *Rogers,* the defendant created a film about two fictional Italian dancers who were called "Ginger and Fred," which was the film's title. Ginger Rogers, a famous dancer who often worked with Fred Astaire, sued under § 43(a) of the Lanham Act, arguing that the film's title falsely implied that she was endorsing or featured in the film.

The court noted that the purchaser of artistic works, "like the purchaser of a can of peas, has a right not to be misled as to the source of the product." *Id.* at 997–98. However, the court concluded that the Lanham Act should be read narrowly to avoid impinging on speech protected by the First Amendment. *Id.* at 998–1000. Thus, the court adopted a balancing test:

> We believe that in general the Act should be construed to apply to artistic works only where the public interest in avoiding consumer confusion outweighs the public interest in free expression. In the context of allegedly misleading titles using a celebrity's name, that balance will normally not support application of the Act unless the title has no artistic relevance to the underlying work whatsoever, or if it has some artistic relevance, unless the title explicitly misleads as to the source of the work.
>
> *Id.* at 999.

Under the facts of *Rogers,* the court concluded that "the slight risk that such use of a celebrity's name might implicitly suggest endorsement or sponsorship to some people is outweighed by the danger of restricting artistic expression." *Id.* at 1000. Accordingly, the court ruled in favor of the movie's producers because the title was artistically relevant to the film, there had been no evidence of explicit misleading as to source, and the risk of confusion was "so outweighed by the interests in artistic expression as to preclude application of the Lanham Act." *Id.* at 1001.

Circuit courts have also applied *Rogers* in cases where trademark law is being used to attack the content—as opposed to the title—of works protected by the First Amendment. In *Cliffs Notes, Inc. v. Bantam Doubleday Dell Publishing Group,* 886 F.2d 490 (2d Cir. 1989), the defendant published humorous versions of "Cliffs Notes" study books and had imitated the plaintiff's trademarked black and yellow covers. *Id.* at 492. The court held that the *Rogers* test was "generally applicable to Lanham Act claims against works of artistic expression" and found that the parody books were protected by the First Amendment because the defendant had not explicitly misled consumers as to the source or content of the books. *Id.* at 495–96.

In *ESS Entertainment 2000, Inc. v. Rock Star Videos, Inc.,* 547 F.3d 1095 (9th Cir. 2008), a scene in the defendant's video game featured the trademark of the plaintiff's entertainment club located in Los Angeles. *Id.* at 1096–98. The Ninth Circuit held that there "is no principled reason why [*Rogers*] ought not also apply to the use of a trademark in the body of the work." *Id.* at 1099. The court found that the defendant's use of the trademark did not explicitly mislead as to the source or content of the video game, and thus the First Amendment protected the defendant's use of the plaintiff's trademark. *Id.* at 1099–1101.

In the case perhaps most similar to the one *sub judice,* the Sixth Circuit addressed a claim of false endorsement under the Lanham Act where an artist had painted a collage of Tiger Woods images. *ETW Corp. v. Jireh Publ'g, Inc.,* 332 F.3d 915, 918–19 (6th Cir. 2003). Woods's publicity company sued the artist, and the court applied the *Rogers* balancing test and found that Woods's image on the painting had artistic relevance to the underlying work and did not explicitly mislead as to the source of the work. As a result, the painting was protected by the First Amendment against a claim of false endorsement.

The University contends that none of those cases are analogous to our current set of facts. It argues that *Cliffs Notes* and *ESS Entertainment* are not applicable because those cases involved parody, whereas Moore's paintings do not. However, neither *Rogers* nor *ETW* dealt with parody, yet the courts in those cases still read the Lanham Act narrowly to avoid First Amendment concerns. Additionally, courts adopting *Rogers* have noted that it is "generally applicable to works of artistic expression," not just parodies. *See ESS Entm't,* 547 F.3d at 1099 ("artistic works"); *ETW,* 332 F.3d at 937 ("artistic works").

The University responds by saying that we should not consider *Rogers* or *ETW* because those cases dealt with rights of publicity, which the University contends are much weaker than trademark rights. However, *Rogers* and *ETW* both dealt also with Lanham Act false endorsement claims, and we have never treated false endorsement and trademark infringement claims as distinct under the Lanham Act.

Therefore, we have no hesitation in joining our sister circuits by holding that we should construe the Lanham Act narrowly when deciding whether an artistically expressive work infringes a trademark. This requires that we carefully "weigh the public interest in free expression against the public interest in avoiding consumer confusion." *Cliffs Notes,* 886 F.2d at 494. An artistically expressive use of a trademark will not violate the Lanham Act "unless the use of the mark has no artistic relevance to the underlying work whatsoever, or, if it has some artistic relevance, unless it explicitly misleads as to the source or the content of the work." *ESS Entm't,* 547 F.3d at 1099.

In this case, we readily conclude that Moore's paintings, prints, and calendars are protected under the *Rogers* test. The depiction of the University's uniforms in the content of these items is artistically relevant to the expressive underlying works because the uniforms' colors and designs are needed for a realistic portrayal of famous scenes from Alabama football history. Also there is no evidence that Moore ever marketed an unlicensed item as "endorsed" or "sponsored" by the University, or otherwise explicitly stated that such items were affiliated with the University. Moore's paintings, prints, and calendars very clearly are embodiments of artistic expression, and are entitled to full First

Amendment protection. The extent of his use of the University's trademarks is their mere inclusion (their necessary inclusion) in the body of the image, which Moore creates to memorialize and enhance a particular play or event in the University's football history. Even if "some members of the public would draw the incorrect inference that [the University] had some involvement with [Moore's paintings, prints, and calendars,] . . . that risk of misunderstanding, not engendered by any overt [or in this case even implicit] claim . . . is so outweighed by the interest in artistic expression as to preclude" any violation of the Lanham Act.

Because Moore's depiction of the University's uniforms in the content of his paintings, prints, and calendars results in no violation of the Lanham Act, we affirm the district court with respect to paintings and prints, and reverse with respect to calendars.

III. MUGS AND OTHER "MUNDANE PRODUCTS"

[The court held that Moore had waived any challenge to the District Court's conclusions that his use of the uniforms on the so-called mundane products was not a fair use and was not protected by the First Amendment. The "mundane products" consisted of "mini-prints, mugs, cups, . . . flags, towels, t-shirts" and other similar products.]

### *NOTES AND QUESTIONS*

1. *New Life Art* reflects a growing consensus around *Rogers v. Grimaldi as the correct* approach to expressive uses of trademarks. Importantly, though *Rogers* itself concerned the use of a name in the title of a film, it has been extended to uses of marks within expressive uses. In *Louis Vuitton Malletier S.A. v. Warner Bros. Entm't Inc.*, 868 F. Supp. 2d 172 (S.D.N.Y. 2012), Louis Vuitton sued the producers of the movie *The Hangover Part II*, alleging that inclusion of a fake Louis Vuitton bag (specifically its Diophy bag) in the movie and a reference to one of the bags as a "Lewis Vuitton" infringed Louis Vuitton's rights. Applying *Rogers v. Grimaldi*, the Southern District of New York rejected Louis Vuitton's claim, finding use of the bag artistically relevant and not explicitly misleading. Louis Vuitton's confusion claims in that case were creative. It argued that (1) that consumers would be confused into believing that the Diophy bag in the movie was a genuine Louis Vuitton bag; and (2) that Louis Vuitton approved the use of the Diophy bag in the film. The court doubted that either claim was cognizable but determined that Louis Vuitton's claim would fail regardless since neither type of confusion would be sufficient to establish that the use was explicitly misleading. *See also Brown v. Electronic Arts, Inc.*, 724 F.3d 1235 (9th Cir. 2013) (applying *Rogers* and insulating from liability use of Jim Brown's likeness in video game).

2. What does it mean for use of a mark to be "artistically relevant"? Must the trademark be integral to the expressive work? Is it enough that the artist simply be able to articulate a connection between the mark and the work? Recognizing the difficulty of this question and the risk that it could pull courts

into the kinds of aesthetic judgments they eschew in copyright, the Ninth Circuit in *Brown* reiterated its view that the level of artistic relevance must simply be "above zero." In *Parks* the Sixth Circuit took a more aggressive approach, finding Outkast's use of Rosa Parks in the title of its song not to be artistically relevant because the song was not about Rosa Parks. *Parks* appears to be a unique case in this respect—most courts have not found this part of the test difficult to meet. See *E.S.S. Entertainment 2000, Inc. v. Rock Star Videos, Inc.*, 547 F.3d 1095 (9th Cir. 2008) (finding video game creator's inclusion of "Pig Pen" gentlemen's club artistically relevant to depiction of Los Angeles neighborhood).

3. *New Life Art* emphasizes that use of the mark in an expressive use is not, by itself, enough to make a use "explicitly misleading," otherwise *Rogers* would be a nullity. What uses would be explicitly misleading under this application? If a court were to find a use explicitly misleading, what remedy would follow? A prohibition on use of the mark within the work, or simply an injunction against the explicitly misleading material?

# CHAPTER 4

# COPYRIGHT PROTECTION

■ ■ ■



---

Copyright protects works of expression. It offers another form of protection for design features, although the availability of protection is limited by copyright's bar against protecting useful articles, which are functional and therefore not copyrightable. As discussed below, courts have struggled to define a workable test to identify when a pictorial, graphic, or sculptural element is separable from a useful article (in which case the separable element can be copyrighted). When Congress enacted copyright protection for architectural works in 1990, it chose to adopt a different test of functionality for architectural works, in order to avoid the problems of applying a separability analysis. In 2017, the Supreme Court finally resolved the longstanding uncertainty over how to determine separability of aesthetic elements from useful articles. This chapter discusses copyright law from the perspective of design and highlights those issues that are most salient in protecting designs under U.S. copyright law.

## A. SUBJECT MATTER, ORIGINALITY, AND FIXATION

We begin by looking at what subject matter may qualify for a copyright and the two basic requirements of copyright, originality and fixation of a work.

### 1. SUBJECT MATTER: WORKS OF AUTHORSHIP

**U.S. Copyright Act, Section 102**

**§ 102. Subject matter of copyright: In general**

(a) Copyright protection subsists, in accordance with this title, in original works of authorship fixed in any tangible medium of expression, now known or later developed, from which they can be perceived, reproduced, or otherwise communicated, either directly or with the aid of a machine or device. Works of authorship include the following categories:

(1) literary works;

(2) musical works, including any accompanying words;

(3) dramatic works, including any accompanying music;

(4) pantomimes and choreographic works;

(5) pictorial, graphic, and sculptural works;

(6) motion pictures and other audiovisual works;

(7) sound recordings; and

(8) architectural works.

(b) In no case does copyright protection for an original work of authorship extend to any idea, procedure, process, system, method of operation, concept, principle, or discovery, regardless of the form in which it is described, explained, illustrated, or embodied in such work.

---

The Copyright Clause of the Constitution gives Congress the power "[t]o promote the Progress of Science and useful Arts, by securing for limited Times to Authors and Inventors the exclusive Right to their respective Writings and Discoveries." U.S. CONST. art. I, § 8, cl. 8. Both the Supreme Court and Congress have taken an expansive view of "Writings." Copyright deals with authors' works of expression—a category that, over time, has grown to include a wide variety of works. Section 102(a) of the

U.S. Copyright Act lists eight non-exhaustive categories of works: (1) literary works; (2) musical works, including any accompanying words; (3) dramatic works, including any accompanying music; (4) pantomimes and choreographic works; (5) pictorial, graphic, and sculptural works; (6) motion pictures and other audiovisual works; (7) sound recordings; and (8) architectural works. Despite their functionality, computer programs are treated as literary works. 17 U.S.C. § 102(a). However, the Copyright Act excludes from protection ideas, facts, and functional elements such as a "procedure, process, system, [or] method of operation." *Id.* § 102(b). As discussed below, design protection figures most prominently in the fifth category of pictorial, graphic, and sculptural works (known as "PGS works"), which often may be incorporated into useful articles that are mass produced, such as clothing, furniture, and household and industrial items.

## 2. ORIGINALITY

In addition to creating a work that falls within the subject matter of copyright, authors must satisfy two other fundamental requirements in order to obtain a copyright: (1) originality and (2) fixation. We discuss each in turn.

### *PROBLEM 4–1*

Georgie is a high school student who enjoys design. Using free online computer-aided design (CAD) software, she designed a toy train engine that can be 3D-printed into a physical toy. The CAD software already had a basic blueprint or wireframe for a toy train engine for users to modify. Using the options and tools of the CAD software, Georgie added the following detail to the train: the choice of colors of the engine, the cow catcher panel in front of the train (a feature she designed from the basic shapes the CAD software provided users to modify), and the size dimensions of the toy for 3D-printing. The manufacturer of the CAD software makes no claim of copyright to any work created by a third party using the software. (1) Does Georgie's 3D-printed toy train engine satisfy originality? (2) Would your answer change if Georgie relied on a photograph she took of an actual train to design her toy train? Consult the following case and notes following the case to analyze the problem.

---

### MESHWERKS, INC. V. TOYOTA MOTOR SALES U.S.A., INC.

528 F.3d 1258 (10th Cir. 2002)

GORSUCH, CIRCUIT JUDGE. This case calls on us to apply copyright principles to a relatively new technology: digital modeling. While fully appreciating that digital media present new frontiers for copyrightable creative expression, in this particular case the uncontested facts reveal that Meshwerks' models owe their designs and origins to Toyota and deliberately do not include anything original of their own; accordingly, we hold that Meshwerks' models are not protected by copyright and affirm.

I. A

In 2003, and in conjunction with Saatchi & Saatchi, its advertising agency, Toyota began work on its model-year 2004 advertising campaign. Saatchi and Toyota agreed that the campaign would involve digital models of Toyota's vehicles for use on Toyota's website and in various other media. These digital models have substantial advantages over the product photographs for which they substitute. With a few clicks of a computer mouse, the advertiser can change the color of the car, its surroundings, and even edit its physical dimensions to portray changes in vehicle styling; before this innovation, advertisers had to conduct new photo shoots of whole fleets of vehicles each time the manufacturer made even a small design change to a car or truck.

To supply these digital models, Saatchi and Toyota hired Grace & Wild, Inc. ("G & W"). In turn, G & W subcontracted with Meshwerks to assist with two initial aspects of the project-digitization and modeling. Digitizing involves collecting physical data points from the object to be portrayed. Meshwerks took copious measurements of Toyota's vehicles by covering each car, truck, and van with a grid of tape and running an articulated arm tethered to a computer over the vehicle to measure all points of intersection in the grid. Based on these measurements, modeling software then generated a digital image resembling a wire-frame model. [T]he vehicles' data points (measurements) were mapped onto a computerized grid and the modeling software connected the dots to create a "wire frame" of each vehicle.

At this point, however, the on-screen image remained far from perfect and manual "modeling" was necessary. Meshwerks personnel fine-tuned or, as the company prefers it, "sculpted," the lines on screen to resemble each vehicle as closely as possible. Approximately 90 percent of the data points contained in each final model, Meshwerks represents, were the result not of the first-step measurement process, but of the skill and effort its digital sculptors manually expended at the second step. For example, some areas of detail, such as wheels, headlights, door handles, and the Toyota emblem, could not be accurately measured using current technology; those features had to be added at the second "sculpting" stage, and Meshwerks had to recreate those features as realistically as possible by hand, based on photographs. Even for areas that were measured, Meshwerks faced the challenge of converting measurements taken of a three-dimensional car into a two-dimensional computer representation; to achieve this, its modelers had to sculpt, or move, data points to achieve a visually convincing result. The purpose and product of these processes, after nearly 80 to 100 hours of effort per vehicle, were two-dimensional wire-frame depictions of Toyota's vehicles that appeared three-dimensional on screen, but were utterly unadorned—lacking color, shading, and other details. [Below] are sample screen-prints of one of Meshwerks' digital wire-frame models [labeled Appendix A].

APPENDIX A

06-4222, Meshwerks v. Toyota

APPENDIX B

06-4222, Meshwerks v. Toyota

With Meshwerks' wire-frame products in hand, G & W then manipulated the computerized models by, first, adding detail, the result of which appeared on screen as a "tightening" of the wire frames, as though significantly more wires had been added to the frames, or as though they were made of a finer mesh. Next, G & W digitally applied color, texture, lighting, and animation for use in Toyota's advertisements. An example of G & W's work product is [included above] as Appendix B. G & W's digital models were then sent to Saatchi to be employed in a number of advertisements prepared by Saatchi and Toyota in various print, online, and television media.

B

This dispute arose because, according to Meshwerks, it contracted with G & W for only a single use of its models—as part of one Toyota television commercial—and neither Toyota nor any other defendant was allowed to use the digital models created from Meshwerks' wire-frames in other advertisements. Thus, Meshwerks contends defendants improperly—in violation of copyright laws as well as the parties' agreement—reused and redistributed the models created by Meshwerks in a host of other media. [The district court granted Toyota's motion for summary judgment and] found that the wire-frame models were merely copies of Toyota's products, not sufficiently original to warrant copyright protection, and stressed that Meshwerks' "intent was to replicate, as exactly as possible, the image of certain Toyota vehicles." Because there was no valid copyright, there could be no infringement.

II

Because Meshwerks obtained registration certificates for its models from the Copyright Office, we presume that it holds a valid copyright. *See* 17 U.S.C. § 410(c). At the same time, defendants may overcome this presumption by presenting evidence and legal argument sufficient to establish that the works in question were not entitled to copyright protection. Because this case comes to us on summary judgment, we review the question whether Meshwerks holds a valid copyright *de novo* and will affirm the district court's judgment only if, viewing all of the facts in the light most favorable to Meshwerks, we are able to conclude that "there is no genuine issue as to any material fact and that [defendants are] entitled to judgment as a matter of law." Fed. R. Civ. P. 56(c).

A

The Constitution authorizes Congress "[t]o promote the Progress of Science and useful Arts, by securing for limited Times to Authors and Inventors the exclusive Right to their respective Writings and Discoveries." U.S. CONST. art. I, § 8, cl. 8. The Supreme Court has emphasized that the power afforded by this provision—namely, to give an author exclusive authority over a work—rests in part on a "presuppos[ition]" that the work contains "a degree of originality." *Feist Publ'ns, Inc. v. Rural Tel. Serv. Co.,* 499 U.S. 340, 346 (1991). Congress has recognized this same point, extending copyright protection only to "*original works* of authorship. . . ." 17 U.S.C. § 102 (emphasis added). Originality, thus, is said to be "[t]he *sine qua non* of copyright." *Feist,* 499 U.S. at 345. That is, not every work of authorship, let alone every aspect of every work of authorship, is protectable in copyright; only original expressions are protected. This constitutional and statutory principle seeks to strike a delicate balance—rewarding (and thus encouraging) those who contribute something new to society, while also allowing (and thus stimulating) others to build upon, add to, and develop those creations. The copyright power is said to exist primarily "not to reward the labor of authors, but to promote the progress of science and the useful arts. . . . To this end, copyright assures authors the right to their original expression, but encourages others to build freely upon the ideas and information conveyed by a work." *Id.* at 349–50.

What exactly does it mean for a work to qualify as "original"? In *Feist,* the Supreme Court clarified that the work must be "independently created by the author (as opposed to copied from other works)." *Id.* at 345. In addition, the work must "possess at least some minimal degree of creativity," though this is not to say that to count as containing a minimal degree of creativity a work must have aesthetic merit in the minds of judges (arguably not always the most artistically discerning lot). As the Court explained through Justice Holmes, even "a very modest grade of art has in it something irreducible, which is one man's alone. That something he may copyright. . . ." *Bleistein v. Donaldson Lithographing Co.,* 188 U.S. 239, 250; *see also Feist,* 499 U.S. at 345 (all that's needed is some creative spark, "no matter how crude, humble, or obvious").[5]

While there is little authority explaining how our received principles of copyright law apply to the relatively new digital medium before us, some lessons may be discerned from how the law coped in an earlier time with a previous revolution in technology: photography.

As Judge Pauley admirably recounted in *SHL Imaging, Inc. v. Artisan House, Inc.,* photography was initially met by critics with a degree of skepticism: a photograph, some said, "copies everything and explains nothing," and it was debated whether a camera could do anything more than merely record the physical world. 117 F. Supp. 2d 301, 307 (S.D.N.Y. 2000). These largely aesthetic debates migrated into legal territory when Oscar Wilde toured the United States in the 1880s and sought out Napoleon Sarony for a series of publicity photographs to promote the event. Burrow-Giles, a lithography firm, quickly copied one of Sarony's photos and sold 85,000 prints without the photographer's permission. Burrow-Giles defended its conduct on the ground that the photograph was a "mere mechanical reproduction of the physical features" of Wilde and thus not copyrightable. *Burrow-Giles,* 111 U.S. at 59. Recognizing that Oscar Wilde's inimitable visage does not belong, or "owe its origins" to any photographer, the Supreme Court noted that photographs may well sometimes lack originality and are thus not *per se* copyrightable. *Id.* ("the ordinary production of a photograph" may involve "no protection" in copyright). At the same time, the Court held, a copyright may be had to the extent a photograph involves "posing the said Oscar Wilde in front of the camera, selecting and arranging the costume, draperies, and other various accessories in said photograph, arranging the subject so as to present graceful outlines, arranging and disposing the light and shade, suggesting and evoking the desired expression. . . ." *Id.* at 60. Accordingly, the Court indicated, photographs are copyrightable, if only to the extent of their *original* depiction of the subject. Wilde's image is not copyrightable; but to

[5] The two pertinent concepts—independent creation and minimal creativity—are intertwined and overlap, at least to some degree: After all, if something qualifies as an independent creation (that is, it is more than a copy) won't it also usually betray some minimal degree of creativity? Still, though the independent test imputed by the creativity requirement is low, it does exist. *Feist,* 499 U.S. at 345, 362. It is thus not the case, as some interpreted Judge Learned Hand to say when he observed that " 'no photograph, however simple, can be unaffected by the personal influence of the author, and no two will be absolutely alike,' " that photographs (or any other works, for that matter) are per se protectable. *See SHL Imaging, Inc. v. Artisan House, Inc.*, 117 F. Supp. 2d 301, 309 (S.D.N.Y. 2000) (quoting *Jewelers' Circular Publ'g Co. v. Key-Stone Publ'g Co.*, 274 F. 932, 934 (S.D.N.Y. 1921) (Hand, J.)).

the extent a photograph reflects the photographer's decisions regarding pose, positioning, background, lighting, shading, and the like, those elements can be said to "owe their origins" to the photographer, making the photograph copyrightable, at least to that extent.

As the Court more recently explained in *Feist,* the operative distinction is between, on the one hand, ideas or facts in the world, items that cannot be copyrighted, and a particular expression of that idea or fact, that can be. "This principle, known as the idea/expression or fact/expression dichotomy, applies to all works of authorship. As applied to a factual compilation," the particular matter at issue in *Feist,* "assuming the absence of original written expression, only the compiler's selection and arrangement may be protected; the raw facts may be copied at will. This result is neither unfair nor unfortunate. It is the means by which copyright advances the progress of science and art." *Feist,* 499 U.S. at 350; *see also id.* at 351 ("In no event may copyright extend to the facts themselves."). So, in the case of photographs, for which Meshwerks' digital models were designed to serve as practically advantageous substitutes, authors are entitled to copyright protection only for the "incremental contribution," *SHL Imaging, Inc.,* 117 F. Supp. 2d at 311, represented by their interpretation or expression of the objects of their attention.

B

Applying these principles, evolved in the realm of photography, to the new medium that has come to supplement and even in some ways to supplant it, we think Meshwerks' models are not so much independent creations as (very good) copies of Toyota's vehicles. All the same, we do not doubt for an instant that the digital medium before us, like photography before it, can be employed to create vivid new expressions fully protectable in copyright.

Key to our evaluation of this case is the fact that Meshwerks' digital wire-frame computer models depict Toyota's vehicles without any individualizing features: they are untouched by a digital paintbrush; they are not depicted in front of a palm tree, whizzing down the open road, or climbing up a mountainside. Put another way, Meshwerks' models depict nothing more than unadorned Toyota vehicles—the car *as* car. *See* Appendix A [above]. And the unequivocal lesson from *Feist* is that works are not copyrightable to the extent they do not involve any expression apart from the raw facts in the world. As Professor Nimmer has commented in connection with the predecessor technology of photography, "[a]s applied to a photograph of a pre-existing product, that bedrock principle [of originality] means that the photographer manifestly cannot claim to have originated the matter depicted therein. . . . The upshot is that the photographer is entitled to copyright solely based on lighting, angle, perspective, and the other ingredients that traditionally apply to that art-form." *Nimmer on Copyright* § 3.03[C][3]. It seems to us that exactly the same holds true with the digital medium now before us: the facts in this case unambiguously show that Meshwerks did not make any decisions regarding lighting, shading, the background in front of which a vehicle would be posed, the angle at which to pose it, or the like—in short, its models reflect none of the decisions that can make depictions of things or facts in the world, whether Oscar Wilde or a Toyota Camry, new expressions subject to copyright protection.

Confirming this conclusion as well is the peculiar place where Meshwerks stood in the model-creation pecking order. On the one hand, Meshwerks had nothing to do with designing the appearance of Toyota's vehicles, distinguishing them from any other cars, trucks, or vans in the world. That expressive creation took place *before* Meshwerks happened along, and was the result of work done by Toyota and its designers; indeed, at least six of the eight vehicles at issue are still covered by design patents belonging to Toyota and protecting the *appearances* of the objects for which they are issued. *See* 35 U.S.C. § 171. On the other hand, how the models Meshwerks created were to be deployed in advertising—including the backgrounds, lighting, angles, and colors—were all matters left to those (G & W, Saatchi, and 3D Recon) who came *after* Meshwerks left the scene. Meshwerks thus played a narrow, if pivotal, role in the process by simply, if effectively, copying Toyota's vehicles into a digital medium so they could be expressively manipulated by others.

Were we to afford copyright protection in this case, we would run aground on one of the bedrock principles of copyright law—namely, that originality, "as the term is used in copyright, means only that the work was independently created by the author (*as opposed to copied from other works*)." *Feist,* 499 U.S. at 345 (emphasis added). Because our copyright laws protect only "original" expression, the reason for refusing copyright protection to copies is clear, "since obviously a copier is not a creator, much less an 'independent' creator." *Patry on Copyright* § 3:28; *see also id.* ("The key is whether original matter in which protection is claimed is the result of plaintiff's ingenuity rather than appropriation of another's material.").

It is certainly true that what Meshwerks accomplished was a peculiar kind of copying. It did not seek to recreate Toyota vehicles outright—steel, rubber, and all; instead, it sought to depict Toyota's three-dimensional physical objects in a two-dimensional digital medium. But we hold, as many before us have already suggested, that, standing alone, "[t]he fact that a work in one medium has been copied from a work in another medium does not render it any the less a 'copy.'" *Nimmer on Copyright* § 8.01[B]. After all, the putative creator who merely shifts the medium in which another's creation is expressed has not necessarily added anything beyond the expression contained in the original.

In reaching this conclusion, we do not for a moment seek to downplay the considerable amount of time, effort, and skill that went into making

Meshwerks' digital wire-frame models. But, in assessing the originality of a work for which copyright protection is sought, we look only at the final *product,* not the process, and the fact that intensive, skillful, and even creative labor is invested in the process of creating a product does not guarantee its copyrightability. In the case before us, there is no doubt that transposing the physical appearances of Toyota's vehicles from three dimensions to two, such that computer-screen images accurately reflect Toyota's products, was labor intensive and required a great amount of skill. But because the end-results were unadorned images of Toyota's vehicles, the appearances of which do not owe their origins to Meshwerks, we are unable to reward that skill, effort, and labor with copyright protection.

The judgment of the district court is affirmed, and defendants' request for attorneys' fees is denied. *So ordered.*

### *NOTES AND QUESTIONS*

1. Toyota obtained design patents for at least 6 of the cars at issue. Do you think Toyota could also obtain copyrights for its cars? Is a Toyota car a copyrightable work of expression?

2. What is the test of originality? How did Meshwerks fail the test in the court's view? Did Meshwerks copy from someone else's work of expression? If so, which work? Did Meshwerks' wire-frame models lack even a modicum of creativity?

3. The court based its decision on its view that the wire-frame models "depict Toyota's vehicles without any individualizing features" and is merely a representation of a "thing" or "fact"? Is this description of the wire-frame model accurate (see above)? Even if accurate, should it matter for originality whether a depiction represents a thing or fact? If Leonard da Vinci were living today, should he be able to get a copyright for new sketches he made of the human body, inventions, or other things? Or should the sketches be disqualified for depicting things?

4. For a critique of *Meshwerks*, see Edward Lee, *Digital Originality*, 14 VAND. J. ENT. & TECH. L. 919, 925–33 (2012). Professor Lee argues that the Tenth Circuit's reasoning is flawed in several key respects, including misreading *Feist*:

> Lost in the sea of the [Tenth Circuit']s string citation is the fact that the Toyota car is not a work of expression. It is a car—an uncopyrightable useful article. That key factual distinction renders irrelevant nearly all of the cases and authorities cited by the Tenth Circuit to support its holding. The *Feist* Court explicitly stated that "independently create" meant not "copied *from other works*." In *Meshwerks*, the Toyota cars are not works of expression—they are useful articles, devices whose designs are inseparable from the functions they serve. Therefore, depicting those useful objects in one's own drawing or representation is not "copying" in the *Feist* sense.

*See also Bleistein v. Donaldson Lithographing Co.,* 188 U.S. 239, 249-50 (1903) ("But even if they had been drawn from the life, that fact would not deprive them of protection. . . . Others are free to copy the original. They are not free to copy the copy.").

5. In *Feist*, the Supreme Court explained that originality does *not* require novelty. "Originality does not signify novelty; a work may be original even though it closely resembles other works so long as the similarity is fortuitous, not the result of copying. To illustrate, assume that two poets, each ignorant of the other, compose identical poems. Neither work is novel, yet both are original and, hence, copyrightable." *Feist Publ'ns, Inc. v. Rural Tel. Serv. Co.* , 499 U.S. 340, 345–46 (1991).

6. How would you compare copyright's originality requirement to design patent's "original" requirement? Does it make sense to have an originality requirement for both forms of IP? Also, does design patent law require novelty?

---

## L. BATLIN & SON, INC. V. SNYDER

536 F.2d 486 (2d Cir. 1976) (en banc)

OAKES, J. Appellants Jeffrey Snyder and Etna Products Co., Inc., his licensee, appeal from a preliminary injunction granted L. Batlin & Son, Inc. (Batlin), compelling appellants to cancel a recordation of a copyright with the United States Customs Service and restraining them from enforcing that copyright. The district court held, 394 F. Supp. 1389 (S.D.N.Y. 1975), as it had previously in *Etna Products Co. v. E. Mishan & Sons*, 75 Civ. 428 (S.D.N.Y. Feb. 13, 1975), that there was "little probability" that appellants' copyright "will be found valid in the trial on the merits" on the basis that any variations between appellants' copyrighted plastic bank and a cast iron bank in the public domain were merely "trivial," and hence appellants' bank insufficiently "original" to support a copyright. 394 F. Supp. at 1390, citing *Alfred Bell & Co. v. Catalda Fine Arts, Inc.*, 191 F.2d 99 (2d Cir. 1951). We agree with the district court and therefore affirm the judgment granting the preliminary injunction.

Uncle Sam mechanical banks have been on the American scene at least since June 8, 1886, when Design Patent No. 16,728, issued on a toy savings bank of its type. [See below Figure. *Ed.*]

**[Uncle Sam bank patented in 1886. *Ed.*]**

The basic delightful design has long since been in the public domain. The banks are well documented in collectors' books and known to the average person interested in Americana. A description of the bank is that Uncle Sam, dressed in his usual stove pipe hat, blue full dress coat, starred vest and red and white striped trousers, and leaning on his umbrella, stands on a four- or five-inch wide base, on which sits his carpetbag. A coin may be placed in Uncle Sam's extended hand. When a lever is pressed, the arm lowers, and the coin falls into the bag, while Uncle Sam's whiskers move up and down. The base has an embossed American eagle on it with the words "Uncle Sam" on streamers above it, as well as the word "Bank" on each side.

Appellant Jeffrey Snyder doing business as "J.S.N.Y." obtained a registration of copyright on a plastic "Uncle Sam bank" in Class G ("Works of Art") as "sculpture" on January 23, 1975. According to Snyder's affidavit, in January, 1974, he had seen a cast metal antique Uncle Sam bank with an overall height of the figure and base of 11 inches. In April, 1974, he flew to Hong Kong to arrange for the design and eventual manufacture of replicas of the bank as Bicentennial items, taking the cast metal Uncle Sam bank with him. His Hong Kong buying agent selected a firm, "Unitoy," to make the plastic "prototype" because of its price and the quality of its work. Snyder wanted his bank to be made of plastic and to be shorter than the cast metal sample "in order to fit into the required price range and quality and quantity of material to be used." The figure of Uncle Sam was thus shortened from 11 to nine inches, and the base shortened and narrowed. It was also decided, Snyder averred, to change the shape of the carpetbag and to include the umbrella in a one-piece mold for the Uncle Sam figure, "so as not to have a problem with a loose umbrella or a separate molding process." The Unitoy representative made his sketches while looking at the cast metal bank. After a "clay model" was made, a plastic "prototype" was approved by Snyder and his order placed in May, 1974. The plastic bank carried the legend "CR Copyright J.S.N.Y." and was assertedly first "published" on October 15, 1974, before being filed with the Register of Copyrights in January, 1975.

Appellee Batlin is also in the novelty business and as early as August 9, 1974, ordered 30 cartons of cast iron Uncle Sam mechanical banks from Taiwan where its president had seen the bank made. When he became aware of the existence of a plastic bank, which he considered "an almost identical copy" of the cast iron bank, Batlin's trading company in Hong Kong procured a manufacturer and the president of Batlin ordered plastic copies also. Beginning in April, 1975, Batlin was notified by the United States Customs Service that the plastic banks it was receiving were covered by appellants' copyright. In addition the Customs Service was also refusing entry to cast iron banks previously ordered, according to the Batlin affidavit. Thus Batlin instituted suit for a judgment declaring appellants' copyright void and for damages for unfair competition and restraint of trade. The sole question on this appeal is whether Judge Metzner abused his discretion in granting Batlin a preliminary injunction. We find that he did not.

This court has examined both the appellants' plastic Uncle Sam bank made under Snyder's copyright and the uncopyrighted model cast iron mechanical bank, which is itself a reproduction of the original public domain Uncle Sam bank. Appellant Snyder claims differences not only of size but also in a number of other very minute details: the carpetbag shape of the plastic bank is smooth, the iron bank rough; the metal bank bag is fatter at its base; the eagle on the front of the platform in the metal bank is holding arrows in his talons while in the plastic bank he clutches leaves, this change concededly having been made, however, because "the arrows did not reproduce well in plastic on a smaller size." The shape of Uncle Sam's face is supposedly different, as is the shape and texture of the hats, according to the Snyder affidavit. In the metal version the umbrella is hanging loose while in the plastic item it is included in the single mold. The texture of the clothing, the hairline, shape of the bow ties and of the shirt collar and left arm as well as the flag carrying the name on the base of the statue are all claimed to be different, along with the shape and texture of the eagles on the side. Many of these differences are not perceptible to the casual observer. Appellants make no claim for any difference based on the plastic mold lines in the Uncle Sam figure which are perceptible.

Our examination of the banks results in the same conclusion as that of Judge Metzner in *Etna Products*, the earlier case enjoining Snyder's copyright, that the Snyder bank is "extremely similar to the cast iron bank, save in size and material" with the only other differences, such as the shape of the satchel and the leaves in the eagle's talons being "by all appearances, minor." Similarities include, more importantly, the appearance and number of stripes on the trousers, buttons on the coat, and stars on the vest and hat, the attire and pose of Uncle Sam, the decor on his base and bag, the overall color scheme, the method of carpetbag opening, to name but a few. After seeing the banks and hearing conflicting testimony from opposing expert witnesses as to the substantiality or triviality of the variations and as to the skill necessary to make the plastic model, the court below stated:

> I am making a finding of fact that as far as I'm concerned, it is practically an exact copy and whatever you point to in this (sic) differences are so infinitesimal they make no difference. All you have proved here by the testimony today is that if you give a man a seven-inch model and you say I want this to come out in a five-inch model, and he copies it, the fact that he has to have some artistic ability to make a model by reducing the seven to the five adds something to it. That is the only issue in this case.

As Judge Metzner went on to say in his opinion, the appellants' plastic version "reproduces" the cast iron bank "except that it proportionately reduces the height from approximately eleven inches to approximately nine inches with trivial variations." The court noted that appellants "went to great pains on the hearing to prove that there were substantial differences between the iron and the plastic articles," and found that there had been no "level of input" such as in *Alva Studios, Inc. v. Winninger*, 177 F. Supp. 265, 267 (S.D.N.Y. 1959) ("great skill and originality" called for in producing an exact scale reduction of Rodin's famous "Hand of God," to museum specifications). The substance of appellee's expert's testimony on which the district judge evidently relied was that the variations found in appellants' plastic bank were merely "trivial" and that it was a reproduction of the metal bank made as simply as possible for the purposes of manufacture. In other words, there were no elements of difference that amounted to significant alteration or that had any purpose other than the functional one of making a more suitable (and probably less expensive) figure in the plastic medium.

What the leading authority has called "the one pervading element prerequisite to copyright protection regardless of the form of the work" is the requirement of originality that the work be the original product of the claimant. 1 M. Nimmer, *The Law of Copyright* § 10, at 32 (1975). This derives from the fact that, constitutionally, copyright protection may be claimed only by "authors." U.S. CONST., art. I, § 8; *Burrow-Giles Lithographic Co. v. Sarony*, 111 U.S. 53, 58 (1884). Thus, "(o)ne who has slavishly or mechanically copied from others may not claim to be an author." 1 M. Nimmer, *supra*, § 6, at 10.2. Since the constitutional requirement must be read into the Copyright Act, the requirement of originality is also a statutory one. *Chamberlin v. Uris Sales Corp.*, 150 F.2d 512 (2d Cir. 1945). It has been the law of this circuit for at least 30 years that in order to obtain a copyright upon a reproduction of a work of art under 17 U.S.C. § 5(h) that the work "contain some substantial, not merely trivial originality. . . ." *Chamberlin*, 150 F.2d at 513.

Originality is, however, distinguished from novelty; there must be independent creation, but it need not be invention in the sense of striking uniqueness, ingeniousness, or novelty, since the Constitution differentiates "authors" and their "writings" from "inventors" and their "discoveries." *Alfred Bell & Co. v. Catalda Fine Arts, Inc.*, 191 F.2d at 100. Originality means that the work owes its creation to the author and this in turn means that the work must not consist of actual copying. *Id.* at 102–03.

The test of originality is concededly one with a low threshold in that "(a)ll that is needed . . . is that the 'author' contributed something more than a 'merely trivial' variation, something recognizably 'his own.' " *Id.* at 103. But as this court said many years ago, "(w)hile a copy of something in the public domain will not, if it be merely a copy, support a copyright, a distinguishable variation will. . . ." *Gerlach-Barklow Co. v. Morris & Bendien, Inc.*, 23 F.2d 159, 161 (2d Cir. 1927).

Necessarily, none of these underlying principles is different in the case of "(r)eproductions of a work of art," 17 U.S.C. § 5(h), from the case of "(w)orks of art . . . ," 17 U.S.C. § 5(g). The requirement of substantial as opposed to trivial variation and the prohibition of mechanical copying, both of which are inherent in and subsumed by the concept of originality, apply to both statutory categories. There is implicit in that concept a "minimal element of creativity over and above the requirement of independent effort." 1 M. Nimmer, *supra*, § 10.2, at 36. While the quantum of originality that is required may be modest indeed, *Herbert Rosenthal Jewelry Corp. v. Grossbardt*, 436 F.2d 315, 316 (2d Cir. 1970), we are not inclined to abandon that requirement, even if in the light of the constitutional and statutory bases therefor and our precedents we could do so.

A reproduction of a work of art obviously presupposes an underlying work of art. Since *Mazer v. Stein*, 347 U.S. 201, 218, (1954) (statuette of Balinese dancer copyrightable despite intended use as lamp base), it has been established that mass-produced commercial objects with a minimal element of artistic craftsmanship may satisfy the statutory requirement of such a work. So, too, a toy which qualifies as a work of art such as the original Uncle Sam mechanical bank may qualify as a "work of art" under Section 5(g). The underlying work of art may as here be in the public domain. But even to claim the more limited protection given to a reproduction of a work of art (that to the distinctive features contributed by the reproducer), the reproduction must contain "an original contribution not present in the underlying work of art" and be "more than a mere copy." 1 M. Nimmer, *supra*, § 20.2, at 93.

According to Professor Nimmer, moreover, "the mere reproduction of a work of art in a different medium should not constitute the required originality for the reason that no one can claim to have independently evolved any particular medium." *Id.* at 94. Professor Nimmer refers to *Doran v. Sunset House Distributing Corp.*, 197 F. Supp. 940 (S.D. Cal. 1961), *aff'd*, 304 F.2d 251 (9th Cir. 1962), as suggesting "the ludicrous result that the first person to execute a public domain work of art in a different medium thereafter obtains a monopoly on such work in such medium, at least as to those persons aware of the first such effort." 1 M. Nimmer, *supra*, § 20.2, at 94. We do not follow the *Doran* case. We do follow the school of cases in this circuit and elsewhere supporting the proposition that to support a copyright there must be at least some substantial variation, not merely a trivial variation such as might occur in the translation to a different medium.

Nor can the requirement of originality be satisfied simply by the demonstration of "physical skill" or "special training" which, to be sure, Judge Metzner found was required for the production of the plastic molds that furnished the basis for appellants' plastic bank. A considerably higher degree of skill is required, true artistic skill, to make the reproduction copyrightable. Thus in *Alfred Bell & Co. v. Catalda Fine Arts, Inc.*, 191 F.2d at 104–05 n.22, Judge Frank pointed out that the mezzotint engraver's art there concerned required "great labour and talent" to effectuate the "management of light and shade . . . produced by different lines and dots . . . ," means "very different from those employed by the painter or draughtsman from whom he copies. . . ." *See also Millworth Converting Corp. v. Slifka*, *supra* (fabric designer required one month of work to give three-dimensional color effect to flat surface). Here on the basis of appellants' own expert's testimony it took the Unitoy representative "(a)bout a day and a half, two days work" to produce the plastic mold sculpture from the metal Uncle Sam bank. If there be a point in the copyright law pertaining to reproductions at which sheer artistic skill and effort can act as a substitute for the requirement of substantial variation, it was not reached here.

Appellants rely heavily upon *Alva Studios, Inc. v. Winninger*, the "Hand of God" case, where the court held that "great skill and originality (were required) to produce a scale reduction of a great work with exactitude." 177 F. Supp. at 267. There, the original sculpture was, "one of the most intricate pieces of sculpture ever created" with "(i)nnumerable planes, lines and geometric patterns . . . interdependent in (a) multi-dimensional work." *Id.* Originality was found by the district court to consist primarily in the fact that "(i)t takes 'an extremely skilled sculptor' many hours working directly in front of the original" to effectuate a scale reduction. *Id.* at 266. The court, indeed, found the exact replica to be so original, distinct, and creative as to constitute a work of art in itself. The complexity and exactitude there involved distinguishes that case amply from the one at bar. As appellants themselves have pointed out, there are a number of trivial differences or deviations from the original public domain cast iron bank in their plastic reproduction. Thus concededly the plastic version is not, and was scarcely meticulously produced to be, an exactly faithful reproduction. Nor is the creativity in the underlying work of art of the same order of magnitude as in the case of the "Hand of God." Rodin's sculpture is, furthermore, so unique and rare, and adequate public access to it such a problem that a significant public benefit accrues from its precise, artistic reproduction. No such benefit can be imagined to accrue here from the "knock-off" reproduction of the cast iron Uncle Sam bank. Thus appellants' plastic bank is neither in the category of exactitude required by Alva Studios nor in a category of substantial originality; it falls within what has been suggested by the amicus curiae is a copyright no-man's land.

Absent a genuine difference between the underlying work of art and the copy of it for which protection is sought, the public interest in promoting progress in the arts indeed, the constitutional demand, *Chamberlin v. Uris Sales Corp., supra* could hardly be served. To extend copyrightability to minuscule variations would simply put a weapon for harassment in the hands of mischievous copiers intent on appropriating and monopolizing public domain work.

To be sure, the test of "originality" may leave a lot to be desired, although it is the only one we have, in that as one scholar has said, the originality requirement does not perform the function of excluding commonplace matters in the public domain from copyright status very effectively. *See* Comment, *Copyright Protection for Mass Produced Commercial Products: A Review of the Developments Following* Mazer v. Stein, 38 U. CHI. L. REV. 807 (1971). In any event, however, the articles should be judged on their own merits, *id.* at 823, and on these merits appellants' claim must fail. Here as elsewhere in the copyright law there are lines that must be drawn even though reasonable men may differ where. Judgment affirmed.

### *NOTES AND QUESTIONS*

1. *Batlin* may be viewed as a case involving the originality standard as applied to a work that draws from another work that is already in the public domain due to the lapse or absence of intellectual property protection. Does the test of originality articulated by the Second Circuit sound different from the general test of originality adopted by the Supreme Court in *Feist*? If so, what might be the reason for the difference?

2. When can a replica of a design that is already in the public domain satisfy the originality standard? Are you persuaded by the Court's attempt to distinguish *Alva Studios, Inc. v. Winninger*, and the replica of the "Hand of God" sculpture?

3. The *Batlin* court characterizes *Alva Studios* as recognizing originality from "an exactly faithful reproduction" of a public domain work of some complexity. Should that reasoning apply to the digital model of the car in *Meshwerks*?

4. In dissent, Judge Meskill argued: "In accord with the purposes of the copyright law to promote progress by encouraging individual effort through copyright protection, we should require only minimal variations to find copyrightability. The independent sculpting of the mold for the plastic bank and the aggregated differences in size and conformation of the figurine should satisfy this standard." Do you agree?

5. The original Uncle Sam bank received a design patent in 1886, which had long since expired by the time of this case. The Copyright Act of 1831, 4 Stat. 436 (1831), did not include sculptural works, so it is doubtful the creator of the Uncle Sam bank had attempted to copyright its design. By the time of this case in 1975, the 1909 Copyright Act, Pub. L. 60–349, was expanded to include "all the writings of an author," broadly construed to include sculptural works. Accordingly, the defendant Snyder was initially able to register a copyright for his plastic bank. What policy reasons might justify the expansion of copyright to include such items?

6. If copyright does not require novelty, why must there be a substantial variation from a preexisting work that is in the public domain in order for the more recent work to be copyrighted?

---

## 3. FIXATION

### *PROBLEM 4–2*

In 1988, Frank wrote a theatrical production involving acrobatic movements performed above and in a pool of water, on stage. He wrote the directions, scenes, choreography, and set design on a legal pad. He called the show *A* (for aqua). Over the years, Frank has hired numerous performers each year to perform in the show. Frank believes in changing the performers in order to bring new life to the show. Each year, the performers are all different. Some years, for example, the cast are all women. In other years, the cast are all minorities. This year, the cast all have red hair. The choreography, set design, and basic performance have remained the same—as memorialized on Frank's yellow pad—since the start of the show, but each year's performers bring a dramatically new look to the show. And, their performances involve some variations from year to year in speed and force of their movements as well as facial expressions. Do Frank's notes on his legal pad constitute a sufficient fixation of the show *A*? If so, should the copyright extend to each year's performances of the show, notwithstanding the variations from year to year? Consult the following section and the case below.

**U.S. Copyright Act, Section 101**

> A work is "fixed" in a tangible medium of expression when its embodiment in a copy or phonorecord, by or under the authority of the author, is sufficiently permanent or stable to permit it to be perceived, reproduced, or otherwise communicated for a period of more than transitory duration. A work consisting of sounds, images, or both, that are being transmitted, is "fixed" for purposes of this title if a fixation of the work is being made simultaneously with its transmission.

In addition to originality, copyright law requires a work that is fixed "by or under the authority of the author." In most instances, fixation will present no problem. An author routinely memorializes her expression on paper, hard drive of a computer, video, or other means. Fixation is rarely ever contested. Some countries do not even require a fixation of the work. Why do you think the United States does? Consider the following discussion.

---

## KELLEY V. CHICAGO PARK DISTRICT

635 F.3d 290 (7th Cir. 2011)

SYKES, CIRCUIT JUDGE.

### I. Background

[Chapman] Kelley is a painter noted for his use of bold, elliptical outlines to surround scenes of landscapes and flowers. In the late-1970s and 1980s, he moved from the canvas to the soil and created a series of large outdoor wildflower displays that resembled his paintings. He planted the first in 1976 alongside a runway at the Dallas-Fort Worth International Airport and the second in 1982 outside the Dallas Museum of Natural History. The wildflower exhibit at the museum was temporary; the one at the airport just "gradually petered out."

In 1983 Kelley accepted an invitation from Chicago-based oil executive John Swearingen and his wife, Bonnie—collectors of Kelley's paintings—to come to Chicago to explore the possibility of creating a large outdoor wildflower display in the area. He scouted sites by land and by air and eventually settled on Grant Park, the city's showcase public space running along Lake Michigan in the center of downtown Chicago. This location suited Kelley's artistic, environmental, and educational mission; it also provided the best opportunity to reach a large audience. Kelley met with the Park District superintendent to present his proposal, and on June 19, 1984, the Park District Board of Commissioners granted him a permit to install a "permanent Wild Flower Floral Display" on a grassy area on top of the underground Monroe Street parking garage in Daley Bicentennial Plaza in Grant Park. Under the terms of the permit, Kelley was to install and maintain the exhibit at his own expense. The Park District reserved the right to terminate the installation by giving Kelley "a 90 day notice to remove the planting."

Kelley named the project "Chicago Wildflower Works I." The Park District issued a press release announcing that "a new form of 'living' art" was coming to Grant Park—"giant ovals of multicolored wildflowers" created by Kelley, a painter and "pioneer in the use of natural materials" who "attracted national prominence for his efforts to incorporate the landscape in artistic creation." The announcement explained that "[o]nce the ovals mature, the results will be two breathtaking natural canvases of Kelley-designed color patterns."

In the late summer of 1984, Kelley began installing the two large-scale elliptical flower beds at the Grant Park site; they spanned 1.5 acres of parkland and were set within gravel and steel borders. A gravel walkway bisected one of the ovals, and each flower bed also accommodated several large, preexisting air vents that were flush with the planting surface, providing ventilation to the parking garage below. For planting material Kelley selected between 48 and 60 species of self-sustaining wildflowers native to the region. The species were selected for various aesthetic, environmental, and cultural reasons, but also to increase the likelihood that the garden could withstand Chicago's harsh winters and survive with minimal maintenance. Kelley designed the initial placement of the wildflowers so they would blossom sequentially, changing colors throughout the growing season and increasing in brightness towards the center of each ellipse. He purchased the initial planting material—between 200,000 and 300,000 wildflower plugs—at a cost of between \$80,000 and \$152,000. In September of 1984, a battery of volunteers planted the seedlings under Kelley's direction.

**Wildflower Works**

When the wildflowers bloomed the following year, Wildflower Works was greeted with widespread acclaim. Chicago's mayor, the Illinois Senate, and the Illinois Chapter of the American Society of Landscape Artists issued commendations. People flocked to see the lovely display—marketed by the Park District as "living landscape art"—and admiring articles appeared in national newspapers. Wildflower Works was a hit. Here's a picture [included above].

For the next several years, Kelley's permit was renewed and he and his volunteers tended the impressive garden. They pruned and weeded and regularly planted new seeds, both to experiment with the garden's composition and to fill in where initial specimen had not flourished. Of course, the forces of nature—the varying bloom periods of the plants; their spread habits, compatibility, and life cycles; and the weather—produced constant change. Some wildflowers naturally did better than others. Some spread aggressively and encroached on neighboring plants. Some withered and died. Unwanted plants sprung up from seeds brought in by birds and the wind. Insects, rabbits, and weeds settled in, eventually taking a toll. Four years after Wildflower Works was planted, the Park District decided to discontinue the exhibit. On June 3, 1988, the District gave Kelley a 90-day notice of termination. [But the two parties worked out one-year permits extending Kelley's exhibit until 1994; afterwards, Kelley's exhibit remained without a permit until 2004 when the District, after giving notice to Kelley, decreased the exhibit to half its size and changed "the elliptical flower beds into rectangles."]

Kelley then sued the Park District for violating his moral rights under VARA. The case proceeded to a bench trial, and the district court entered judgment for the Park District on the VARA claim and for Kelley on the contract claim.

II. Discussion

[T]he district court's conclusion misunderstands the originality requirement. Originality is "the touchstone of copyright protection today," an implicit constitutional and explicit statutory requirement. *Feist Publ'ns, Inc. v. Rural Tel. Serv. Co.*, 499 U.S. 340, 347, 346 (1991). Despite its centrality in our copyright regime, the threshold for originality is minimal. The "requisite level of creativity is extremely low; even a slight amount will suffice. The vast majority of works make the grade quite easily, as they possess some creative spark." *Id.*

The district court took the position that Wildflower Works was not original because Kelley was not "the first person to ever conceive of and express an arrangement of growing wildflowers in ellipse-shaped enclosed area[s]." This mistakenly equates originality with novelty; the law is clear that a work can be original even if it is not novel. *Feist*, 499 U.S. at 345 ("Originality does not signify novelty; a work may be original even though it closely resembles other works so long as the similarity is fortuitous, not the result of copying."). No one argues that Wildflower Works was copied; it plainly possesses more than a little creative spark.

The judge was also at a loss to discover "what about the exhibit is original. Is it the elliptical design? The size? The use of native instead of non-native plants? The environmentally-sustainable gardening method to which 'vegetative management system' apparently refers?" It is true that common geometric shapes cannot be copyrighted. See U.S. COPYRIGHT OFFICE, COMPENDIUM II: COPYRIGHT OFFICE PRACTICES § 503.02(a)–(b) (1984); 2 PATRY § 4:17 (2010). And "[i]n no case does copyright protection for an original work of authorship extend to any idea, procedure, process, system, method of operation, concept, principle, or discovery, regardless of the form in which it is described, explained, illustrated, or embodied in such a work." 17 U.S.C. § 102(b).

The Park District suggests that Wildflower Works is an uncopyrightable "method" or "system," and is also ineligible because its design uses simple elliptical shapes. The first of these arguments is not well-developed; the second is misplaced. Although Wildflower Works was designed to be largely self-sustaining (at least initially), it's not really a "method" or "system" at all. It's a garden. And Kelley is seeking statutory protection for the garden itself, not any supposed "system" of vegetative management encompassed within it. Regarding the use of elliptical shapes, an author's expressive combination or arrangement of otherwise noncopyrightable elements (like geometric shapes) may satisfy the originality requirement.

The real impediment to copyright here is not that Wildflower Works fails the test for originality (understood as "not copied" and "possessing some creativity") but that a living garden lacks the kind of authorship and stable fixation normally required to support copyright. Unlike originality, authorship and fixation are explicit constitutional requirements; the Copyright Clause empowers Congress to secure for "authors" exclusive rights in their "writings." U.S. CONST. art 1, § 8, cl. 8. The originality requirement is implicit in these express limitations on the congressional copyright power. *See Feist*, 499 U.S. at 346 (The constitutional reference to "authors" and "writings" "presuppose[s] a degree of originality."). The Supreme Court has "repeatedly construed all three terms in relation to one another [or] perhaps has collapsed them into a single concept"; therefore, "[w]ritings are what authors create, but for one to be an author, the writing has to be original." 2 PATRY § 3:20.

"Without fixation," moreover, "there cannot be a 'writing.' " *Id.* § 3:22. A work is "fixed" in a tangible medium of expression "when its embodiment in a copy or phonorecord . . . is sufficiently permanent or stable to permit it to be perceived, reproduced, or otherwise communicated for a period of more than transitory duration." 17 U.S.C. § 101. As William Patry explains:

> Fixation serves two basic roles: (1) easing problems of proof of creation and infringement, and (2) providing the dividing line between state common law protection and protection under the federal Copyright Act, since works that are not fixed are ineligible for federal protection but may be protected under state law. The distinction between the intangible intellectual property (the work of authorship) and its fixation in a tangible medium of expression (the copy) is an old and fundamental and important one. The distinction may be understood by examples of multiple fixations of the same work: A musical composition may be embodied in sheet music, on an audio-tape, on a compact disc, on a computer hard drive or server, or as part of a motion picture soundtrack. In each of the fixations, the intangible property remains a musical composition.

2 PATRY § 3:22 (internal quotation marks omitted).

Finally, "authorship is an entirely human endeavor." *Id.* § 3:19 (2010). Authors of copyrightable works must be human; works owing their form to the forces of nature cannot be copyrighted. *Id.* § 3:19 n. 1; *see also* U.S. COPYRIGHT OFFICE, COMPENDIUM II: COPYRIGHT OFFICE PRACTICES § 503.03(a) ("[A] work must be the product of human authorship" and not the forces of nature.) (1984); *id.* § 202.02(b).

Recognizing copyright in Wildflower Works presses too hard on these basic principles. We fully accept that the artistic community might classify Kelley's garden as a work of postmodern conceptual art. We acknowledge as well that copyright's prerequisites of authorship and fixation are broadly defined. But the law must have some limits; not all conceptual art may be copyrighted. In the ordinary copyright case, authorship and fixation are not contested; most works presented for copyright are unambiguously authored and unambiguously fixed. But this is not an ordinary case. A living garden like Wildflower Works is neither "authored" nor "fixed" in the senses required for copyright. *See Toney v. L'Oreal USA, Inc.*, 406 F.3d 905, 910 (7th Cir. 2005) ("A person's likeness—her persona—is not authored and it is not fixed.").

Simply put, gardens are planted and cultivated, not authored. A garden's constituent elements are alive and inherently changeable, not fixed. Most of what we see and experience in a garden—the colors, shapes, textures, and scents of the plants—originates in nature, not in the mind of the gardener. At any given moment in time, a garden owes most of its form and appearance to natural forces, though the gardener who plants and tends it obviously assists. All this is true of Wildflower Works, even though it was designed and planted by an artist.

Of course, a human "author"—whether an artist, a professional landscape designer, or an amateur backyard gardener—determines the initial arrangement of the plants in a garden. This is not the kind of authorship required for copyright. To the extent that seeds or seedlings can be considered a "medium of expression," they originate in nature, and natural forces—not the intellect of the gardener—determine their form, growth, and appearance. Moreover, a garden is simply too changeable to satisfy the primary purpose of fixation; its appearance is too inherently variable to supply a baseline for determining questions of copyright creation and infringement. If a garden can qualify as a "work of authorship" sufficiently "embodied in a copy," at what point has fixation occurred? When the garden is newly planted? When its first blossoms appear? When it is in full bloom? How—and at what point in time—is a court to determine whether infringing copying has occurred?

In contrast, when a landscape designer conceives of a plan for a garden and puts it in writing—records it in text, diagrams, or drawings on paper or on a digital-storage device—we can say that his intangible intellectual property has been embodied in a fixed and tangible "copy." This writing is a sufficiently permanent and stable copy of the designer's intellectual expression and is vulnerable to infringing copying, giving rise to the designer's right to claim copyright. The same cannot be said of a garden, which is not a fixed copy of the gardener's intellectual property. Although the planting material is tangible and can be perceived for more than a transitory duration, it is not stable or permanent enough to be called "fixed." Seeds and plants in a garden are naturally in a state of perpetual change; they germinate, grow, bloom, become dormant, and eventually die. This life cycle moves gradually, over days, weeks, and season to season, but the real barrier to copyright here is not temporal but essential. The essence of a garden is its vitality, not its fixedness. It may endure from season to season, but its nature is one of dynamic change.

Because Kelley's garden is neither "authored" nor "fixed" in the senses required for basic copyright, it cannot qualify for moral-rights protection under VARA. For the foregoing reasons, we AFFIRM the judgment in favor of the Park District on the VARA claim; we REVERSE the judgment in favor of Kelley on the contract claim and REMAND with instructions to enter judgment for the Park District.

### *NOTES AND QUESTIONS*

1. What is the test of fixation? How did Kelley fail the test in the court's view? If Kelley drew up plans depicting his exhibit in his proposal submitted to Chicago, why did not those plans provide a sufficient fixation of the work? For other types of works, such as an architectural work, choreographic work, or musical work, writing down the building plan, dance routine, or musical notes easily satisfies the fixation requirement. Did the fact that the work involved a living garden affect the court's analysis? If so, should human dancers performing a choreographic work affect the analysis of whether it is fixed?

2. What are the purposes of requiring a fixation of the work? Would those purposes be undermined if the court had found that Kelley's work was fixed?

3. For further critique of *Kelley*, see Roberta R. Kwall, *The Lessons of Living Gardens and Jewish Process Theology for Authorship and Moral Rights*, 14 VAND. J. ENT. & TECH. L. 889, 906 (2012) (arguing that a better test of fixation would require "substantial compliance" that allows room for minimal changes of a work over time, including changes in a garden or a performance of a dance).

4. How do design patent law and trademark law respectively handle the issue of fixation? Do they have a requirement of fixation or something similar that addresses the purposes of fixation?

5. Could Kelley have obtained a design patent or trademark for the design of his garden?

---

## B. PICTORIAL, GRAPHIC, AND SCULPTURAL WORKS

Now that we have an understanding of the two basic prerequisites for a work of authorship to qualify for a copyright, originality and fixation, we can focus on the area that most often involves an issue of design. Copyright law protects works of expression by authors. In some respect, every work has a certain "design," whether a novel, musical composition, or software program. However, design is especially salient today in industries that produce consumer products. Indeed, nearly every successful product these days—ranging from Apple computers, to Michael Kors clothing and Kohler faucets and sinks, to household items sold at Target—incorporate some element of design. Copyright law typically encounters these design issues in the class of pictorial, graphic, and sculptural ("PGS") works.

Section 101 of the Copyright Act defines "pictorial, graphic, and sculptural works" as including "two-dimensional and three-dimensional works of fine, graphic, and applied art, photographs, prints and art reproductions, maps, globes, charts, diagrams, models, and technical drawings, including architectural plans." 17 U.S.C. § 101.

But the Act then excludes utilitarian features in the following way: "Such works shall include works of artistic craftsmanship insofar as their form but not their mechanical or utilitarian aspects are concerned; the design of a useful article, as defined in this section, shall be considered a pictorial, graphic, or sculptural work only if, and only to the extent that, such design incorporates pictorial, graphic, or sculptural features that can be identified separately from, and are capable of existing independently of, the utilitarian aspects of the article." U.S. Copyright Act, § 101. "A 'useful article' is an article having an intrinsic utilitarian function that is not merely to portray the appearance of the article or to convey information. An article that is normally a part of a useful article is considered a 'useful article.'" *Id.*

Thus, in analyzing whether the design of a certain product can by copyrighted, one must ask two questions:

(1) Does the pictorial, graphic, or sculptural work entail or embody a useful article? If not, the work can be potentially copyrighted if it is an original work of authorship.

(2) However, if it is a useful article, one must ask if the aesthetic feature is separable from the utilitarian aspects of the article. If the aesthetic and utilitarian aspects are inseparable, then there can be no copyright. But, if they are separable, the aesthetic feature can be copyrighted to the extent it is an original work of authorship.

Courts struggled for many years in elaborating a workable test of separability. The lower courts adopted several different tests, and the Supreme Court eventually rejected all of them.

### *PROBLEM 4–3*

Alvar, a Finnish designer, was hired by Keene Corp. to design a mannequin head that had the "hungry look of high-fashion, runway models."

The mannequin is to be used by hair and makeup artists to practice hair styles and makeup on the mannequin head. Keene gave Alvar some general instructions about making the mannequin head the standard size of a female head to hold a wig, but gave him complete freedom on how to create the "hungry look." Alvar designed the mannequin head, which he named "Mara," in the figure on the left below:

Mara

Liza

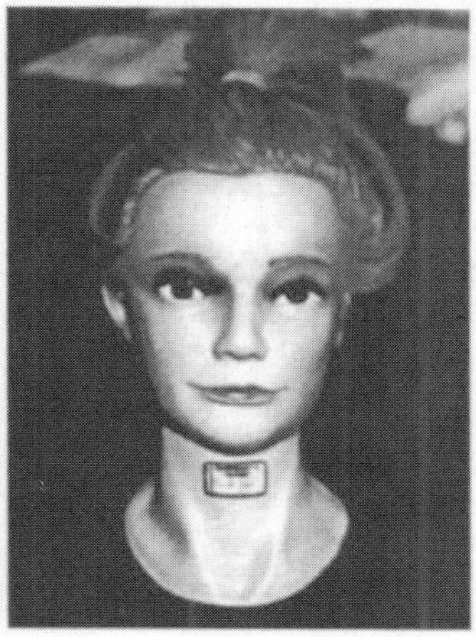

Chow Products copied the Mara design without permission from Keene or Alvar and sold it as a cheaper, competing mannequin head called Liza (shown above on the right). Keene owns the U.S. intellectual property rights to the Mara mannequin head under the agreement with Alvar. Keene now hires you for legal advice on whether its Mara head is copyrightable, so that Keene can sue Chow for copyright infringement. Consult the following two sections on useful articles and separability.

---

## 1. IS THE WORK A USEFUL ARTICLE?

The first part of the useful article/PGS work inquiry asks whether the product entails a useful article? If not, the product design can be potentially copyrighted if it is an original work of authorship. Even though this first inquiry is easier to apply than the separability analysis, courts have sometimes struggled in applying the test of useful article.

### HART V. DAN CHASE TAXIDERMY SUPPLY CO.

86 F.3d 320 (2d Cir. 1996)

CALABRESI, CIRCUIT JUDGE. In *Carol Barnhart Inc. v. Economy Cover Corp.,* 773 F.2d 411, 418–19 (2d Cir. 1985), we held that mannequins of human torsos were not copyrightable sculptural works. The parties before us today dispute whether the Copyright Act protects not human forms, but rather forms designed to hold up fish skins. This case therefore presents a modest question: Is taxidermy different? We hold that it is.

## I. BACKGROUND

The plaintiffs are designers of taxidermy mannequins, which are used to mount animal skins. The plaintiffs registered their creations with the United States Copyright Office, and claim that the defendant, Dan Chase Taxidermy Supply Co. ("Dan Chase"), is infringing their copyrights by selling exact duplicates of their products.

After an evidentiary hearing, the district court concluded that almost all of the animal mannequins at issue (bear, moose, sheep, deer, steer, and antelope) had enough artistic detail to be copyrightable. The only exceptions were fish mannequins. The fish, the court found, had "no meaningful detail . . . that is not commanded by the idea of a realistic fish." Accordingly, it held that the fish "exemplif[ied] the merger of idea and expression" and were not copyrightable. The court dismissed the plaintiffs' claims with regard to the fish and directed that the case proceed to trial to determine whether the other animal mannequins had, in fact, been copied by Dan Chase.

## II. DISCUSSION

Since the plaintiffs registered their fish mannequins with the U.S. Copyright Office, their works enjoy a presumption of protection, 17 U.S.C. § 410(c), and Dan Chase bears the burden of proving that the registered copyrights are invalid, *Barnhart,* 773 F.2d at 414.

The Copyright Act covers "[p]ictorial, graphic, and sculptural works" which include "three-dimensional works of fine, graphic, and applied art, . . . diagrams, [and] models . . . includ[ing] works of artistic craftsmanship insofar as their form but not their mechanical or utilitarian aspects are concerned." 17 U.S.C. § 101. The Act does not, however, protect "useful articles"—that is, articles "having an intrinsic utilitarian function that is not merely to portray the appearance of the article or to convey information." *Id.* A useful article will "be considered a pictorial, graphic, or sculptural work only if, and only to the extent that, such design incorporates pictorial, graphic, or sculptural features that can be identified separately from, and are capable of existing independently of, the utilitarian aspects of the article." *Id.*

Mannequins straddle the line between utilitarian and sculptural works, and so one is tempted to describe them as "useful sculptures." On the one hand, the district court accepted testimony that each sculptor's "intent and purpose in creating the animal mannequins at issue was to make lifelike forms and to capture his or her individual perception of the animals." 884 F. Supp. at 74. Such testimony supports the view that the mannequins are artistic expressions that qualify as protectable "sculptural works." Yet the products indisputably serve a very practical purpose: They act as a mount for animal skins. *Id.* This characteristic suggests that they may be no more than "useful articles," and, as such, not copyrightable. In fact, however, many objects are both useful and works of artistic craftsmanship. Even useful articles, moreover, can gain copyright protection for any "physically or conceptually separable" artistic features. *Barnhart,* 773 F.2d at 418.

The district court in this case, however, did not decide whether the fish mannequins were useful articles, and if they were, whether they nevertheless had any "physically or conceptually separable" artistic features that were copyrightable. (It merely noted that "most" of the animal forms in dispute were not useful articles, 884 F. Supp. at 74, and that "many" of the forms also had conceptually separable artistic aspects, *id.* at 75.) Instead, it held that "even if the fish mannequins are sculptural works or have artistic separable parts, the fish mannequins . . . are not copyrightable" because "there are [so] few ways in which to express the idea of a realistic fish body in a mannequin [that] the expression merges with the idea." *Id.* at 77.

A. Merger of Idea and Expression

We have explained the merger doctrine in the following way: "The fundamental copyright principle that only the expression of an idea and not the idea itself is protectable has produced a corollary maxim that even expression is not protected in those instances where there is only one or so few ways of expressing an idea that protection of the expression would effectively accord protection to the idea itself." *Kregos v. Associated Press,* 937 F.2d 700, 705 (2d Cir. 1991) (citation omitted); *see* 17 U.S.C. § 102(b) ("In no case does copyright protection . . . extend to any idea. . . ."). But, having recognized that the concept of merger differs from the question of infringement, we nevertheless indicated our strong preference for considering, in the context of the infringement inquiry rather than in that of copyrightability, the issue of whether an idea inevitably "merges" with its expression. *Kregos,* 937 F.2d at 705.

We hold that the district court invoked the merger doctrine prematurely. It is true that *Kregos* did not categorically forbid district courts from reaching merger questions before hearing evidence about substantial similarity. There may be highly unusual cases in which virtually all of an idea's possible expressions are before a district court at the copyrightability stage. In such rare cases it may perhaps be possible to determine the merger issue while deciding whether a given expression is copyrightable. But we agree with *Kregos* that this is very unlikely and therefore adhere to our strong preference that the question be decided only after all the evidence of substantial similarity is before the court.

### B. Useful Articles

Dan Chase urges us to affirm anyway, arguing that fish mannequins are "useful articles" and hence are not entitled to copyright protection regardless of merger. It relies primarily on our decision in *Barnhart,* in which we found that styrene human torsos used to display blouses and sweaters were not copyrightable. In that case, the parties had stipulated that the torsos were "useful articles," 773 F.2d at 414, that were designed "to display clothes," *id.* at 418. Taking this concession as our starting point, we concluded that the torsos did not possess separable aesthetic or artistic features, and that nothing about them was therefore copyrightable. Dan Chase argues that the fish mannequins serve the same purpose as the torsos did in *Barnhart*—they act as a mount for skin or clothing. In both cases, Dan Chase says, the "display" function dictates the shape of the mannequin.

We do not agree that *Barnhart* mandates a finding that fish mannequins are "useful articles" undeserving of copyright protection. First, in *Barnhart,* we had no occasion to question the parties' stipulation that the human torsos were "useful articles." But, even apart from the stipulation, we do not believe that the *Barnhart* torsos can be analogized to the fish in this case. In *Barnhart,* the headless, armless, backless styrene torsos were little more than glorified coat-racks used to display clothing in stores. The torsos were designed to present the clothing, not their own forms. In taxidermy, by contrast, people look for more than a fish skin; they wish to see a complete "fish." The superficial characteristics of the fish, such as its color and texture, are admittedly conveyed by the skin, but the shape, volume, and movement of the animal are depicted by the underlying mannequin. Whether the fish is shown as resting, jumping, wiggling its tail, or preparing to munch on some plankton, is dictated by the mannequin and by its particular form, not by the skin. 884 F. Supp. at 74 (crediting expert testimony that "a taxidermist buys a mannequin which expresses the pose, attitude and appearance of the animal that will satisfy his or her customer").

In short, the fish mannequin is designed to be looked at. That the fish mannequin is meant to be viewed clothed by a fish skin, rather than naked and on its own, makes no difference. The function of the fish form is to portray its own appearance, and that fact is enough to bring it within the scope of the Copyright Act. 17 U.S.C. § 101; *accord Superior Form Builders v. Dan Chase Taxidermy Supply Co.,* 74 F.3d 488 (4th Cir. 1996) (distinguishing *Barnhart* and holding that mammal taxidermy mannequins are "sculptural works" rather than "useful articles" because their utilitarian aspects serve "merely to portray the appearance" of the animal).

We conclude that fish mannequins, even if considered "useful articles," are useful insofar as they "portray the[ir] appearance." 17 U.S.C. § 101.

That makes them copyrightable. Accordingly, we vacate the judgment and remand the case.

### *NOTES AND QUESTIONS*

1. What is the test to determine a useful article? If a work of expression is not a useful article, can it be copyrighted?

2. Is the Second Circuit's treatment of the human torso mannequins in *Carol Barnhart* and the fish mannequins in *Hart* consistent?

3. The Second Circuit discusses but does not consider the merger doctrine. Can you explain the merger doctrine? Does it make a difference whether a court considers it as a question of copyrightability or infringement?

4. *Costumes and masks.* The Copyright Office treats costumes and masks differently. Costumes are useful articles because they also provide clothing for the body, according to the Copyright Office. As such, costumes cannot be copyrighted unless they have "separately indentifiable pictorial and/or sculptural authorship." By contrast, the Copyright Office treats masks as *not* useful articles because masks are "merely to portray the appearance" of what the masks portray—thereby falling outside the Copyright Act's definition of useful articles. Masks do not serve as clothing. The Copyright Office treats masks as copyrightable works if they have "minimum pictorial and/or sculptural authorship." If both a costume and mask are sold together as a unit, the Copyright Office "will register the 'work' on the basis of the copyrightable authorship in the mask." Copyright Office, Library of Congress, Registrability of Costume Designs, 56 FR 56530 (1991). Do these distinctions make sense? (After we consider the *Star Athletica* decision below, consider whether the Copyright Office should alter its approach in any way.)

5. *Fashion design.* The Copyright Office has been generally unreceptive to copyright claims for garment designs, including everyday apparel, historical dress, and uniforms. The Office maintains that such garments are useful articles. However, "separately identifiable pictorial representations of designs imposed upon the garment" may be copyrightable if they satisfy the separability analysis. "A two-dimensional design applied to the surface of the clothing may be registered, but this claim to copyright is generally made by the fabric producer rather than the garment or costume designer. Moreover, this claim . . . is ordinarily made when the two-dimensional design is applied to the textile fabric and before the garment is cut from the fabric." Copyright Office, Library of Congress, Registrability of Costume Designs, 56 FR 56530 (1991).

6. Congress has considered proposals to provide a limited form of protection to fashion designs. Innovative Design Protection and Piracy Prevention Act (IDPPPA) (S.3728) was a bill proposed in 2010 and reintroduced as the Innovative Design Protection Act in 2012 (S. 3523). It would amend Chapter 13 of the Copyright Act, which currently only protects boat designs ("the design of a vessel hull, deck, or combination of a hull and deck," 17 U.S.C. § 1301(a)) and grant a 3-year protection for new and original fashion designs. Unlike copyright, fashion design protection would require novelty or something new.

In order to qualify for protection, the design must have "unique, distinguishable, non-trivial and non-utilitarian variation over prior designs." The Act would also create a defense based on independent creation of the same design. Congress has yet to pass the bill, and it appears to have stalled. Should Congress pass the bill? Reconsider the debate between Professors Raustiala and Sprigman versus Professors Hempill and Suk from Chapter 1.

---

## 2. IF SO, IS THE PICTORIAL, SCULPTURAL, OR GRAPHIC ELEMENT SEPARABLE FROM THE USEFUL ARTICLE?

If a useful article is involved, the second part of the inquiry asks whether the aesthetic feature is separable from the utilitarian aspects of the article. Courts struggled for many years to devise a workable test that can identify when something is separable. In 2017, the Supreme Court finally decided the issue in *Star Athletica, L.L.C. v. Varsity Brands, Inc.*

### MAZER V. STEIN

347 U.S. 201 (1954)

MR. JUSTICE REED delivered the opinion of the Court. This case involves the validity of copyrights obtained by respondents for statuettes of male and female dancing figures made of semivitreous china. The controversy centers around the fact that although copyrighted as 'works of art,' the statuettes were intended for use and used as bases for table lamps, with electric wiring, sockets and lamp shades attached.

Respondents are partners in the manufacture and sale of electric lamps. One of the respondents created original works of sculpture in the form of human figures by traditional clay-model technique. From this model, a production mold for casting copies was made. The resulting statuettes, without any lamp components added, were submitted by the respondents to the Copyright Office for registration as 'works of art' or reproductions thereof under § 5(g) or § 5(h) of the copyright law, and certificates of registration issued. Sales (publication in accordance with the statute) as fully equipped lamps preceded the applications for copyright registration of the statuettes. Thereafter, the statuettes were sold in quantity throughout the country both as lamp bases and as statuettes. The sales in lamp form accounted for all but an insignificant portion of respondents' sales.

Petitioners are partners and, like respondents, make and sell lamps. Without authorization, they copied the statuettes, embodied them in lamps and sold them.

The instant case is one in a series of reported suits brought by respondents against various alleged infringers of the copyrights, all presenting the same or a similar question. Petitioners, charged by the present complaint with infringement of respondents' copyrights of reproductions of their works of art, seek here a reversal of the Court of Appeals decree upholding the copyrights. Petitioners in their petition for certiorari present a single question:

> 'Can statuettes be protected in the United States by copyright when the copyright applicant intended primarily to use the statuettes in the form of lamp bases to be made and sold in quantity and carried the intentions into effect?
>
> 'Stripped down to its essentials, the question presented is: Can a lamp manufacturer copyright his lamp bases?'

The first paragraph accurately summarizes the issue. The last gives it a quirk that unjustifiably, we think, broadens the controversy. The case requires an answer, not as to a manufacturer's right to register a lamp base but as to an artist's right to copyright a work of art intended to be reproduced for lamp bases. As petitioners say in their brief, their contention 'questions the validity of the copyright based upon the actions of respondents.' Petitioners question the validity of a copyright of a work of art for 'mass' production. 'Reproduction of a work of art' does not mean to them unlimited reproduction. Their position is that a copyright does not cover industrial reproduction of the protected article. Thus their reply brief states:

> 'When an artist becomes a manufacturer or a designer for a manufacturer he is subject to the limitations of design patents and deserves no more consideration than any other manufacturer or designer.'

It is not the right to copyright an article that could have utility under § 5(g) and (h), note 1, *supra*, that petitioners oppose. Their brief accepts the copyrightability of the great carved golden saltcellar of Cellini but adds:

> 'If, however, Cellini designed and manufactured this item in quantity so that the general public could have salt cellars, then an entirely different conclusion would be reached. In such case, the salt cellar becomes an article of manufacture having utility in addition to its ornamental value and would therefore have to be protected by design patent.'

It is publication as a lamp and registration as a statue to gain a monopoly in manufacture that they assert is such a misuse of copyright as to make the registration invalid.

No unfair competition question is presented. The constitutional power of Congress to confer copyright protection on works of art or their reproductions is not questioned. Petitioners assume, as Congress has in its enactments and as do we, that the constitutional clause empowering legislation 'To promote the Progress of Science and useful Arts, by securing for limited Times to Authors and Inventors the exclusive Right to their respective Writings and Discoveries', Art. I, § 8, cl. 8, includes within the term 'Authors' the creator of a picture or a statue. The Court's consideration will be limited to the question presented by the petition for the writ of certiorari. In recent years the question as to utilitarian use of copyrighted articles has been much discussed.

In answering that issue, a review of the development of copyright coverage will make clear the purpose of the Congress in its copyright legislation. In 1790 the First Congress conferred a copyright on 'authors of any map, chart, book or books already printed'. Later, designing, engraving and etching were included; in 1831 musical composition; dramatic compositions in 1856; and photographs and negatives thereof in 1865.

The Act of 1870 defined copyrightable subject matter as:

> '* * * any book, map, chart, dramatic or musical composition, engraving, cut, print, or photograph or negative thereof, or of a painting, drawing, chromo, *statue, statuary, and of models or designs intended to be perfected as works of the fine arts'.* (Emphasis supplied.)

The italicized part added three-dimensional work of art to what had been protected previously. In 1909 Congress again enlarged the scope of the copyright statute. The new Act provided in § 4:

> 'That the works for which copyright may be secured under this Act shall include all the writings of an author.'

Some writers interpret this section as being coextensive with the constitutional grant, but the House Report, while inconclusive, indicates that it was 'declaratory of existing law' only. Section 5 relating to classes of writings in 1909 read as shown in the margin with subsequent additions not material to this decision. Significant for our purposes was the deletion of the fine-arts clause of the 1870 Act. Verbal distinctions between purely aesthetic articles and useful works of art ended insofar as the statutory copyright language is concerned.

The practice of the Copyright Office, under the 1870 and 1874 Acts and before the 1909 Act, was to allow registration 'as works of the fine arts' of articles of the same character as those of respondents now under challenge. Seven examples appear in the Government's brief amicus curiae. In 1910, interpreting the 1909 Act, the pertinent Copyright Regulations read as shown in the margin. Because, as explained by the Government, this regulation 'made no reference to articles which might fairly be considered works of art although they might also serve a useful purpose,' it was reworded in 1917 as shown below. The amicus brief gives sixty examples selected at five-year intervals, 1912–1952, said to be typical of registrations of works of art possessing utilitarian aspects. The current pertinent regulation, published in 37 CFR, 1949, § 202.8, reads thus:

> 'Works of art (Class G)—(a)—In General. This class includes works of artistic craftsmanship, in so far as their form but not their mechanical or utilitarian aspects are concerned, such as artistic jewelry, enamels, glassware, and tapestries, as well as all works belonging to the fine arts, such as paintings, drawings and sculpture. * * * '

So we have a contemporaneous and long continued construction of the statutes by the agency charged to administer them that would allow the registration of such a statuette as is in question here.

The successive acts, the legislative history of the 1909 Act and the practice of the Copyright Office unite to show that 'works of art' and 'reproductions of works of art' are terms that were intended by Congress to include the authority to copyright these statuettes. Individual perception of the beautiful is too varied a power to permit a narrow or rigid concept of art. As a standard we can hardly do better than the words of the present Regulation, § 202.8, *supra*, naming the things that appertain to the arts. They must be original, that is, the author's tangible expression of his ideas. Compare *Burrow-Giles Lithographic Co. v. Sarony*, 111 U.S. 53, 59–60. Such expression, whether meticulously delineating the model or mental image or conveying the meaning by modernistic form or color, is copyrightable. What cases there are confirm this coverage of the statute.

But petitioners assert that congressional enactment of the design patent laws should be interpreted as denying protection to artistic articles embodied or reproduced in manufactured articles. They say:

> 'Fundamentally and historically, the Copyright Office is the repository of what each claimant considers to be a cultural treasure, whereas the Patent Office is the repository of what each applicant considers to be evidence of the advance in industrial and technological fields.'

Their argument is that design patents require the critical examination given patents to protect the public against monopoly. Attention is called to *Gorham Mfg. Co. v. White*, 14 Wall. 511, 20 L. Ed. 731, interpreting the design patent law of 1842, 5 Stat. 544, granting a patent to anyone who by 'their own industry, genius, efforts, and expense, may have invented or produced any new and original design for a manufacture * * * .' A pattern for flat silver was there upheld. The intermediate and present law differs little. 'Whoever invents any new, original and ornamental design for an article of manufacture may obtain a patent therefor, * * * ' subject generally to the provisions concerning patents for invention. § 171, 66 Stat.

805, 35 U.S.C.A. § 171. As petitioner sees the effect of the design patent law:

> 'If an industrial designer cannot satisfy the novelty requirements of the design patent laws, then his design as used on articles of manufacture can be copied by anyone.'

Petitioner has furnished the Court a booklet of numerous design patents for statuettes, bases for table lamps and similar articles for manufacture, quite indistinguishable in type from the copyrighted statuettes here in issue. Petitioner urges that overlapping of patent and copyright legislation so as to give an author or inventor a choice between patents and copyrights should not be permitted. We assume petitioner takes the position that protection for a statuette for industrial use can only be obtained by patent, if any protection can be given.

As we have held the statuettes here involved copyrightable, we need not decide the question of their patentability. Though other courts have passed upon the issue as to whether allowance by the election of the author or patentee of one bars a grant of the other, we do not. We do hold that the patentability of the statuettes, fitted as lamps or unfitted, does not bar copyright as works of art. Neither the Copyright Statute nor any other says that because a thing is patentable it may not be copyrighted. We should not so hold.

Unlike a patent, a copyright gives no exclusive right to the art disclosed; protection is given only to the expression of the idea—not the idea itself. Thus, in *Baker v. Selden*, 101 U.S. 99, the Court held that a copyrighted book on a peculiar system of bookkeeping was not infringed by a similar book using a similar plan which achieved similar results where the alleged infringer made a different arrangement of the columns and used different headings. The distinction is illustrated in *Fred Fisher, Inc. v. Dillingham, D.C.*, 298 F. 145, 151, when the court speaks of two men, each a perfectionist, independently making maps of the same territory. Though the maps are identical each may obtain the exclusive right to make copies of his own particular map, and yet neither will infringe the other's copyright. Likewise a copyrighted directory is not infringed by a similar directory which is the product of independent work. The copyright protects originality rather than novelty or invention—conferring only 'the sole right of multiplying copies.' Absent copying there can be no infringement of copyright. Thus, respondents may not exclude others from using statuettes of human figures in table lamps; they may only prevent use of copies of their statuettes as such or as incorporated in some other article. Regulation § 202.8, *supra*, makes clear that artistic articles are protected in 'form but not their mechanical or utilitarian aspects.' See *Stein v. Rosenthal, D.C.*, 103 F. Supp. 227, 231. The dichotomy of protection for the aesthetic is not beauty and utility but art for the copyright and the invention of original and ornamental design for design patents. We find nothing in the copyright statute to support the argument that the intended use or use in industry of an article eligible for copyright bars or invalidates its registration. We do not read such a limitation into the copyright law.

"The copyright law, like the patent statutes, makes reward to the owner a secondary consideration." *United States v. Paramount Pictures*, 334 U.S. 131, 158. However, it is "intended definitely to grant valuable, enforceable rights to authors, publishers, etc., without burdensome requirements; 'to afford greater encouragement to the production of literary (or artistic) works of lasting benefit to the world.' " *Washingtonian Pub. Co. v. Pearson*, 306 U.S. 30, 36.

The economic philosophy behind the clause empowering Congress to grant patents and copyrights is the conviction that encouragement of individual effort by personal gain is the best way to advance public welfare through the talents of authors and inventors in 'Science and useful Arts.' Sacrificial days devoted to such creative activities deserve rewards commensurate with the services rendered. Affirmed.

### *NOTES AND QUESTIONS*

1. This case involved the prior 1909 Copyright Act, which did not contain the language regarding separability that the 1976 Copyright Act now includes. Does the Supreme Court adopt a separability analysis to decide whether the statuette is copyrightable? How would you characterize the Court's approach?

2. Some commentators have characterized the decision as exemplifying physical separability: If a pictorial, sculptural, or graphic element can be physically separated from the useful article, such as the statuette from the rest of the lamp, that PGS element can be copyrighted. Do you think this is a helpful way to characterize *Mazer v. Stein*? The Supreme Court would later address—and reject—this characterization in *Star Athletica*, discussed below.

3. The Supreme Court discusses the issue of how design patents and copyrights might both be implicated by an item. Does the Court adopt the election approach requiring selection of only one form of IP protection or the overlapping approach, allowing more than one form of IP protection? Do you agree with the Court's approach?

4. What is a fundamental difference between the requirements for a design patent and those for a copyright? Which law, design patent or copyright, is it easier for an item to qualify for?

---

Over time, the lower courts developed different tests of separability. The Second Circuit was the first circuit to grapple with the issue. It eventually adopted the "design process" test as elaborated in Professor Robert Denicola's article, *Applied Art and Industrial Design: A Suggested Approach to Copyright in Useful Articles*, 67 MINN. L. REV. 707 (1983). The Second Circuit focused on the subjective thought process of the designer in selecting design elements. Design choices "reflecting the designer's artistic judgment exercised independently of functional influences" satisfied conceptual separability. *Brandir Int'l, Inc. v. Cascade Pacific Lumber Co.*, 834 F.2d 1142, 1145 (2d Cir. 1987). However, if the design choices were "significantly influenced by functional considerations," no separability existed. *Id.* at 1146. The Second Circuit test influenced other circuits, some of which adopted it or variations of it. Other circuits departed from it (as summarized below in note 2 following the case below). The Supreme Court finally stepped in.

## STAR ATHLETICA, L.L.C. V. VARSITY BRANDS, INC.

137 S. Ct. 1002 (2017)

Justice THOMAS delivered the opinion of the Court. Congress has provided copyright protection for original works of art, but not for industrial designs. The line between art and industrial design, however, is often difficult to draw. This is particularly true when an industrial design incorporates artistic elements. Congress has afforded limited protection for these artistic elements by providing that "pictorial, graphic, or sculptural features" of the "design of a useful article" are eligible for copyright protection as artistic works if those features "can be identified separately from, and are capable of existing independently of, the utilitarian aspects of the article." 17 U.S.C. § 101.

We granted certiorari to resolve widespread disagreement over the proper test for implementing § 101's separate-identification and independent-existence requirements. We hold that a feature incorporated into the design of a useful article is eligible for copyright protection only if the feature (1) can be perceived as a two- or three-dimensional work of art separate from the useful article and (2) would qualify as a protectable pictorial, graphic, or sculptural work—either on its own or fixed in some other tangible medium of expression—if it were imagined separately from the useful article into which it is incorporated. Because that test is satisfied in this case, we affirm.

### I

Respondents Varsity Brands, Inc., Varsity Spirit Corporation, and Varsity Spirit Fashions & Supplies, Inc., design, make, and sell cheerleading uniforms. Respondents have obtained or acquired more than 200 U.S. copyright registrations for two-dimensional designs appearing on the surface of their uniforms and other garments. These designs are primarily "combinations, positionings, and arrangements of elements" that include "chevrons . . . , lines, curves, stripes, angles, diagonals, inverted [chevrons], coloring, and shapes." At issue in this case are Designs 299A, 299B, 074, 078, and 0815:

Design 299A

Design 299B

Design 074

Design 078

Design 0815

Petitioner Star Athletica, L.L.C., also markets and sells cheerleading uniforms. Respondents sued petitioner for infringing their copyrights in the five designs.

II

The Copyright Act establishes a special rule for copyrighting a pictorial, graphic, or sculptural work incorporated into a "useful article," which is defined as "an article having an intrinsic utilitarian function that is not merely to portray the appearance of the article or to convey information." 17 U.S.C. § 101. The statute does not protect useful articles as such. Rather, "the design of a useful article" is "considered a pictorial, graphical, or sculptural work only if, and only to the extent that, such design incorporates pictorial, graphic, or sculptural features that can be identified separately from, and are capable of existing independently of, the utilitarian aspects of the article."

Courts, the Copyright Office, and commentators have described the analysis undertaken to determine whether a feature can be separately identified from, and exist independently of, a useful article as "separability." In this case, our task is to determine whether the arrangements of lines, chevrons, and colorful shapes appearing on the surface of respondents' cheerleading uniforms are eligible for copyright protection as separable features of the design of those cheerleading uniforms.

### A

As an initial matter, we must address whether separability analysis is necessary in this case. Respondents argue that "[s]eparability is only implicated when a [pictorial, graphic, or sculptural] work is the 'design of a useful article.'" They contend that the surface decorations in this case are "two-dimensional graphic designs that appear on useful articles," but are not themselves designs of useful articles. Under this theory, two-dimensional artistic features on the surface of useful articles are "inherently separable."

This argument is inconsistent with the text of § 101. The statute requires separability analysis for any "pictorial, graphic, or sculptural features" incorporated into the "design of a useful article." "Design" refers here to "the combination" of "details" or "features" that "go to make up" the useful article. 3 OXFORD ENGLISH DICTIONARY 244 (def. 7, first listing) (1933) (OED). Furthermore, the words "pictorial" and "graphic" include, in this context, two-dimensional features such as pictures, paintings, or drawings. *See* 4 *id.*, at 359 (defining "[g]raphic" to mean "[o]f or pertaining to drawing or painting"); 7 *id.*, at 830 (defining "[p]ictorial" to mean "of or pertaining to painting or drawing"). And the statute expressly defines "[p]ictorial, graphical, and sculptural works" to include "two-dimensional ... works of ... art." § 101. The statute thus provides that the "design of a useful article" can include two-dimensional "pictorial" and "graphic" features, and separability analysis applies to those features just as it does to three-dimensional "sculptural" features.

### B

We must now decide when a feature incorporated into a useful article "can be identified separately from" and is "capable of existing independently of" "the utilitarian aspects" of the article. This is not a free-ranging search for the best copyright policy, but rather "depends solely on statutory interpretation." *Mazer v. Stein*, 347 U.S. 201, 214 (1954). We thus begin and end our inquiry with the text, giving each word its "ordinary, contemporary, common meaning." *Walters v. Metropolitan Ed. Enterprises, Inc.*, 519 U.S. 202, 207 (1997) (internal quotation marks omitted). We do not, however, limit this inquiry to the text of § 101 in isolation. "[I]nterpretation of a phrase of uncertain reach is not confined to a single sentence when the text of the whole statute gives instruction as to its meaning." *Maracich v. Spears*, 133 S. Ct. 2191, 2203 (2013). We thus "look to the provisions of the whole law" to determine § 101's meaning. *United States v. Heirs of Boisdore*, 8 How. 113, 122 (1849).

The statute provides that a "pictorial, graphic, or sculptural featur[e]" incorporated into the "design of a useful article" is eligible for copyright protection if it (1) "can be identified separately from," and (2) is "capable of existing independently of, the utilitarian aspects of the article." § 101. The first requirement—separate identification—is not onerous. The decisionmaker need only be able to look at the useful article and spot some two- or three-dimensional element that appears to have pictorial, graphic, or sculptural qualities. *See* 2 PATRY § 3:146, at 3–474 to 3–475.

The independent-existence requirement is ordinarily more difficult to satisfy. The decisionmaker must determine that the separately identified feature has the capacity to exist apart from the utilitarian aspects of the article. *See* 2 OED 88 (def. 5) (defining "[c]apable" of as "[h]aving the needful capacity, power, or fitness for"). In other words, the feature must be able to exist as its own pictorial, graphic, or sculptural work as defined in § 101 once it is imagined apart from the useful article. If the feature is not capable of existing as a pictorial, graphic, or sculptural work once separated from the useful article, then it was not a pictorial, graphic, or sculptural feature of that article, but rather one of its utilitarian aspects.

Of course, to qualify as a pictorial, graphic, or sculptural work on its own, the feature cannot itself be a useful article or "[a]n article that is normally a part of a useful article" (which is itself considered a useful article). § 101. Nor could someone claim a copyright in a useful article merely by creating a replica of that article in some other medium—for example, a cardboard model of a car. Although the replica could itself be copyrightable, it would not give rise to any rights in the useful article that inspired it.

The statute as a whole confirms our interpretation. The Copyright Act provides "the owner of [a] copyright" with the "exclusive righ[t] . . . to reproduce the copyrighted work in copies." § 106(1). The statute clarifies that this right "includes the right to reproduce the [copyrighted] work in or on any kind of article, whether useful or otherwise." § 113(a). Section 101 is, in essence, the mirror image of § 113(a). Whereas § 113(a) protects a work of authorship first fixed in some tangible medium other than a useful article and subsequently applied to a useful article, § 101 protects art first fixed in the medium of a useful article. The two provisions make clear that copyright protection extends to pictorial, graphic, and sculptural works regardless of whether they were created as freestanding art or as features of useful articles.

This interpretation is also consistent with the history of the Copyright Act. In *Mazer*, a case decided under the 1909 Copyright Act, the respondents copyrighted a statuette depicting a dancer. The statuette was intended for use as a lamp base, "with electric wiring, sockets and lamp shades attached." 347 U.S., at 202.

Two of *Mazer*'s holdings are relevant here. First, the Court held that the respondents owned a copyright in the statuette even though it was intended for use as a lamp base. *See id.*, at 214. In doing so, the Court approved the Copyright Office's regulation extending copyright protection to works of art that might also serve a useful purpose. *See ibid.* (approving 37 C.F.R. § 202.8(a) (1949) (protecting "works of artistic craftsmanship, in so far as their form but not their mechanical or utilitarian aspects are concerned")).

Second, the Court held that it was irrelevant to the copyright inquiry whether the statuette was initially created as a freestanding sculpture or as a lamp base. 347 U.S., at 218–219 ("Nor do we think the subsequent registration of a work of art published as an element in a manufactured article, is a misuse of copyright. This is not different from the registration of a statuette and its later embodiment in an industrial article"). *Mazer* thus interpreted the 1909 Act consistently with the rule discussed above: If a design would have been copyrightable as a standalone pictorial, graphic, or sculptural work, it is copyrightable if created first as part of a useful article.

Shortly thereafter, the Copyright Office enacted a regulation implementing the holdings of *Mazer*. *See* 1 NIMMER § 2A.08[B][1][b] (2016). As amended, the regulation introduced the modern separability test to copyright law:

> "If the sole intrinsic function of an article is its utility, the fact that the article is unique and attractively shaped will not qualify it as a work of art. However, if the shape of a utilitarian article incorporates features, such as artistic sculpture, carving, or pictorial representation, which can be identified separately and are capable of existing independently as a work of art, such features will be eligible for registration." 37 C.F.R. § 202.10(c) (1960) (punctuation altered).

Congress essentially lifted the language governing protection for the design of a useful article directly from the post-*Mazer* regulations and placed it into § 101 of the 1976 Act. Consistent with *Mazer*, the approach we outline today interprets §§ 101 and 113 in a way that would afford copyright protection to the statuette in *Mazer* regardless of whether it was first created as a standalone sculptural work or as the base of the lamp.

C

In sum, a feature of the design of a useful article is eligible for copyright if, when identified and imagined apart from the useful article, it would qualify as a pictorial, graphic, or sculptural work either on its own or when fixed in some other tangible medium.

Applying this test to the surface decorations on the cheerleading uniforms is straightforward. First, one can identify the decorations as features having pictorial, graphic, or sculptural qualities. Second, if the arrangement of colors, shapes, stripes, and chevrons on the surface of the cheerleading uniforms were separated from the uniform and applied in another medium—for example, on a painter's canvas—they would qualify as "two-dimensional ... works of ... art," § 101. And imaginatively removing the surface decorations from the uniforms and applying them in another medium would not replicate the uniform itself. Indeed, respondents have applied the designs in this case to other media of expression—different types of clothing—without replicating the uniform. The decorations are therefore separable from the uniforms and eligible for copyright protection.

The dissent [of Justice Breyer] argues that the designs are not separable because imaginatively removing them from the uniforms and placing them in some other medium of expression—a canvas, for example—would create "pictures of cheerleader uniforms." This is not a bar to copyright. Just as two-dimensional fine art corresponds to the shape of the canvas on which it is painted, two-dimensional applied art correlates to the contours of the article on which it is applied. A fresco painted on a wall, ceiling panel, or dome would not lose copyright protection, for example, simply because it was designed to track the dimensions of the surface on which it was painted. Or consider, for example, a design etched or painted on the surface of a guitar. If that entire design is imaginatively removed from the guitar's surface and placed on an album cover, it would still resemble the shape of a guitar. But the image on the cover does not "replicate" the guitar as a useful article. Rather, the design is a two-dimensional work of art that corresponds to the shape of the useful article to which it was applied. The statute protects that work of art whether it is first drawn on the album cover and then applied to the guitar's surface, or vice versa. Failing to protect that art would create an anomaly: It would extend protection to two-dimensional designs that cover a part of a useful article but would not protect the same design if it covered the entire article. The statute does not support that distinction, nor can it be reconciled with the dissent's recognition that "artwork printed on a t-shirt" could be protected.

To be clear, the only feature of the cheerleading uniform eligible for a copyright in this case is the two-dimensional work of art fixed in the tangible medium of the uniform fabric. Even if respondents ultimately succeed in establishing a valid copyright in the surface decorations at issue here, respondents have no right to prohibit any person from manufacturing a cheerleading uniform of identical shape, cut, and dimensions to the ones on which the decorations in this case appear. They may prohibit only the reproduction of the surface designs in any tangible medium of expression—a uniform or otherwise.[2]

D

Petitioner and the Government raise several objections to the approach we announce today. None is meritorious. Petitioner first argues that our reading of the statute is missing an important step. It contends that a feature may exist independently only if it can stand alone as a copyrightable work and if the useful article from which it was extracted would remain equally useful. In other words, copyright extends only to "solely artistic" features of useful articles. Because the uniforms would not be equally useful without the designs, petitioner contends that the designs are inseparable from the "utilitarian aspects" of the uniform. Brief for Petitioner 50. The Government raises a similar argument, although it reaches a different result. It suggests that the appropriate test is whether the useful article with the artistic feature removed would "remai[n] similarly useful." Brief for United States as Amicus Curiae 29 (emphasis added). In the view of the United States, however, a plain white cheerleading uniform is "similarly useful" to uniforms with respondents' designs. *Id.*, at 27–28.

The debate over the relative utility of a plain white cheerleading uniform is unnecessary. The focus of the separability inquiry is on the extracted feature and not on any aspects of the useful article that remain after the imaginary extraction. The statute does not require the decisionmaker to imagine a fully functioning useful article without the artistic feature. Instead, it requires that the separated feature qualify as a nonuseful pictorial, graphic, or sculptural work on its own.

Of course, because the removed feature may not be a useful article—as it would then not qualify as a pictorial, graphic, or sculptural work—there necessarily would be some aspects of the original useful article "left behind" if the feature were conceptually removed. But the statute does not require the imagined remainder to be a fully functioning useful article at all, much less an equally useful one. Indeed, such a requirement would

---

[2] The dissent suggests that our test would lead to the copyrighting of shovels. But a shovel, like a cheerleading uniform, even if displayed in an art gallery, is "an article having an intrinsic utilitarian function that is not merely to portray the appearance of the article or to convey information." 17 U.S.C. § 101. It therefore cannot be copyrighted. A drawing of a shovel could, of course, be copyrighted. And, if the shovel included any artistic features that could be perceived as art apart from the shovel, and which would qualify as protectable pictorial, graphic, or sculptural works on their own or in another medium, they too could be copyrighted. But a shovel as a shovel cannot.

deprive the *Mazer* statuette of protection had it been created first as a lamp base rather than as a statuette. Without the base, the "lamp" would be just a shade, bulb, and wires. The statute does not require that we imagine a nonartistic replacement for the removed feature to determine whether that feature is capable of an independent existence.

Petitioner's argument follows from its flawed view that the statute protects only "solely artistic" features that have no effect whatsoever on a useful article's utilitarian function. This view is inconsistent with the statutory text. The statute expressly protects two- and three-dimensional "applied art." § 101. "Applied art" is art "employed in the decoration, design, or execution of useful objects," WEBSTER'S THIRD NEW INTERNATIONAL Dictionary 105 (1976) (emphasis added), or "those arts or crafts that have a primarily utilitarian function, or . . . the designs and decorations used in these arts," RANDOM HOUSE DICTIONARY 73 (1966) (emphasis added); *see also* 1 OED 576 (2d ed. 1989) (defining "applied" as "[p]ut to practical use"). An artistic feature that would be eligible for copyright protection on its own cannot lose that protection simply because it was first created as a feature of the design of a useful article, even if it makes that article more useful.

Indeed, this has been the rule since *Mazer*. In holding that the statuette was protected, the Court emphasized that the 1909 Act abandoned any "distinctions between purely aesthetic articles and useful works of art." 347 U.S., at 211. Congress did not enact such a distinction in the 1976 Act. Were we to accept petitioner's argument that the only protectable features are those that play absolutely no role in an article's function, we would effectively abrogate the rule of *Mazer* and read "applied art" out of the statute.

Because we reject the view that a useful article must remain after the artistic feature has been imaginatively separated from the article, we necessarily abandon the distinction between "physical" and "conceptual" separability, which some courts and commentators have adopted based on the Copyright Act's legislative history. *See* H.R. Rep. No. 94–1476, p. 55 (1976). According to this view, a feature is physically separable from the underlying useful article if it can "be physically separated from the article by ordinary means while leaving the utilitarian aspects of the article completely intact." COMPENDIUM [OF U.S. COPYRIGHT OFFICE PRACTICES] § 924.2(A) (3d ed. 2014); *see also Chosun Int'l, Inc. v. Chrisha Creations, Ltd.*, 413 F.3d 324, 329 (C.A.2 2005). Conceptual separability applies if the feature physically could not be removed from the useful article by ordinary means. *See* COMPENDIUM § 924.2(B); *but see* 1 P. Goldstein, COPYRIGHT § 2.5.3, p. 2:77 (3d ed. 2016) (explaining that the lower courts have been unable to agree on a single conceptual separability test); 2 PATRY §§ 3:140–3:144.40 (surveying the various approaches in the lower courts).

The statutory text indicates that separability is a conceptual undertaking. Because separability does not require the underlying useful article to remain, the physical-conceptual distinction is unnecessary.

We hold that an artistic feature of the design of a useful article is eligible for copyright protection if the feature (1) can be perceived as a two- or three-dimensional work of art separate from the useful article and (2) would qualify as a protectable pictorial, graphic, or sculptural work either on its own or in some other medium if imagined separately from the useful article. Because the designs on the surface of respondents' cheerleading uniforms in this case satisfy these requirements, the judgment of the Court of Appeals is affirmed. *It is so ordered.*

Justice BREYER, with whom Justice KENNEDY joins, dissenting.

I agree with much in the Court's opinion. But I do not agree that the designs that Varsity Brands, Inc., submitted to the Copyright Office are eligible for copyright protection. Look at the designs that Varsity submitted to the Copyright Office. You will see only pictures of cheerleader uniforms. And cheerleader uniforms are useful articles. A picture of the relevant design features, whether separately "perceived" on paper or in the imagination, is a picture of, and thereby "replicate[s]," the underlying useful article of which they are a part. Hence the design features that Varsity seeks to protect are not "capable of existing independently o[f] the utilitarian aspects of the article." 17 U.S.C. § 101.

I

The relevant statutory provision says that the "design of a useful article" is copyrightable "only if, and only to the extent that, such design incorporates pictorial, graphic, or sculptural features that can be identified separately from, and are capable of existing independently of, the utilitarian aspects of the article." But what, we must ask, do the words "identified separately" mean?

Consider the explanation that the House Report for the Copyright Act of 1976 provides. It says:

> "Unless the shape of an automobile, airplane, ladies' dress, food processor, television set, or any other industrial product contains some element that, *physically or conceptually*, can be identified as separable from the utilitarian aspects of that article, the design would not be copyrighted . . . ." H. R. Rep., at 55 (emphasis added).

These words suggest two exercises, one physical, one mental. Can the design features (the picture, the graphic, the sculpture) be physically removed from the article (and considered separately), all the while leaving the fully functioning utilitarian object in place? If not, can one nonetheless conceive of the design features separately without replicating a picture of the utilitarian object? If the answer to either of these questions is "yes," then the design is eligible for copyright protection. Otherwise, it is not.

An example will help. Imagine a lamp with a circular marble base, a vertical 10-inch tall brass rod (containing wires) inserted off center on the base, a light bulb fixture emerging from the top of the brass rod, and a lampshade sitting on top. In front of the brass rod a porcelain Siamese cat sits on the base facing outward. Obviously, the Siamese cat is physically separate from the lamp, as it could be easily removed while leaving both cat and lamp intact. And, assuming it otherwise qualifies, the designed cat is eligible for copyright protection.

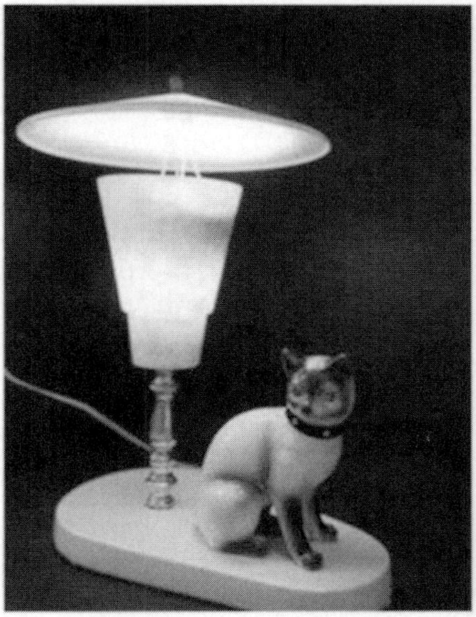

Fig. 1

Fig. 2

Now suppose there is no long brass rod; instead the cat sits in the middle of the base and the wires run up through the cat to the bulbs. The cat is not physically separate from the lamp, as the reality of the lamp's construction is such that an effort to physically separate the cat and lamp will destroy both cat and lamp. The two are integrated into a single functional object, like the similar configuration of the ballet dancer statuettes that formed the lamp bases at issue in *Mazer v. Stein*, 347 U.S. 201 (1954). But we can easily imagine the cat on its own, as did Congress when conceptualizing the ballet dancer. *See* H.R. Rep., at 55 (the statuette in Mazer was "incorporated into a product without losing its ability to exist independently as a work of art"). In doing so, we do not create a mental picture of a lamp (or, in the Court's words, a "replica" of the lamp), which is a useful article. We simply perceive the cat separately, as a small cat figurine that could be a copyrightable design work standing alone that does not replicate the lamp. Hence the cat is conceptually separate from the utilitarian article that is the lamp. The pair of lamps pictured at Figures 1 and 2 illustrate this principle.

By way of contrast, Van Gogh's painting of a pair of old shoes, though beautifully executed and copyrightable as a painting, would not qualify for a shoe design copyright. *See* fig. 3. Courts have similarly denied copyright protection to objects that begin as three-dimensional designs, such as measuring spoons shaped like heart-tipped arrows, candleholders shaped like sailboats, and wire spokes on a wheel cover. None of these designs could qualify for copyright protection that would prevent others from selling spoons, candleholders, or wheel covers with the same design. Why not? Because in each case the design is not separable from the utilitarian aspects of the object to which it relates. The designs cannot be physically separated because they themselves make up the shape of the spoon, candleholders, or wheel covers of which they are a part. [O]ne cannot easily imagine or otherwise conceptualize the design of the spoons or the candleholders or the shoes without that picture, or image, or replica being a picture of spoons, or candleholders, or wheel covers, or shoes. The designs necessarily bring along the underlying utilitarian object. Hence each design is not conceptually separable from the physical useful object.

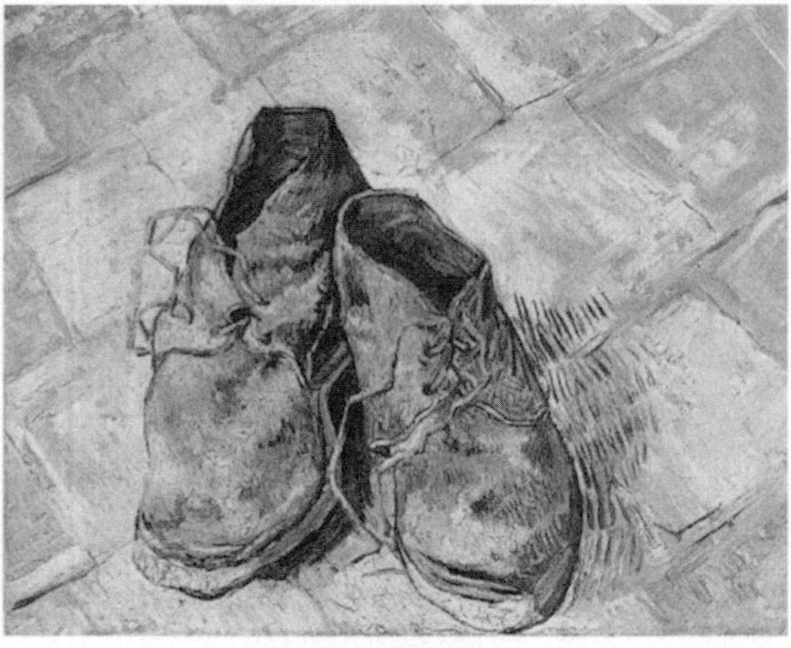

Fig. 3: Vincent Van Gogh, "Shoes"

The upshot is that one could copyright the floral design on a soupspoon but one could not copyright the shape of the spoon itself, no matter how beautiful, artistic, or esthetically pleasing that shape might be: A picture of the shape of the spoon is also a picture of a spoon; the picture of a floral design is not. *See* Compendium § 924.2(B).

II

To ask this kind of simple question—does the design picture the useful article?—will not provide an answer in every case, for there will be cases where it is difficult to say whether a picture of the design is, or is not, also a picture of the useful article. But the question will avoid courts focusing primarily upon what I believe is an unhelpful feature of the inquiry, namely, whether the design can be imagined as a "two- or three-dimensional work of art." That is because virtually any industrial design can be thought of separately as a "work of art": Just imagine a frame surrounding the design, or its being placed in a gallery. Consider Marcel Duchamp's "readymades" series, the functional mass-produced objects he designated as art. *See* fig. 4. What design features could not be imaginatively reproduced on a painter's canvas? Indeed, great industrial design may well include design that is inseparable from the useful article—where, as Frank Lloyd Wright put it, "form and function are one." F. Wright, AN AUTOBIOGRAPHY 146 (1943) (reprint 2005). Where they are one, the designer may be able to obtain 15 years of protection through a design patent. *See also* McKenna & Strandburg, *Progress and Competition in Design*, 17 STAN. TECH. L. REV. 1, 48–51 (2013). But, if they are one, Congress did not intend a century or more of copyright protection.

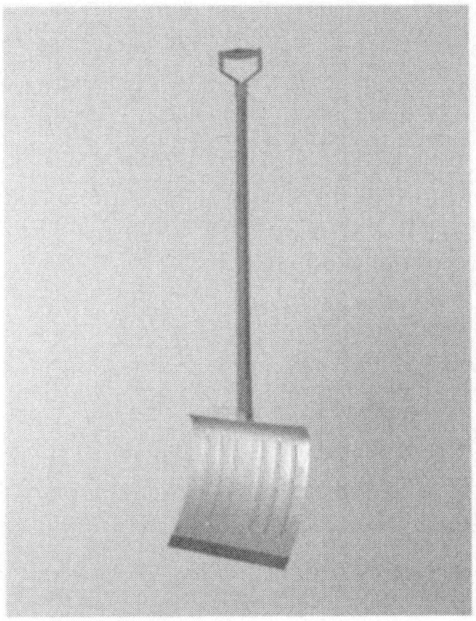

Fig. 4: Marcel Duchamp,
"In Advance of the Broken Arm"

IV

If we ask the "separateness" question correctly, the answer here is not difficult to find. The majority's opinion, in its appendix, depicts the cheerleader dress designs that Varsity submitted to the Copyright Office. Can the design features in Varsity's pictures exist separately from the utilitarian aspects of a dress? Can we extract those features as copyrightable design works standing alone, without bringing along, via picture or design, the dresses of which they constitute a part?

Consider designs 074, 078, and 0815. They certainly look like cheerleader uniforms. That is to say, they look like pictures of cheerleader uniforms, just like Van Gogh's old shoes look like shoes. I do not see how one could see them otherwise. Designs 299A and 2999B present slightly closer questions. They omit some of the dresslike context that the other designs possess. But the necklines, the sleeves, and the cut of the skirt suggest that they too are pictures of dresses. Looking at all five of Varsity's pictures, I do not see how one could conceptualize the design features in a way that does not picture, not just artistic designs, but dresses as well.

Were I to accept the majority's invitation to "imaginatively remov[e]" the chevrons and stripes as they are arranged on the neckline, waistline, sleeves, and skirt of each uniform, and apply them on a "painter's canvas," that painting would be of a cheerleader's dress. The esthetic elements on which Varsity seeks protection exist only as part of the uniform design—there is nothing to separate out but for dress-shaped lines that replicate the cut and style of the uniforms. Hence, each design is not physically separate, nor is it conceptually separate, from the useful article it depicts, namely, a cheerleader's dress. They cannot be copyrighted.

I fear that, in looking past the three-dimensional design inherent in Varsity's claim by treating it as if it were no more than a design for a bolt of cloth, the majority has lost sight of its own important limiting principle. One may not "claim a copyright in a useful article merely by creating a replica of that article in some other medium," such as in a picture. That is to say, one cannot obtain a copyright that would give its holder "any rights in the useful article that inspired it."

With respect, I dissent.

## *NOTES AND QUESTIONS*

1. *Separability.* What test of separability did the Supreme Court adopt? How, if at all, is it different from the Second Circuit's approach in *Brandir*, summarized above? Do you think it would be easier or harder to show separability under the Supreme Court's test? Do you agree with Justice Breyer's dissent and the problems he identifies with the Court's test? Is Breyer's test of separability better?

2. *Lower courts' and other tests of separability.* The Sixth Circuit, in *Star Athletica*, provided a summary of the various tests of separability:

> (1) **The Copyright Office's Approach:** "A pictorial, graphic, or sculptural feature satisfies [the conceptual-separability] requirement only if the artistic feature and the useful article could both exist side by side and be perceived as fully realized, separate works—one an artistic work and the other a useful article." COMPENDIUM III § 924.2(B).
>
> (2) **The Primary-Subsidiary Approach:** A pictorial, graphic, or sculptural feature is conceptually separable if the artistic features of the design are "primary" to the "subsidiary utilitarian function." *Kieselstein-Cord,* 632 F.2d at 993.
>
> (3) **The Objectively Necessary Approach:** A pictorial, graphic, or sculptural feature is conceptually separable if the artistic features of the design are not necessary to the performance of the utilitarian function of the article. *Carol Barnhart, Inc. v. Economy Cover Corp.,* 773 F.2d 411, 419 (2d Cir. 1985).
>
> (4) **The Ordinary-Observer Approach:** A pictorial, graphic, or sculptural feature is conceptually separable if "the design creates in the mind of the ordinary[, reasonable] observer two different concepts that are not inevitably entertained simultaneously." *Id.* at 422 (Newman, J., dissenting).
>
> (5) **The Design-Process Approach:** A pictorial, graphic, or sculptural feature is conceptually separable if the "design elements can be identified as reflecting the designer's artistic judgment exercised independently of functional influences." *Brandir,* 834 F.2d at 1145; *see also Pivot Point Int'l Inc. v. Charlene Prods.,* 372 F.3d 913, 930-31 (7th Cir. 2004); Robert C. Denicola, *supra,* at 741–45.
>
> (6) **The Stand-Alone Approach:** A pictorial, graphic, or sculptural feature is conceptually separable if "the useful article's functionality remain[s] intact once the copyrightable material is separated." *Pivot Point,* 372 F.3d at 934 (Kanne, J., dissenting).
>
> (7) **The Likelihood-of-Marketability Approach:** A pictorial, graphic, or sculptural feature is conceptually separable if " 'there is substantial likelihood that even if the article had no utilitarian use it would still be marketable to some significant segment of the community simply because of its aesthetic qualities.' " *Galiano v. Harrah's Operating Co.,* 416 F.3d 411, 419 (5th Cir. 2005) (quoting 1 NIMMER ON COPYRIGHT § 2.08[B][3]).
>
> (8) **Patry's Approach:** There no need to engage in a separability analysis if (A) the work is the design of a three-dimensional article, and (B) the design is not of a "useful article." 2 PATRY ON COPYRIGHT § 3:145. When determining whether pictorial, graphic, or sculptural features are protectable under the Copyright Act, the

focus should be on whether those pictorial, graphic, or sculptural aspects are separable from the "utilitarian *aspects* " of the article, not the "article" because "the protected features need not be capable of existing apart from the article, only from its functional aspects." *Id.* § 3:146. This task requires two additional steps. *Id.* First, the court "must be able to discern pictorial, graphic, or sculptural features." *Id.* Second, the pictorial, graphic, or sculptural features "must be capable of existing as *intangible* features independent of the utilitarian *aspects* of the useful article, not independent of the whole article. . . ." *Id.* This necessitates asking "whether the pictorial, graphic, or sculptural features are dictated by the form or function of the utilitarian aspects of the useful article." *Id.* If form or function—rather than aesthetics—dictates the way that the pictorial, graphic, or sculptural features appear, then those pictorial, graphic, and sculptural features are not capable of existing independently of the utilitarian aspects of the useful article. *Id.*

(9) **The Subjective-Objective Approach:** Conceptual separability is determined by balancing (A) "the degree to which the designer's subjective process is motivated by aesthetic concerns"; and (B) "the degree to which the design of a useful article is objectively dictated by its utilitarian function." *See* Barton R. Keyes, Note, *Alive and Well: The (Still) Ongoing Debate Surrounding Conceptual Separablility in American Copyright Law*, 69 OHIO ST. L.J. 109, 141 (2008). "The first factor requires courts to consider the degree to which aesthetic concerns, as opposed to functional ones, motivate the designer." *Id.* The second factor considers whether "the design is mostly dictated by function" or "hardly dictated by function at all." *Id.* at 142. If the design of the useful article "is mostly dictated by function," then that fact "weigh[s] against conceptual separability, and therefore, against copyright protection." *Id.* If the design "is hardly dictated by function at all" then that fact "weigh[s] in favor of a finding of conceptual separability." *Id.*

799 F.3d 468 (6th Cir. 2015), *rev'd*, 137 S. Ct. 1002 (2017). Do you prefer any of the above tests to the one adopted by the Supreme Court? Which test do you think provides the best way to determine separability of pictorial, graphic, or sculptural works?

3. The Supreme Court rejected the approaches of the lower courts in several respects. First, and most importantly, the Court did not adopt any test from a lower court, despite plenty of alternatives to choose from. Instead, without even discussing the various tests of the lower courts, the Court fashioned its own test from the language of the Copyright Act. Second, the Court rejected the distinction between physical and conceptual separability that some courts had adopted. Can you explain why? Third, the Court recognized two different requirements of separability based on the language "[1] can be identified separately from, and [2] are capable of existing independently of, the

utilitarian aspects of the article," whereas the lower courts had conflated the two into one requirement. 17 U.S.C. § 101 (bracketed numbers added).

4. *Imagined*. A key part of the separability test is whether the feature can be imagined as a pictorial, graphic, or sculptural work separate from the useful article in which it is incorporated. Does the Court explain from what perspective a court is to imagine? Ordinary observer? Reasonable person? Ordinary person skilled in the art?

5. *Section 113(a)*. How does the Court explain the purpose of § 113(a), which states: "Subject to the provisions of subsections (b) and (c) of this section, the exclusive right to reproduce a copyrighted pictorial, graphic, or sculptural work in copies under section 106 includes the right to reproduce the work in or on any kind of article, whether useful or otherwise." In her concurrence in the judgment, Justice Ginsburg argued that Varsity Brands' designs at issue were, in fact, two-dimensional works that were later reproduced onto Varsity's uniforms. If Justice Ginsburg's characterization is accurate, should the case have been decided under § 113(a)?

6. For an insightful discussion of useful articles and separability, see Jane C. Ginsburg, *"Courts Have Twisted Themselves Into Knots": U.S. Copyright Protection for Applied Art*, 40 COLUM. J.L. & ARTS 1 (2016).

## *PROBLEM 4–4*

David Levine designed a sleek, curved design for a bike rack, shown below:

Under the Supreme Court's test of separability, is the bike rack design copyrightable?

## C. ARCHITECTURAL WORKS

### *PROBLEM 4–5*

Emilia, an architect, designed and constructed the building in Figure 1 below in 2017. She describes its key features as consisting of "(1) alternating concave and convex sections; (2) three prominent elevator shafts that protrude above the roof of the building; (3) rounded building ends; (4) constant radius curves; (5) holes in the building; (6) a twin tower design; (7) see-through floor plans; (8) a circular plaza; (9) a central fountain; and (10) a rooftop pool and landscape elements." The building design won an award from a prominent architectural magazine. (1) Is Emilia's building design copyrightable as an architectural work? (2) Don designed the building in Figure 2 below. He admits seeing Emilia's building (from public view) before he created his building, but insists that he did not infringe Emilia's copyright (assuming her design is copyrightable). Is Don's building design substantially similar to Emilia's and therefore infringing? Consult the following two cases and notes.

**Figure 1. Emilia's building design**

**Figure 2. Don's building design**

---

Another type of work that prominently involves design is an architectural work. In 1990, Congress amended the Copyright Act to recognize copyright for architectural works. Prior to 1990, architectural plans could be copyrighted as pictorial or graphic works, but the actual buildings were not protected. Therefore, a third party could copy the design of a building simply by looking at the building itself without violating the copyright to the architectural plan. By contrast, the Copyright Act now protects the design of the building. Section 101 defines an "architectural work" as "the design of a building as embodied in any tangible medium of expression, including a building, architectural plans, or drawings. The work includes the overall form as well as the arrangement and composition of spaces and elements in the design, but does not include individual standard features." 17 U.S.C. § 101.

Instead of the separability approach that applies to PGS works, Congress chose instead to avoid the difficulties of separability analysis. Legislative history suggests that Congress intended to exclude only those elements that are "functionally required" in the design of a building. The House Committee on the Judiciary described functionality as follows: "If such [original] design elements are present, a second step is reached to examine whether the design elements are functionally required. If the design elements are not functionally required, the work is protectible without regard to physical or conceptual separability." H.R. Rep. No. 101–735 (1990) reprinted in 1990 U.S.C.C.A.N. 6935, 6951–52.

## SHINE V. CHILDS

382 F. Supp. 2d 602 (S.D.N.Y. 2005)

MUKASEY, DISTRICT JUDGE. Plaintiff Thomas Shine sues David M. Childs and Skidmore, Owings & Merrill, LLP (SOM) for copyright infringement. Shine alleges that he created designs for an original skyscraper which Childs saw and later copied in the first design plan for the Freedom Tower at the World Trade Center (WTC) site. Defendants move to dismiss the Complaint, or alternatively for summary judgment. For the reasons explained below, defendants' motion for summary judgment is granted in part and denied in part.

I.

The facts viewed in the light most favorable to the plaintiff, are as follows. In fall 1999, Shine was a student in the Masters of Architecture Program at the Yale School of Architecture. As part of the required curriculum in his program, he took a studio class on skyscrapers taught by renowned architect Cesar Pelli. The object of this studio was to create a design proposal for a monumental skyscraper that would be built on West 32nd Street in Manhattan and used by the media during the 2012 Olympic Games; the building was to be adjacent to the proposed West Side stadium.

During the first half of October 1999, Shine developed a preliminary model for his design, which he refers to as "Shine '99" for the purposes of this litigation. Plaintiff describes Shine '99 as a tower that tapers as it rises, with "two straight, parallel, roughly triangular sides, connected by two twisting facades, resulting in a tower whose top [is] in the shape of a parallelogram."

By the end of the fall 1999 semester, Shine had developed a more sophisticated model of his design, entitled "Olympic Tower." Shine describes this structure as "a twisting tower with a symmetrical diagonal column grid, expressed on the exterior of the building, that follows the twisting surface created by the floor plates' geometry." According to Shine, the column grid he designed gives rise to "an elongated diamond pattern, supporting a textured curtain wall with diamonds interlocking and protruding to create a crenelated appearance."

On or about December 9, 1999, Shine presented his designs for Olympic Tower to a jury of experts invited by the Yale School of Architecture to evaluate and critique its students' work. During a 30-minute presentation to the panel, Shine explained his tower's structural design, and displayed different structural and design models (including Shine '99), renderings, floor plans, elevations, sections, a site plan, and a photomontage giving a visual impression of the tower's exterior. Defendant Childs was on the panel, and he praised Olympic Tower during the presentation, as did the other luminaries evaluating Shine's work. When the review was completed, Shine was applauded by the jury and other visitors, which, according to Shine, is "highly unusual" at a student's final review. After the presentation, Childs approached Shine, complimented Shine's color pencil rendering of Olympic Tower, and invited Shine to visit after his graduation.

Childs' favorable reaction to Olympic Tower was also documented in *Retrospecta,* an annual alumni magazine[3] published by the Yale School of Architecture featuring selected works by the school's current students. The 1999–2000 edition of *Retrospecta* featured a large composite photographic rendering of Olympic Tower set against an imaginary New York sunset, in addition to smaller inset photographs of two of Shine's models of the tower. Favorable comments from the panel members were printed next to the photographic rendering, including the following compliment from Childs: "It is a very beautiful shape. You took the skin and developed it around the form—great!" Shine does not allege that he had any contact with Childs after the December 1999 panel evaluation. However, he does claim that Childs' design for the Freedom Tower, unveiled four years later, infringed Shine '99 and Olympic Tower.

Childs did not begin work on the Freedom Tower until summer 2003. In order to choose the best possible design for the rebuilt WTC, the Lower Manhattan Development Corporation and the Port Authority of New York and New Jersey held an architectural competition in 2002 and 2003, in search of a master WTC site plan. In February 2003, Studio Daniel Libeskind's plan entitled "Memory Foundations" was selected as the winning design. In summer 2003, WTC developer Larry Silverstein asked Childs, who is a Consulting Design Partner at SOM, to begin working as

---

[3] Because Childs is an alumnus of the Yale School of Architecture, he presumably received a copy of this issue of *Retrospecta.* However in his Answer, Childs denies that he ever saw a copy of the issue referenced by Shine in the Complaint. (Durschinger Aff. Ex. D, ¶ 12).

design architect and project manager for the tallest building at the proposed new WTC site as conceptualized by Libeskind—the building that later would be called the Freedom Tower. Libeskind was to serve as collaborating architect during the initial concept and schematic design phases. In spite of what was described as a "difficult marriage" between Childs and Libeskind, a design for the Freedom Tower was completed within six months, and was presented to the public at a press conference at Federal Hall in lower Manhattan on December 19, 2003. At this presentation, SOM and Childs displayed six large computer-generated images of the Freedom Tower; two scale models of the Tower; and a computer slide show detailing the Tower's design principles. They also distributed a press packet containing six images of the proposed Tower.

As described by Shine, this version of the Freedom Tower "tapers as it rises and has two straight, parallel, roughly triangular facades on opposite sides, with two twisting facades joining them." Shine alleges that this design is substantially similar to the form and shape of Shine '99, and that it incorporates a structural grid identical to the grid in Olympic Tower, as well as a facade design that is "strikingly similar" to the one in Olympic Tower. Apparently, others at the Yale School of Architecture noticed the similarity between the Freedom Tower and Shine's design: According to plaintiff's expert, Yale Professor James Axley, several days after Childs unveiled the design for the Freedom Tower, one of Shine's original models for Olympic Tower "was retrieved from archival storage and placed on the desk of the Dean of the School of Architecture."

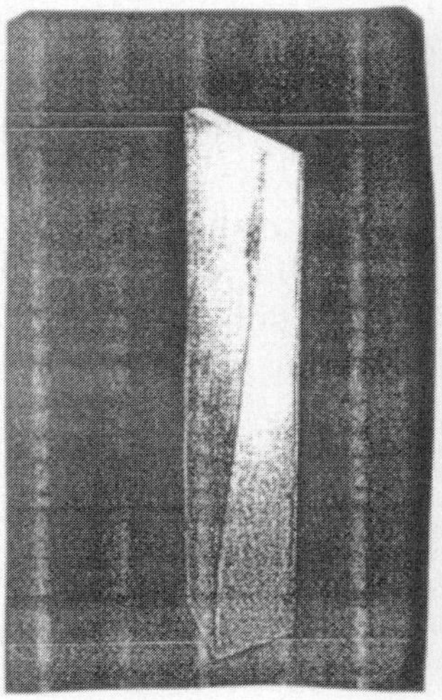
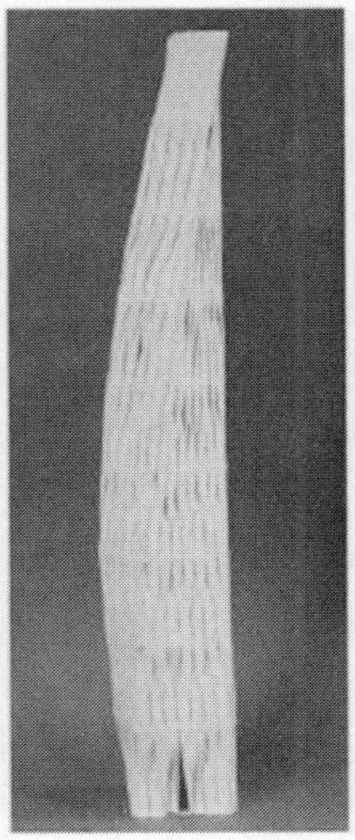
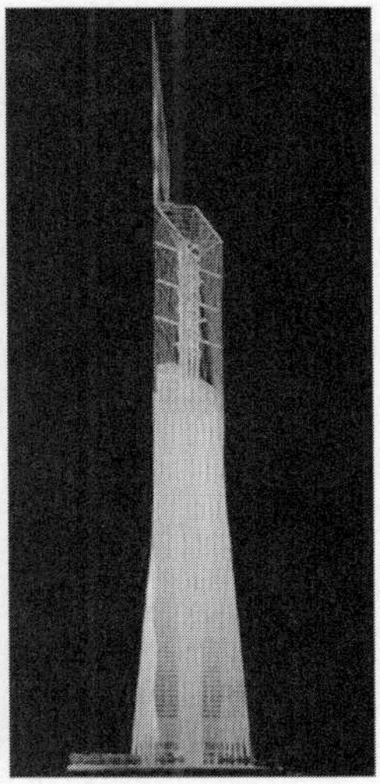

**Shine's 99 design** **Shine's Olympic Tower** **Childs' Freedom Tower**

Shine registered Olympic Tower as an architectural work with the U.S. Copyright Office on March 30, 2004, and did the same for Shine '99 on

June 24, 2004. He filed the Complaint in this action on November 8, 2004, claiming that defendants copied his designs without his permission or authorization, and stating that defendants distributed and claimed credit for his designs "willfully and with conscious disregard" for his rights in his copyrighted works.

Shine requests an injunction to prevent further infringement by defendants, as well as actual damages and defendants' profits realized by their infringement. Defendants move to dismiss the Complaint, or alternatively for summary judgment, claiming that Shine's works are not original and not worthy of protection, and further arguing that there is no substantial similarity between either work and the Freedom Tower.

It should be noted that in June 2005, after law enforcement authorities, among others, objected to the Freedom Tower's original design, Childs, SOM, and Libeskind unveiled a substantially redesigned version of the Tower. The alleged infringing design apparently has been scrapped and is unlikely to be constructed. The new version has, at least to this court's untrained eye, little similarity to either of Shine's copyrighted works, and the court assumes that Shine makes no claim that it infringes his works. Because the alleged infringing design may never be constructed, Shine's actual damages in this action may be reduced, and he may be unable to show the need for an injunction. But because defendants' original design for the Freedom Tower remains in the public domain, Shine's infringement claim stands.

II.

To prevail, plaintiff must prove " '(1) ownership of a valid copyright, and (2) copying of constituent elements of the work that are original.' " *Williams [v. Crichton],* 84 F.3d 581, 587 (2d Cir. 1996) (quoting *Feist Publ'ns, Inc. v. Rural Tel. Serv. Co.,* 499 U.S. 340, 361 (1991)). To prove copying of original elements of his work, in addition to showing originality, plaintiff must demonstrate both that defendants actually copied his works, and that such copying was illegal because there is substantial similarity between each of his works and the alleged infringing work—the Freedom Tower.

A. Architectural Works Under the Copyright Act

Prior to 1990, the United States did not allow structures to be copyrighted, except those few that did not serve any utilitarian purpose. However, in 1989, the United States became a party to the Berne Convention for the Protection of Literary and Artistic Works, which required protection for " 'three dimensional works relative to . . . architecture.' " *See id.* (quoting Berne Convention for the Protection of Literary and Artistic Works, revised at Paris, July 24, 1971, art. 2, 828 U.N.T.S. 221). Membership in the Berne Convention required the United States to protect works of architecture; therefore, in 1990, Congress amended the Copyright Act, adding the Architectural Works Copyright Protection Act (AWCPA), which included architectural works as a new category of copyrightable material.

The AWCPA defines an architectural work as:

> the design of a building as embodied in any tangible medium of expression, including a building, architectural plans, or drawings. The work includes the overall form as well as the arrangement and composition of spaces and elements in the design, but does not include individual standard features.

17 U.S.C. § 101. Defendants cite various portions of the legislative history of the AWCPA to argue that Shine's models are not architectural works meriting copyright protection. They claim that Shine's works are preliminary or conceptual, and do not meet the standard of a "design of a building." They argue also that plans for the "design of a building" may be protected only if a building actually could be constructed from the plans.

Defendants cite no cases to support their reading of the AWCPA. The statute nowhere states or implies that only designs capable of construction are worthy of protection. Although our Circuit has not specifically articulated the standard by which an architectural design is to be evaluated under the Copyright Act, when considering pictorial, graphic, and sculptural (PGS) works, also protected by the Act, *see* 17 U.S.C. § 101, it has twice noted that plans or designs not sufficiently detailed to allow for construction still may be protected. This reasoning should apply equally to architectural works, because our Circuit also has held that " '[i]n general, architectural works are subject to the same standards that apply to other copyrightable works.' " *Attia v. Soc'y of the N.Y. Hosp.*, 201 F.3d 50, 53 n.3 (2d Cir. 1999) (quoting 1 Nimmer § 2.20[A]). It is true that "generalized ideas and concepts pertaining to the placement of elements, traffic flow, and engineering strategies," or in other words, "ideas and concepts," are not worthy of protection. *Id.* at 57. However, once a design includes "specific expression and realization of . . . ideas," copying constitutes infringement. *Sparaco v. Lawler, Matusky & Skelly Eng'rs LLP*, 303 F.3d 460, 469 (2d Cir. 2002).

Both Shine '99 and Olympic Tower are worthy of protection under the AWCPA. Shine '99 is a scale model of a twisting tower: Two of the tower's sides are smooth and taper straight toward the top creating a roughly triangular shape; the other two sides twist and taper as they rise, and one of those sides features four graded setbacks or levels that narrow as the tower rises. The top of the tower forms a parallelogram. Shine '99, although certainly a rough model, is more than a concept or an idea; it is a distinctive design for a building. As explained above, whether a tower actually could be constructed from this model is irrelevant. Defendants argue that the shape and form of Shine '99 are so rudimentary and standard that protecting it would be akin to protecting a particular geometric shape, such as "an ellipse, a pyramid, or an egg." However, the AWCPA protects "the design of a building as embodied in any tangible medium of expression . . . [including] the overall form as well as the arrangement and composition of spaces and elements in the design. . . ." 17 U.S.C. § 101. Individual arguably "standard" elements of Shine '99, such as its twist or its setbacks, might not be worthy of protection, but the arrangement and composition of the various elements in the model do at least arguably constitute the "design of a building" under the AWCPA.

The same is true for Olympic Tower, which is a much more intricate and detailed design than Shine '99. The copyrighted Olympic Tower materials include two models of the tower, one of the building's internal supports and one of its external appearance. Both models show that the building twists on all four sides; comparing the models reveals that the internal diamond-shaped grid supporting the tower is reflected and repeated in the external "skin" on its facade—a design that Childs commented on during his evaluation of Shine's work. Shine also copyrighted elevation sketches of the tower to display the building's core at different levels, a photomontage of what the building might look like against the New York sky, as well as what appears to be a sketch of the undulating triangular grid design for the exterior, of the building. The detailed and specific materials Shine copyrighted for Olympic Tower certainly constitute the "design of a building," and qualify it as an architectural work under the AWCPA.

### B. Originality

Defendants next claim that neither Shine '99 nor Olympic Tower is sufficiently original to warrant protection under the AWCPA. Using the House Committee Report on the AWCPA as their guide, defendants argue for a two-step analysis of the originality and functionality of an architectural work: First, the House Report noted, the work in question should be examined for the presence of original design elements. If such elements exist and are not functionally required, the Report concluded, then the work is protectable. Following this framework, defendants argue that no single part of Shine's work is original; that any parts that might be original are functionally required to support its design and therefore unprotectable; and that the arrangement of the various design elements featured in Shine's work is a compilation not meriting protection under existing law.

In this analysis, defendants fly high and fast over the large body of Supreme Court and Second Circuit case law on originality and copyright infringement, as well as the text of the AWCPA, which states that "the overall form as well as the arrangement and composition of spaces and elements in the design" of an architectural work may be the subject of a valid copyright. 17 U.S.C. § 101. First, defendants fail to acknowledge that plaintiff's "certificates of [copyright] registration constitute prima facie evidence of the validity not only of their copyrights, but also of the originality of [the] works." *Boisson v. Banian, Ltd.*, 273 F.3d 262, 268 (2d Cir. 2001); *see also* 17 U.S.C. § 410(c). It is also true, however, that originality is "the sine qua non of copyright," *Feist,* 499 U.S. at 345, and if a work is not original, then it is not protectable. If a certain element within a work is not original, that element is not protectable "even if other elements, or the work as a whole, warrant protection." *Boisson,* 273 F.3d at 268.

Plaintiff need not clear a high bar in order for his architectural works to qualify as original:

> In the copyright context, originality means the work was independently created by its author, and not copied from someone else's work. The level of originality and creativity that must be shown is minimal, only an "unmistakable dash of originality need be demonstrated, high standards of uniqueness in creativity are dispensed with."

*Folio Impressions, Inc. v. Byer California,* 937 F.2d 759, 764–65 (2d Cir. 1991) (quoting *Weissmann v. Freeman,* 868 F.2d 1313, 1321 (2d Cir. 1989)). Additionally, our Circuit has held that "a work may be copyrightable even though it is entirely a compilation of unprotectible elements." *Knitwaves [v. LollyTogs Ltd.],* 71 F.3d 996, 1003–04 (2d Cir. 1995).

If the court followed defendants' suggestion and analyzed the elements of plaintiff's works separately, comparing only those elements that are copyrightable to those present in the designs for the Freedom Tower, as our Circuit noted, "we might have to decide that there can be no originality in a painting because all colors of paint have been used somewhere in the past." *Id.* at 1003.

Following this analysis, both Shine '99 and Olympic Tower at least arguably are protectable and original. It is true that, as defendants' expert points out, twisting towers have been built before. Towers with diamond-windowed facades have been built before. Towers with support grids similar to the one in Olympic Tower have been built before. Towers with setbacks have been built before. But defendants do not present any evidence that the particular combinations of design elements in either Shine '99 or Olympic Tower are unoriginal. These works each have at least the mere "dash of originality" required for copyrightability, not to mention that they both have been copyrighted, and therefore are prima facie original.

Defendants argue also that any original aspect of Olympic Tower's facade is functionally required by the support grid utilized by Shine, and therefore unprotectable. However, Shine's expert disputes this contention. Therefore, even if certain of the original design elements of Olympic Tower are dictated by functionality and therefore not copyrightable—a proposition for which there is no apparent support in the case law or the AWCPA—a material issue of fact on this matter remains for trial.

## FRANK BETZ ASSOCIATES, INC. V. SIGNATURE HOMES, INC.

2010 WL 1373268, No. 3:06–0911 (March 29, 2010)

JOHN T. NIXON, SENIOR DISTRICT JUDGE. This is a copyright infringement case brought against Defendants Signature Homes, Inc., Brian Burns, and Signature Partnership, LLC's ("Signature Defendants") by Plaintiff Frank Betz Associates, Inc. ("Betz"). Signature Defendants have also filed a Third Party Complaint against Third Party Defendants Christopher L. Turner, Turner Designs, and Turner Designs, Inc.'s (collectively referred to as "Turner Defendants"). After granting in part and denying in part the Parties' summary judgment motions, the Court granted Signature Defendants' Motion to Separate Trial. A bench trial on the issue of the functionality was held in this Court on August 11–12, 2009. For the following reasons, the Court finds that Plaintiff has met its burden of persuasion and therefore ENTERS JUDGMENT in favor of Plaintiff on the question of functionality.

### I. PROCEDURAL AND FACTUAL BACKGROUND

At issue in this case are eleven stock single-family home plan designs distributed and marketed by Betz ("the Betz Designs"). Betz asserts thirteen counts of copyright infringement against Signature Defendants Specifically, Betz alleges that Signature published, distributed, marketed, and advertised thirteen home plans based upon the Betz Designs and marketed, advertised, and sold houses built from the Betz Designs. Betz is seeking permanent injunctive relief, destruction of the infringing copies, and damages. Per this Court's August 7, 2009 Clarification Order, the bench trial proceeded on the narrow question of the protectible, non-functional elements of Plaintiff's designs.

### II. FINDINGS OF FACT AND CONCLUSIONS OF LAW

#### A. Copyright in Architectural Works

The Copyright Act protects original works of authorship fixed in a tangible medium of expression, including architectural works. 17 U.S.C. § 102(a) (1990). Before the 1990 Amendment to the Copyright Act, architectural plans received very minimal protection as "pictorial, graphic, and sculptural works" subject to the "useful article doctrine," 1–2 *Nimmer on Copyright* § 2.08, and architectural buildings that served a utilitarian purpose, such as houses, received no protection. *Id.* at § 2.20. The 1990 Amendment to the Copyright Act, also called the Architectural Works Copyright Protection Act, added a new category of protectible "architectural works" defined as:

> the design of a building as embodied in any tangible medium of expression, including a building, architectural plans, or drawings. The work includes the overall form as well as the arrangement and composition of spaces and elements in the design, but does not include individual standard features.

*Id.* (citing 17 U.S.C. § 101). While standard features are not protected, "the creator's independent selection and arrangement of component parts into an overall, original design" may be protected. 1–2 *Nimmer* § 2.20 (internal citation omitted). The expressions "overall form" and "standard features" are designed to give the court guidance "regarding the nature of the protected matter" in what must be an ad hoc extent of protection analysis. *Id.* (citing H.R. Rep. No. 101–735 (1990)). Architectural works created on or after December 1, 1990, qualify for this protection. *Id.*

The owner of a copyright has the exclusive right to, among other rights not applicable here: (1) reproduce the copyrighted work; (2) prepare derivative works; (3) distribute copies of the work; and (4) publically display the work. 17 U.S.C. § 106. To bring a claim of infringement of any of these exclusive rights, a plaintiff must demonstrate both "(1) ownership of a valid copyright; and (2) copying of constituent elements of the work that are original." *Stromback v. New Line Cinema,* 384 F.3d 283, 293 (6th Cir. 2004) (citing *Feist Publ'ns, Inc. v. Rural Tel. Serv. Co.,* 499 U.S. 340, 361 (1991)). Plaintiff's claim of ownership of valid copyrights in the eleven Betz Designs was granted in summary judgment.

To prove the second prong of the *Feist/Stromback* infringement analysis, a plaintiff must first show copying. As is often the case, when there is no direct evidence of copying, a plaintiff may establish an inference of copying by showing: "(1) access to the allegedly-infringing work by the defendant(s) and (2) a substantial similarity between the two works at issue." *Kohus v. Mariol,* 328 F.3d 848, 854 (6th Cir. 2002). Access is defined as "having a reasonable opportunity to [view] the plaintiff['s] work and thus having the opportunity to copy." *Stromback,* 384 F.3d at 293. The Sixth Circuit has adopted a two-part test for substantial similarity: (1) "identifying which aspects of the artist's work, if any, are protectible by copyright"; and (2) "determining whether the allegedly infringing work is 'substantially similar' to the protectible elements of the artist's work." *Id.* at 294.

As to what is protectible under copyright, architectural works, as their own subject matter category under the Copyright Act, are unique. While no longer hindered by the physical or conceptual separability test of pictorial, graphic, and sculptural works, courts must weigh function when considering architectural works infringement. *See* 1–2 *Nimmer* § 2.20 (the legislative history affords protection for architectural works only when the design elements are not functionally required). The Legislative History of the 1990 Amendment sets forth a two part functionality test in which the

Court must: (1) determine whether there are original design elements present, including overall shape and interior architecture; and, if so, (2) examine whether the design elements are functionally required. H.R. Rep. No. 101–735. Non-functionally required elements will be protected without considering physical or conceptual separability. 1–2 *Nimmer* § 2.20 at n. 29. After establishing the protectible elements of an architectural work, if any, the Plaintiff must then prove copying. *See Kohus,* 328 F.3d at 854.

In determining the protectible aspects of the architectural work, the Court must first identify whether there are original design elements present, including overall shape and interior architecture. 1–2 *Nimmer* § 2.20 at n. 29. While the case law is little help in guiding the Court as to what, if any, constitute original design elements of an architectural plan, *see Tiseo Architects, Inc. v. B & B Pools Service & Supply Co.,* 495 F.3d 344, 347 (6th Cir. 2007); *La Resolana Architects, PA. v. Reno, Inc.,* 555 F.3d 1171, 1179 (10th Cir. 2009); *Oravec v. Sunny Isles Luxury Ventures, L.C.,* 527 F.3d 1218, 1225–27 (11th Cir. 2008): *T-Peg, Inc., et al. v. Vermont Timber Works, Inc., et al.,* 459 F.3d 97, 113–14 (1st Cir. 2006), the Legislative History of the 1990 Amendment indicates that standard features not contemplated for protection under the definition of architectural works include "common windows, doors, or other staple building components." H.R. Rep. No. 101–735. "[T]he arrangement and composition of spaces and elements in the design," including interior architecture, however, may qualify as an original design element. *Id.* This Court found, in its Order on the Parties' summary judgment motions, that the eleven Betz designs display original design elements in the way that their standard features are arranged.

The second prong of the protectibility test for architectural works is an examination of whether the design elements are functionally required. *See* 1–2 *Nimmer* § 2.20 at n. 29. While both the originality and the non-functionality of a copyrighted work are presumptively established by the copyright registration, *Lexmark Intern., Inc. v. Static Control Components, Inc.,* 387 F.3d 552, 534 (6th Cir. 2004), Plaintiff has put forth evidence to convince the Court, and Defendants have not tendered sufficient rebuttal evidence to refute, that the overall design and arrangement of the eleven Betz Designs are not functionally required, although they contain functional elements, and are therefore protectible under copyright.

The Legislative History indicates that the Architectural Works Copyright Act specifically contemplated protection for buildings that perform a function—for example, habitable or useful structures such as houses, office buildings, and churches—while instructing courts to examine whether original design elements of those buildings are functionally required or functionally determined. H.R. Rep. No. 101–735. Non-functionally required elements will be protected without considering physical or conceptual separability. *See* 1–2 *Nimmer* § 2.20 at n. 29.

Plaintiff has shown that although the component parts of a house, as captured in a house plan, perform certain functions, the overall design and arrangement of those component parts is not functionally required. Defendant's expert witness James Edwards conceded that the only things required for a house to function as a house are four walls, a roof, and an entrance/exit. Edwards further explained that a designer's choices as to the internal arrangement of a house plan are not functionally required. Plaintiff's expert witness agreed that although elements of the Betz designs were functional, each design's particular arrangement was not functionally required. Just as someone using a kaleidoscope mixes standard colors into a new pattern, there are certain common features that go into a house design—a kitchen, bathroom, bedrooms—and the designer moves each of those elements into an original, potentially protectible arrangement.

While both experts agree that some outside constraints, including market demands, dictate aspects of home plan designs, the Court does not find that these external considerations undermine protection for the plans as a whole. There is no standard for house plans. Building codes constrain the ultimate design of a house, and while zoning or historic preservation ordinances may affect the exterior design, they do not dictate the interior arrangement of rooms. Plaintiff's witness Eric Taylor explained that when designing plans, Betz considers the changing taste of the middle class and strives for a "sweet spot where the majority of buyers are" in terms of house square footage and expectations concerning number of bedrooms and amenities. The number of bedrooms for any design may be limited, to some extent, by square footage and, likewise, the width and depth of the lot may influence a design. However, courts routinely protect modern architectural structures and plans, including commercial homes, possessing the minimal amount of originality required by copyright. *See, e.g., Axelrod v. Cherveny Architects, P.C. v. Winmar Homes,* No. 2:05–cv–711–ENV–ETB, 2007 WL 708798, at *9 (E.D.N.Y. March 6, 2007). And the fact that the creator of a house plan factored marketability into the design renders the plan no less worthy of protection than a pop song designed for mass appeal.

Defendants argue that courts should be particularly wary of granting copyright protection to non-custom residential housing where creativity is often *de minimus,* there is a vast, existing body of public domain material, and the adverse consequences of overprotection could be serious. *See Patry on Copyright,* § 3:1:08. Yet, according to the legislative history, "[e]vidence that there is more than one method of obtaining a given functional result may be considered in evaluating . . . the scope of protection." H.R. Rep. No. 101–735. The sheer number of Betz designs as issue and the number of designs cited by the experts in their testimony point to the various ways that even the features shared by these designs—such as number of bedrooms—may be arranged in original ways. These designs display the minimum amount of originality necessary for protection under the

Copyright Act. *See id.* Although comprised of functional elements, the Betz designs do not rise to the level of functionality such that copyright protection cannot be extended to them. As discussed in the legislative history: "creativity in architecture frequently takes the form of a selection, coordination, or arrangement of unprotected elements into an original, protectable whole." *Id.; see also Sturdza v. United Arab Emirates,* 281 F.3d 1287, 1296 (D.C. Cir. 2002) ("protectible expression may arise through the ways in which artists combine even unprotectible elements"). Plaintiff has established that the overall design and arrangement of the Betz Designs are not functionally required, and are therefore protectible under copyright. Judgment is ENTERED for Plaintiff Betz on the issue of the functionality of the Betz Plans. It is so ORDERED.

### *NOTES AND QUESTIONS*

1. *Originality.* Do you think Shine's design for the Olympic Tower satisfies originality? What elements, if any, are original? The House Committee on the Judiciary noted: "The phrase 'arrangement and composition of spaces and elements" recognizes that: (1) creativity in architecture frequently takes the form of a selection, coordination, or arrangement of unprotectible elements into an original, protectible whole; (2) an architect may incorporate new, protectible design elements into otherwise standard, unprotectible building features; and (3) interior architecture may be protected.'" H.R. Rep. No. 101–735 (1990) reprinted in 1990 U.S.C.C.A.N. 6935, 6949.

2. *Functionality.* The *Shine* court does not consider whether the design elements are functional, leaving that issue for trial. Do you think "the original design elements of Olympic Tower are dictated by functionality"? What would you consider to determine if a design element is "functionally required"? Does the *Betz* decision provide some guidance on how to determine functionality? Is this test of functionality easier to apply than the test of conceptual separability for PGS works? Other courts have taken a more expansive view of what is considered functional in architectural works. *See, e.g., Zalewski v. Cicero Builder Dev., Inc.*, 754 F.3d 95, 105-06 (2d Cir. 2014) (considering efficiency concerns—including "design elements attributable to building codes, topography, structures that already exist on the construction site, or engineering necessity"—to be functional).

3. How does this test of functionality for architectural designs compare to the test for functionality for design patents and for trademarks?

4. What is the definition of "architectural work"? If a person sketched a design of a house, would it qualify as an architectural work even before the house is built? What if the house is never built or the design defies the principles of engineering and could not possibly be built as designed? Hint: consider the *Shine* case.

5. *Building.* The Copyright Office regulation defines "building" in the following way: "The term building means humanly habitable structures that are intended to be both permanent and stationary, such as houses and office

buildings, and other permanent and stationary structures designed for human occupancy, including but not limited to churches, museums, gazebos, and garden pavilions." 37 C.F.R. § 202.11(b)(2). The regulation excludes "[s]tructures other than buildings, such as bridges, cloverleafs, dams, walkways, tents, recreational vehicles, mobile homes, and boats."

6. *Individual standard features.* The Copyright Office includes "windows, doors, and other staple building components" as examples of individual standard features that are not copyrightable as an architectural work. 37 C.F.R. § 202.11(d).

7. *Effective date of AWCPA.* The U.S. granted copyright protection for architectural works created on or after Dec. 1, 1990. The preexisting architectural works were not protected with one exception. The Act extended protection for architectural works that had been embodied in unpublished plans before Dec. 1, 1990, but that had not been built. However, to receive copyright, the architectural works must have been built by Dec. 31, 2002. Prior to the Architectural Works Copyright Protection Act (AWCPA), architectural plans and models received copyright protection as pictorial, graphic, or sculptural works. (Plans and models can still receive copyright protection today as PGS works.) But the copyright for plans and models did not extend to the physical structure of a building (a useful article). Thus, if a person copied the design of a building by looking at the physical structure of the building, the copyright for the architectural plan would not be infringed. *See Nat'l Med. Care, Inc. v. Espiritu,* 284 F. Supp. 2d 424, 435 (S.D.W.Va. 2003). However, now with copyright for architectural works, the copyright for the work may be infringed. The scope of protection is broader.

8. *Section 120 exemption.* The Copyright Office has two important limitations to the copyright for architectural works:

> (a) Pictorial Representations Permitted.—The copyright in an architectural work that has been constructed does not include the right to prevent the making, distributing, or public display of pictures, paintings, photographs, or other pictorial representations of the work, if the building in which the work is embodied is located in or ordinarily visible from a public place.
>
> (b) Alterations to and Destruction of Buildings.—Notwithstanding the provisions of section 106 (2), the owners of a building embodying an architectural work may, without the consent of the author or copyright owner of the architectural work, make or authorize the making of alterations to such building, and destroy or authorize the destruction of such building.

17 U.S.C. § 120. Why do you think Congress included these exemptions only for architectural works and not other types of works, such as public sculptures?

---

## D. COPYRIGHT OWNERSHIP AND WORKS MADE FOR HIRE

### *PROBLEM 4–6*

Amanda is in the process of opening a cupcake shop called Bliss. She hired Raven, a freelance web designer who is just starting in web design, to design a website for Bliss for a payment of $2,000. Amanda discussed her vision for the website with Raven and was actively involved in plans for the design of the website. She told her ideas to Raven, "I would like pink and white to be the dominant colors, with Instagram-style photographs of my cupcakes prominently sliding through the center of the home page every few seconds. The look should be clean, minimalist, and focus on the cupcakes in the photographs that I will provide you." Raven took Amanda's ideas and wrote the computer code necessary to give expression to Amanda's ideas in a beautifully designed website. Amanda and Raven did not have a written agreement for the website design. Excluding the photographs (for which Amanda owns the copyrights), who owns the copyright to the website design? Hint: Is the website design a work made for hire or not? To answer this problem, consider the following discussion and case. Assume that Amanda and Raven would not be considered joint authors. Consider the following discussion and case.

**U.S. Copyright Act, Section 101**

A "work made for hire" is—

> (1) a work prepared by an employee within the scope of his or her employment; or
>
> (2) a work specially ordered or commissioned for use as a contribution to a collective work, as a part of a motion picture or other audiovisual work, as a translation, as a supplementary work, as a compilation, as an instructional text, as a test, as answer material for a test, or as an atlas, if the parties expressly agree in a written instrument signed by them that the work shall be considered a work made for hire. For the purpose of the foregoing sentence, a "supplementary work" is a work prepared for publication as a secondary adjunct to a work by another author for the purpose of introducing, concluding, illustrating, explaining, revising, commenting upon, or assisting in the use of the other work, such as forewords, afterwords, pictorial illustrations, maps, charts, tables, editorial notes, musical arrangements, answer material for tests, bibliographies, appendixes, and indexes, and an "instructional text" is a literary, pictorial, or graphic work prepared for publication and with the purpose of use in systematic instructional activities. * * *

**U.S. Copyright Act, Section 201**

(b) Works Made for Hire.—

> In the case of a work made for hire, the employer or other person for whom the work was prepared is considered the author for purposes of this title, and, unless the parties have expressly agreed otherwise in a written instrument signed by them, owns all of the rights comprised in the copyright.

---

A key question in situations involving employees and independent contractors is who owns the copyright. The Copyright Act has a special provision for "works made for hire." 17 U.S.C. § 201. An independent contractor who creates a work typically owns the copyright to her work. However, the parties can, by a written agreement signed by them, agree to treat the work as a work made for hire, in which case the person who hired the independent contractor is the copyright owner and even the author. Such "specially commissioned works" are limited to 9 types of works: "(1) a contribution to a collective work, (2) a part of a motion picture or other audiovisual work, (3) a translation, (4) a supplementary work, (5) a compilation, (6) an instructional text, (7) a test, (8) answer material for a test, or (9) an atlas." *Id.* § 101.

By contrast, employee creators are not typically treated as the authors of works they create within the scope of their employee. Instead, employers are considered both the authors and the copyright owners of the works created by their authors. *Id.* This treatment occurs by operation of law and no written agreement is necessary.

## JUSTMED, INC. V. BYCE

600 F.3d 1118 (9th Cir. 2009)

BETTY B. FLETCHER, CIRCUIT JUDGE: At the heart of this case is a dispute over whether a small technology start-up company owns the source code developed for its product. Its informal employment practices raise questions as to whether defendant-appellant Michael Byce was an employee when he developed the source code.

### I

Joel Just and Michael Byce are former brothers-in-law who together developed the idea of a digital audio larynx, a device to help laryngectomees—individuals whose larynxes have been surgically removed—produce clearer speech. Both have degrees in electrical engineering and experience working in the computer industry. Initially, the two began discussing the idea in 1994 on a family vacation. Just and Byce brainstormed ideas for how to advance such devices—in particular how to produce a hands-free device, rather than one that required the user to hold the device against the throat—and, in 1995, they applied for a patent as co-inventors of a "system and method for monitoring the oral and nasal cavity," which was issued to them in 1998.

Byce worked on the project between 1995 and 1998, but no one did any further work on the device from 1999—when Byce's wife, the sister of Just's wife Ann, unexpectedly died—until 2003. Then, in 2003, Joel and Ann Just formed JustMed, Inc., based in Beaverton, Oregon, to continue development of the product. Just recruited a former business associate, Jerome Liebler, to help work on the idea. He offered founders' options to Byce, and Byce ultimately invested $25,000 in return for 130,000 shares. Byce also accepted a position on JustMed's board of directors, serving with the Justs.

Just and Liebler worked full time developing a new hardware prototype and writing source code for the product.[1] Liebler wrote a majority of the code, working at his home on his own computers. The code was never released outside of the company, and notices on the code stated that it was copyrighted by JustMed, although the code was not registered with the United States Copyright Office. Since it was not yet producing a product, the company operated financially by selling shares to family members and by relying on loans from the Justs. Just and Liebler did not receive a cash salary and instead were compensated with shares of stock.

By the summer of 2004, JustMed had a marketable product called "JusTalk." Liebler, however, moved to Kentucky, making it difficult for him to continue his work on the product. At the same time, Byce expressed interest in becoming more involved with the company. Liebler was still drawing half of his salary, but agreed to have the whole package—at that point, $90,000 per year, paid as 15,000 shares per month, each share valued at 50 cents—transferred to Byce and to have Byce take over development of the source code.

At trial, Just testified that Byce was hired as an employee to replace Liebler, who was also an employee, and that Byce agreed to be paid a salary in shares of stock. Byce, on the other hand, testified that while he expected to be adequately compensated in shares upon transferring ownership of the source code, he never understood himself to be an employee and had no "explicit knowledge" that he was accruing shares as compensation.

JustMed and Byce had no written employment agreement. Byce never filled out an I–9 employment verification form or, until 2005, a W–4 tax withholding form. At most, Just documented Byce's salary and duties in a notebook that he kept, although the notation indicating when Byce started was not recorded until several months after Byce began working on the source code. Although Byce began full-time work on the source code in

[1] Source code is code written in a programming language that is readable by humans. Object code is produced by rendering those same programming instructions in a binary form that the computer can read, a process known as compiling.

September 2004 and began accruing JustMed stock in October, he never received share certificates for the stock he received as compensation. Indeed, the company generally did not keep formal records other than a series of notebooks Just maintained to track conversations and events. While Byce worked for JustMed, the company did not issue Byce a W–2 wage statement form, withhold taxes, or pay workers' compensation or unemployment insurance. Nor did the company provide benefits for Byce or report his employment to the state. Just testified that he did not think much of this was necessary because he thought of Byce as a JustMed "executive," and because JustMed was modeled on prior startup technology businesses that Just had been involved with, where employees were paid exclusively in stock and the stock was never reported as income because of its uncertain value.

Although Byce was carrying on Liebler's duties, Byce operated differently, because he did not live and work in Oregon as Liebler had. Instead, Byce worked from his home in Boise, Idaho, using his own computer. Just provided Byce with the original code created by Liebler and various materials necessary to Byce's development work, including JusTalk units, schematics, data sheets, batteries, chargers, assemblers, source code, and headsets. Byce set his own hours, often working late into the night, and Just did not tell him how to spend his days. As Byce developed new versions of the source code, he would e-mail the new version to Just, who would compile it and load it onto the JusTalk to evaluate its performance. Whereas Just had previously worked side-by-side with Liebler, Just and Byce often communicated by phone or e-mail, and occasionally would meet in Boise or Portland or somewhere in between. The two exchanged ideas and discussed the functionality of the code, as well as improvements that needed to be made. Just, admittedly a poor programmer, never made changes to the source code, and by the time this dispute arose, Byce had substantially rewritten the source code Liebler had developed. According to Byce, only 21 lines of code from the last version Liebler worked on remained, out of approximately 3500 to 4000 lines total.

While he was working on the source code, Byce was included in the company profile brochure and had a JustMed business card. He was alternatively referred to as the "Director of Research and Development" and the "Director of Engineering," the latter title supplied by Byce himself. Although he was primarily working on the source code, Byce also updated the company Web site and attended conferences, marketing meetings, and demonstrations on behalf of JustMed.

Because he was not earning money, Byce was living on credit, and by May 2005 he was worried about his financial situation. He told Just that he would soon need cash. In response, Just agreed to have JustMed pay Byce half in cash and half in shares. Byce filled out a W–4 form, and the company issued three checks for him as payment for May, June, and July

2005. Byce, however, never cashed the checks. At this point, Byce became concerned that Just did not view him as an equal in the corporation. In order to protect what he perceived as his intellectual property, Byce changed the copyright statement on the software, so that it now read "Copyright (c) Mike Byce 2005" instead of copyright JustMed.

Then, while Byce was working in the Oregon office two days before Just was scheduled to meet with a potential merger or buy-out partner, Byce deleted all copies of the source code from JustMed's computers. Byce testified that he made the decision after seeing a spreadsheet showing a large disparity between the number of shares Byce owned and those shares that the Justs and Liebler owned. In its memorandum decision, the district court found that Byce deleted the code to gain leverage over Just in Byce's efforts to acquire a greater share of the company. The next day, Byce raised with Just the disparity in ownership between Byce and the other primary shareholders. The two talked for several hours, but Just declined to give additional shares to Byce. During this conversation, Byce did not mention that he had deleted the source code from JustMed's computers.

Just still had a recent version of the object code loaded on a JusTalk unit, but after flying to Chicago for his demonstration meeting, Just could not get the unit to work. Hoping this was a curable problem, Just tried to recompile the source code on his laptop and then load it onto the unit, only to discover that he no longer had a copy of the source code. Just called Byce about the missing code, but Byce claimed to have assumed "revision control," meaning that he had removed the source code to insure that no one else would make changes to it.

Only upon returning to Oregon did Just realize that Byce had deleted the source code from all of JustMed's computers. Just was able to recover some prior versions of the source code files, but not the most recent one. Byce later returned the latest version of the source code, with some of the programmer's notes removed, but only after JustMed filed suit against Byce and the Idaho state court issued a temporary restraining order.[2] Because Just did not trust the code he received from Byce, JustMed has since worked from older versions of the code to develop the device.

JustMed filed suit in state court, and Byce removed the case to federal court, asserting that it required determination of ownership of the software under the Copyright Act. After a bench trial, the district court found in favor of JustMed and held that Byce was an employee when he wrote the software, so that JustMed owned the copyright to the software. The court

[2] Programmer's notes or comments are annotations within the source code that comment on the source code and try to make it easier to understand. While such comments are typically ignored by the compiler or interpreter when compiling source code because they do not affect the operation of the object code, several of JustMed's witnesses testified that they considered the comments part of the software.

also found Byce liable for misappropriation of a trade secret, conversion, and breach of his fiduciary duty. This timely appeal followed.

III

A

Under the Copyright Act of 1976, copyright ownership "vests initially in the author or authors of the work." 17 U.S.C. § 201(a). An exception exists, however, for "works made for hire," in which case "the employer or other person for whom the work was prepared is considered the author" and owns the copyright, unless there is a written agreement to the contrary. *Id.* § 201(b). As it is relevant here, a "work made for hire" is "a work prepared by an employee within the scope of his or her employment." 17 U.S.C. § 101. Thus, whether Byce owns the source code copyright turns on whether he was an employee of JustMed or an independent contractor.

The Supreme Court has explained that absent any textual indications to the contrary, when Congress uses the terms "employee," "employer," or "scope of employment," it means to incorporate principles from the general common law of agency. *Community for Creative Non-Violence v. Reid*, 490 U.S. 730, 740–41 (1989) (*CCNV*). Accordingly, "the hiring party's right to control the manner and means by which the product is accomplished" is the central inquiry here. *CCNV*, 490 U.S. at 751. Factors relevant to this inquiry include: the skill required for that occupation, the source of the instrumentalities and tools, the location of the work, the duration of the relationship between the parties, whether the hiring party has the right to assign additional projects to the hired party, the extent of the hired party's discretion over when and how long to work, the method of payment, the hired party's role in hiring and paying assistants, whether the work is part of the regular business of the hiring party, whether the hiring party is in business, the provision of employee benefits, and the tax treatment of the hired party. *Id.* at 751–52 (citing Restatement (Second) of Agency § 220(2) (1958)). Because "the common-law test contains no shorthand formula or magic phrase that can be applied to find the answer, all of the incidents of the relationship must be assessed and weighed with no one factor being decisive." *Nationwide Mut. Ins. Co. v. Darden,* 503 U.S. 318, 324 (1992) (quoting *NLRB v. United Ins. Co. of Am.,* 390 U.S. 254, 258 (1968)) (quotation marks and alteration omitted).

Byce argues on appeal that the district court improperly weighed the factors and ignored crucial facts, especially JustMed's tax treatment of Byce, the failure to provide him with benefits, the failure to fill out appropriate employment forms, the lack of any written agreement regarding Byce's employment or salary, and the lack of stock certificates for shares Byce was accruing.

However, taking the various factors into account, we conclude that the district court did not err in finding that Byce was an employee. In particular, the contemplated duration of the relationship, the tasks Byce did for JustMed, the fact that Byce earned a salary from JustMed, and the nature of JustMed's business all support the finding that Byce was an employee. While no one factor is decisive, we draw some guidance in weighing the factors from JustMed's status as a technology start-up company. The evidence of the way JustMed operates gives support to the finding that Byce was an employee. Admittedly, some of the factors that Byce points to support his position, but mostly they are entitled to little weight when viewed in light of the way JustMed conducts its business.

JustMed hired Byce primarily to work on the JusTalk software, but he was not hired for a specific term or with a discretely defined end product in mind. *Cf. CCNV,* 490 U.S. at 753 (independent contractor hired for single task of producing sculpture). JustMed continuously worked on the source code to improve its effectiveness and capability. Although Byce's work on the source code lasted only nine months, it was halted not because the code's development had reached a logical termination point but because of the parties' dispute. Thus, the fact that the parties contemplated a relationship of indefinite duration cuts in favor of finding Byce an employee.

Byce did other work for JustMed as well. He updated the company's Web site and demonstrated the JusTalk units at tradeshows. Byce had previously worked on the Web site when he acted only as a director and shareholder for the company, but his continued work on tasks besides programming indicates JustMed could have assigned additional projects to Byce. Moreover, his formal title indicates that he had broad duties within JustMed, as well as a relationship with the company that was intended to be permanent.

JustMed hired Byce to replace Liebler, an employee, and paid him the same salary that Liebler received.[5] At trial Byce disputed that there was any agreement as to how he would be paid, and Byce continues to argue that the lack of a written agreement regarding salary and the lack of stock certificates undermine the salience of this factor. But the district court did not find credible Byce's inability to recall what he was being paid and how. Although independent contractors are often paid upon completion of a specific job, *see CCNV,* 490 U.S. at 753 (independent contractor was to be paid upon completion of sculpture), Byce was paid a regular monthly salary in the same way as other JustMed employees. This weighs heavily in favor

---

[5] While an employer's designation of a person as an employee or independent contractor is not always relevant because employers often have an incentive to designate an individual as one or the other, both Liebler and JustMed believed they had an employee-employer relationship. *See* Restatement (Second) of Agency § 220(2)(I) (listing parties' subjective conceptions of the relationship as one factor in master-servant determination). This fact cuts in favor of similarly finding Byce an employee, as he essentially stepped into Liebler's role. That Byce replaced Liebler also indicates that the JusTalk software was an ongoing concern for the company, not a discrete project that JustMed expected Byce to simply finish and be done with.

of finding him an employee, even though much of the salary came in the form of stock.

Also militating in favor of JustMed is the fact that its primary business was the development and marketing of the JusTalk device. Byce's work was integral to JustMed's regular business, since the JusTalk cannot work without functioning software. *Cf. Aymes,* 980 F.2d at 863 (finding programming work for swimming pool company not part of the firm's regular business but stating that "work done by a computer programmer employed by a computer software firm would be done in the firm's regular business"). Indeed, there is evidence that JustMed tried to sell consumers on the JusTalk precisely by emphasizing that the software could constantly be updated. It seems highly unlikely that JustMed would leave such an important, continuous responsibility to an independent contractor who would terminate his relationship with the company upon completing a working version of the software.

While some factors initially seem to favor Byce, on closer examination they are insufficient to find him an independent contractor. It is true, for example, that Just did not exercise much control over the manner and means by which Byce created the source code. However, this is not as important to a technology start-up as it might be to an established company. Byce was an inventive computer programmer expected to work independently. The business model and Byce's duties do not require that the project be completed in a particular manner or that Just continuously oversee Byce's work, so long as JustMed eventually found itself with a marketable product. Moreover, Just did have some input into Byce's work on the software, even if it was given by e-mail and phone.

The nature of the business and the work similarly means that Byce's ability to set his own hours and the fact that he worked from home are not particularly relevant. As a programmer, Byce could, in essence, ply his craft at any time and from any place without significant impairment to its quality or his ability to meet JustMed's needs. So although physical separation between the hiring party and the worker is often relevant to determining employment status, it is less germane in light of the kind of work Byce was doing. Of course, computer programming is a skilled profession, which weighs in favor of finding Byce not an employee, but given the other factors and the fact that JustMed's regular business requires it to employ programmers, we find this far from conclusive.

Byce's strongest argument turns on JustMed's failure to pay benefits and fill out the appropriate employment forms, and JustMed's tax treatment of Byce. Some courts have relied heavily on these factors as "highly probative of the true nature of the employment relationship." *See Aymes,* 980 F.2d at 861, 863–64 ("[E]very case since [*CCNV*] that has applied the test has found the hired party to be an independent contractor where the hiring party failed to extend benefits or pay social security taxes."). There is a danger, however, in relying on them too heavily, because they do not bear directly on the substance of the employment relationship—the right to control. In this case, the factors do not decisively favor Byce, especially when one considers JustMed's business model.

We note Byce did eventually fill out a W–4 form and have taxes withheld once he started receiving paychecks from JustMed. The tax treatment here is therefore more ambiguous than in other copyright cases where courts have relied on the hiring party's treatment of the hired party as an independent contractor—for example, by not withholding taxes and by giving the hired party 1099 forms—and only later asserted that the individual was an employee. While an inherent unfairness exists in a company claiming a worker to be an independent contractor in one context but an employee in another, that is not the case here.

JustMed's treatment of Byce with regard to taxes, benefits, and employment forms is more likely attributable to the start-up nature of the business than to Byce's alleged status as an independent contractor. The indications are that other employees, for example Liebler, were treated similarly. Insofar as JustMed did not comply with federal and state employment or tax laws, we do not excuse its actions, but in this context the remedy for these failings lies not with denying the firm its intellectual property but with enforcing the relevant laws.

As a small start-up company, JustMed conducted its business more informally than an established enterprise might. This fact can make it more difficult to decide whether a hired party is an employee or an independent contractor, but it should not make the company more susceptible to losing control over software integral to its product. Weighing the common law factors in light of the circumstances and JustMed's business, we conclude that the district court did not err in holding that Byce was an employee and that the source code was a work made for hire. [The court's opinion on the remaining issues is omitted. *Ed.*]

### *NOTES AND QUESTIONS*

1. When Byce started programming for JustMed in the summer of 2004, did he receive any income or fill out a W–4 tax withholding form that year? Did he work from home or at JustMed? Do you think Byce was an employee of the company in 2004? Did his status change in 2005? When did he create the computer program?

2. What policies are served by applying the work-made-for-hire doctrine to employee works? Could one policy be to help employers reduce transaction costs of having to obtain transfer of copyrights from their employees for works created within the scope of employment? If so, why might some countries reject the work-made-for-hire doctrine (as some countries do, for example, in Europe)?

3. Neither design patent law nor trademark law has a work-made-for-hire doctrine. In the patent context, courts recognize that employees who are hired to invent typically assign their patent rights to their employers by implied contract. *See Teets v. Chromalloy Gas Turbine Corp.*, 83 F.3d 403, 407 (Fed. Cir. 1996). In the trademark context, the work-made-for-hire doctrine is not relevant. Trademark rights are typically established through use of the mark in commerce (not mere creation of a mark). Whoever uses the mark in commerce—typically, the business on its products or services—will establish trademark rights.

---

## E. FORMALITIES: REGISTRATION TO LITIGATE (BUT NOT TO OBTAIN) COPYRIGHT

Authors do not have to apply for a copyright, in contrast with a design patent. Although trademarks are created under the common law based simply on use, federal registration, a type of formality, is very common to secure national scope of protection and federal remedies. By contrast, copyrights automatically extend to original works of authorship once they are fixed in a tangible medium of expression. However, for works whose country of origin is the United States (unpublished works created by U.S. citizens or residents, or works first published in the United States), registration of copyright in the Copyright Office is a precondition to file a copyright lawsuit in federal court. 17 U.S.C. § 411. From 2008 to 2012, roughly 460,000 works were registered on average each year.[14] Although significant, the number of registered works probably pales in comparison to the millions of copyrighted works created each year.

In addition, timely registration is a precondition for a copyright owner to be eligible for an award of statutory damages (discussed below) and attorneys' fees. The copyright owner must register the copyright for a work in the Copyright Office *before* the defendant's infringement has started. If the registration occurs after the infringement has started, then statutory damages are not available for recovery in that case. There is an exception: a copyright owner gets a 3-month grace period after the date of first publishing a work; the owner may still recover statutory damages for infringement that started during that 3-month period as long as the owner registers the copyright within the 3-month period. *See* 17 U.S.C. § 412.

### *NOTES AND QUESTIONS*

1. Is it an advantage to be able to obtain a copyright without having to apply for it? Assuming it is, then why might one nonetheless apply for a design patent or register a trade dress to protect the design of the same item? Hint: might

---

[14] Dotan Oliar et al., *Copyright Registrations: Who, What, When, Where, and Why*, 92 TEXAS L. REV. 2211, 2220 (2014).

copyright's separability analysis factor into the calculus? Another possible answer lies with the scope of protection of the respective IP. Independent creation of the same or similar work is not considered copyright infringement. But, for design patents and trade dress, independent creation does not immunize a defendant from possible infringement.

2. *Orphan works*. One potential problem with the lack of formalities in copyright law is that it may exacerbate the problem of orphan works. Orphan works are works for which the author or copyright owner is not readily identifiable due, for example, to the passage of time, death of the author, or demise of a corporate author. The "orphan" status deters members of the public from utilizing the works, which are still subject to copyright but for which one cannot locate a copyright holder to obtain a license. A number of commentators argue that requiring registration for copyrighted works would help to reduce the number of orphan works. For example, one could require authors or copyright owners to maintain their information in a copyright registry. *See* David R. Hansen, Kathryn Hashimoto, Gwen Hinze, Pamela Samuelson & Jennifer M. Urban, *Solving the Orphan Works Problem for the United States*, 37 COLUM. J.L. & ARTS 1, 48–50 (2013). Do you agree with this proposal?

3. *Berne Convention*. One impediment to imposing a registration requirement is that the Berne Convention prohibits countries from imposing such formalities on works of foreign origin: "The enjoyment and the exercise of these rights shall not be subject to any formality." Berne Conv. art. 5(2). Scholars have debated different schemes that may or may not run afoul of this prohibition in Berne. *See, e.g.*, *id.* at 50; Jane C. Ginsburg, *Berne Forbidden Formalities and Mass Digitization*, 96 B.U. L. REV. 745 (2016); Christopher Jon Sprigman, *Berne's Vanishing Ban on Formalities*, 28 BERKELEY TECH. L.J. 1565 (2013).

---

## F. SCOPE OF COPYRIGHT PROTECTION

Now that we have learned what types of works fall within the subject matter of copyright and the requirements and the lack of formalities for obtaining copyrights, we can turn to the scope of copyright protection. As you study this section, consider how the scope of copyright protection compares to design patents and trade dress protection. The exclusive rights for each IP form affect the scope of protection. In § 106, the Copyright Act recognizes 6 exclusive rights. As mentioned above, one difference in the scope of copyright is that copyright does not prohibit the independent creation of the same or similar design, whereas design patents and trade dress do not recognize such a limitation. Other differences lie in the type and number of exceptions to the respective IP form. Copyright has more exceptions than the other IP forms (although a complete discussion of them goes beyond the scope of this casebook). *See* 17 U.S.C. §§ 107–122. In this section, we focus on the basic test of copyright infringement.

## 1. EXCLUSIVE RIGHTS

Section 106 of the Copyright Act grants authors the following exclusive rights:

(1) to reproduce the copyrighted work in copies or phonorecords;

(2) to prepare derivative works based upon the copyrighted work;

(3) to distribute copies or phonorecords of the copyrighted work to the public by sale or other transfer of ownership, or by rental, lease, or lending;

(4) in the case of literary, musical, dramatic, and choreographic works, pantomimes, and motion pictures and other audiovisual works, to perform the copyrighted work publicly;

(5) in the case of literary, musical, dramatic, and choreographic works, pantomimes, and pictorial, graphic, or sculptural works, including the individual images of a motion picture or other audiovisual work, to display the copyrighted work publicly; and

(6) in the case of sound recordings, to perform the copyrighted work publicly by means of a digital audio transmission. 17 U.S.C. § 106.

For the purposes of design, the first three rights—reproduction of a work in copies, preparing derivative works, and public distribution of copies of a work—are the most relevant. This casebook focuses on the first right, the basic right of reproduction, which protects against the copying of the work. Copyright extends to not only verbatim copies of a work commonly called "knock-offs," but also copies that are substantially similar.

## 2. INFRINGEMENT

### *PROBLEM 4–7*

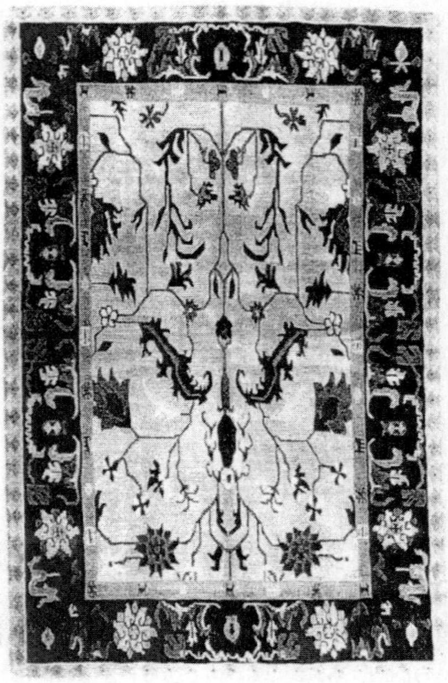

**Figure 3. Tori's rug design (plaintiff's)** **Figure 4. Dre's rug design (defendant's)**

Tori designed the rug in Figure 3 above. Tori copied some design elements from two other rugs (below in Figures 5 and 6) that are in the public domain and are not protected by copyright. First, Tori scanned the designs of the two public domain rugs into a computer program. Then, she removed some of the design elements from the rug in Figure 5 to open the space in the center of the design, reconfigured the remaining elements, and elongated the design in order to create an open or less cluttered feeling. In contrast with the rug design in Figure 5, Tori created an asymmetrical pattern: the pattern on the top half is not symmetrical to the one on the bottom half, in contrast to both public domain patterns. However, she admittedly copied several elements and some of the arrangement of the public domain rug design in Figure 5.

For the primary border of her rug, Tori adapted the primary border of the public domain rug in Figure 6. She simplified the original border by removing the smaller elements and maintaining the larger, primary ones in order to open the space between them. Tori also inserted a thin, minor border inspired by "Gebbah" Persian carpets, which are also in the public domain. That border features "primitive" animal stick figures evenly spaced around the rug. She also created a thin, minor border consisting of castle-like forms side-by-side around the outermost edge of the rug.

**Figure 5. Persian rug in public domain** **Figure 6. Indian rug in public domain**

Tori's rug became very popular and had phenomenal sales. During the height of Tori's sales, Barbara designed the rug in Figure 4 above. Barbara was aware of Tori's rug, but insists she did not infringe Tori's copyright because the main elements of Tori's rug are already in the public domain. Tori sues Barbara for infringement. (1) What are the elements of Tori's rug design that are protected by copyright? (2) Did Barbara infringe those protected elements? To answer this problem, consult the *L. Batlin & Sons, Inc. v. Snyder* case above, as well as the following two cases.

---

## LAUREYSSENS V. IDEA GROUP, INC.

964 F.2d 131 (2d Cir. 1992)

OAKES, CHIEF JUDGE: At issue in this trade dress and copyright infringement case are similarities between two sets of foam rubber puzzles. The puzzles produced by the parties contain six pieces with a variety of notches cut into each of their four edges. By interlocking the notched edges, the puzzles can be assembled either in a flat form in a rectangular frame or into a three-dimensional hollow cube. The more intrepid puzzler can piece together more challenging multi-puzzle combinations such as a larger cube or other three-dimensional figures including a beam of two or three cubes joined in a line, a cross of five cubes, and a star comprised of pieces from six cube puzzles. One set of puzzles is marketed under the name

HAPPY CUBE. The HAPPY CUBE puzzles were designed by Dirk Laureyssens and are produced, distributed, exported from Europe, and marketed in the United States through a number of entities including I Love Love Company, N.V., Creative City Limited, and Extar Corporation (collectively "Laureyssens"). The competing set is marketed under the name SNAFOOZ by Idea Group, Inc., a California corporation ("Idea Group").

For the reasons set forth below, we reverse the district court's decision to grant a preliminary injunction based on trade dress infringement under section 43(a) of the Lanham Act and under the New York common law of unfair competition, and affirm the district court's decision to deny a preliminary injunction based on copyright infringement.

I.

Dirk Laureyssens, a designer of various toys and puzzles, first began creating cube puzzles in 1985. Over the next few years, he refined his cube puzzle designs by selecting puzzle pieces which would not only permit assembly in flat and cube form, but which also were aesthetically pleasing. Six puzzle designs emerged, each of which contains pieces with edges that are five notch-widths to a side.[1] By 1991, Laureyssens had filed certificates of copyright registration with the Copyright Office in Washington for each of his six designs. The certificates indicate that the nature of authorship claimed consists of the shape of the pieces; the certificates also refer to earlier filings with the Copyright Office in 1987 and 1988 which also covered his puzzle designs.

Laureyssens introduced his puzzles for sale in the United States at the 1988 International Toy Fair held in New York City. Subsequently, he decided to market them on his own under the name CUBE-IT. After his counsel discovered a trademark conflict, prior to the 1990 International Toy Fair in New York, Laureyssens changed the name of the puzzles to HAPPY CUBE. HAPPY CUBE puzzles come in six colors and each is named after a well-known city. The yellow puzzle is named Tokio [sic], the green New York, the purple Brussels, the orange Amsterdam, the blue Milano, and the red Paris. By design, some of the puzzles are harder to assemble than others. [You may view the design of the Happy Cube at http://happysolver.sourceforge.net/. *Ed.*]

Since their introduction in the United States market, Laureyssens claims to have sold 103,000 puzzles, 90,000 of which were marketed in the HAPPY CUBE packaging. Raphael Berkien, the chief executive officer of Laureyssens' exclusive United States distributor Extar Corporation, declared in an affidavit that sales since 1988 were worth $50,000, but one week later was unable to substantiate the figure during his deposition.

[1] A notch-width is equal to the thickness of the puzzle material. The notch-width must be equal to the thickness of the puzzle material in order to join two pieces smoothly in the perpendicular alignment.

Berkien also claims to have orders for an additional 250,000 puzzles, and to have entered into an agreement with an organization possessing a nationwide sales force of 40 sales representatives, each of whom apparently committed to selling 100,000 puzzles per month. Following the original appearance at the 1988 American International Toy Fair in New York, Laureyssens exhibited the puzzles at toy and novelty shows across the country where leaflets in the style of the packaging were distributed. Laureyssens also advertised the puzzles in various trade publications, such as the New York Toy Fair Directory.

The first conflict between Laureyssens and Idea Group arose at the 1990 American International Toy Fair in New York City. During the fair, Dirk Laureyssens discovered that Idea Group was manufacturing and marketing identical puzzles called SNAFOOZ. After receiving cease and desist letters from Laureyssens' counsel, Idea Group acknowledged on March 19, 1990 that "our puzzle apparently was copied from a sample obtained through your French distributor or licensee and, in its present form, cannot be marketed in the U.S. without your permission."

The president of Idea Group was approached by Mr. Berkien of Extar Corporation approximately one month after the Toy Fair about the possibility of Idea Group marketing the Laureyssens puzzles in the United States. Apparently, Berkien was unaware of the recent dispute between Dirk Laureyssens and Idea Group until a few hours before he was supposed to meet with Idea Group. After a few weeks of negotiations, however, the parties failed to reach an agreement.

Following the breakdown of negotiations with Laureyssens, Idea Group decided to develop its own version of the flat-to-cube puzzle series, utilizing pieces whose edges were six notch-widths in length rather than five. Late in July 1990, an executive vice president of Idea Group contacted a graduate student in computer science at the Massachusetts Institute of Technology, Eric Brewer, and described the new series of puzzle designs that Idea Group was hoping to market. Brewer then met with the executive vice president who provided him with two of the old SNAFOOZ Puzzles and discussed the nature of the computer program Idea Group desired. An agreement was reached in August 1990, and the graduate student completed the work for Idea Group a few weeks later. Brewer stated in an affidavit that he designed the new series entirely from scratch, utilizing the old SNAFOOZ Puzzles only to gain an understanding of the desired product and to calibrate the difficulty of his puzzle designs against the five notch-width designs of the Laureyssens puzzles. [You may view the Snafooz design at http://puzzle-solutions.enygmo.com/put-together/_58-snafooz-green.php. *Ed.*]

After receiving the designs from Brewer, Idea Group made arrangements to manufacture the new SNAFOOZ puzzles. From September 1990 to February 1991, Idea Group received approximately

300,000 SNAFOOZ puzzles from its manufacturer in Korea. In preparation for the maiden exhibition of the new six-notch width SNAFOOZ puzzles at the 1991 American International Toy Fair in New York City, Idea Group conducted a direct mail campaign to potential customers, and placed advertisements in the 1991 Toy Fair Directory and other trade publications.

During the 1991 American International Toy Fair in February, Laureyssens paid a visit to Idea Group's showroom but made no effort to stop Idea Group from selling the SNAFOOZ puzzles at the fair. At the end of the fair, Laureyssens met with representatives from Idea Group in his counsel's office, but made no demand on Idea Group to cease and desist from infringing on his copyrights or the HAPPY CUBE trade dress.

In April 1991, Laureyssens instituted this action against Idea Group seeking, *inter alia,* to enjoin Idea Group from infringing Laureyssens' copyrights and trade dress by distributing the SNAFOOZ puzzles. On July 31, 1991, the district court issued an opinion denying Laureyssens' motion for a preliminary injunction based on copyright infringement, but granting Laureyssens' motion on the grounds that Idea Group's flat-form, shrink wrapped SNAFOOZ packaging raises a serious question of trade dress infringement under section 43(a) of the Lanham Act and under the New York common law of unfair competition. A corresponding order issued on August 7, 1991 preliminarily enjoined Idea Group from "marketing its SNAFOOZ puzzles . . . in flat form and in transparent packaging, unless the puzzle package contains an assembled SNAFOOZ puzzle." This appeal and cross-appeal followed. [The court of appeals' analysis of the trademark and unfair competition claims is omitted. *Ed.*]

C. Copyright infringement

In order to establish a claim for copyright infringement, a plaintiff must show ownership of a valid copyright and the defendant's infringement by unauthorized copying. It is now an axiom of copyright law that actionable copying can be inferred from the defendant's access to the copyrighted work and substantial similarity between the copyrighted work and the alleged infringement. We have recently explained this recitation to mean that a plaintiff must first show that his work was actually copied by proving "access and substantial similarity between the works." *See Folio Impressions,* [*Inc. v. Byer California*, 937 F.2d 759, 765 (2d Cir. 1991)]. The plaintiff then must show that the copying amounts to an "improper" or "unlawful" appropriation, *Arnstein v. Porter*, 154 F.2d 464, 468 (2d Cir. 1946), by demonstrating that substantial similarities relate to protectible material. *See Folio Impressions*, 937 F.2d at 765; *see also* Latman, *"Probative Similarity" as Proof of Copying: Toward Dispelling Some Myths in Copyright Infringement*, 90 COLUM. L. REV. 1187, 1191–1204 (1990) (clarifying that copyright infringement claims involve consideration of similarity at two different stages of the analysis—actual copying and improper appropriation).

The presence of a "substantial similarity" requirement in both prongs of the analysis—actual copying and whether the copying constitutes an improper appropriation—creates the potential for unnecessary confusion, especially because a plaintiff need not prove *substantial* similarity in every case in order to prove actual copying. For these reasons, we wish to restate some of our previous explanations of the requirements for proving actionable copying in copyright infringement cases. A plaintiff must first show that his or her work was actually copied. Copying may be established either by direct evidence of copying or by indirect evidence, including access to the copyrighted work, similarities that are probative of copying between the works, and expert testimony. If actual copying is established, a plaintiff must then show that the copying amounts to an improper appropriation by demonstrating that substantial similarity to protected material exists between the two works.

In the case at hand, with respect to proof of actual copying, Idea Group does not dispute that it had access to the HAPPY CUBE puzzles.[8] Furthermore, after examining pieces of the HAPPY CUBE and SNAFOOZ puzzles, we find similarities in their shapes which are probative of copying and which at least raise a question of actual copying. The central concern in this appeal, then, is whether the district court properly determined that no serious question exists of unlawful appropriation of protected material.

The test for unlawful appropriation to prove infringement of another's copyright asks whether substantial similarity as to protectible material exists between the works at issue. To that end, we determine in most cases whether "the ordinary observer, unless he set out to detect the disparities, would be disposed to overlook them, and regard their aesthetic appeal as the same." *Peter Pan Fabrics, Inc. v. Martin Weiner Corp.*, 274 F.2d 487, 489 (2d Cir. 1960). However, where a design contains both protectible and unprotectible elements, we have held that the observer's inspection must be more "discerning," ignoring those aspects of a work that are unprotectible in making the comparison. *Folio Impressions*, 937 F.2d at 765–66.

The district court applied the more discerning ordinary observer test for substantial similarity of *Folio Impressions,* concluding that this was the appropriate test because only the shapes of the HAPPY CUBE puzzle pieces are protected by Laureyssens' copyrights. In doing so, the district court excluded from its consideration of substantial similarity the fact that both sets of designs involve "a hollow cube puzzle formed from six pieces

[8] Idea Group, in fact, gave two of their original SNAFOOZ puzzles, which admittedly were copies of the HAPPY CUBE puzzles, to the graduate student hired to design the new SNAFOOZ puzzles.

with rectilinear interlocking projections which can also be assembled into a flat three-piece-by-two-piece form."

Laureyssens argues that it was clearly erroneous for the district court to exclude any portion of the Laureyssens design because Laureyssens created the puzzles independently, thereby rendering the entire puzzle design "original" under the standard of *Feist Publications, Inc. v. Rural Tel. Serv. Co.*, 499 U.S. 340 (1991). We disagree. "[T]he protection granted to a copyrightable work extends only to the particular expression of an idea and never to the idea itself." *Durham Industries, Inc. v. Tomy Corp.*, 630 F.2d 905, 912 (2d Cir. 1980) (quoting *Reyher v. Children's Television Workshop*, 533 F.2d 87, 90 (2d Cir.), *cert. denied,* 429 U.S. 980, (1976)). In the case at hand, in order to express the idea of a perfect hollow cube puzzle that can also be assembled in flat form, a designer must use pieces that interlock through fingers and notches cut at right angles. Indeed, Idea Group presented evidence of two different patents that were obtained for flat-to-cube puzzles in 1974 and 1975; both were created prior to Laureyssens' work. Therefore, we think the district court was correct in concluding that the Laureyssens copyright extends only to his particular expression of the idea of a flat-to-cube puzzle, manifested in the particular shapes of his puzzle pieces.

Finally, Laureyssens argues that the district court misapplied even the more discerning ordinary observer test for substantial similarity because Laureyssens contends that any differences between the shapes of the puzzle pieces reflect only a proportional enlargement of the puzzle pieces.

Here, the designs of the puzzle pieces at issue have as their purpose the creation of a puzzle which can be assembled in either cube or flat form. The question, then, is whether the ordinary observer would consider a design change in the shapes of the pieces from five notch-widths per edge to six notch-widths per edge as effectuating essentially the same puzzle challenge with pieces that have somewhat wider notches and fingers, or as effectuating a completely different expression of a flat-to-cube puzzle.

We think that an ordinary observer would conclude that the design change to six notch-widths per edge in the shapes of the SNAFOOZ puzzle pieces results in a qualitatively different challenge to the puzzler. A side-by-side visual comparison of the pieces comprising the green HAPPY CUBE and the purple SNAFOOZ—the two puzzles with the most pieces that are supposedly similar—provides the clearest evidence of the different ways in which the HAPPY CUBE and SNAFOOZ puzzles express the idea of a flat-to-cube: three of the six pieces in each puzzle share some similarities, none are virtually identical, and the remaining three are quite different. Based on this observation, we think the ordinary observer comparing the shapes of the pieces would conclude that SNAFOOZ is a bona fide redesign of the idea of a flat-to-cube puzzle. If the ordinary observer were asked to compare side-by-side two common cardboard 500-piece jigsaw puzzles depicting the American flag where the two puzzles were configured differently, and assuming that the copyright did not protect the particular depiction of the flag, we certainly think the observer would conclude that the allegedly infringing jigsaw puzzle was simply a different expression of the idea of a jigsaw puzzle.

Our belief that the SNAFOOZ puzzles are not unlawful appropriations of the HAPPY CUBE designs is reinforced by the testimony of the graduate student who designed the SNAFOOZ puzzles. He stated in his affidavit that he generated a computer program from scratch to create flat-to-cube puzzles that could also be assembled in multi-puzzle combinations with six notch-widths per edge. Declaration of Eric Brewer ("I can state without equivocation that I designed the SNAFOOZ Puzzles, along with their solutions and the solutions for all of the complex shapes . . . without any reference to the Five-Segment Puzzles (other than to play with them); I started from scratch.").

For these reasons, we conclude that the district court did not abuse its discretion in deciding that the SNAFOOZ puzzles pose no serious question of unlawful appropriation, and accordingly, of copyright infringement with respect to the protectible elements of Laureyssens' copyrights in his HAPPY CUBE designs.

### *NOTES AND QUESTIONS*

1. What is the test to prove copyright infringement? Do you agree with the result reached by the court in applying the test to the two puzzles, the Happy Cube and the defendant's Snafooz?

2. Is there a difference between probative and substantial similarities in the test for copyright infringement?

3. Is there a difference between the ordinary observer and the more discerning observer? Do you think an ordinary observer would not find substantial similarities between the two puzzles? What about the more discerning observer?

4. How did Idea Group attempt to "design around" Laureyssens' copyrighted Happy Cube? Do you think that process is a good one for businesses to adopt? Or is it risky?

5. Should the configuration of cube puzzles be copyrightable? Or are they useful articles, systems, or methods of operation?

6. Laureyssens was not the first to design a cube puzzle. As the district court discussed, Sukeo Tsurumi and Gerald Allen Freedman obtained design patents for cube puzzles in 1975 and 1974, respectively. Laureyssens' cube was different in having five units per edge, but similar to the two prior cubes in having 6 pieces with rectilinear interlocking edges.

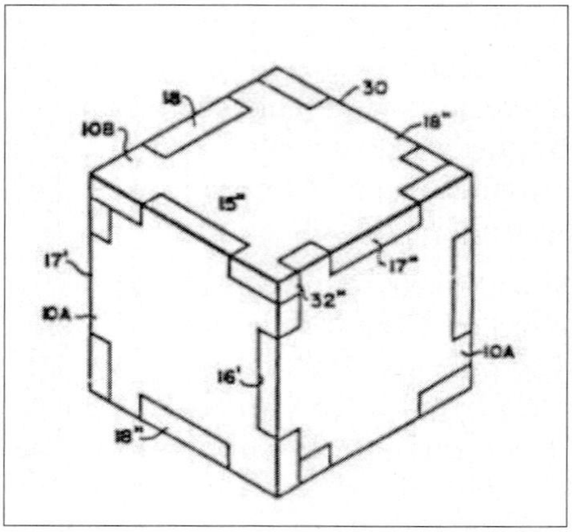

Tsurumi cube

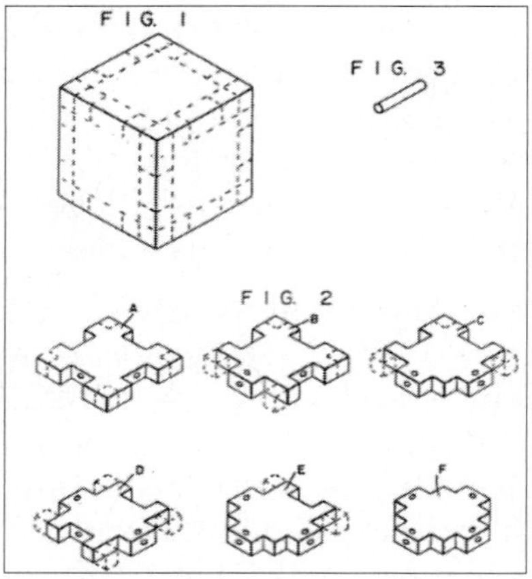


Freedman cube

Given the similarities to the two prior cubes, the district court ruled: "The cube puzzle and the patents discussed above, particularly the Tsurumi Patent, are sufficient to establish that Laureyssens was not the first person to conceive and design a hollow cube puzzle formed from six pieces with rectilinear interlocking projections which also can be assembled into a flat three-piece-by-two-piece form, and hence these aspects of his puzzles do not fall within the scope of his copyright. Therefore, to the extent that the SNAFOOZ Puzzles are also flat-to-cube puzzles with rectilinear interlocking projections, any similarities between them and the Laureyssens Puzzles is not the result of 'illicit' copying of protectible elements of Laureyssens' works. In other words, the fact that the pieces of both types of puzzles are squares with right-angled fingers and notches cut in the edges may not be taken as evidence of substantial similarity. Rather, the inquiry must focus on whether there is similarity with regard to the original aspect of Laureyssens' works, the shapes of the pieces." 768 F. Supp. at 1054.

---

## NOLA SPICE DESIGNS, L.L.C. v. HAYDEL ENTERPRISES, INC.

783 F.3d 527 (5th Cir. 2015)

STEPHEN A. HIGGINSON, CIRCUIT JUDGE: This case concerns the intersection between intellectual property rights and a Mardi Gras tradition. Haydel Enterprises appeals the district court's grant of summary judgment to Nola Spice Designs and Raquel Duarte on claims of trademark infringement, unfair competition, trademark dilution, copyright infringement, and unfair trade practices. We affirm.

FACTS AND PROCEEDINGS

During Mardi Gras parades in New Orleans, parade "krewes" throw strands of plastic beads to onlookers, who, in turn, have created "bead dogs" by twisting these strands into the shape of a dog. Haydel Enterprises ("Haydel") owns Haydel's Bakery in New Orleans, which makes and sells pastries and cakes, including its popular king cake sold during the Mardi Gras season. In 2008, Haydel commissioned an artist to design a mascot, which was named "Mardi Gras Bead Dog." On October 13, 2009, and December 1, 2009, the United States Patent and Trademark Office ("PTO") issued two trademark registrations to Haydel for, respectively, the phrase "MARDI GRAS BEAD DOG" and its bead dog design. The design consists of a "stylized dog wearing a beaded necklace, with the dog being formed by a series of spheres designed to look like Mardi Gras style beads. The dog has two eyes and a nose, all formed by smaller beads." [See figure below. *Ed.*] Both registrations cover king cake pastries, jewelry, and clothing (shirts, hats, and baby jumpsuits). Haydel sells these items in its New Orleans store, online, and through its licensee Fleurty Girl, a New Orleans retailer. In September 2012, Haydel obtained a certificate of copyright registration for its work titled "Bead Dog" in "photograph(s), jewelry design, 2-D artwork, sculpture." Haydel has acknowledged that its mascot "brings to mind the traditional bead dog" made of Mardi Gras beads. Nevertheless, Haydel asserts that its mascot and its use of the phrase "Mardi Gras Bead Dog" differ from the Mardi Gras tradition in key respects, which we will discuss.

In May 2012, Raquel Duarte formed Nola Spice Designs, which sells jewelry and accessories, including necklaces and earrings featuring bead dog trinkets. Duarte twists each bead dog by hand from beads and wire, following the same general method that she used to make bead dogs as a child during Mardi Gras. By contrast, the bead dogs in Haydel's jewelry are made of sterling silver. Duarte sells her jewelry on the Internet under titles that include the phrase "bead dog," but not "Mardi Gras bead dog."

Haydel learned of Duarte's bead dogs through Haydel's customers. In August 2012, Haydel sent Nola Spice Designs a letter noting Haydel's trademark and copyright in "the bead dog design," and demanding, *inter alia,* that Nola Spice Designs "remove from [its] website all display, mention of or reference to the bead dog design," and "cease any and all promotion, sale, and/or use" of materials incorporating the bead dog design. In October 2012, Nola Spice Designs filed a complaint against Haydel seeking (1) a declaratory judgment that Nola Spice Designs's activities do not violate the Lanham Act, 15 U.S.C. § 1051 *et seq.*, or any other trademark law; (2) the cancellation of Haydel's trademarks under 15 U.S.C. § 1119; and (3) damages for unfair trade practices under the Louisiana Unfair Trade Practices Act ("LUTPA"), La. Rev. Stat. Ann. § 51:1401 *et seq.* Haydel asserted counterclaims against Nola Spice Designs and filed a third-party complaint against Duarte, seeking injunctive relief and damages.

On August 28, 2013, the district court granted in part and denied in part the motion for summary judgment filed by Nola Spice Designs and Duarte (collectively, "Nola Spice") and denied Haydel's motion for summary judgment.

V. Copyright Infringement

The district court relied on the merger doctrine in granting summary judgment to Nola Spice on Haydel's copyright infringement claim. The merger doctrine is based on the statutory prohibition against copyright protection for ideas. *See* 17 U.S.C. § 102(b). "If an idea is susceptible to only one form of expression, the merger doctrine applies and § 102(b) excludes the expression from the Copyright Act." *Veeck v. S. Bldg. Code Cong. Int'l, Inc.*, 293 F.3d 791, 801 (5th Cir. 2002). However, examples of bead dogs in the record make clear that the idea of a bead dog may be expressed in various ways. The merger doctrine therefore does not alone preclude a finding of copyright infringement. Still, "we may affirm the district court's decision on any ground supported by the record, even if it was not the basis for the judgment." *Terrebonne Parish Sch. Bd.,* 310 F.3d at 878. We find that the grant of summary judgment was appropriate based on the absence of substantial similarity between Haydel's and Nola Spice's bead dogs.

While the question of substantial similarity "typically should be left to the factfinder, summary judgment may be appropriate if the court can conclude, after viewing the evidence and drawing inferences in a manner most favorable to the nonmoving party, that no reasonable juror could find substantial similarity." *Peel & Co. v. Rug Mkt.*, 238 F.3d 391, 395 (5th Cir. 2001). To assess substantial similarity, we have often cited the following test: "[A] side-by-side comparison must be made between the original and the copy to determine whether a layman would view the two works as 'substantially similar.'" *Creations Unlimited, Inc. v. McCain*, 112 F.3d 814, 816 (5th Cir. 1997) (per curiam). However, where the copyrighted work contains unprotectable elements, the first step is to distinguish between protectable and unprotectable elements of the copyrighted work. This determination should be based on the perspective of a "layman" or "ordinary observer." Our precedents also support consideration of the importance of the copied protectable elements to the copyrighted work as a whole.

Haydel's Sculpture

Haydel's Design Mark

Haydel's Jewelry

Nola Spice's Jewelry

Traditional Bead Dog Trinket

Applying these principles to Haydel's claim, we first identify the unprotectable elements in Haydel's bead dog design, which is manifested most clearly in sculpture form. Haydel concedes that its bead dog design is a "derivative" work, meaning that it is "based upon one or more preexisting works." 17 U.S.C. § 101. "The copyright in a . . . derivative work extends only to the material contributed by the author of such work, as distinguished from the preexisting material employed in the work, and does not imply any exclusive right in the preexisting material." *Id.* § 103(b). Haydel concedes that the body of its bead dog design is unprotectable as preexisting material because it mimics the body of a traditional bead dog. Haydel nevertheless contends that its "original contributions include, among other things, the selection and arrangement of a necklace, nose, eyes, and a tail, all made of smaller beads." However, anatomical features on replicas of animals are ideas not entitled to copyright protection. As for the "necklace" in Haydel's design, the ring of spheres around the neck of Haydel's bead dog may be characterized as a *collar.* Collars on dogs, like anatomical features, are common ideas that belong to the public domain. Still, while the idea of eyes, a nose, a tail, and a collar are not protectable, the manner in which Haydel expresses these features may be protectable, as long as that expression is original and not dictated by the underlying idea.

We now compare Nola Spice's bead dog to the protectable elements of Haydel's bead dog, assuming the perspective of an ordinary observer and considering the significance of the protectable elements to Haydel's work as a whole. [See figures above. *Ed.*] Haydel argues that only some of Nola Spice's bead dogs are infringing and identifies examples in the record. Focusing on the protectable elements of Haydel's design, the similarity between Nola Spice's and Haydel's bead dogs is the expression of the collar as a ring of small spheres. As for the differences, the torso of Haydel's bead dog has three spheres, while the torso of Nola Spice's bead dog has one sphere. The spheres that make up Haydel's bead dog are pressed together, whereas visible wire connects the spheres that make up Nola Spice's bead dogs. Whereas the tail of Haydel's bead dog consists of two spheres and no wire, the tails of Nola Spice's bead dogs include a curled wire, either alone or atop one or two spheres. Likewise, the noses of Nola Spice's bead dogs include a curled wire, either alone or atop a single sphere, while the nose of Haydel's bead dog is a single sphere. Unlike Haydel's bead dog, Nola Spice's bead dogs do not have eyes. No reasonable juror could conclude that Nola Spice's bead dogs bear a substantial similarity to the way in which the eyes, nose, and tail are expressed in Haydel's bead dog. Indeed, Haydel focuses its argument on the collar, conceding that its "copyright infringement claim is narrow. Only to the extent that Nola Spice copied Haydel's original expression by, at least adding a necklace made of smaller beads to what would otherwise look like a dog trinket made of larger beads, has Nola Spice infringed Haydel's copyrighted expression." We must therefore decide whether the collar on Nola Spice's bead dogs could suffice to support a finding of substantial similarity in the mind of a reasonable juror.

Because the idea of a collar is unprotectable, only its expression as a string of spheres is relevant to the analysis of substantial similarity. As a threshold matter, we question whether using bead-shaped spheres for a bead dog's collar is sufficiently original to merit copyright protection. *See Feist Publ'ns, Inc.,* 499 U.S. at 348 ("[C]opyright protection may extend only to those components of a work that are original to the author."). Although the requirement of originality demands only a "creative spark, no matter how crude, humble or obvious," the level of creativity must be more than "trivial." *Id.* at 345, 359. Even if a bead-shaped collar possesses the requisite creative spark, its minimal originality counsels against a finding of substantial similarity. In addition, the collar is both qualitatively and quantitatively insignificant in relation to Haydel's work as a whole, which is designed to represent a traditional bead dog trinket and is dominated by unprotectable elements. In light of these considerations, no reasonable jury could find substantial similarity based solely on Haydel's expression of a collar.

Haydel argues that the "best evidence" of substantial similarity consists of statements by the Haydel family that its customers were confused about the relationship between Nola Spice's bead dogs and Haydel's mascot. Haydel points to a sworn statement by David Haydel, Sr.

that he "personally heard several customers of Haydel's Bakery asking whether Nola Spice Designs sells Haydel's MARDI GRAS BEAD DOG jewelry and telling our staff that they (the customers) believed that Nola Spice Designs sold Haydel's MARDI GRAS BEAD DOG jewelry." This vague allegation of consumer confusion by a self-interested party possesses little probative value. More important, any confusion by Haydel's customers would have stemmed from a comparison of the two bead dog designs in their entirety, and would therefore have been based largely on unprotectable elements. Given that the substantial similarity analysis requires a focus on protectable elements, Haydel's evidence of confusion does not raise a genuine issue for trial. Because no reasonable jury could conclude that Nola Spice's and Haydel's bead dogs are substantially similar in protectable expression, the district court properly granted summary judgment to Nola Spice on Haydel's copyright infringement claim. [The court of appeals' analysis of the other claims is omitted. *Ed.*]

## *NOTES AND QUESTIONS*

1. Do you think the district court was correct in applying the merger doctrine to bead dogs? The court of appeals disagreed that merger applied to the facts of this case. Would there be a difference in the result if the court of appeals agreed with the district court and applied the merger doctrine to Haydel's bead dog? If so, what's the difference in ruling on merger versus substantial similarity?

2. Do you agree with result reached by the Fifth Circuit in applying the test of substantial similarity? Is the Fifth Circuit's test of substantial similarity different from the Second Circuit's test in *Laureyssens*? Would the result be different under the Second Circuit's test?

3. Should consumer confusion be relevant to determining whether the two products are substantially similar under copyright law? Or is consumer confusion an inquiry best left for trademark law?

4. One difficulty both *Laureyessens* and *Nola Spice Designs* present is a designer's incorporation of designs elements that are already in the public domain and not protected by copyright. Copyright can extend to the new (original) elements a designer adds to the public domain elements, including the selection and arrangement of elements. Do you think this approach to copyright would work well with industries or areas of design that involve a high percentage of public domain elements, such as arguably the culinary and fashion industries? Is part of the problem with allowing copyright for culinary dishes or fashion designs that so many basic design features in those industries—traditional dishes and designs (e.g., pasta and polka dots)—are already in the public domain?

## 3. LIMITATIONS AND EXCEPTIONS

The Copyright Act contains numerous exceptions to copyright in Section 107 through 122. In addition, as discussed already, copyright excludes other matter, such as functional elements through various doctrines. In this section, we discuss three important limitations to copyright: (1) the first sale doctrine, (2) fair use, and (3) the idea-expression dichotomy.

### a. First Sale Doctrine (Exhaustion)

An important limitation on the scope of the exclusive right of public distribution is provided by the first sale doctrine, codified in § 109 of the Copyright Act. It states in part: "the owner of a particular copy or phonorecord lawfully made under this title, or any person authorized by such owner, is entitled, without the authority of the copyright owner, to sell or otherwise dispose of the possession of that copy or phonorecord." 17 U.S.C. § 109(a). The first sale doctrine is also known as exhaustion—which occurs when the copyright owner's distributional rights to a particular copy of her work is extinguished or "exhausted" in the stream of commerce.

#### *PROBLEM 4–8*

Katrina is an artist who creates colorful artwork. She sells some of her artwork as prints, 8.5 by 11 inches in size. Ruben purchased a bulk of 100 copies of Katrina's prints from the museum store where Katrina sells her work. He then used Katrina's prints as the covers of ordinary binders that had clear plastic on the front to insert a piece of paper. The paper or print can be inserted and removed from the plastic binder cover. On the website Etsy, Ruben started selling the binders, with Katrina's colorful prints as covers. He did so without permission from Katrina. Katrina sues Ruben for copyright infringement. What result? Consult Section 109(a) of the Copyright Act and the following case.

---

## OMEGA S.A. v. COSTCO WHOLESALE CORP.

776 F.3d 692 (9th Cir. 2015)

NELSON, SENIOR CIRCUIT JUDGE: This case involves two big commercial players: Costco Wholesale Corporation ("Costco"), a discount warehouse, and Omega S.A. ("Omega"), a global purveyor of luxury watches. Omega appeals the district court's decisions granting summary judgment and attorney's fees to Costco. We have jurisdiction pursuant to 28 U.S.C. § 1291, and we affirm.

I. Background

Omega manufactures luxury watches in Switzerland, which it distributes around the world. One of Omega's high end watches, the Seamaster, sometimes bears an engraving of the Omega Globe Design ("Omega Globe"). Omega obtained a copyright for the Omega Globe in March 2003. Omega began selling some Seamaster watches with engraved reproductions of the Omega Globe in September 2003.

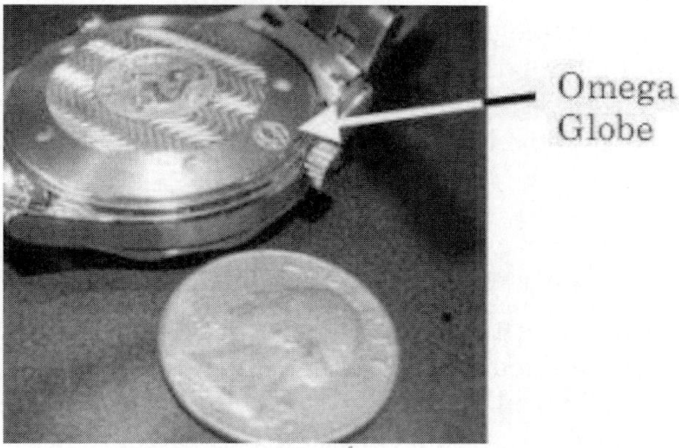


**[Photograph by Aaron Moss. *Ed.*]**

Omega distributes its watches, including the Seamaster, through authorized distributors and dealers throughout the world, including the United States. In 2003, Costco and Omega discussed the possibility of Costco carrying Omega watches. The parties did not come to an agreement and Costco never became an authorized Omega retailer.

In 2004, Costco purchased 117 Seamaster watches bearing the Omega Globe on the so-called "gray market." *Omega S.A. v. Costco Wholesale Corp.*, 541 F.3d 982, 984 (9th Cir. 2008) ("*Omega I*"), *abrogated by Kirtsaeng v. John Wiley & Sons, Inc.*, 133 S. Ct. 1351 (2013). First, Omega sold the watches to authorized foreign distributors. *Id.* Next, unidentified third parties purchased the watches and sold them to ENE Limited, a New York company. *Id.* Costco purchased the watches from ENE Limited. *Id.* Costco then sold 43 of those watches to its members in California. Omega undoubtedly authorized the initial sale of the watches but did not approve the importation of the watches into the United States or Costco's later sale of the watches. *Id.*

Omega sued Costco for copyright infringement, specifically the importation of copyrighted work without the copyright holder's permission, 17 U.S.C. § 602. The district court granted summary judgment to Costco based on the first sale doctrine. *Omega I*, 541 F.3d at 984–85 (explaining that the first sale doctrine, codified at 17 U.S.C. § 109(a), means that once a copyright owner consents to the sale of particular copies of work, that same copyright owner cannot later claim infringement for distribution of those copies). We reversed the district court and remanded because our precedent held that the first sale doctrine did not apply to copies of copyrighted works that had been produced abroad. *Id.* at 990 (discussing *BMG Music v. Perez*, 952 F.2d 318 (9th Cir. 1991)). The Supreme Court granted certiorari, and an equally divided Court summarily affirmed. *Costco Wholesale Corp. v. Omega, S.A.*, 562 U.S. 40 (2010) (per curiam).

On remand, the district court again granted summary judgment to Costco, finding that Omega misused its copyright of the Omega Globe to expand its limited monopoly impermissibly. The district court also granted Costco attorney's fees in the amount of $396,844.17. Omega appeals both the district court's copyright misuse judgment and the attorney's fee award.

III. Discussion

A. First Sale Doctrine

While briefing in this matter was pending, the Supreme Court revisited the first sale doctrine in *Kirtsaeng*, 133 S. Ct. at 1355.[1] In that case, the Court considered 'first sale' doctrine applies to protect a buyer or other lawful owner of a copy (of a copyrighted work) lawfully manufactured abroad." *Id.* In other words, the Court asked whether the purchaser of the copyrighted work can "bring that copy into the United States (and sell it or give it away) without obtaining permission to do so from the copyright owner[.]" *Id.* The Court held that the answer was yes, and, thus, the " 'first sale' doctrine applies to copies of a copyrighted work lawfully made abroad." *Id.* at 1355–56.

Kirtsaeng explained that copyright distribution and importation rights expire after the first sale, regardless of where the item was manufactured or first sold. *Id.* Kirtsaeng interpreted 17 U.S.C. § 109(a), the first sale statutory provision, without overruling prior Supreme Court precedent, *see Trans World Airlines, Inc. v. Hardison*, 432 U.S. 63, 73 n.8 (1977) (explaining judgment from an equally divided Supreme Court is not precedent), and its holding is therefore fully retroactive and applies here, *Rivers v. Roadway Express, Inc.*, 511 U.S. 298, 312–13 (1994).

It is clear, then, that Omega has no infringement cause of action against Costco. Omega's only allegation is that Costco violated Omega's copyright-based importation and distribution rights by selling gray market watches without a prior authorized first sale in the United States. Omega

---

[1] The concurrence argues both that copyright misuse is the only issue presented to the court and that we should have ordered the parties to file supplemental briefing on Kirtsaeng. The first sale issue is properly before us. First, Costco raised the first sale doctrine based on the intervening decision in Kirtsaeng in a filing with the court prior to oral argument. Moreover, at oral argument, Costco's first argument, made extensively, was that we can and should affirm on Kirtsaeng. Because the parties litigated the first sale issue extensively the first time this case was before us, and because the holding in Kirtsaeng is so clear, there was no need for supplemental briefing.

concedes that it authorized a first sale of the watches in a foreign jurisdiction. Omega's right to control importation and distribution of its copyrighted Omega Globe expired after that authorized first sale, and Costco's subsequent sale of the watches did not constitute copyright infringement. *Kirtsaeng*, 133 S. Ct. at 1366; 17 U.S.C. § 109(a). Thus, application of the first sale doctrine disposes of Omega's claim, resolves this case in Costco's favor, and conclusively reaffirms that copyright holders cannot use their rights to fix resale prices in the downstream market. *Bobbs-Merrill Co. v. Straus*, 210 U.S. 339, 350–51 (1908); *see also Kirtsaeng*, 133 S. Ct. at 1366 (noting the "absurd result" that would exist if a copyright owner could exercise downstream control after authorizing a first sale). AFFIRMED.

## *NOTES AND QUESTIONS*

1. Why do you think Omega asserted a copyright claim instead of a trademark claim? Hint: might it relate to trademark's treatment of exhaustion? Do you think the Omega watch itself could be copyrighted? What was Omega trying to achieve by putting the tiny Globe Design on the back of its watches?

2. Does the holding of *Kirtsaeng* in interpreting the first sale doctrine result in national or international exhaustion for copyright law? Does an authorized first sale of a copy of a work abroad result in exhaustion of the copyright owner's distributional right over that copy in the U.S. (international exhaustion)? Or is the first sale doctrine limited to authorized sales or manufacture of the works in the U.S. (national exhaustion)?

3. *Copyright misuse.* The district court ruled that Omega's attempt to use the copyright on the small Globe Design on the back of its watches was a misuse of copyright: "Omega misused its copyright of the Omega Globe Design by leveraging its limited monopoly in being able to control the importation of that design to control the importation of its Seamaster watches," which themselves were uncopyrightable. 2011 WL 8492716, No. CV 04–05443, at *2 TJH (C.D. Cal. Nov. 9, 2011). Concurring in the judgment, Judge Wardlaw agreed with the district court: "The watchmaker's anticompetitive acts promoted neither the broad public availability of the arts nor the public welfare. Instead, they eliminated price competition in the retail market for Omega watches and deprived consumers of the opportunity to purchase discounted gray market Omega watches from Costco." 776 F.3d at 705–06. Although the majority of the Ninth Circuit decided the case on other grounds (the first sale doctrine), do you think Omega's strategy should also be deemed to be copyright misuse?

4. Assume that Omega had design patents on the Seamaster watch that was the subject of this lawsuit and those design patents were still in force. Do you think design patent law would consider Omega's distributional rights to be exhausted as well for authorized first sales of its watches abroad? Would it

make sense for copyright, trademark, and patent to adopt the same approach to exhaustion?

---

### b. Fair Use

Fair use is one of the most important exceptions to copyright. Courts first developed the doctrine in deciding copyright cases. Later, Congress codified the doctrine in the 1976 Copyright Act, which states:

> **§ 107. Limitations on exclusive rights: Fair use**
>
> Notwithstanding the provisions of sections 106 and 106A, the fair use of a copyrighted work, including such use by reproduction in copies or phonorecords or by any other means specified by that section, for purposes such as criticism, comment, news reporting, teaching (including multiple copies for classroom use), scholarship, or research, is not an infringement of copyright. In determining whether the use made of a work in any particular case is a fair use the factors to be considered shall include—
>
> (1) the purpose and character of the use, including whether such use is of a commercial nature or is for nonprofit educational purposes;
>
> (2) the nature of the copyrighted work;
>
> (3) the amount and substantiality of the portion used in relation to the copyrighted work as a whole; and
>
> (4) the effect of the use upon the potential market for or value of the copyrighted work.
>
> The fact that a work is unpublished shall not itself bar a finding of fair use if such finding is made upon consideration of all the above factors.

#### *PROBLEM 4–9*

Richard Prince is an appropriation artist. This style of art is known for copying or appropriating pre-existing works of others and re-using them in some way. Prince copied a photograph (shown below in Figure 7) from a book of photographs by photographer Patrick Cariou. Cariou's photograph was 8.5 by 11 inches in size. Prince increased the size of his copy of Cariou's photograph to 100.5 by 104.5 inches and altered the photograph by adding—using Photoshop—a photograph of a guitar he copied from the Internet. Using his computer program, Prince also added blue circles to the face of the person shown in Cariou's photograph. Prince sold his artwork (shown in Figure 8 below) for $1 million. Cariou sues Prince for infringement. Prince raises a defense of fair use. Consulting Section 107 and the following two cases, analyze whether a court should find a fair use by Prince. Would your answer change if

Prince admitted during his testimony that he was "not trying to create anything with a new meaning or a new message"?

**Figure 7. Patrick Cariou photograph**

**Figure 8. Richard Prince artwork**

---

## GAYLORD V. UNITED STATES

595 F.3d 1364 (Fed. Cir. 2010)

MOORE, CIRCUIT JUDGE. Mr. Frank Gaylord appeals the decision of the United States Court of Federal Claims that a stamp issued by the United States Postal Service made fair use of a copyrighted work, specifically, soldier sculptures in formation constituting part of the Korean War Veterans Memorial (Memorial). Because the court erred when it determined that the stamp made fair use of Mr. Gaylord's work, but it correctly determined that the government was not a joint author and that the AWCPA did not bar an infringement suit, we affirm-in-part, reverse-in-part, and remand for a determination of damages.

BACKGROUND

This case arises from the Postal Service's decision to issue a 37-cent stamp depicting a portion of the Memorial. The path from the concept of the Memorial to the creation of the stamp spans more than 15 years. In 1986, Congress enacted legislation to erect a memorial in Washington, D.C. to honor veterans of the Korean War. Authorization of Memorial, Pub.L. No. 99–572, § 1, 100 Stat. 3226 (1986). The legislation authorized the American Battle Monuments Commission (Commission) to establish the Memorial, and the Commission sponsored a contest to select the designer of the Memorial. A team from the Pennsylvania State University (the Penn

State Team) won the contest with a proposal to create 38 larger-than-life granite soldiers in formation. According to the Penn State Team, "[f]rom a distance, one [would see] the Memorial as an elusive, dream-like presence of ghostly figures moving across a remote landscape." Although its original concept undoubtedly influenced the design of the Memorial, the Penn State Team eventually withdrew from the project.

The Army Corps of Engineers selected Cooper-Lecky Architects, P.C. (Cooper-Lecky) as the prime contractor for the creation, construction, and installation of the Memorial. Cooper-Lecky sponsored a competition to select the sculptor for the Memorial. Mr. Gaylord, a nationally recognized sculptor, won the contest.

In 1990, Mr. Gaylord began work on the project. Although the Penn State Team's proposal called for 38 granite soldiers, "the final design featured 19 stainless steel statues representing a platoon of foot soldiers in formation," referred to as The Column. Mr. Gaylord prepared successively larger models of the soldiers, transforming them along the way in response to critiques and suggestions by Cooper-Lecky, members of the Korean War Veterans Memorial Advisory Board (VAB), and the Commission on Fine Arts (CFA). Once Mr. Gaylord completed models for the soldiers, they were cast in stainless steel and installed at the site of the Memorial on the National Mall in Washington, D.C. At the suggestion of a member of the VAB, Mr. Gaylord staggered the statues, thereby creating the composition of The Column. Cooper-Lecky, the VAB, and the CFA all participated in incorporating The Column into the Memorial, which also includes landscaping, a mural, and granite plates representing the reflection of rice paddies at the soldiers' feet. A picture of The Column—taken on a sunny day—is below.

Mr. Gaylord received five copyright registrations relating to the soldier sculptures from 1990 to 1995. Each certificate listed Mr. Gaylord as the sole author.

In 1995, shortly after the Memorial was dedicated, a photographer named John Alli took a photograph of the Memorial as a retirement gift for his father, a veteran of the Korean War. Mr. Alli visited the Memorial on five or six occasions, taking photographs at various times of year and day. One such visit occurred in January 1996 just after a snowstorm. Over the course of about two hours on that cold winter morning, Mr. Alli took about 100 photographs of the Memorial, including photographs of individual soldiers, from various angles using different exposures and lighting conditions. Mr. Alli selected one of his photographs for his father's retirement gift. The photograph, titled "Real Life," is reproduced below. No one questions that Mr. Alli is entitled to his own copyright protection in his photograph as a derivative work.

Mr. Alli decided to sell prints of the photograph. He therefore sought permission from the copyright owner of the underlying work, eventually locating Mr. Lecky of Cooper-Lecky, who held himself out as the "outright" owner of the copyright. Mr. Alli agreed to pay a 10% royalty on sales of prints of his photographs to a licensing entity established by Mr. Lecky. Mr. Lecky did not notify Mr. Gaylord about the agreement with Mr. Alli.[2]

In 2002, the Postal Service decided to issue a 37-cent stamp commemorating the 50th anniversary of the armistice of the Korean War. The Postal Service selected Mr. Alli's photograph for the stamp and paid him $1500 for its use. Mr. Alli told the Postal Service that it would need the permission of the owner of the copyright of the underlying work and referred the Postal Service to Mr. Lecky. The Postal Service issued the stamp, titled "Korean War Veterans Memorial." The stamp features Mr. Alli's photo and depicts 14 of the 19 soldier sculptures (see below).

[2] In 2006, Mr. Gaylord sued Mr. Alli for copyright infringement. Mr. Alli settled the dispute and agreed to pay Mr. Gaylord 10% of his net sales.

The Postal Service produced approximately 86.8 million stamps before retiring the stamp on March 31, 2005. The Postal Service acknowledged that it received over $17 million from the sale of nearly 48 million stamps. It was estimated that in 2003, the Postal Service generated $5.4 million from the sales of stamps to collectors who did not use the stamps to send mail. In addition, the Postal Service sold retail goods such as commemorative panels and framed art featuring images of the stamp. It did not seek or obtain Mr. Gaylord's permission to use the sculptures in the stamp or in any related retail goods.

Mr. Gaylord sued the government in the Court of Federal Claims on July 25, 2006, alleging infringement of his copyright. On June 16–20, 2008, the Court of Federal Claims conducted a trial, at which the government argued that the stamp made fair use of the work, excepting it from copyright liability. The Court of Federal Claims determined that Mr. Gaylord was the sole copyright owner of The Column and that The Column did not qualify as an architectural work under the AWCPA. However, the Court of Federal Claims also determined that the government was not liable for copyright infringement because the government's use of The Column was fair use. Mr. Gaylord appeals the court's decision as to fair use, and the government challenges the court's determinations of ownership and the inapplicability of the AWCPA.

DISCUSSION

I. Fair Use

Fair use of a copyrighted work "for purposes such as criticism, comment, news reporting, teaching (including multiple copies for classroom use), scholarship, or research, is not an infringement of copyright." 17 U.S.C. § 107. "The fair use doctrine thus 'permits [and requires] courts to avoid rigid application of the copyright statute when, on occasion, it would stifle the very creativity which the law is designed to foster.'" *Campbell v. Acuff-Rose Music, Inc.,* 510 U.S. 569, 577 (alteration in original) (citation omitted).

Fair use is a mixed question of law and fact. *Harper & Row, Publishers, Inc. v. Nation Enter.,* 471 U.S. 539, 560 (1985). Because "the doctrine is an equitable rule of reason, no generally applicable definition is possible, and each case raising the question must be decided on its own facts." *Id.* at 560 (citation omitted). Section 107 requires courts to consider four nonexclusive factors when evaluating fair use:

> (1) the purpose and character of the use, including whether such use is of a commercial nature or is for nonprofit educational purposes;
>
> (2) the nature of the copyrighted work;
>
> (3) the amount and substantiality of the portion used in relation to the copyrighted work as a whole; and
>
> (4) the effect of the use upon the potential market for or value of the copyrighted work.

17 U.S.C. § 107. Each factor is "to be explored, and the results weighed together, in light of the purposes of copyright." *Campbell,* 510 U.S. at 577.

A. Purpose and Character of the Infringing Use

When evaluating the purpose and character of the use, one must consider "whether the new work merely 'supersede[s] the objects' of the original creation or instead adds something new, with a further purpose or different character, altering the first with new expression, meaning, or message; it asks, in other words, whether and to what extent the new work is 'transformative.' " *Id.* at 579. Although "transformative use is not absolutely necessary for a finding of fair use, the goal of copyright, to promote science and the arts, is generally furthered by the creation of transformative works. Such works thus lie at the heart of the fair use doctrine's guarantee of breathing space within the confines of copyright." *Id.* (citation omitted).

As a preliminary matter, we note that the inquiry must focus on the purpose and character of the stamp, rather than that of Mr. Alli's photograph. The stamp does not reflect any "further purpose" than The Column. *See Campbell,* 510 U.S. at 579. As the Court of Federal Claims found, both the stamp and The Column share a common purpose: to honor veterans of the Korean War.

Works that make fair use of copyrighted material often transform the purpose or character of the work by incorporating it into a larger commentary or criticism. For example, in *Blanch v. Koons,* an artist incorporated a copyrighted photograph of a woman's feet adorned with glittery Gucci sandals into a collage "commenting on the 'commercial images . . . in our consumer culture.' " 467 F.3d 244, 248 (2d Cir. 2006). The court determined that this was fair use in part because the collage was transformative. *Id.* at 252–53. It reasoned that the collage and the photo had "sharply different" purposes and that the collage was intended to be a "commentary on the social and aesthetic consequences of mass media." *Id.*

We conclude that the stamp does not transform the character of The Column. Although the stamp altered the appearance of The Column by adding snow and muting the color, these alterations do not impart a different character to the work. To the extent that the stamp has a surreal character, The Column and its soldiers themselves contribute to that character. Indeed, the Penn State Team suggested that the Memorial have a "dream-like presence of ghostly figures." Capturing The Column on a cold morning after a snowstorm—rather than on a warm sunny day—does not transform its character, meaning, or message. Nature's decision to snow cannot deprive Mr. Gaylord of an otherwise valid right to exclude.

Analysis of the purpose and character of the use also includes whether the "use is of a commercial nature or is for nonprofit educational purposes." 17 U.S.C. § 107. The Postal Service acknowledged receiving $17 million from the sale of nearly 48 million 37-cent stamps. An estimated $5.4 million in stamps were sold to collectors in 2003. The stamp clearly has a commercial purpose. Because the stamp did not have a further purpose or different character, and because it had a commercial use, we conclude that this factor weighs strongly against fair use.

B. Nature of the Copyrighted Work

We next consider the nature of the copyrighted work, The Column. "This factor calls for recognition that some works are closer to the core of intended copyright protection than others, with the consequence that fair use is more difficult to establish when the former works are copied." *Campbell,* 510 U.S. at 586. Relevant to this factor, courts consider: "(1) whether the work is expressive or creative, such as a work of fiction, or more factual, with a greater leeway being allowed to a claim of fair use where the work is factual or informational, and (2) whether the work is published or unpublished, with the scope for fair use involving unpublished works being considerably narrower." *Blanch,* 467 F.3d at 256.

We see no clear error in the Court of Federal Claims' finding that The Column is expressive and creative. However, it noted that "when a creative work has been copied, the second factor may be of limited utility to the fair use analysis where the challenged work is transformative." *Id.* (citing *Blanch,* 467 F.3d at 257). In this case, the stamp did not use The Column in a transformative manner—the purpose and character of the use were identical. Thus, we see no reason to discount the expressive and creative nature of The Column. Although The Column is part of a national monument—perhaps the epitome of a published work—given the overall creative and expressive nature of the work, we conclude that this factor weighs against fair use.

C. The Amount and Substantiality of the Portion Used

The third factor concerns whether "the amount and substantiality of the portion used in relation to the copyrighted work as a whole . . . are reasonable in relation to the purpose of the copying." *Campbell,* 510 U.S. at 587. Courts consider both the quantity and quality of the materials used. *Id.*

As to the quantity, the Court of Federal Claims found that the stamp depicted a substantial number (14 of the 19) of the soldier sculptures, weighing against fair use. As to the quality, the court determined that "Mr. Alli and the Postal Service used variables to lessen the quality and importance of 'The Column' and to alter the expression of the Stamp," changing "the qualitative message of 'The Column.' " The court concluded that while the use of many of the soldier statues weighed against fair use, the weight of this factor was "somewhat mitigated" by the quality and importance of the statues to the stamp.

We agree that the government's use of many of the soldiers in the stamp weighs against fair use, however, we disagree that the weight is mitigated by the quality and importance of The Column to the stamp. The Column constitutes the focus—essentially the entire subject matter—of the stamp. The stamp itself is titled "Korean War Veterans Memorial." Although the snow and muted coloring lessen the features of the soldier sculptures, the stamp clearly depicts an image of The Column. Thus, we conclude that this factor weighs against fair use.

### D. Market Impact

The fourth fair use factor is "the effect of the use upon the potential market for or value of the copyrighted work." 17 U.S.C. § 107. This factor requires courts to consider "whether unrestricted and widespread conduct of the sort engaged in by the defendant . . . would result in a substantially adverse impact on the potential market." *Campbell,* 510 U.S. at 590 (quoting 3 M. Nimmer & D. Nimmer, *Nimmer on Copyright* § 13.05[A][4] (1993)). "In evaluating this factor, a court must consider not only the primary market for the copyrighted work, but the current and potential market for derivative works." *Twin Peaks* [*Productions, Inc. v. Publications Int'l Ltd.*], 996 F.2d 1366, 1377 (2d Cir. 1993).

The Court of Federal Claims found that the stamp caused no harm to either the value of The Column or the market for derivative works. It noted that Mr. Gaylord conceded that the stamp actually increased the value of The Column. *Id.* The court further determined that the stamp did not impact Mr. Gaylord's prior efforts to market derivative works, and that it was not likely to impact such efforts in the future because the stamp was an inadequate market substitute for The Column. *Id.* at 70–71. The court therefore concluded that this factor weighed in favor of fair use.

We see no clear error in the court's determination that the stamp has not and will not adversely impact Mr. Gaylord's efforts to market derivative works of The Column. Thus, we agree that this factor favors fair use.

E. No Fair Use

Weighing the factors, we conclude that the government's use of The Column in the stamp was not a fair use. Even though the stamp did not harm the market for derivative works, allowing the government to commercially exploit a creative and expressive work will not advance the purposes of copyright in this case. [The court of appeals affirmed the remaining parts of the Court of Federal Claims' decision finding that the government was not a joint author and the Memorial was not an architectural work.]

NEWMAN, Circuit Judge, dissenting. The Court of Federal Claims decided the case on the ground of fair use, holding that the depiction of the Korean War Veterans Memorial on the postage stamp is a "transformative" work. The court explained that the image on the stamp has a "new and different character" from the sculpture at the Memorial, depicting a "surrealistic environment with snow and subdued lighting where the viewer is left unsure whether he is viewing a photograph of statutes or actual human beings." Mr. Alli's photograph was further edited by the Postal Service, to amplify the stark effect of the snowy image.

Clear error has not been shown in the Court of Federal Claims' factual findings supporting the statutory factors of fair use. A transformative work is generally deemed a fair use of a copyrighted work. This finding of fair use of itself establishes the right of the United States to use a picture of the Memorial on a United States postage stamp, without liability for copyright infringement.

The Contracting Officer observed that the contractors' assertion of copyright "unreasonably and unfairly impact[s] the end users of the Memorial," and "produce[s] a chilling effect on the public's ability to use the [Memorial] as intended." Final Decision of the Engineers Contracting Officer of the U.S. Army Engineer District, Baltimore, February 23, 2000 at 7. The use for governmental purposes of a photograph of the Korean War Veterans Memorial, a public monument that was designed and built with public money, is unambiguously covered by the contract and statutes under which this Memorial was built. The court errs in its holding that Mr. Gaylord is entitled to damages for copyright infringement.

## *NOTES AND QUESTIONS*

1. *Purpose of use.* How much weight did the court place on the issue of whether the U.S. Postal Service's use of an image of The Column on its stamp was transformative? Is the court's finding of a lack of a transformative use or purpose consistent with its later conclusion that the stamp was not a substitute for the actual work or derivatives of the work? Does Judge Newman have a valid point in dissent? The Supreme Court explained the first factor as follows: "The central purpose of this investigation is to see, in Justice Story's words, whether the new work merely 'supersede[s] the objects' of the original creation,

*Folsom v. Marsh*, *supra*, at 348; or instead adds something new, with a further purpose or different character, altering the first with new expression, meaning, or message; it asks, in other words, whether and to what extent the new work is 'transformative.'" *Campbell v. Acuff-Rose Music, Inc.*, 510 U.S. 569, 578–79 (1994).

2. *Market impact.* Gaylord acknowledged the stamp *increased* the value of his sculptural work, The Column. How would you weigh the fact that Gaylord suffered no market harm to his work from the U.S. Postal Service's stamp? Do you agree with the court's balancing of the four fair use factors?

3. Would it have made a difference if The Column were an architectural work? (Hint: review the section on architectural works above.)

4. *Design.* Do you think the fair use doctrine is helpful to designers who wish to copy, as a fair use, some design elements of other works? For example, could a competitor claim a fair use in copying some of the cheerleading patterns in Problem 4–3 above (assuming they are copyrightable)? Or does the case-by-case determination of fair use based on a balancing of 4 factors provide cold comfort to designers who hope to make legitimate fair uses?

---

## LOUIS VUITTON MALLETIER S.A. v. HAUTE DIGGITY DOG, LLC

464 F. Supp. 2d 495 (E.D. Va. 2006), *aff'd*, 507 F.3d 252 (4th Cir. 2007)

JAMES C. CACHERIS, DISTRICT JUDGE. This matter comes before the Court on Plaintiff's and Defendants' cross-motions for summary judgment. This "dog of a case" gave the Court a great amount of facts to chew upon and applicable law to sniff out. Nonetheless, having thoroughly gnawed through the record, this Court finds that no material dispute of fact remains, and summary judgment is appropriate on all counts. For the following reasons, the Court will deny Plaintiff's motion and grant Defendants' motion.

### I. Background

Plaintiff, Louis Vuitton Malletier S.A., ("LVM") is a manufacturer of luxury consumer goods, including luggage and handbags. In 1896, LVM created a Monogram Canvas Pattern Design mark and trade dress, which includes, *inter alia,* an entwined L and V monogram with three motifs and a four pointed star, and is used to identify its products. In 2002, Vuitton introduced a new signature design in collaboration with Japanese designer Takashi Murakami. LVM manufactures a limited number of high-end pet products, such as leashes and collars that range in price from $250 to $1600.

Plaintiff filed this action on March 24, 2006 against Defendants Haute Diggity Dog, LLC ("HDD"), Victoria Dauernheim, and Woofies, LLC d/b/a

Woofie's Pet Boutique. HDD is a company that markets plush stuffed toys and beds for dogs under names that parody the products of other companies. HDD sells products such as Chewnel # 5, Dog Perignon, Chewy Vuiton, and Sniffany & Co. in pet stores, alongside other dog toys, bones, beds, and food, and most are priced around $10. [Some of the dog toys may be viewed at http://www.hautediggitydog.com/collections/toys/products/white-chewy-vuiton-purse, and at https://www.hautediggitydog.com/collections/toys/products/checker-chewy-vuiton-bones. *Ed.*] Plaintiff's complaint specifically refers to HDD's use of the mark "Chewy Vuiton" and alleges that this mark, as well as other marks and designs that imitate Plaintiff's trademarks and copyrights, violate Plaintiff's trademark, trade dress, and copyright rights. Plaintiff and Defendants have filed cross-motions for summary judgment. These motions are currently before the Court. [The court's analysis of the trademark claims is omitted. *Ed.*]

B. Defendants' Fair Use Defense

Defendants next argue that, even if a valid and enforceable copyright is owned by LVM, Defendants' use of the LVM design is a non-infringing, fair use of the copyrighted material for the purpose of parodying the LVM design. The Supreme Court has developed a test to determine fair use, by which courts are to consider by a totality of the circumstances: (1) purpose and character of the use, including whether such use is of a commercial nature or is for nonprofit educational uses; (2) nature of the copyrighted work; (3) amount and substantiality of the portion used in relation to the copyrighted work as a whole; (4) the effect of the use upon potential market for or value of the copyrighted work. *Campbell v. Acuff-Rose Music, Inc.*, 510 U.S. 569, 577 (1994). Fair use is an affirmative defense with the burden of proof on the defendant. *Id.* at 590.

This Court must first consider the purpose and character of the use. Commercial use is one factor to be considered in determining fairness, and is not by itself presumptively unfair. *Id.* at 591. Parody, even when done for the purpose of commercial gain, can be a fair use, as the Supreme Court has stated specifically that it is more likely that "the new work [a parody] will not affect the market for the original in a way cognizable under this factor, that is, by acting as a substitute for it." *Id.* at 591. In this case, the use of similar marks and name in a line of dog chew toys and beds parodies the high-end fashion status of LVM's products in a market that LVM does not participate—the market for pet toys and beds. This Court finds that the use of similar markings and colors to those copyrighted by LVM for Chewy Vuiton products is a parody.

The next element, nature of the copyrighted work (creative) is a less-important factor for a parody case and "not much help" in separating infringers from parodies. *Id.* at 586. Therefore, this Court will not address nature of the copyrighted work, other than to acknowledge that it is a creative design.

This Court will finally consider the amount and substantiality of the portion used in relation to the copyrighted work as a whole. The Supreme Court held that in a parody case, the parody itself necessarily springs from recognizable allusion to its object through distorted imitation. Its art lies in the tension between a known original and its parodic twin. When parody takes aim at a particular original work, the parody must be able to "conjure up" at least enough of that original to make the object of its critical wit recognizable. *Id.* at 588.

In this case, the name "Chewy Vuiton" is an obvious wordplay on the name Louis Vuitton, and the superimposed C and V on the logo are intended to "conjure up" enough of the Louis Vuitton logo in order to make the object of its wit—a humorous play on Louis Vuitton's high-end image in the form of dog toys—recognizable. The parody is not possible unless the logo and name are similar to those of Plaintiff, and therefore such parody constitutes a fair use in this respect.

Finally, this Court considers interference with the potential market for plaintiff's original and derivative works caused by Defendants' actions. First, the market overlap between Plaintiff and Defendants is tenuous. Louis Vuitton's primary market is for high-end women's apparel, not pet toys. As explained *supra,* Plaintiff does sell some pet items, but not toys or beds, and only in a limited, high-end market. Second, Plaintiff has offered no evidence of interference with potential markets or control of its copyrights. Defendants, on the other hand, have presented deposition testimony and an expert declaration indicating that there has been no effect on LVM's potential markets or control of its copyrights. For the foregoing reasons, summary judgment should be granted for the Defendants.

### *NOTES AND QUESTIONS*

1. How does a parody use of a copyrighted work affect the fair use analysis? Is a parody considered transformative under the first factor? Does a parody affect the remaining three factors?

2. The Supreme Court defined parody as follows: "For the purposes of copyright law, the nub of the definitions, and the heart of any parodist's claim to quote from existing material, is the use of some elements of a prior author's composition to create a new one that, at least in part, comments on that author's works." *Campbell v. Acuff-Rose Music, Inc.,* 510 U.S. 569, 580 (1994). The Court also established a low threshold for courts to apply: "The threshold question when fair use is raised in defense of parody is whether a parodic character may reasonably be perceived. Whether, going beyond that, parody is in good taste or bad does not and should not matter to fair use. As Justice Holmes explained, '[i]t would be a dangerous undertaking for persons trained only to the law to constitute themselves final judges of the worth of [a work], outside of the narrowest and most obvious limits. At the one extreme some works of genius would be sure to miss appreciation.' " *Id.* at 582 (citation

omitted). Under this test, do you think the Chewy Vuitton dog toy was a parody?

3. Why do you think copyright law privileges parodies under fair use? How do parodies promote learning or knowledge? Can you think of examples of parodies that provided you with a better understanding of an issue?

---

### c. Idea v. Expression Dichotomy and Functional Elements

#### U.S. Copyright Act Section 102(b)

> (b) In no case does copyright protection for an original work of authorship extend to any idea, procedure, process, system, method of operation, concept, principle, or discovery, regardless of the form in which it is described, explained, illustrated, or embodied in such work.

### BAKER V. SELDEN

101 U.S. 99 (1879)

MR. JUSTICE BRADLEY delivered the opinion of the Court. Charles Selden, the testator of the complainant in this case, in the year 1859 took the requisite steps for obtaining the copyright of a book, entitled "Selden's Condensed Ledger, or Bookkeeping Simplified," the object of which was to exhibit and explain a peculiar system of bookkeeping. In 1860 and 1861, he took the copyright of several other books, containing additions to and improvements upon the said system. The bill of complaint was filed against the defendant, Baker, for an alleged infringement of these copyrights. The latter, in his answer, denied that Selden was the author or designer of the books, and denied the infringement charged, and contends on the argument that the matter alleged to be infringed is not a lawful subject of copyright.

The book or series of books of which the complainant claims the copyright consists of an introductory essay explaining the system of bookkeeping referred to, to which are annexed certain forms or banks, consisting of ruled lines, and headings, illustrating the system and showing how it is to be used and carried out in practice. This system effects the same results as bookkeeping by double entry, but, by a peculiar arrangement of columns and headings, presents the entire operation, of a day, a week, or a month on a single page or on two pages facing each other, in an account book. The defendant uses a similar plan so far as results are concerned, but makes a different arrangement of the columns, and uses different headings. If the complainant's testator had the exclusive right to the use of the system explained in his book, it would be difficult to contend that the defendant does not infringe it, notwithstanding the difference in his form of arrangement; but if it be assumed that the system is open to public use, it seems to be equally difficult to contend that the books made and sold by the defendant are a violation of the copyright of the complainant's book considered merely as a book explanatory of the system. Where the truths of a science or the methods of an art are the common property of the whole world, any author has the right to express the one, or explain and use the other, in his own way. As an author, Selden explained the system in a particular way. It may be conceded that Baker makes and uses account books arranged on substantially the same system, but the proof fails to show that he has violated the copyright of Selden's book, regarding the latter merely as an explanatory work, or that he has infringed Selden's right in any way, unless the latter became entitled to an exclusive right in the system.

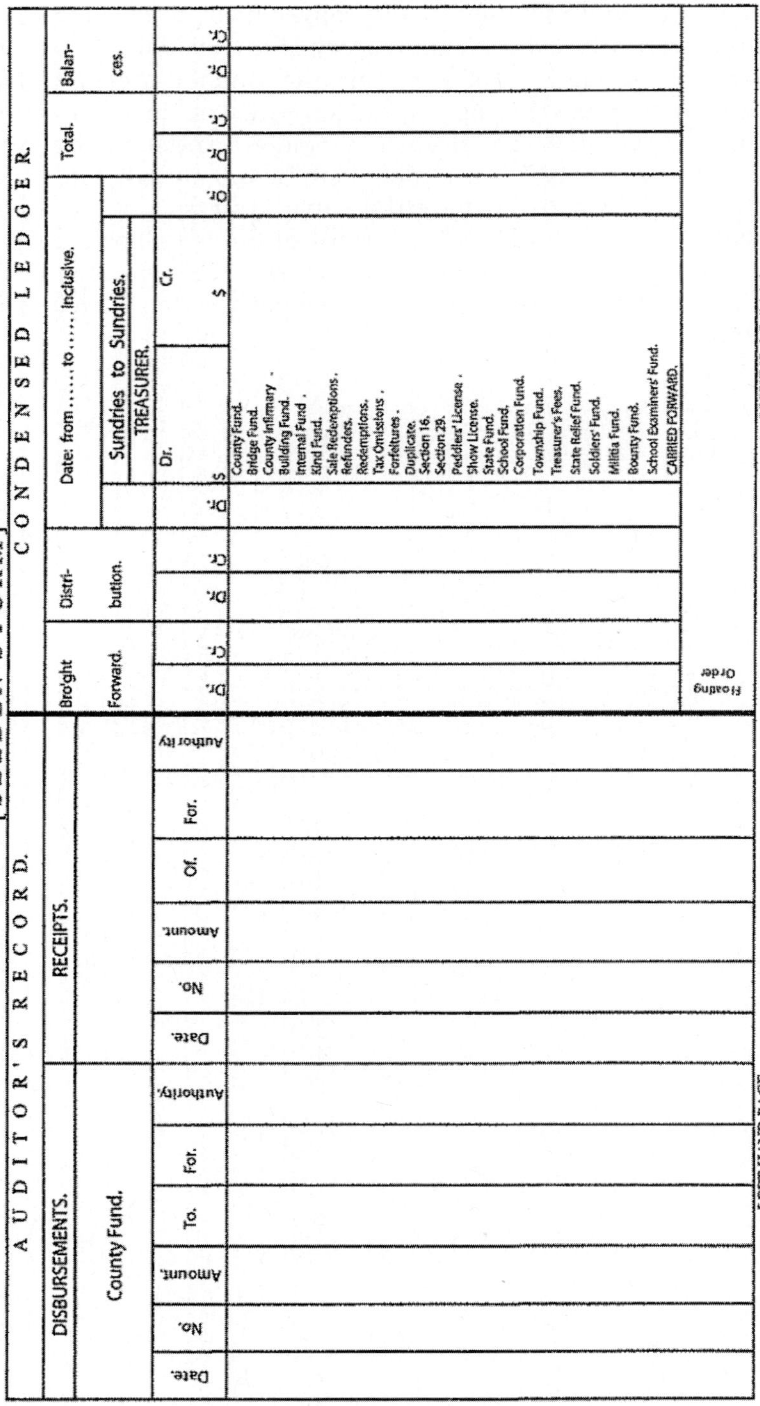

[SELDEN'S FORM]

AUDITOR'S RECORD.

DISBURSEMENTS. County Fund.

| Date. | No. | Amount. | To. | For. | Authority. |
|---|---|---|---|---|---|

RECEIPTS.

| Date. | No. | Amount. | Of. | For. | Authority. |
|---|---|---|---|---|---|

LEFT HAND PAGE

CONDENSED LEDGER.

| Brog'ght Forward. | | Distribution. | | Date: from ...... to ...... inclusive. Sundries to Sundries. TREASURER. | | | | Total. | | Balances. | |
|---|---|---|---|---|---|---|---|---|---|---|---|
| Dr. | Cr. | Dr. | Cr. | Dr. | Dr. $ | Cr. $ | Cr. | Dr. | Cr. | Dr. | Cr. |

County Fund.
Bridge Fund.
County Infirmary.
Building Fund.
Internal Fund.
Kind Fund.
Sale Redemptions.
Refunders.
Redemptions.
Tax Omissions.
Forfeitures.
Duplicate.
Section 16.
Section 29.
Peddlers' License.
Show License.
State Fund.
School Fund.
Corporation Fund.
Township Fund.
Treasurer's Fees.
State Relief Fund.
Soldiers' Fund.
Militia Fund.
Bounty Fund.
School Examiners' Fund.
CARRIED FORWARD.

Floating Order

RIGHT HAND PAGE

[Forms are recreated from Baker's brief by Pamela Samuelson. *Ed.*]

[BAKER'S FORM.]

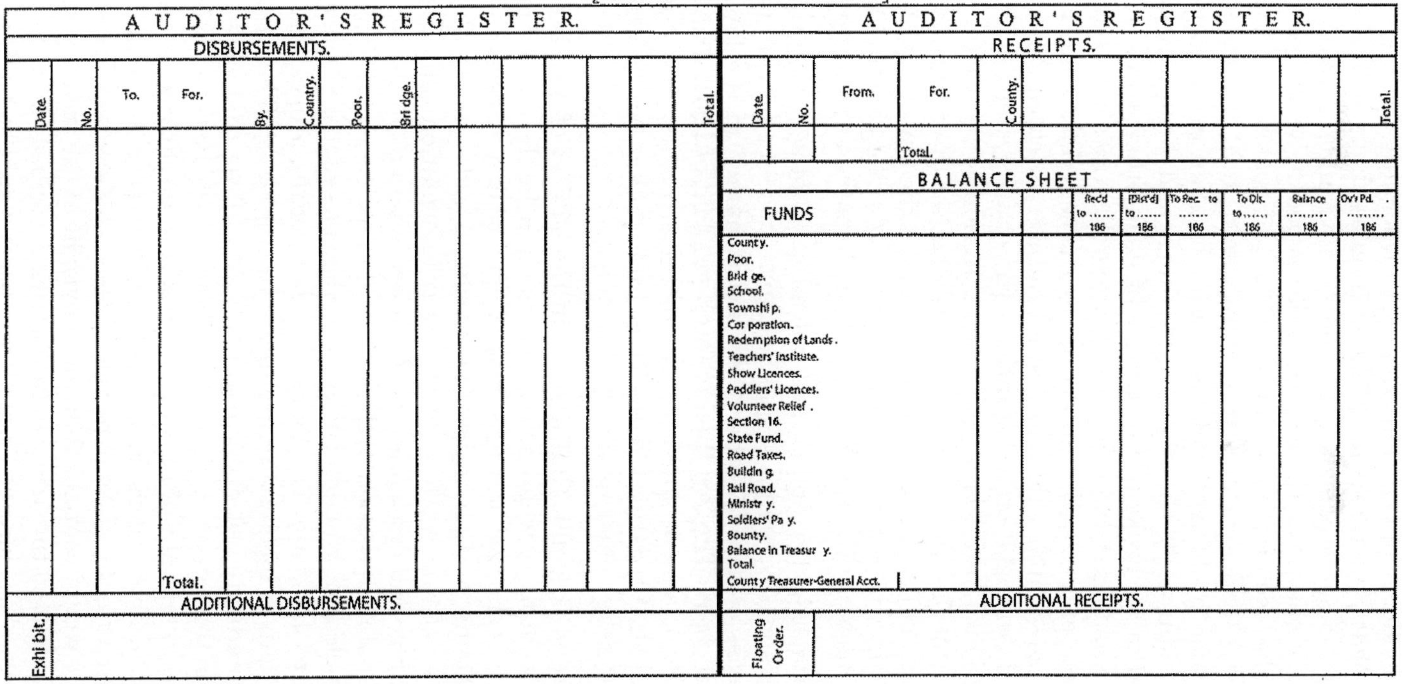

AUDITOR'S REGISTER.

DISBURSEMENTS.

| Date. | No. | To. | For. | By. | Country. | Poor. | Bri dge. | | | | | | | Total. |
|---|---|---|---|---|---|---|---|---|---|---|---|---|---|---|
| | | | Total. | | | | | | | | | | | |

ADDITIONAL DISBURSEMENTS.

Exhi bit.

AUDITOR'S REGISTER.

RECEIPTS.

| Date. | No. | From. | For. | County. | | | | | | | Total. |
|---|---|---|---|---|---|---|---|---|---|---|---|
| | | | Total. | | | | | | | | |

BALANCE SHEET

| FUNDS | | | Rec'd to ...... 186 | [Dist'd] to ...... 186 | To Rec. to ....... 186 | To Dis. to...... 186 | Balance .......... 186 | Ov'r Pd. ......... 186 |
|---|---|---|---|---|---|---|---|---|
| County. | | | | | | | | |
| Poor. | | | | | | | | |
| Brid ge. | | | | | | | | |
| School. | | | | | | | | |
| Townshi p. | | | | | | | | |
| Cor poration. | | | | | | | | |
| Redemption of Lands. | | | | | | | | |
| Teachers' Institute. | | | | | | | | |
| Show Licences. | | | | | | | | |
| Peddlers' Licences. | | | | | | | | |
| Volunteer Relief . | | | | | | | | |
| Section 16. | | | | | | | | |
| State Fund. | | | | | | | | |
| Road Taxes. | | | | | | | | |
| Buildin g. | | | | | | | | |
| Rail Road. | | | | | | | | |
| Ministr y. | | | | | | | | |
| Soldiers' Pa y. | | | | | | | | |
| Bounty. | | | | | | | | |
| Balance in Treasur y. | | | | | | | | |
| Total. | | | | | | | | |
| Count y Treasurer-General Acct. | | | | | | | | |

ADDITIONAL RECEIPTS.

Floating Order.

The evidence of the complainant is principally directed to the object of showing that Baker uses the same system as that which is explained and illustrated in Selden's books. It becomes important, therefore, to determine whether, in obtaining the copyright of his books, he secured the exclusive right to the use of the system or method of bookkeeping which the said books are intended to illustrate and explain. It is contended that he has secured such exclusive right because no one can use the system without using substantially the same ruled lines and headings which he was appended to his books in illustration of it. In other words, it is contended that the ruled lines and headings, given to illustrate the system, are a part of the book, and as such are secured by the copyright, and that no one can make or use similar ruled lines and headings, or ruled lines and headings made and arranged on substantially the same system, without violating the copyright. And this is really the question to be decided in this case. Stated in another form, the question is whether the exclusive property in a system of bookkeeping can be claimed under the law or copyright by means of a book in which that system is explained? The complainant's bill, and the case made under it, are based on the hypothesis that it can be.

It cannot be pretended, and indeed it is not seriously urged, that the ruled lines of the complainant's account book can be claimed under any special class of objects, other than books, named in the law of copyright existing in 1859. The law then in force was that of 1831, and specified only books, maps, charts, musical compositions, prints, and engravings. An account book, consisting of ruled lines and blank columns, cannot be called by any of these names unless by that of a book.

There is no doubt that a work on the subject of bookkeeping, though only explanatory of well known systems, may be the subject of a copyright, but then it is claimed only as a book. Such a book may be explanatory either of old systems or of an entirely new system, and, considered as a book, as the work of an author, conveying information on the subject of bookkeeping, and containing detailed explanations of the art, it may be a very valuable acquisition to the practical knowledge of the community. But there is a clear distinction between the book as such and the art which it is intended to illustrate. The mere statement of the proposition is so evident that it requires hardly any argument to support it. The same distinction may be predicated of every other art as well as that of bookkeeping. A treatise on the composition and use of medicines, be they old or new; on the construction and use of ploughs, or watches, or churns; or on the mixture and application of colors for painting or dyeing; or on the mode of drawing lines to produce the effect of perspective—would be the subject of copyright; but no one would contend that the copyright of the treatise would give the exclusive right to the art or manufacture described therein. The copyright of the book, if not pirated from other works, would be valid without regard to the novelty, or want of novelty, of its subject matter. The novelty of the art or thing described or explained has nothing to do with the validity of the copyright. To give to the author of the book an exclusive property in the art described therein when no examination of its novelty has ever been officially made would be a surprise and a fraud upon the public. That is the province of letters patent, not of copyright. The claim to an invention or discovery of an art or manufacture must be subjected to the examination of the Patent Office before an exclusive right therein can be obtained, and it can only be secured by a patent from the government.

The difference between the two things, letters patent and copyright, may be illustrated by reference to the subjects just enumerated. Take the case of medicines. Certain mixtures are found to be of great value in the healing art. If the discoverer writes and publishes a book on the subject (as regular physicians generally do), he gains no exclusive right to the manufacture and sale of the medicine; he gives that to the public. If he desires to acquire such exclusive right, he must obtain a patent for the mixture as a new art, manufacture, or composition of matter. He may copyright his book if he pleases, but that only secures to him the exclusive right of printing and publishing his book. So of all other inventions or discoveries.

The copyright of a book on perspective, no matter how many drawings and illustrations it may contain, gives no exclusive right to the modes of drawing described, though they may never have been known or used before. By publishing the book without getting a patent for the art, the latter is given to the public. The fact that the art described in the book by illustrations of lines and figures which are reproduced in practice in the application of the art makes no difference. Those illustrations are the mere language employed by the author to convey his ideas more clearly. Had he used words of description instead of diagrams (which merely stand in the place of words), there could not be the slightest doubt that others, applying the art to practical use, might lawfully draw the lines and diagrams which were in the author's mind, and which he thus described by words in his book.

The copyright of a work on mathematical science cannot give to the author an exclusive right to the methods of operation which he propounds, or to the diagrams which he employs to explain them, so as to prevent an engineer from using them whenever occasion requires. The very object of publishing a book on science or the useful arts is to communicate to the world the useful knowledge which it contains. But this object would be frustrated if the knowledge could not be used without incurring the guilt of piracy of the book. And where the art it teaches cannot be used without employing the methods and diagrams used to illustrate the book, or such as are similar to them, such methods and diagrams are to be considered as necessary incidents to the art, and given therewith to the public—not given for the purpose of publication in other works explanatory of the art, but for the purpose of practical application.

Of course these observations are not intended to apply to ornamental designs or pictorial illustrations addressed to the taste. Of these it may be said that their form is their essence, and their object, the production of pleasure in their contemplation. This is their final end. They are as much the product of genius and the result of composition as are the lines of the poet or the historian's period. On the other hand, the teachings of science and the rules and methods of useful art have their final end in application and use, and this application and use are what the public derive from the publication of a book which teaches them. But as embodied and taught in a literary composition or book, their essence consists only in their statement. This alone is what is secured by the copyright. The use by another of the same methods of statement, whether in words or illustrations, in a book published for teaching the art would undoubtedly be an infringement of the copyright.

Recurring to the case before us, we observe that Charles Selden, by his books, explained and described a peculiar system of bookkeeping, and illustrated his method by means of ruled lines and blank columns, with proper headings on a page or on successive pages. Now whilst no one has a right to print or publish his book, or any material part thereof, as a book intended to convey instruction in the art, any person may practice and use the art itself which he has described and illustrated therein. The use of the art is a totally different thing from a publication of the book explaining it. The copyright of a book on bookkeeping cannot secure the exclusive right to make, sell, and use account books prepared upon the plan set forth in such book. Whether the art might or might not have been patented is a question which is not before us. It was not patented, and is open and free to the use of the public. And of course, in using the art, the ruled lines and headings of accounts must necessarily be used as incident to it.

The plausibility of the claim put forward by the complainant in this case arises from a confusion of ideas produced by the peculiar nature of the art described in the books which have been made the subject of copyright. In describing the art, the illustrations and diagrams employed happen to correspond more closely than usual with the actual work performed by the operator who uses the art. Those illustrations and diagrams consist of ruled lines and headings of accounts, and it is similar ruled lines and headings of accounts which, in the application of the art, the bookkeeper makes with his pen, or the stationer with his press, whilst in most other cases the diagrams and illustrations can only be represented in concrete forms of wood, metal, stone, or some other physical embodiment. But the principle is the same in all. The description of the art in a book, though entitled to the benefit of copyright, lays no foundation for an exclusive claim to the art itself. The object of the one is explanation; the object of the other is use. The former may be secured by copyright. The latter can only be secured, if it can be secured at all, by letters patent.

In *Drury v. Ewing,* 1 Bond, 540, which is much relied on by the complainant, a copyright was claimed in a chart of patterns for cutting dresses and basques for ladies, and coats, jackets, &c., for boys. It is obvious that such designs could only be printed and published for information, and not for use in themselves. Their practical use could only be exemplified in cloth on the tailor's board and under his shears—in other words, by the application of a mechanical operation to the cutting of cloth in certain patterns and forms. Surely the exclusive right to this practical use was not reserved to the publisher by his copyright of the chart. Without undertaking to say whether we should or should not concur in the decision in that case, we think it cannot control the present.

The conclusion to which we have come is that blank account books are not the subject of copyright, and that the mere copyright of Selden's book did not confer upon him the exclusive right to make and use account books, ruled and arranged as designated by him and described and illustrated in said book. The decree of the circuit court must be reversed and the cause remanded with instructions to dismiss the complainant's bill, and it is. *So ordered.*

### *NOTES AND QUESTIONS*

1. What is the holding of *Baker v. Selden*? Were the accounting forms of Selden copyrightable?

2. *Idea-expression; merger doctrine; systems.* Some commentators attribute the basic principle of copyright law that ideas are not copyrightable (only the expression is) to *Baker v. Selden*. Another doctrine associated with the case is the merger doctrine: even original expression (e.g., a form) may not be copyrighted if there are two few ways to express the same idea (e.g., double-entry bookkeeping). In addition, others contend that *Baker* is better understand as a case prohibiting the copyrighting of a useful system (and forms necessary to perform the system). For further discussion, see Pamela Samuelson, *Why Copyright Law Excludes Systems and Processes from the Scope of Its Protection*, 85 TEX. L. REV. 1921, 1923 (2006–2007) (interpreting *Baker v. Selden* as a case barring useful systems from copyright, but not a case originating the idea-expression dichotomy).

3. Section 102(b) of the Copyright Act reflects at least some of the teachings of the case: copyright law does not extend to "any idea, procedure, process, system, method of operation, concept, principle, or discovery, regardless of the form in which it is described, explained, illustrated, or embodied in such work." Do you think these principles are relevant to analyzing whether industrial designs are copyrightable? For example, do you think designs embody ideas? If so, what if there are too few ways to express a certain idea embodied in a design.

4. *Blank forms.* Another facet of *Baker v. Selden* is its origin of the so-called "blank forms" doctrine. The Copyright Offices takes the position: "Blank forms, such as time cards, graph paper, account books, diaries, bank checks,

scorecards, address books, report forms, order forms and the like, which are designed for recording information and do not in themselves convey information." 37 C.F.R. § 202.1(c) (2006).

5. Does *Baker v. Selden* run counter to the overlapping IP rights approach we have seen in other contexts? Why might utility patents present a different situation than design patents, militating against allowing overlapping IP rights?

---

## G. REMEDIES

Copyright law affords copyright owners a full panoply of potential remedies if they prevail in proving, in court, infringements of their works by defendants. The following section discusses injunctions and damages.

### 1. PRELIMINARY AND PERMANENT INJUNCTIONS

Section 502 gives courts the discretion to "grant temporary and final injunctions on such terms as it may deem reasonable to prevent or restrain infringement of a copyright." In the past, courts routinely granted preliminary injunctions (before a trial while the case was litigated) to copyright owners if they showed (1) a probability of success on the merits and (2) that they will suffer irreparable harm in the absence of a preliminary injunction. Courts typically presumed irreparable harm if there was infringement. However, in a patent case, the Supreme Court disagreed with this presumption and held that injunctive relief is a matter of equity and courts must consider the following four equitable factors before awarding an injunction:

> A plaintiff must demonstrate: (1) that it has suffered an irreparable injury; (2) that remedies available at law, such as monetary damages, are inadequate to compensate for that injury; (3) that, considering the balance of hardships between the plaintiff and defendant, a remedy in equity is warranted; and (4) that the public interest would not be disserved by a permanent injunction.

*eBay, Inc. v. MercExchange, L.L.C.,* 547 U.S. 388, 390 (2006). Courts have applied the *eBay* factors to copyright cases, as well as to determining both preliminary and permanent injunctions. Consider the following case.

## FLEXIBLE LIFELINE SYSTEMS, INC. v. PRECISION LIFT, INC.

654 F.3d 989 (9th Cir. 2011)

PER CURIAM:

### BACKGROUND

John Tollenaere formed Precision [Lift] in the 1990s to market a helicopter rescue lift product he had patented. In or around 2000, Precision expanded its business to include sales of aircraft maintenance stands and platforms for fixed- and rotorwing aircraft.[1] Precision did not manufacture any of its own stands or platforms. Rather, Precision sold stands or platforms manufactured by others, even though it claims that it also had the ability to independently design aircraft maintenance stands. In early 2001, Precision again sought to increase its business and became the sole distributor for aircraft maintenance stands designed and manufactured by West Coast Weld Tech, Inc. ("West Coast").

West Coast allowed Precision to use the technical drawings of the stands manufactured by West Coast in order for Precision to market the stands, but West Coast always claimed ownership of the drawings.[2] All of the drawings at issue were stamped by West Coast as its confidential and proprietary information. West Coast never transferred or sold ownership of the drawings, or any of its intellectual property, to Precision.

In July of 2008, Precision and West Coast entered into a joint venture to compete for a United States Air Force contract to manufacture and sell maintenance stands for C–130 Hercules aircraft.

In 2009, West Coast encountered significant financial problems. Unable to continue operating on its own, West Coast sold the majority of its assets, including much of its intellectual property, to Flexible. In particular, the purchase agreement specified that "ALL drawings, details, production schedules, etc. for design, construction and installation of maintenance platforms for aircraft and land vehicles" were included in the purchase. After the purchase, Flexible continued what had been West Coast's work on the final C–130 drawings and forwarded them to the Air Force in December 2009. Meanwhile, Precision asked Flexible to discuss formalizing their continuing business relationship in light of Flexible's purchase of West Coast's assets.

---

1 Maintenance stands and platforms are used by aircraft maintenance personnel to stand on when working on aircraft. They provide greater stability and an easier base from which to work than a ladder. Due to the varied size and shape of different aircraft, maintenance stands come in a variety of sizes, shapes, and configurations. In addition, while there are generic stands available, stands and platforms are sometimes specifically designed to fit a particular aircraft. This dispute involves stands and platforms specifically designed for a particular aircraft.

2 As will be shown, Flexible is the plaintiff here because West Coast sold its assets, including the rights to the drawings at issue, to Flexible in 2009.

On January 27, 2010, Flexible responded to Precision's requests to formalize their business relationship by advising Precision that Flexible was not interested in continuing a joint venture. Flexible presented Precision with alternate proposals, including one by which Precision would become a sales agent for Flexible's products. Rather than proceed with either of Flexible's proposals, Precision found another joint venture partner to take West Coast's place in the C–130 maintenance stand bid proposal. Precision joined with Carbis, one of Flexible's competitors, and submitted a final bid for the project totaling over $61 million. Flexible did not submit a bid of its own for the proposal. The Air Force eventually awarded the contract to another competitor at a contract price approximately $9.5 million higher than Precision's bid, likely due to the dispute between Precision and Flexible as to the ownership of the drawings. Precision protested the award, but the Air Force ultimately denied the protest.

In the meantime, Flexible filed applications to register the drawings it had purchased from West Coast, and the Copyright Office granted the registrations effective June 23, 2010. Flexible then filed its complaint and an application for injunctive relief to enjoin Precision from using Flexible's intellectual property on the C–130 bid. The district court denied the motion for a temporary restraining order, but set a hearing on the preliminary injunction. Prior to the hearing, Flexible filed an amended application for injunctive relief, expanding the scope of the relief sought to include enjoining Precision from using any of the drawings for maintenance stands for aircraft other than the C–130. In both its application and supplemental application, Flexible argued only that it was entitled to a presumption of irreparable harm and did not offer any evidence of actual harm that it was likely to suffer in the absence of an injunction. The district court held a hearing on the preliminary injunction application on October 14 and 19, 2010. Following the hearing, the court granted the injunction except as to the use of the drawings for the C–130 bid.

## DISCUSSION

### II. STANDARD FOR PRELIMINARY INJUNCTIVE RELIEF

The Copyright Act provides that a court "may . . . grant temporary and final injunctions on such terms as it may deem reasonable to prevent or restrain infringement of a copyright." 17 U.S.C. § 502(a). Thus, injunctive relief to prevent copyright infringement is available as an equitable remedy in the court's discretion. In order to obtain preliminary injunctive relief, a plaintiff "must establish that he is likely to succeed on the merits, that he is likely to suffer irreparable harm in the absence of preliminary relief, that the balance of equities tips in his favor, and that an injunction is in the public interest." *Marlyn Nutraceuticals, Inc. v. Mucos Pharma GmbH & Co.,* 571 F.3d 873, 877 (9th Cir. 2009) (quoting *Winter,* 555 U.S. 7, 129 S. Ct. 365, 374 (2008)). This is commonly referred to as the "four-factor test."

A. Presumption of Irreparable Harm

We have long held that irreparable harm can be presumed in a copyright infringement case upon a showing of a likelihood of success on the merits by the copyright owner.[3] Based on our precedent, the district court granted the preliminary injunction after finding a likelihood of success on the merits, without inquiring into whether Flexible would actually suffer any irreparable harm absent relief. Instead, the district court relied solely on the presumption of irreparable harm, citing our 2003 decision *Elvis Presley* [*Enterprises, Inc. v. Passport Video*], 349 F.3d 622 (9th Cir. 2013). According to Precision, after the Supreme Court's *eBay* and *Winter* decisions in 2006 and 2008, this circuit's long-standing practice of presuming irreparable harm upon the showing of likelihood of success on the merits in a copyright infringement case is no longer good law. Precision is correct. As we prophetically proclaimed in *Elvis Presley* that "[t]he King is dead," 349 F.3d at 624, referring to Elvis Presley the man, today we proclaim that the "*King*" is dead, referring to *Elvis Presley* the case—to the extent it supported the use of a presumption of irreparable harm in issuing injunctive relief.

1. *eBay Inc. v. MercExchange, L.L.C.*

In *eBay,* the Supreme Court reviewed a request for a permanent injunction after a jury found eBay had infringed MercExchange's patent. The district court refused to issue an injunction notwithstanding the infringement, finding "that a 'plaintiff's willingness to license its patents' and its 'lack of commercial activity in practicing the patents' would be sufficient to establish that the patent holder would not suffer irreparable harm." *eBay,* 547 U.S. at 393 (quoting *MercExchange, L.L.C. v. eBay, Inc.,* 275 F. Supp. 2d 695, 712 (E.D. Va. 2003)). The Federal Circuit reversed the district court, "applying its 'general rule that courts will issue permanent injunctions against patent infringement absent exceptional circumstances.' " *Id.* at 391 (quoting *MercExchange, L.L.C. v. eBay, Inc.,* 401 F.3d 1323, 1339 (Fed. Cir. 2005)).

The Supreme Court stated that the district court's "categorical rule" regarding irreparable harm "cannot be squared with the principles of equity adopted by Congress." *eBay,* 547 U.S. at 393. However, by applying a "general rule," the Federal Circuit had "departed in the opposite direction [as the district court] from the four-factor test." *Id.* The Court explained that "[j]ust as the district court erred in its categorical denial of injunctive relief, the Court of Appeals erred in its categorical grant of such relief." *Id.* at 394. The Court was very clear that even where infringement had been

[3] We were not alone in presuming harm. Indeed, nearly thirty years ago the prevailing view among the circuits was that "[a] copyright plaintiff who [made] out a prima facie case of infringement [was] entitled to a preliminary injunction without a detailed showing of irreparable harm." *Apple Computer, Inc. v. Franklin Computer Corp.,* 714 F.2d 1240, 1254 (3d Cir. 1983) (citing 3 *Nimmer on Copyright* § 14.06[A], at 14–50, 14–51 & n.16 (collecting authorities)).

proven, a plaintiff may not be granted injunctive relief until he satisfies the four-factor test, which includes demonstrating irreparable injury. *Id.*

Flexible tries to distinguish *eBay* on the grounds that *eBay* involved patent infringement, not copyright infringement, and argues that the presumption remains valid for a copyright infringement case. However, the Court's reasoning in *eBay* cannot be so narrowly read. The Court based its conclusions on principles of equity, citing the Patent Act's authorization to grant an injunction "in accordance with the principles of equity." *Id.* at 392. The Court made clear that these principles apply equally to copyright infringement by discussing the Copyright Act and drawing parallels between patent and copyright protection throughout its analysis. It explained that its "approach is consistent with our treatment of injunctions under the Copyright Act," *id.,* and noted that "[l]ike the Patent Act, the Copyright Act provides that courts 'may' grant injunctive relief 'on such terms as it may deem reasonable to prevent or restrain infringement of a copyright,' " *id.* (quoting 17 U.S.C. § 502(a)). The Court emphasized that it "has consistently rejected invitations to replace traditional equitable considerations with a rule that an injunction automatically follows a determination that a copyright has been infringed," and based on its experience in copyright cases, similarly rejected the invitation to adopt a categorical rule in patent infringement cases. *Id.* at 392–93. Thus, under *eBay,* a presumption of irreparable harm is equally improper in a case based on copyright infringement as it is in a case based on patent infringement.

Nor does the fact that *eBay* concerned a permanent injunction rather than a preliminary injunction sufficiently distinguish the cases to result in a different outcome. The Supreme Court has been more than clear on this point. *Amoco Prod. Co. v. Gambell,* 480 U.S. 531, 546 n. 12. Indeed, the *eBay* Court relied on a preliminary injunction case in reaching its holding. 547 U.S. at 391 (citing *Amoco,* 480 U.S. at 54). Thus, we conclude that *eBay* applies with equal force to preliminary injunction cases as it does to permanent injunction cases.

2. *Winter v. Natural Resources Defense Council, Inc.*

If we harbored any doubts about the applicability of *eBay* in the preliminary injunction context, they have been dispelled by the Supreme Court's decision in *Winter.* In *Winter,* the Supreme Court reaffirmed the equitable nature of the four-factor framework and applied it to a case involving a preliminary injunction. The district court had issued an injunction restricting the U.S. Navy's ability to conduct war readiness exercises off the coast of Southern California, and the Ninth Circuit affirmed. *Natural Res. Def. Council, Inc. v. Winter,* 518 F.3d 658, 697 (9th Cir. 2008). We held that the district court need only find a *possibility* of irreparable harm to issue an injunction and rejected the Navy's argument that any claim of irreparable injury was merely speculative. *Id.*

The Supreme Court reversed, holding that "the Ninth Circuit's 'possibility' standard is too lenient." *Winter,* 555 U.S. at 22. The Court explained that its "frequently reiterated standard requires plaintiffs seeking preliminary relief to demonstrate that irreparable injury is *likely* in the absence of an injunction." *Id.* (emphasis original). The Court clarified that "[i]ssuing a preliminary injunction based only on a possibility of irreparable harm is inconsistent with our characterization of injunctive relief as an extraordinary remedy that may only be awarded upon a clear showing that the plaintiff is entitled to such relief." *Id.* Thus, *Winter* reaffirms the principles relied upon in *eBay:* a plaintiff must satisfy the four-factor test in order to obtain equitable injunctive relief, even if that relief is preliminary.

C. Presuming Irreparable Harm Is Now Impermissible

We conclude that presuming irreparable harm in a copyright infringement case is inconsistent with, and disapproved by, the Supreme Court's opinions in *eBay* and *Winter. Id.* at *4. Thus, our long-standing precedent finding a plaintiff entitled to a presumption of irreparable harm on a showing of likelihood of success on the merits in a copyright infringement case, as stated in *Elvis Presley* and relied on by the district court, has been effectively overruled. In other words, "*Elvis* has left the building." Accordingly, we hold that even in a copyright infringement case, the plaintiff must demonstrate a likelihood of irreparable harm as a prerequisite for injunctive relief, whether preliminary or permanent.

The district court, albeit reasonably in light of our precedent, relied solely on the presumption of irreparable harm to issue its injunction. Applying our reading of *eBay* and *Winter* to this case, reliance on a presumption of irreparable harm was error. Flexible must demonstrate a likelihood of irreparable harm in order to obtain injunctive relief.

We believe the better course is to remand to allow the district court to make the requisite factual determinations regarding irreparable harm and apply those factual findings to the four-factor framework to determine whether injunctive relief is warranted. Accordingly, we vacate the injunction and remand to the district court for further proceedings consistent with this opinion.

## *NOTES AND QUESTIONS*

1. Why do you think courts presumed irreparable harm in copyright cases under an approach that persisted for thirty years? Did this approach advantage one side? If so, does *eBay* restore a more level playing field? How do you think *eBay* will affect settlement of lawsuits?

2. Under what circumstances do you think courts might strike the balance of *eBay* factors against granting an injunction? Should courts look at the magnitude of actual harm to the plaintiffs? Whether defendants may have

been acting under a belief that their conduct was not infringing? The public's interest in continued access to the infringing copies? Based on the description of facts above, do you think the court should grant a preliminary injunction?

3. *Impoundment and disposition of infringing articles*. Section 503 of the Copyright Act grants courts the authority to impound (or hold) during the litigation of a case all allegedly infringing articles; "all plates, molds, matrices, masters, tapes, film negatives, or other articles by means of which such copies of phonorecords may be reproduced"; and "records documenting the manufacture, sale, or receipt of things involved in any such violation, provided that any records seized under this subparagraph shall be taken into the custody of the court." 17 U.S.C. § 503. If the copyright owner prevails in proving infringement, "the court may order the destruction or other reasonable disposition of all copies or phonorecords found to have been made or used in violation of the copyright owner's exclusive rights, and of all plates, molds, matrices, masters, tapes, film negatives, or other articles by means of which such copies or phonorecords may be reproduced." *Id.*

---

## 2. ACTUAL DAMAGES, INFRINGER'S PROFITS, AND STATUTORY DAMAGES

### *PROBLEM 4–10*

Cassie is a fashion designer who designed a dress with a colorful floral pattern. She registered the floral pattern in the U.S. Copyright Office on March 25, 2017. The dress, which was sold in stores starting on April 1, 2017 for $100, was a big hit with consumers. Maura Maker, a discount store, copied Cassie's floral pattern and sold cheap "knock-off" versions for $25. Maura Maker sold 1 million "knock-off" dress. Cassie now sues Maura Maker for infringement. If Cassie elects to seek statutory damages, what is the maximum award Cassie can obtain? Would it better for her to seek actual damages? Consider the following discussion.

---

Getting a monetary award of damages is often a major reason for a copyright owner's decision to bring a lawsuit. Section 504 of the Copyright Act recognizes two types of damage awards: (1) actual damages and infringer's profits and (2) statutory damages. A prevailing party can receive only one type of damage award—either actual damages or statutory damages. As discussed below, statutory damages are often (though not always) the more attractive option to copyright owners.

*Actual Damages and Profits*. Copyright owners who prevail in their infringement lawsuits are entitled to receive monetary awards for damages they actually suffered. The basic measure is the loss of the fair market value of the copyright. Plaintiffs typically show such a loss by the profits they lost due to the infringement or the licensing fees or royalties lost from the defendant's unauthorized use. Proving the loss of a reasonable royalty has become a popular method for actual damages.

In addition, prevailing copyright owners are entitled to the infringer's profits from exploiting infringing copies, but the recovery cannot be duplicative of the actual damages. Section 504(b) limits the recovery of profits to "any profits of the infringer that are attributable to the infringement and are not taken into account in computing the actual damages." In other words, no double counting. The section sets forth the burden of proving an infringer's profits in a way that splits the burden between the parties: "In establishing the infringer's profits, the copyright owner is required to present proof only of the infringer's gross revenue, and the infringer is required to prove his or her deductible expenses and the elements of profit attributable to factors other than the copyrighted work." 17 U.S.C. § 504(b).

*Statutory Damages.* Instead of actual damages and profits, prevailing copyright owners "may elect, at any time before final judgment is rendered, to recover . . . an award of statutory damages for all infringements involved in the action." 17 U.S.C. § 504(c)(1). However, statutory damages are available only if the copyright owner registered her work in the Copyright Office before the defendant's infringement started. 17 U.S.C. § 412. There is a grace period of three months for a copyright to register a published work. If an infringement occurs after the first publication of a work, the copyright owner is eligible to receive statutory damages as long as she registered her work within three months of the first publication. *Id.*

The Copyright Act establishes a range of statutory damages from $750 to $30,000 per work infringed. *Id.* The range increases up to $150,000 per work if the court finds the defendant's infringement was willful. The range decreases to as low as $200 per work if the court finds the defendant "was not aware and had no reason to believe that his or her acts constituted an infringement of copyright." *Id.* § 504(c)(2).

Statutory damages can increase very quickly if the defendant infringed several works. For example, a college student engaged in music file sharing and shared recordings of 30 works online. A jury awarded the copyright owner $675,000 in statutory damages based on a selection of $22,500 damages for each musical work the defendant infringed. *See Sony BMG Music Entertainment v. Tenenbaum*, 719 F.3d 67 (1st Cir. 2013). Seem harsh? Consider another jury's award of $1.5 million ($62,500 statutory damages per work times 24 musical works) against the defendant, a mother who engaged in music file sharing. The award finally awarded after several new trials that was upheld on appeal was "only" $222,000. *See Capitol Records, Inc. v. Thomas-Rasset*, 692 F.3d 899, 903–04 (8th Cir. 2012). Under the Due Process clause, a statutory damage award is unconstitutional only if it is "so severe and oppressive as to be wholly disproportioned to the offense and obviously unreasonable." *Id.* at 908 (quoting *St. Louis, I. M. & S. Ry. Co. v. Williams*, 251 U.S. 63, 67 (1919)). This is a very high standard to meet. An award of statutory damages does not have to be proportional to the actual damages suffered from defendant's infringement. Instead, the court may consider the award in light of "the interests of the public, the numberless opportunities for committing the offense, and the need for securing uniform adherence to [federal law]." *Id.* Under this test, both awards of $675,000 and $222,000 for music file sharing 30 and 24 works, respectively, were upheld on appeal.

### *NOTES AND QUESTIONS*

1. Among intellectual property laws, statutory damages under copyright are unique. Why do you think Congress authorized them for copyright but not for other intellectual property, such as patents or trademarks? Should statutory damages be available for other IP remedies?

2. In what circumstances do you think a prevailing copyright owner would prefer actual damages? What about statutory damages? Is it simply based on which would be the larger potential amount?

---

## H. COPYRIGHT TERMS

### *PROBLEM 4–11*

Bronderville Company created a new toy on November 20, 2010. The toy hit store shelves on August 10, 2011. Assume the toy is copyrightable. When does the copyright for the toy expire? Give the exact date. Consult the following discussion.

---

Copyrights last a long time, making them potentially more attractive in terms of their duration for rights holders than patents. Only trademarks, which have indefinite duration, can last longer than copyrights. The Copyright Act covers duration in Sections 302 through 305. The provisions are somewhat complicated because the method by which the term of copyright is computed is different depending on if the work was created and copyrighted before or after January 1, 1978, the effective date of the 1976 Act.

*Works copyrighted under the 1909 Act.* For works published and copyrighted before January 1, 1978, the 1909 Act granted all copyrighted works a basic term of 28 years and a possible renewal term of 28 years. In 1998, Congress passed the Sonny Bono Copyright Term Extension Act, which extended the renewal term (which Congress had already extended several times) to 67 years for a total of 95 years of copyright. *See* 17 U.S.C.

§ 304. Given the long duration of copyright, many works published when the 1909 Act was in force (all the way back to 1923) are still under copyright in the United States today.

*Works created under the 1976 Act.* In order to join the Berne Convention, Congress changed the method by which the basic term of copyright is computed to the life of the author plus 50 years. In 1998, the Sonny Bono Act extended the term to the life of the author plus 70 years. Thus, for works created by individual authors on or after January 1, 1978, the copyrights for those works last the life of the author plus 70 years. 17 U.S.C. § 302(a). If several authors create a work jointly, the copyright lasts the life of the last surviving author plus 70 years. *Id.* § 302(b). For works created within the scope of employment, which are treated as works made for hire, the employer is considered to be the author and copyright owner (absent a written agreement to the contrary). Thus, works created by employees of corporations within the scope of their employment typically fall within the work made for hire doctrine. The copyright for works made for hire last for 95 years from publication of the work or 120 years from creation, whichever expires first. *Id.* § 302(c).

*Computing terms.* Section 305 treats as all terms as expiring at "the end of the calendar year in which they would otherwise expire." Accordingly, all copyrights should expire at the end of December 31. For example, Amanda Author wrote a song on June 18, 2001 and later died on August 15, 2016. Her copyright would expire at the end of December 31, 2086. Likewise, Movie Studio created a movie on June 18, 2001 and published it on February 14, 2002. The studio's copyright would expire at the end of December 31, 2097.

There always remains a possibility that Congress will extend the terms of copyrights, including for existing copyrighted works. Congress has extended the terms of copyrights several times, the last time in 1998 under the Sonny Bono Copyright Term Extension Act. The Copyright Clause of the Constitution gives Congress the power "[t]o promote the Progress of Science and useful Arts, by securing for limited Times to Authors and Inventors the exclusive Right to their respective Writings and Discoveries." The Supreme Court has interpreted "limited Times" to require a finite number—a requirement that gives Congress much discretion to extend the terms of copyrights in the future. *See Eldred v. Ashcroft*, 537 U.S. 186 (2003). Does the term of copyright provide an attractive feature for protecting designs? Or does it impair the process of design?

# CHAPTER 5

# THE EU COMMUNITY DESIGN RIGHT AND INTERNATIONAL APPROACHES

■ ■ ■



---

In today's global market, businesses and multi-national corporations often seek protection for the designs of their products in many countries. In this chapter, we examine design protection in the European Union, which has a more advanced, *sui generis* form of protection specifically for designs. Indeed, the EU has been a leader in design protection. We also briefly examine two international agreements relevant to design protection, the Hague Agreement Concerning International Registration of Industrial Designs and the TRIPS Agreement. In studying the EU approach to design protection, consider whether you think the U.S. or EU approach is better.

# A. EU COMMUNITY DESIGN PROTECTION

## 1. RELEVANT LAWS

The EU has two sets of laws governing design protection: (1) the Community Design Regulation (CDR), along with an Implementing Regulation (CDIR), both enacted in 2002, and (2) a design Directive, enacted in 1998, that attempts to harmonize the national laws of EU members for protection of designs registered in national offices of EU members. The CDR establishes a uniform design law that applies directly in EU members, whereas the Directive must be implemented by the national laws of EU members. We outline both EU laws below, but focus on the CDR in the sections that follow.

### a. Community Design Regulation (CDR)

The advantage of design protection under the CDR is that it establishes a unified, EU-wide, transnational protection in all EU members—similar to the Community Trade Mark (CTM). Instead of having to seek protection under the laws of each EU member, an entity can obtain uniform, EU-wide protection for designs, including transnational remedies for infringement under the CDR. The Regulation itself recognizes the efficiency such a transnational system creates: "This calls for the creation of a Community design which is directly applicable in each Member State, because only in this way will it be possible to obtain, through one application made to the Office for Harmonisation in the Internal Market (Trade Marks and Design) in accordance with a single procedure under one law, one design right for one area encompassing all Member States." Council Regulation (EC), No. 6/2002 of 12 December 2001 on Community designs, para. 5.

The CDR recognizes two levels of protection depending on whether the design has been registered for protection in the Office for Harmonisation in the Internal Market (OHIM), the EU agency located in Alicante, Spain that oversees design registrations along with registrations for the Community Trade Mark. Since March 23, 2016, the Office has been renamed the EU Intellectual Property Office (EUIPO). For ease of reference, we will refer to the Office interchangeably as both OHIM and EUIPO, given that the Office has been commonly referred to as OHIM. The two levels of protection are:

(1) A registered Community design (RCD) in OHIM receives a 5-year term of protection from the date of filing, renewable with payment of fees for a total of 5 terms or 25 years from the date of filing. CDR, art. 12.

(2) By contrast, unregistered Community designs (UCD) in the EU receive only 3 years of protection starting from the date a design is disclosed or made available to the public. *Id.* art. 11. There is no renewal term. Drafters of the CDR believed the shorter protection for unregistered

designs would be especially useful for industries (such as fashion and textile) that produce many designs lasting only short periods of time: "Some of those sectors produce large numbers of designs for products frequently having a short market life where protection without the burden of registration formalities is an advantage and the duration of protection is of lesser significance." CDR, para. 16.

**Table 1. Comparison of EU Registered and Unregistered Community Design**

| | **Registered Community Design** | **Unregistered Community Design** |
|---|---|---|
| **Term** | 5-year term of protection from the date of filing | 3 years of protection starting from the date a design is disclosed to the public |
| **Renewal** | Yes, renewal for a total of 5 terms or 25 years from date of filing | No |
| **Public disclosure** | Must apply for registration before a public disclosure of design, except designer gets a 1-year grace period starting from her own public disclosure of design | Public disclosure of design starts UCD protection |
| **Rights** | Same rights<br>Independent creation by third parties is no defense | Same rights<br>Independent creation by third parties is a defense |

As Table 1 above summarizes, the decision whether to register a design or rely instead on the unregistered Community design may depend on how long a term of protection is desired. For some designs (such as in fashion) that do not typically last long in the market, the 3-year term of the UCD may suffice. However, if a longer term is necessary, then the RCD seems the better option, especially given the chance of renewal of the term. But, in order to maintain the novelty of the design (discussed in depth below), one must seek registration in EUIPO *before* the design is publicly disclosed by third parties. The designer's own public disclosures are subject to a 1-year grace period: the designer has 1 year following her first public disclosure of the design within which to file for the RCD. CDR, art. 7(2). The grace period does not apply to unregistered designs—the clock starts ticking with any public disclosure of an unregistered design.

### b. 1998 Directive on the Legal Protection of Designs

The EU also has a directive from 1998 setting forth common standards for the protection of registered designs under the national laws of EU members; however, national protection of unregistered designs, such as under the United Kingdom's approach, are not regulated by the Directive. *See* Directive 98/71/EC of the European Parliament and of the Council of 13 October 1998 on the legal protection of designs. The national registrations governed by the Directive are handled by the national offices in each EU member. The CDR does not displace national design laws or national protections in EU members, so it is possible and perhaps common for an entity to seek protection under both the CDR (EU-wide protection) and national design protections in EU members (national protection). The approach is similar to how the Community Trade Mark and national trademarks coexist in the EU. Both the CDR and CTM take a unitary approach and establish one EU-wide form of intellectual property (design right and trade mark right, respectively) that encompass the entire EU. By contrast, each EU member has its own national laws that may recognize design and trademark rights that are national in scope. Our focus in this chapter will be on the EU-wide protection under the CDR, given its popularity.

## 2. FORMALITIES AND REGISTRATION IN EUIPO

Those who seek to register a Community design must do so in the EU Intellectual Property Office (EUIPO), formerly known as OHIM. EUIPO has a convenient e-filing system (https://euipo.europa.eu/rcd/efiling/wizard.htm?execution=e1s1), with a registration fee of 350 Euros (in 2017). According to the Office, it registers approximately 85,000 designs annually.

Notably, the EUIPO does *not* examine the design against the prior art or any of the substantive requirements in Articles 4 to 8 of the CDR. Instead, the Office examines only the formal requirements for filing (CDR, art. 45), the satisfaction of the definition of design (*id.* art. 47), and potential violations of public policy or morality that might result from registration. In this respect, EUIPO follows a "registration"—not "examination"—approach, which makes for a quicker process. EUIPO also has a "Fast Track" application process, which the Office claims can result in a registration within two working days. The applicant can file in any of the 24 official languages of EU members. Once registered, the design registration is published. Third parties can then challenge the validity of the registration through a challenge filed in EUIPO or as a counterclaim to the registrant's infringement claim in a Community design court (*id.* art. 24). If a Community design is declared invalid, it becomes null and void retroactively back to the beginning of its term (*id.* art. 26).

The drawings in a design application are very important. As the United Kingdom Supreme Court explained:

> Article 3(a) of the Principal Regulation identifies what is meant by "design", and, unsurprisingly, it refers to the appearance, which is expressed to include a number of different factors, all, some or one of which can be included in a particular registered design. It is, of course, up to an applicant as to what features he includes in his design application. He can make an application based on all or any of "the lines, contours, colours, shape, texture . . . materials . . . and/or . . . ornamentation" of "the product" in question. Further, he can make a large number of different applications, particularly as the Principal Regulation itself provides that applications for registration have to be cheap and simple to make. As Lewison J. put it in *Procter & Gamble Co v. Reckitt Benckiser (UK) Ltd* [2006] EWHC 3154 (Ch), [2007] F.S.R. 13, at [48], "[t]he registration holder is entitled to choose the level of generality at which his design is to be considered. If he chooses too general a level, his design may be invalidated by prior art. If he chooses too specific a level he may not be protected against similar designs". So, when it comes to deciding the extent of protection afforded by a particular Community registered design, the question must ultimately depend on the proper interpretation of the registration in issue, and in particular of the images included in that registration.
>
> Accordingly, it is right to bear in mind that an applicant for a design right is entitled, within very broad limits, to submit any images which he chooses. Further, in the light of art. 36(6), an applicant should appreciate that it will almost always be those images which exclusively identify the nature and extent of the monopoly which he is claiming. As Dr. Martin Schlötelburg, the co-ordinator of OHIM's Designs Department, has written, "the selection of the means for representing a design is equivalent to the drafting of the claims in a patent: including features means claiming them"—The Community Design: First Experience with Registrations [2003] EIPR 383, at p. 385.

*Magmatic Ltd v. PMS Int'l Group PLC*, [2016] UKSC 12, [2016] R.P.C. 11.

## 3. REQUIREMENTS FOR COMMUNITY DESIGN PROTECTION

Article 3 defines "design" as follows: "The *appearance* of the whole or a part of a product resulting from the features of, in particular, the lines, contours, colours, shape, texture and/or materials of the product itself and/or its ornamentation." CDR, art. 3 (emphasis added). Thus, design is visual—the appearance of a product. A basic requirement for Community design protection is that the design is visible—it has an appearance.

Accordingly, ideas, smells, music, and sounds do not qualify as designs because they do not have any appearance.

Article 4 of the CDR sets forth the basic requirements for design protection: "A design shall be protected by a Community design to the extent that it is *new* and has *individual character*." CDR, art. 4(1) (emphasis added). In addition, Article 8 bars protection of design features that are dictated solely by their technical function. *Id.* art. 8. However, the EU does not contain a requirement of ornamentality as U.S. design patent law does (as discussed above in Chapter 1). These three basic requirements of the CDR are examined below.

### a. Novelty

#### *PROBLEM 5–1*

Based on an application filed on April 14, 2016, Unleash Time Company registered the design of a watch (depicted below in Figure 1) that can be worn around the neck or wrist by use of a lanyard. In Figure 1, the claimed design is indicated by the solid lines; however, dotted lines are not within the scope of the claimed design. A third party filed in the EUIPO an application for a declaration of invalidity of the registered design. The third party submitted a published catalogue photo from 2001 that showed a watch with a lanyard for sale in the EU (see Figure 2); the catalogue was distributed to the public in EU countries in 2001. How should the EUIPO rule as to the novelty of Unleash Time Company's design? Should the registration be invalidated? Consider the following provision and case.

**Figure 1. Unleash Time Company** **Figure 2. Prior art from 2001**

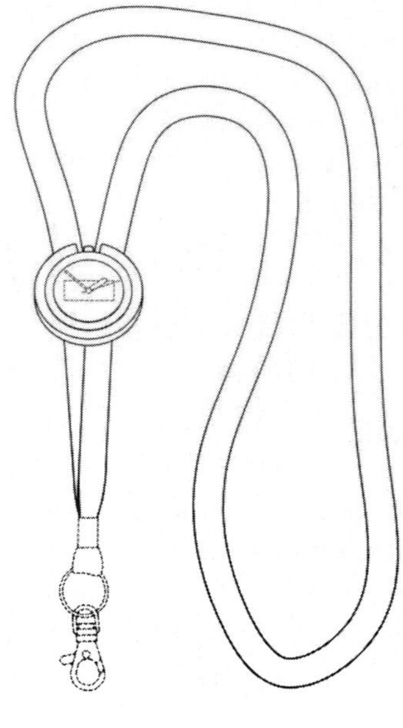

**Community Design Regulation, Article 5**

**Novelty**

1. A design shall be considered to be new if no identical design has been made available to the public:

(a) in the case of an unregistered Community design, before the date on which the design for which protection is claimed has first been made available to the public;

(b) in the case of a registered Community design, before the date of filing of the application for registration of the design for which protection is claimed, or, if priority is claimed, the date of priority.

2. Designs shall be deemed to be identical if their features differ only in immaterial details.

**Article 7**

**Disclosure**

1. For the purpose of applying Articles 5 and 6, a design shall be deemed to have been made available to the public if it has been published following registration or otherwise, or exhibited, used in trade or otherwise disclosed, before the date referred to in Articles 5(1)(a) and 6(1)(a) or in Articles 5(1)(b) and 6(1)(b) [Article 6 pertains to individual character and is discussed later. *Ed.*], as the case may be, except where these events could not reasonably have become known in the normal course of business to the circles specialised in the sector concerned, operating within the Community. The design shall not, however, be deemed to have been made available to the public for the sole reason that it has been disclosed to a third person under explicit or implicit conditions of confidentiality.

2. A disclosure shall not be taken into consideration for the purpose of applying Articles 5 and 6 and if a design for which protection is claimed under a registered Community design has been made available to the public: (a) by the designer, his successor in title, or a third person as a result of information provided or action taken by the designer or his successor in title; and (b) during the 12-month period preceding the date of filing of the application or, if a priority is claimed, the date of priority.

3. Paragraph 2 shall also apply if the design has been made available to the public as a consequence of an abuse in relation to the designer or his successor in title.

---

Novelty is a basic requirement for designs to receive protection under the CDR, for both unregistered and registered designs. For unregistered designs, the critical period to examine is "before the date on which the design for which protection is claimed has first been made available to the public." CDR, art. 5(1)(a). For registered designs, the critical period is "before the date of filing of the application for registration of the design for which protection is claimed, or, if priority is claimed, the date of priority." *Id.* art. 5(1)(b). (We will discuss priority dates under the Paris Convention at the end of this chapter.) If an identical design has already been made available to the public during the respective time periods above, it constitutes prior art that defeats the novelty of any subsequent identical design, thereby disqualifying the subsequent identical design from design protection under the CDR.

Article 7 explains which disclosures constitute public disclosures—and which do not. The provision states that "a design shall be deemed to have been made available to the public if it has been [i] published following registration or otherwise, or [ii] exhibited, [iii] used in trade or [iv] otherwise disclosed, before the date referred to in Articles 5(1)(a) and 6(1)(a) or in Articles 5(1)(b) and 6(1)(b), as the case may be." *Id.* art. 7(1) (bracketed numbers added). However, there is an exception for disclosures in circumstances "where these events could not reasonably have become known in the normal course of business to the circles specialised in the sector concerned, operating within the Community." Disclosures in such circumstances do not constitute public disclosures. *Id.* Nor do disclosures that are made "to a third person under explicit or implicit conditions of confidentiality," such as under a non-disclosure agreement. *Id.*

Article 7 also establishes a 12-month grace period for registered designs. CDR, art. 7(2). Designers have effectively one year to make disclosures of their designs before they must register their designs—or else lose eligibility for registered design protection. As the General Court of the EU explained, this grace period is intended "to offer a creator or his successor in title the opportunity to market a design, for a period of 12 months, before having to proceed with the formalities of filing." *Liu v. OHIM*, No. T–813/14, at para. 21. "Accordingly, during this period, the creator or his successor in title can ascertain that the design concerned is a commercial success before incurring the costs relating to registration, without fear that the disclosure that takes place at that time may be successfully raised during any invalidity proceedings brought after the possible registration of the design concerned." *Id.*, at para. 22. However, if a designer makes a disclosure of the design and fails to apply for registration within the 1-year period, the designer is disqualified from registering that design under the CDR and must rely on the shorter, 3-year protection for unregistered designs—which starts to run as soon as the design is first made available to the public. Thus, a would-be registrant who misses the registration of a design within the 12-month grace period after publicly disclosing the design would have only 2 years of protection remaining for the unregistered design.

The following case discusses how novelty is tested between two designs, specifically examining the issue whether the only differences between competing designs are "immaterial," the standard set forth in Article 5(2) of the CDR. If two designs are identical and any differences between them only immaterial, then the prior design constitutes prior art that defeats the novelty of the subsequent design. In the case below, the "design relates to signboards that are typically made of lightweight cardboard and may be folded like an accordion, and are used at group events, such as sporting events, by a person clutching it at the shorter sides with his hands and holding it high above his head." The General Court had to consider whether the design in question was novel in light of the prior art.

## ARGO DEVELOPMENT AND MANUFACTURING LTD V. OHIM

General Court, European Union
Case T–41/14 (28 January 2015)

On 20 March 2010, Clapbanner Ltd filed an application for registration of a Community design with the Office for Harmonisation in the Internal Market (Trade Marks and Designs) (OHIM), pursuant to Council Regulation (EC) No. 6/2002 of 12 December 2001 on Community designs (OJ 2002 L 3, p. 1). The design for which registration was sought ('the contested design') is represented as follows:

On the day the application for registration was filed, the contested design was registered under No. 1 684 325–0001 and published in *Community Designs Bulletin* No. 173/2010 of 5 August 2010. It is intended to be applied to 'advertising articles' in Class 20–03 of the Locarno

Agreement Establishing an International Classification for Industrial Designs of 8 October 1968, as amended. On 20 April 2011, the applicant, Argo Development and Manufacturing Ltd, applied to OHIM for a declaration that the contested design was invalid, based on Articles 4 to 6 of Regulation No. 6/2002.

In support of its application for a declaration of invalidity, the applicant relied on the Community designs registered on 26 September 2007 under Nos. 796 446–0001 to 796 446–0004 in respect of 'advertising articles' in Class 20–03 of the Locarno Agreement, as amended. Those designs are set out below:

—design No. 796 446–0001:

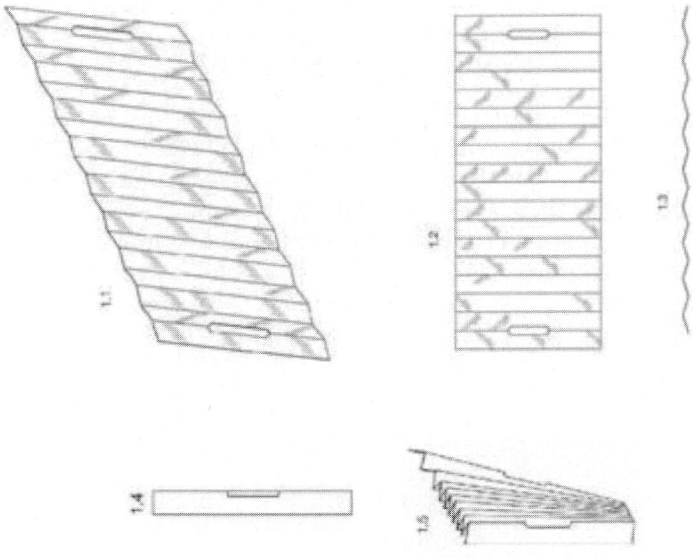

—design No. 796 446–0002:

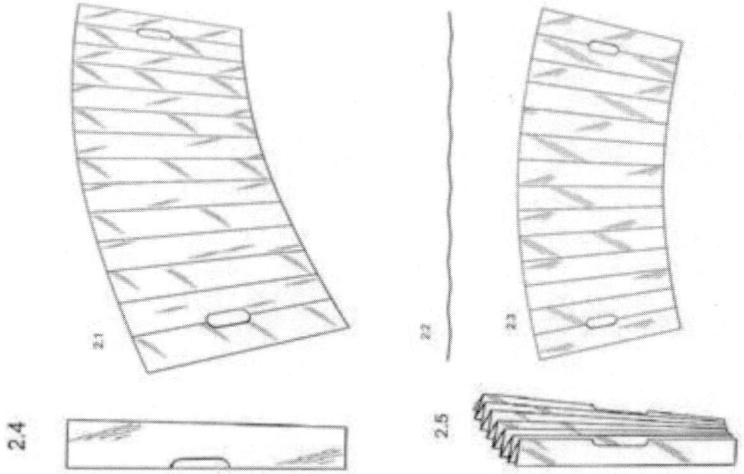

—design No. 769 446–0003:

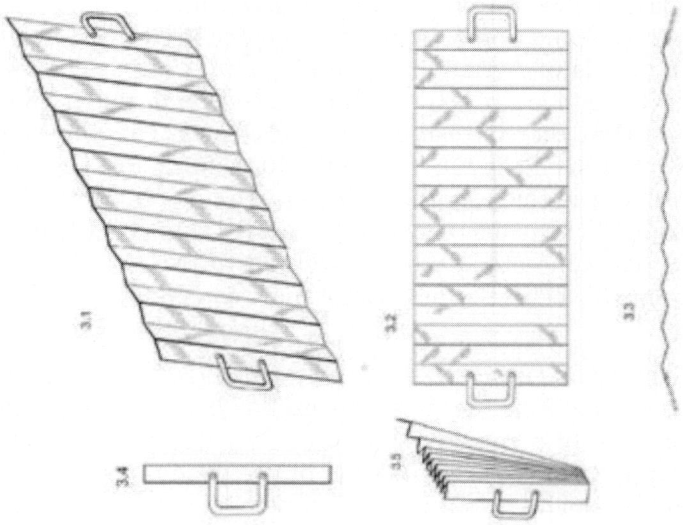

—design No. 796 446–0004:

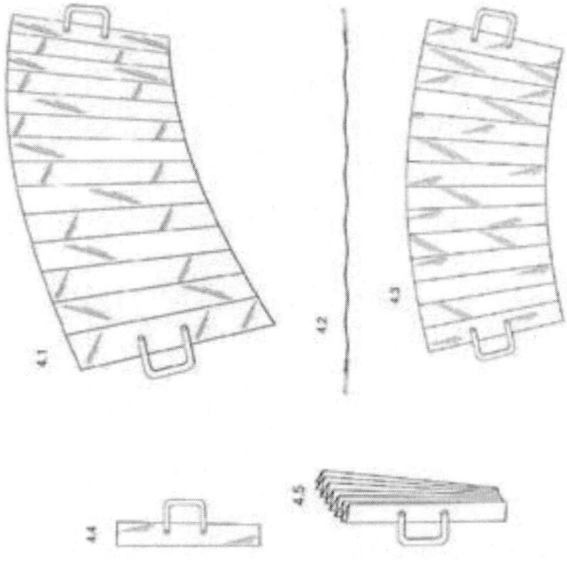


By decision of 20 March 2012, the Invalidity Division granted the application for a declaration of invalidity and declared the contested design invalid on the basis of Article 25(1)(b) of Regulation No. 6/2002, read in conjunction with Article 6 of that regulation. In that decision, the Invalidity Division found that the contested design was new. On the other hand, it took the view that the design lacked individual character. On 18 May 2012, Clapbanner filed a notice of appeal under Articles 55 to 60 of Regulation No. 6/2002 against the decision of the Invalidity Division. By decision of 22 October 2013 ('the contested decision'), the Third Board of Appeal of OHIM upheld that appeal. [The General Court now considers the appeal of that decision. *Ed.*]

Under Article 5(1)(b) of Regulation No. 6/2002, a design is to be considered to be new if no identical design has been made available to the public, in the case of a registered Community design, before the date of filing of the application for registration of the design for which protection is claimed, or, if priority is claimed, the date of priority. Under Article 5(2) of Regulation No. 6/2002, designs are to be deemed to be identical if their features differ only in immaterial details.

The applicant claims that any features of the contested design that may not be considered to be strictly identical to the corresponding features of the earlier designs constitute minor immaterial details. More specifically, the applicant claims that the contested design differs from the earlier designs only in immaterial details, namely its handles.

In the present case, it should be observed that the contested design and the earlier designs are not identical as regards the handles of the products represented therein. As the Board of Appeal correctly pointed out in the contested decision, the handles represented in the contested design consist of a perforated area that can be pressed out. In comparison, the handles represented in the earlier designs are cut out (designs Nos. 796 446–0001 and 796 446–0002) or added on to the cardboard signboard (designs Nos. 796 446–0003 and 796 446–0004).

Those differences cannot be considered to be immaterial details since they are perceptible when the earlier designs and the contested design are placed side by side. Accordingly, the Board of Appeal was fully entitled to conclude, in the contested decision, that the contested design was new within the meaning of Article 5 of Regulation No. 6/2002. [The Court's analysis of individual character is excerpted below. *Ed.*]

### *NOTES AND QUESTIONS*

1. What test does the General Court use to evaluate whether Clapbanner's design was not new in light of the prior designs registered in 2007 (Nos. 796 446–0001 to 796 446–0004)? Were the differences in the designs of the competing handles material or immaterial? How does the Court determine if a difference is immaterial? Do you agree with the Court's conclusion?

2. How does the test for novelty under the CDR compare to the test for novelty under U.S. design patent law (discussed in Chapter 2)? Which test, if any, is more favorable to a designer seeking to protect a design?

3. Should the law protect only new designs? At least for U.S. design patents and the EU Community design, the answer is yes. But what about trade dress and copyright protection? Why do they protect design features without requiring novelty? Is that a flaw?

4. *EU Courts.* The General Court of the European Union is a division within the Court of Justice of the European Union (CJEU), the highest court for the EU that interprets and decides EU law and handles referrals of questions from courts in EU members regarding the correct interpretation of EU law. The General Court has jurisdiction over matters brought against EU institutions, such as OHIM. The General Court has 28 judges, one from each EU member, who typically decide cases on panels of 5 or 3 judges, but, in some cases, just one judge or in the Grand Chamber (15 judges). For more, visit the Court's website: http://curia.europa.eu/jcms/jcms/Jo2_7033/en/.

---

## b. Individual Character

### *PROBLEM 5–2*

Cookie Monster Company filed an application in EUIPO to register the design of a cookie, depicted below. Cookie Monster's cookie had a layer of filling inside the cookie that was not visible when the cookie was intact. Consumers looking at the cookie do not see the filling until they take a bite of the cookie, which is delicious.

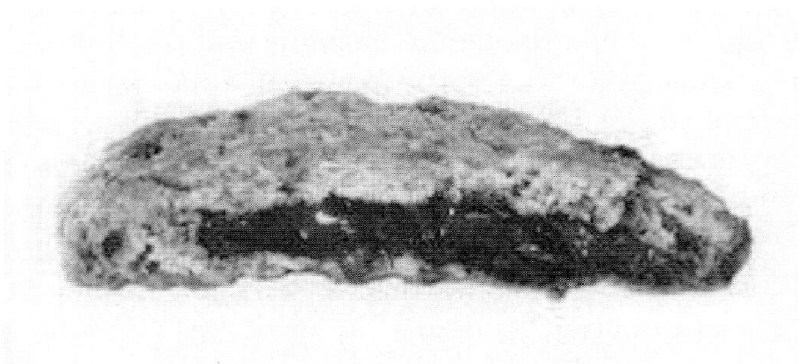

**Cookie Monster Cookie**

Arielle Cookies challenged Cookie Monster's application on the ground that the cookie design lacked individual character because Cookie Monster's cookies' overall impression on the informed user was no different from many cookies that have been sold for many years in the past. As prior art, Arielle pointed to the following cookies below, all of which have been sold for many years and some of which had filling inside:

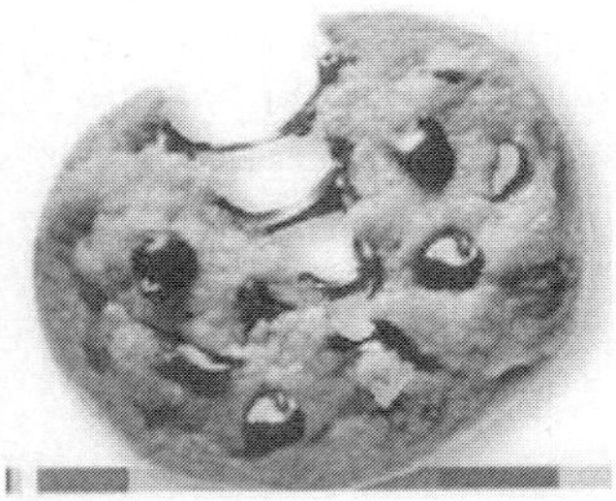

Please advise EUIPO on how to determine if Cookie Monster's cookie has individual character, specifically answering these questions: (1) Should the inside of Cookie Monster's cookie be considered a part of the design in determining whether the overall impression of the cookie has individual character? (2) Who is the informed user in this case? and (3) Comparing the overall impression of Cookie Monster's cookie to the prior art cookies, do Cookie Monster's cookies have individual character? To answer these questions, consider Article 6 and the discussion below.

---

In addition to being new, a design must have "individual character" to qualify for protection as registered or unregistered designs. The General Court has interpreted this requirement as applying to only design features of a product that are *visible*. *See Biscuits Poult SAS v. OHIM*, No. T–494/12 (Sept. 9, 2014). Features of a product that are not visible are not considered in evaluating the product's overall impression. Article 4(2) expressly requires visibility of component parts of a complex product during normal use of the product in order for the design of the component parts to be eligible for consideration of individual character. CDR, art. 4(2). Even though Article 4(1) does not have a similar, express requirement of visibility for all (non-complex) products generally, the General Court has interpreted it as to so require. What policy might underlie the requirement that a design feature be visible? Does the internal design not matter, no matter how elegant?

In comparing a design to prior designs, OHIM and courts compare individual products instead of piecing together a mosaic of features from different products. In other words, the point of comparison is between the design in question and each prior art, considered individually, not collectively. As the Court of Justice explained, "[I]n order for a design to be considered to have individual character, the overall impression which that design produces on the informed user must be different from that produced on such a user not by a combination of features taken in isolation and drawn from a number of earlier designs, but by one or more earlier designs, taken individually." *Karen Millen Fashions Ltd v. Dunnes Stores*, C–345/13, para. 35 (June 19, 2014). This approach contrasts with how U.S. courts allow, to some extent, the combination of different prior art—a single primary reference of the design, plus secondary references used to supplement the primary reference—in determining whether a design is nonobvious, as discussed above in the chapter on design patents. Which approach do you think is better to identifying designs that merit protection? Should prior art be combined or be treated individually?

In addition to the visibility requirement, courts also typically examine the informed user and the freedom of the designer in selecting design features in order to determine if a design has individual character, as the provision and case below discuss.

**Community Design Regulation, Article 6**

**Individual character**

1. A design shall be considered to have individual character if the overall impression it produces on the informed user differs from the overall impression produced on such a user by any design which has been made available to the public:

(a) in the case of an unregistered Community design, before the date on which the design for which protection is claimed has first been made available to the public;

(b) in the case of a registered Community design, before the date of filing the application for registration or, if a priority is claimed, the date of priority.

2. In assessing individual character, the degree of freedom of the designer in developing the design shall be taken into consideration.

---

## ARGO DEVELOPMENT AND MANUFACTURING LTD V. OHIM

General Court, European Union
Case T–41/14 (28 January 2015)

[The disputed designs of signboards are discussed in the section above on novelty. In this part, the Court considers whether the Board of Appeal was correct in finding that the contested design had individual character. *Ed.*]

Under Article 6(1)(b) of Regulation No. 6/2002, a registered Community design is to be considered to have individual character if the overall impression it produces on the informed user differs from the overall impression produced on such a user by any design which has been made available to the public before the date of filing the application for registration or, if a priority is claimed, the date of priority. Article 6(2) of Regulation No. 6/2002 states that, in assessing individual character, the degree of freedom of the designer in developing the design is to be taken into consideration. Furthermore, it is apparent from Article 6(1)(b) of Regulation No. 6/2002 and settled case-law that the assessment of whether a design has individual character is determined by the overall impression that it produces on the informed user.

For the purposes of examining the individual character of the contested design, it must be assessed whether the Board of Appeal erred when it (i) defined the nature of the product to which the contested design applies, (ii) defined the informed user of the design, (iii) assessed the designer's degree of freedom in the development of the design and (iv) compared the overall impressions produced on the informed user by the designs at issue.

*The nature of the product to which the contested design applies*

It is apparent from recital 14 in the preamble to Regulation No. 6/2002 that, when assessing whether a design has individual character, account should be taken of the nature of the product to which the design is applied or in which it is incorporated, and in particular, the industrial sector to which it belongs. It is common ground, and it is moreover confirmed by the examination of the file relating to the proceedings before OHIM, forwarded to the Court in accordance with Article 133(3) of its Rules of Procedure, that the contested design applies to a rectangular cardboard signboard divided into pleats, which can be folded like an accordion, and that the signboard can be used in an unfolded position in order to convey a message or, in a folded position, to produce a sound effect.

*The informed user*

According to the case-law, the concept of the 'informed user' must be understood as lying somewhere between that of the average consumer, applicable in trade mark matters, who need not have any specific knowledge and who, as a rule, makes no direct comparison between the trade marks at issue, and the sectoral expert, who is an expert with detailed technical expertise. Thus, the concept of the 'informed user' may be understood as referring, not to a user of average attention, but to a particularly observant one, either because of his personal experience or his extensive knowledge of the sector in question. In the present case, the Board of Appeal found that the informed users are both the persons who use those signboards at group events and the bodies which buy those signboards and then distribute them to the persons participating in those group events. That assessment, which the applicant does not dispute, is untainted by error and should, therefore, be confirmed.

*The designer's degree of freedom*

The designer's degree of freedom in creating a design is determined, inter alia, by the constraints of the features imposed by the technical function of the product or an element thereof, or by statutory requirements applicable to the product to which the design is applied. Those constraints result in a standardisation of certain features, which will thus be common to the designs applied to the product concerned.

In the present case, the applicant disputes the Board of Appeal's assessment that the designer has a very limited degree of freedom as regards the shape of the signboards represented in the designs at issue and as regards the division of those signboards into accordion-like foldable pleats. It claims that the Board of Appeal erred in concluding that the only feature that had to be taken into consideration in the present case was the handles of the signboards. In this connection, first, it should be recalled that it is common ground that the contested design applies to a rectangular cardboard signboard, divided into pleats, which can be folded like an accordion. It is also common ground that such a signboard is used, when unfolded, to convey a message and, when folded, to make noise when the end user claps it, inter alia, against his hand.

Second, as regards the shape of the contested design, it must be observed that the applicant has not shown that there is 'ample opportunity to create a different design' for an advertising article consisting of a cardboard signboard designed to be waved at group events and to make noise when the user claps it, inter alia, against his hand. Moreover, as the Board of Appeal observed, the rectangle is the most obvious shape for an advertising signboard, since it offers more writing space and enables the user to hold it comfortably without obstructing his vision. In addition, the rectangular shape, which enables the drawing of foldable cardboard pleats of an identical size, is the appropriate shape if those pleats are to produce noise when they enter into contact with each other. Accordingly, in the contested decision, the Board of Appeal was justified in taking the view that the rectangular shape was not an aspect of the design in relation to which the designer had much freedom of choice.

Thirdly, as regards the division of the signboard into cardboard pleats that can be folded like an accordion, the applicant asserts, without demonstrating, that other methods of folding are conceivable in order to enable a signboard to fulfil its function. Moreover, it should be observed, as did the Board of Appeal, that folding the signboard like an accordion is a method that enables the cardboard signboard to be folded and unfolded in a quick and practical manner. In addition, folding the signboard like an accordion is the only method of folding capable of producing the sound effect sought by the designer of a product such as the one represented in the contested design. Thus, only the snap of numerous cardboard pleats against each other, in particular, when in contact with the user's hand, enables a sufficient sound to be made for the sound to be propagated. Accordingly, the Board of Appeal was correct in finding that the designer's degree of freedom was almost non-existent as regards the division of the cardboard signboard into accordion-like foldable pleats.

Therefore, the Board of Appeal did not make an error of assessment in finding that the rectangular shape of the cardboard signboard and its division into accordion-like foldable pleats constituted two features in relation to which the designer had a very limited degree of freedom. The Board of Appeal was also fully entitled to take the view that the handles were the only part of the signboards in relation to which the designer had some creative freedom.

*The comparison of the overall impressions*

The applicant claims that the overall impression produced by the contested design does not differ from that produced by the earlier designs. It submits that, in assessing the overall impression produced by the contested design, the signboard as a whole as represented should be taken into consideration and not the signboard's handles alone. Moreover, it is important to take into consideration the manner in which the product is used. Lastly, the applicant submits that when the signboard is used, the differences in the shape of the handles will not be noticed by the informed user. In this connection, in the first place, it should be pointed out that, having regard to the conclusions drawn as to the designer's degree of freedom, the Board of Appeal was justified in taking the view that the aspect of the handles plays an essential role in the overall impression produced by the designs at issue on the informed user. In the second place, and as the applicant states, the overall impression produced by a design on the informed user must necessarily be determined also in the light of the manner in which the product in question is used.

However, it should be recalled that the signboards represented in the designs at issue can be used in an unfolded position or in a folded position. As regards the use of the signboards in an unfolded position, the applicant's argument that the minor differences that characterise the handles will not be visible cannot be accepted. First, the aspect of the handles will be visible when the signboard represented in the contested design is first used, inasmuch as, in contrast to the use of the signboards represented in the earlier designs, the use of the signboard represented in the contested design in an unfolded position will first require pressure to be applied to the perforated area in order to form the handles. Second, the documents submitted during the proceedings before OHIM by the applicant itself show that users can hold the signboards at issue in different ways. Users will thus not necessarily hold the signboards at issue with all of their fingers but may only use some of them, which will result in the aspect of the handles being exposed.

As regards the use of the signboards represented in the designs at issue in a folded position, it should be noted that, in order to produce a noise, the user will be required to hold the end of the folded signboard in one hand and to clap the other end of the folded signboard against, for example, the palm of his other hand. Thus, when used in this way, the products represented in the earlier designs will reveal a slot in the middle of the pleats at the edges of the signboard (designs Nos. 796 446–0001 and 796 446–0002) or handles added on to the middle of those pleats (designs

Nos. 796 446–0003 and 796 446–0004). By contrast, when used in a folded position in order to make noise, the product represented in the contested design will not reveal any handle if the user has not pressed on the perforation, or, if the user has already done so, will reveal a simple semi-circular opening.

Therefore, the applicant's argument that the aspect of the handles will not be visible when the products represented in the designs at issue are used must be rejected.

In the third place, the applicant states that the handles that appear in the contested design are positioned in the same place as the handles found in the earlier designs and that those handles have the same dimensions. It adds that the minor differences as to the way in which the handles have been depicted in the designs at issue cannot have an impact on the overall impression produced on the informed user. As regards the earlier designs Nos. 796 446–0003 and 796 446–0004, the applicant's argument that the handles are in the same place in the designs at issue is manifestly not well founded in so far as, inter alia, the handle in the contested design is represented as a line of perforations to be pressed out, whereas the handle is attached in the earlier designs. Moreover, as the Board of Appeal indicated in paragraph 29 of the contested decision, the aspect of the handles in the earlier designs Nos. 796 446–0003 and 796 446–0004 is completely different from that of the handles represented in the contested design.

Accordingly, taking into consideration the very limited degree of freedom of the designer as regards the rectangular shape of the cardboard signboard and its division into accordion-like foldable pleats, and having regard to the differences noted in the paragraph above as regards the handles depicted in the designs, the contested design produces, on the informed user, an overall impression different from that of the earlier designs Nos. 796 446–0003 and 796 446–0004.

As regards the earlier designs Nos. 796 446–0001 and 796 446–0002, it must be observed that the handle is cut out in those designs whereas it is represented as a line of perforations to be pressed out in the contested design. Moreover, the handle that appears in those earlier designs has an oblong shape, whereas it has a semi-circular shape in the contested design. Lastly, the applicant's argument that the handles are in the same place in the designs at issue must be rejected in so far as, as the Board of Appeal observed in paragraph 29 of the contested decision, the handle depicted in the contested design occupies the penultimate foldable pleat at the edge of the signboard, whereas it occupies two foldable pleats in the earlier designs. It should be added that, for that reason and by contrast with the product represented in the contested design, the products represented in the earlier designs will reveal a slot in the middle of the pleats at the edge of the signboard when they are used in a folded position. Lastly, even if that difference in positioning might go unnoticed by the informed user, as contemplated by the Board of Appeal, that circumstance would not modify the overall impression produced by the designs at issue on the informed user.

Accordingly, following an overall assessment and taking into consideration the designer's very limited degree of freedom as regards the rectangular shape of the cardboard signboard and its division into accordion-like foldable pleats, it must be held that the aspect of the handles in the contested design is sufficiently different from that of the handles in the earlier designs Nos. 796 446–0001 and 796 446–0002 to produce a different overall impression on the informed user. In the light of the foregoing, it must be held that the Board of Appeal did not make an error of assessment in finding that the contested design produced, on the informed user, an overall impression different from that of the earlier designs.

### *NOTES AND QUESTIONS*

1. *Informed user.* Article 6 states that a design has "individual character" if "the overall impression it produces on the informed user *differs* from the overall impression produced on such a user by any design which has been made available to the public." CDR, art. 6 (emphasis added). In this case, the Court identifies the nature of the product and then who the "informed user" of the product would be. Who is the informed user in this case, according to the Court?

2. *Designer's degree of freedom.* Next, the Court examined the designer's degree of freedom in creating the design. How does the designer's degree of freedom affect the analysis? For example, if, as the Court here found, that a designer did not have much freedom in designing several aspects of the design (e.g., because of "the constraints of the features imposed by the technical function of the product or an element thereof"), which side does that tend to favor? In other words, did the "very limited degree of freedom" help or hurt the applicant Clapbanner's claim for design protection in the Court's analysis of individual character? Do you agree with the Court's reasoning in this regard? (Remember this approach when we discuss functionality below.)

3. *Comparison of overall impressions of designs.* Finally, the Court compared the overall impressions of the designs from the prior art and in the application. Were they different? If so, in what respects?

4. How does the examination of individual character differ from the novelty examination? Is there much of a difference?

5. How does individual character under the CDR compare to U.S. design patent law's requirement of nonobviousness? Which requirement, if any, is easier for a designer to satisfy? Do you think it's easier for a design to be considered nonobvious under U.S. law or to have individual character under EU law? In answering these questions, consider the scope of prior art considered either individually or in combination, the person's perspective by

which the prior art and the design in question are to be judged, the designer's degree of freedom (or lack thereof), and any other factors the U.S. and EU laws consider to be relevant. Go back to the cases on nonobviousness in Chapter 2 and review the approach to nonboviousness. One useful exercise would be to apply the standard of individual character to those cases, and the standard of nonobviousness to *Argo* above. Do you think the results would be any different?

6. *No ornamentality requirement*. Recall that U.S. design patent law requires an "ornamental design." 17 U.S.C. § 171(a). The CDR lacks such a requirement. Which approach do you think is better for design protection?

---

### c. Non-Functional

#### *PROBLEM 5–3*

Lego obtained a RCD on its interlocking toy bricks, depicted below. The brick has eight circular ridges on the top that snap into the underside of another brick. By snapping the bricks together, children can build toy structures, such as a house. Matrix Toys has now challenged Lego's RCD on the grounds that the design of the toy brick is functional. (1) How should the EUIPO rule on functionality? (2) What if Lego had obtained a European patent on the same toy brick and the patent had expired (but Lego is seeking a renewal of its RCD past the 20-year patent term)? Do you think the EUIPO or a court should give weight to the expired patent as evidence of the functionality of the toy brick? Consider the following provision and discussion.

**Lego brick**

**Community Design Regulation, Article 8**

**Designs dictated by their technical function and designs of interconnections**

> 1. A Community design shall not subsist in features of appearance of a product which are solely dictated by its technical function.
>
> 2. A Community design shall not subsist in features of appearance of a product which must necessarily be reproduced in their exact form and dimensions in order to permit the product in which the design is incorporated or to which it is applied to be mechanically connected to or placed in, around or against another product so that either product may perform its function.
>
> 3. Notwithstanding paragraph 2, a Community design shall under the conditions set out in Articles 5 and 6 subsist in a design serving the purpose of allowing the multiple assembly or connection of mutually interchangeable products within a modular system.

The final basic requirement for EU design protection is that the design is not functional. Article 8 of the CDR defines functionality as applying to "features of appearance of a product which are *solely* dictated by its technical function." CDR, art. 8(1) (emphasis added). Notice that a high standard of functionality is required: the feature in question must be "*solely dictated* by its technical function," in order for the functionality bar to apply. Implicit in this approach is recognition that some design features may be both ornamental and functional, and still qualify for design protection. Moreover, functionality under the CDR focuses on *technical* function, not what might be characterized as aesthetic function (e.g., a clothing design that produces a slimming appearance). Article 8 also has a functionality provision for designs of parts that interconnect with other parts or products to perform a function. Such elements are considered functional: "A Community design shall not subsist in features of appearance of a product which must necessarily be reproduced in their exact form and dimensions in order to permit the product in which the design is incorporated or to which it is applied to be mechanically connected to or placed in, around or against another product so that either product may perform its function." *Id.* art. 8(2).

---

## LINDNER RECYCLINGTECH V. FRANSSONS VERKSTADER AB

OHIM, Third Board of Appeal
Case R 690/20073 (Oct 22, 2009)

[The appellant Lindner, which filed an application for declaration of invalidity against the contested RCD owned by Franssons, identifies five characteristic features of the contested RCD for chaff cutters used for shredding materials, depicted below, that Lindner asserts are purely functional. You can view some of Franssons' shredders at http://franssons.com/en/products/. *Ed.*]

The rotor is in the form of a cylinder having grooves in planes perpendicular to the rotation axis of the cylinder, the grooves having essentially the same width as the elevations between the grooves (feature A);

Knives are arranged along two parallel lines (feature B);

The two parallel lines are V-shaped (feature C);

The knives along one of the parallel lines are arranged within the grooves (feature D);

The knives along the other parallel line are arranged on the elevations (feature E).

According to the appellant [Lindner], all five of the aforesaid 'characteristic features' pursue a purely technical function. The V-shaped knives (feature C) ensure that the material introduced into the shredder is guided into the middle of the rotor. They also ensure that material is shredded successively, and not all at the same time. This means that the shredder operates more quietly and thus complies more easily with government regulations which protect workers against excessive noise. The appellant attempts to explain the technical function of features A, B, D and E by means of the following sketch showing the cutting region of two different shredders:

Fig. 1a

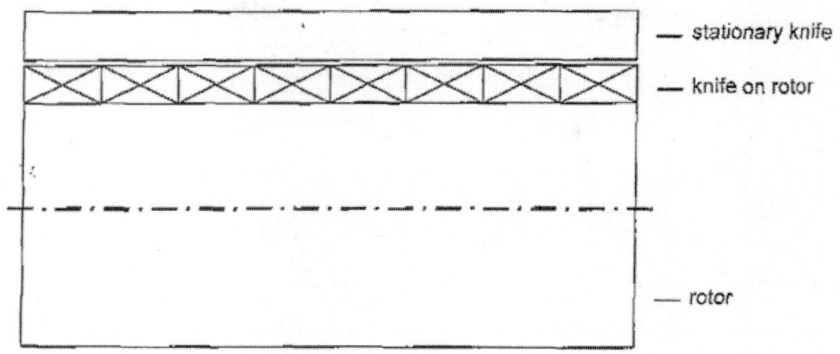


Fig. 2a

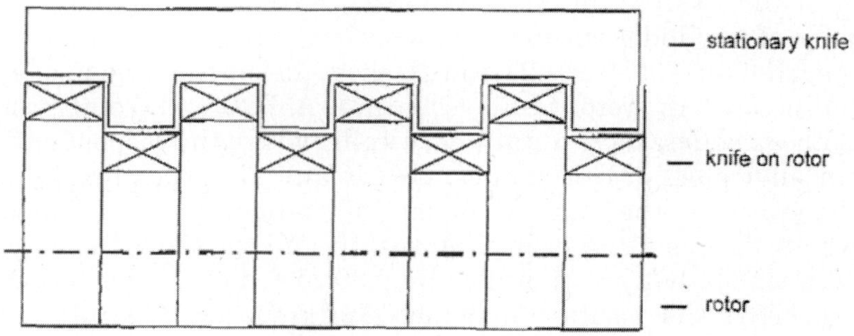


Fig. 1b

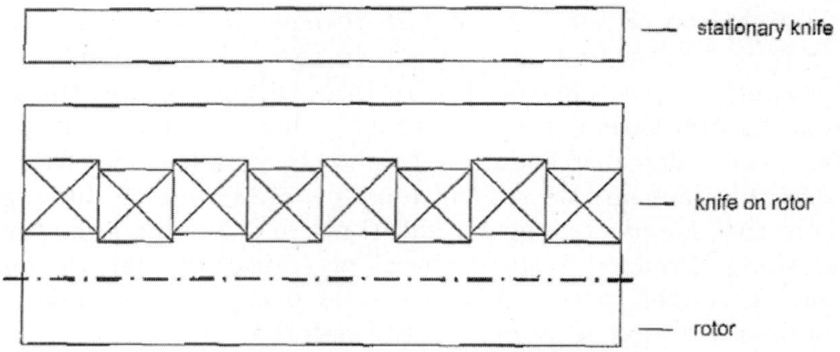

Fig. 2b

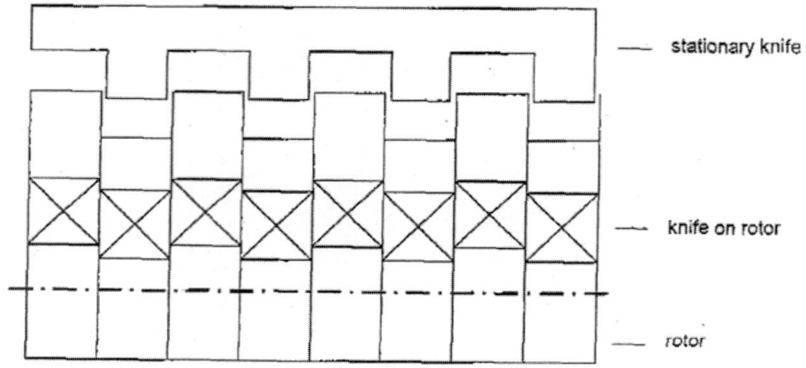


Figures 1a and 1b show the cutting region of a first shredder having a rotor in the form of a cylinder without grooves, on which the knives are arranged in two parallel lines. Figures 2a and 2b show the cutting region of a second shredder in which the rotor displays features A, B, D and E of the contested RCD. Both shredders have a stationary knife (which the respondent prefers to call an 'anvil steel' or Gegenstück in German). The shredding takes place when the knives on the rotor are facing the stationary knife. This position is shown in figures 1a and 2a. Figures 1b and 2b show the rotors in a position in which they are approximately 90° (i.e. a quarter of a revolution) before reaching the position in which the knives of the rotor face the stationary knife. In the position shown in figures 1b and 2b a gap is present between the rotor and the stationary knife. Material which is smaller than the gap can fall through it, even if it has not been shredded to the intended size. A comparison of figure 1b and 2b reveals that the gap in the first shredder is much bigger than the gap in the second shredder (i.e. the shredder which displays features A, B, D and E). Moreover, the shape of the gap in the first shredder is rectangular, whereas the gap in the second shredder has a 'labyrinth' shape. Owing to the smaller size of the gap in the second shredder and its labyrinth shape, only material having a size which is in the intended range can fall through the gap and larger pieces of material are shredded to the intended size. In particular, the design of the second shredder means that pieces of material that have a large extension in one direction cannot fall through the gap.

The respondent attempts to refute the appellant's arguments about the technical function of the design by arguing as follows: 'The RCD design has been chosen to tune with the relatively low speed rotation of the rotor; therefore the stretched out V-form has been chosen. The 'larger' pattern the better conception of it when [in] rotation. A zig-zag form has the same good technical function, but it is harder to identify when [in] rotation; one can also chose other angles of the V-form, for instance one that covers only 90 percent of the rotor surface. These alternatives offer a successive shredding ability and they are not significantly different as to the technical function when compared with a rotor wherein the V-shape covers 180 percent or a zig-zag shape. Lindners apparently fails to realise, that non-successive shredding can be done only when the knives are arranged in a straight line. A 90-degree arrangement or a zig-zag shaped arrangement is not louder than the RCD V-shape arrangement.'

Both parties have submitted various items of evidence to back up their assertions.

The interpretation of Article 8(1) CDR (and of the corresponding provision in Article 7(1) of Council Directive 98/71/EC on the legal protection of designs) is highly controversial. Similar provisions existed in the designs legislation of several Member States prior to harmonization of the law by Directive 98/71. The assumption has generally been made that the purpose of such provisions is to prevent design rights from being used to obtain monopolies over technical solutions without meeting the relatively stringent conditions laid down in patent law. Two contrasting views have been canvassed in the legal literature. One view holds that a technical necessity exception, such as that contained in Article 8(1) CDR applies only if the technical function cannot be achieved by any other configuration; if the designer has a choice between two or more configurations, the appearance of the product is not solely dictated by its technical function. That theory—known as the multiplicity-of-forms theory—is defended by some German authors (see, for example, P. Schramm, *Der europaweite Schutz des Produktdesigns, Nomos Verlagsgesellschaft, Baden-Baden* 2005, at p. 242 et seq., and U. Ruhl, *Gemeinschaftsgeschmacksmuster: Kommentar*, Carl Heymanns Verlag, Köln-Berlin-München 2007, at p. 169 et seq.) and was formerly followed by the French courts (see D. Cohen, *Le droit des dessins et modèles*, 2nd edition, *Economica*, Paris 2004, at p. 22). Advocate General Ruiz-Jarabo suggested in *Philips v. Remington* (Case C–299/99, [2002] ECR I–5475, at paragraph 34 of the Opinion) that Article 7(1) of the Designs Directive (and therefore obviously Article 8(1) CDR) should be interpreted in that manner. He stated: '. . . a functional design may, none the less, be eligible for protection if it can be shown that the same technical function could be achieved by another different form.' The Advocate General's comment is clearly an obiter dictum since *Philips v. Remington* was a case on the interpretation of Article 3(1)(e) of Council Directive 89/104/EEC of 21 December 1988 to approximate the laws of the Member States relating to trade marks ('TMD'). Article 3(1)(e) TMD excludes from trade mark protection 'signs which consist exclusively of the shape of goods which is necessary to obtain a technical result'.

The multiplicity-of-forms theory has been adopted by courts in the United Kingdom (see the judgment of 28 July 2006 of the Court of Appeal in *Landor & Hawa International Ltd v. Azure Designs Ltd* [2006] EWCA

Civ 1285) and Spain (Juzgado de lo Mercantil PTO Número Uno de Alicante, Auto No. 267/07, 20 November 2007, in *Silverlit Toys Manufactory Ltd v. Ditro Ocio 2000 SL and others*.

There is none the less a major flaw in the multiplicity-of-forms theory. If it is accepted that a feature of a product's appearance is not 'solely dictated by its function' simply because an alternative product configuration could achieve the same function, Article 8(1) CDR will apply only in highly exceptional circumstances and its very purpose will be in danger of being frustrated. That purpose, as was noted above, is to prevent design law from being used to achieve monopolies over technical solutions, the assumption being that such monopolies are only justified if the more restrictive conditions imposed by patent law (and in some countries by the law of utility models) are complied with. If a technical solution can be achieved by two alternative methods, neither solution is, according to the multiplicity-of-forms theory, solely dictated by the function of the product in question. This would mean that both solutions could be the subject of a design registration, possibly held by the same person, which would have the consequence that no one else would be able to manufacture a competing product capable of performing the same technical function (see W. Cornish and D. Llewelyn, *Intellectual Property: Patents, Copyright, Trade Marks and Allied Rights*, 5th edition, London, Sweet & Maxwell 2003, at p. 549). This leads to the conclusion that the multiplicity-of-forms theory cannot be correct.

The principal alternative, discussed by academic authors, to the multiplicity-of-forms theory has its origin in English case law. The case of *Amp v. Utilux* [1971] FR 572 concerned the interpretation of a provision of the Registered Designs Act 1949 which denied protection to the features of a design that were solely dictated by a product's technical function. The House of Lords held that a product's configuration was solely dictated by its technical function if every feature of the design was determined by technical considerations. The striking similarity between section 1(3) of the 1949 Act and Article 8(1) CDR does not of course mean that the approach of the House of Lords in *Amp v. Utilux* must necessarily be adopted in relation to the Community provision. Indeed, as was noted above in paragraph 29, the multiplicity-of-forms theory has now been adopted by the English Court of Appeal in *Landor & Hawa International v. Azure Designs*. Thus the Court of Appeal must have thought that the approach taken in *Amp v. Utilux* was no longer valid, following harmonization, in spite of the similar wording of the Community provisions and the 1949 Act. The approach taken in *Amp v. Utilux* would, however, have the advantage of allowing the purpose of Article 8(1) CDR to be achieved. No one would be able to shut out competitors by registering as Community designs the handful of possible configurations that would allow the technical function to be realised. This may explain why the French courts, which formerly espoused the multiplicity-of-forms theory, began to abandon that theory at the beginning of the 21st century in favour of an interpretation which closely resembles the *Amp v. Utilux* approach.

In addition to being supported by a teleological interpretation, the approach discussed in the previous paragraph is also supported by the wording of Article 8(1) CDR. That provision denies protection to features of a product's appearance that are 'solely dictated by its technical function'. Those words do not, on their natural meaning, imply that the feature in question must be the only means by which the product's technical function can be achieved. On the contrary, they imply that the need to achieve the product's technical function was the only relevant factor when the feature in question was selected.

Good design involves two fundamental elements: the product must perform its function and it should be pleasant to look at. In the case of some products, such as pictures and ornaments, their very function is to please the eye. In the case of other products, such as the internal working parts of a machine, the visual appearance is irrelevant. That is why the Community design legislation denies protection to component parts that are not visible in normal use. In the case of most products the designer will be concerned with both the functional and the aesthetic elements. That applies also to large items of industrial equipment, such as shredders for use in recycling plants. The shredder must, in the first place, perform its function effectively and safely and without creating excessive noise, but it is also desirable that the shredder should be pleasing to the eye and thus enhance the working environment of the people who operate it and see it in use. For that reason there is no objection in principle to granting design protection to industrial products whose overall appearance is determined largely, but not exclusively, by functional considerations.

The significance of limiting protection to the visual appearance of products is that aesthetic considerations are in principle capable of being relevant only when the designer is developing a product's visual appearance. Most of the time the designer will be concerned with both elements of good design: functionality and eye appeal. In some cases functionality will be the dominant preoccupation of the designer. The need to make a product that works will be uppermost in the designer's mind and will largely determine the appearance of the product. As long as functionality is not the only relevant factor, the design is in principle eligible for protection. It is only when aesthetic considerations are completely irrelevant that the features of the design are solely dictated by the need to achieve a technical solution. This is not, it must be stressed, tantamount to introducing a requirement of aesthetic merit into the legislation. It is simply recognition of the obvious fact that when aesthetics are totally irrelevant, in the sense that no one cares whether the product looks good, bad, ugly or pretty, and all that matters is that the product functions well, there is nothing to protect under the law of designs.

It follows from the above that Article 8(1) CDR denies protection to those features of a product's appearance that were chosen exclusively for the purpose of designing a product that performs its function, as opposed to features that were chosen, at least to some degree, for the purpose of enhancing the product's visual appearance. It goes without saying that these matters must be assessed objectively: it is not necessary to determine what actually went on in the designer's mind when the design was being developed. The matter must be assessed from the standpoint of a reasonable observer who looks at the design and asks himself whether anything other than purely functional considerations could have been relevant when a specific feature was chosen.

The appellant identified five characteristic features of the design. The respondent has not disputed that these are the most important features of the design. They could fairly be described as the essential features of the design. If all five of those features were solely dictated by the technical function of the step rotor, the design must be declared invalid, under Article 25(1)(b) in conjunction with Article 8(1) CDR.

The appellant gave a detailed, coherent and convincing explanation of the technical function of each of the five features and showed how each feature had been selected in such a way as to improve the shredding process. The respondent's attempts to rebut those arguments can only be described as inadequate. In the passage quoted above the respondent recognizes that the design was chosen 'to tune with the relatively low speed rotation of the rotor'. He goes on to state that a 'zig-zag form has the same good technical function, but it is harder to identify when [in] rotation'. He then points out that certain alternative configurations could achieve the same technical result. The respondent's own statements show that the design was chosen purely for technical reasons.

The affidavit by Mr Gradin does little to refute the view that the contested RCD was designed solely with a view to enhancing the technical performance of the shredder. The bold statement that the V-shape was chosen for mainly aesthetical reasons is scarcely credible. The statement that a zig-zag configuration would be more effective from a technical point of view is surprising: it is hard to believe that a technical advantage would be surrendered in favour of aesthetical considerations in the case of a piece of industrial equipment that might only be visible through a mirror or with the aid of a camera. In fact Mr Gradin concedes that the V-shape might have the advantage of centering the shredding process but claims that the downside of this is that more strain is put on the centrally placed teeth. What he appears to be saying is that the design represents an engineering compromise, which may well be true of most industrial designs. Something is gained, something is lost. The designer takes into account conflicting technical considerations and strives to come up with a product that has the best overall technical performance. The fact that the designer accepts a technical drawback (X) for the sake of a technical advantage (Y), knowing that he cannot have both X and Y, does not mean that the design has not been solely dictated by the technical function of the product. On the contrary, it strongly implies that nothing but the technical function of the product was relevant to the development of the design.

The respondent produces a declaration signed by Mr Jan Olsson of Bjerkens Patent Bureau KB. Mr Olsson refers to a commentary on the provision of Swedish law that implements Article 7(1) of Directive 98/71. He states that, according to this commentary, the law does not exclude 'protection of a product that lacks any aesthetical quality'. Thus, argues Mr Olsson, it is possible to protect solely functional designs. He goes on to state that it is possible 'that such details of the appearance of a product that are dictated solely by its technical function, together compose a design that [it] is possible to protect, although the particular details in themselves cannot be protected'.

The views expressed in Mr Olsson's declaration are problematical. They could, if accepted, deprive Article 7(1) of the Directive and Article 8(1) CDR of any purpose and content. Those provisions might just as well be deleted from the legislation. It is true that there is no ban on the protection of designs that lack any aesthetic quality. Such a requirement is not imposed because it is notoriously difficult to make an objective evaluation of aesthetic merit. Article 7(1) of the Directive and Article 8(1) CDR deny protection to certain designs, not because they lack aesthetic merit but because aesthetic considerations play no part in the development of the designs, the sole imperative being the need to design a product that performs its function in the best possible manner. That may fairly be said of the contested RCD. No one cares whether such a product looks good, bad or indifferent because no one spends much time looking at it. All that matters is that the product performs its function properly. Every essential feature of the design has been chosen with a view to achieving the best possible technical performance. Those features were therefore solely dictated by the product's technical function. It follows that the contested RCD must be declared invalid under Article 25(1)(b) in conjunction with Article 8(1) CDR.

## *NOTES AND QUESTIONS*

1. What is the test to determine if a design feature is functional under Article 8(1) of the CDR? Did OHIM endorse the multiplicity-of-forms approach or a different approach? Can you explain the respective approaches to functionality OHIM considered (based on what different EU members had adopted), as well as the advantages or disadvantages of each approach?

2. Does the designer's subjective intent in choosing a design matter in determining whether it is functional? Did OHIM evaluate Franssons' explanation of why it chose certain design features?

3. Under the test adopted by OHIM, was the contested design functional? Do you agree with the result?

4. Do you agree that "good design" principles (both functional and aesthetic goals) are relevant to large industrial equipment, such as the shredders in this case? Do you agree that "the shredder should be pleasing to the eye"?

5. How does the EU approach to functionality compare to treatment of functionality by U.S. design patent law, trademark law, and copyright law? Which approach, if any, makes it more likely to find a design to be functional? Which approach provides the best way to screen out functional designs?

6. *Patented features.* In a case involving whether Lego could assert a trade mark on its lego brick after the patent for it expired, the Court of Justice viewed the patent as evidence of functionality: "When the shape of a product merely incorporates the technical solution developed by the manufacturer of that product and patented by it, protection of that shape as a trade mark once the patent has expired would considerably and permanently reduce the opportunity for other undertakings to use that technical solution." *Lego Juris A/S v. Office of Harmonisation in the Internal Market (Trade Marks and Design)*, para. 46, Case C–48/09 (14 September 2010).

7. For further discussion of functionality, see Jason J. Du Mont & Mark D. Janis, *Functionality in Design Protection Systems*, 19 J. INTELL. PROP. L. 261 (2012).

---

## 4. DESIGN PROTECTION

### a. Designer and Ownership

Article 14 sets forth ownership of the Community design: "The right to the Community design shall vest in the designer or his successor in title." CDR, art. 14. Likewise, Article 18 recognizes a recognizes a right of attribution for the designer: "The designer shall have the right, in the same way as the applicant for or the holder of a registered Community design, to be cited as such before the Office and in the register." *Id.* art. 18. When more than one designer is involved in creating a design, all of the designers share the RCD jointly. The CDR also follows the work-made-for-hire doctrine, recognizing that designs created by employees within the scope of their employment are owned by the employers—"unless otherwise agreed or specified under national law." *Id.* art. 14. This approach is similar to U.S. copyright law, which (as discussed in the prior chapter) also recognizes a default rule of work-made-for-hire for employees.

### b. Exclusive Rights and Infringement

*Registered designs.* The CDR recognizes several exclusive rights. The scope of these rights varies depending on whether the design was registered. For RCDs, Article 19 recognizes: "A registered Community design shall confer on its holder the exclusive right to use it and to prevent any third party not having his consent from using it. The aforementioned use shall cover, in particular, the [1] making, [2] offering, [3] putting on the market, [4] importing, [5] exporting or [6] using of a product in which the design is incorporated or to which it is applied, or [7] stocking such a product for those purposes." CDR, art. 19 (bracketed numbers added). Even if the defendant independently created the same design, the RCD still protects against such uses of the design.

*Unregistered designs.* By contrast, the UCD recognizes the same exclusive rights, but is limited to copying of the protected design by third parties. Independent creation of the same design by third parties is allowed, in other words. "The contested use shall not be deemed to result from copying the protected design if it results from an independent work of creation by a designer who may be reasonably thought not to be familiar with the design made available to the public by the holder." CDR, art. 19(2).

*Scope of protection.* Article 10 describes the scope of protection according to the overall impression a competing design would have on the informed user of the produce: "The scope of the protection conferred by a Community design shall include *any design which does not produce on the informed user a different overall impression.*" CDR, art. 10(1) (emphasis added). The analysis is very similar to consideration of the individual character of a design, in order to obtain protection. "In assessing the scope of protection, the degree of freedom of the designer in developing his design shall be taken into consideration." *Id.* art. 10(2). Thus, if a designer had practically no freedom to design a certain element that was similar to a protected design, a similar competing design that incorporated that element would be less likely to be considered infringing simply based on that element.

## MAGMATIC LTD V. PMS INTERNATIONAL GROUP PLC

UK Supreme Court
[2016] UKSC 12, [2016] R.P.C. 11.[15]

LORD NEUBERGER: (with whom LORD SUMPTION, LORD CARNWATH, LORD HUGHES and LORD HODGE agree). This appeal concerns an alleged infringement of Community registered design No. 43427–0001 ("the CRD"), which is owned by the appellant, Magmatic Ltd. The CRD consists of six images prepared by a 3D Computer Assisted Design ("CAD") program, in monochrome, with grey-scale shading and distinct tonal contrasts. These are two of those images:

[15] Crown copyright, reproduced under Open Government License, http://www.nationalarchives.gov.uk/doc/open-government-licence/version/3/.

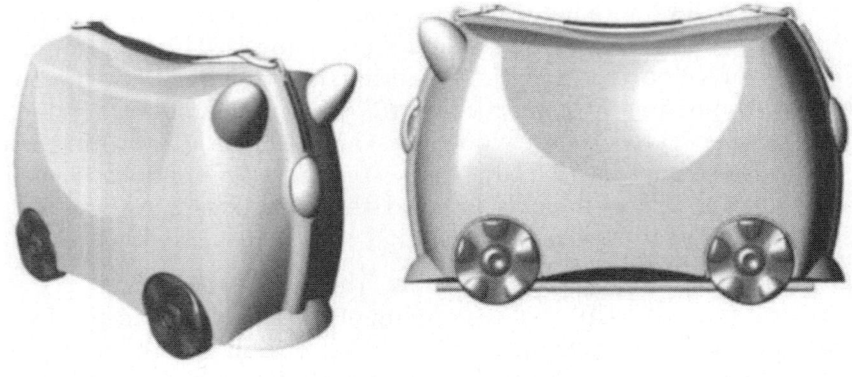

**Registered design of Magmatic**

Although it might appear from these images that the horns, and possibly the front and rear clasps, are differently shaded from the body, it is clear from the six images, viewed collectively, that they are the same light grey shade as the rest of the body, whereas the wheels and spokes, the strap on the top and the strips in the front and the rear are shaded black.

Magmatic's founder, Robert Law, won a prize in 1998 for a design of a ride-on suitcase for children. It had four wheels and a handle, and was known as the "Rodeo". He updated the design, which he then applied to register at the Office for Harmonization in the Internal Market ("OHIM"), who published it on 28 October 2003 as the CRD, with the express indication that the product depicted in the six images is for use as "suitcases".

Since May 2004, Magmatic has (initially through a licensee and since 2006 by itself) manufactured and sold ride-on suitcases for children under the trade mark "Trunki", whose shape is very similar indeed to that shown on the CRD. The Trunki case was initially marketed with the body and strap one colour, the horns and wheels another colour, and the strips, clasps and wheel-spokes a third colour, but without ornamentation. Subsequent models had slightly different colouring and included ornamentation. Two examples of such subsequent models, which are based on images which are contained in Community registered designs, applied for in 2010 by Magmatic, are shown below. The images included in these later registrations included both coloured CADs with markings and drawings with markings. Two of those registered designs included CADs shown below:

**Trunki registered design by Magmatic**

The first example has a red body, with black horns, nose, spots, bottom front, strip, handles, and wheels, and a white centre to the nose and white spokes. The second example is coloured orange, with horns, front feet, nose and wheels which are white, but with black markings, nose centre, spokes, handles and strip.

In February 2013, Magmatic issued proceedings seeking damages and an injunction against the respondent, PMS International Group plc, alleging that PMS was importing into, and selling in, the United Kingdom and Germany a "Kiddee Case" which infringed the CRD. These are two examples of a Kiddee Case:

**Kiddee Case by PMS International Group**

It will be noted that in each example, the Kiddee Case is a suitcase with a number of features similar to the CRD; for instance, it is designed to look like an animal, with a wheel at each of its four bottom corners, and has a clasp at the front, and a saddle-shaped top so that it can be ridden on. On the other hand, it has differences from the CRD, such as being brightly coloured (in the first example it has two main colours, namely, red and black, and in the second example it is orange), and with eyes in the front, and (in the first example) a group of large spots or circles towards the rear and (in the second example) stripes and whiskers, and having an unsculptured ridge and covered wheels. There are some aspects of the Kiddee Case which can be said to cut both ways in terms of similarity with the CRD: for instance it has two protuberances at the front, but they are antennae or ears rather than horns, and, while it has a ridge along the front, centre and rear, the ridge has a different shape from that of the CRD.

*Community Design Right*

Commission Regulation (EC) No. 2245/2002 ("the Implementing Regulation") implements the Principal Regulation. Article 4(1) of the Implementing Regulation states that the "representation of the design shall consist in a graphic or photographic reproduction of the design, either in black and white or in colour". Up to seven different views of the design are permitted. Reflecting art. 36 of the Principal Regulation, art. 4(1)(c) of the Implementing Regulation states that "no explanatory text, wording or symbols, other than the indication 'top' . . . may be displayed". And art. 4(1)(e) provides that the images accompanying an application to register a design "shall be of a quality permitting all the details of the matter for which protection is sought to be clearly distinguished . . . for entry in the Register of Community Designs".

As Jacob L.J. said in *Procter & Gamble Co v. Reckitt Benckiser (UK) Ltd* [2007] EWCA Civ 936, [2008] F.S.R. 8, at [3]:

"The most important things in a case about registered designs are:

(1) the registered design;

(2) the accused object; and

(3) the prior art.

And the most important thing about each of these is what they look like." And he said that "[t]he point of protecting a design is to protect that design as a design. So what matters is the overall impression created by it: will the user buy it, consider it or appreciate it for its individual design?"

*The proceedings: first instance*

After setting out the facts, Arnold J. made a number of initial findings before turning to the crucial issue of whether the Kiddee Case "produce[s] on the informed user a different overall impression" from the CRD.

Arnold J. addressed the question whether, when comparing the Kiddee Case with the CRD, "the graphical designs on the surface of the Kiddee Case are to be ignored" and concluded that they were, because the "CRD is evidently for the shape of the suitcase, and the proper comparison is with the shape of the Kiddee Case". He then identified and discussed the detailed similarities and differences between the CRD and the Kiddee Case. In particular, he identified 11 items of similarity including "[t]wo horns/protrusions located at the top of the front of the case", and six features of the Kiddee Case which were absent from the CRD, although he said that two of the six, namely "[p]rominent animal markings" and "[e]yes at front" were to be ignored, as the registration in this case "was for a shape", as he had explained. Arnold J. said that "the informed user would notice both similarities and differences", but that what mattered was "how those similarities and differences would affect the informed user's overall impression", and identified the differences as being "(i) the more rounded contours of the Kiddee Case around the seating area . . . , (ii) the covered wheels of the Kiddee Case, . . . (iii) the more flared areas . . . around the clasps and (iv) the absence of [a] lip [at the bottom of front and rear]" in the Kiddee Case.

Were it not for the Rodeo, he would have had "little hesitation" in holding that the Kiddee Case "produced the same overall impression" as the CRD, Arnold J. described himself as "rather more doubtful", given that the scope of protection to be afforded to the CRD was reduced by the prior art of the Rodeo. Nonetheless, he concluded that:

> "Despite the differences between the Kiddee Case and the CRD, the overall impression the Kiddee Case creates shares the slimmer, sculpted, sophisticated, modern appearance, prominent ridge and horn-like handles and clasps looking like the nose and tail of an animal which are present in the CRD, but which are absent from the Rodeo. Moreover, neither the Kiddee Case nor the CRD have anything like the handle which is a prominent feature of the Rodeo."

*The proceedings: the Court of Appeal*

PMS appealed to the Court of Appeal solely on the issue of whether the Kiddee Case infringed the CRD. For reasons given by Kitchin L.J., with which Moses and Black L.JJ. agreed, the appeal was allowed—[2014] R.P.C. 24. Kitchin L.J. considered that Arnold J. [in finding infringement] had erred in two respects [discussed below. *Ed.*]. Magmatic now appeals to this court.

*The Court of Appeal's first criticism: the horned animal appearance*

So far as the first criticism mentioned above is concerned, Kitchin L.J.'s statements that the overall impression given by the CRD is that of a horned animal is clearly right. Further, it is not a factor to which Arnold J. specifically referred when carrying out the exercise of comparing the CRD and the Kiddee Case. Having conducted a detailed analysis of the similarities and differences between the CRD and the Kiddee Case, he rightly focussed on "the overall impression." In that paragraph, he identified specific items of difference, but, crucially, he did not mention the horns on the images of the CRD, let alone the horned animal appearance of those images.

In addition, while he rightly referred to "the overall impression," Arnold J. did not mention in that paragraph the fact that the CRD images present as a horned animal. It is true that he observed that the Kiddee Case "shares" the "horn-like handles" of the CRD, which may at first sight appear to undermine the criticism. However, it appears to me that this observation actually supports the view that the judge did not consider the horned animal impression of the CRD as being particularly distinctive for present purposes, because he wrongly seems to have treated the antennae and ears of the Kiddee Case as "horn-like". It is also true that, as Magmatic argues, Arnold J. observed that the horns form an important part of the CRD's appearance and that the clasps look much more like the nose and tail of an animal, but these were comments made when comparing the CRD with the Rodeo not with the Kiddee Case, and, in any event, they were directed to detail, not to overall impression. Accordingly, I consider that the Court of Appeal was justified in its first criticism of the trial judge.

*The Court of Appeal's second criticism: decoration of the Kiddee Case*

Kitchin LJ. disagreed with Arnold J. when it came to the question of the decoration on the Kiddee Case. Kitchin LJ. was of the view that the fact that the CRD image was "not adorned with any . . . imagery" reinforced the impression it gave of "a horned animal with a nose and a tail". By contrast, he said, "the impression" which the shape in the first example of the Kiddee Case creates is "clearly influenced by the two tone colouring of the body and the spots on its flanks", so that "it looks like a ladybird and the handles on its forehead look like antennae". This, he said, effectively reinforced the conclusion that the Kiddee Case produced on the informed user a completely different overall impression from the horned animal embodied in the CRD design. The same conclusion, he said, applied to the second example of the Kiddee Case, as "[t]he stripes on its flanks and the whiskers on either side of its nose immediately convey to the informed user that this is a tiger with ears. It is plainly not a horned animal."

In my view, the point which Kitchin LJ. was making in this second criticism was that the absence of decoration on the CRD reinforced the horned animal impression made by the CRD. In other words, he considered that it supported what I have called his first criticism of Arnold J.'s judgment. In my view, there is limited force in this point, in that, unless the decoration had been positively distracting in nature, such as flashing lights, it would have been unlikely to have much effect in diluting the horned animal impression made by the CRD. However, I accept that the point has some force, in the sense that, unless it included items such as eyes and a mouth, any decoration could well detract from the animal impression, and, even if it consisted of such items, it could be said to distract the observer's attention from the horns.

Magmatic, however, argued that this second criticism raised a significant question of principle, namely whether the absence of ornamentation can, as a matter of law, be a feature of a registered design, and, if so, whether it was a feature of the CRD in this case. Magmatic further argued, with the support of the Comptroller General, that this question is one which should be referred to the CJEU as it is neither acte clair nor acte éclairé. I do not agree with either argument.

As I have sought to explain, when making his second criticism, Kitchin LJ. was not raising a free-standing contention that a feature of the CRD was that it contained no decoration. In the first place, that is not what Kitchin L J. said. Secondly, if it had been what he had intended, it would not have been expressed as part of the first criticism. Both points appear clear from his judgment, namely that it would be wrong "to eliminate the decoration on the accused design from . . . consideration entirely because it significantly affects how the shape itself strikes the eye, and the overall impression it gives. At least in the case of this particular registered design, the global comparison necessarily requires account to be taken of the context in which the accused shape appears."

In those circumstances, anything I say as to whether a Community Design can include an absence of decoration, would be obiter. Nonetheless, it is worth expressing some views on the topic, as it was fully canvassed. First, despite Magmatic's argument to the contrary, it seems plain to me that absence of decoration can, as a matter of principle, be a feature of a registered design. Simplicity or minimalism can notoriously be an aspect of a design, and it would be very curious if a design right registration system did not cater for it.

Secondly, whether absence of ornamentation is a feature of a particular design right must turn on the proper interpretation of the images on the registered design. Thirdly, I accept that it may sometimes be hard to decide if absence of ornamentation is a feature of a particular registered design, because art. 36(3) of the Principal Regulation and art. 4(1) of the Implementing Regulation preclude any verbal descriptions. Fourthly, if absence of ornamentation is a feature of a registered design, that does not mean that because an item has ornamentation, it cannot, for that reason alone, infringe the registered design in question: it merely means that the fact that an allegedly infringing item has ornamentation is a factor which can be taken into account when deciding whether or not it does infringe that design.

Two domestic cases are worth mentioning in this connection. In *Procter & Gamble*, the registered design was illustrated by line drawings, which were clearly concerned purely with external shape. Both Lewison J. ([2007] F.S.R. 13) and the Court of Appeal held, as Jacob L.J. put it at [2008] F.S.R. 8, at [40], that "[t]he registration is evidently for a shape. The proper comparison is with the shape of the alleged infringement. Graphics on that (or on the physical embodiment of the design) are irrelevant." Many line drawings simply show a physical shape, as in *Procter & Gamble*, but while they can show colouring and decoration, they are generally less appropriate for that purpose than photographs or CAD images, which can easily show subtle shadings and contours, as well as decoration, such as colours and ornamentation. Accordingly, while each Community Registered Design image must be interpreted in its own context, a line drawing is much more likely to be interpreted as not excluding ornamentation than a CAD image. That is consistent with what Dr Schlötelburg wrote in the article from which I have already quoted, namely that "[b]asically, the broadest claims can be achieved by drawings showing only the contours of the design. In contrast, a photo specifies not only the shape, but the surface structure and the material as well, thereby narrowing the scope of protection accordingly"—[2003] EIPR 383, at p. 385.

If, as in the case of the CRD, an applicant for a Community Registered Design elects to submit CADs of an item, whose main body appears as a uniform grey, but which has a black strip, a black strap and black wheels, the natural inference is that the components shown in black are intended to be in a contrasting colour to that of the main body. That conclusion is reinforced by the short passages from Dr Schlötelburg's article cited above. It is also supported, as Kitchin L.J. pointed out, by the fact that other features such as the clasps or the horns are not shown in a contrasting colour. It was argued by Magmatic that the wheels were shown black because they had a specific function, but I find that unconvincing: there is no logical connection between the colour and the function, and it does not explain the black strip.

Accordingly, I consider that Kitchin L.J. was right in concluding that the CRD claimed not merely a specific shape, but a shape in two contrasting colours—one represented as grey and the other as black on the images, and that Arnold J. was correspondingly wrong in holding that the CRD was a claim simply for a shape. Once one concludes that a registered design claims not just a three dimensional shape, but a three dimensional shape in two contrasting colours, one colour for the body and another colour (or possibly other colours) for specified components, then it seems to me that it must follow that, when one compares the allegedly infringing article with that design on a "like for like" basis, one must take into account the colouring on that article. If the predominant colour of the first example of the Kiddee Case shown above was the front part and was coloured red, then one would presumably compare it with the CRD on the basis that the CRD was principally coloured red, but that the wheels and spokes, strap and strips of the CRD were in a contrasting colour, and the Kiddee Case was differently coloured.

*Conclusions*

The effect of this analysis is that the Court of Appeal was right to hold that the design claimed in this case was for a wheeled suitcase in the shape of a horned animal, but that it was not a claim for the shape alone, but for one with a strap, strips and wheels and spokes in a colour (or possibly colours) which contrasted with that of the remainder of the product. Given that the Court of Appeal was right to hold that Arnold J. misdirected himself in the respects discussed above, I consider that they were, to put it at its lowest, entitled to hold that the judge materially misdirected himself, and that the Court of Appeal should reconsider the question of infringement for itself. For the reasons given above, because the Court of Appeal addressed the question of infringement on the correct basis in law, this court should be very slow indeed to interfere with their conclusion that the Kiddee Case did not infringe the CRD. I see no grounds for questioning Kitchin L.J.'s conclusion, even if I considered that another judge (or even I) might have reached a different conclusion.

I should perhaps add that, while it may be little comfort to Magmatic, I think I would have reached the same conclusion. It is a conclusion I would have reached with some regret, as the conception of the Trunki, a ride-on wheeled case which looks like an animal, seems to have been both original and clever; as Arnold J. said, "[t]here is no dispute that the Trunki was an innovative design" and it "has won numerous awards and has been a significant commercial success." Furthermore, it appears clear that Mr Beverley of PMS conceived the idea of manufacturing a Kiddee Case as a result of seeing a Trunki, and discovering that a discount model was not available. Unfortunately for Magmatic, however, this appeal is not concerned with an idea or an invention, but with a design.

## *NOTES AND QUESTIONS*

1. What is the test to determine if a Community registered design is infringed? Is the test one that can be applied with consistency? Or do you think it runs the risk of being too subjective?

2. Do line drawings, CAD drawings, or photographs of the design affect the analysis of infringement? Is there a difference among the three, in terms of scope of the design? How, if at all, did CAD images affect the Court's analysis?

3. Did the UK Supreme Court agree with the Court of Appeal's conclusion that the RCD in this case was not infringed by PMS International? Do you agree?

4. How would you compare the test of infringement of a Community registered design to the infringement analysis for U.S. design patents, trademarks, and copyrights? Would a better test for design protection focus on substantial similarity? Or would that test give too much protection to a design? For a comparison of infringement analysis under U.S. design patent law versus EU design right, see Dana Beldiman & Paolo Beconcini, *The Final Impression*

*Counts: Seeking Common Ground in Design Patent Infringement*, 97 J. PAT. & TRADEMARK OFF. SOC'Y 551 (2015).

5. *Minimalist design*. The UK Supreme Court discusses how the absence of decoration can be a design feature, such as in a minimalist design. Recall the Tenth Circuit's analysis, in *Meshwerks* (discussed above in the copyright chapter), of the "unadorned" digital model of the Toyota car as not reflecting sufficient creative choice. Would the result in *Meshwerks* be different under UK Supreme Court's approach: in other words, should the unadorned aspect of the digital model of the car be considered to reflect a specific design choice?

---

### c. Exceptions and Exhaustion

**Community Design Regulation**

**Article 20**

**Limitation of the rights conferred by a Community design**

1. The rights conferred by a Community design shall not be exercised in respect of: (a) acts done privately and for non-commercial purposes; (b) acts done for experimental purposes; (c) acts of reproduction for the purpose of making citations or of teaching, provided that such acts are compatible with fair trade practice and do not unduly prejudice the normal exploitation of the design, and that mention is made of the source.

2. In addition, the rights conferred by a Community design shall not be exercised in respect of: (a) the equipment on ships and aircraft registered in a third country when these temporarily enter the territory of the Community; (b) the importation in the Community of spare parts and accessories for the purpose of repairing such craft; (c) the execution of repairs on such craft.

**Article 21**

**Exhaustion of rights**

The rights conferred by a Community design shall not extend to acts relating to a product in which a design included within the scope of protection of the Community design is incorporated or to which it is applied, when the product has been put on the market in the Community by the holder of the Community design or with his consent.

As indicated above in Article 20(1), reproductions of designs for citation and teaching uses must comply with 3 conditions: (1) "they must be compatible with fair trade practice," (2) "not unduly prejudice the normal exploitation of the design," and (3) "mention is made of the source." In addition, Article 22 recognizes an exception to RCDs for prior users of the design who used, in good faith, the same design *before* the filing date of the registrant's application or the priority date. Such prior users can continue to exploit the design as they had before, without the need for a license. CDR, art. 22.

The CDR follows a principle of EU-wide exhaustion in Article 21. Under this approach, the design owner's right to control subsequent distributions of goods containing its protected design cease—or are "exhausted"—once the owner has consented to the sale or putting of the goods on the market in the EU.

#### d. Enforcement and Remedies

The Community Design Regulation establishes a unitary right that applies across the entire EU and is subject to one uniform EU law. An attractive feature of both the RCD and UCD is that EU-wide injunctions and damages can be obtained in an infringement lawsuit. Enforcement of rights occurs in Community design courts as designated by EU members, pursuant to Article 80 of the CDR. Community design courts have exclusive jurisdiction over Community design infringement actions, actions for declaration of invalidity of a UCD, and counterclaims for declaration of invalidity of a RCD. The European Commission publishes a list of Community design courts for EU members at http://eur-lex.europa.eu/legal-content/DE/TXT/?uri=uriserv:OJ.C_.2014.332.01.0004.01.ENG.

#### e. Duration

A RCD lasts 5 years from the date of filing of the application, once the registration is granted by OHIM. CDR, art. 12. A registrant may elect to obtain, with the payment of fees, 4 renewal periods for a total of 25 years of protection. *Id.*

A UCD lasts 3 years "from the date on which the design was first made available to the public within the Community." CDR, art. 11. The CDR defines "made available to the public" as follows: "a design shall be deemed to have been made available to the public within the Community if it has been published, exhibited, used in trade or otherwise disclosed in such a way that, in the normal course of business, these events could reasonably have become known to the circles specialised in the sector concerned, operating within the Community." *Id.* However, a design is not public if the only disclosure is "that it has been disclosed to a third person under explicit or implicit conditions of confidentiality." *Id.*

## B. INTERNATIONAL TREATIES

Next, we consider two important international agreements related to design protection: (1) the Hague Agreement Concerning International Registration of Industrial Designs ("the Hague Agreement") and (2) the Agreement on Trade Related Aspects of Intellectual Property of the World

Trade Organization ("TRIPS Agreement"). The Hague Agreement establishes a streamlined international application for design protection in now 66 countries (including the United States starting in 2015), while the TRIPS Agreement sets forth minimum standards of design protection that all 164 WTO countries must adopt.

## 1. INTERNATIONAL APPLICATIONS UNDER THE HAGUE AGREEMENT CONCERNING INTERNATIONAL REGISTRATION OF INDUSTRIAL DESIGNS

The Hague Convention provides a system through which applicants can file, in the International Bureau of WIPO, a single international application for design protection in 66 countries that are members of the Convention. Hague System applications are typically filed electronically, directly through WIPO's website (http://www.wipo.int/hague/en/how_to/file/file.html), although they also may be filed indirectly in national offices of members. Up to 100 designs (belonging to the same class under the Locarno Classification) may be registered in one application. The United States joined the Geneva Act of the Hague Agreement on May 13, 2015. U.S. design patent applications filed on or after May 13, 2015 have a term of 15 years from issuance. The EU joined the Geneva Act in 2008, which means that one can select the EU registered Community design in Hague's international application just as one can select national design protection in Hague members.

Today, two different versions of Hague are in effect depending on which act a member joined: the 1960 Act (http://www.wipo.int/wipolex/en/details.jsp?id=12528) and the 1999 Act (Geneva). For simplicity, we will describe the more recent 1999 Geneva Act (http://www.wipo.int/wipolex/en/details.jsp?id=12531). Both Acts are governed by a common set of regulations (http://www.wipo.int/wipolex/en/treaties/text.jsp?file_id=355960).

The Hague System application offers great efficiency. An applicant can file one international application in one language (English, French, or Spanish) in the International Bureau (IB) of WIPO, while designating the intent to seek an extension of protection in up to 66 members of Hague. The IB of WIPO (which also handles international trademark applications under the Madrid System) examines the application to meet the necessary formalities requirements and, if approved, publishes the international registration in the weekly *International Designs Bulletin* (http://www.wipo.int/haguebulletin/?locale=en). Notably, the IB does not undertake a substantive novelty review of the design—that is left up to each country designated in the application. Each national office (whose country the application has designated for extension of protection) then has 6 months to decide whether to grant the design protection or not—according to the national law of each country. Under the 1999 Act, countries that have an examining office or an opposition procedure have up to 12 months from the publication of the international registration to make a decision (Rule 18(1)(b)). Failure of a national office to decide within the prescribed time results in the automatic grant of protection in that country. Hague Agreement art. 14(2). The International Register then reflects the countries that have accepted the design for protection for each design that has been subject to international registration in the Hague System.

Registered designs are searchable via the Hague Express database at http://www.wipo.int/designdb/hague/en/index.jsp. WIPO also collects "a world-wide collection of industrial design data, including WIPO Hague registrations and information from participating national offices" at the Global Design Database of WIPO, at http://www.wipo.int/designdb/en/index.jsp. For example, the following light switch designs of Ingelec were registered in 2004:

**Figure 3. Registered Designs of Light Switches of Ingelec**

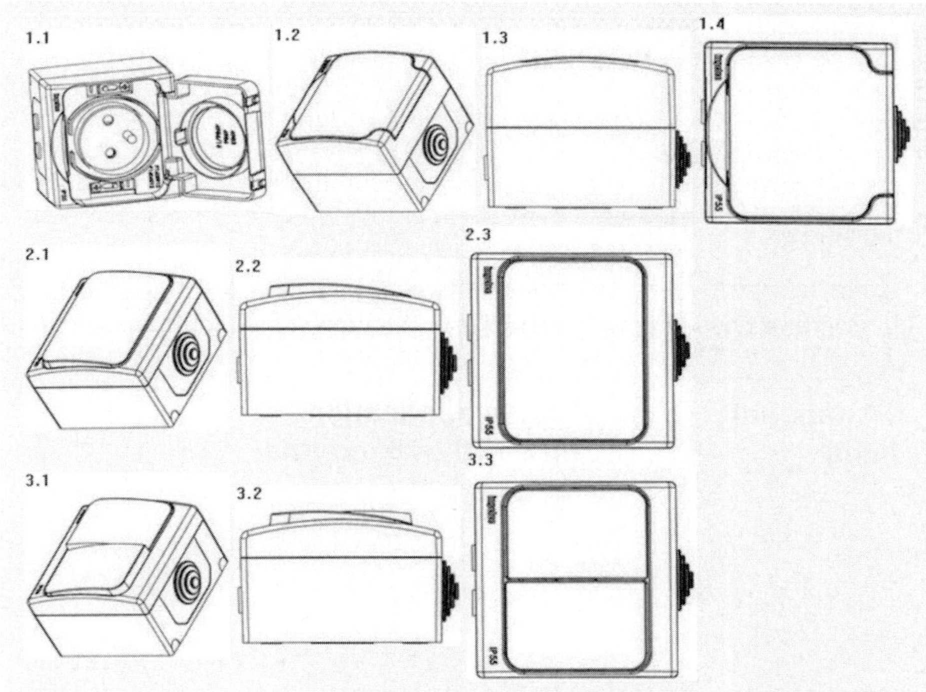


You can read the registration at http://www.wipo.int/designdb/hague/en/showData.jsp?KEY=DM/065983. As the registration indicates, Ingelec, a Moroccan based company, obtained registrations in Israel, the Benelux countries, Switzerland, Cote D'ivoire, Germany, France, Greece, and Senegal. It has a Paris priority date of Sept. 20, 2004 based on a Moroccan filing.

Members of the Paris Convention allow a period of priority for applications, including design, trademarks, and patents. *See* Paris Conv., art. 4. For industrial designs, the period is 6 months from the filing of the first application on the same design. Under Paris priority, an applicant may claim the benefit of its first filed application date to apply to all foreign filings in other Paris members for the same design within that 6 month period. For example, imagine that Alicia files a design patent application in the USPTO, and, within 6 months of the U.S. filing date, decides to file an international application under the Hague System. As depicted in Figure 4 below, Alicia may claim her U.S. filing date (the priority date) for the international application that was filed within the 6-month Paris priority period. *See* Hague Agreement, art. 6 (Geneva Act of July 2, 1999).

**Figure 4. National and Hague Applications with Paris Priority**

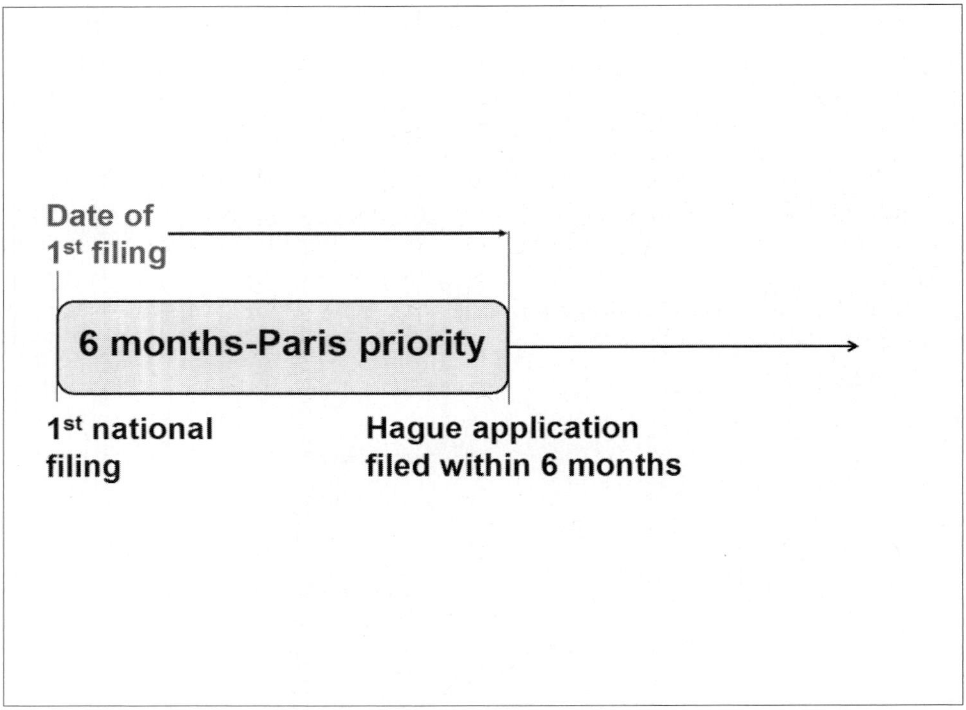


## *NOTES AND QUESTIONS*

1. If you are seeking design protection, when might you opt for filing a Hague System application first instead of a national application? Likewise, when do you think it might be better to file a national registration first and then decide within 6 months whether to pursue an international filing? Hint: what advantage, if any, does 6 extra months provide?

2. Similar international systems for filing applications exist for patents and for trademarks. The Patent Cooperation Treaty (PCT) currently has 152 members, while the Madrid Union (for trademarks) has 114 countries. Until recently, industrial design protection was not as heavily sought—which might explain why the Hague System has only 66 members. The United States joined only in 2015. Given the growing popularity of design protection among businesses, one would expect the membership of Hague to increase.

3. The Hague system ultimately relies on national protections (or regional protection in the case of the EU) for designs, instead of one international protection decided under a uniform law. What are the advantages and disadvantages of the Hague system versus an international system that is unitary and uniform in approach? Given the similarities and differences between the U.S. design patent and EU design right, do you think it would be feasible for countries eventually to agree on a uniform system of design protection? Would such an international approach be desirable?

---

## 2. MINIMUM STANDARDS OF PROTECTION UNDER TRIPS AGREEMENT

The Agreement on Trade Related Aspects of Intellectual Property Rights (TRIPS Agreement) sets forth minimum standards of protection for seven different forms of intellectual property, including industrial designs. All WTO countries are obligated to provide protection at least at the minimum standard; countries are free to go above the minimum standard and provide additional protection.

The requirements for design protection in the TRIPS Agreement are relatively modest. Only two provisions—Articles 25 and 26—relate to protection for industrial designs.

**TRIPS Agreement. Article 25**

**Requirements for Protection**

1. Members shall provide for the protection of independently created industrial designs that are new or original. Members may provide that designs are not new or original if they do not significantly differ from known designs or combinations of known design features. Members may provide that such protection shall not extend to designs dictated essentially by technical or functional considerations.

2. Each Member shall ensure that requirements for securing protection for textile designs, in particular in regard to any cost, examination or publication, do not unreasonably impair the opportunity to seek and obtain such protection. Members shall be free to meet this obligation through industrial design law or through copyright law.

**Article 26**

**Protection**

1. The owner of a protected industrial design shall have the right to prevent third parties not having the owner's consent from making, selling or importing articles bearing or embodying a design which is a copy, or substantially a copy, of the protected design, when such acts are undertaken for commercial purposes.

2. Members may provide limited exceptions to the protection of industrial designs, provided that such exceptions do not unreasonably conflict with the normal exploitation of protected industrial designs and do not unreasonably prejudice the legitimate interests of the owner of the protected design, taking account of the legitimate interests of third parties.

3. The duration of protection available shall amount to at least 10 years.

Article 25 sets forth the basic minimum standard of protection for industrial designs. WTO countries must protect "independently created industrial designs that are new or original." TRIPS art. 25(1). The provision gives WTO members the discretion of adopting the following standard for "new or original": "Members may provide that designs are not new or original if they do not significantly differ from known designs or combinations of known design features." *Id.* In addition, WTO members may adopt the following standard of functionality, a doctrine that disqualifies protection of functional features: "Members may provide that such protection shall not extend to designs dictated essentially by technical or functional considerations." *Id.*

Article 25(2) is a special provision for textile designs. Given the short life cycle of many textile designs, WTO members must ensure a process for protection "in particular in regard to any cost, examination or publication, do not unreasonably impair the opportunity to seek and obtain such protection." *Id.* art. 25(2). Countries are allowed to meet this requirement through either copyright law or industrial design protection. *Id.* Copyright law typically does not require any formalities, given the prohibition against formalities under the Berne Convention. Likewise, design protection in some countries is based on a quick "registration" system, such as for the EU Community design registration.

Article 26 recognizes the minimum standard for exclusive rights for design protection: "The owner of a protected industrial design shall have the right to prevent third parties not having the owner's consent from making, selling or importing articles bearing or embodying a design which is a copy, or substantially a copy, of the protected design, when such acts are undertaken for commercial purposes." *Id.* art. 26(1). Notice that the minimum standard covers only unauthorized *commercial* exploitation of protected designs.

In addition, countries may recognize exceptions to design protection, provided that the exceptions meet the 2-step test set forth in Article 26(2): "such exceptions (1) do not unreasonably conflict with the normal exploitation of protected industrial designs and (2) do not unreasonably prejudice the legitimate interests of the owner of the protected design, taking account of the legitimate interests of third parties."

Finally, the minimum term of protection for design protection is 10 years. But countries are given discretion to have more than one term that "amount[s] to at least 10 years," such as two terms of 5 years. *Id.* 26(3). Do the U.S. design patent and registered Community design satisfy this TRIPS minimum standard of protection?

### *NOTES AND QUESTIONS*

1. Do the EU Community Design Regulation's standard for novelty and U.S. design patent law's standard for novelty satisfy the TRIPS minimum standard for "new or original"?

2. How do the EU Community Design Regulation's standard for functionality and U.S. design patent law's standard for functionality compare to the TRIPS minimum standard for functionality?

3. Review the exceptions to the Community design in Article 20 of the CDR above. Do you think they satisfy the two-step test of TRIPS Article 26?

4. Why do you think TRIPS limits the exclusive rights for design protection to commercial exploitation ("when such acts are undertaken for commercial purposes"), whereas TRIPS contains no such commercial limitation for the exclusive rights of patents (Article 28)?

# CHAPTER 6

# REVIEW PROBLEMS

■ ■ ■

In this chapter, we offer several problems to review the lessons from the previous chapters. These problems should help you review the materials and test your knowledge of the various forms of design protection.

## *PROBLEM 6–1*

Tesla Motors designs electric cars. It has designed a sports utility vehicle (SUV) called the X, as depicted in the Figures below. Tesla touts the X as follows: "Model X is the safest, fastest and most capable sport utility vehicle in history. With all-wheel drive and a 100 kWh battery providing 289 miles of range, Model X has ample seating for seven adults and all of their gear. And it's ludicrously fast, accelerating from zero to 60 miles per hour in as quick as 2.9 seconds. Model X is the SUV uncompromised." Photographs of the X car can be found at https://www.tesla.com/modelx and below. For this problem, assume that the Model X has not yet been marketed or sold to the public.

### A. Design of X Car

Elon Musk, the founder and CEO of Tesla, has hired your law firm to provide legal advice on whether the design of the X car be protected under U.S. law, as well as under the EU Community design. In answering this question, you should discuss (1) whether the X car falls within the eligible subject matter of the respective IP protections, (2) whether the X car can meet the substantive requirements of the respective IP protections, (3) whether the X car design would face problems of functionality under the respective IP protections, and (4) whether one type of IP protection is strategically better for Tesla to seek. Musk, while brilliant, is not that familiar with the differences among design patents, trademarks, copyrights, and the Community design, so he'd like your assessment of not only the legal requirements but also the business advantages that each IP form might offer. Please note any factual issues (if any) that require further research.

FIG. 1

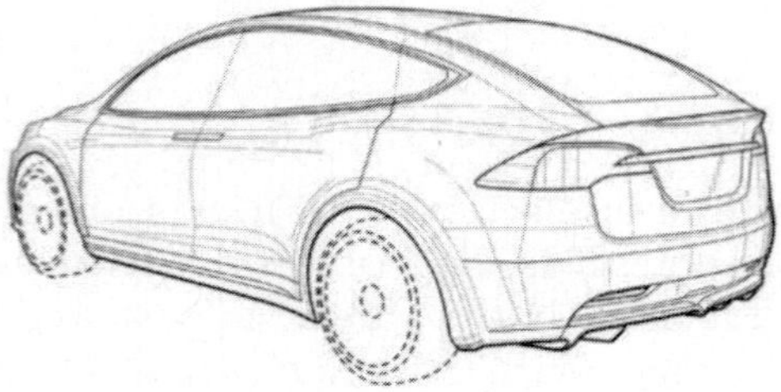

FIG. 2

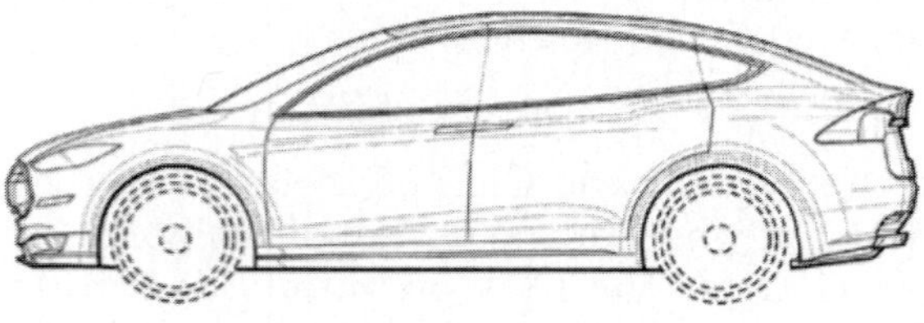

FIG. 3

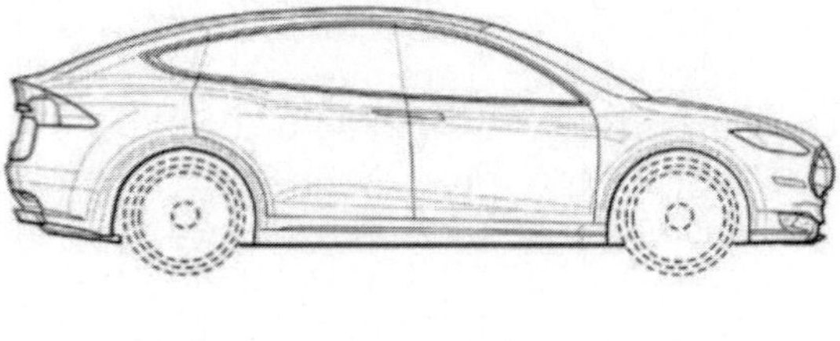

FIG. 4

FIG. 5

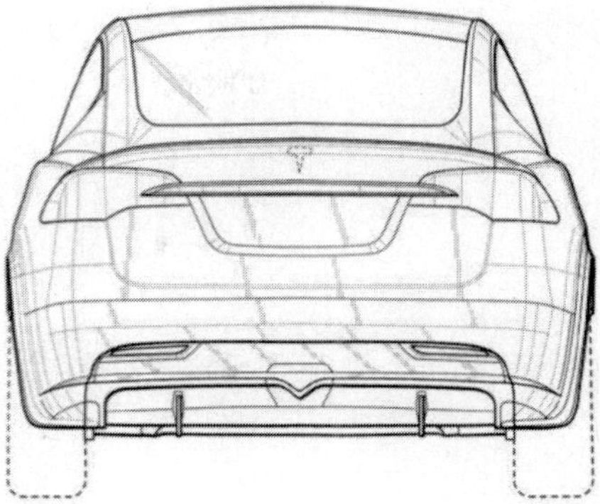

FIG. 6

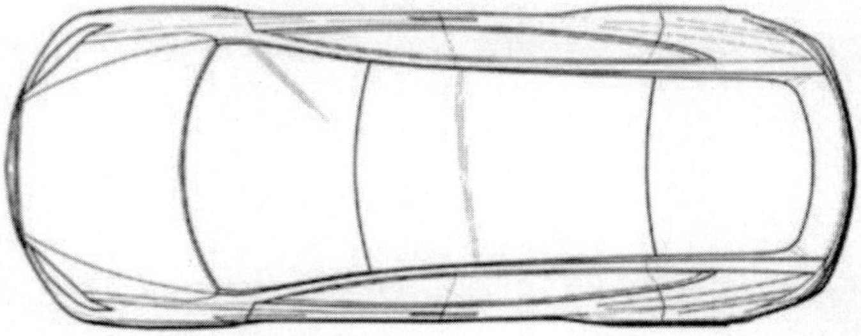

FIG. 7

B. Design of the X Doors

One of the most interesting features of the X car are the doors, which Tesla calls "Falcon wing doors." They are dual hinged (both at the roof of the car where the door connects and in the middle of the door, which folds) and they open upward, instead of out, thereby allowing parking in tight spaces. You can see a demonstration of the Falcon wing doors opening at https://youtu.be/3iWWkVWUxis. The doors are similar to "gull wing" doors first pioneered by Mercedes Benz in the 1950s, but the typical gull-wing doors are only single-hinged at the roof (so the doors themselves do not hinge in the center). Diagrams of the motion of Tesla's door are shown in the Figures below. Musk believes the X doors are unique and distinctive—adding a "wow" factor to the X car unlike anything in the car industry today. He'd like to get not only a utility patent on the dual-hinged door, but also design protection for the distinctive upward-hinging motion by which the doors open. Another law firm is preparing the application for the utility patent. He'd like you to analyze the design protection issues answering the following: (1) whether the upward-hinging motion of the X doors falls within the eligible subject matter of the respective IP protections, (2) whether the upward-hinging motion of the X doors can meet the substantive requirements of the respective IP protections, (3) whether the upward-hinging motion of the X doors would face problems of functionality under the respective IP protections, and (4) whether one type of IP protection is strategically better for Tesla to seek. Please note any factual issues (if any) that require further research.

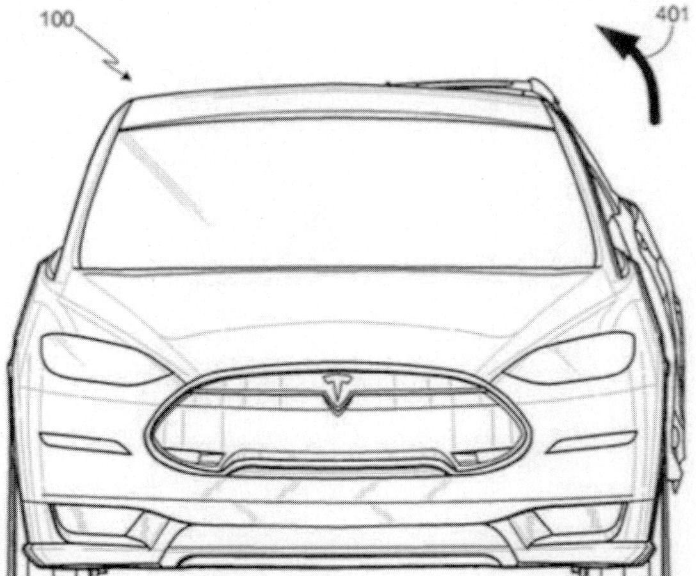

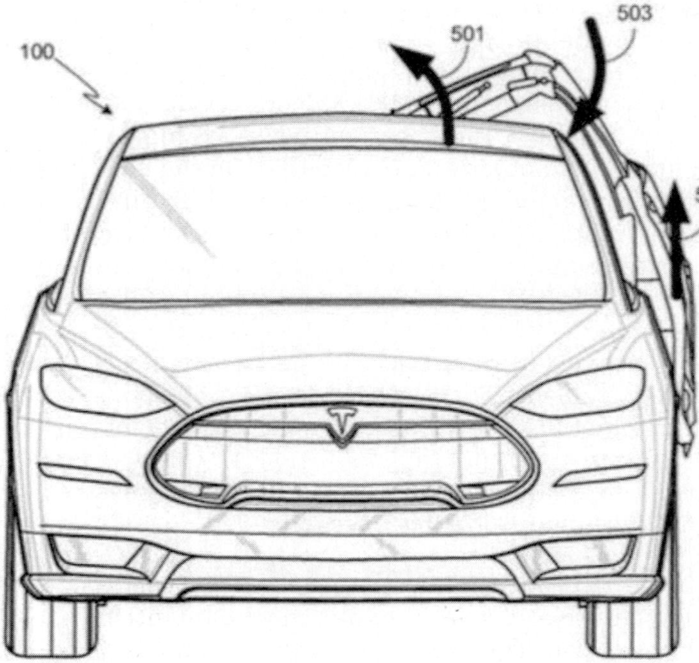
100
501
503
505

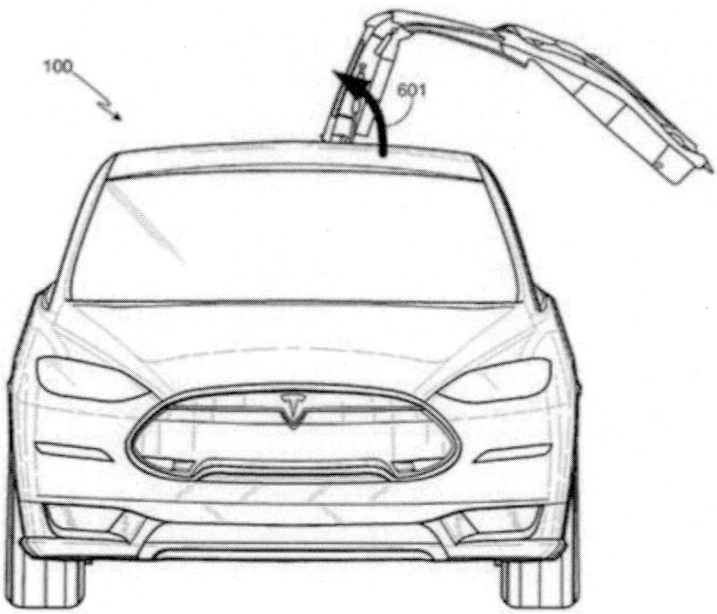
100
601

### *PROBLEM 6–2*

Apple designs and sells consumer electronic equipment. In April 2015, Apple introduced the Apple Watch. The Apple Watch was a commercial success, selling over 12 million watches at an average price of $500. The Apple Watch is much more than a digital watch. Apple describes the Apple Watch as follows: "Track and share your activity. Measure your workouts. Monitor your health. And stay connected to the people and information you care about most." The Apple Watch also has a distinctive look, much like Apple's other products. Before releasing the Apple Watch, Apple filed a series of design patent applications covering the design. The applications have begun to issue as patents. Below is Figure 1 in United States Patent No. D737,157 ("the '157 patent."), assigned to Apple. Figure 1 illustrates the design of a watch and woven nylon (plastic) band. All lines in Figure 1 are solid lines.

Sasio is a multinational electronics developer and manufacturer. Sasio sells digital watches in countries around the world, as well as calculators, digital cameras, phones, and electronic musical instruments. In late 2016, Sasio introduced a new digital watch, called the iShock, in the U.S. and ten countries in the EU. The watch was called the iShock because the watch was extremely durable. The face of the iShock can withstand 25 pounds of force, hence the name. The band of the iShock is made from a black resin that is different from the woven nylon of the Apple Watch in both texture and tensile strength. The iShock is a traditional electronic watch. It includes a calendar, lap timer, alarm, countdown, dual time, etc., but has none of the smart watch features of the Apple Watch such as exercise counters or ability to communicate with other electronic devices. Nonetheless, there are certain physical similarities between the layout of the Apple Watch and the Sasio iShock. Below are images of the Apple Watch (via the '157 patent) and the Sasio iShock.

Figure 1 of '157 Patent

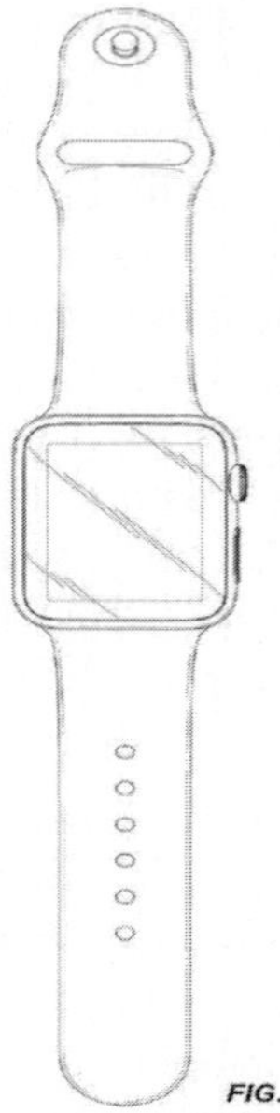

FIG. 1

Sasio iShock

A. U.S. Design Patent

Apple sues Sasio for patent infringement in the Eastern District of Texas. You are hired by Sasio to aid in its defense. Sasio provides to you two prior art watches that were sold in the United States by the mid-2000s. Images of those watches, both sold by another watch manufacturer, SIMEX, are illustrated below.

**SIMEX Prior Art 1**

**SIMEX Prior Art 2**

**Apple '157 Patent**

FIG. 1

Please advise Sasio on who is likely to prevail on the issue of validity and infringement in Apple's U.S. lawsuit. If Apple prevails, what are the likely remedies it could seek?

B. EU Registered Community Design

Apple also obtained registered Community designs for the Apple Watch within the Paris priority period after its first application in the United States. Apple also files suit against Sasio in the EU to enforce its RCD. Please advise Sasio on who is likely to prevail on the issue of validity and infringement of Apple's RCD in Apple's EU lawsuit. Does Apple stand a better chance of prevailing under the U.S. design patent or EU Community design? If Apple prevails, what are the likely remedies it could seek in the EU? Based on your analysis in A and B, would you advise Sasio to litigate the case or to pursue settlement with Apple?

### *PROBLEM 6–3*

Puff Daddy Inc. has designed a smoking accessory called the Dragon Puff. The Dragon Puff has an ergonomic sleeve that holds a conventional disposal lighter. A retractable poker hinges from one of the bottom corners to use in mixing tobacco or other substances in a pipe or other container. The other corner has a tamper to pack down a substance in a pipe or other container. The body is contoured for hemp wick to be wrapped around it. Puff Daddy Inc. obtained a design patent on the Dragon Puff, as well as a registered Community design. Puff Daddy submitted the following drawings in both the USPTO and EUIPO. The broken lines showing a cigarette lighter in the figures depicts an intended use for the lighter holder and tool that form no part of the claimed design.

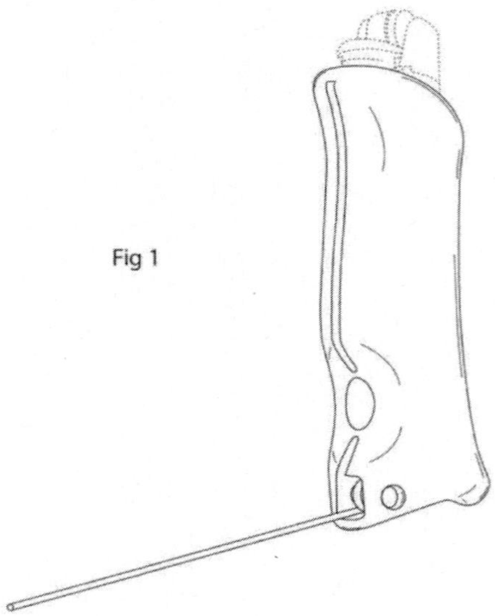

Fig 1

Figure 1 above is a top perspective view of the lighter holder and tool showing a poker extended therefrom.

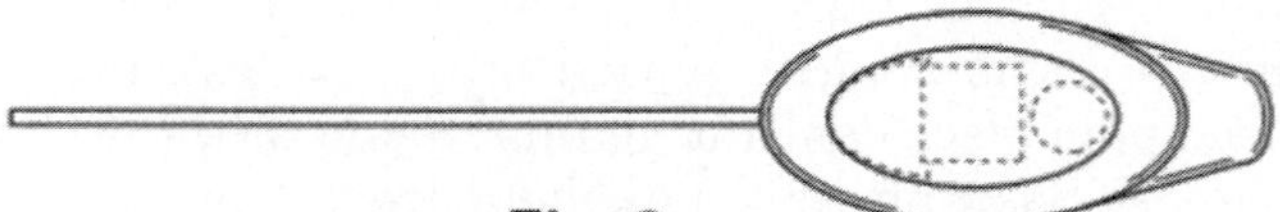

Fig 2

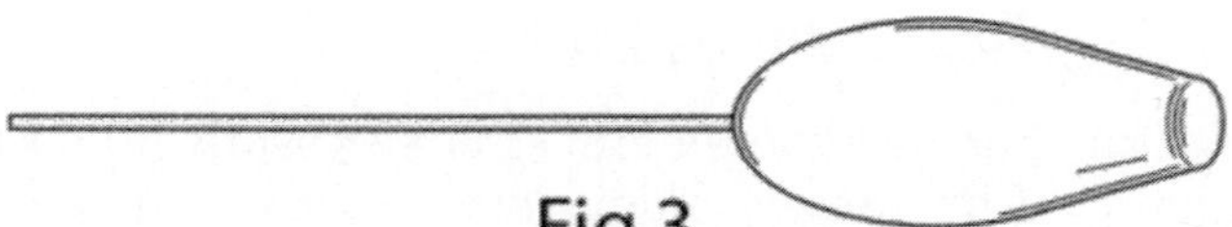

Fig 3

Figure 2 is a top plan view thereof. Figure 3 is a bottom plan view thereof.

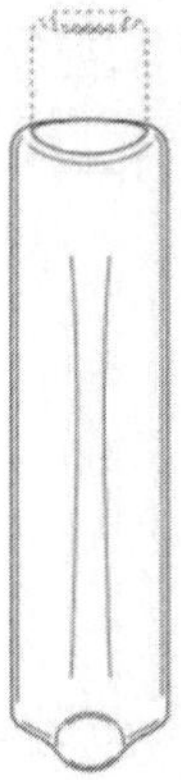

Fig 4

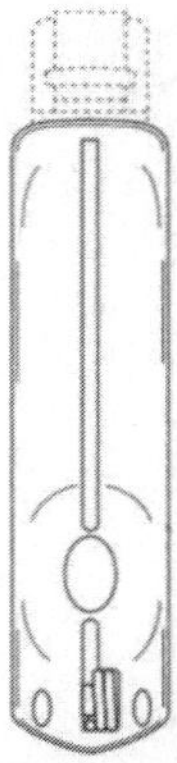

Fig 5

Figure 4 above is a rear elevational view thereof. Figure 5 is a front elevational view thereof.

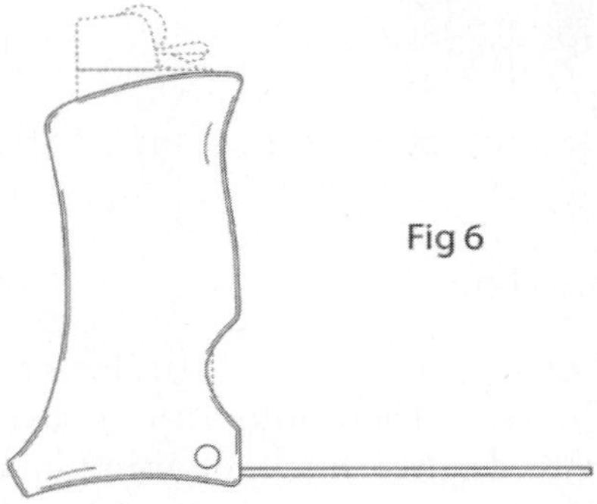

Fig 6

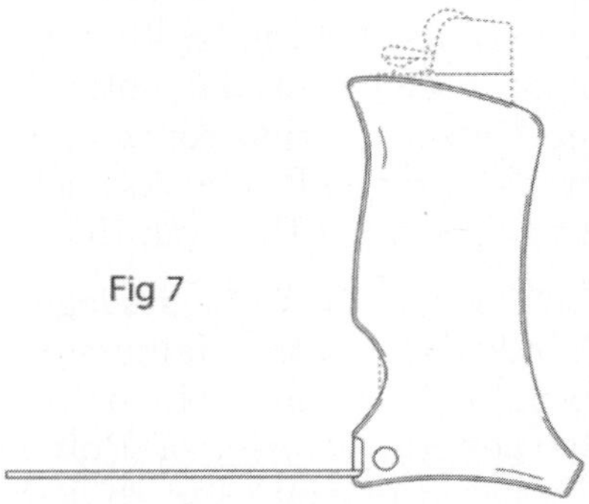

Fig 7

Figure 6 above is a right side elevational view thereof; and Figure 7 is a left side elevational view thereof.

Puff Daddy Inc. began selling its Dragon Puff in the U.S. and Europe to great commercial success, especially in Washington, Oregon, California, Nevada, Alaska, Colorado, and Maine, as well as the Czech Republic, the Netherlands, and Portugal. A photograph of the Dragon Puff as it is sold for $7.95 in the U.S. and 6,95 Euros in the EU is shown in the photograph below on the left:

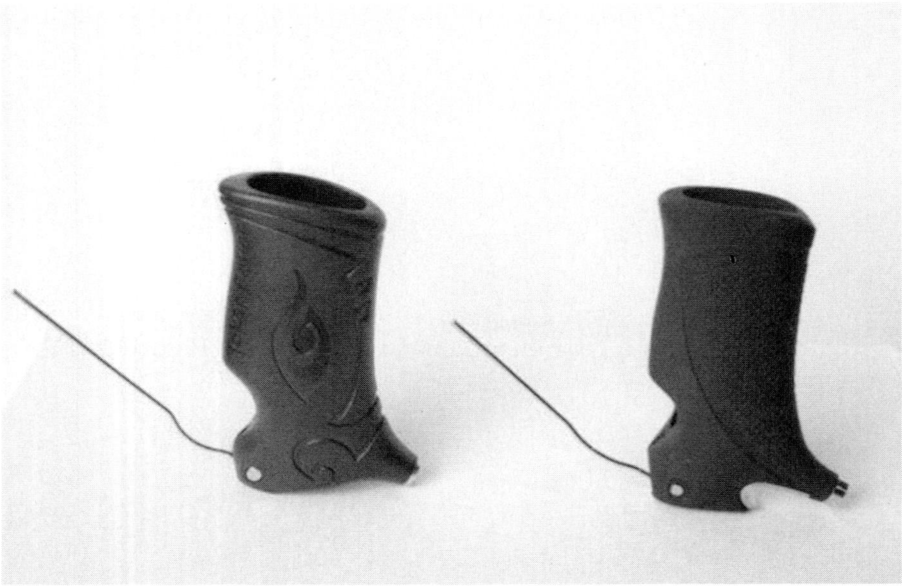

**Dragon Puff** **All of the Lights**

Canye East Co. has begun selling a similar smoking accessory called All of the Lights, as shown in the photograph above on the right. Like the Dragon Puff, All of the Lights has an ergonomic sleeve that holds a conventional disposal lighter, a retractable poker that hinges from one of the bottom corners to use in mixing tobacco, and a tamper to pack down a substance in a pipe. The body of All of the Lights is also contoured for hemp wick to be wrapped around it. However, one noticeable difference with All of the Lights is that the bottom portion contains a curved element that serves as a bottle opener; the Dragon Puff lacks such a feature. Canye sells the device for $4.99 in the U.S. and 4 Euros in the EU.

Puff Daddy Inc. has hired you to pursue its legal claims against Canye East Co. Evaluate Puff Daddy's potential claims under U.S. design patent, trade dress, and copyright law, as well under the EU registered Community design. The general counsel of Puff Daddy is particularly concerned about Canye's potential argument that the Dragon Puff design is functional. In your analysis of the potential claims, include a comparison of the various IP laws and identify which, if any, provides a greater chance for the Dragon Puff to be considered nonfunctional in design and, ultimately, to prevail in establishing infringement.

# INDEX

References are to Pages